D1552829

POLITICAL GLOBALIZATION

A New Vision of Federal World Government

James A. Yunker

University Press of America,® Inc.
Lanham · Boulder · New York · Toronto · Plymouth, UK

Copyright © 2007 by
University Press of America,® Inc.
4501 Forbes Boulevard
Suite 200
Lanham, Maryland 20706
UPA Acquisitions Department (301) 459-3366

Estover Road
Plymouth PL6 7PY
United Kingdom

Library of Congress Control Number: 2007930034
ISBN-13: 978-0-7618-3845-6 (clothbound : alk. paper)
ISBN-10: 0-7618-3845-7 (clothbound : alk. paper)

CONTENTS

LIST OF FIGURES

LIST OF TABLES

PREFACE

The seed that ultimately grew into this book germinated over 45 years ago, during the winter of 1961-1962. At that time I was a freshman college student, of thoroughly conventional background and beliefs, at Fordham University in New York City. To the extent that I thought about world government at all, I dismissed the possibility as, at best, a misguided and thoroughly utopian delusion, and at worst, a despicable communist plot to destroy freedom and democracy throughout the world. During the early 1960s, the Cold War was rapidly approaching its peak level of intensity, and I sincerely believed (although I hoped that it would never be necessary to make the choice) that it would be better to be dead than Red. If a world government were established, I had no doubt that the international communist movement would exert every effort to gain complete control over it. And should this effort be successful, I had no doubt also that human existence throughout the world would be reduced to the lowest level of oppression and misery—an awful realization of rampant totalitarianism as described in George Orwell's nightmarish novel *1984*.

But by the end of my freshman year, I had completely changed my opinion of world government. From my former opinion that it was both quite infeasible and highly undesirable, I had migrated 180 degrees to the opinion that it was both quite feasible and highly desirable. The emotional impact of this fundamental change in my belief system was easily the equivalent of religious conversion. It was an epiphany of the highest order. The immediate catalyst to the chain of thought leading to this diametrical reversal was a casual reading of *The Power Elite* by the noted sociologist C. Wright Mills. Exactly what it was about the Mills treatise that precipitated this drastic reappraisal I cannot say. While Mills was definitely leftwing in his basic ideological orientation, he was by no means a genuine radical. His purpose was not to preach the need for major social transformations, either domestic or international, but rather merely to put people on their guard against excessive manipulation by the "power elite" of wealthy capitalists, corporation executives, high military officers and government officials—what Dwight D. Eisenhower was to call the "military-industrial complex." In my case, however, recognition of the possibility that my prior thinking might have been to some extent manipulated by those with an especially strong interest in the status quo thoroughly disturbed me, and thoroughly dislodged my previously orderly structure of conventional political and economic judgments. The winter and spring of 1962 was a period of intense intellectual activity, the culmination of which was a fairly comprehensive vision of pragmatic market socialism as a steppingstone to world government.

The title of this book refers to a "new vision" of federal world government. While the vision will be new to most readers, it is obviously not, after 45 years of gradual, evolutionary development on my part, a "new vision" to me. Yet the plan of world government developed herein is not unduly precise, and I trust that it is not guilty of the sin of "premature specificity." The reader might wonder, therefore, why it has taken more than four decades for the author to produce this book. An explanation is in order, and I will endeavor to provide it by outlining briefly the intellectual odyssey that led up to this point.

The blueprint for world government set forth in this book is sufficiently constrained and limited that it could conceivably have been implemented back in the 1960s, at the height of the Cold War. Fundamental to the plan are two key provisions: (1) that member nations retain perpetually the right to secede (withdraw) from the world federation at their own unilateral discretion; (2) that member nations retain perpetually the right to maintain whatever military forces and armaments under their direct control they desire, up to and including strategic nuclear weapons. No doubt if such a world government had been established in the 1960s, both the USA and the USSR, and their various friends and allies, would have maintained virtually the same military machines they did in reality. The short-term threat of nuclear holocaust would have been unaffected.

However, the institutions and procedures of the world government might have been more conducive to meaningful dialogue and cooperation than were the institutions and procedures of the existing United Nations. Quite likely there would have been more rapid progress toward ideological disengagement and accommodation, and the Cold War might have come to an end in the late 1970s or early 1980s rather than in the early 1990s. Had that happened, humanity would have been spared a great deal of military expense and war-risk. Resources that were actually allocated to military uses might instead have been allocated to economic development, and as a result the economic gap between the richest nations and the poorest nations might today be much smaller. But as the saying goes, that is water under the bridge, and there is no point in bemoaning lost opportunities. The important thing is not to waste the opportunities we have today.

The specific institutional and procedural details envisioned for the Federal Union of Democratic Nations proposed in this book were not part of the initial vision. At its earliest stage of development, the world government component of the overall vision was quite vague and indistinct. The thrust of the initial vision was the creation of relatively uniform ideological and economic conditions throughout the world. Should the ideological and economic conditions become sufficiently homogeneous, no great ingenuity would be needed to formulate a workable plan of world government. As mentioned above, the initial vision was that of pragmatic market socialism as a steppingstone to world government. Actually pragmatic market socialism was the first steppingstone; the second steppingstone was a very large-scale global economic development program—what is designated in this book as the "World Economic Equalization Program" (WEEP). Pragmatic market socialism was intended as a bridge over the ideological gap between the communist nations and noncommunist nations. The World Economic Equalization Program was intended to close the economic gap between the rich nations and the poor nations.

The scenario which I envisioned, as an optimistic young college student in the early 1960s, was approximately as follows. Pragmatic market socialism (or some variant of the same basic idea) would be recognized by both the communist and noncommunist nations as a viable and desirable socioeconomic system, and would thereupon be adopted by all or most nations. The resulting tremendous de-escalation of ideological controversy would lead quickly to major disarmament programs. Disarmament would free up a tremendous amount of economic resources previously devoted to military uses, and all or most of these resources would be invested in a World Economic Equalization Program. The WEEP would be a gigantic, world-wide economic development program financed by foreign aid contributions from the rich nations. It would be similar to the Marshall Plan of the post-World War II period, only on a far larger scale both geographically and financially.

Concurrently with the initiation of the WEEP, a limited world government would be established. The WEEP and the world government were viewed as complementary initiatives. The WEEP would increase the success probability of the world government, and simultaneously the world government would increase the success probability of the WEEP. I fully recognized, even in the first rush of enthusiasm, that there could be no guarantees that even if the scenario proceeded according to plan, the outcome would be favorable. Even assuming basic ideological uniformity throughout the world (the end of the confrontation between communist and noncommunist ideology), the World Economic Equalization Program might easily be a complete fiasco, in which case it would soon be terminated, and, very likely, the world government dissolved. My position was then (and remains today) that if humanity makes the effort of initiating both a WEEP and a world government, there will be a *higher probability* of a favorable long-term outcome for human civilization on this planet. We cannot assure positive outcomes; but we can increase the likelihood of positive outcomes.

In view of the collapse and dissolution of the Soviet Union in 1991, it seems extremely probable that pragmatic market socialism is no longer necessary for providing a bridge between communism and noncommunism. Although it is apparently an academic matter at this point, a brief description of the pragmatic market socialist concept is merited. Within the overall controversy between proponents and opponents of communism, there were (and remain—since communism is by no means extinct in the contemporary world) three principal subcontroversies: (1) proponents of communism maintain that socialism (public ownership of capital) is preferable to capitalism (private ownership of capital), opponents maintain the opposite; (2) proponents of communism maintain that central planning of the economy is efficient and effective, opponents maintain the opposite; and (3) proponents of communism maintain that governments controlled by oligarchic communist parties are politically necessary and even desirable, opponents maintain the opposite. Prior to the winter of 1961-1962, I had always assumed, with a confidence bordering on dogmatism, that the opponents of communism were correct on all three sub-controversies: that capitalism was preferable to socialism, that market allocation was preferable to central planning, and that democracy was preferable to oligarchy.

But now that I was subjecting my prior beliefs to a far more searching scrutiny than I had ever done in the past, I had a sudden inspiration on this matter—an inspiration that soon developed into a near-certainty. The inspiration was that while the opponents of communism were correct on two of the three points of dispute, they were *not* correct on the remaining point. Specifically, while it was true that democracy is preferable to oligarchy, and it is also true that market allocation is preferable to central planning, it is *not* true that capitalism is preferable to socialism. In other words, a democratic market socialist system would possess significant advantages over a democratic market capitalist system. While democratic market capitalism as practiced in the leading noncommunist nations was superior to the oligarchic planned socialism practiced in the leading communist nations, the reason for this was the superiority of market allocation over central planning and the superiority of democracy over oligarchy—not the superiority of capitalism over socialism. If other things could be held equal, i.e., the political condition of democracy and the economic condition of free market allocation, socialism would be superior to capitalism. In other words, democratic market socialism would be superior to democratic market capitalism. This assumes, of course, that socialism (public ownership of capital) is compatible with both market allocation and political democracy. I became convinced that such compatibility is not only theoretically possible, but is practically possible in the real world through the instrumentality of pragmatic market socialism.

At about the same time (as a freshman college student) that I encountered *The Power Elite* by C. Wright Mills, I encountered another pivotal figure in my intellectual development: Oskar Lange. During the dark days of the Great Depression in the 1930s, Lange had published in the *Review of Economic Studies* (a reputable theoretical journal) an essay entitled "On the Economic Theory of Socialism." In this essay, Lange outlined a plan for market socialism: a system that would combine public ownership of capital (socialism) with free market determination of most prices and production quantities. Such a system would not be prey to the inefficiencies of overly centralized economic planning such as was then being implemented in the Soviet Union. Prior to Lange, most orthodox socialists and orthodox economists, although poles apart on most issues, nevertheless agreed on one point: that socialism and the free market were contradictory concepts, and that the term "market socialism" (had anyone used it) would have been an oxymoron. Within the mainstream of 1930s Western neoclassical economics, Lange was regarded as a "brilliant young economist" who had made numerous impressive contributions to economic theory and econometrics. Therefore, when he asserted that contrary to prevailing opinion at the time, socialism and the free market *could* be combined successfully, this assertion could not readily be dismissed on grounds that its author was ignorant and/or mentally deficient. Following Lange, mainstream economists granted the possibility (grudgingly) of a market socialist economic system which would probably be at least somewhat more efficient and successful than the centrally planned socialist economic system of the USSR. Lange's insight had a much larger impact on me than it had on the typical mainstream economist. To me, this was no "theoretical curiosity." Rather it held potentially enormous significance since it pointed the way to an ideological reconciliation between East and West.

But almost as soon as I discovered Lange's work on market socialism, I concluded that many specific aspects of his scheme were probably impractical. For example, Lange proposed that, in general, production decisions of firm managers be guided by marginal cost pricing. Marginal cost pricing, while familiar to economists, is foreign to almost all real-world business decision-making. My "improvement" on Lange in this area was to propose that production decisions of firm managers be guided by profit maximization, the same goal which animates most real-world business decision-making. Similar adjustments were made in other areas. By the time I graduated from college in 1965, I had already developed a fairly detailed alternative market socialist blueprint designated "pragmatic market socialism" to distinguish it from "Langian market socialism."

The basic idea was that pragmatic market socialism would work almost identically to contemporary capitalism, with the key exception that capital property return generated by the business operations of large corporations would be returned, not mostly to a minority of wealthy capitalists as under capitalism, but to the overall labor force via a social dividend supplement to ordinary wage and salary income. Public ownership would be confined to large, established corporations; private ownership would be retained for small business and entrepreneurial business (i.e., business enterprises still being managed by their founder/owners). The latter exemption would address the concern that property income is an essential incentive to entrepreneurial endeavor. Whatever proportion of the total property return is an incentive to entrepreneurial endeavor under capitalism (a very small proportion in fact) would remain an incentive to entrepreneurial endeavor under pragmatic market socialism. Although I had effectively abandoned Langian market socialism as a practical reform proposal, it was expedient, in view of Lange's reputation, to do my Ph.D. dissertation ("The Administrative Costs of Langian Socialism") on his blueprint. But once I was awarded my Ph.D. from Northwestern University in 1971, I filed away my dissertation with a feeling of great relief that I would no longer have to waste time and energy on what was essentially a dead end proposal.

Thereafter, throughout the nearly 40 years of my career as an academic economist, I have devoted a very large proportion of my intellectual resources to developing the economic and political case for pragmatic market socialism. Despite the fact that the conclusions I reached contested the conventional consensus that any and all socialist endeavors, even market socialist endeavors, must necessarily be less efficient and/or dynamic than contemporary capitalism, I managed to publish quite a lot on the subject from the 1970s through the 1990s, including four books and over 20 articles in various scholarly journals. Among the small minority of economists who have noticed this work, the verdict seems to be that while I make an "interesting" case for pragmatic market socialism, the case is far from being sufficiently compelling to seriously challenge the overwhelming popular consensus in favor of capitalism.

In my own judgment, that consensus is not based on objective examination of the socialist alternative to capitalism, but rather manifests an emotional reaction to the horrific episode of unbridled tyranny during Joseph Stalin's dominion in the USSR. In the light of that horrific episode, most people have concluded that any form of public ownership socialism is too risky even to be contemplated. Arguments that the Stalinist terror was not caused by public ownership socialism, in and of itself, are not so much rejected as simply ignored. Perhaps this will change in the future; but until it does, prospects for public ownership socialism, outside of the remaining communist nations, are virtually nil.

During the years I labored on pragmatic market socialism, my principal motivation was not the relatively minor potential improvement in the socioeconomic situation within the industrialized nations that might have been realized by the implementation of pragmatic market socialism. I was realistic enough to recognize that a relatively minor economic reform could at most yield relatively minor benefits. The principal motivation was the possibility that the implementation of pragmatic market socialism in the West could have led to ideological reconciliation between East and West. The abandonment by the Western capitalist nations of capitalism and their adoption of socialism would have (hopefully) inspired the abandonment of central planning and the one-party state by the Eastern communist nations, and their adoption of respectively free market economies and multi-party democracy. The West would have evolved from democratic market capitalism to democratic market socialism; the East would have evolved from oligarchic planned socialism to democratic market socialism. From different starting points, both would have arrived at the ending point of democratic market socialism. This compromise solution to the ideological confrontation would have (hopefully) laid the basis for the World Economic Equalization Program and a world government.

Now, of course, most of the world seems to be converging on democratic market capitalism. A handful of communist nations, most notably the People's Republic of China, continue to uphold socialism and the one-party state. (It cannot be said, incidentally, that they continue to uphold central planning: the "responsibility system" in the contemporary PRC is almost unrecognizably distant from the classical socialist central planning developed in the USSR under Stalin.) The expectation among most people is that within the foreseeable future, the remaining communist nations will follow in the footsteps of the ex-USSR and the Eastern European nations, and renounce both socialism and the one-party state. Although any usefulness of pragmatic market socialism as an ideological bridge seems to have been eliminated by developments, I do not regret unduly the time and effort I spent over the last three decades developing and defending the concept. Pragmatic market socialism represents a worthwhile potential reform of the socioeconomic system, especially in the industrially advanced nations, and perhaps eventually it will be recognized as such.

But the important point is that ideological controversy has diminished tremendously throughout the world now that Marxist ideology no longer guides Russia and the other successor republics of the USSR. In consequence of the transformation, a very considerable amount of disarmament has taken place, and the probability of a devastating nuclear world war taking place within the immediate future seems to have reached an almost negligibly low level. There is no doubt that this is a time for great rejoicing among all humanity. Although the ideological impediment to world government is not dead, it certainly seems to be moribund. Unfortunately, the same cannot be said of the economic impediment to world government. But that impediment can also be overcome, although it will require some time and effort to do so.

The principal reason why it took 40 years to evolve this book from the initial insights of the winter of 1961-1962 is that for most of that time, I devoted most of my energy to work on pragmatic market socialism. I regarded the West's uncritical adherence to capitalism as the "logjam," so to speak, preventing the further economic and political progress of humanity. If that logjam could be broken up, then the flow of progress could be resumed: ideological reconciliation leading to disarmament leading to reallocation of economic resources from military purposes to global economic development ("swords into plowshares"). A world government would assist in the acceleration of global economic development, while at the same time global economic development would assist in the stabilization of world government. The economic and political aspects would interact in a mutually reinforcing, snowballing process toward a very high level of worldwide economic prosperity and a very stable and effective world government. Secure foundations would have been laid for the further progress of human civilization. But the whole scenario depended on first getting the populations of the leading Western nations to perceive the virtues of pragmatic market socialism (or some near-equivalent market socialist system). Of course, there was an analogous "logjam" on the other side of the ideological gap: i.e., the East's uncritical adherence to central planning and oligarchic governance. But since I personally had been born in the West, I reasoned that I could do nothing directly toward the correction of mistakes being made in the East. My hope was that if the West would take the initiative and start constructing an ideological bridge toward the East, the East would be inspired to construct the rest of the bridge from its side.

As it turned out, however, an ideological bridge was not necessary. The postwar policy of containment finally worked as intended. Ideological compromise between East and West was unnecessary, because in the end the East was compelled into ideological capitulation to the West, and thereupon in effect admitted that it had been in error all along on all three issues: capitalism versus socialism, market versus plan, and democracy versus oligarchy. Or at least the USSR, by far the most powerful of the communist nations, underwent an ideological capitulation in the early 1990s. In my personal judgment, of course, the USSR threw out the baby (socialism) along with the bath water (central planning and political oligarchy). But on the whole the event greatly improved the future prospects of humanity, since the reduction in nuclear war-risk immensely outweighed any possible advantages of democratic market socialism over democratic market capitalism.

A skeptic might find in this account grounds for disregarding the proposals put forward in this book for a World Economic Equalization Program and a limited world government tentatively designated the Federal Union of Democratic Nations. The skeptic could point to the fact that I, the author, spent decades trying to find a solution to the problem of ideological conflict—a problem that ultimately "solved itself" by means of the USSR's repudiation and abandonment of communism. Quite possibly, therefore, the problem of world economic inequality will "solve itself" without need for the intervention of a World Economic Equalization Program. Also quite possibly, the international system will soon achieve—assuming it has not already achieved—a very high level of safety and security without the foundation of a world government.

It would be futile for me to deny that these are indeed *possibilities*. They are both obviously "possible." But it is also obviously possible that a World Economic Equalization Program might greatly assure and hasten progress toward worldwide prosperity, and that a world government might greatly increase the level of worldwide safety and security, both currently and into the future. Anything is "possible"—the difficulty is in determining the relative *probabilities* of different outcomes under different courses of action. One of the fundamental themes of this book is that we cannot reliably determine the effects of a global economic development program and a global government unless we actually implement these things. Only actual experiment will provide useful information; anything less is mere speculation of very limited value. Certainly the evidence from an actual experiment could be quite unfavorable to the proposals of this book. The global economic development program might turn out to be a giant boondoggle that would have no perceptible improving effect on the living standards of the general populations of the poorer nations. And the global government might be so paralyzed by unending acrimonious debate that it will accomplish nothing. If these unfortunate outcomes were to come to pass, the global economic development program would be phased out, and the global government would be dissolved. But at least lessons would have been learned that would be useful to the future economic and political development of human civilization. I will argue in this book that given a reasonable amount of restraint and prudence in designing them, neither the direct costs nor the implied risks of these two initiatives (a global economic development program and a global government) would be excessive, given the potentially immense benefits.

But, it might be objected, if my own personal efforts to awaken interest in democratic market socialism in general and pragmatic market socialism in particular, have been so manifestly unsuccessful, on what basis can it be expected that efforts to awaken interest in global economic development and world government will be any more successful? After all, the great majority of the human population at the present time is just as skeptical of global economic development (through the mechanism of foreign aid), and of world government, as it is of socialism (in the pure sense of public ownership of capital property). As I see it, the fundamental practical impediment against the implementation of pragmatic market socialism or any other form of democratic market socialism was, and remains, the fact that there is an identifiable group of losers.

Specifically, that group would be the wealthy capitalists—individuals whose personal income is dominated by such property income components as dividends, interest and capital gains. Although there would be a considerable amount of financial compensation for capital property surrendered into public ownership, the compensation would not be so generous as to preclude any reduction in the living standards of wealthy capitalists. It may well be that those wealthy capitalists whose living standards would be lowered comprise less than 5 percent of the population, while the other 95 percent of the population would be financially benefited by social dividend distribution of capital property income. It may well be that the reduction of the living standards of that 5 percent would be fairly modest. But the fact remains that there would be some reduction in living standards for 5 percent of the population—there would be an identifiable group of losers. And that particular group, owing to its great wealth, wields disproportionate influence in political decision-making within even the most democratic polities. This disproportionate influence may well have been what actually checkmated pragmatic market socialism—not any inherent defects of the proposal.

On the other hand, with respect to the proposals presented herein for a World Economic Equalization Program and a limited world government (the Federal Union of Democratic Nations), there is no identifiable group of losers. Everyone in the world, from the wealthiest capitalists of the economically advanced nations to the poorest peasants of the less developed regions, stands to gain. The gains would be in terms of both higher material welfare and greater psychological peace of mind. Many people in the richer nations of the contemporary world will be especially skeptical that either a World Economic Equalization Program or a world government could possibly be consistent with the maintenance of their own high living standards. Given the fact that the great majority of the human population in the world today have quite low living standards, would not a democratically controlled world government be very likely to establish a global welfare state under which the populations of the rich nations would be heavily taxed in order to provide generous welfare benefits to the populations of the poor nations? This scenario I refer to as the "Crude Redistribution" scenario (the capitalization of the initial letters is intended because of the profound significance of the concept). A possible tendency toward Crude Redistribution in a democratically controlled world government cannot be denied and must not be minimized. Now that the ideological impediment to world government has been dramatically reduced by the ending of the Cold War, the economic impediment, as manifested in the tendency toward Crude Redistribution, is by far the most important remaining impediment. This problem must be addressed—and it must be addressed decisively and persuasively.

A twofold strategy is proposed for dealing with and overcoming the economic impediment to world government. The first component of the strategy is to design the world government in such a way that it would be difficult if not impossible for the poor nations to impose Crude Redistribution on the rich nations. I already mentioned two key provisions for ensuring this: the right of secession, and the right of nations to maintain whatever military forces and armaments they feel are necessary. The second right is the effective guarantor of the first right. Thus if the world government starting moving toward Crude Redistribution, the rich nations would simply depart from the government, and they would possess the military power to ensure that their wishes were respected.

In addition to this, the legislative branch of the Federal Union of Democratic Nations would utilize a "dual voting" mechanism under which measures would have to be approved on the basis of both the population vote and the material vote. In the population vote, the voting weight of each representative would be proportional to the population being represented, thus in this vote the populous poorer nations would be dominant. In the material vote, the voting weight of each representative would be proportional to Federal Union revenues derived from the representative's district, thus in this vote the less populous richer nations would be dominant. Thus the only measures capable of passage would be those on which both the rich nations and the poor nations could achieve a reasonable degree of consensus. The rich nations would be able to block moves toward Crude Redistribution, while at the same time the poor nations would be able to block measures of which they disapprove, perhaps because they appear to reestablish conditions of colonial exploitation, or perhaps because they appear to embody unduly restrictive environmental regulations. Hopefully this voting provision will forestall such drastic eventualities as nations seceding from the world government under threat of war if their departure is opposed. Of course, the dual voting mechanism might result in a deadlocked legislature and an ineffective world government. But if so, the situation would be no worse than the various deadlocks of the present time owing to the fact that there is no effective source of governance in the world above the national governments (the United

Nations clearly does not qualify as such).

This first component of the strategy (dual voting in the world government legislature, and the retained national rights to secession and armaments) is the short-term solution to the problem of world economic inequality. The long-term solution to the problem is to eliminate the inequality. This is where the World Economic Equalization Program (WEEP) comes into play. But, the skeptic will surely ask, how can one possibly eliminate the problem of world economic inequality without engaging in Crude Redistribution? My response is that over a significant but not excessively lengthy period of time (perhaps 50 years), it would be possible to eliminate the problem of world economic inequality on the basis of "Common Progress." (Once again, capitalization of initial letters is appropriate in view of the fundamental importance of the concept.)

The Common Progress concept is that throughout the operation of the global economic development program, living standards in *all* nations of the world, rich and poor, would continue to advance (progress would be "common" to all). However, the *rate of increase* of living standards in the rich nations would be somewhat lower in order that the *rate of increase* of living standards in the poor nations could be higher. Transfers from the rich nations to the poor nations would definitely not consist of current consumption output. Rather the transfers would consist of "generalized capital," a term which I have coined to encompass three separate types of capital: business physical capital (plant and machinery used by business enterprises); social overhead capital (roads, schools, hospitals, etc., built under public auspices); and human capital (knowledge and skills inculcated in the labor force by means of education and training). The rate of increase in the generalized capital stocks of the rich nations would be reduced in order that the rate of increase in the generalized capital stocks of the poor nations be increased. Thus Common Progress, in contrast to Crude Redistribution, would be a politically acceptable means of moving toward the reduction of world economic inequality to an acceptable level equivalent to the inequality level presently existing within politically stable nations.

At this point, the skeptic will surely object that in view of the failure of foreign aid in the past to significantly ameliorate the problem of world economic inequality, there is absolutely no basis for thinking that an expansion of foreign aid will do so. This is like saying that because a pinprick will not fell an elephant, there is no reason to expect a bullet to fell an elephant. The reason why foreign aid has not cured the problem is that in the past the amount of foreign aid has been inadequate to the task. This proposition may be supported by more than theoretical speculation. In Chapter 6, "A World Economic Equalization Program," I present results from computer simulation of a model (the "WEEP model") of global economic development under conditions of massive foreign aid transfers from the rich nations to the poor nations. What is so remarkable about these results is that they not only show rapid economic progress being made in the poor nations but at the same time rapid economic progress continues in the rich nations. Comparison of these projected results with projected results if there were no global economic development program (i.e., foreign aid maintained at the current low levels) demonstrates that the WEEP does in fact impose a cost on the rich nations in terms of a lower rate of growth—but the diminution in growth is so minor as to be veritably unnoticeable. Living standards in the rich nations would continue to rise at a very good rate despite the aid program.

The results suggest that the notion of "Common Progress" is by no means unattainable in the real world. Needless to emphasize, results from computer simulation of a simplified model of the world economy will not necessarily accurately forecast real-world results. All these results do is to demonstrate the possibility of dramatic economic progress. They suggest that it would be worthwhile to make the effort: to initiate a real-world WEEP in the hope that it will be effective. If this hope is disappointed, then the experiment would be discontinued. The populations of the rich nations would then have clear consciences because the futility of real-world economic equalization will have been demonstrated by means of a definitive experiment.

The basic results shown in Chapter 6 herein were preceded in the economics literature by two articles and a book. My first article on the subject, entitled "A World Economic Equalization Program: Results of a Simulation," appeared in the *Journal of Developing Areas* in January 1976. The WEEP model in that case was comprised of only six "regions" defined in terms of per capita income. This was followed by "A World Economic Equalization Program: Refinements and Sensitivity Analysis," published in *World Development* in August 1988. This second article added a rudimentary validation analysis (determining how closely model results fit real-world results) and fairly extensive sensitivity analysis (determining how the simulation results are affected by changes in the numerical values of model parameters). But it retained the six per capita income regions. My book *Common Progress: The Case for a World Economic Equalization Program*, published in 2000, is based on simulation results from a far more disaggregated model comprised of 140 nations rather than six per capita income regions. It also contains far more elaborate validation and sensitivity analyses. Notwithstanding their various technical differences, the two articles and the book are agreed on the same fundamental point: that a sufficiently large foreign development assistance effort could greatly accelerate economic progress in the poor nations without seriously retarding economic progress in the rich nations. They all agree that the Common Progress scenario is within the realm of possibility. They all agree that it might be possible to entirely overcome the economic impediment to world government within a reasonably abbreviated period of historical time in the order of 50 years. This would be the long-term solution to the problem of world economic inequality which so much vexes us today.

While the great majority of my intellectual effort over the past 40 years has been devoted to trying to find a solution to the ideological problem through pragmatic market socialism and trying to find a solution to the economic problem through the World Economic Equalization Program, I did devote some effort to reflecting on the possible shape of the world government to be made possible by ideological harmonization and economic equalization. Although ideological harmonization could be achieved almost overnight by means of appropriate attitude adjustments, the economic gap would obviously take an extended period of time to overcome even assuming that a massive global economic development program was in operation. During that period of time, tendencies toward Crude Redistribution would be an ever-present threat. My initial thought was that at first only the economically advanced nations would be full members of the world government (i.e., voting members) while the poorer nations would be associate (non-voting) members. But within a fairly short period of time, I scrapped the notion of full and associate members of the world government in favor of the three fundamental provisions already outlined: (1) member nations to retain the right of secession; (2) member nations to retain the right to armaments; and (3) the dual voting system in the world government legislature. These and other basic characteristics of the world government were first set forth in a lengthy unpublished manuscript dating from the 1972-1973 academic year: a book with the working title *The Grand Convergence: Economic and Political Aspects of Human Progress.*

At the time I composed *The Grand Convergence*, I was a junior-level faculty member with a freshly minted Ph.D., a heavy teaching load, and a negligible publication record. With great optimism and much youthful enthusiasm, I set out to codify the grand scenario of pragmatic market socialism leading to ideological harmonization, ideological harmonization leading to disarmament, a global economic development program, and world government. As it turned out, I was not yet ready for such a comprehensive and ambitious project. The result was dogmatic, diffuse, unfocused and far too long. Although I never quite completed the entire book, the typescript ran to over 950 pages, without counting dozens of additional pages to be devoted to tables and charts. I approached a few publishers with the project in the spring of 1973, but not surprisingly they declined interest. As a junior-level, untenured faculty member at that time, it was important, for purposes of preserving my academic career, to accumulate some publications, and so I turned my attention to articles. Many of them were on market socialism but by no means all. Between the early 1970s and the present, I have published around 75 articles, of which only around 20 are on market socialism. Intellectual curiosity has taken me in a number of directions, and the majority of my articles have nothing to do with such visionary projects as pragmatic market socialism, global economic development, or world government. No doubt this is another factor in the long gestation between my initial enlightenment in the winter of 1961-1962 and this book. *The Grand Convergence* laid out the entire vision, but a very large proportion of the entire manuscript dealt with the subject of pragmatic market socialism, which at the time I hoped would be the instrument for breaking up the "logjam" in the river of human progress. I did get a certain limited amount of "mileage" out of that specific material. In the mid-

1970s I shortened and refined it, and after a long and frustrating search for a publisher, it eventually appeared in 1979 under the title *Socialism in the Free Market*. This book attracted no attention either at the time or thereafter.

By the mid-1980s, I felt that I was ready for another effort at a book. The emphasis on market socialism was clearly manifested by the working title: *Pragmatic Market Socialism: An Economic and Political Appraisal*. This was a far more professionally competent and focused production, to some extent because by this time I had published several substantial articles on market socialism in the periodical literature. The third and shortest part of the manuscript dealt with the possible role of pragmatic market socialism as a potential ideological bridge between East and West, and thereby as a potential steppingstone to world government. This was part of the "political" appraisal of pragmatic market socialism, as opposed to the "economic" appraisal. Most of my journal articles on market socialism focused on narrowly defined economic questions, although I did eventually publish two articles on the ideological dimension: "Ideological Harmonization as a Means of Promoting Authentic Détente: A False Hope?" (*Coexistence*, 1982), and "New Prospects for East-West Ideological Convergence: A Market Socialist Viewpoint" (*Coexistence*, 1993). In addition, I published one article that went beyond ideological harmonization to the world government itself: "Practical Considerations in Designing a Supernational Federation" (*World Futures*, 1985).

Getting back to the book *Pragmatic Market Socialism: An Economic and Political Appraisal*, the typescript for this amounted to 1,300 pages by the time I approached the publishers in the spring of 1988. Most of them immediately cited excessive length as a reason for declining interest. By the fall of 1988 I reluctantly concluded that the manuscript as it then existed was unpublishable. Not only was length a problem, but in addition to that, the advent of the reformer Mikhail Gorbachev in the Soviet Union promised to drastically revise the international situation. It was beginning to look as though pragmatic market socialism might not be needed after all as an ideological bridge between East and West and a first step in the direction of world government. Should the USSR and its Eastern European satellite nations abandon communism and become fully democratic market capitalist nations, then ideological harmonization would have been achieved without benefit of pragmatic market socialism. Such an outcome would have seemed veritably miraculous only a few years previously, but by the latter 1980s it was recognized by everyone as a very strong possibility.

In response both to the length problem and to the epochal transitions then occurring in the world, I developed two successor manuscripts from *Pragmatic Market Socialism*. Material from the approximately 1,150 pages on pragmatic market socialism was radically condensed into a book entitled *Socialism Revised and Modernized: The Case for Pragmatic Market Socialism*, published by Praeger in 1992. Material from the approximately 150 pages on world government was considerably expanded into a book entitled *World Union on the Horizon: The Case for Supernational Federation*, published by University Press of America in 1993. By the time these books appeared, the USSR had been dissolved and it was generally agreed that the Cold War was, if not completely dead, at least moribund. Although it was by now quite clear that the role for pragmatic market socialism as an ideological bridge was virtually extinct, the sheer force of momentum kept me contributing on the subject throughout most of the 1990s. I felt that I had a few more things to say on the subject, and in addition to half a dozen articles, I published three more books on market socialism: *Capitalism versus Pragmatic Market Socialism: A General Equilibrium Evaluation* (Kluwer, 1993), *Economic Justice: The Market Socialist Vision* (Rowman & Littlefield, 1997), and *On the Political Economy of Market Socialism: Essays and Analyses* (Ashgate, 2001). This last was not original work, but was a compilation of 14 previously published articles on market socialism that had originally appeared between 1975 and 1997. One other task remained prior to my commencing work on another book—the present book—on world government. That task was further computer simulation work using the WEEP model. This work was published in 2000 in the book *Common Progress*, mentioned earlier.

Much of the substance of the present book was in fact included in my 1993 book entitled *World Union on the Horizon: The Case for Supernational Federation*. For example, the proposal for a Federal Union of Democratic Nations in that book parallels the proposal for a Federal Union of Democratic Nations in this book. The WEEP model simulation results reported in Chapter 4 of *World Union* (based on the 1988 *World Development* article) parallel the WEEP model results reported in Chapter 6 of this book (based on the 2000 Praeger book). To my disappointment, *World Union on the Horizon* attracted very little attention, either at the time of publication or thereafter. I was, however, somewhat gratified that Derek Heater, in his 1996 historical survey of world government thinking (*World Citizenship and Government: Cosmopolitan Ideas in the History of Western Political Thought*) devoted a few pages to *World Union*, and described its world government proposal as "meaty and original." But to my knowledge, Prof. Heater's comments are the only reference to the Federal Union proposal ever to have appeared in either the popular or professional literature on international relations and organization.

On what do I base my present hopes that *Political Globalization* will not meet with the same fate of "instant oblivion" that met *World Union on the Horizon*? First and foremost, as a result of its background *World Union* devoted quite a bit of attention to pragmatic market socialism as a potential bridge over the ideological gap between East and West. By the time was the book was circulated to publishers in the early 1990s, the Cold War was widely considered to be at an end, and there was no further apparent need for an ideological bridge (even assuming one had been feasible). So the book seemed dated and out of touch with current events. This book, in contrast, focuses almost exclusively on the economic and nationalistic impediments to world government on the presumption that the ideological impediment is virtually extinct.

In addition to its misplaced emphasis, the earlier book devoted almost no attention to comparing and contrasting the Federal Union of Democratic Nations proposal to other world government proposals, thus possibly generating the misapprehension that the Federal Union proposal was not fundamentally innovative. This book goes into considerable detail on the historical background of the world government concept, and also on the "conventional" world government proposal of the post-World War II era, which envisions a militarily dominant world government operating among totally disarmed member nations. I fully agree with world government skeptics that such a plan, if implemented, would likely be a one-way ticket to global tyranny.

But if the evaluation of world government is in terms of a limited world government rather than an omnipotent world government, then the danger of global tyranny would be reduced to an acceptable level—a level well beneath the danger of eventual nuclear holocaust brought on by the sovereign nation-state system of today. While the short-term nuclear war-risk has been greatly reduced by the decline of the Cold War, there are still large stockpiles of operational nuclear weapons in today's world, and our long-term prospects—in light of the repeated lessons of history—are not so rosy. In the final analysis, there is no avoiding risk of some kind. If we do not form a world government, there is a greater risk of eventual nuclear holocaust. If we do form a world government, there is a greater risk of global tyranny. But I will argue herein that if the world government is properly designed, the latter risk will be minimal.

Finally, my exposition of the case for world government in *World Union on the Horizon* was mostly rather abstract and lacking in empirical content (perhaps the unconscious result of my own educational background and teaching credentials in economic theory). The present book endeavors to flesh out the abstract arguments with a considerable amount of historical and political detail. Many topical discussions in the book are quite independent of other topical discussions. So it is certainly not necessary to read the entire book in order to attain a good grasp of its nature and contents. In a strictly logical sense, a goodly amount of the descriptive and narrative material contained in this book does not bear directly and unambiguously on the basic question of whether or not a world government would be a good thing. But the fact is that this question cannot be answered by means of logical argumentation based on universally accepted empirical realities. In the end, one must make an intuitive judgment based on a great mass of what can only be described, using a legal term, as "circumstantial evidence." Nevertheless, it is my hope that this book will awaken many of its readers to the potential advantages that may reside in federal world government, in the same way that I myself was awakened to these potential advantages in that long-ago winter of 1961-1962.

James A. Yunker
Macomb, Illinois
April 2007

PART I

A NEW APPROACH
TO WORLD GOVERNMENT

1

FEDERAL WORLD GOVERNMENT:
INTRODUCTION AND OVERVIEW

Aspirations among humanity toward federal world government became greatly intensified during the hundred year period, now part of history, known as the twentieth century. The devastating experiences of World War I (1914-1918) and World War II (1939-1945) brought into sharp focus two fundamental realities. First, self-righteously sovereign nation-states are strongly predisposed toward confrontation and warfare among one another, and the great strength of this predisposition limits the effectiveness of diplomatic maneuvers intended to preserve or restore a stable balance of power. Second, owing to dramatic progress in science and technology, in combination with the size and economic power of the largest nation-states, the sheer destructiveness of warfare has reached tremendous proportions far beyond anything witnessed throughout all prior human history. The destruction of two Japanese cities, Hiroshima and Nagasaki, by atomic bombs at the end of World War II, foretold of possible future wars of a level of destructiveness, conceivably, so overwhelming as to set the human race sliding irrevocably downward toward physical extinction.

In the years immediately following World War II, interest in world government reached a peak unprecedented in history. Just as the largest national governments had established peaceful and secure conditions over huge territories and vast populations, so too a world government might be able to establish peaceful and secure conditions over the entire face of the planet. Such an outcome was especially urgent in view of the apparent capacity of nuclear weapons not merely to devastate human civilization, but to terminate it. Unfortunately, as a consequence of the Cold War conflict that rapidly developed during the post-World War II years between the communist East and the noncommunist West, interest in world government soon declined. Amid post-war chaos, the communist ideological movement flourished. The Soviet Union exploited its military occupation of Eastern Europe to forcibly install communist governments in several countries. At the same time, it provided military assistance to communist forces in China, enabling the establishment of the People's Republic of China in 1949. Inasmuch as the communist movement aspired toward the revolutionary overthrow of the capitalist socioeconomic system throughout the world, these developments aroused intense anxiety throughout the noncommunist West. It was widely feared that a world government, if established, would quickly be subverted by the communists and turned into a tool of communist expansion. At the same time, the communists entertained an exactly analogous apprehension: that a world government would quickly be turned into a reactionary tool for the overthrow of communist regimes in Russia, China and elsewhere. Given the pressures and anxieties of the time, it is not surprising that the world government movement quickly lost momentum.

As the Cold War progressed throughout the second half of the twentieth century, apprehensions that a world state, if established, would quickly become an instrument toward the imposition of communistic totalitarianism, were increasingly supplemented by a second apprehension of great seriousness. This is the apprehension that a world state, if it were established, would become an instrument toward the imposition of a worldwide welfare state through which the populations of the rich nations would be impoverished. A world state, it is feared, might well impose confiscatory taxation on the rich nations (the United States, Japan, the Western European nations, and so on) for the purpose of providing welfare benefits to the populations of the poor nations of Asia, Africa and Latin America (the "Third World"). This could happen even if—or perhaps *especially* if—the world state was democratically organized, in view of the fact that the "teeming masses" of the Third World greatly outnumber the populations of the relatively small number of rich, noncommunist nations of the "First World." This potential problem of world government has come into much sharper focus as a result of the Cold War. According to the Marxist theory underpinning communist ideology, the coming socialist revolution will directly and dramatically benefit the impoverished proletariat. Since the impoverished proletariat is especially numerous in the nations of the Third World, the Second World nations (the Soviet Union, Red China, and their allies and satellites) looked to these nations for potential future support. As a result, the First World nations became far more conscious of the economic gap than they had ever been in the past. Greater awareness of this gap contributed to apprehensions that the principle of redistribution of income, widely accepted within nations (up to a limited point), might be extended to the international arena if all of humanity were to be politically united within a single world government.

Thus, in the minds of the populations of the First World nations, world government came to be perceived as a potential threat to their welfare even greater than the threat of unrestricted nuclear warfare. This latter threat was (and is), after all, not all that great—according to the predominant contemporary consensus. True, a full-scale nuclear war, if it were to take place, would be unimaginably horrible and destructive. But (according to the consensus logic) there is an extremely small—almost microscopically small—probability that such a war will ever take place. Nuclear weapons are sufficiently abundant, and delivery systems are sufficiently reliable, that conditions of Mutual Assured Destruction (MAD) have been achieved. The costs of nuclear war would be so overwhelming to all nations involved, including those initiating the war, that no national leader will ever seriously contemplate launching such a war. Nuclear disaster would be so huge, so terrible, and so universal, that owing to the fundamental rationality of mankind it will never occur. Of course, the possibility exists that this reasoning, as conventional and widespread as it may be, represents merely wishful thinking, and that when it is finally recognized as such (in the wake of nuclear disaster), it will be too late.

Humanity has not yet experienced a nuclear world war, but most of us believe that we have a fairly clear idea of what would be involved—and it would not be pleasant. Nevertheless, we believe that there are "fates worse than death," even worse than the especially horrible deaths that would be occasioned by nuclear world war. In the minds of most citizens of the United States, for example, to live under a communistic socioeconomic system would be worse than death. Equally so, it would be worse than death to live under the noxious burden of confiscatory taxation for purposes of funding a worldwide welfare state. The option of helping to establish, and then participating in a world government, is rejected by the U.S. population on grounds that to do so would substantially increase the probability of being subjected to communism and/or confiscatory taxation at some point in the future.

Strictly speaking, it is not an either-or choice. Presumably at least a few people in the United States would opt for the communist socioeconomic system, and/or confiscatory taxation, if it were *an absolute certainty* that the only alternative to these was nuclear world war. But, of course, it is *not* an absolute certainty that nuclear world war will occur if the U.S. population declines to establish a communist socioeconomic system, or declines to support a worldwide welfare state. Equally, it is *not* an absolute certainty that nuclear world war will occur if the U.S. population does not help to establish, and does not participate in, a world government. What is involved, in rejecting the world government possibility, is a calculated risk. The people of the United States (along with most of the rest of the world population) have presumably carefully weighed up the relative costs and benefits of a world government, along with their respective probabilities, and have concluded that their future prospects are more favorable without a world government in existence than with one in existence.

A MISCALCULATED RISK

I will argue in this book that this particular calculated risk has been badly miscalculated. In actual fact, the future prospects of humanity would be appreciably better with a functioning world government in place than without one. Furthermore, what is true of humanity as a whole is true of the human populations of each and every nation in the world. This is true of the rich nations, the poor nations, the large nations, the small nations, the noncommunist nations, the communist nations, the ex-communist nations, the Christian nations, the Islamic nations, the Hindu nations, the Buddhist nations—and if there are some nations that do not fit into any of the above categories, it is also true of those nations. Federal world government should be the next step taken in the political development of human civilization. For the first time in human history, we have the incentive and we have the means to establish a benign and effective world government. If we wait for "more propitious circumstances" to establish such a government, at best we will be significantly retarding human progress relative to what might be achieved, and at worst, we may inflict upon ourselves a disastrous future that will be even more tragic for being unnecessary.

The argument advanced herein relies only to a very minor extent on the traditional accusation among world federalists that humanity is seriously underestimating both the cost of nuclear world war and the probability that such a war will occur within the near future if we persist with the sovereign nation-state system of today. Although I personally believe that both the costs and the probability of nuclear war are being somewhat underestimated (albeit I would leave out the "within the near future" part), the ineffectiveness of this argument has been convincingly demonstrated by recent history. Even at the height of the Cold War, when the nuclear threat was obviously far greater than it is at the present time, world federalists tried in vain in muster support for world government by brandishing the prospect of nuclear holocaust. In the judgment of the overwhelming majority of the population, in all walks of life and throughout the world, nuclear holocaust constituted an acceptable risk, as weighed against the greater risks inherent in world government. Following the collapse and dissolution of the USSR in 1991, the near-term threat of nuclear war has greatly receded, hence appeals for world government based on this threat will be even less effective than they were throughout the Cold War period. Therefore, relatively little reference will be made herein to the threat of nuclear war.

The argument advanced herein instead relies primarily on the proposition that humanity is seriously *over*estimating the risks that would be involved in world government. I hasten to add that this is true only of a *properly designed* world government. If one imagines a strongly authoritative and highly activist world government, a government that would interact with the governments of the component nation-states exactly as the federal government of the contemporary United States interacts today with the governments of the 50 component states, then there would indeed exist a very substantial probability of a disastrous outcome. If we imagine a world government possessed of a monopoly on nuclear weapons, it could, under extreme circumstances, threaten uncooperative nation-states with mass destruction should they persist in opposing the established policy of the world government. Even if nuclear weapons have been abolished, a world government possessed of a monopoly on conventional heavy weaponry would be in basically the same position as one possessed of a monopoly on nuclear weaponry. If we further imagine that the high officials of this world government have been democratically elected by the world population, most of whom are desperately poor by the standards of a handful of wealthy nations, it is not too difficult to perceive the possibility that the world government might decide that it would be beneficial to this impoverished majority to carry out very substantial income redistribution financed by heavy taxation of the handful of wealthy nations.

Should this handful of wealthy nations refuse to pay the heavy tax assessments required by the redistribution program, the world government could threaten them with nuclear destruction. Or, presuming the world government refrains from anything so barbaric as threats of nuclear destruction, or is unable to make such threats because nuclear weapons have been abolished, it could threaten the wealthy nations with invasion by an army equipped with machine guns, tanks and heavy artillery. If the only forces at the disposal of the wealthy nations consisted of police units equipped with small arms, these nations would be virtually helpless in the face of such a threat. No doubt pockets of armed resistance would remain in the wealthy nations, but these would be gradually whittled down by hordes of secret police and internal security forces unleashed by the world government. Dissidents of all kinds, whether engaged in armed resistance or mere verbal opposition, would be rounded up and shipped off to concentration camps for re-education—or elimination. The final outcome would be a nightmarish period of terror and oppression comparable to that experienced by the Soviet people during the worst years of Stalinist tyranny.

Certain democratic nations, such as India, show a high level of political stability today despite the long-term persistence of a very high level of economic inequality. A fairly strong case might be made, therefore, that this particular scenario would be extremely unlikely to materialize even if a potential future world government *did* possess a monopoly on both nuclear weapons and conventional heavy weapons, and even if the economic gap which exists today *were* to persist into the remote and indefinite future. But the probability of such a scenario under those circumstances, while it might be small, would certainly not be negligible. Similar conflicts of interest might also develop on matters unrelated to economic living standards: on matters such as ideological, religious or cultural differences. As a result, it is absolutely necessary that any proposed world government, in order to be seriously contemplated, be subject to appropriate limitations and constraints designed to safeguard the vital interests of the various national populations, and to reduce the probability of a totalitarian outcome to an acceptably low level. The fundamental thesis of this book is that, contrary to presently dominant opinion, a world government can and should be established—a world government that would represent an acceptable compromise between the competing objectives of protecting the essential short-term interests of the various national populations, and at the same time favoring the essential long-term interests of the entire human population.

The world government proposal which I shall outline and develop in this book is for a world state somewhere between the United Nations of today, an organization that is essentially little more than an assemblage of speech-making ambassadors, and the full-scale, highly authoritative, extremely centralized state entity conceived by the typical world federalist from the latter 1940s (the immediate post-World War II period) through to the present time. The United Nations is certainly a step in the right direction, and its existence and operations have certainly yielded some benefits to humanity. But it was founded just as the Cold War between East and West was beginning, and the constraints on it that were necessitated by the realpolitik of that period effectively hobbled it as an instrument for peace in the contemporary world. At the same time, those world federalists who envision the instantaneous elimination of the threat of nuclear holocaust, as well as the threat of major wars fought with conventional weapons, through the foundation of a very strong, very dominant world government, are indeed hopelessly naive and unrealistic. Those world federalists may eventually be proved correct in their contention that what is actually naive and unrealistic is the conventional belief that the sovereign nation-state system of the contemporary world can be allowed to go on indefinitely into the remote future without the occurrence of disastrous wars. But if they are proved correct in this, it will be through the occurrence of those wars, and then, of course, it will be too late. Until those wars actually occur, it is most unlikely that the human race will recognize in them a threat equal to or greater than the threat of totalitarianism imposed by an all-powerful world state—unless it can be demonstrated that a properly designed world state need not entail a serious threat of totalitarianism.

What the human race as a whole has not yet recognized is that a world state does not have to be all-powerful in order to make a worthwhile contribution to the future prospects of human civilization. The specific world government proposal that will form the basis for the general consideration and evaluation herein of the world government possibility, is tentatively designated the Federal Union of Democratic Nations. The use of the word "democratic" in the proposed name should not be taken to imply that membership would be restricted to nations that *presently* implement high standards of democratic accountability—but merely that all member nations *intend* to implement these standards. The Federal Union would be a legitimate state entity: it would have a capital city and a permanent organization, its high officials would be directly elected by the citizens, it would possess the power to make binding laws and to levy mandatory taxes, it would raise and maintain military forces, and it would display the conventional emblems and trappings of state authority.

On the other hand, it would be subject to several key restrictions that are certainly not typical of the nation-states of today. Two such restrictions are especially important. First, the member nation-states of the Federal Union of Democratic Nations would possess the permanent and inalienable right to peaceful and unopposed secession from the Federal Union at their own unilateral discretion. Second, the member nation-states of the Federal Union of Democratic Nations would possess the permanent and inalienable right to maintain military forces under their direct control of whatever strength and weaponry (including nuclear weaponry) is deemed necessary and appropriate by the governments of these nation-states. There are certain other characteristics of the proposed Federal Union of Democratic Nations that depart from the normal characteristics of present-day nation-states, and that would serve to weaken its authority and effectiveness relative to its component nation-states. But these two are the most important.

To the typical, conventionally-minded world federalist of today, these two characteristics of the proposed world government—the right of member nation-states to secede at any time, and the right of member nation-states to maintain whatever military forces and weaponry they wish to—would doubtless be deemed thoroughly unacceptable. In the minds of "traditional" world federalists, such characteristics would surely defeat the purpose of world government. Such a world government, to their way of thinking, would not represent a significant, meaningful, worthwhile advance beyond the United Nations of today, an institution that has proven, beyond a reasonable doubt, its incapacity to significantly reduce the danger of warfare. In order to be truly effective in abolishing warfare, the world government would have to maintain a monopoly, or near-monopoly, on heavy weaponry, and it would also have to be ready at all times to return errant nation-states to the fold.

It must be made clear from the outset that the present proposal for world government is not addressed primarily to those who already believe in the cause of world government. At the present time, those individuals who advocate world government represent a tiny, veritably microscopic fraction of the total human population—a tiny fraction regarded by the majority as hopelessly ignorant, foolish and/or misguided, as simplistic enthusiasts pursuing impossible utopias. I would anticipate that most current proponents of world government (who are, in fact, far more intelligent, sensible and realistic than is commonly supposed) will grasp the essential nature of the case for world government that I am offering, and will recognize its basic validity, somewhat more readily and quickly than will the typical opponent of world government. But if the case can be grasped and appreciated *only* by those who already advocate world government, then nothing will have been accomplished. A tiny and impotent minority will remain a tiny and impotent minority. What I am trying to do in this book is to reach beyond that tiny minority, out into the mainstream of human thinking, to revise and reshape the consensus understanding, perception and evaluation among all humanity of world government. Therefore, it is not a major problem that most world federalists of the present day will not immediately recognize and appreciate the contribution to the future prospects of human civilization that could be made by the proposed Federal Union of Democratic Nations.

THE VISION OUTLINED

At the present time, both the proponents and the opponents of world government tend to envision world government as an extremely powerful and activist state entity in international affairs. Proponents see this power and activism as a positive development because it would very quickly and drastically reduce the threat of warfare, especially nuclear warfare. Opponents see this power and activism as a negative development, because it would very quickly and drastically increase the possibility of oppression of various national populations by the world government. Neither perception would apply to a world government which would merely be *somewhat* powerful and activist—not *extremely* powerful and activist.

The Federal Union of Democratic Nations being put forward for consideration in this book is based on a fundamentally novel and original perception of the nature and purposes of world government. The idea underlying the Federal Union is not to instantly achieve a radical improvement in the current operation of human civilization. The idea is rather to lay a firmer and more reliable foundation on which to base future progress. The fundamental proposition which I shall argue in this book is that the expected rate of future progress of human civilization will be higher if a world government along the lines of the proposed Federal Union of Democratic Nations is established, than if no such government is established. It is emphatically *not* part of this fundamental proposition that the foundation of a world government would *directly and immediately* improve the human condition. A world government would be no more and no less than an investment in the future.

For as long as there have been advocates of world government, skeptics have dismissed them as deluded visionaries building castles in the sky, proposing impossible utopias, and longing for imaginary paradises on the earthly plane. Although this typical perception of world federalists by conventional-minded skeptics is exaggerated, I will not waste much effort contesting it. In any event, there is certainly more than a little justification for this perception. No doubt in the past most world federalists were indeed prone to concentrate far too much on the putative benefits to be derived from world government, to the exclusion of any careful consideration of possible problems and perils. In addition, they tended either to be excessively vague about the institutional framework of world government, or, at the opposite extreme, they produced detailed constitutions for world government based too closely on those of existing national governments, constitutions that failed to take into account the special difficulties confronting the successful establishment of a world government. In evaluating the charge of utopianism, however, we must also take into account the historical circumstances, the existing state of the world at any point in time. Conceivably it was legitimate, as of 1900, to brand world federalists as "deluded utopians" whose views could safely be ignored. Conceivably it was still legitimate to do this as of 1950. This does not mean that it was still legitimate to do this as of 2000, or that it is still legitimate to do this today. Between 1950 and 2000 the world changed dramatically. Between 1900 and 2000 the changes were still more dramatic. What might well have been "utopian" in 1900 or in 1950 might not be at all "utopian" today.

Of course, utilization of the "utopian" epithet by opponents of world government is in reality a slur and a smear, an effort to derail calm, logical and rational contemplation of the concept through appeal to prejudice and preconception. It is in the same basic category as utilization of such terms as "police state" and "giant bureaucracy" to describe the imagined characteristics of a world government. The term "utopia" connotes a polity so harmonious and well-ordered that its citizens would be permanently exhilarated and euphoric, in the same psychic state associated with the heavenly paradise promised by many of the great religions of the world. Without speculating on the likelihood or unlikelihood of this condition being achieved by individual human beings following their respective deaths, I will state here, without qualification or equivocation, that it is my absolute belief that this condition will never, ever be achieved by any individual human being within his/her temporal lifespan—even if a world government is indeed established. Relative to the imaginable (but impossible) condition of heavenly bliss, the long-term improvement in the human condition which would be brought about by the foundation of a world government, would be modest indeed. But this fact does not diminish the importance of the strong possibility that world government would most likely significantly improve the long-term human condition *relative to what it is likely to be* if no world government is ever established.

Critics of world government desirous of conducting the debate more fairly and impartially, with less reliance on prejudices and preconceptions which may be fundamentally invalid, might consider the term "impossible," rather than "utopian," to describe the world government concept. "Impossible" is not so loaded a term as "utopian"—although it is still somewhat loaded. This because if something is truly, literally impossible, then there would be no point in considering whether it is desirable or undesirable. But clearly, a world government is not truly, literally impossible. Humanity could certainly establish such a government, although if the critics are correct, we would soon regret the action. In order to conduct the debate in the fairest and most impartial manner, critics of world government should assert that such a government would be "undesirable." This gets to the heart of the matter. This allegation invites calm, logical and rational contemplation of the world government possibility. Why, we are encouraged to ask, is it undesirable? And why might it be, to the contrary, desirable? These are the legitimate questions that need to be addressed, considered, discussed and resolved if we are to arrive at a reasonably reliable and valid judgment on the issue of world government.

One of the major obstacles to focused, sensible discussion of the world government idea is the multiplicity of plans for world government which have been put forward over the course of time. Plans for world government especially proliferated during the tumultuous twentieth century. Unfortunately for the cause of world government, most if not all of these plans merely extrapolated existing patterns of federal national government into the international realm. The basic idea was merely to employ the basic political structure of the United States of America, for example, as a template for the proposed political structure of a future United States of the World. In other words, little if any consideration was given to possible institutional structures and operational principles for coping with the well-known obstacles to world government: ideological conflicts, the economic gap, and the force of nationalism, among others.

The Federal Union of Democratic Nations under consideration here does in fact incorporate a number of specific institutional structures and operational principles intended to cope with various obstacles, real and imagined, to world government. But I certainly do not want to commit the sin of "premature specificity" (as Richard Falk has termed it), thus I will refrain from such things as a draft constitution and detailed organizational specifics. On the other hand, to enable a coherent, organized and focused consideration of the world government possibility in general, I deem it essential that the reader have a fairly clear and precise understanding of the specific world government proposal being advanced. Therefore, a reasonably detailed institutional, operational proposal will be described early in the book (in Chapter 2), so that there will be a solid basis for the discussion to follow. I will now provide a brief preliminary overview of that proposal.

The Federal Union of Democratic Nations would be a full-fledged state entity, comprised of legislative, executive and judicial branches. It would have a capital city, and a standing armed force termed the Union Security Force. Elections for high positions in the government would be on a quinquennial basis (once every five years). The legislature would be a unicameral body, designated the Union Chamber of Representatives, consisting of approximately 200 Union Representatives, directly elected by the populations of their respective districts for terms of five years. The Union Chamber would have the power to make laws and issue policy directives within its area of authority, as well as the power to alter and amend the annual financial budget prepared by the executive branch. The head of the executive branch would be designated the Union Chief Executive, an individual elected by popular vote of the entire Union population for a term of ten years. The Union Chief Executive would be responsible for preparing budgets, for enforcing laws and implementing policy directives approved by the Union Chamber of Representatives, and (through direction of the Union Security Force) for maintaining the internal peace and external security of the Union. The judicial branch of the Federal Union would be known as the Union High Court, composed of 25 Union Justices, five of whom would be elected in each quinquennial election for terms of 25 years. The Union High Court would serve as a court of last appeal on those matters within its area of authority, including the constitutionality of legislation and policy directives passed by the Union Chamber of Representatives.

Although a unicameral legislature is envisioned for the world government legislature, some of the virtues of bicameralism would be captured by a proposed "dual voting system." Whenever a vote is taken in the Union Chamber of Representatives, the measure being considered would have to be approved by a majority, possibly a 60 percent majority, on two different bases: the population basis and the material basis. In the population vote, the weight given to the vote of each particular Union Representative would be proportional to the population of his/her Union district, relative to the total population of the Federal Union. In the material vote, the weight given to the vote of each particular Union Representative would be proportional to the financial revenues derived from his/her Union district, relative to the total financial revenues of the Federal Union. In computing revenues derived from specific Union districts, the general tax revenues from each district would be combined with "directed contributions" made on a voluntary basis by the nation or nations within that district. Directed contributions would be allocated to specific programs of the Federal Union at the direction of the contributing nations: such specific programs might include space exploration, pollution abatement, or the World Economic Equalization Program (described below). Union Representatives from the rich nations would be disproportionately represented in the material vote, while Union Representatives from populous poorer nations would be disproportionately represented in the population vote. Since measures would have to be approved on both the material basis and the population basis, only measures on which rich nations and poor nations could achieve a reasonable degree of consensus would have a chance of being approved by the Union Chamber of Representatives.

As far as the power of taxation itself is concerned, as opposed to the voluntary directed contributions which could be of any amount desired by the contributing member nation-states, this power would be subject to certain restrictions, the most binding of which would be contained in a Transitional Codicil, a supplement to the Union Constitution to remain in effect for the first 50 years of the Federal Union's existence. For example, the Transitional Codicil might specify that tax liabilities on member nations be initially limited to no more than five percent of total national output of each member nation, rising at a rate of one percent per decade to a maximum of ten percent at the end of the 50-year transitional period.

Federal Union revenues would be used to finance the operations of the several components of the executive branch. A Ministry of Security would direct the operations of the Union Security Force. A Ministry of the Interior would assume a number of functional operations such as the collection and reporting of statistics currently handled by the World Bank, and would take responsibility for such specialized agencies of the United Nations as the Universal Postal Union. A Ministry of External Development would direct the space exploration program. Especially important in the initial decades of the Federal Union of Democratic Nations would be the World Development Authority, the Union agency responsible for the World Economic Equalization Program.

The World Economic Equalization Program (WEEP) set forth herein is envisioned as a complementary initiative to the Federal Union of Democratic Nations. They are logically separate initiatives, but are very closely related in a practical sense. The World Economic Equalization Program would transfer large quantities of new investment resources from the rich nations to the poor nations, for purposes of building up the productive capabilities of the latter nations. These transfers would *absolutely not* consist of any final consumption commodities such as food, clothing, consumer electronics, or entertainment. They would be strictly confined to augmentation of generalized capital stocks in the recipient nations. Financial resources provided by the WEEP could be utilized for the following purposes, and the following purposes only: (1) purchase and installation of physical plant and machinery; (2) training and education of the labor force; and (3) augmentation of social overhead capital such as roads, railways, harbors, airports, schools and hospitals. Financial resources provided by the rich nations would be far more substantial than their economic development assistance expenditures of the past; however, they would be not so substantial as to reduce living standards in the rich nations, nor would they even be so substantial as to cause a significant decrease in the rate of rise of living standards in the rich nations. The program would be initiated and conducted on an explicitly experimental basis. That is to say, if after a reasonable period of time, say 10 to 15 years, it became evident that the program *was not* dramatically increasing living standards in the poor nations, and/or that it *was* significantly decreasing living standards in the rich nations, then the program would be quickly downsized or even terminated.

The collapse and dissolution of the USSR in 1991 dealt what will hopefully prove to be a decisive blow to ideological conflict as a barrier to world government. That historic event was occasioned by what amounted to a mere shift in mental attitude. Unlike the ideological gap, the economic gap cannot be abrogated by a mere "shift in mental attitude" of the sort that brought the Cold War to a sudden and most welcome end. The economic gap is dependent on very real and tangible factors. The poor nations have very limited generalized capital resources relative to those of the rich nations. Generalized capital resources cannot be brought into existence by "shifts in mental attitude." Self-reliance is a virtue, and most people in the rich nations today feel that it is the sole responsibility of the poor nations to provide their own generalized capital through saving and investment. Unfortunately, world economic history up to the present time has generated a situation whereby it is extremely unlikely that the economic gap will ever be eliminated, or even appreciably narrowed within the foreseeable future, unless the rich nations convey very large amounts of investment resources to the poor nations. The special conditions which in the past led to dramatic economic progress in the rich nations (e.g., the opening up of the North American landmass to Western European colonization) no longer exist, nor will they ever again exist. The economic gap is likely to be permanent unless the rich nations make a conscious policy decision to provide the productive resources to the poor nations necessary to close it.

A fundamental component of the overall argument for world government advanced in this book is the proposition that, despite the very formidable size of the current economic gap, it could in fact be overcome within a relatively brief period of historical time (something on the order of 50 years), by a sufficiently massive and coordinated economic development assistance effort. This effort, termed herein the World Economic Equalization Program, would be somewhat analogous to the post-World War II Marshall Plan, only on a much larger scale and pursued over a much longer time horizon. At the appropriate point in the following, I shall discuss detailed evidence derived from a computer simulation model of the world economy that suggests that a dramatic acceleration in the rate of growth of living standards in the poor nations could be achieved at the very minor cost of a slight retardation in the *rate of growth* of living standards in the rich nations. The cost to the rich nations would *not* be a decline in their living standards, nor even a noticeable decline in the rate of growth of their living standards. In other words, the material cost would be virtually unnoticeable.

Aside from its intrinsic humanitarian value, the elimination of the economic gap between rich and poor nations would doubtless assist the cause of international harmony in the absence of a world government, and it would similarly improve the political stability of a world government should one be established. While the precise degree of improvement might be debated, it seems obvious that there would be at least an appreciable amount of improvement. Thus there would be a benefit. Of course, benefits must be weighed against costs. Even very large benefits might not be desirable if the costs of achieving them are very large. On the other hand, even rather modest benefits might be desirable if the costs of achieving them are very small. What I will argue is that the costs to the rich nations of achieving a high degree of economic equalization over the entire world would be very minor. In view of the virtually trivial costs, it does not matter if the benefits are not obviously and necessarily enormous.

An important question might occur to the reader at this point, assuming it has not already done so. Would it not be wiser, it might be asked, to undertake the World Economic Equalization Program *prior to* the formation of a Federal Union of Democratic Nations, with the intention of establishing the latter only if the former proves to be successful. That way, worldwide political unity would be established if and only if a solid basis were laid for it in the form of worldwide economic equality. This would be a safer, more cautious, more conservative approach, one less likely to degenerate into conflict and possible warfare.

Personally, I believe that a World Economic Equalization Program, on the sufficiently massive scale necessary to achieve success, would be very desirable in its own right, without any reference to the possibility of world government. I would be overjoyed to see such a program undertaken, even if there were no simultaneous move to establish a world government. But at the same time, I would be even more overjoyed to see *both* the World Economic Equalization Program and the Federal Union of Democratic Nations simultaneously launched. To my mind, these two initiatives are extremely complementary, in the sense that initiation of a world government would greatly increase the probability that the world economic development effort would be pursued long enough and vigorously enough to achieve success, while at the same time initiation and pursuit of the world economic development effort would greatly increase the stability and survival probability of the world government.

There is no doubt whatsoever that whether a world government exists or does not exist, the World Economic Equalization Program envisioned here would generate a tremendous amount of complaint and opposition among conservative elements in the rich nations. As much as it might be argued that the effect of the program on the rich nations is only a slight retardation in the long-term growth rate, these elements will focus their attention narrowly on the absolute amounts of the transfers, which will inevitably be tremendous. Opponents of the program will be predictably appalled and outraged by the prospect of tremendous amounts ("billions and billions" of dollars—possibly "trillions and trillions") being "poured out" to benefit "foreigners." Charity begins at home, they will cry, we should be using these resources to solve "our own" social problems, to enable "our own people" to achieve a better standard of living. These complaints will become especially strident during periods of business recession, when the short-term growth rate slows or even reverses. It is practically inevitable that recessionary periods will occur during the several decades that will be required to complete the world economic development effort.

In my judgment, there is a far greater probability that these inevitable problems will be overcome, and the World Economic Equalization Program continued until it has achieved full success, if the program is being supported by an existent, active, functioning Federal Union of Democratic Nations. The Federal Union would make the endeavor larger than "mere economics." It would make it far more clear and tangible that the ultimate purpose of the effort is not merely to provide the poorer populations with better food and more automobiles than they have now, but to achieve a more perfect sense of community over the entire world, in order that the costs and anxieties associated with conflict and warfare may be greatly reduced both in our own time and in that of our descendents. It is not a matter of logical necessity, but rather of psychological feasibility and practical expediency, that world government and world economic development go hand in hand.

A SCIENTIFIC APPROACH

Proponents of major social policy innovations in the past have tended to be extremely confident that the benefits of these innovations would far outweigh the costs. Or if they had any doubts on this score, they kept these doubts to themselves. They argued the virtues of their proposals with an enthusiasm bordering on fanaticism, and dismissed critics and opponents as either mental incompetents or hypocrites in the pay of "vested interests." If they were heeded and their proposals implemented, then, normally, unanticipated adverse consequences would quickly surface, so that the net benefits of the transition would be less than expected, sometimes far less than expected.

In some cases, the proposed cure was indubitably far worse than the disease. One thinks immediately of Karl Marx, who proclaimed the socialist millennium with all the faith and zeal that one normally associates with religious fanatics. Within a few decades of Marx's death, what should have been the workers' paradise of the Soviet Union was transformed into a totalitarian nightmare presided over by Joseph Stalin, who may not have been a monster to begin with, but who had certainly evolved into one by the time of his death. No doubt Stalin, who died comfortably enough of old age in 1953 after slaughtering millions of his own countrymen, never experienced any significant self-doubt. No doubt he convinced himself that his own personal survival and continued undisputed leadership of the Soviet Union was hastening the glorious socialist millennium promised by Karl Marx. From the ideas and idealism of Karl Marx to the concentration camps and firing squads of Joseph Stalin—such can be the disastrous outcome of sympathetic concern for all humanity and innovative social thinking.

As a result of the real-world disaster initiated by the social theories and prescriptions of Karl Marx, as well as a host of similar experiences throughout human history, a large proportion of both the intelligentsia and the general human population have today lapsed into unimaginative conservatism and thoughtless opposition to almost any significant social transformation. This is most unfortunate, since continued social innovation and progress is probably no less important to the further development of human civilization, and to the further enhancement of individual human existence, than continued scientific innovation and progress. However, in light of past history, it is incumbent upon proposers of social innovations to think very carefully about such innovations, to be quite detailed and specific in their formulation, to be quite thorough and balanced in considering possible flaws and problems, and, above all, to be properly circumspect and restrained in presenting the case for these innovations.

Therefore, I need to state here and now, without qualification or equivocation, that as a matter of fact, I personally am *not* completely certain that the effect of a potential future World Economic Equalization Program, or of a potential future Federal Union of Democratic Nations, would be favorable. It is extremely important, in my view, that if either one or both of these initiatives is actually undertaken in the real world, it would be on a tentative, provisional and experimental basis. It would be useless to deny that a non-negligible possibility exists that the World Economic Equalization Program would be a complete failure, that there would be little acceleration in the growth rates of the poor nations and/or a serious decline in the economic condition of the rich nations. If that happens (after a reasonable trial period of at least 10 to 15 years), then the program should be cut back drastically or terminated altogether. It would be equally useless to deny that a non-negligible possibility exists that the Federal Union of Democratic Nations might be a complete failure, for a variety of reasons, including continued pursuit of a World Economic Equalization Program which is clearly failing to achieve its mission. If that happens (again after a reasonable trial period), nations should withdraw from the Federal Union, until finally, having been reduced to an impotent rump state, the Federal Union voluntarily terminates its own existence. Such a dissolution would be sad and unfortunate, and an ill omen for the future of humanity. But peaceful dissolution would obviously be preferable to violent dissolution. If dissolution does occur, then humanity would be back to where we are today—sadder and wiser, but otherwise none the worse for wear.

It is an absolutely central component of this proposal for a world government that the world government implement an absolutely pure and unadulterated "open door" policy with respect to membership. The Federal Union must always remain ready to admit new nations to membership in the Union, and it must always remain equally ready to allow member nations to depart from the Union whenever they desire to do so. These principles must be clearly and unequivocally stated in the constitution that establishes the Union. The constitution must not only enshrine the permanent right of each member nation to withdraw from the Union at its own unilateral discretion, but it must also enshrine the permanent right of each member nation to maintain whatever military forces and armament it desires, including nuclear. These military forces and weapons would provide a practical guarantee and a tangible safeguard for the constitutional right of free secession from the Union. These two interrelated reserved rights of the member nations are essential to the effective initiation of the Federal Union— owing to these reserved rights, a large number of nations, including the larger and more powerful nations, will be willing to join the Union. Conceivably there could even be universal membership by all nations right from the start. Of course, the hope would be that the Federal Union would evolve smoothly and favorably, so that the member nations would become progressively more confident and would gradually reduce their directly controlled military forces. The hope is also that the reserved right of secession would, in due course, become nothing more than a historical curiosity, since the benefits of maintaining membership in the Federal Union would be so clear and compelling to every national population that secession would become politically unthinkable.

The formation of a world government along the lines of the proposed Federal Union of Democratic Nations should be looked upon as no more and no less than *a scientific experiment*. Such an experiment is the one and only way we have for achieving truly reliable, convincing and compelling evidence on the potential performance of world government. Whether a world government would be a success or a failure simply cannot be determined, to any reasonably satisfactory level of certitude, on the basis of theoretical speculations and hypothetical musings based on the past history of human civilization. The current situation is simply too novel, too unprecedented, and too unparalleled for past history to provide more than circumstantial and inconclusive indications. The fact is that the only means by which we may ascertain whether a world state would make a positive contribution to the future development of human civilization is to set up a world state and then observe the outcome. What is needed is not more words but rather experimental *action*.

Whether progress has been achieved, in a fundamental social welfare sense, through the historical evolution of the institutions and operations of human civilization, might be debated by reasonable people. Most of us believe, for example, that the principle of representative democracy does in fact constitute a meaningful advance over the principle of absolute monarchy. But it cannot be proven, in a mathematically or logically rigorous sense, that the average level of human happiness and self-realization is higher today under representative democracy than it was in the past under absolute monarchy. But where historical progress *has* been achieved, surely and incontestably, is in the area of science and technology. It cannot be reasonably disputed that a world in which automobiles and computers exist, is farther along than a world in which these things did not exist. Note that the argument is *not* that automobiles and computers necessarily increase human welfare in any meaningful way (though most of us believe they do). The argument is simply that automobiles and computers represent incontestable scientific and technical advance.

And the point is simply that an essential component of scientific and technical advance has always been the experimental method. Throughout the history of science and technology, fruitless abstract disputations over factual propositions have very often been resolved more or less conclusively and definitively by means of properly designed laboratory experiments. These disputations could never have been, and would never have been, settled by means of logical argumentation and a priori reasoning, even if that argumentation and reasoning had been continued indefinitely. In the final analysis, disagreements could only be overcome by making reference to *facts*. Speculations, conjectures, hypotheses, and theories are not necessarily factually accurate. Factual accuracy of abstract propositions can never be compellingly demonstrated in the absence of factual demonstrations. In the absence of experimentation, it is very doubtful that science and technology would ever have been capable of bringing forth such marvels as automobiles and computers.

What this means, in terms of the fundamental thesis of this book, is that we will never be able to compellingly demonstrate either the desirability or the undesirability of federal world government without actually establishing a federal world government. This proposition may seem strange to the reader at first, because neither the proponents nor the opponents of world government in the past have been sufficiently aware of it. Or if they were aware of it, they apparently feared that explicit recognition and discussion of this point could have weakened the case they were attempting to put forward, pro or con, on world government. But upon reflection, the reader will hopefully acknowledge the high level of plausibility which characterizes the proposition. Of course, even if the reader is prepared to assent to the proposition that only a real-world experiment with world government is likely to yield compelling evidence on the performance of world government, he or she might still regard such an experiment as far too risky to be undertaken. What I am attempting to do in this book is to show that a real-world experiment with a *properly designed* world government would not in fact entail excessive risk, especially in view of the great benefits that might be garnered if the experiment is successful.

Of course, it would clearly be dishonest to assert that there would be *absolutely no risk* involved in an experimental foundation of a federal world government, even one as "properly designed" as the proposed Federal Union of Democratic Nations. Risk is unavoidable at all levels of human existence. Whatever course of action (or inaction) is taken, there are inevitable risks. A psychotic person might decide stay in bed every morning, as a means of avoiding such risks as killing himself by falling in the bathroom, or being killed while driving to work. But as any sane person realizes, this strategy is untenable. The notion of "avoiding all risks," clearly, is an insane notion. Sometimes we *must* take risks. And sometimes we *should* take risks. So it is with world government. At the present moment in history, the risks involved in *not* establishing a world government are arguably much greater than the risks involved in doing so.

However, honesty also dictates the acknowledgement of another uncongenial reality with respect to active risk-taking. "Active" risk-taking is involved in *taking* a certain action; "passive" risk-taking is involved in *not taking* an action. A calculated active risk, prior to the action being taken, might be fully sensible: the expected payoff to the individual if the action is taken might be very much greater than the expected payoff if the action is not taken. However, owing to bad luck, the actual outcome of taking the action might be disastrous. Thus the sane person who gets out of bed in the morning to go to the bathroom and then drive to work, might kill himself in a bathroom fall—or if the bathroom is survived, he might then be killed in a traffic accident on the way to work.

Equally bad luck might befall human civilization even if humanity does follow the active course of establishing a federal world government. Despite all the precautions and safeguards, such a government might actually become the mechanism which generates the very nuclear world war it was intended to forestall. I make this point not because I believe that it is a sensible argument against world government, but because I wish to reduce to a minimum the sensibility of the accusation that this particular advocacy of world government is based upon "idealistic and unrealistic" thinking. The thinking from which this advocacy of world government proceeds, is in fact solidly rooted in a realistic perception of the facts as we presently know them: the facts of human psychology, the facts of human history, the facts of the planetary habitat, the facts of science and technology, and the facts of decision-making under uncertainty. It is realism to acknowledge that no strategy exists that will absolutely guarantee a favorable long-term outcome for human civilization. But it is also realism to acknowledge that under certain circumstances, the risks of inaction are actually greater than the risks of action.

Needless to emphasize, in the past major social innovations have rarely if ever been proposed in experimental terms. Rarely have the proposers of such innovations offered arguments which could be easily satirized as equivalent to: "Try it—you *might* like it!" Neither have the opponents of these innovations considered it advisable to express their arguments in anything less than terms of complete certainty. However, to those in the middle of the dispute, to those whose judgment inclines them in one direction or the other but *not strongly* in one direction or the other, the perception may be that the proposed innovation may be worthwhile as a means of establishing once and for all, by experimental means, whether or not the innovation is, on the whole, socially beneficial.

It may be found, after the innovation is adopted, that its overall effect is unfavorable. In that case, the innovation could and should be repealed, revoked, discontinued. An interesting case of this sort in United States history was the imposition of a national ban on the production, transportation and sale of alcoholic beverages from 1920 through 1933. The ban was the outcome of long-term organized efforts, dating back to the early nineteenth century, to limit the consumption of alcohol and thereby to curb the various social problems generated by drunkenness. Section 1 of the proposed 18th Amendment to the United States Constitution, submitted by Congress to the states in 1917, stated: "After one year from the ratification of this article the manufacture, sale, or transportation of intoxicating liquors within, the importation thereof into, or the exportation thereof from the United States and all territory subject to the jurisdiction thereof for beverage purposes is hereby prohibited." The Amendment was ratified by the requisite number of states by early 1919. Enforcement legislation entitled the National Prohibition Act (popularly known as the "Volstead Act") was passed by Congress on Oct. 28, 1919, over the veto of President Woodrow Wilson. The ban went into effect on January 29, 1920.

Within a short period of time, the costs of "legislating morality" became obvious. Millions of otherwise law-abiding citizens ignored the ban, resulting in a thriving illegal black market supplied by organized crime. Violence erupted in the streets as rival gangs fought to gain control over the illicit but lucrative trade. Corruption spread widely through the enforcement agencies as some of the abundant revenues were diverted to bribes to gain the complicity of the police. The quality of illegal alcohol degenerated, leading to much death and disability among the consuming public. Anyone who wonders what the "war on alcohol" was like during the 1920s has only to look at the "war on drugs" being waged today. After a decade of experience suggesting that in this case the cure was worse than the disease, the pendulum of public opinion swung against prohibition. The onslaught of the Great Depression in 1930 may have put the final nail in prohibition's coffin. To the other arguments against prohibition was now added the assertion that a legal liquor industry would add thousands of new, legal jobs paying taxable income. Another argument at that time might have been that legalized alcohol would help people to cope peaceably with the new economic adversity: clearly, drunkenness might be preferable to the insurrection being preached by the newly socialized Soviet Union. In any event, by the early 1930s the repeal movement was in full swing. The 21st Amendment to the U.S. Constitution, whose principal purpose was simply the repeal of the 18th Amendment, was ratified before the end of 1933. And that marked the end of what President Herbert Hoover referred to as "the noble experiment."

Whether the episode had been noble or ignoble, Hoover's use of the term "experiment" is informative. Throughout the many decades prior to the 1920s during which the controversy had raged, advocates and opponents of prohibition had speculated endlessly about the probable effects of a national ban on alcoholic drink. Advocates forecast the moral regeneration of a nation no longer plagued by intoxication and alcoholism. Opponents forecast a narrow and joyless existence presided over by puritanical religious zealots. But no one *really* knew what would happen. When the pro-prohibition forces finally got the upper hand and pushed through the national ban, the anti-prohibition forces howled their lamentations. As it turned out, they should have shouted their hosannas. Within ten years, the compelling evidence provided by actual experience with prohibition swung the overwhelming weight of public opinion over to the anti-prohibition side of the controversy.

Skeptics of world government today should keep this historical incident well in mind. Assuming they are correct, then very shortly after the formation of a world government, its disadvantages and liabilities will begin to manifest themselves in a very clear and obvious manner. Perhaps, despite all the admonitions and warnings against attempting to make the world state into an instrument for the radical redistribution of current income, the high officials of the world state will set themselves resolutely toward this course of action. Against opposition to this policy, they will threaten to unleash the military and police forces of the world state. Clear evidence would then exist that the apprehensions and anticipations of world government skeptics are fully on-target. If this were to happen, then the world state would dissolve very quickly and very completely. Just as prohibition was abandoned as soon as its disadvantages could no longer be reasonably denied, so too the world state would be abandoned. It would be a very long time—if ever—before humanity would ever again consider experimenting with world government.

Of course, I myself do not believe that there is any significant possibility that were a world government to be established, its high leadership would be so foolish and misguided as to pursue policies which would inevitably be strongly opposed by substantial national populations. I have cited the example of prohibition of alcohol in the United States from 1920 through 1933 only to suggest that the formation of a world government need not be a final, definitive and irrevocable step. If a potential future world government were to be as unsuccessful in practice as was the policy of prohibition of alcohol in the United States during the 1920s, then that world government would quickly follow the same path as that followed by prohibition—into rapid and complete oblivion.

But at the same time, most students of social policy recognize in the experience of prohibition in the United States during the 1920s an atypical case. The rule is that innovative social policies—policies which are finally adopted after decades of vociferous controversy and bitter resistance—are successful rather than unsuccessful. Of all of the amendments to the United States Constitution, for example, only the 18th was later repealed because its effects were obviously perverse. The 13th Amendment, abolishing slavery, has not as yet had to be repealed. Nor has the 19th, which granted the right to vote to women. If a world government is established in the real world, I am very confident that it will very quickly be acknowledged as a positive development by all but a small handful of extremely inflexible and reactionary mentalities. The key point is, however, that my own personal confidence on this score is *not* a vital component of the case to be made for world government. What *is* a vital component of this case is that it would not be impossible, nor even especially difficult, to dissolve a world government that was not developing in a positive way.

THE CHICKEN OR THE EGG?

For the most part, academic specialists in international organization do not consider that world government will become feasible at any point in the foreseeable future, and therefore deem it unworthy of detailed consideration. Most discussions of world government in the professional literature are sketchy outlines of the progress of the concept in the history of ideas, to which is appended a cursory dismissal as far as the contemporary real world in concerned. The usual basis for the dismissal is the assertion that the contemporary human population is far too heterogeneous and diverse—economically, religiously, and ideologically—for peacefully attained universal political unity to be feasible. According to this conventional viewpoint, the only kind of state entity capable of encompassing and controlling such diversity would be a ruthlessly totalitarian regime determined to crush and annihilate any and all vestiges of dissent and resistance. In the well-known formulation of Kenneth Waltz, the degree of coercion necessary to hold a political system together is positively related to the heterogeneity of the population. The current world population is highly diverse—ergo, only a brutal totalitarian regime could hold its various components in check. In the following typical passage (from *Man, the State and War*, 1959, p. 228), Waltz applies the principle to suggest the unwisdom of contemplating world government:

> Yet in the international as in the domestic sphere, if anarchy is the cause [of monstrous behavior], the obvious conclusion is that government is the cure... The problem, however, becomes a practical one. The amount of force needed to hold a society together varies with the heterogeneity of the elements composing it. World federalists write as though the only alternatives before us were unity or death. "World government is necessary and therefore possible," Robert Maynard Hutchins avers. But demonstrating the need for an institution does not bring it into existence. And were world government attempted, we might find ourselves dying in the attempt, or uniting and living a life worse than death.

In Chapter 18 of the 1971 edition of *Swords into Plowshares*, Inis L. Claude subjects the notion of world government to a somewhat more thorough critique than it usually receives in the international organization literature. Claude's argument may be summarized as follows: World government would either be useless or it would be intolerable. If it were such a weak federation that it could not suppress wars among member nations, or between members and nonmembers, there would be no value in it. On the other hand, if it were given enough power to suppress wars among nations, it would almost certainly constitute an intolerable tyranny. The latter is seen as the more serious defect, and the point is stated as follows (p. 430):

The problem of power looms large with respect to any governmental system adequate to cope with the elements of disorder and discord in the international community. If a global regimen is to have sufficient power to fulfill its task, questions of profound gravity arise: who will exercise and control the force of the community, in accordance with what conception of justice, within what constitutional limits, with what guarantees that the limits will be observed? These are not questions that can be readily answered, but they are crucial for the threat of global tyranny lurks in unsatisfactory answers. In terms of Western liberalism, the problem is not to get just any kind of world government—Hitler and Stalin were only the most recent of a long series of leaders who would have been glad to provide that—but to get a system of world order that is compatible with the political ideals of the democratic heritage.

In *The Nature and Function of International Organization* (2nd edition, 1967), Stephen Goodspeed explains the impracticality of world government as follows (pp. 662-663):

While the arguments of the world government enthusiasts have great appeal on the surface, a number of them are open to serious question. Those who still demand the immediate remaking of the United Nations into even a limited world government oversimplify the problem by not assessing fully the manner in which governments are made, nor do they recognize the basic meaning of sovereignty. All evil cannot be eradicated simply be revising the Charter or devising a new constitution. Constitutions follow upon a society which has grown used to common institutions, a community attached to certain norms and interests. It is from this communal society that governments and constitutions spring. The community is developed first, and the constitution, the laws, and the administration come afterwards...

The way in which the United States was created is often cited as an argument in favor of the theory of world federalism. When carefully scrutinized, this analogy breaks down. The thirteen colonies meeting in convention did not constitute thirteen separate sovereignties preparing to join together as one. They had fought a war together and possessed the same moral convictions, the same loyalties, a common heritage, and similar political institutions... The colonial people existed as a community before the establishment of the United States, just as a world community must be created before the erection of a world state.

If, in some desperate effort to solve the problems dividing the Soviets and the Western world, the United Nations were to be transformed into some form of world government with the General Assembly made a legislature based on the democratic principles of popular representation and majority rule, could it succeed in the absence of a majority possessed of common values, interests, and goals? The answer is a categorical "no" since struggle between East and West would not dissolve merely because the setting was changed. The possibility of establishing a limited world government is at the present time as remote as it has been for centuries.

What do these quotations—typical of numerous similar "analyses" of world government to be found throughout the academic literature on international organization—have in common? To begin with, they are unimaginative and superficial. Their authors seem fully oblivious to the possibility that a limited world government—a world government subject to sufficient and adequate constraints to preclude it from establishing an intolerably totalitarian hegemony over the nations of the world—could nevertheless make a meaningful and useful contribution to the future evolution of the international community. On what reasonable basis, for example, does Inis L. Claude assert that unless a world government were to possess a virtual monopoly on heavy weaponry, it would be "useless" as an instrument for the suppression of wars between nations? A world government might not possess a virtual monopoly on heavy weaponry, but it might possess enough of such weaponry to give serious pause to potential aggressor nations. Moreover, the simple existence of a world government, even were several of its member nations to remain heavily armed, would create moral and psychological pressures toward peaceful and cooperative behavior among member nations. Surely these negative viewpoints on world government would not be so complacently dogmatic were their authors to have given any serious consideration to proposals for limited world government along the lines of the Federal Union of Democratic Nations. The authors assume that a meaningful world government must necessarily be all-powerful, and that an all-powerful government must necessarily be despotic. This simplistic formula conveniently spares these authorities from the onerous responsibility for any sort of serious thinking about the world government possibility.

Another striking commonality of the above quotations is that they are based firmly on the Cold War conditions which prevailed from the end of World War II in 1945 until the collapse and dissolution of the Soviet Union in 1991. Each of these three authors takes it as a given that a primary problem with world government—if not *the* primary problem with world government—is that communist national leaders would endeavor to subvert the world government and transform it into an instrument for the expansion of communism. None of the authors feel it necessary to explain the disadvantages of communism. They merely assume that their readers are sufficiently aware of recent history (specifically the dictatorships of Adolf Hitler in Germany and of Joseph Stalin in Russia) to be sensitive to the threat of totalitarianism. With the sentence: "And were world government attempted, we might find ourselves dying in the attempt, or uniting and living a life worse than death," Kenneth Waltz expresses the standardized Cold War judgment that it would be better to be dead than Red. With the sentence: "In terms of Western liberalism, the problem is not to get just any kind of world government—Hitler and Stalin were only the most recent of a long series of leaders who would have been glad to provide that—but to get a system of world order that is compatible with the political ideals of the democratic heritage," Inis L. Claude effectively smears world government by portraying the likes of Adolf Hitler and Joseph Stalin as putative endorsers of the concept. And in answering a rhetorical question concerning the feasibility of world government with a "categorical no," Stephen Goodspeed explains that the "struggle between East and West would not dissolve merely because the setting was changed." Anyone who is aware of the collapse and dissolution of the Soviet Union in 1991 realizes that in order to retain a reasonable amount of relevance, such quotations as these need to be revised rather substantially. What is really quite surprising, however, is the very limited alteration to be found in typical "analyses" of world government in the international organization literature in the years following 1991. Although there is less explicit reference to and reliance on apprehensions about "communist world domination," the same basic ideas are there: world government as a one-way street toward devastating civil war or nightmarish tyranny. Obviously mental inertia is a powerful force—just as formidable, in its context, as the force of physical inertia.

A third commonality of these quotations is their insistence that the essential *precondition* for successful world government is the attainment of a very high degree of socioeconomic homogeneity and psychological consensus among humanity. These authors seem to be fully unaware and oblivious of two critical issues pertaining to the relationship between social uniformity and political unity: the *continuous nature* of the relationship, and the *interactive nature* of the relationship. First, the relationship between social uniformity and political unity at any one point in time is a smooth and continuous relationship: the higher the degree of social uniformity achieved, the higher the level of political unity that may be established. To have a *very high* level of political unity in a world government—that is to say, an extremely strong, centralized and authoritative world government—we would need a very high level of social uniformity. This book does not advocate any such world government. If we are content, as we should be, with a *reasonable* level of political unity at the global level—that is to say, with a limited world government such as the Federal Union of Democratic Nations under consideration herein—then we would *not* need a very high level of social uniformity. Second, the relationship between social uniformity and political unity over a period of time is an interactive and mutually reinforcing relationship: the mere existence of political unity, albeit weak in the beginning, tends gradually to generate a higher level of social uniformity, and as social uniformity increases, it in turn permits a higher level of political unity. Thus the relationship over time between social uniformity and political unity is not static but dynamic; a mutually reinforcing, snowballing process is created which over time will tend toward a high (albeit far from "complete") level of both social uniformity and political unity.

Consider the traditional question: Which came first—the chicken or the egg? What makes the question absurd, and therefore humorous, is that *neither* the modern chicken nor the modern egg came first. The modern chicken-egg-chicken progression is the result of millions of years of slow, evolutionary development with roots in the primeval slime. Those who argue that it is necessary to have a high level of social homogeneity prior to having an effective state are equivalent to those who would argue, in response to the chicken-egg question, that since chickens come out of eggs, then the egg came first. The problem with this argument, obviously, is that it is also true that eggs come out of chickens. If we take social and attitudinal homogeneity to be the egg, and the effectiveness of state organization (i.e., political unity) to be the chicken, the direct relevance of the chicken-egg question to the present discussion becomes clear. A population that is politically united within the same state organization tends to become, over time, more socially and attitudinally homogeneous. Similarly, as a given population becomes more socially and attitudinally homogeneous, its state organization tends to become more effective (among other reasons, because it expends less resources on enforcing the majority will upon recalcitrant minorities). There is an ongoing, progressive, interactive, mutually reinforcing, snowballing process between the social and attitudinal homogeneity of a given population, and the effectiveness of the state organization in which it is politically united.

In terms of the chicken-egg analogy, the "egg" which we have at the present time (the level of social homogeneity throughout the contemporary world), and the "chicken" which is capable of coming forth from this egg (the level of political unity which could be achieved by a world government established at the present point in history), are both fairly primitive versions of what we eventually hope to realize. The ancient egg and the ancient chicken were virtually unrecognizable relative to their modern counterparts. But we should not allow the best to be the enemy of the good. It is certainly true that the world government that we could establish today would be far short of the utopian ideal that might be imagined. Such a world government would not directly and immediately banish the threat of nuclear holocaust, would not directly and immediately banish such equally serious threats as excessive population growth and accelerating environmental degradation. But these facts should not obscure the high probability that a world government *would* establish a more secure foundation for long-term efforts toward the reduction of such threats as nuclear war, excessive population growth and accelerating environmental degradation.

PROS AND CONS OUTLINED

Now that some of the preconceptual underbrush has been cleared away, we are in a better position to engage in rational deliberation on the question of whether the establishment of a world government in the near future would be a desirable or an undesirable initiative. The world government under consideration here would not nearly as strongly centralized and highly authoritative as are the presently existing national governments of the "major powers" such as the United States and the Russian Federation. On the other hand, the Federal Union of Democratic Nations being proposed in this book, while not being "all-powerful" in any sense, would nevertheless be a legitimate state authority with considerable power and influence. What, then, would be the major advantages of such a world government, and what would be the major disadvantages? We will look first at the advantages and then at the disadvantages.

At or near the top of every list of "benefits of world government" composed by advocates of world government throughout the twentieth century has been reduced risk of major warfare. This benefit has both a utilitarian and a psychological dimension. The destruction, suffering and death *not* experienced by humanity because a certain war is *not* fought can be classified as a utilitarian benefit. But there is also a psychological benefit involved in the lower level of apprehension and anxiety experienced by individual human beings less subject to the risk of warfare. No doubt the excessive confidence evinced by many if not most past proponents of world government that world government would instantly relegate the threat of major warfare to a negligible level has had an adverse impact on the real-world credibility and effectiveness of the concept. Too much has been promised, and the net effect of what are regarded by most as ridiculously unrealistic promises has been to seriously weaken the sensibility of the world government concept. Therefore, it is important that this particular benefit not be overstated. The only avenue by which an actual world government could immediately suppress all armed conflict and warfare would be to endow it with a virtual monopoly on heavy weaponry and large-scale military forces. But such a world government has no chance of being established in the real world within the foreseeable future because of the serious danger that would exist that it would utilize its military power to impose a despotic global hegemony. A limited world government—one that would be obliged to share control over heavy weaponry and large-scale military forces with the national governments—is the only kind of world government that has a reasonable chance of being established within the relatively immediate and foreseeable future.

Such a limited world government would not necessarily be able to abolish warfare everywhere in the world. At least not immediately. Major national powers might decide not to join the Federal Union of Democratic Nations at the time of its initial foundation. These major powers might retain nuclear weapons, and at some future time, owing to adverse developments, they might be "forced" or "obliged" to use these weapons on each other. They might also be "forced" or "obliged" to use these weapons on member nations of the Federal Union. Whether or not the Federal Union ought to have nuclear weapons under its own direct control would be a matter for future consideration. Once it has been decided by a sufficient number of nations to establish a world government, many practical questions would arise, of which one of the more important would be whether the world government's directly controlled military force should have a nuclear capability. Whether or not the world government is permitted direct control over nuclear weapons, it seems inevitable that several national governments, even if they decide to join the world government, will retain nuclear weapons under their own direct control for an extended period into the future. Thus the threat of future nuclear wars, while diminished, would certainly not be completely abrogated by the foundation of a world government.

Ever since the development of nuclear weapons in 1945, and their use against the unfortunate Japanese cities of Hiroshima and Nagasaki in the same year, the possibility of a nuclear world war has haunted humanity. But in the decades following 1945, humanity gained much added experience with conventional warfare: various wars between Israel and the Arab states, the Korean War, the Vietnam conflict, the Afghanistan conflict, the war between Iran and Iraq, the first and second Gulf War, as well as a host of smaller international wars. In addition, a large number of devastating civil wars have occurred: in China, Laos, Cambodia, Somalia, Angola, Ethiopia, Nigeria, Rwanda, the former Yugoslavia, and so on. To those who are killed and wounded in these non-nuclear conflicts, and to those who live in fear of being killed or wounded in them, the difference between nuclear war and conventional war is purely abstract. Of course, there is a large difference from the point of view of the entire human race: conventional wars are far more "affordable" than nuclear wars. Nevertheless, while conventional wars do not pose a fundamental threat to the existence of human civilization, they are clearly an evil which all reasonable people wish to see minimized.

It is also clear to most reasonable people that a world government—assuming the danger that it would degenerate into a global tyranny can be averted—would significantly reduce the prevalence and intensity of conventional international and civil wars throughout the world. But it is important not to exaggerate this potential benefit of world government. Eventually the world government might become sufficiently powerful (in a non-tyrannical way) that armed conflict, whether among nations or within nations, would be completely deterred because of the recognition among all those tempted to initiate such conflicts that they would be instantly met by overwhelming force on the part of the world government. Today in the United States, for example, whatever the conflicts of interest which might emerge between the contiguous Midwestern states of Illinois and Indiana, the governors of these two states never even consider the possibility of resolving these conflicts of interest by force of arms. It is certainly to be hoped that in the long run an analogous situation will be achieved among nations, so that India and Pakistan, for example, will refrain from taking up arms against one another for the same reason that Illinois and Indiana refrain from taking up arms against one another today. But this situation may take a long time to develop, even if a world government is established and operates successfully.

One of the most plausible scenarios for the failure and dissolution of a future Federal Union of Democratic Nations, aside from the possibility that it will attempt to establish a highly egalitarian worldwide welfare state, is that it will become embroiled in localized conflict situations among or within nonmember nations. Let us imagine, for example, a future localized conflict situation analogous to the 1980-1988 Iran-Iraq war or the 1991-1994 civil war in Bosnia. Humanitarian appeals are made to the Federal Union government to intervene to halt the carnage. The Federal Union government accedes to these appeals and sends "peacekeeping" military forces into the theater of conflict. More often than not, participants in localized conflict situations are fanatically self-righteous and in a thoroughly desperate frame of mind. More than likely the peacekeeping soldiers will find themselves fired upon by one or both sides of the local conflict. Soon the growing casualty lists will be a dominant concern of the member nations providing the peacekeeping troops. Critics will charge that the "foreigners" in control of the world government are carelessly sacrificing battalions of our

young people in wars on the other side of the world—involving nasty foreign
people who mean nothing to us and unworthy foreign causes which mean less
than nothing to us—just to satisfy their own lust for personal glory and acclaim.
If the Federal Union is unwise enough to persist in the intervention, many of the
nations providing peacekeeping troops will withdraw from the Union just so that
they can withdraw their troops from costly intervention in a repugnant localized
conflict situation.

If a major localized conflict situation involving nonmember nations emerges
within the first few decades after the foundation of the Federal Union of Democratic Nations, it would probably be best if the appeals for humanitarian intervention were disregarded and the Federal Union remained uninvolved. In the short
run there would be too much of a risk that a costly intervention would erode
support for the Union sufficiently to cause defections by important member nations. It could be argued that if the intervention were sufficiently massive, it
would achieve its aim of halting the conflict and disarming the participants at
minimal cost since the latter would recognize the futility of resisting such a massive force. This argument is analogous to the argument that if the United States
had deployed a force of five million soldiers in South Vietnam in 1965, the
North Vietnamese would have recognized the futility of their aspiration toward
unification and would have desisted from their military effort. It will never be
determined whether a force of five million soldiers would have had the effect
desired by the United States in 1965, because it was politically impossible for
the U.S. government at that time to undertake such an enormous commitment.
Similarly, it would quite likely be politically impossible for a potential future
world government to undertake a sufficiently enormous military intervention into
a localized conflict situation as to induce the participants to desist peaceably and
lay down their arms. Conceivably in the long run, after 50 or 100 years of successful operation by the world government, it will have generated enough support and commitment throughout the world that it *would* in fact be willing and
able to undertake enormous commitments to suppress localized conflict situations. Its willingness and ability to do so would then operate as a powerful deterrent to such situations. But this is looking forward to the relatively remote future.

Although avoidance of future warfare has always dominated the case presented by advocates of world government, there are certainly other aspects of
this case. A world government would considerably facilitate organization and
coordination of human activity on a global scale. Just as there are technical
economies of scale in the production of economic commodities, so too there are
administrative economies of scale in the production of public goods and services. For example, a world government would foster effective coordination of
humanity's continuing effort to break free of the gravitational shackles of planet
earth, and to expand outward among the planets of our own solar system, and
later, hopefully, among the solar systems of other stars. A world government
would bring about a higher level of global standardization in weights and measures, currency, and accounting principles. A world government would hasten the

development of a common language understood by all or at least a large majority of the global population. As argued earlier, a world government would increase the probability that a World Economic Equalization Program would be pursued long enough and vigorously enough to achieve a reasonable degree of homogeneity in economic living standards throughout the world. A world government would make a significant contribution to humanity's long-term effort to lower the rate of world population growth and to retard the rate of world environmental degradation.

The objective of avoidance of war, and these various other objectives not directly concerned with war, are of course very closely interrelated. Successful pursuit of the other objectives will reduce the probability of warfare, and the longer and more completely warfare is avoided, the more successful will be the pursuit of the other objectives. For example, if those economic resources which would otherwise have been invested in preparations for wars, and then in the fighting of wars, are instead invested in a space exploration program which unites humanity in a common purpose, the unifying effect of this alternative investment will further reduce the perceived need for military investments, further reduce the probability of warfare, and enable the investment of still greater resources in the space exploration program. Space exploration, while it has tremendous symbolic importance even in the short run, is unlikely to yield any significant material benefits for the present generation of humanity. It is rather a very long-term investment in the future of the human race, and the principal material payoff (if there is any) will be to generations yet unborn. With respect to many other objectives of the world government, however, tangible material benefits may reasonably be anticipated even for the present generation of humanity. This would be the case, for example, with respect to the closely related efforts and programs intended to establish better control over population growth and environmental degradation.

In previously discussing the key benefit of world government that it would reduce the future costs imposed on humanity by war, I emphasized the importance of not exaggerating this benefit, lest a legitimate basis be provided for charges that serious advocacy of world government betrays only utopian delusions. As enunciated herein, the argument is merely that world government would significantly reduce the probability of future warfare, not that it would definitely and totally abrogate warfare from humanity's future. It is likewise essential not to exaggerate the potential contribution of world government in matters not directly and immediately related to the probability and costs of warfare. For example, it cannot be promised that a world government would "solve" the interrelated problems of population growth and environmental degradation. Similarly, it cannot be promised that a World Economic Equalization Program under the auspices of a world government would necessarily make a significant dent on world economic inequality.

In fact, overly ambitious and enthusiastic policies of the world government in dealing with the problems of global human civilization could easily bring about its downfall. The problems of global human civilization are deeply rooted in the realities of human nature and human psychology, the implication of which is that any proposed "solution" to these problems, which is arguably in the long-term interest of the entire human population, will be perceived by substantial groups within this population as being contrary to their own specific short-term self-interest. Thus most people in the rich nations will at first presume that a World Economic Equalization Program on the scale proposed herein must necessarily reduce their own living standards. Only if these people can be convinced that such a program does *not* constitute a serious threat to their own short-term wel- fare will they be likely to accurately perceive and properly appreciate the long-term advantages of the program to the entire human race. Similarly, any proposed measures to control population growth and/or to reduce the rate of exploitation of the natural environment will be perceived by some as an imposition upon their basic human rights. In order to survive in the short run, and thus to make a significant long-term contribution to the future destiny of human civilization, the world government will have to be very cautious and circumspect with respect to policies and programs intended to cope with such difficult and sensitive problems as rapid population growth and environmental degradation.

Another point worthy of mention in this regard is that there are certain inescapable limits on the amount of cultural, psychological and attitudinal uniformity among humanity which is possible. Any effort to go beyond these limits would instantly cause the total or near-total dissolution of the world federation. An important example of this is religion. Historically, religious differences have been implicated in a tremendous amount of violent conflict among humanity: the holy wars of Islamic expansion, the Crusades, and the wars of the Protestant Reformation, to name only a few of the more dramatic cases. Religion, in and of itself, did not create the conflicts of interest which ultimately led to warfare, but religion was instrumental in transforming what would otherwise have been manageable conflicts of interest amenable to peaceful compromise and accommodation into violent confrontations and open warfare. Optimally therefore—as far as reducing the propensity toward violence and warfare is concerned—the entire human race should subscribe to the same religion. The trouble is that religion is inherently a matter of faith and not reason. This means that there is absolutely no way that humanity can determine, by means of rational intellectual reasoning based on dispassionate examination of the available empirical evidence, which elements of religious doctrine are valid, and which are not. What this means in terms of world government is that if such a government desires to survive, it must be absolutely neutral with respect to religion, in word and deed, in law and policy, now and forever.

Religious differences are the most obvious example of cultural differences which obviously, from the historical record, are capable of aggravating hostility and generating conflict. There are many other such differences which are equally impervious to reduction or modification in the foreseeable future. But these differences need not constitute an insuperable impediment to world government—

so long as the world government is sufficiently tolerant in its attitude and modest in its laws and policies regarding such differences. Over the centuries, humanity has made great progress in learning a very important lesson concerning cultural differences: that it is intolerably costly and burdensome to allow these differences to generate armed conflict and warfare. Moreover, humanity now recognizes certain types of cultural diversity as healthy and fully beneficial. Religious fanaticism is hardly extinct in the modern world, nor is the enlistment of religious faith by demagogues and cynics as an instrument for violently pursuing their own material interests. But the contribution of religious faith to rampant hostility and armed conflict is on the decline (9/11 to the contrary). An existent, functioning world government would in all probability assist and accelerate this trend.

Let us turn now to the cons on world government, to the perceived difficulties and salient objections that, up to the present time, have prevented humanity from moving forward to the establishment of a legitimate, full-fledged world government. There are several ways in which we might categorize these difficulties and objections. For example, Frederick L. Schuman, in his magisterial advocacy of world government *The Commonwealth of Man* (1952), writes as follows (p. 468): "The antifederalist case, reduced to bare bones, holds that world government, federal or otherwise, is either undesirable or unnecessary or irrelevant or impossible, or all four together." This categorization is as good as any, and will serve as an organizational basis for the following comments. In briefly outlining the positive case for world government in the foregoing, I have been careful not to overstate the potential benefits that might reasonably be anticipated. The various qualifications and caveats I have discussed above amount in effect to a partial statement of the case against world government, especially under the rubric of "irrelevancy." It is only fair that in outlining the negative case against world government, I do not overstate the weight and seriousness of the potential costs. Therefore, after stating and briefly discussing each objection, I will offer a brief summary of the counter-argument to be made by a proponent of world government. Throughout this book, a consistent effort will be made to underpin and substantiate these counter-arguments. I will take up each of the four objections mentioned by Schuman in what I consider to be the order of increasing sensibility and importance.

The charge that world government is "irrelevant" is based on the proposition that the establishment of an institutional structure of world government will not, in and of itself, constitute a solution of any major problem confronting humanity. Even if a world government were to come about, there would still be poverty and hunger throughout the world, population would continue to expand and the natural environment would continue being squeezed, human beings would still be hostile toward one another and would still express this hostility through violent aggression. The problems of humanity are too deep-rooted to be solved by means of adding another layer of political organization at the top. For these problems to be solved, billions of individual human beings have to change their habits of thought and behavior. And if and when that happens, the appropriate solutions to the various problems of human civilization will be rapidly implemented by the national governments. For example, if it is indeed the case that only strong anti-natalist policies will save humanity from disastrous overpopulation of the planet, if and when this is recognized by billions of individual human beings, then strongly anti-natalist policies will be implemented by the nations. The existence of a world government will neither help nor hinder in the solution of the problems of human civilization—it is in fact irrelevant to these problems.

Now it is obviously true that the legal formalities of initiating a world government, the construction of buildings to house the agencies of this government, and the hiring of personnel to staff these agencies, will not, in and of themselves, accomplish anything constructive toward solving the problems of human civilization. If the personnel of the world government were to go to their offices each day and spend all day reading novels or playing cards, then the world government would indeed be fully irrelevant. But few people seriously expect that lassitude and inactivity among the personnel of the world government would constitute a fundamental problem. Rather the typical expectation is that these personnel would be very active and energetic—although in the view of world government skeptics, the activity and energy would probably be misguided and counter-productive.

Of course, the irrelevancy argument may be reworked to enhance its plausibility, but in so doing it would be transformed into the very different argument that world government would be undesirable. For example, the allegation that a world government "would not affect the likelihood of war" does not make sense as an argument against world government unless it is elaborated along the lines that "the civil wars that would be generated by a world government would be worse than the international wars generated by the sovereign nation-state system." This makes logical sense (although it is probably not empirically true), but then the argument is essentially that world government would be undesirable. For another example, the allegation that a world government "would not affect the likelihood of environmental disaster brought on by overpopulation" does not make sense unless it is elaborated along the lines that "the massive and stifling bureaucracy entailed by world government would make the achievement of control over population growth less likely rather than more likely." Once again, this makes logical sense (although it is probably not empirically true), but then again the argument is essentially that world government would be undesirable.

The argument against world government that it is irrelevant blends gradually into the argument that world government is "unnecessary." Both arguments have in common the proposition that world government will not cure world problems. The main difference is that the irrelevancy argument has a pessimistic connotation while the unnecessity argument has an optimistic connotation. The implication of irrelevancy is that the problems of human civilization which we know today will be with us always and forever, whether or not we establish a world government. The implication of unnecessity is that the problems of human civilization which we know today will eventually be overcome, even if we never establish a world government. The latter argument emphasizes the great progress which has been made, particularly in recent decades, in the cultivation of attitudes of mutual toleration and respect throughout the world. The growth of appropriate attitudes is making the achievement of peace, prosperity and progress fully possible without the need for world government. The growth of appropriate attitudes is not attributed entirely, in this view, to advances in human kindness and altruism. Rather, to a large extent, this growth is attributable to the tremendous twentieth century advances in the actual and potential destructiveness of warfare, especially after the development of hydrogen bombs and long-range ballistic missile delivery systems. As a consequence of these advances, mankind has awakened at last to the unacceptability of unrestrained warfare. Of necessity, we must love our fellow man, and a world government is therefore no longer important to the cultivation of this love.

A basic weakness of both the irrelevancy argument and the unnecessity argument is that neither one of them argues toward the *undesirability* of world government. If, as the proponents of the irrelevancy argument maintain, human civilization cannot escape the problems of war, poverty, overpopulation, environmental decay, and so on, by means of establishing a world government, this does not necessarily mean there would be a positive evil in establishing such a government. Besides, it can never be known absolutely that world government would actually be useless as an instrument for coping with the problems of human civilization. If the proponents of irrelevancy are correct, then while it is true that a world government will do no good, it is also true that it will do no harm. The question emerges: What is the harm in trying?

Turning to the unnecessity argument, if, as the proponents of this argument maintain, human civilization will overcome the problems of war, poverty, overpopulation, environmental decay, and so on, without establishing a world government, again this does not necessarily mean there would be a positive evil in establishing such a government. Besides which, any serious reliance on this argument betrays exactly the sort of innocent optimism and naïve utopianism which has always been a standard accusation made against proponents of world government. This is not to say that no meaningful evidence exists to support a reasonable degree of optimism regarding the future destiny of human civilization. For example, nuclear weapons have been in existence for well over a half-century, and although most of this period witnessed a virulent Cold War confrontation between the communist and noncommunist ideological systems, no nuclear war occurred. But to jump from the fact that humanity has so far been fortunate, to the conclusion that potential nuclear war in the future is not to be greatly feared, is very much contrary to common sense, and amounts to the elevation of mere wishful speculation to the status of plausible hypothesis. Moreover, if the strict form of the unnecessity argument against world government were indeed correct, this would imply the invalidity of the far more serious argument against world government that it is undesirable. In the matter of nuclear war, the contention of the undesirability argument is that there is a much greater danger of nuclear civil war if a world government is established, than there is of nuclear international wars among sovereign nation-states if a world government is not established. But according to the unnecessity argument, there is no danger of any nuclear war in any event because its consequences would be so terrible. This speculation (an extremely dubious speculation) would apply to nuclear civil wars within a world state no less than it would to nuclear international wars between sovereign nation-states.

The charge that world government is "impossible" is based on the proposition that what has been empirically true in the past (that mankind has not established a world government) will necessarily remain true into the remote and unforeseeable future. Despite all the arguments and admonitions of proponents of world government over the years, decades, and even centuries, there has never been even a very distant approach (according to this argument) to the actual achievement of a world government in the real world. What is abundantly clear is that the prejudices and preconceptions against world government among the vast majority of the human population are so strongly and deeply entrenched that very few individuals in the past have ever taken the time and trouble to think seriously about world government, and the same thing will continue to be true into the indefinite future. In the strictest form of this argument, *it does not matter* if the rational and logical case for world government is in fact sound, and that in actual fact the interests of humanity would be well served by the establishment of a world government. The actual truth of the issue is irrelevant, according to the strict form, because in some matters humanity is not guided to any appreciable extent by logic and rationality.

Clearly the impossibility argument, in its strictest form, is not only untenable but an insult to the intelligence and rationality of humanity. It is certainly true that some things are definitely, literally and inalterably impossible. It is impossible for the sum of 2 plus 2 to equal 5. It is impossible for any physical object, animate or inanimate, to be free of the force of gravity. It is impossible for the polar ice caps to melt overnight, or for the oceans to evaporate in an instant (unless our sun explodes). It is impossible for human beings to live to the age of 250 years. It is impossible for human beings to flap their arms and fly like birds, or to breathe water like fish so that they can survive underwater indefinitely without artificial breathing apparatus. Many things are impossible in the strict sense. Given the time and inclination, one could fill a large book with things which are impossible in a strict sense. But the formation by humanity of a world government is not one of them.

The impossibility argument against world government is frequently invoked by world government skeptics, but rarely are they employing the strictest sense of the argument. When skeptics say that "world government is impossible now and will remain so into the remote and unforeseeable future," what they actually mean is that "world government is *undesirable* now and will remain so into the remote and unforeseeable future—and for that reason, owing to the rationality and common sense of humanity, world government is *impossible* now and will remain so into the remote and unforeseeable future." Only if the impossibility charge is directly supported by the undesirability charge does it carry any weight. Any legitimate sensibility of the impossibility proposition—owing to the fact that it is obviously *not* definitely, literally and inalterably impossible for humanity to establish a world government—must lie in the proposition that a world government would be undesirable. Therefore, the impossibility argument is not independent of, but is fully dependent upon, the undesirability argument. Paradoxically, any actual sensibility of the impossibility argument relies completely on the rationality, rather than the irrationality, of mankind.

The foregoing discussion has hopefully made it clear that once we penetrate beyond the level of superficial analysis, three of the four arguments against world government (that world government is irrelevant, unnecessary, and impossible) are perceived to have very little sensibility when isolated from the fourth argument: that world government would be undesirable. The essence of the matter, therefore, lies in the alleged undesirability of world government.

In explicating the alleged undesirability of world government, critics rely mostly on the proposition that owing to the deep divisions within humanity in terms of race, religion, language, ideology and economic status, establishment of a world government would very likely lead to one of two equally terrible outcomes: a repressive totalitarian regime, or a disastrous civil war. A democratic world government not only would not necessarily forestall these adverse outcomes, but might facilitate them. Any decisions or policies democratically determined according to the majority will possess a tremendous amount of legitimacy—to the majority. The notion that every human being possesses certain "natural rights" beyond restriction by democratic decision-making is an idealistic abstraction which thus far has had rather limited impact within human societies. In the real world, natural rights are defined by state authority, and human history is replete with instances in which state authority has weighed very heavily on the individual human beings composing the society. Tyranny need not involve oligarchic rule: under some plausible circumstances, the majority can impose over various minorities just as odious a tyranny as that imposed by a non-benevolent dictator.

A world government (continuing with this line of thought) would open the door wide to a tremendous amount of repression and oppression, with the attendant risks of violent revolution and civil war. Inevitably, individual nations would attempt to impose their own social and cultural preferences on the world government, and thereby on all other nations. Even under the best-case scenario, this would lead to such perpetual bickering and wrangling within the world government that its practical effectiveness in dealing with global issues would be negligible. What is far more likely, given sufficient time, is that eventually one or another faction of nations would become dominant in the world government, with the consequence that the world government would then endeavor to impose the preferences of the dominant faction on all member nations. At this point, two outcomes would be possible. If the world government has retained a monopoly on heavy weaponry, including nuclear weaponry, it would impose its will on nations which are not part of the dominant faction by force and threat of force. The other possibility—which would be operative if the world government has *not* maintained a monopoly on heavy weaponry—is that those nations unwilling to submit to a world government under the control of a dominant faction of nations would secede from the world federation with the warning (perhaps implicit rather than explicit) that any effort to forcibly prevent secession will be met with the full force of the heavy armament under the seceding nations' control. If the world government does not oppose the departure of these nations, then its membership will have been so depleted that the experiment in world government will be seen as nothing more than a very costly exercise in futility. If the world government does oppose the departure of these nations, the result will be a civil war of catastrophic proportions.

Of course I will have a great deal to say in the following pages that suggests, directly or indirectly, the very dubious plausibility of this overall scenario of world government as the operative instrumentality of the downfall of human civilization. At this point, therefore, I will confine myself to a very brief critical comment. World government skeptics, in developing this scenario (usually in a very perfunctory and unsatisfactory manner) rarely take cognizance of the very obvious objection that the actual risk of the envisioned disasters would depend very greatly on the institutional structures and procedures of the world government. There have been many proposals for world government, and these proposals differ widely in critical respects. For example, the Federal Union of Democratic Nations proposed herein envisions the member nations retaining, by explicit constitutional authorization, both the permanent and inalienable right to secession, and the permanent and inalienable right to maintain military forces equipped with nuclear weaponry. While it is true that this specific aspect of the Federal Union proposal is not typical of world government proposals, it is hardly a matter of great subtlety and ingenuity. Many world government skeptics are recognized academic and journalistic experts in international relations and organization. Therefore, they ought to be aware of such possibilities, and they ought to keep them in mind and make reference to them when assessing the world government possibility.

Another problem with the "world government leading to disaster" scenario is that it does not trouble to show that the threat of disaster would be *greater* with a world government than without a world government. It has already been thoroughly demonstrated by modern history that the sovereign nation-state system is capable of generating a prodigious amount of conflict and warfare. No world government was implicated in World War I, nor was one implicated in World War II, nor was one implicated in the post-World War II Cold War which very nearly generated a nuclear World War III which would have devastated human civilization. The question arises with respect to the danger of war: How much worse could it get? With respect to the danger of totalitarian oppression, it should be well noted that the principles and practices of totalitarian oppression were not invented by a world government. These principles and practices have been well developed by various national governments. More often than not, totalitarian oppression within nations has been associated with the stresses and strains imposed on nations by rivalry with other nations. For example, it is very difficult to imagine that Joseph Stalin would have achieved such a remarkable level of dictatorial control over the Soviet Union if both its general population and its ruling Communist Party elite had not been so concerned about the possibility of invasion by hostile capitalist nations. Again, it is very difficult to imagine that Adolf Hitler would have achieved such a remarkable level of dictatorial control over Germany if its people had not been so disgruntled by their military defeat in World War I. These are the most dramatic examples of inflamed nationalism paving the way to totalitarian dictatorship, but there are others. In general, the more that leaders of nations are able to inculcate fear and loathing of foreign nations within their own countrymen, the more likely these leaders are to attain dictatorial power and oppressive control. If there is no higher political authority in the world than the nation-state, there is nothing to check this propensity. Once again the question arises, now with respect to the danger of totalitarian oppression: How much worse could it get?

Skeptics of world government conjure up vague and indistinct visions of nations attempting to gain control over the world government, and then using that control to impose their own preferences on other nations to whom these preferences are repugnant and intolerable. But what exactly are these "preferences"? Is it seriously proposed that the Christian nations, for example, will attempt to foist Christianity on the Muslim nations? Or that the Muslim nations will attempt to foist Islam on the Christian nations? The Islamic holy wars of expansion had run their course many hundreds of years ago. The lesson that they taught adherents of Islam was that no matter how much blood was shed and treasure wasted, there was no possibility of imposing the worship of Allah on the entire world population. A similar lesson was taught to the adherents of Christianity by the Crusades. The virtue of tolerance is not natural to humanity, but the vicissitudes of history have taught the great majority of humanity that the only alternative to tolerance is endless loss and suffering. Of course, the tragic occurrences of September 11, 2001, constitute powerful testimony to the fact that religious fanaticism—while less important today than in the past—is by no means extinct in the modern world. But while modern adherents to the ancient Muslim cause of jihad have proved themselves capable of extremely destructive acts of terrorism, they are not sufficiently numerous to induce the governments of the Islamic nations to openly pursue jihad as national policy.

And leaving aside these "preferences," by exactly what means and mechanisms is it proposed that any sub-group of nations could succeed in "gaining control" over a world government? There is never any serious discussion and analysis of these means and mechanisms. Is this because these means and mechanisms are so self-evident as to make discussion and analysis superfluous? Or is it because serious discussion and analysis of these means and mechanisms might make their dubiousness and improbability self-evident? And if we do (for the sake of argument) imagine that some nations in the world are so absolutely determined to impose their own preferences on other nations that they will go to great lengths to gain control over a world government in order to accomplish this objective, what is there to discourage or prevent these nations from pursuing the odious and disruptive policy of trying to impose their own preferences on other nations within the sovereign nation-state system of today? In other words, on what basis, exactly, is it proposed that certain nations which *will not* be troublemakers under the sovereign nation-state system of today *will* become troublemakers if a world government exists?

While the primary objection to world government among skeptics has always been that world government would set the stage for totalitarian repression and/or disastrous civil war, a secondary objection worthy of mention is that a world government would generate such a huge and overwhelming bureaucracy as to stifle the individual and small-group initiative on which the progress of human civilization so much depends. National governments (according to the argument) have shown themselves capable of producing prodigious bureaucracies whose intrusive regulations and prohibitions operate as a heavy deadweight burden on the various national societies. It follows that since the territory and population of a world government would be so much more extensive than that of even the largest nation-state, it will inevitably produce an even more prodigious bureaucracy. The costs of government bureaucracies at the national level are already dire; at the supernational level, the costs of a world government bureaucracy would clearly be disastrous.

Now it is well-known to anyone with even a cursory familiarity with sociological literature that in Max Weber's seminal work on the subject, a "bureaucracy" is simply any large-scale organization incorporating specialization, division of labor, and hierarchical stratification. By this neutral definition, somewhat over 90 percent of the labor force in an advanced, industrialized nation is employed in bureaucracies of one sort or another. Bureaucracies in this general sense include, in addition to government agencies, business enterprises at all but the smallest scale of operation, plus a very wide spectrum of nonprofit, nongovernmental organizations (NGOs) comprising religious administrations, special interest groups, and voluntary associations. Outside of the professional sociological literature, of course, the term "bureaucracy" is widely utilized in a pejorative sense to refer to any large-scale government organization whose operations impede the discretionary autonomy of individual citizens. The classic example of bureaucracy in this negative sense are various tax-collecting agencies, such as the U.S. Internal Revenue Service. Except to a tiny minority of veritably unhinged ideological fanatics, it is obvious that some amount of bureaucracy is necessary to the operation of society.

Turning to the relationship between world government and government bureaucracy, this relationship is not simple and straightforward. It is undeniable, of course, that a newly founded world government would require the creation of some additional bureaucratic agencies. But quite likely these bureaucratic agencies would take over some of the functions and responsibilities of existing national government bureaucracies, so that the total overhead costs of government administration, adding together national and supernational costs, will not be greatly increased. Of course, one of the fundamental objectives of world government is to reduce the likelihood of conflict and warfare, so that total military expenditures over all nations, including those at the national and those at the supernational level, may be reduced without diminishing the security of individual human beings. It is well known that some of the biggest and most costly of the national government bureaucracies of the present day are the military establishments of the various nations. World government is a plausible avenue toward the reduction of this deadweight burden.

There is a reasonable expectation, in any event, that the additional bureaucracies necessitated by the world government would make a positive contribution to human civilization in their own right, without reference to the possibility that world government would reduce the aggregate military overhead costs of worldwide human civilization. In rational historical perspective, bureaucracy is simply the administrative organization of cooperation and coordination, and the story of progress throughout the ages has largely been the story of advancing cooperation and coordination. For example, an individual genius such as Thomas Edison, working in solitary splendor in his laboratory, may invent marvels such as the electric light bulb. But this invention would have been useless to humanity in the absence of large-scale business organizations (bureaucracies) devoted to the production and marketing of light bulbs. With respect to government bureaucracies which do not produce and market commercial commodities, their contribution may not be as obvious, but it is not necessarily less worthwhile.

Government-supported bureaucracies do not suddenly mushroom up out of the earth because of the self-interest of their personnel in remunerative and undemanding employment. Each of them has a purpose and a mission of service to the larger society. If we look, for example, at the various bureaucratic agencies of the United States federal government, they all had their historical origins as instruments for the amelioration of some problem. The U.S. Army and the U.S. Navy were originally established to avert the "problem" of conquest by and subjugation to foreign powers. Without these bureaucracies, the United States would certainly have quickly resumed its former status as a colonial possession of Great Britain. The U.S. Department of Agriculture played an important role in the agricultural productivity growth that led to the current condition in which less than ten percent of the national workforce feeds the entire nation. The Federal Bureau of Investigation makes it far more difficult for criminals to elude justice by simply crossing state lines. The Food and Drug Administration helped to curb a brisk trade in useless patent medicines. If there were no U.S. Internal Revenue Service to collect taxes from less conscientious taxpayers, the more conscientious taxpayers would have to shoulder a much heavier burden. And so on. All these bureaucracies serve worthwhile purposes, and it would be the same with whatever additional bureaucracies are needed to support the worthwhile purposes of a potential future world government.

In any event, the strong possibility exists that alleged concerns about potential bureaucratic overload under world government represent a form of psychological displacement. If objections to world government are based primarily on the possibility that people in the disfavored nations (typically imagined by the objector to include his or her own nation) will be hounded by the secret police, it might make the objector seem to be paranoiac. Or if objections to world government are based primarily on the possibility that people in the disfavored nations (again typically imagined by the objector to include his or her own nation) will be subjected to extortionate taxation to support lavish welfare benefits for the people of poorer nations, this might make the objector seem to be selfish. But if objections are based largely on "bureaucracy," this absolves the objector of possible odors of paranoia or selfishness.

The above discussion merely scratches the surface of a full-scale evaluation of the pros and cons of world government. It is hardly intended to settle the matter one way or the other. But hopefully enough has been said up to this point to open the mind of the reader to possibilities which may not have been fully appreciated heretofore, and to enable the recognition that a very serious case may be made in favor of establishing a federal world government within the relatively near future—a much more serious case than is widely recognized at the present time. The balance of this book is devoted to the presentation of this case.

2

A Pragmatic Blueprint
for World Government

Appeals for world government have sometimes been accompanied by specific institutional proposals, but more often have not. Some of the best-known, most elaborate and most adamant appeals for world government, such as *The Anatomy of Peace* (1945) by Emery Reves and *The Commonwealth of Man* (1952) by Frederick Schuman, are entirely devoid of any specific institutional proposals. These works lambaste in great detail and most unmercifully the notion that reliable international security may be achieved by any means short of world government—and yet they are completely silent on how that government ought to be organized. One possible inference that might be taken from such works is that the specific institutional details are immaterial, since *any* world government would be better than no world government. Obviously, this particular inference will not appeal to a great many people. Another possible inference is that surely it is not beyond the intellectual powers of humanity to devise a workable institutional blueprint for benign and effective world government. But if this is so, why do not authors such as Reves and Schuman exercise their own intellectual powers to provide at least a rough blueprint?

In perusing the works of Emery Reves and Frederick Schuman, as well as many others of a similar nature, one is likely to be reminded of Karl Marx's intemperate tirades against the capitalist economic system, tirades that were unaccompanied by any significant development of a specific socialist alternative. As is well known, Marx disdained the task of "writing recipes for the social chefs of the future" on grounds that any socialist system was bound to be superior to the capitalist system. The subsequent history of socialism in the USSR and elsewhere has clearly demonstrated, to the satisfaction of the large majority of humanity, that the socialist cure is in fact worse than the capitalist disease. It is possible, of course, that there could be forms of socialism that would perform better than did the Soviet system. In the judgment of advocates of various plans of democratic market socialism, for example, it would be possible to combine the socialist principle of public ownership of capital property with both the principle of free market allocation and the principle of democratic accountability of government. Be that as it may, what the history of the USSR has demonstrated beyond a reasonable doubt is that socialism, in and of itself, as defined by public ownership of all or most capital property, is by no means *sufficient* to establish a social system preferable to the capitalist social system.

In the same way, world government is by no means sufficient to establish global conditions preferable to those currently prevailing under the sovereign nation-state system. The world government cure *could* be worse than the international anarchy disease. It follows, therefore, that any appeal for world government which is not based on a specific blueprint for world government, is likely to be quite unpersuasive. In order to avoid this problem, the present world government appeal will be based on a fairly detailed world government proposal. Although appeals for world government unaccompanied by specific proposals outnumber appeals that are indeed accompanied by specific proposals, there has in fact been a sufficient number of the latter put forward throughout the course of modern history as to constitute an important obstacle to focused consideration of world government. The assets and liabilities of one particular plan of world government might be very much different from those of another. Some plans of world government might be considerably more promising than others. I hope to persuade the reader that the plan of world government that forms the focus of this book is in fact substantially more promising than previously enunciated blueprints for world government.

The decision on whether or not to establish a world government must be based on the statistically expected outcome were a world government to be established, relative to the statistically expected outcome were a world government *not* to be established. If a world government is *not* established, there would be a higher probability of nuclear world war and a lower probability of global tyranny. If a world government *is* established, there would be a lower probability of nuclear world war and a higher probability of global tyranny. This much is more or less indisputable, but the point which I want to emphasize here is that presuming a world government *is* established, the probability that this government would degenerate into a global tyranny is strongly dependent on the government's specific institutional structure.

While a detailed blueprint is necessary, it would be a mistake to commit the sin of "premature specificity"—of getting bogged down in an excessive amount of detail. Therefore, among various other limitations, no proposed constitution for a world government will be provided here. In many important areas, I will provide no more than rough indications. I should also emphasize that, aside from a handful of absolutely fundamental components of the overall proposal (such as the right of member nations to withdraw legally and peacefully from the world federation), the specific nomenclature and institutional/operational proposals put forward herein are intended only to be suggestive, tentative, conditional and provisional—simply to provide a basis for discussion. If the reader finds some of these details distasteful or even unacceptable, I hope that this will not lead to rejection of the overall concept. A great many details set forth below could very easily be altered without appreciably affecting the overall thrust of the proposal.

FEDERAL UNION FUNDAMENTALS

Our objective is to formulate a plan for an international political entity that would go qualitatively beyond the United Nations of today, an international organization which is primarily just a debating society composed of ambassadors from fully sovereign nations, but at the same time would be significantly less centralized and cohesive than is the typical nation-state of today. We want to achieve a happy medium between the competing objectives of a world state sufficiently powerful and authoritative to have an important impact on the future evolution of global governance, and at the same time a world state sufficiently limited and constrained as not to represent a serious threat of degenerating into a global tyranny.

The proposed Federal Union of Democratic Nations, founded on the basis of a Federal Union Constitution, would be a full-fledged, genuine, legitimate state entity with clearly defined geographical boundaries (assuming some non-member nations), a permanent and continuous governmental structure, the power to levy taxes and enact binding legislation, and the authority to maintain standing military forces under its direct command. As the name suggests, it would be a federal rather than a unitary form of government. This means that the member nations would maintain their separate identities, governments and cultures, and would retain substantial independence, autonomy and sovereignty in all matters that do not impinge heavily on the welfare of other member nations. No officials of existing national governments would be either appointed or approved by the supernational government; rather these officials would be elected or appointed by whatever means are currently employed.

The Federal Union Constitution would comprise five principal sections: (1) nature and purposes of the Union; (2) the three branches of government (legislative, executive and judicial); (3) powers and responsibilities of the supernational government; (4) rights and responsibilities of nations; (5) rights and responsibilities of citizens. It would also include a Transitional Codicil to remain in effect for the first several decades of operation of the Federal Union. Two absolutely essential components of the articles concerning rights and responsibilities of nations would be: (1) the permanent and inalienable right of a member nation to withdraw peacefully from the Federal Union; and (2) the permanent and inalienable right of a member nation to maintain under its direct control whatever military forces and armaments it deems necessary. These two substantive rights would be the practical guarantors of other national rights.

The name of the union implies that the member nations would all be democratic in nature. A fairly generous interpretation of the word "democratic" may be necessary, lest too many nations be denied membership on the basis that they are not sufficiently democratic. In a general sense, "democracy" implies that the government is responsive to the preferences of the people. But more specifically, it implies that high government officials are elected by the people in regular, open, and contested elections, and that the people enjoy strong and effective rights of free speech, free press, and free political organization. A substantial number of nations in the world today—even some that proclaim themselves to be "democratic"—do not exhibit these characteristics. For example, the People's Republic of China is today regarded by many people as a political oligarchy under the effective control of a handful of high officials of the Communist Party of China. But it would not be advisable to exclude a nation as large and important as China from the Federal Union on grounds that it is insufficiently democratic. If China is a member nation of the Federal Union of Democratic Nations, there would be stronger and more effective psychological pressure on the leadership to implement democratic reforms, than there would be if China were not a member nation. The same is true of smaller nations that at the present time are not internally democratic in the strong sense. The long-run objective would be to have every nation maintaining very high domestic standards of democratic accountability of the government—but this long-run objective will be better served if considerable flexibility is practiced in the short run.

The supranational federation would implement what has become a fairly standard tripartite division of government power among legislative, executive and judicial branches. The legislative branch would consist of a unicameral Union Chamber of Representatives of about 200 members; the executive branch would be headed by a Union Chief Executive; and the judicial branch, composed of 25 justices, would be known as the Union High Court. It is proposed that world government elections be held on a quinquennial basis (every five years), and that the highest officials of all three branches be democratically elected directly by the citizens. It is an absolutely central element of the plan that no high-level Federal Union officials would be appointed by the national governments, nor would they be subject to any direct control by the national governments. Naturally, as citizens of specific member nations, Federal Union officials would be fully cognizant of the special interests of their respective nations. This provides sufficient recognition of the interests of nations.

The regional components of the Federal Union would comprise between 100 and 200 Union Districts, of roughly equivalent population. These Union Districts quite possibly would have little or no administrative significance, but might merely be regions from which legislators are elected. Some large nations would contain several Union Districts; on the other hand, several smaller nations might be needed to comprise a single Union District. For the most part, nations in the same Union District would be territorially contiguous—but not necessarily. In some cases, historical, economic or cultural factors may override geographical proximity. For example, one obvious possibility would be the combination of a large number of very small island nations from around the world in one single Union District.

Each Union District would elect a single Union Representative to the Union Chamber of Representatives every five years. The entire population of the Union would elect a Union Chief Executive, the head of the executive branch of the supranational government, every 10 years. Finally, the elections of the 25 Union

Justices serving on the Union High Court would be staggered: the term of office of a Union Justice would be 25 years, so that one fifth of the members of the Court would be elected in each quinquennial election.

The supernational government would possess the standard symbols and trappings of state authority: a flag, an anthem, an oath of allegiance, emblems, formal protocols, a capital city, and so on and so forth. Of these symbols and trappings, perhaps the single most important would be the capital city. The capital city of the Federal Union of Democratic Nations should not merely be a locus for the operations of the various branches of the supernational government; in addition to that it should be developed into one of the great tourist attractions of the world. To assist this purpose the Federal Union capital should be located close to a major existing city that is already an important tourist attraction. This should be a city of fairly central location (in a world sense), and it should also be a city of great historical and cultural significance. Another criterion is that the city should neither be in a very wealthy First World nation nor in a very poor Third World nation. One obvious possibility is Athens, Greece.

The Federal Union complex should be developed on the remote outskirts of the selected city, in order that its development not be excessively constrained by existing structures. To begin with, the government buildings should be large and impressive. They should be grouped around an expansive, park-like mall (as in Washington, D.C.), decorated with numerous monuments, fountains and ponds. Also around this mall should be sited several large museums covering various dimensions of human endeavor from the fine arts to space exploration. Not far away from the mall should be two additional attractions much favored by tourists: a large zoo and botanical garden; and a major theme park along the lines of the various Disneyworlds. The tourist trade should be assiduously cultivated by means of luxurious hotels and fine restaurants, as well as by theaters, concert halls, opera houses, markets, shopping centers, and so on.

As the capital city would be filled, from one end to the other, with a plethora of flags, emblems and other symbols of the Federal Union of Democratic Nations, it would hopefully inspire its many visitors with the humane and civilizing spirit of supernational unity. In the first decades of the Federal Union of Democratic Nations, it is quite possible that many visitors to the capital city will be citizens of non-member nations. It is essential that these visitors be favorably impressed, and that they return home as supporters of entry into the Union.

Outside the capital city of the Federal Union, there should be a high level of visibility of the Union—within reason. It would not be good, for example, to have loudspeakers in public squares blasting out slogans accompanied by martial music, or to interrupt regular programming on radio and television for special bulletins on the activities of the supernational government and the statements and proclamations of its various officials. That sort of thing, of course, was associated with the worst dictatorships of the twentieth century, and no doubt would be severely counterproductive if not completely disastrous. More helpful would be such significant yet relatively unobtrusive things as establishing a supernational holiday to commemorate the foundation of the Union, flying the supernational flag over national government buildings and sports arenas, singing the supernational anthem before sports events and other public occasions, and the like.

Of critical importance in the long term would be the attitudes toward world government inculcated in children. Primary and secondary school educators should be encouraged to impart a generally positive viewpoint on the Federal Union to their students. This does not mean preaching mindless celebration of and enthusiasm for the Union. Problems and difficulties—of which there will assuredly be an abundance—should be clearly acknowledged and discussed. But it should also be maintained that unless there emerges incontrovertible evidence to the contrary, people should assume that the Federal Union is on the whole making a positive contribution to human welfare.

There are a number of areas in which supernational and national observances should occur simultaneously for an extended period of time following the foundation of the Union, but with the expectation that in the very long term the supernational observances will eventually supersede the national observances. Patience and caution must obviously be exercised in these matters: trying to push too far too quickly could lead to a reaction which might jeopardize the continued participation of important nations in the Federal Union. The general rule in pursuing the long-term goal is to maintain perpetual flexibility and toleration with respect to matters in which diversity is either inevitable or has no seriously adverse bearing on practical economic and political issues, but to work gradually toward uniformity in other matters.

An important example of the former is religion. Whether this is the result of divine purpose or of human nature, humanity has developed a large number of religious systems: Judaism, Christianity, Islam, Hinduism and Buddhism, to name only some of the more important. Within each of the major categories there are normally several sub-categories. It is almost definitional that religious belief systems cannot be confirmed or contradicted by any conceivable appeal to either logical reasoning or empirical reality. Many if not most religious belief systems offer the believer some form of solace against the apparent personal extinction implied by the physical realities of death and decay: for example, that the spiritual soul's awareness, perception and reasoning will continue onward into an afterlife following the death of the physical body. In view of the fact that personal survival may be at stake, religious beliefs are often accompanied by strong emotions and great determination to suppress opposed religious beliefs. No doubt it would be desirable, from the point of view of peace and tranquillity, if humanity were to organize a universal ecumenical council with the purpose of specifying the tenets of a single "true" religion acceptable to all people in the world. The futility of such an undertaking will be obvious to most reasonable individuals. Thus, religious diversity is apparently inevitable into the foreseeable future. What this means is that if it is to survive, the Federal Union must exercise complete impartiality with respect to religion, and it must practice an uncompromising separation of church and state.

While religion is an example of a matter in which diversity seems inevitable, but which need not have any adverse effect on the practical economic and political operations of the Union, language is an example of a matter in which considerable diversity exists at the present time, but this is a form of diversity which is neither inevitable nor neutral in its effects on economic and political operations. This is an area in which the Federal Union should indeed press forward—albeit at a gradual and unhurried pace—toward less diversity and more homogeneity. History has clearly demonstrated that a common language is a powerful force in support of both political unity and economic prosperity. It has equally clearly demonstrated that different languages are frequently a potent divisive force: more often than not, the curse of separatism (as in Canada's province of Quebec) is linguistically based. As a speaker of English, my own judgment on this matter is possibly biased. Nevertheless, it is certainly arguable that in view of the present widespread dissemination of the English language throughout the world, there are compelling arguments of practicality, convenience and expedience in favor of the adoption of English as the official language of the Federal Union of Democratic Nations.

There are several languages besides English that are widely spoken throughout the world, which would make it very difficult to specify the second official language. And once a second official language had been allowed, the arguments would be endless for a third, a fourth, and so on. The operations of the Union would be in danger of bogging down in a multilingual morass. A possible compromise to facilitate the adoption of English as the sole official language of the Federal Union might be to require schoolchildren in English-speaking nations to study some other language to the same extent and intensity that schoolchildren in other nations study English. According to the ancient proverb, "Misery loves company": thus the knowledge that schoolchildren in English-speaking nations were being subjected to the mental strain of studying another language no less than their own children, might provide a sufficient amount of psychological solace to non-English speakers to induce them to accept English as the sole official language of the Federal Union. Even if this compromise were acceptable to most nations, it would probably require a period of many decades, if not many centuries, before the overwhelming majority of humanity becomes fluent in a single language.

It is a conventional policy of a modern nation-state to maintain a free trade area within its national boundaries. The close ties which this policy facilitates between all parts of the nation are not only economically beneficial, but they also augment psychological feelings of unity and shared purpose. Despite decades of multilateral conferences and bilateral negotiations, first under the GATT rubric (General Agreement on Tariffs and Trade) and now under the WTO rubric (World Trade Organization), the various legal and financial impediments erected by individual nations against international trade and investment remain a very significant drag on the development of the global economy. Therefore a primary task of the Federal Union during its early decades would be to oversee the full and comprehensive dismantling of various national impediments (tariffs, import quotas, and so on) to the free flow of physical commodities and financial capital between member nations. This will not necessarily be an easy task, since in some cases tariff revenues constitute a significant source of national government revenue, while in other cases protection against foreign competition is very much in the financial interest of influential individuals and organizations. Owing to these factors, it may require a substantial period of time before the domestic free trade objective is achieved.

It is also a conventional policy of a modern nation-state to maintain a high level of internal population mobility. This is also economically beneficial, both to individual citizens and to the nation as a whole, as well as augmenting psychological feelings of unity and shared purpose among the population. Unfortunately, this particular characteristic of the typical modern nation-state cannot be quickly and easily emulated by the Federal Union of Democratic Nations. The immigration barriers that have been established by the rich nations to restrain the flow of migrants from the poor nations must be kept in force until the successful completion of the World Economic Equalization Program. The opinion is almost universal among economists that the abolition of immigration restrictions under the current condition of wide economic disparities between nations would lead to a massive wave of migration from the poor nations to the rich nations, and that the probable result of such a massive wave would be a drastic reduction in the average living standards of the rich nations. The potential dangers from unrestricted immigration may be exaggerated but they certainly cannot be ignored. Therefore the elimination of barriers to human mobility within the Federal Union will have to await successful completion of the WEEP. This would entail a period of at least several decades, possibly longer.

THE THREE BRANCHES OF GOVERNMENT

There are three fundamental aspects of governance: the making of laws, the enforcement of laws, and the interpretation and adjudication of laws. Although the word "law" normally implies a regulation or restriction of individual or organizational behavior, it may also pertain to the budgetary allocation and expenditure of government revenues on such things as schools, highways, police and fire protection, and national defense. According to the separation of powers principle, generally deemed a bulwark of democracy, responsibility for these three fundamental aspects of governance should be subdivided among three separate and organizationally distinct branches of government, each staffed and administered independently by its own personnel. The legislative branch makes the laws, the executive branch enforces the laws, and the judicial branch interprets and adjudicates the laws. The idea is that the division of government powers makes it less likely that "bad laws" will become operational. If the legislative branch unwisely passes a bad law, for example, that law might be rendered ineffective if the executive branch wisely declines to enforce it, or if the judicial branch either wisely overturns it entirely on constitutional grounds, or wisely interprets it in a manner which thwarts the unwise intentions of the legislature.

Although the separation of powers principle envisions the full independence of all three branches of government from one another, in the real world some branches of government are often indirectly controlled by other branches. For example, under the parliamentary form of government, the highest executive officers (the ministers) are elected by the legislative branch. For another example, under the presidential form of government, the highest judges of the judicial branch are appointed by the executive branch, subject to the approval of the legislative branch. The proposal put forward here for the three branches of government of the Federal Union of Democratic Nations, envisions the fullest possible autonomy and independence of the three branches of government, by means of regular, contested elections for the highest positions within each of the three branches. Elections would be held every five years, that is, on a quin-quennial basis. No doubt it would be convenient to have elections in years divisible by five: e.g., in 2020, 2025, 2030, 2035, and so on. Elections would either be "0 year elections" (2020, 2030, etc.) or "5 year elections" (2025, 2035, etc.). In "5 year elections," each of the approximately 200 Union Districts would elect its Union Representative to a 5-year term, and 5 seats on the 25-seat Union High Court would be up for election to 25-year terms. With respect to the Union Justices, they might be elected by the entire population of the Federal Union without regard to the candidates' Districts of residence, or they might be associated with specific Union Districts in order to guarantee representation of each District on the Union High Court. The "0 year elections" would be the same as the "5 year elections" except for the fact that in the former, the entire population of the Federal Union would also elect a single Union Chief Executive to head the executive branch.

The Legislative Branch

The legislative branch of the world government would be a Union Chamber of Representatives consisting of representatives elected from the Union Districts. The principal functions of the Union Chamber of Representatives would include the following: (1) to debate and vote on permanent legislation or policy directives proposed internally or by the Union Chief Executive; (2) to debate and vote on major personnel appointments by the Union Chief Executive, including all Cabinet-level positions; (3) to debate, amend and vote on the budget presented by the Union Chief Executive; (4) to impeach and remove members of the legislative and/or judicial arms of the government who are found guilty of serious criminal or constitutional offenses. There would be one Union Representative from each Union District. The salary and benefits of Union Representatives should be commensurate with their important responsibilities and high prestige—that is to say, they should be very generous.

The question of how many Union Districts—and therefore how many Union

Representatives—there should be, will be a matter for very careful consideration. I have been using "approximately 200" for this number, but this is merely a suggestion. Of course, a case could be made for a much larger legislature, of 300, 400 or even more members. Many national legislatures throughout the world consist of several hundred members. For example, the United States Congress comprises a House of Representatives with 435 members and a Senate with 100 members, for a total of 535 members. The standard justification for a large legislature is that it permits the representation of a large number of diverse economic interests and political viewpoints. However, the obvious problem with a very large number of legislators, particularly if they represent a very wide array of economic interests and political viewpoints, is that it hampers the achievement of consensus and the determination of action. The degree of social and economic heterogeneity among the population of the Federal Union of Democratic Nations will obviously be very great, far surpassing the social and economic heterogeneity within any particular member nation. This heterogeneity clearly poses a problem as far as the attainment of agreement is concerned. It is generally believed that in most cases, the fewer individuals are involved in making a decision, the less difficult it is to reach an agreement. One way of coping with the problem of heterogeneity, therefore, is to have a legislature with a relatively limited number of members. On the other hand, if the legislature consisted of only 20, 30, or even 50 members, this would seem to be too small a number. The number 200 might be deemed a happy medium between the competing objectives of a legislature large enough to represent a reasonable amount of diversity, yet small enough to allow the sort of personal acquaintance and interaction among the legislators that would facilitate achieving consensus.

Another mechanism for coping with heterogeneity would be the unicameral nature of the proposed world government legislature. Bicameral legislatures, of course, are a time-honored institutional mechanism for guaranteeing an acceptable minimum amount of representation for diverse regions or interests. The major disadvantage of bicameralism, however, is that it tends to make governmental decision-making slow and unwieldy, and thus to retard the progressive development of social policy. Although there might be compelling reasons for bicameralism at one point in historical time, sometimes the historical development of a state over a long period of time erodes these reasons. For example, the British Parliament was originally constituted in the 14th century as a House of Commons, representing the non-aristocratic population, and a House of Lords, representing the aristocratic population. With the gradual advance of democratic principles in Britain over the centuries, the authority of the House of Lords was steadily curtailed, until at the present time it is little more than a superfluous and anachronistic relic of past history.

For another example, when the United States was founded, Congress was divided into two houses, the House of Representatives and the Senate, so that the smaller states in terms of population would have an equal amount of representation in one of the two houses (in this case the Senate). But it is difficult to see how this system truly preserves the interests today of very lightly populated states such Delaware and Wyoming. As of the 1990s, there were seven states out of fifty in the United States with a population under 1,000,000. These seven small states are overwhelmingly outvoted in the Senate as well as in the House of Representatives. Does this mean that these seven states are discriminated against and oppressed by the remaining 43 states? There is no evidence that anything of the kind is occurring. It follows that the bicameral nature of the U.S. Congress in fact serves no essential purpose today as far as guaranteeing an equitable distribution of political power across the states is concerned. On the other hand, more than two centuries of U.S. history have brought to light no obvious and serious harm in having a two-house legislature. Therefore this institutional arrangement has continued on throughout U.S. history, and will probably continue onward into the indefinite future. One lesson to be learned from this is that if conditions are propitious (e.g., the population is relatively homogeneous, there is a minimum of conflicts of interest among regions, etc.), then the precise institutional forms of a particular government may not be a matter of great consequence.

As of the 1990s, there were something over 200 sovereign and independent nations in the world. I have proposed herein that the number of Union Districts be approximately 200. The juxtaposition of these two numbers might suggest that it would be natural to define each Union District as corresponding to a single nation. However, owing to the tremendous disparity of population over the contemporary nations of the world, such an arrangement would seem patently absurd to most people. It would mean that there would be one Union Representative from China, a nation with a population over one billion persons, and at the same time one Union Representative from Monaco, a nation of less than 50,000 persons. Therefore, it is envisioned that Union Districts would *not* coincide with nations. In the case of larger nations, more than one Union District would be encompassed within the national boundaries. In the case of smaller nations, several nations would be required to form one Union District.

On the other hand, we would not want the Union Districts to be defined in such a way that they all have approximately the same population. For if we were to do this, the most populous nations would be disproportionately represented. To illustrate, at the present time, the People's Republic of China contains over 20 percent of the world's population. If the Union Chamber of Representatives were to number 200 representatives from Union Districts of approximately equal population, there would be approximately 40 representatives from China. This seems to be too high a number from a single nation, even if that nation is by far the most populous in the world. Another problem with requiring all Union Districts to have nearly the same population is that it would mean that a great many nations would not have even one complete Union District within their boundaries. World population as of the year 2000 was estimated to be approximately 6 billion persons. If we assume 200 Federal Union Districts, the average population over the Districts (had there been a Federal Union in existence in

2000) would have been 30 million persons. As of 2000, of the 200-odd sovereign and independent nations in the world, only 33 had populations of 30 million or greater. One possibility would be to specify that every nation with a population over a specified minimum (such as 5 million) would have at least one complete Union District within its borders, while for nations with populations substantially over 5 million, the relationship between population and number of Union Districts would be specified in such a way that the number of Union Districts would be a positive but diminishing function of population. For example, if we divided each national population (for the year 2000) by 5,000,000, raised the result to the power of .35, and rounded the result downward to the nearest integer, then China and India would each have 6 Union Districts, the United States 4, the next 7 most populous nations would have 3 Union Districts each, the next 21 most populous nations would have 2 Union Districts each, and the next 79 most populous nations would have 1 Union District each, for a total of 158 Union Districts. This would allow 117 nations to have at least one full Union District within their borders. The remaining 42 Union Districts would be allocated over the remaining nations, which number approximately 90.

It is certainly conceivable that some nations will decline to join the Federal Union of Democratic Nations on grounds that owing to their small populations, they would not have representatives in the Union Chamber of Representatives devoted exclusively to their own national interests. If this is an issue for a substantial number of small nations, one way to deal with it would be to inflate the number of Union Districts, and hence the number of Union Representatives in the Chamber. It is to be hoped that this course will not be necessary. In cases where smaller nations have to "share" their Union Representative with other nations, every effort would be made to ensure that the nations thus sharing one representative will be homogeneous in important respects, so that their national interests would be uniform. Also, as will become apparent below when we take up the issue of voting weights of Union Representatives, the voting weight of any particular nation in the Union Chamber of Representatives would be unrelated to how many representatives that nation has in the Chamber. But in the final analysis, it must be recognized that there is no possible way to determine representation in the Chamber, and voting weights of Union Representatives, to ensure that every citizen of every potential member nation will be happy.

Quite possibly a significant number of nations will in fact decline membership in the Federal Union for one reason or another—including the reason with which we are here concerned. This need not compromise the effectiveness of the Union as far as its larger purposes are concerned. If some nations stay out of the Union because they are worried that their interests will not be adequately served, that would be unfortunate, but it is not necessarily a serious problem. There were 50 nations as of the 1990s which had populations less than 1,000,000, while almost 20 nations out of this 50 had populations less than 100,000. If a number of these small nations were to stay out of the Union, the Union could carry on without them. It is to be hoped that it would quickly become apparent—after the

Federal Union is established and has been operating for a few years—that its smaller member nations are not encountering any special difficulties on account of their small population size, and this fact would induce the holdout smaller nations to join the Union.

Up to the present time, three conventional principles have been prevalent in legislative decision-making throughout the nations of the world: (1) bicameralism as a means of guaranteeing that minority interests (usually based on regional subdivisions or aristocratic status) exercise adequate and appropriate weight in legislative decision-making; (2) within each legislative house, one-person-one-vote; and (3) within each legislative house, majority rule. All of these principles are straightforward, easy to understand, and have worked well in practice over a wide range of nations throughout a long period of historical time. However, it is quite possible that these principles can be improved upon. The Federal Union of Democratic Nations would mark a major step forward in the political evolution of human civilization. The increasing sophistication of human civilization should be reflected in the increasing sophistication of the institutions of political decision-making. Therefore, I shall suggest here two fairly obvious innovations with respect to the determination of legislative decisions in the world state.

First, while the legislature would be unicameral, a "dual voting" system would be utilized to ensure adequate and appropriate weight in legislative decisions for both the populations of the rich nations and the populations of the poor nations. This would mark a break with both the bicameral principle and the one-person-one-vote principle. Second, the majority needed to approve legislation on both the population basis and the material basis, would be significantly in excess of the traditional standard of anything over 50 percent. The criterion suggested here is 60 percent. That is to say, passage of any measure by the Union Chamber of Representatives would require a 60 percent majority in both the population vote and the material vote. This marks a break with the majority rule principle—this principle would be replaced by something that might be termed the "substantial majority rule" principle. The specification of a substantial majority to approve legislation is an effort to cope with the inevitably wide diversity of viewpoints and interests within the Federal Union.

According to the dual voting principle, the vote of each Union Representative on a particular matter would be weighted in two different ways in two conceptually distinct votes. In the population vote, the weight of each Union Representative's vote would be equal to the proportion of his/her Union District's population to the total population of the Federal Union. Thus, if the population of a given Union District is 1/100th of the total population, the vote of that District's representative would be weighted as 1 in 100 in the population vote. In the material vote, the weight of each Union Representative's vote would be equal to the proportion of total Federal Union revenues raised in his/her Union District during the previous budgetary period. Thus, if 1/10th of the Federal Union's total revenues were raised in a particular Union District in the previous budgetary period, then the vote of that District's Union Representative would be weighted as 1 in 10 in the material vote. The voting weight of a particular Union Representative would have nothing to do with how many Union Representatives there are. If there were 200 Union Representatives, for example, neither in the population vote nor in the material vote would a given Union Representative's voting weight be 1 in 200. The voting weight of a particular Union Representative would rather depend on what that individual was representing: in the population vote, it would be the number of people there are in the representative's Union District, and in the material vote it would be the amount of Federal Union revenues derived from that representative's Union District. Table 2.1 lists the 30 nations potentially having the greatest weights in the population vote on the left, and the 30 nations potentially having the greatest weights in the material vote on the right.

These percentages are based on 2000 population and per capita income data for 207 nations that were independent as of 2000, derived mostly from the World Bank. The appendix to this chapter contains two tables giving data for all these nations. The first of these tables (Table 2.A.1) lists the 207 nations in alphabetical order, and provides for each nation 2000 Gross Domestic Product per Capita (GDPPC), Population (POP), and Gross Domestic Product (GDP). GDP is obtained by multiplying GDPPC and POP. The second appendix table (Table 2.A.2) lists all 207 nations in descending order of population (on the left) and GDP (on the right). Figures are given for national population as a percentage of total world population, and for national GDP as a percentage of total world GDP. If there had been a Federal Union of Democratic Nations in operation in 2000, and if all 207 nations had been members, the population percentages would have been the voting weights of Union Representatives from each respective nation in the population vote, while the GDP percentages would have been the voting weights of the same Union Representatives from each respective nation in the material vote (as discussed below, national tax liability would be based on GDP). Table 2.1 shows the first 30 nations from the full listing in Table 2.A.2. There would be some divergence between these potential weights as of 2000, and those that would hold if and when a Federal Union of Democratic Nations is established in the future. But they probably give a good idea of relative magnitudes.

The most obvious short-term motivation for the dual voting principle is to impede possible efforts by populous poorer nations to impose radical redistribution on rich nations, and also to impede the rich nations from passing legislation that is unacceptable to the poor nations for one reason or another—for example, because they would tend toward the re-imposition of the exploitative economic conditions of the colonial era. But it is important to realize that if, as hoped, the World Economic Equalization Program is successful, then the proportion of Union revenues raised in a given District would tend to become equal to the District's population, and this motivation would become irrelevant. At that point, no systematic differences would be observed between the population and the material votes.

TABLE 2.1
Potential Voting Weights of 30 Nations in the
Federal Union Chamber of Representatives,
based on 2000 Population and GDP

Population Basis		Material Basis	
Nation	% of Total	Nation	% of Total
China	20.923958	United States	26.641876
India	16.837864	Japan	16.820686
United States	4.666398	Germany	7.925874
Indonesia	3.487508	France	5.192075
Brazil	2.824302	United Kingdom	3.827953
Russian Federation	2.412422	Italy	3.563292
Pakistan	2.288532	China	3.076632
Bangladesh	2.172017	Brazil	2.330514
Nigeria	2.103401	Spain	2.077271
Japan	2.102738	Canada	2.049928
Mexico	1.623684	Korea, Rep.	1.826241
Germany	1.361551	Netherlands	1.457874
Vietnam	1.301432	India	1.380170
Philippines	1.252660	Australia	1.352292
Turkey	1.082163	Mexico	1.106489
Ethiopia	1.065672	Russian Federation	1.056750
Egypt, Arab Rep.	1.060335	Switzerland	0.992418
Iran, Islamic Rep.	1.055164	Belgium	0.934750
Thailand	1.006503	Argentina	0.868798
United Kingdom	0.990110	Sweden	0.818518
France	0.976073	Austria	0.785830
Italy	0.956152	Indonesia	0.618390
Congo, Dem. Rep.	0.844410	Denmark	0.607898
Ukraine	0.820427	Turkey	0.605238
Myanmar	0.791390	South Africa	0.504440
Korea, Rep.	0.783534	Norway	0.504096
South Africa	0.709382	Thailand	0.503760
Colombia	0.701067	Finland	0.490300
Spain	0.654091	Hong Kong, China	0.486820
Poland	0.640583	Poland	0.482755

The Executive Branch

The function of the executive branch of the Federal Union of Democratic Nations would be to enforce legislation passed by the Union Chamber of Representatives, and to administer the various agencies of the supernational government in conformance with policy directives passed by the Chamber. The executive arm of the Federal Union of Democratic Nations would be guided by a "Union Chief Executive," an official elected by majority vote of the entire population of the Union every other quinquennial election for a term of ten years. If the Federal Union achieves its desired objective, this individual would ultimately be acknowledged as the paramount political leader of the entire human population. It is clear that a major factor determining the survival and success of the potential Federal Union of Democratic Nations would be the energy, determination, intelligence, patience, and good judgment of its Chief Executives.

In designing the executive branch of the world government, our desire is to achieve an appropriate balance between the competing objectives of a strong executive authority that would enhance the effectiveness of the government, and a restrained executive authority that would obstruct possible tendencies toward totalitarianism. The basic safeguard against the emergence of global totalitarianism are the constitutional provisions allowing member nation-states to secede from the Union, and to maintain whatever independent military forces they deem necessary under their direct control. These two reserved rights of the member nation-states provide a high level of assurance against totalitarianism, but they obviously weaken the effectiveness of the Union. In light of this basic weakening tendency, it may be appropriate, as a counterweight to this tendency, to design the world government in such a way as to enhance the authority of the executive branch. One provision serving this end is the relatively long term of office specified for the Union Chief Executive: ten years. This is much longer than the typical presidential term of office within most nations.

In the standard system of checks and balances among the three basic branches of government (legislative, executive and judicial), the highest executive official often exercises some form of veto power over the enactments of the legislative branch. In the interest of both a strong executive branch of the world government, and the overall stability of that government, the Union Chief Executive should exercise a comprehensive and powerful veto authority. The authority should not pertain only to legislative acts and budget authorizations in their entirety, but in addition to specific components of such acts and authorizations. In addition to this, the Union Chief Executive might be given the power to suspend legislation previously approved by both the legislative and executive branches, but the application of which was generating serious unforeseen problems. Existing legislation suspended by the executive branch would not necessarily be permanently abolished, but rather would be returned to the legislative branch for "review and revision."

The veto power of the executive branch, possibly supplemented by a suspension power as just outlined, establishes a check on the power of the legislative branch. Another standard power that establishes a countervailing check on the power of the executive branch is that of impeachment and removal from office. In the Federal Union of Democratic Nations, this power would be exercised jointly by the Union Chamber of Representatives (the legislative branch) and the Union High Court (the judicial branch). Grounds for impeachment would include suspected criminal offenses, flagrant disregard of the decisions of the legislative or judicial branches of government, and/or personal behavior that demeans the dignity and degrades the prestige of the office. The authority to impeach the Union Chief Executive would rest with the Union Chamber of Representatives. Once impeached, the Union Chief Executive would be tried before the Union High Court, which could convict or acquit.

The activities of the Federal Union of Democratic Nations would be organized under ten agencies, whose directors (termed "ministers"), nominated by the Union Chief Executive and approved by the Chamber of Representatives, would comprise the Cabinet. The ten agencies would be as follows: (1) Ministry of the Interior; (2) Ministry of Finance; (3) Ministry of Justice; (4) Ministry of Science; (5) Ministry of Education; (6) Ministry of Planning; (7) Ministry of External Development; (8) Ministry of Security; (9) Ministry of Non-Union Affairs; (10) World Development Authority. Some indications of the kinds of activities in which these agencies might engage are as follows.

Ministry of the Interior. This ministry would endeavor to administer and develop the physical substructure of the planetary habitat, in terms of both natural resources and capital infrastructure. It would be the logical repository for activities in support of international commerce and communication: construction, maintenance and operation of airports, seaports, international roads, railroads, cables and pipelines, as well as satellites. It could also incorporate a number of existing autonomous specialized agencies affiliated with the present-day United Nations, agencies such as the Universal Postal Union, the World Meteorological Organization, the International Maritime Organization and the International Civil Aviation Organization. This ministry would also be responsible for dismantling trade barriers within the Federal Union—or at least keeping these barriers as low as possible—through the activities of the incorporated World Trade Organization. Finally, the ministry's statistical division could handle the collection and dissemination of various statistical data currently provided by the World Bank and the United Nations.

Ministry of Finance. This ministry would be responsible for a large part of the financial operations of the Federal Union of Democratic Nations. It would administer the collection of tax revenues and the disbursement of appropriated funds. However, the Ministry of Finance would not encompass the World Development Authority (described below), which would be a separate Federal Union agency, with separate financing pertaining exclusively to the World Economic Equalization Program (WEEP). The WEEP would be a temporary operation, to be phased out once the poor nations have achieved an acceptable level of economic prosperity. The Ministry of Finance, in contrast, would be involved with permanent financial operations of the Federal Union.

Ministry of Justice. This ministry would be concerned with the implementation and enforcement of Federal Union laws and regulations. It would incorporate some form of armed police organization—an organization not to be confused with the Union Security Force incorporated into the Ministry of Security. The Union's police organization would be concerned exclusively with violations of Union law by private individuals and organizations, as opposed to government organizations. It would endeavor to bring individuals responsible for these violations to trial in the court system. The court system would comprise the existing court systems of nations and localities, possibly supplemented by an additional court system operated by the Federal Union.

Ministry of Science. This ministry would endeavor to lay a basis for the continuation and acceleration of the rate of technological progress on which depends the future progress of human civilization. Although the Ministry of Science would operate a few laboratories and research facilities of its own, to a large extent its responsibilities would lie in the dissemination of scientific and technological information emanating from existing research operations in nations around the world. It might also provide financial support for private and governmental research operations. It may become involved in legal aspects of scientific and technological endeavors: for example, in the creation of a world-wide patent code.

Ministry of Education. This ministry would endeavor to facilitate the educational development of humanity. For the most part its participation in educational activity would be indirect and integrative, because all of the nations of the world have already established elaborate educational systems. A major objective of the Ministry of Education would be the achievement and maintenance of universal literacy. A secondary objective would be to achieve universal fluency and literacy in the English language, which has been proposed earlier as the sole official language of the Federal Union of Democratic Nations on grounds of convenience and expediency.

Ministry of Planning. This ministry would have nothing to do with direct economic planning of the sort that was long favored in the ex-Soviet Union and some other communist nations. Rather it would operate as a permanent, large-scale "think tank," which would carefully analyze and evaluate various policy concepts and proposals emanating in embryonic form from legislators and executives in the supernational government. Its analytical reports would then become inputs into practical decision-making by these legislators and executives.

Ministry of External Development. If we look far enough ahead into the future, to a time when the frustrating and perilous predicaments, entanglements and complications that presently plague the human race will hopefully have been consigned forever to history, we recognize in the illimitable expanse of outer space which envelops our small planet Earth, an immense horizon beckoning insistently to humanity. Perhaps the dreams of interstellar expansion that mankind has nourished for generations are doomed never to be achieved—there are, of course, immense technical problems involved. But it is one of the ineffable characteristics of humanity to want to undertake any great task which appeals to the imagination. Therefore the Federal Union of Democratic Nations should sponsor a very vigorous program of research and development aimed at achieving practical means of manned space travel. The Ministry of External Development would be assigned exclusively to this purpose. Although individual member nations would be free to undertake space exploration on their own account, hopefully most space exploration would soon be centralized under the aegis of the Federal Union Ministry of External Development. This seems to be an area in which duplication of effort might be particularly costly. Another reason for consolidating the effort would be to put the world government at the center of attention in this exciting and inspiring area of human endeavor.

Ministry of Security. The Ministry of Security would be the civilian agency with authority over the Union's armed forces, termed the Union Security Force. Just how large and heavily armed the Union Security Force will need to be would depend on future circumstances which are impossible to predict at this point in time. The long-term purpose of the Federal Union of Democratic Nations, of course, is to establish such a spirit of toleration, cooperation and common purpose throughout human civilization as to completely eliminate large-scale armed conflict among humanity. Unfortunately, such a spirit cannot be developed overnight. Quite possibly, not all nations will join the Federal Union at the time of its founding. Almost certainly, numerous nations which do join the Federal Union at the time of its founding will maintain substantial military forces under their own control. The Union will need an armed force to protect small and/or lightly armed member nations against possible aggression.

Ministry of Non-Union Affairs. This ministry will handle relations between the Federal Union of Democratic Nations and non-member nations. In the early period of the Federal Union's operation, quite possibly a substantial number of nations will abstain from membership. Hopefully, most of these nations will enter the Union once its benign and beneficial nature becomes apparent from experience. However, even in the long run, considering how many nations there are, it seems quite possible that at least a few nations might remain permanently separate from the Union. Whether the number of non-member nations is inconsequential or otherwise, the Federal Union will need an agency dedicated to maintaining peaceful and cooperative relations with these nations.

World Development Authority. Of the ten principal administrative agencies of the executive branch of the Federal Union of Democratic Nations, only the World Development Authority (WDA) will be, of its nature, of a temporary nature. The WDA's mission would be to coordinate the global economic development program designated the World Economic Equalization Program (WEEP). Conceivably this agency could operate separately and autonomously from the Federal Union, with a fully independent budgetary apparatus. It would probably be desirable, however, that this agency be subject to some measure of democratic control through the world government. The World Development Authority would continue on as a major operation until the World Economic Equalization Program has achieved a satisfactory degree of equalization among the living standards of the nations of the world. At that point, it might be succeeded by a Ministry of Economic Development concerned merely with the general advance of living standards within all nations of the world, as opposed to the equalization of living standards across nations.

The Judicial Branch

The judicial branch of the Federal Union of Democratic Nations would be designated the Union High Court. The primary functions of this body would be as follows: (1) deciding on the validity of legal challenges to various legislation or administrative policies of the Federal Union brought by individuals or national governments on grounds that such legislation or policies violate either the letter or the spirit of the Federal Union constitution; (2) ruling on challenges to national and lower level legislation and policies on grounds that such legislation or policies violate individual rights guaranteed by the Federal Union constitution; (3) adjudication of disputes between national governments. Over the past century there has been some development of international courts, and the Union High Court would logically take over existing activities of courts such as the present-day International Court of Justice. There would be, however, a paramount distinction. Existing international courts have little or no authority with which to enforce their judgments. Since compliance with decisions of these courts is essentially voluntary, there is rather little incentive for contesting parties to submit their disputes to them. The High Court of the Federal Union of Democratic Nations, on the other hand, as the judicial component of a functioning world government equipped with both police and military forces, would exercise far more effective authority. Submission of serious disputes between nations to this world tribunal would not be a voluntary matter, nor would compliance with its judgments be a voluntary matter.

On the other hand, the effective authority of the Union High Court over the entire world would not begin to compare with the effective authority today of the U.S. Supreme Court within the United States—for the same reason that the Federal Union of Democratic Nations would not exercise the same level of effective authority over the entire world that the federal government of the United States exercises within the United States. To begin with, quite likely a substantial number of nations in the world will not choose to become charter members of the Federal Union. What degree of informal authority the Federal Union might exercise over non-member nations is quite uncertain. It would depend largely on how many non-member nations there are, and how much internal cohesion and joint determination exists among the member nations. Moreover, in rendering its judgments, the Union High Court would have to take into account the fact that a sufficiently incensed member nation could legally depart from the Union. The Court might feel that while ideal legal orthodoxy dictates one decision, another decision might be advisable on grounds of expediency. This is hardly to say that expediency should invariably take precedence over ideal legality, not to mention ideal morality.

According to the conventional viewpoint, it is appropriate that a supreme court enjoy a substantial degree of continuity and stability, so that its concern for tradition and basic principle might serve as a beneficial restraint on the legislative and executive branches, since the latter branches are often perceived as more susceptible to the forces of short-term political expediency. Stability would be promoted by the provision for staggered elections: only one fifth of the membership of the Union High Court would be elected in each quinquennial election. The provision of a 25-year term for elected Union Justices should render them more or less immune from considerations of short-term political expediency. Such immunity might be still further enhanced by stipulating that Union Justices may serve one term only. This would not constitute a "term limit" in the usual sense owing to the fact that the standard term of a quarter century would consume a substantial fraction of the working career of the average person. In fact, such a lengthy term raises the question of what to do if a Union Justice dies or wishes to retire before the expiration of his/her term. One possibility is that Union Justices be allowed to name their own successors for the completion of their terms in office, these successors being named in a written testament to be implemented in the event of the Union Justice's death, incapacitation, or voluntary retirement.

CRITICAL LIMITATIONS AND AUTHORIZATIONS

The Federal Union constitution, whether it be long and verbose or short and pithy, should at a minimum contain two critical limitations on the Federal Union of Democratic Nations, and at the same time two critical authorizations of the Federal Union of Democratic Nations. The two critical constitutional limitations would be: (1) all member nations of the Federal Union are to possess the permanent and inalienable right to withdraw from the Federal Union at any time at their own unilateral discretion; (2) all member nations of the Federal Union are to possess the permanent and inalienable right to maintain whatever military forces under their direct control they deem appropriate, equipped with whatever weaponry (including nuclear weapons) they deem appropriate. The two critical constitutional authorizations would be: (1) the Federal Union would possess full and comprehensive authority to levy taxes on nations for the purpose of financially funding its activities; (2) the Federal Union would possess the authority to maintain substantial military forces armed with heavy weaponry. Let us consider these critical limitations and authorizations.

National Right of Secession

One of the most fundamental objections to the proposal for a world federation being put forward herein is that any state entity that was not prepared to forcibly prevent the departure of its subsidiary units would lack what is perhaps the most basic and essential characteristic of a state. It is quintessential, in this view, of a state entity that it be completely determined to preserve its territorial integrity at all costs. However commonplace this viewpoint might be at the present time, it is not a correct and valid viewpoint. A state, whether it be at the national or the supernational level, can be a legitimate, genuine, authentic, and highly effective political organization in the absence of any determination to utilize force to suppress independence movements in subsidiary regions.

Think, for example, of the nation of Canada. A very large and important province in Canada, the province of Quebec, has been toying seriously with the possibility of independence for several decades. The major basis for this separatist leaning is the fact that the predominant language among the population of Quebec is French, whereas the predominant language among the population of the rest of Canada is English. No knowledgeable person, either in Quebec, or in the rest of Canada, or in the rest of the world, expects that if Quebec does in fact ultimately declare its independence, the national government of Canada will employ its armed forces to keep Quebec within the Canadian federation. But the expectation that potential secession would not be opposed by military force does not mean that Canada is any less a nation. If Quebec leaves Canada, Canada would carry on as a nation with its 11 remaining provinces and territories, which together account for approximately 85 percent of the present Canadian land area, and approximately 75 percent of the present Canadian population. Although the loss of 15 percent of its land area and 25 percent of its population would not be a happy event for English-speaking Canadians, one consolation might be that it would no longer be necessary for the nation to maintain two official languages.

What I would suggest is that if and when it is founded in the future, the Federal Union of Democratic Nations would regard possible secessions by individual nations much as the English-speaking population of Canada presently regards possible secession by the province of Quebec: as an unfortunate and undesirable eventuality that is certainly to be avoided if at all possible—but nevertheless as survivable and certainly not worth the costs that would be involved in its forcible prevention. There is actually no alternative to taking this attitude if the world government is to be established in the first place, and, assuming it is established, that it will survive for any appreciable period of time. The membership door must be left open permanently, and traffic must be permitted to move freely through this door in both directions. The only limitation on this national right should be that independence must be approved by a majority of the population in a democratic referendum. This would be to ensure that it is the entire national population which desires independence, and not a minority which has achieved temporary control over the national government.

If the Federal Union evolves as intended, within a relatively brief period there would be strong economic, social, political and psychological links between the member nations and the supernational federation. Leaving the federation would be by no means costless to the nation, even though it would not have to fight for its independence. For one thing, leaving the Federal Union would take the newly independent nation out of the common market within the Union. As a non-member nation, its exports to Federal Union member nations would be subject to some degree of tariff imposition. We have seen, in the evolution of the European Community, the decisive importance which access to a free trade area can come to have even to nations with a long history and a strong tradition of nationalistic individuality.

Admittedly, it may require a certain amount of mental flexibility and imagination to fully comprehend how a world government could be tolerant and flexible with respect to the membership, and yet be a meaningful and effective state organization. When we reflect on the concept of "independence," a variety of images and scenarios come to mind, based on both historical and current events. These images and scenarios certainly do not suggest that the condition of independence is either won or lost without the accompaniment of force either on a large scale or a small scale.

Individual citizens, of course, do not have the right to declare themselves independent of the political authority of the locality in which they reside, so that they are no longer subject to the various laws and taxes established by that authority. Occasionally, small groups of citizens who hold personal ownership rights over a certain area of land will proclaim a sovereign and independent state entity located on that area of land. This is typically a form of protest against prevailing laws, taxes, or both. If the "founding fathers" of these mini-states do not soon desist, they usually end up either in prison or mental asylums. Normally such endeavors are not viewed very sympathetically by the great majority of citizens. Clearly, if such endeavors were tolerated, and thereupon proliferated on a large scale, society would soon descend to a quasi-anarchic condition.

When it comes, however, to large political entities declaring their independence from still larger political entities in which they had previously been incorporated, this is no trivial matter. Human history is filled with wars fought to gain or prevent independence. War has played a critical role no less in the devolution of large state entities as in their evolution. Contemporary viewpoints on specific wars of independence vary depending on both the individual and on the circumstances of the war. For example, most American citizens today regard the Revolutionary War of 1775 to 1783, which secured the independence of the thirteen original American colonies from Britain, to have been a triumphant and unquestionably beneficial episode not merely for the United States but for world civilization as a whole. British citizens today, while not usually inclined to dispute the benefits, understandably tend to be less enthusiastic about them. At the same time, most American citizens today regard the U.S. Civil War of 1861 to 1865, which forcibly prevented the Southern states from leaving the Union, to also have been a triumphant and unquestionably beneficial episode not merely for the United States as a whole, but for the Southern states as well. Citizens of the Southern states today, while not usually inclined to dispute the benefits, understandably tend to be less enthusiastic about them.

More often than not throughout history, wars of independence have been fought by the populations of certain regions against those large political entities known as "empires." The American Revolutionary War, for example, was fought to attain the independence of the American colonies from the British empire. Throughout history, both the construction and the destruction of empires have typically been accompanied by violence and bloodshed. One of the major obstacles to the formation of a world state in our time is the extremely widespread preconception that a real-world world state would be equivalent to an empire. According to the standard dictionary definition, an "empire" is a political organization incorporating a wide diversity of peoples and subsidiary political units. The standard dictionary definition does *not* state that an empire governs without the consent of the governed, engages in exploitation of most of the incorporated peoples, and relies heavily on force and the threat of force to maintain compliance with its dominion. Nevertheless, the word "empire," in the minds of most people, carries strong connotations of exactly these characteristics. This is understandable since, throughout history, empires have often— indeed, almost always—exhibited these characteristics. This is not to say that empires were always and everywhere an evil institution that worsened the condition of every included human individual other than a tiny elite at the top of the hierarchy. In some cases, empires were able achieve peaceful cooperation over a wide range of subsidiary political units that otherwise would have been in continuous conflict with one another. True, the empire which incorporated these previously squabbling principalities was normally undemocratic, but so also were the component principalities normally undemocratic. The establishment of an empire often simply replaced numerous small local oligarchies with one big centralized oligarchy. Little was lost to the typical citizen in terms of effective political freedom; while peace was gained. Despite their bad reputation today, it is plausibly arguable that, historically speaking, empires advanced the cause of human civilization far more than they hindered it.

Be that as it may, at this point in time, it is clear that a world government will only be possible if most people can be convinced that such a government would be nothing like any of the numerous empires which have come and gone throughout human history. The critical distinction between the Federal Union of Democratic Nations envisioned here, and the typical historical empire, is that the former would be democratically accountable to the entire population of the Union. The right to vote would be held by every adult citizen, with the exception of the insane and convicted criminals. All three branches of government (legislative, executive and judicial) would be headed by individuals elected by the citizens in free and open elections. Empires, on the other hand, have been democratically accountable only to a small minority of their populations—if any at all. In extremely centralized cases, which have been the rule rather than the exception, empires were governed by "emperors" equivalent to kings in the era of absolute monarchy, or to dictators in the modern era. In some cases, there might be some elements of democratic procedure in the determination of high positions in the imperial government. But if so, the right to participate in these procedures would be held only by a relatively small minority of those governed by the empire. For example, in the later period of the British colonial empire, within Britain itself, Parliament, an elective body, became steadily more powerful while at the same time the electorate was steadily broadened in terms of the population of the British Isles. The electorate was *not* broadened, however, to include as voting citizens the native population of Britain's various overseas colonies.

An interesting "what if" historical question, in this context, is the following: Would the American Revolutionary War have taken place if elected representatives from the American colonies had been seated as voting members of the British Parliament? Quite possibly not, in view of the fact that one of leading slogans of the restive colonists, during the years leading up to the Revolutionary War, was "No taxation without representation!" There were two principal problems with adding Members of Parliament from the American colonies during that era. The first was distance: the American colonies were physically separated from the British government in London by the Atlantic Ocean, the crossing of which entailed a dangerous ocean voyage of several weeks' duration. Thus it would have been clumsy obtaining input from the American colonies on legislation applying in both the British Isles and the American colonies. The second problem may have been even more serious: this was the problem that the democratic principle was still quite feeble in the era of the American Revolution. Property requirements for the franchise kept all but a small minority of the population of the British Isles from voting in Parliamentary elections. Parliament itself was still relatively weak vis-a-vis the monarch, and the reigning British monarch of the time, George III, was determined that policy toward the American colonies should mainly be set by the monarchy rather than Parliament. Therefore, there were never any voting representatives from the American colonies in the British Parliament, the American Revolutionary War commenced, it ground onward for several years, and at its conclusion Britain recognized the independence of the American colonies. Shortly afterwards the colonies organized themselves into the United States of America.

When we compare the circumstances of the American Revolutionary War with those which would prevail were a world government to be established along the lines of the proposed Federal Union of Democratic Nations, we recognize that it would be virtually impossible for the circumstances which led to the American Revolutionary War to be replicated. There are not one but two reasons for this. First, the world government would be democratically accountable to its entire population throughout the world via free and open elections for high government positions. There would be no such thing as "taxation without representation." Owing to the tremendous advances in transportation and communications since the time of the American Revolutionary War, there would be no problems of coordination in having representatives from all parts of the world sitting in the Federal Union's legislative body. In today's world, representatives from even the remotest nations could travel to the Federal Union's capital city in one or two days. Communications among all parts of the world are virtually instantaneous. For example, using the Internet, Union Representatives from distant nations could participate in discussions and votes in the Union Chamber of Representatives without being physically present in the Union capital city. None of this was technically possible at the time of the American Revolutionary War.

Second, all member nations would hold an explicit constitutional right to secession (withdrawal) from the world federation. It is hardly unimaginable that the world federation—despite being democratically accountable, or perhaps even *because* it is democratically accountable—would implement legislation and policies completely unacceptable to some nations. The fact that certain legislation and policies are desired by a substantial majority on both the population voting basis and the material voting basis by no means guarantees that they would be not be completely unacceptable to the populations of some nations. If that happened, these nations would be able to peacefully depart the Federal Union. It is difficult to imagine that the American colonies would have been impelled to fight for their independence in 1775 if they had had voting representatives in the British Parliament at that time. It is even more difficult to imagine that if Britain had had a written constitution in 1775 which stated that the American colonies had a right to declare their independence at any time, and the American colonies had chosen to exercise that right, the British government would nevertheless have employed military force to try to block independence.

Now let us move the time frame of U.S. history forward from the 1770s to the 1860s. The U.S. Civil War of 1861-1865 was one of the bloodiest and most destructive wars of the 19th century. For skeptics of world government, the U.S. Civil War provides an instructive lesson on the probable fate of a future world government. Prospects for the success of the United States in 1788 (the year of the final ratification of the present U.S. Constitution) were highly auspicious. The thirteen original states of United States shared a common language, a common heritage, geographical contiguity, and had cooperated closely in waging the war for independence. And yet, despite all of these advantages, after only a little over seven decades of operation, the United States was engulfed in a bitter civil war brought about by the effort of the Southern states to establish their independence. How clear it is, therefore, say skeptics of world federation, that if such a federation were established, it would very quickly dissolve and degenerate into bitter civil war. The only means of avoiding this outcome would be to completely disarm the member nations and give the world government a monopoly on heavy armaments. But to do that would open the door wide to global tyranny. It follows that world government must be avoided if we are to preserve ourselves from the vicissitudes of both civil war and global tyranny.

There are two major flaws in the argument that a world government would necessarily follow the path followed by the United States to the Civil War of 1861-1865. First, the constitution of the world federation proposed here (the Federal Union of Democratic Nations), in contrast to the United States Constitution, would explicitly allow member nations to declare their independence from the world federation at any time they desire. The U.S. Constitution was silent on the issue of whether member states would or would not be permitted to secede peacefully from the United States. Had the U.S. Constitution explicitly stated that any move by a state toward independence would be forcibly suppressed, it is quite possible that the Southern states, being fully aware of the fact that they would have to fight hard to achieve independence, would have been more conciliatory and susceptible to compromise. At the time the U.S. Constitution was formulated, however, there was a great deal of apprehension about the federal government being too strong, and therefore putting into the Constitution an explicit anti-secession provision might have eliminated any possibility of ratification. On the other hand, had the U.S. Constitution explicitly stated that any move by a state toward independence would be unopposed by the federal government, it is quite possible that the Northern states, being fully aware of the fact that they would have no legal right to oppose secession, would have been more conciliatory and susceptible to compromise. Whether the U.S. Constitution had explicitly forbidden secession or explicitly condoned secession, quite probably the conflict between the Northern and Southern states would not have escalated to the point where secession actually occurred. It follows, therefore, that the provision in the Federal Union constitution explicitly allowing secession by member nations will, in all likelihood, prevent the escalation of conflicts to the point where actual secessions occur. And this provision, at the same time, makes it highly unlikely that in the unfortunate event that secessions *do* occur, they will be opposed with military force.

The second flaw in the argument that a potential world federation will follow the path the United States followed into civil war, is that it neglects the over-riding role that the institution of slavery played in the degeneration of relations between the Northern and Southern states to the point of secession and civil war. What was not foreseen by the U.S. founding fathers was that the rise of cotton cultivation for export in the Southern states, during the early decades of the republic, would greatly enhance the profitability of slavery, thus giving that reprehensible institution a new lease on life. At the time the U.S. Constitution went into effect, it was widely assumed that the United States would fairly quickly follow the lead of the rest of the civilized world and abolish slavery. It was assumed that the abolition would be peaceful, because of the marginal profitability of slavery. Unfortunately, the invention of the cotton gin by Eli Whitney greatly changed the business calculus of slavery. Soon, the manifest conflict between the political ideals of liberty and equality on which the nation was supposedly founded, and the economic self-interest of the Southern planta-tion owners, resulted in continuing acrimonious controversy which bedeviled the young republic. The small minority of wealthy Southern plantation owners was able to enlist the support of the entire white Southern population by making good use of the old and reliable bugaboo of "domination of our affairs by outsiders." The slavery issue became a bitter moral issue, with each side accusing the other of base and unworthy motivations. When the Southern states eventually declared their independence, it was not because they were in immediate fear that slavery would be abolished by Abraham Lincoln's new Republican presidential adminis-tration, but rather because they simply could not tolerate any more questioning and criticizing of slavery—and Lincoln's administration would certainly engage in a great deal of questioning and criticizing of slavery. And when the Northern states went to war to prevent Southern independence, it was not primarily to preserve the Union, as such, but rather to thwart the selfish and immoral determination of the Southern gentry to perpetuate the evil and demeaning institution of slavery. It was the incendiary issue of slavery which made the U.S. Civil War of 1861-1865 inevitable—not the innate unwillingness of state entities to permit subsidiary entities to establish their independence.

At the present moment in world history, there is no political issue on the horizon that will be as controversial and emotional, over the next several decades, as was the slavery issue in American politics in the decades leading up to the Civil War. There is no nation on the face of the globe, of course, in which slavery is legal. This is hardly to say that full racial equality has been achieved in every nation of the world. But the principle of full racial equality is accepted by almost all properly educated people, and gradual progress is being made in most nations toward the practical implementation of this principle. Humanity seems to have made peace with itself on the matter of religion. None of the major organized religions in the world today has on its agenda the suppression of all other religions throughout the world. Within some nations, there is serious adverse discrimination against adherents to religions other than the dominant religion, and in a handful of nations the union of church and state has reached a point where these nations may be described as "theocracies." But even in the handful of nations in which governance is dominated by clerics, there is no serious policy or intention to export this system to other nations.

Until very recently, the ideological controversy between communism and noncommunism was a major factor in world politics. In fact, if at some point during the Cold War from the 1950s through the 1980s, accident or miscalculated brinkmanship had ignited a nuclear holocaust which destroyed human civilization, ideological disagreement over the issue of social ownership of capital property could have been plausibly cited as the decisive factor in bringing about the disaster. It can certainly be said that from the world perspective, the issue of socialism was just as pivotal and potentially explosive during the latter half of the twentieth century, as was the issue of slavery in the United States during the first half of the nineteenth century. But with the abandonment of socialism and communism by the USSR in the 1990s, ideological controversy has become a dramatically less important factor in international politics. Even the handful of nations which continue their adherence to communistic socialism, are no longer determined to export this social system to other nations.

The fact that there are no political controversies in the world today comparable to the slavery controversy in the nineteenth century and the socialism controversy in the twentieth century, makes it much less likely that a world federation established at the present time will follow the same path that the early United States followed to the Civil War of 1861-1865. This does not imply, however, that worldwide human civilization in the future will remain forever free of political controversies within or among nations of such intensity and emotionalism as to generate armed conflict and warfare. One of the reasons why we should form a world federation now—while we have the chance—is to forestall the development of such controversies in the future. The Federal Union of Democratic Nations would be a major force for the peaceful elimination of unacceptable institutions and practices (such as slavery). At the same time—and more importantly—it would be a major force for the permanent maintenance of toleration and flexibility in areas where no compelling evidence exists for the superiority of one form over another: examples here include the varieties of religion, and social versus private ownership of capital property.

National Right of Armament

The standard view among "world government traditionalists" is that the establishment of the world state would be accompanied by the immediate and total disarmament of nations. Most weapons of mass destruction (such as nuclear weapons) would be dismantled and destroyed, but a small proportion would be taken over by the military arm of the world government. With the nations deprived of heavy armament, presumably the world government would not require much military power to maintain peace and order. No longer would human civilization lie in the shadow of world war and/or nuclear holocaust. The problem perceived by the vast majority of the human population with this scenario, however, is that while human civilization would no longer lie in the shadow of nuclear holocaust, it *would* now lie in the shadow of global tyranny imposed by a totalitarian world government. It has been convincingly demonstrated, through the several decades of the Cold War during which the human population operated under a very real and present threat of virtually instantaneous nuclear annihilation, that the nuclear peril, in and of itself, will not induce the nations to disarm and pledge their fealty to a world government. If disarmament of the nations is made a precondition for and a necessary concomitant of world government, then the conclusion seems inevitable that world government truly is impossible—now and probably forever.

Therefore, it is an absolutely indispensable component of the present proposal for a Federal Union of Democratic Nations that the member nations possess a permanent and inalienable right to maintain whatever military forces and weapons—including nuclear weapons—that they feel it necessary to maintain, for as long as they feel it necessary. The hope is that slowly and gradually, nations will voluntarily disarm, until at some future point the armaments of nations will be reduced to a very low level which could legitimately be described as inconsequential. But the objective of major disarmament (as opposed to "complete" disarmament—which may forever be impossible) would be a very long-term goal of the Federal Union, to be pursued in a relaxed, tolerant, flexible and unhurried manner. The important thing is not that weapons of mass destruction not exist—but that they not be used. Of course, if they don't exist, they cannot be used. But it is virtually inconceivable, in both today's world and the world of the foreseeable future, that weapons of mass destruction can be made to disappear. The continued existence of these weapons appears virtually inevitable. But continued non-use of these weapons is an achievable objective. Continued non-use of these weapons into the remote future will be more likely if humanity establishes a world federation along the lines of the Federal Union of Democratic Nations, than if it does not do so.

The notion of reducing the threat of war through formal disarmament treaties among nations came into prominence in the latter part of the nineteenth century. The immediate impetus to this was the arms competition which developed among the major European powers in the wake of German unification at the time of the Franco-Prussian War of 1871. By the 1890s, all the major European powers, not just the superpowers, found it necessary to maintain large-scale military forces armed with increasingly sophisticated and destructive weaponry. To the more perceptive and prescient people of the period, the arms competition, in and of itself, was increasing the threat of war. And, of course, if war *did* occur among nations with such formidable military forces, the costs would be enormous. Toward the end of the nineteenth century, therefore, appeals for international measures to slow or even halt the accumulation of military power were becoming increasingly common. But it was not until the leader of a major European power, Czar Nicholas II of Russia, called for an international conference to control armaments that one actually took place.

Two Hague Disarmament Conferences were held, in 1899 and 1907, but a planned third conference was cancelled because the would-be conferees were busily fighting World War I (1914-1918), a devastating conflict very nearly as horrible as had been warned by those who saw the Hague Conferences as a shining ray of hope amid thickening war clouds. World War I did not terminate human civilization, as had been forecast by some alarmists, but it certainly imposed a great deal of needless pain, suffering, death and destruction upon human civilization. Although all of the major military powers participated in the Hague Conferences, little of substance was accomplished. The two Hague Conferences not only did not forestall the advent of World War I, but they did not noticeably reduce the carnage of that conflict. No agreements were reached limiting machine guns and other automatic weapons, artillery, bombs, airplanes, capital ships or submarines. No agreements could have been reached regarding tanks, which were invented later on, during the course of World War I. A few minor agreements regarding weaponry were reached, but these had little perceptible impact on the evolution of warfare in the First World War. Despite an agreement not to use poison gas, poison gas was in fact utilized. A ban on aerial bombardment from balloons was observed, but this was only because airplanes and dirigibles proved to be far more effective means for the delivery of bombs than the unpowered balloons envisioned by the Conference agreement. Even if detailed provisions for the limitation of weapons of mass destruction had been agreed to at the First and Second Hague Conferences, it is doubtful that they would have had any effect. There was no provision for the enforcement of any of the agreements reached, and amid the increasing rancor and tension of the pre-1914 years, the agreements would almost certainly have been ignored.

The futility of the Hague Conferences provides a lesson on the limited effectiveness of disarmament efforts—in and of themselves—in those situations where nothing is done (or can be done) to alleviate the root causes of hostility and conflict among nations. In medical terms, disarmament efforts are an effort to treat symptoms of the disease, as opposed to treating the disease itself. The disease in this case is the normal suspicion, distrust, hostility and conflict that naturally emerges from a system of sovereign and independent nation-states, all of whom are keenly aware of their self-perceived rightful and legitimate national interests, and all of whom are determined that deadly force can and will be utilized against any nation which presumes to frustrate these interests. Arms races are a consequence of bad attitudes. On an irregular but continuing basis, these bad attitudes become inflamed in one or more nations to the point of what might be described as a "nationalistic fever," and these nations begin behaving in what other nations view as a hostile and aggressive manner. In response, these other nations soon develop reciprocal nationalistic fevers of their own.

In an atmosphere of rampant hostility and distrust, with an arms competition in full swing, disarmament negotiations accomplish little of value. These negotiations do not address the fundamental issues dividing nations, but rather merely the derivative military aspect of the confrontation. Even were a strong will toward disarmament to exist, there are very serious practical obstacles to reaching arms limitation and/or reduction agreements. One obstacle is the possibility that one side will secretly violate the agreement ("cheat"), thus giving it a decisive advantage over the other side when war finally occurs. The solution to this problem, as perceived by disarmament experts, lies in some kind of inspection or surveillance system. The problem is that extremely reliable inspection or surveillance systems—sufficient to deter even the most determined and amoral nation—have never existed, and probably never will exist.

But even if there were no possibility whatever that a certain nation could successfully cheat on a disarmament agreement, there are further obstacles. A second obstacle is the great variety and complexity of modern weapons systems, together with uncertainty as to how they will perform on the future battlefield. This makes it virtually impossible to find a numerical formula which will guarantee a certain balance of power among the participants. A third obstacle is the rapid rate of technological advance in weaponry. So even if a numerical formula *could* be found which would guarantee a certain balance of power with *current* weapons, the development of *new* weapons will soon upset that balance. The upshot of this is that if nothing occurs to alleviate the fundamental sources of conflict among nations, disarmament efforts are very unlikely to have a significant effect on either the probability or the costs of warfare. Various agreements may be signed and even implemented, but these agreements have an almost imperceptible effect on the overall military power of the contracting nations. It is not that nations participating in an arms competition would not prefer to reduce the costs of armaments. It is rather that owing to the lack of confidence and trust among nations, each nation is concerned that if it agrees to and carries out significant disarmament, this will somehow present other nations with decisive advantages if and when war breaks out.

The post-World War I history of the twentieth century provides further evidence on the limited effectiveness of disarmament efforts in the absence of progress toward the amelioration of basic sources of conflict. During the two decades separating World War I (1914-1918) from World War II (1939-1945), the major powers, shocked by what they had done to themselves in 1914-1918, endeavored to forestall a repetition of the catastrophe. Unfortunately, they left fully intact the root cause of the "Great War": the sovereign nation-state system. They established a League of Nations, but this was not a functional world government, but merely a formalized and institutionalized international alliance. The long history of international alliances in human affairs had demonstrated their frailty when one or more major participants—as normally occurs in the evolving course of events—decides that it is no longer in their immediate national interest to participate. The United States decided, for example, even before the League was formally established, that participation would not be in its immediate national interest. The fact that the United States was not a member of the League of Nations hobbled that organization from the beginning.

In retrospect, one of the more fatuous projects of the interwar period was the Kellogg-Briand Pact of 1928, signed by a host of nations, large and small, renouncing war as an instrument of foreign policy. (Many nations attached qualifications regarding defensive wars and/or wars to preserve "vital national interests.") Among the 63 signatories to the Kellogg-Briand Pact were Germany, Italy and Japan, nations which a short while later instigated World War II. The Pact provided an object lesson in the fact that solemn statements of commendable principles may have little or no effect on the outcome, presuming no change in the substantive conditions which tend to generate violations of these commendable principles. Specifically, the sovereign nation-state system tends to generate violations of the commendable principles of international brotherhood and world peace. Solemn statements by sovereign nation-states upholding these principles, in the absence of any fundamental alteration of the sovereign nation-state system, are unlikely to accomplish anything much.

The interwar period also witnessed several multilateral disarmament conferences in the tradition of the Hague Conferences. These were held variously in Washington, London and Geneva. The Washington conferences of the early 1920s endeavored to set limits on the number of battleships in the navies of the great powers. These capital ships were regarded by the disarmament experts of the time as especially promising candidates for arms limitation agreements, owing both to the huge costs of production, and to the virtual impossibility of concealing these huge ships. A 1924 treaty established a 5-5-3 ratio as between Britain, the United States and Japan. That is, for every 5 battleships possessed by Britain and the United States, Japan could have 3 battleships. When in the 1930s, the Japanese government was swept away by the concept of a Japanese quasi-empire in Asia (the "East Asia Co-Prosperity Sphere"), it withdrew from disarmament negotiations and commenced building all the battleships it wanted. In any event, naval warfare in the Pacific theater during World War II established the dominance of the aircraft carrier, a type of capital ship ignored by the naval disarmament conferences of the 1920s. Those conferences also neglected submarines, which were a major factor in both the Atlantic and Pacific theaters during World War II.

In 1932, after nearly ten years of preliminary discussions under the auspices of the League of Nations, a World Disarmament Conference was commenced in Geneva. The intention was to establish numerical limitations on all types of weapons: land, sea and air. Any and all hope quickly foundered on the determination of Germany, controlled from January 1933 onward by Adolf Hitler, to throw off the arms limitations imposed by the Treaty of Versailles. Hitler ordered the German delegation home from the Geneva disarmament conference, withdrew Germany from the League of Nations, and commenced a massive and comprehensive rearmament drive. The rise to power of Adolf Hitler in Germany in the early 1930s carried several lessons, one of which is that unless a defeated nation in war is absolutely crushed by the victors, it is more than likely that revanchist impulses toward revenge and redress will impel that nation toward a renewal of the conflict. In retrospect, the interwar period was merely a truce in one long war by which Germany and its various allies endeavored to revise the balance of world power. World War I and World War II are sometimes referred to as "the German wars," because the decisive factor in both cases was German policy. A very important lesson in world politics may be derived from the German wars. The lesson is that so long as the sovereign nation-state system remains basically unmodified, it does not matter if almost all nations behave in a prudent and reasonable manner in pursuing their national interests— if even *one* nation pursues its national interests in a reckless and unreasonable manner, then catastrophic warfare is likely to eventuate.

The aftermath of World War II was, in important respects, a carbon copy of the aftermath of World War I. Humanity was shocked and horrified by what it had just done to itself, and was determined to avoid future repetitions of catastrophic warfare. The advent of nuclear weapons intensified the sense of urgency. Prior to nuclear weapons, few had taken seriously the warning by peace advocates that civilization itself could be destroyed by modern warfare. In light of what atomic bombs had done to the Japanese cities of Hiroshima and Nagasaki in 1945, these warnings were taken far more seriously than they had been previously. Despite intensified apprehensions regarding the potential consequences of unrestricted warfare, however, humanity regretfully concluded that no viable alternative existed to the sovereign nation-state system. The post-World War I League of Nations was replaced by the post-World War II United Nations, an organization based on essentially the same principles as the defunct League. The only major difference was that the United States was a charter member and moving force behind the United Nations, whereas it had declined to join the League.

Just as hopes for major disarmament in the interwar period eventually foundered on German intransigence, hopes for major disarmament in the postwar period foundered on Russian intransigence. Germany had been forcibly disarmed after World War I, and more than a decade passed before it commenced the rearmament program which contributed to the genesis of World War II. Russia, on the other hand, was a member of the victorious "Grand Alliance" of World War II. At the end of the war, it was armed to the teeth, and owing to the vituperous ideological conflict with the non-communist nations in which Russia was embroiled, it was most disinclined to disarm. By 1950, Russia was a nuclear power, and by 1960 it was well advanced in missile technology. By the early 1960s the basic groundwork had been laid for instantaneous nuclear Armageddon. Both sides disposed large numbers of extremely powerful nuclear bombs on extremely reliable rocket-powered delivery devices. The potential time frame for making critical decisions shrank down to a few minutes. If there were telemetric indications of a ballistic missile attack by the other side, only a few minutes would be available to decide how to respond. Most likely the response would have been a massive missile counterattack, because all missiles not immediately launched were likely to be destroyed in place.

For more than 30 years, humanity lived in the shadow of nuclear destruction, of catastrophe far beyond anything experienced in the past, of an unimaginable setback so comprehensive and devastating as quite possibly to set humanity sliding irretrievably back toward barbarism or even physical extinction. The surreal quality of this waking nightmare was intensified by a bevy of chilling acronyms:

ICBM —	Intercontinental Ballistic Missile
SLBM —	Submarine-Launched Ballistic Missile
SSBM —	nuclear powered ballistic missile submarine
MIRV —	Multiple Independently Targetable Reentry Vehicle
ACM —	Advanced Cruise Missile
MRBM —	Medium Range Ballistic Missile
INF —	Intermediate Range Nuclear Forces
ABM —	Anti-Ballistic Missile
NORI —	Nuclear Operational Readiness Inspection
SAC —	Strategic Air Command
SDI —	Strategic Defense Initiative

And perhaps the most chilling of all:

MAD —	Mutually Assured Destruction

Amid the grim acronyms were two of a more optimistic nature: SALT and START. SALT originally stood for "Strategic Arms Limitation Talks," but after 1972 when the first agreement was signed by the United States and the USSR after several years of negotiation, this was amended to "Strategic Arms Limitation Treaty." START stands for "Strategic Arms Reduction Treaty," the first of which was signed in 1991 and the second in 1993.

The SALT agreements were signed and implemented while the Cold War was still at its height. (Although SALT II was never formally ratified by the U.S. Senate owing to the 1979 Soviet incursion into Afghanistan, its provisions were respected by both sides.) Two factors seem to have been instrumental in making these agreements possible. First, the development of very capable surveillance satellites by the U.S. made it unlikely that the Soviet Union could successfully cheat on the imposed missile limitations. Second, it was generally believed by both sides that the existing sizes of nuclear arsenals, in view of the destructive power of these weapons, was more than adequate to deter the other side. Although the SALT treaties were definitely a step in the right direction, their significance should not be over-estimated. Just as the naval arms limitation agreements of the 1920s had little apparent impact on the destructiveness of the Second World War, quite possibly the nuclear weapons agreements of the 1970s would have had little apparent impact on the destructiveness of the Third World War—had one occurred. The carnage wrought by 10,000 nuclear explosions might not have been perceptibly less than what would have been wrought by 20,000 nuclear explosions.

The rapid decline of the Cold War in the aftermath of the collapse and disintegration of the Soviet Union in 1991 has certainly improved the odds on substantial arms reduction by the two nuclear superpowers, the United States and the Russian Federation, either with or without benefit of a formal treaty. The START II treaty, between the same two nuclear superpowers as the SALT treaties, was quite ambitious, calling for the elimination of two thirds of existing nuclear warheads and all land-based multiple warhead ballistic missiles. However, START II, signed by George Bush and Boris Yeltsin in early 1993, has not been fully ratified and implemented. As of the end of the 1990s, there were five nations in the world with major nuclear arsenals, plus another eight nations with declared or undeclared nuclear capabilities. According to a 1998 report from the National Resources Defense Council (*Taking Stock: Worldwide Nuclear Deployments*), as of the end of 1997, Russia had 22,500 nuclear warheads, the United States 12,070, France 500, China 450 and Britain 380. No doubt there has been some reduction since then, but it is safe to say that there are still plenty of operational nuclear weapons in the world, more than enough to inflict catastrophe on human civilization should they be utilized. This is the situation at the present time, and it is likely to remain true for at least the next several decades.

If the 1993 START II treaty were to be fully implemented, this would leave the United States and Russia each with several thousand nuclear warheads, together with the means to deliver them to their targets anywhere in the world. If and when that point is reached, would there be further substantial reductions? It would be rash to expect further reductions if there are no fundamental changes in the world order (i.e., the sovereign nation-state system). Russia has to consider, for example, the possibility of a resurgent Germany tempted by the huge Russian land area and natural resource base in the same way that Hitler was tempted. A

Russian nuclear capability will help ensure that Germany continues to resist such temptations. The United States has to consider, for example, that there are masses of poor people in the world, many of them living in Mexico and the Latin American nations to the south of Mexico. Mexico, of course, suffered what it might tend to regard as outrageous injustices at the time of the Mexican-American War of 1848. A U.S. nuclear capability will help ensure that Mexico does not contemplate redressing the injustices of the Mexican-American War, nor that the impoverished people of Latin America do not contemplate a forcible redistribution of wealth by means of a land invasion of the continental United States—an invasion possibly aided and abetted by the remaining communist nations of the Far East, most notably the People's Republic of China. Are these paranoid delusions? Possibly so, but if so, these delusions would explain why—more than 15 years following the supposed demise of the Cold War—both the United States and the Russian Federation feel it necessary to maintain nuclear arsenals numbering in the thousands of warheads.

The same rationale that justifies the United States and Russia maintaining large nuclear arsenals would justify many other nations doing the same. Several nations have already taken the step. Hindu India and Muslim Pakistan have been at odds over Kashmir ever since independence and partition in 1948. Relations between India and China have also been none too warm over the years. China, as the number two power in the communist camp, felt it needed nuclear weapons—for the same reason that Britain and France in the noncommunist camp felt they needed them. Since China had nuclear weapons, India felt it needed them. Because India had nuclear weapons, Pakistan felt it needed them. Israel needs nuclear weapons to deter the surrounding Arab nations. Therefore, the surrounding Arab nations may need nuclear weapons lest Israel become expansionist. Bosnia may need nuclear weapons to protect itself against Serbia, and vice versa. And so it goes. Most nations of the world have signed the Nuclear Nonproliferation Treaty of 1968. But that treaty is a slender reed on which to depend, because for a number of nations there are compelling reasons to acquire at least a minimum nuclear capability. These nations may not be dissuaded forever from taking this route. After all, it could be seen as a form of hypocrisy for the nuclear superpowers to preach against nuclear weapons—after all, if they truly believed in what they preach, they would divest themselves of these weapons. As more and more smaller nations acquire nuclear weapons, it makes it more and more difficult for the major nuclear powers to reduce their arsenals.

This is a difficult situation, and I am certainly not saying that the establishment of a world government along the lines of the Federal Union of Democratic Nations would quickly and radically transform the situation. The proposed Federal Union would allow its member nations to maintain whatever armaments they desire under their own direct control. At the same time, there is no guarantee that the Federal Union would succeed. Quite possibly, after a brief "honeymoon period," the various conflicts of interest among the member nations—conflicts of interest which we see constantly at work in the world today—would reassert themselves and cause the departure from the Union of several important member nations. If secession were to become sufficiently popular, this could well lead to the remaining Federal Union dissolving itself in despair. Under the circumstances, nations today could not place undue reliance on the Federal Union to protect them against both historical and potential adversaries. It seems inevitable, therefore, that militarily powerful nations—even if they join the Federal Union with a certain amount of commitment and enthusiasm—will exercise their right to maintain substantial military forces. We can expect nuclear powers, large and small, to remain nuclear powers.

This is not a problem—in the sense that it is not an argument against world government. We are confronted with a choice between an armed world without a world government in operation, or an armed world with a world government in operation. The hope of every informed and reasonable person in the world today is that as international hostility and tension gradually fade, the level of armaments maintained by the nations will gradually decline. Both the threat of war and the potential destructiveness of war, it is hoped, will slowly subside to what might be termed an inconsequential level. The argument that I am putting forward here is that an operational world government will both increase the probability of this potential outcome, and accelerate progress toward its realization. The world state would facilitate the processes of communication and accommodation among the nations which further the cause of benign global governance. At the same time, it would provide a potent symbol of the brotherhood of mankind and of the high aspirations of human civilization. With a functioning world government in operation, we would have a better chance of realizing, within a reasonable period of historical time, our aspiration toward a world without war and the fear of war.

Supernational Taxation Authority

We have specified that the Federal Union of Democratic Nations shall possess what is perhaps the most fundamental and definitive characteristic of a state entity: namely, the power to tax. But the power to tax, as we all know, is the power to destroy. And we also know that a fundamental and definitive characteristic of a tyrannical state entity is the imposition of exorbitant taxes. But at the same time, we recognize that a state entity deprived of a meaningful and significant power of taxation is unlikely to be effective. Human nature being what it is, if taxes were voluntary instead of compulsory, most people would choose not to pay them. Therefore, we need to formulate the taxation authority of the supernational federation in such a way that the federation would have a reliable source of income, while at the same time the possibilities for disintegrative conflicts and confrontations would be minimized. One very important issue is whether the Federal Union should collect its tax revenues from individual citizens and/or business enterprises, or rather from the national governments of member nations. Another important issue concerns the appropriate basis for taxation at the supernational level. Let us consider each of these in turn.

Within nations, taxes are almost invariably collected from private households and business enterprises, rather than from lower levels of government. For example, in the United States the national government does not collect taxes from the state governments, the state governments do not collect taxes from the county governments, and the county governments do not collect taxes from the town and city governments within the county borders. Rather all four levels of government—national, state, county and local (town/city)—separately collect taxes from the private households and business enterprises within their respective borders. This fiscal situation, which has evolved historically, seems questionable from an efficiency standpoint. From an efficiency standpoint, the most attractive solution would seem to have all taxes collected either by the highest level of government or by the lowest level. In the former case, the highest level of government, having collected all the taxes, would allocate a part of tax revenue to lower levels of government using formulas based on population and other factors. In the latter case, the lowest level of government, having collected all the taxes, would pass along a part of tax revenue to the next highest level, which in turn would pass along a part to the next highest level, and so on up to the national government. The question arises why this apparently efficient system is not utilized.

One reasonably plausible principle that would explain this is that it is appropriate that each level of government, in order to allow different allocations in different areas according to local preferences, be separately responsible for raising revenue sufficient to support whatever public goods and services are provided by that level of government. For example, one town might prefer to spend relatively more on its local public school system, and another town relatively less. Another possibility has to do with enforcement of taxation. One unifying characteristic of any government is the possession and disposition of armed force. Even small towns have police departments. Every county in the United States, even the most rural, has its sheriff's department. Among the duties of the armed forces of governments is to ensure compliance with tax legislation, i.e., the payment of taxes. In contrast with governments, private households and business enterprises typically possess and control little or no armed force. In the final analysis, this disproportion with respect to armed force is what guarantees that taxes will be paid. If we envision a situation in which higher levels of government collected taxes from lower levels of government, the failure of a lower level of government to pay its due to the higher level of government might lead to a confrontation between the armed forces of the lower and higher levels of government. Such confrontations will be avoided if each level of government collects its own taxes from unarmed private households and business enterprises.

This line of thought suggests that in order to avoid potential confrontations between the supernational government and the national governments should the latter be, for whatever reason, reluctant to turn over the required tax payments to the former, the supernational government should not collect tax revenues from national governments, but rather from private households and business enterprises. Private households and business enterprises would not have the armed force necessary to successfully resist arrest and imprisonment of those responsible for non-payment of taxes. However, there are two serious problems with having the supernational government collect tax revenues from private households and business enterprises—even though this is the standard pattern for all lower levels of government. First, it would involve the supernational government in direct financial dealings with a tremendous number of very diverse private households and/or business enterprises. There would be a very substantial administrative cost of collecting taxes from hundreds of millions of taxpayers. The second problem with direct taxation of private households and business enterprises by the world government is that in all probability this would *not* be a reliable means for avoiding confrontations between the world government and the national governments. If relations between the world government and a specific member nation sour to the point where its national government does not want to pay taxes to the world government, it would not matter if the world government were collecting these taxes from private households and business enterprises within the nation's borders rather than from the national government itself—the national government might still forcibly intervene to prevent its private households and business enterprises from paying these taxes.

Therefore, the proposal put forward here for world government taxes is that they be levied directly on the national governments of the member nations. This would cut the administrative costs of tax collection to a bare minimum. However, it does bring up the question of what could be done in the event of non-payment of taxes by national governments. Anyone with the slightest acquaintance with the financial history of the United Nations is well aware of the fact that the primary means by which member nations of the U.N. demonstrate their dissatisfaction with and/or contempt for that organization is through non-payment of assessments. Generations of politicians in the United States, for example, have found that it is often helpful to their careers to pander to xenophobic tendencies among the voters by opposing the payment of U.N. assessments. If this same pattern emerges after the foundation of the Federal Union of Democratic Nations, it would bode very ill for the prospects of the Union. Our principal hope that this will not happen lies in the fact that the Federal Union of Democratic Nations would be a much more serious attempt to achieve worldwide political unity than was the United Nations.

The United Nations came into being at a time when the world was beset by bitter and irreconcilable ideological conflict among the superpowers. As a consequence, it was designed from the start merely to provide a permanent forum for non-binding discussions and consultations among ambassadors appointed by national governments. The main advantage of the U.N. from the standpoint of the rich and powerful nations, such as the United States, was (and remains) that it gives their ambassadors the opportunity to instruct representatives of other nations as to why policies that are in the interest of the rich and powerful nations are also in the interest of all other nations. The main disadvantage of the U.N. from the standpoint of the rich and powerful nations is that they are inevitably subjected to a certain amount of verbal flak from ambassadors from other nations who are not inclined to fully accept the positions taken by the rich and powerful nations. This flak is reported in the media and is particularly objectionable to the more xenophobic citizens of the rich and powerful nations. Some politicians court the favor of these citizens by opposing payment of assessments. But the United Nations was fatally flawed from the beginning, and its primary importance has always been symbolic rather than practical.

However, I am not suggesting that the Federal Union should rely only on its status and prestige to induce the national governments of the member nations to pay their taxes. There has to be some practical enforcement mechanism by which non-paying member nations would be seriously disadvantaged. Obviously, however, the enforcement mechanism would be tempered by the permanent and inalienable right of member nations to withdraw from the Federal Union at their own unilateral discretion. Tax enforcement has to be sufficiently rigorous to cause immediate and serious difficulties for non-paying member nations, yet not so severe as to cause a substantial number of nations to depart from the Union. The standard tax enforcement tool of lower level governments is the arrest and imprisonment of those individuals responsible for non-payment of taxes. This tool should be available to the world government, because in some cases it might be a practical means of enforcement. For example, if we imagine non-payment by a relatively small nation in which the national government has become extremely unpopular with the citizens of that nation, it might be possible to peacefully arrest the highest executive officials of that nation. In more normal cases, however, the decision of a national government not to pay taxes to the world government would enjoy a high level of support among the national population. Of course, if this is the case, it seems very likely that this nation would simply declare its independence from the Federal Union. But for the sake of discussion, let us imagine a case in which a certain nation is unwilling to pay its taxes, yet wishes to retain its membership. Of course, the Federal Union ought to possess the authority to expel member nations who are seriously in arrears with respect to payment of taxes. But this relatively drastic action should not be considered before less severe measures have been exhausted.

The primary means of dealing with non-payment of taxes by member nations should be the imposition of financial penalties on the citizens of that nation and on business enterprises with operations in that nation. These penalties would be imposed outside the boundaries of the non-paying nations. Citizens of a non-paying nation traveling outside the nation would be subject to special assessments. Commodities produced in that nation and marketed in other nations would also be subject to special assessments. The intention is that private citizens and business enterprises subjected to these costly and inconvenient assessments would thereupon put pressure on the national government to pay its tax obligations to the supernational government. Presumably it would not be practical for a national government in this situation to send its military forces into other nations to forestall the imposition of these special assessments. Presumably, therefore, it would not take very long for such a nation either to withdraw from the Federal Union, or to make arrangements for payment of its back taxes.

Of course, no one enjoys paying taxes. This is true of private households and business enterprises today in paying taxes to various levels of government from the local to the national. It would be no less true of national governments in the future in paying taxes to the world government. There is a natural disintegrative tendency set into motion by the imposition and enforcement of taxes, whatever the level of government assessing them. National governments and lower-level governments have proved their capability to overcome these disintegrative tendencies. But these same tendencies at the supernational level might pose a serious threat to the continued existence of the Federal Union of Democratic Nations. If the Union is to survive and succeed, it will be necessary to keep the tax burden on the citizens of the Union to a reasonable minimum. In this context, it is very important to recognize that there would be two important additional sources of revenue, besides taxation, for the Federal Union of Democratic Nations. One of these, much utilized today by national and lower-level governments, is the issuance of bonds. The other, which would be unique to government at the supernational level, would be the "directed contribution."

A "directed contribution" would be a voluntary, non-obligatory payment made by a national government to the supernational government, outside of normal taxes, for the support of certain programs and projects of the supernational federation specified by the national government. The term "contribution" manifests the voluntary nature of the payment, and the term "directed" manifests the fact that the utilization of the payment would be determined by the national government making the payment. This mechanism would provide an avenue for the adequate financing of programs and projects about which some nations are more enthusiastic than other nations. For example, space exploration might be a Federal Union program that would enjoy a higher level of support in the rich member nations than in the poor member nations. With respect to the determination of the voting weight of a Union Representative in the material vote, it would be determined by the sum of tax payments and directed contributions. In the material vote, recall, the voting weight of a representative from a particular Union District would be equal to the proportion of total Union revenues realized from that district.

Turning now to the question of the basis for taxes to support the supernational federation, as in the case of the levying of taxes, there would be important distinctions between the supernational government and the national and lower-level governments. The economic basis for taxes within nations is wide and varied. There are taxes on household income and business profits, there are sales taxes on either the number of physical units sold or on the total revenue derived from the sale of physical units, there are taxes on the value of residential and commercial real estate, as well as on other forms of personal and business property, there are taxes on imports, exports, and international financial flows, there are taxes on estates, financial gifts, and financial inheritances. Wherever money and/or commodities change hands, or property exists in any form, the tax authorities are likely to be in attendance. Rates of taxation sometimes depend significantly on taxpayer characteristics and circumstances. A well-known example is the progressive income tax on household income, according to which households with higher incomes pay a higher proportion of their incomes in taxes. Contemporary systems of taxation within nations tend to be very elaborate and complicated, the result of generations of political negotiation and legal maneuvering among the taxpayers, the tax authorities, and their supporting lawyers and accountants.

Despite the tremendous amount of time and effort over the decades and the centuries which have gone into the development of tax systems at the national and lower levels, any sort of close inspection of these systems produces a strong impression of both inequity and inefficiency. The Federal Union of Democratic Nations proposed here would be a novel and innovative political institution, started from scratch and built from the ground up. It need not and should not emulate the apparently needless irrationalities and inefficiencies of lower levels of government. It follows that its tax system should be quite simple and straight-forward. Accordingly, let us propose that its sole tax base be the measured monetary value of output of its member nations. There are a number of basic measures of national income accounting that might be used: Gross National Product (GNP), Gross Domestic Product (GDP), National Income (NI), etc. The only obvious requirement would be that whatever measure is utilized be consistently measured over nations. As any economist who has become involved in national income comparisons among nations will verify, this will not necessarily be easy. However, thanks to the efforts of the World Bank and other international agencies over the last several decades, much progress has been made in compiling comparable economic statistics over a large range of nations. These statistics, of course, are not perfectly accurate, but they are sufficiently accurate to form a legitimate basis for tax policy.

The "Transitional Codicil" to the Federal Union constitution has been mentioned from time to time in the preceding. This would be an appendix to the constitution to remain in effect during the first few decades of the Union's existence, possibly for 50 years. The Codicil would specify certain temporary restrictions and limitations on the world government which are necessary to make the world government acceptable to the cautious and suspicious nations of the present day, but which, if continued beyond the initial adjustment period, would unduly hamper the flexibility and effectiveness of the world government in the long run. One of the most important provisions of the Transitional Codicil would pertain to the tax authority of the Federal Union. This provision would limit both the tax base and the tax rate. The tax base would be strictly confined to the national income of the member nation. No other financial or physical basis could be specified for the taxes to be paid to the supernational government. My suggestion for the tax rate is that it be confined to a maximum of five percent for the first decade of Federal Union operation, thereafter rising at the rate of one percent per decade, until at the end of five decades of operation it would stand at ten percent. This does not necessarily mean that the expenditures of the world government would be five percent of member nation national income in the first decade, six percent in the second decade, and so on. Recall that the Federal Union would have two additional sources of revenue besides tax revenue: bond issues and directed contributions. The tax stipulation of the Transitional Codicil would merely require that *tax* revenue be no more than five percent of member nation national income in the first decade, no more than six percent in the second decade, and so on. If adequately supported by directed contributions, Federal Union expenditures could be substantially in excess of five percent of member national income in the first decade, six percent in the second decade, and so on.

After the Transitional Codicil has expired, the world government, with the support of the member nations, might alter the tax system, expanding both the base and the rate. The possibility that the world government would eventually increase the proportion of income which it takes in tax revenues to a substantially higher level than the highest level permitted by the Transitional Codicil, does not necessarily imply that the overall tax burden on the typical household within the Union would be increased. Government tax revenues as a percentage of national income, taking into account all levels of government from the national downwards, are already approaching 50 percent in a number of nations. Obviously, it would be possible to go beyond the optimal proportion of income spent publicly, and obviously, we do not want to do this. This principle holds now, in the absence of world government; it would hold equally in the future if there were a world government.

Assuming world government comes about, and that it manages to get past the initial difficulties and becomes fully accepted as a useful component of overall human governance in general and global governance in particular, at that point there might occur a gradual transfer of some functions of the national governments and lower-level governments to the supernational government. Households would continue to pay the same taxes, but a smaller proportion of these taxes would go to support the operations of national and lower level governments, and a higher proportion to support the operations of the supernational government. Although it is imperative to give full and deliberate consideration to the principle of subsidiarity in deciding on the allocation of governmental responsibilities (whatever government functions may be efficiently and equitably performed by lower levels of government, should in fact be performed by those lower levels), certainly there are some functions of government which would be performed significantly more efficiently and/or equitably at the supernational level than at lower levels. Once the world government has established that it is a benign and democratically accountable political entity, certain issues regarding the allocation of government responsibilities among the various levels of government could be examined in a calm and rational manner.

Supernational Armament Authority

It is customary that state entities possess military forces: these military forces protect the citizen body from outside aggression and they also deter (at least potentially) the citizen body from engaging in warfare among itself. Aside from its utilitarian purposes, the possession of a military force carries potent symbolic significance as a key defining characteristic of a political entity. An unarmed political entity would be at somewhat the same disadvantage, in its dealings with other political entities, as would a person wearing no clothing in his/her dealings with other persons. It is therefore proposed that the Federal Union of Democratic Nations possess a military force, to be called the Union Security Force (USF). The USF would be administered by a civilian authority in the form of the Ministry of Security, an agency of the executive branch.

Of course, the disposition of armed force by a political entity is intended to preserve peace and security, it is intended to deter aggression and violence perpetrated from within or without, it is intended to be of a preventive rather than a curative nature. It is a bitter irony when, as often has happened throughout history, these intentions fail, and the military forces and armaments which were supposed to maintain peace, are instead utilized in war. The death and destruction that ensue in the course of warfare are then directly proportional to the size and armaments of the military forces involved. The paradox is that the greater the size and strength of military forces, the higher will be their deterrent effect against armed conflict—but in the event that war occurs despite this deterrent effect, the more horrific will be the slaughter. In the past, this paradox has not been considered a serious argument against national governments main-taining substantial military forces—except to a small minority of uncompro-mising pacifists. Neither should it be considered, in the future, a serious argument against a potential supernational government maintaining substantial military forces.

It should be taken as a given that the Federal Union of Democratic Nations will possess a substantial military apparatus. But exactly how large its military forces should be, exactly what sort of weaponry they should possess, and exactly how the USF should be organized and administered, are difficult questions requiring a great deal of careful thought and reflective deliberation. The Federal Union would be a unique and unprecedented political form in human affairs. In addition, there are many questions about its circumstances and conditions that cannot be answered at the present time. For example, how many nations will choose to become charter members of the world federation, and what forces will they choose to maintain under their direct control? What military forces will be maintained by those nations not choosing to become charter members of the world federation? How much economic progress will be made at the world level? What will be the course of religious and ideological developments: will increasing toleration and flexibility be the rule, or might there be retrograde movements which will intensify religion and/or ideology as contributing factors to hostility, suspicion and strife among humanity? And so on and so forth. We must also take into special account, in designing the military component of the world state, the fears and apprehensions that are so widespread among humanity at the present time that such a state would tend to become, gradually or quickly as the case may be, an instrument of oppression and tyranny. The proper military force of the world government is obviously an exceptionally delicate and difficult issue. The proposals described in the following are merely suggestions.

The Union Security Force of the Federal Union of Democratic Nations would comprise land, sea, and air forces, and it would be armed with the entire range of weaponry from small arms through to strategic nuclear weapons. The number of military personnel in this force, and the quantity of weaponry with which they would be armed, would be substantial—but exact numerical figures cannot be specified at this time. The exact numerical figures would depend on conditions and circumstances which cannot be predicted in advance. An especially important question concerns nuclear weapons. I would suggest that the nuclear capability directly controlled by the Federal Union be of more than a token level, but less than the capabilities of the nuclear superpowers of the present day, the United States and the Russian Federation. An appropriate capability might be on the order of the present-day nuclear capabilities of Britain or France. Of course, it should be recalled that under some circumstances, the nuclear capabilities of member nations might be put at the disposal of the world government. For example, even if the United States and the Russian Federation chose to become charter members of the world federation, they would in all probability maintain substantial nuclear forces under their direct control for an indefinite period following formation of the union. Thus the Federal Union would *potentially* control a major nuclear capability, even though its *directly* controlled nuclear capability might be minor.

With respect to outside aggression, the ultimate objective of the Federal Union would of course be universal membership by all the nations of the earth, and were this objective to be eventually achieved there would be no danger of outside aggression by other nations. However, even if the human race were to achieve complete political unity, there will always exist the possibility, however remote, of conflict with intelligent nonhuman species emanating from other solar systems. Although most of the abundant "war of the worlds" speculation produced by science fiction writers from H. G. Wells on down seems patently preposterous, there is perhaps just enough substance to these scary visions to postulate a Ministry of Security and a Union Security Force as permanent components of the supernational state, even were complete participation in the Union and perfect internal harmony to be achieved. In the near term, however, such a force might more plausibly be necessary to deter aggression against member nations by non-member nations. It is of course fairly probable that not all nations of the earth will join the Federal Union upon its formation. Moreover, member nations of the Federal Union would be guaranteed the right of secession from the Union, so that some nations might withdraw from the Union at some point after initially joining it. Until the long-term goal of universal membership has been achieved, the threat of aggression by non-member nations against member nations would continue, and this threat would justify a Union Security Force.

It is proposed that any and all military forces financially supported by national governments at their own discretion be considered, in a pro forma sense, component units of the Union Security Force. In addition to nationally funded military units not subject to direct control by the Federal Union government, the Federal Union would financially support some Union Security Force units of its own, these latter units being subject to direct control by the Federal Union government. The uniforms, insignia, code of conduct, and basic weaponry would be very similar across all units of the Union Security Force. The primary outward distinction would be that personnel of nationally funded units would wear shoulder patches depicting the national flag, while personnel of Union funded units would wear shoulder patches depicting the Federal Union flag.

In the absence of common dangers, the units of the Union Security Force supported by a particular nation, which would be stationed on its own territory and which would be composed almost entirely of its own citizens, would serve as guarantees of independent action by the nation should it decide to secede from the Federal Union because it deems certain Union policies or actions to be intolerably prejudicial to its national interests. Of course, the possibility would exist that if a particular nation announced its secession from the Union, the supernational government would ignore the formal guarantees of the right of secession contained in the Union Constitution, and would send its units of the Union Security Force into battle against the nation's own military units. In this case, a nuclear civil war might well ensue. This possibility, however grim, is sufficiently improbable that it does not constitute a serious argument against the foundation of a world state. This is because the threat of nuclear war eventually occurring among sovereign and independent nations, if a world state is *not* established, would almost certainly be significantly greater than the threat of nuclear war occurring among member nations of a world state, if one *is* established. Now that nuclear weapons have been manufactured in large quantities and are dispersed among a substantial number of nations, it will probably require a prolonged period of historical time before the threat of nuclear war subsides to a truly negligible level. For the moment, we cannot completely eliminate the threat of nuclear war. What we can do, however, is to take an action—specifically the foundation of a world federation—that would greatly accelerate long-term progress toward the eventual extinction of this threat.

One of the important purposes of a nation-state is to deter armed conflicts between subsidiary governments representing component localities. Thus, for example, the national government of the United States would not allow the different component states to go to war with one another. If necessary, United States military forces commanded by the federal government would be employed to suppress such a conflict. But to those who are personally familiar with life in the contemporary United States, the notion that the state governments would contemplate making war on one another is simply inconceivable. The ideal of national unity has become so strongly rooted in the United States that state leaders never in their wildest dreams imagine using armed force to resolve various disputes and controversies with other states. It is simply taken for granted that these disputes and controversies will be resolved peacefully by some type of negotiation, arbitration, or adjudication. This psychological attitude is possible because the citizens of the United States harbor very little emotional allegiance to their respective states: rather their emotional allegiance is almost entirely bestowed upon the nation. Thus, armed conflicts between states are not so much deterred by the existence of the United States military forces which would forcibly suppress such conflicts were they to occur (although such forcible suppression would indeed be inevitable); rather they are principally forestalled by the absence of emotional allegiance in citizens to their respective states.

Moreover, the strong spirit of national unity which is common to the populations of all the states guarantees that all the other states—embodied in the federal government of the United States—would come to the assistance of any one state threatened by aggression from a foreign nation. It is virtually impossible for other nations to "divide and conquer," as far as the individual states of the United States are concerned. There is very little question but that an attack on any one state would immediately be deemed by the other states as an attack on all states. This unity of purpose and complete mutual resolution greatly enhances the safety and security of each one of the 50 individual states comprising the United States. There is great strength to be had in numbers—presuming that dysfunctional instincts toward shortsighted selfishness have been supplanted by beneficial instincts toward farsighted cooperativeness and mutual support.

The long-term goal of the Federal Union of Democratic Nations would be to achieve an analogous situation in the international sphere: that is, to bring about a condition under which the citizens of the Union would harbor rather little emotional allegiance to their respective nations, but would rather bestow most such allegiance upon the Federal Union as a whole. A strong spirit of supernational unity would operate very much as does a strong spirit of national unity: it would render armed conflicts among member nations of the Federal Union extremely unlikely, while at the same time it would render the member nations of the Federal Union highly impervious against the threat of military aggression by non-member nations. If a point is reached at which it is obvious to any non-member nation that an attack on any member nation will incur the full military weight of the Union Security Force, including all national as well as supernational component units, then no such attacks will be contemplated. The lengthy process of evolution by which such a condition might eventually be achieved would involve a complex interplay between real factors (such as the supernational federation's military forces) and psychological factors (the important symbolic impact of the very existence of the supernational federation).

The most difficult question regarding the use of force by the Federal Union of Democratic Nations concerns possible applications of force outside the boundaries of the Federal Union. Should the military power of the Union Security Force be used to suppress large-scale armed conflicts within or among *non-member* nations? Throughout the Cold War era and beyond, there have been a number of humanitarian disasters throughout the world: some of the nations involved include Cambodia, Somalia, Bosnia-Herzegovina, and Rwanda. None of these conflicts involved international aggression, but rather intense civil wars motivated by various ideological, religious, ethnic and tribal factors. These episodes witnessed complete disregard for and abrogation of all civilized notions of human rights. Should the world stand by quietly while innocent people are dispossessed and dispersed, tortured and mistreated, maimed and murdered? This question has been asked at the time of each and every major humanitarian disaster over the last few decades. Generally speaking, however, intervention in such situations by outside forces under specific nations, or under such multinational bodies as NATO or the United Nations, has been rather limited.

If we look forward to a future in which a world government along the lines of the Federal Union of Democratic Nations has become an existent, functioning component of international relations, then if and when humanitarian disasters in non-member nations occur, it is inevitable that many citizens of the Federal Union will demand that the Union Security Force be utilized to restore peace and order in the affected nations. Notwithstanding that these calls reflect worthy ideals and commendable principles, I would strongly suggest that any and all calls for military intervention be examined in an extremely cautious and conservative manner. Intervention should only be undertaken if there is strong evidence that the costs would be relatively minor. The thing to be avoided at all costs is for the populations of large and important member nations to begin to believe that their own soldiers are being used heedlessly as cannon fodder by incompetent and callous officers from other nations. This would most definitely spur secessionist impulses within these nations.

For those who would decry a passive stance by the supernational federation toward humanitarian disasters occurring in non-member nations, I would offer two consoling considerations. First, these episodes provide useful instruction in the persistence and harmfulness of those negative human characteristics and motivations which it is the long-run purpose of the Federal Union to bring under control. Second, a passive stance, in the event of humanitarian disasters in non-member nations during the early period of the Federal Union, is only a temporary expedient to get the world federation over the difficult early period during which its stability and permanence would be problematical. Later on, once the spirit of supernational patriotism has achieved the critical minimum at which no further serious doubt would exist on the basic feasibility and desir-ability of world government in the long term, then that government might well become far more activist and willing to make significant sacrifices to protect human rights anywhere and everywhere in the world.

Appendix to Chapter 2

TABLE 2.A.1
Gross Domestic Product per Capita (GDPPC) in 1995 U.S. $, Population (POP), and Gross Domestic Product (GDP), for 207 Nations in 2000 (Alphabetical Order)

Nation	GDPPC	POP	GDP
Afghanistan	258	26,550,000	6,849,900,000
Albania	899	3,411,000	3,067,942,173
Algeria	1,606	30,399,250	48,818,776,028
American Samoa	7,779	65,440	509,057,760
Andorra	18,130	67,000	1,214,710,000
Angola	506	13,134,000	6,646,773,178
Antigua/Barbuda	9,138	68,000	621,360,227
Argentina	7,933	37,032,000	293,769,503,719
Armenia	976	3,803,000	3,711,194,596
Aruba	7,779	101,000	785,679,000
Australia	23,838	19,182,000	457,254,933,738
Austria	32,763	8,110,240	265,715,460,473
Azerbaijan	506	8,049,000	4,071,467,320
Bahamas, The	13,928	303,000	4,220,122,453
Bahrain	9,297	691,000	6,424,227,000
Bangladesh	373	131,050,000	48,906,097,896
Barbados	8,282	267,000	2,211,292,957
Belarus	2,760	10,005,000	27,618,289,548
Belgium	30,830	10,252,000	316,070,061,055
Belize	3,141	240,000	753,736,582
Benin	414	6,272,000	2,597,648,867
Bermuda	7,779	63,000	490,077,000
Bhutan	532	805,000	428,433,637
Bolivia	952	8,328,700	7,925,702,552
Bosnia/Herzegovina	1,526	3,977,000	6,068,221,366
Botswana	3,951	1,602,000	6,329,665,485
Brazil	4,624	170,406,000	788,024,491,286
Brunei	29,837	338,000	10,084,906,000
Bulgaria	1,503	8,166,960	12,276,756,314
Burkina Faso	252	11,274,000	2,841,620,336
Burundi	141	6,807,000	957,718,289
Cambodia	297	12,021,230	3,564,614,229
Cameroon	675	14,876,000	10,043,553,554
Canada	22,541	30,750,000	693,148,902,832
Cape Verde	1,519	441,000	669,927,396
Cayman Islands	7,779	35,000	272,265,000
Central African Rep.	339	3,717,000	1,258,457,684
Chad	218	7,694,000	1,676,049,309
Channel Islands	22,176	149,000	3,304,224,000

Table 2.A.1 continued—

Nation	GDPPC	POP	GDP
Chile	5,354	15,211,300	81,445,296,137
China	824	1,262,460,032	1,040,311,757,946
Colombia	2,290	42,299,300	96,864,147,436
Comoros	436	558,000	243,168,492
Congo, Dem. Rep.	806	50,948,000	41,064,088,000
Congo, Rep.	841	3,018,000	2,539,397,403
Costa Rica	3,912	3,811,000	14,907,870,917
Cote d'Ivoire	743	16,013,000	11,890,021,941
Croatia	5,146	4,380,000	22,537,899,521
Cuba	1,618	11,188,000	18,102,184,000
Cyprus	14,063	757,000	10,645,748,662
Czech Republic	5,311	10,273,300	54,561,471,219
Denmark	38,521	5,336,000	205,550,619,781
Djibouti	783	632,000	494,902,868
Dominica	3,371	73,000	246,052,399
Dominican Republic	2,062	8,373,000	17,263,582,637
Ecuador	1,425	12,646,000	18,021,318,763
Egypt, Arab Rep.	1,226	63,976,000	78,421,518,398
El Salvador	1,752	6,276,000	10,995,272,369
Equatorial Guinea	1,599	457,000	730,540,217
Eritrea	155	4,097,000	635,238,675
Estonia	4,431	1,369,000	6,066,494,219
Ethiopia	116	64,298,000	7,450,896,213
Faeroe Islands	7,779	45,000	350,055,000
Fiji	2,395	811,900	1,944,428,547
Finland	32,024	5,177,000	165,786,872,859
France	29,811	58,892,000	1,755,613,768,813
French Polynesia	19,896	235,000	4,675,502,168
Gabon	4,378	1,230,000	5,384,938,198
Gambia, The	370	1,303,000	482,734,818
Georgia	499	5,024,000	2,504,667,609
Germany	32,623	82,150,000	2,680,002,394,238
Ghana	413	19,306,000	7,978,279,325
Greece	13,105	10,560,000	138,386,325,000
Greenland	29,588	56,200	1,662,845,600
Grenada	3,832	98,000	375,506,141
Guam	7,779	154,500	1,201,855,500
Guatemala	1,558	11,385,300	17,741,769,138
Guinea	603	7,415,000	4,474,210,276
Guinea-Bissau	210	1,199,000	251,498,959
Guyana	941	761,000	716,169,232
Haiti	367	7,959,000	2,922,574,773
Honduras	711	6,417,000	4,563,115,227
Hong Kong, China	24,218	6,797,000	164,609,998,232
Hungary	5,425	10,022,000	54,371,444,441
Iceland	31,304	281,000	8,796,470,650
India	459	1,015,923,008	466,681,601,891

Table 2.A.1 continued—

Nation	GDPPC	POP	GDP
Indonesia	994	210,420,992	209,098,309,070
Iran, Islamic Rep.	1,649	63,664,000	104,985,573,055
Iraq	2,590	23,263,840	60,253,345,600
Ireland	27,741	3,794,000	105,247,946,070
Isle of Man	21,546	75,000	1,615,950,000
Israel	17,067	6,233,210	106,383,290,751
Italy	20,885	57,690,000	1,204,867,818,984
Jamaica	1,785	2,633,000	4,701,168,789
Japan	44,830	126,870,000	5,687,635,127,695
Jordan	1,616	4,886,810	7,899,300,489
Kazakhstan	1,512	14,869,000	22,487,360,485
Kenya	328	30,092,000	9,876,112,117
Kiribati	561	90,700	50,881,919
Korea, Dem. Rep.	1,295	22,268,000	28,837,060,000
Korea, Rep.	13,062	47,275,000	617,513,067,383
Kuwait	13,546	1,984,400	26,880,300,636
Kyrgyz Republic	885	4,915,000	4,350,488,071
Lao PDR	450	5,279,000	2,376,370,816
Latvia	2,597	2,372,000	6,160,158,704
Lebanon	2,891	4,328,000	12,510,729,607
Lesotho	551	2,035,000	1,122,163,513
Liberia	1,035	3,130,000	3,239,550,000
Libya	8,546	5,290,000	45,208,340,000
Liechtenstein	28,877	32,000	924,064,000
Lithuania	2,056	3,695,000	7,596,791,902
Luxembourg	56,372	438,400	24,713,483,088
Macao, China	15,244	438,000	6,676,662,838
Macedonia, FYR	2,530	2,031,000	5,137,982,744
Madagascar	246	15,523,000	3,815,492,100
Malawi	169	10,311,000	1,738,786,618
Malaysia	4,797	23,270,000	111,616,918,359
Maldives	1,933	276,000	533,415,450
Mali	288	10,840,000	3,119,073,375
Malta	10,223	390,000	3,986,981,045
Marshall Islands	1,602	52,000	83,325,925
Mauritania	496	2,665,000	1,320,978,966
Mauritius	4,429	1,186,140	5,253,422,168
Mayotte	1,229	145,000	178,205,000
Mexico	3,819	97,966,000	374,140,979,550
Micronesia, Fed. Sts.	1,735	118,100	204,942,396
Moldova	636	4,282,000	2,721,554,940
Monaco	20,720	32,000	663,040,000
Mongolia	428	2,398,000	1,026,989,897
Morocco	1,370	28,705,000	39,323,502,301
Mozambique	191	17,691,000	3,380,380,656
Myanmar	1,229	47,749,000	58,683,521,000
Namibia	2,408	1,757,000	4,230,113,050

Table 2.A.1 continued—

Nation	GDPPC	POP	GDP
Nepal	241	23,043,000	5,560,337,150
Netherlands	30,966	15,919,000	492,955,682,408
Netherlands Antilles	2,893	215,000	621,995,000
New Caledonia	17,432	212,700	3,707,764,382
New Zealand	17,548	3,830,800	67,222,017,966
Nicaragua	466	5,071,000	2,361,034,108
Niger	203	10,832,000	2,196,720,873
Nigeria	254	126,910,000	32,184,396,140
Northern Mariana Is.	2,893	72,000	208,296,000
Norway	37,954	4,491,000	170,451,817,488
Oman	5,716	2,395,000	13,689,820,000
Pakistan	516	138,080,000	71,277,546,621
Palau	6,726	19,000	127,787,599
Panama	3,279	2,856,000	9,365,118,246
Papua New Guinea	927	5,130,000	4,756,020,996
Paraguay	1,700	5,496,000	9,344,438,479
Peru	2,368	25,661,000	60,774,169,207
Philippines	1,167	75,580,000	88,231,586,411
Poland	4,223	38,650,000	163,235,689,526
Portugal	12,794	10,008,000	128,039,390,648
Puerto Rico	3,581	3,920,000	14,037,520,000
Qatar	13,756	584,890	8,045,746,840
Romania	1,460	22,435,000	32,748,480,689
Russian Federation	2,455	145,555,008	357,322,299,743
Rwanda	242	8,508,000	2,056,942,067
Samoa	1,440	170,000	244,877,841
San Marino	23,985	27,000	647,595,000
Sao Tome/Principe	341	148,000	50,415,291
Saudi Arabia	6,729	20,723,150	139,437,819,470
Senegal	609	9,530,000	5,806,050,709
Seychelles	7,000	81,230	568,640,660
Sierra Leone	147	5,031,000	741,494,138
Singapore	28,230	4,018,000	113,426,421,363
Slovak Republic	4,160	5,401,790	22,471,032,298
Slovenia	11,659	1,988,000	23,177,334,852
Solomon Islands	643	447,000	287,335,414
Somalia	647	8,778,000	5,679,366,000
South Africa	3,985	42,800,992	170,568,149,650
Spain	17,798	39,465,000	702,394,678,477
Sri Lanka	860	19,359,000	16,657,681,013
St. Kitts and Nevis	6,830	41,000	280,040,710
St. Lucia	3,968	156,000	619,051,456
St. Vincent /Grenadines	2,771	115,000	318,621,763
Sudan	319	31,095,000	9,921,853,864
Suriname	994	417,000	414,355,878
Swaziland	1,476	1,045,000	1,542,838,791
Sweden	31,206	8,869,000	276,768,387,150

Table 2.A.1 concluded—

Nation	GDPPC	POP	GDP
Switzerland	46,737	7,180,000	335,569,640,625
Syrian Arab Rep.	839	16,189,000	13,578,446,678
Tajikistan	386	6,170,000	2,381,055,120
Tanzania	190	33,696,000	6,418,594,406
Thailand	2,805	60,728,000	170,338,229,674
Togo	327	4,527,000	1,478,565,200
Tonga	1,768	100,200	177,177,904
Trinidad/Tobago	5,123	1,301,000	6,664,596,745
Tunisia	2,470	9,563,500	23,622,606,157
Turkey	3,134	65,293,000	204,651,328,155
Turkmenistan	1,377	5,198,940	7,156,601,745
Uganda	348	22,210,000	7,728,045,006
Ukraine	896	49,501,000	44,352,397,485
United Arab Emirates	20,634	2,905,080	59,943,420,720
United Kingdom	21,667	59,738,900	1,294,358,662,586
United States	31,996	281,550,016	9,008,507,306,079
Uruguay	6,115	3,337,000	20,404,601,389
Uzbekistan	485	24,752,000	12,006,648,462
Vanuatu	1,177	197,000	231,788,175
Venezuela, RB	3,300	24,170,000	79,771,780,906
Vietnam	356	78,522,704	27,933,943,928
Virgin Islands (U.S.)	7,779	121,000	941,259,000
West Bank/Gaza	1,365	2,966,000	4,049,983,933
Yemen, Rep.	314	17,507,160	5,496,029,022
Yugoslavia, Fed. Rep.	1,240	10,637,000	13,187,310,344
Zambia	392	10,089,000	3,958,732,645
Zimbabwe	621	12,627,000	7,837,598,321
ALL NATIONS	5,604	6,033,562,312	33,813,336,367,597

TABLE 2.A.2
Potential Voting Weights of 207 Nations in the
Federal Union Chamber of Representatives,
based on 2000 Population and GDP

Population Basis		Material Basis	
Nation	% of Total	Nation	% of Total
China	20.923958	United States	26.641876
India	16.837864	Japan	16.820686
United States	4.666398	Germany	7.925874
Indonesia	3.487508	France	5.192075
Brazil	2.824302	United Kingdom	3.827953
Russian Federation	2.412422	Italy	3.563292
Pakistan	2.288532	China	3.076632
Bangladesh	2.172017	Brazil	2.330514

Table 2.A.2 continued—

Population Basis		Material Basis	
Nation	% of Total	Nation	% of Total
Nigeria	2.103401	Spain	2.077271
Japan	2.102738	Canada	2.049928
Mexico	1.623684	Korea, Rep.	1.826241
Germany	1.361551	Netherlands	1.457874
Vietnam	1.301432	India	1.380170
Philippines	1.252660	Australia	1.352292
Turkey	1.082163	Mexico	1.106489
Ethiopia	1.065672	Russian Federation	1.056750
Egypt, Arab Rep.	1.060335	Switzerland	0.992418
Iran, Islamic Rep.	1.055164	Belgium	0.934750
Thailand	1.006503	Argentina	0.868798
United Kingdom	0.990110	Sweden	0.818518
France	0.976073	Austria	0.785830
Italy	0.956152	Indonesia	0.618390
Congo, Dem. Rep.	0.844410	Denmark	0.607898
Ukraine	0.820427	Turkey	0.605238
Myanmar	0.791390	South Africa	0.504440
Korea, Rep.	0.783534	Norway	0.504096
South Africa	0.709382	Thailand	0.503760
Colombia	0.701067	Finland	0.490300
Spain	0.654091	Hong Kong, China	0.486820
Poland	0.640583	Poland	0.482755
Argentina	0.613767	Saudi Arabia	0.412375
Tanzania	0.558476	Greece	0.409266
Sudan	0.515367	Portugal	0.378665
Canada	0.509649	Singapore	0.335449
Algeria	0.503836	Malaysia	0.330097
Kenya	0.498744	Israel	0.314619
Morocco	0.475755	Ireland	0.311262
Afghanistan	0.440039	Iran, Islamic Rep.	0.310486
Peru	0.425304	Colombia	0.286467
Uzbekistan	0.410239	Philippines	0.260937
Venezuela, RB	0.400593	Chile	0.240867
Malaysia	0.385676	Venezuela, RB	0.235918
Iraq	0.385574	Egypt, Arab Rep.	0.231925
Nepal	0.381914	Pakistan	0.210797
Romania	0.371837	New Zealand	0.198803
Korea, Dem. Rep.	0.369069	Peru	0.179734
Uganda	0.368108	Iraq	0.178194
Saudi Arabia	0.343465	United Arab Emirates	0.177277
Sri Lanka	0.320855	Myanmar	0.173551
Ghana	0.319977	Czech Republic	0.161361
Australia	0.317922	Hungary	0.160799
Mozambique	0.293210	Bangladesh	0.144636
Yemen, Rep.	0.290163	Algeria	0.144377

Table 2.A.2 continued—

Population Basis		Material Basis	
Nation	% of Total	Nation	% of Total
Syrian Arab Rep.	0.268316	Libya	0.133700
Cote d'Ivoire	0.265399	Ukraine	0.131168
Netherlands	0.263841	Congo, Dem. Rep.	0.121443
Madagascar	0.257278	Morocco	0.116296
Chile	0.252111	Romania	0.096851
Cameroon	0.246554	Nigeria	0.095183
Kazakhstan	0.246438	Korea, Dem. Rep.	0.085283
Angola	0.217682	Vietnam	0.082612
Ecuador	0.209594	Belarus	0.081679
Zimbabwe	0.209279	Kuwait	0.079496
Cambodia	0.199239	Luxembourg	0.073088
Guatemala	0.188699	Tunisia	0.069862
Burkina Faso	0.186855	Slovenia	0.068545
Cuba	0.185429	Croatia	0.066654
Mali	0.179662	Kazakhstan	0.066504
Niger	0.179529	Slovak Republic	0.066456
Yugoslavia, Fed. Rep.	0.176297	Uruguay	0.060345
Greece	0.175021	Cuba	0.053536
Malawi	0.170894	Ecuador	0.053296
Czech Republic	0.170269	Guatemala	0.052470
Belgium	0.169916	Dominican Republic	0.051056
Zambia	0.167215	Sri Lanka	0.049264
Hungary	0.166104	Costa Rica	0.044089
Portugal	0.165872	Puerto Rico	0.041515
Belarus	0.165822	Oman	0.040486
Tunisia	0.158505	Syrian Arab Rep.	0.040157
Senegal	0.157950	Yugoslavia, Fed. Rep.	0.039000
Sweden	0.146994	Lebanon	0.036999
Somalia	0.145486	Bulgaria	0.036307
Rwanda	0.141011	Uzbekistan	0.035509
Dominican Republic	0.138774	Cote d'Ivoire	0.035164
Bolivia	0.138040	El Salvador	0.032518
Bulgaria	0.135359	Cyprus	0.031484
Austria	0.134419	Brunei	0.029825
Azerbaijan	0.133404	Cameroon	0.029703
Haiti	0.131912	Sudan	0.029343
Chad	0.127520	Kenya	0.029208
Guinea	0.122896	Panama	0.027697
Switzerland	0.119001	Paraguay	0.027635
Burundi	0.112819	Iceland	0.026015
Hong Kong, China	0.112653	Qatar	0.023795
Honduras	0.106355	Ghana	0.023595
El Salvador	0.104018	Bolivia	0.023440
Benin	0.103952	Jordan	0.023361
Israel	0.103309	Zimbabwe	0.023179

Table 2.A.2 continued—

Population Basis		Material Basis	
Nation	% of Total	Nation	% of Total
Tajikistan	0.102261	Uganda	0.022855
Paraguay	0.091090	Lithuania	0.022467
Slovak Republic	0.089529	Ethiopia	0.022035
Denmark	0.088439	Turkmenistan	0.021165
Libya	0.087676	Afghanistan	0.020258
Lao PDR	0.087494	Macao, China	0.019746
Turkmenistan	0.086167	Trinidad/Tobago	0.019710
Finland	0.085803	Angola	0.019657
Papua New Guinea	0.085024	Bahrain	0.018999
Nicaragua	0.084047	Tanzania	0.018982
Sierra Leone	0.083384	Botswana	0.018719
Georgia	0.083268	Latvia	0.018218
Kyrgyz Republic	0.081461	Bosnia/Herzegovina	0.017946
Jordan	0.080994	Estonia	0.017941
Togo	0.075030	Senegal	0.017171
Norway	0.074434	Somalia	0.016796
Croatia	0.072594	Nepal	0.016444
Lebanon	0.071732	Yemen, Rep.	0.016254
Moldova	0.070970	Gabon	0.015925
Eritrea	0.067904	Mauritius	0.015537
Singapore	0.066594	Macedonia, FYR	0.015195
Bosnia/Herzegovina	0.065915	Papua New Guinea	0.014066
Puerto Rico	0.064970	Jamaica	0.013903
New Zealand	0.063492	French Polynesia	0.013827
Costa Rica	0.063163	Honduras	0.013495
Armenia	0.063031	Guinea	0.013232
Ireland	0.062882	Kyrgyz Republic	0.012866
Central African Rep.	0.061605	Namibia	0.012510
Lithuania	0.061241	Bahamas, The	0.012481
Albania	0.056534	Azerbaijan	0.012041
Uruguay	0.055307	West Bank/Gaza	0.011977
Liberia	0.051876	Malta	0.011791
Congo, Rep.	0.050020	Zambia	0.011708
West Bank/Gaza	0.049158	Madagascar	0.011284
United Arab Emirates	0.048149	Armenia	0.010976
Panama	0.047335	New Caledonia	0.010965
Mauritania	0.044170	Cambodia	0.010542
Jamaica	0.043639	Mozambique	0.009997
Mongolia	0.039744	Channel Islands	0.009772
Oman	0.039695	Liberia	0.009581
Latvia	0.039313	Mali	0.009224
Lesotho	0.033728	Albania	0.009073
Macedonia, FYR	0.033662	Haiti	0.008643
Slovenia	0.032949	Burkina Faso	0.008404
Kuwait	0.032889	Moldova	0.008049

Table 2.A.2 continued—

Population Basis		Material Basis	
Nation	% of Total	Nation	% of Total
Namibia	0.029120	Benin	0.007682
Botswana	0.026551	Congo, Rep.	0.007510
Estonia	0.022690	Georgia	0.007407
Gambia, The	0.021596	Tajikistan	0.007042
Trinidad/Tobago	0.021563	Lao PDR	0.007028
Gabon	0.020386	Nicaragua	0.006983
Guinea-Bissau	0.019872	Barbados	0.006540
Mauritius	0.019659	Niger	0.006497
Swaziland	0.017320	Rwanda	0.006083
Fiji	0.013456	Fiji	0.005750
Bhutan	0.013342	Malawi	0.005142
Guyana	0.012613	Chad	0.004957
Cyprus	0.012546	Greenland	0.004918
Bahrain	0.011453	Isle of Man	0.004779
Djibouti	0.010475	Swaziland	0.004563
Qatar	0.009694	Togo	0.004373
Comoros	0.009248	Mauritania	0.003907
Equatorial Guinea	0.007574	Central African Rep.	0.003722
Solomon Islands	0.007409	Andorra	0.003592
Cape Verde	0.007309	Guam	0.003554
Luxembourg	0.007266	Lesotho	0.003319
Macao, China	0.007259	Mongolia	0.003037
Suriname	0.006911	Burundi	0.002832
Malta	0.006464	Virgin Islands (U.S.)	0.002784
Brunei	0.005602	Liechtenstein	0.002733
Bahamas, The	0.005022	Aruba	0.002324
Iceland	0.004657	Belize	0.002229
Maldives	0.004574	Sierra Leone	0.002193
Barbados	0.004425	Equatorial Guinea	0.002161
Belize	0.003978	Guyana	0.002118
French Polynesia	0.003895	Cape Verde	0.001981
Netherlands Antilles	0.003563	Monaco	0.001961
New Caledonia	0.003525	San Marino	0.001915
Vanuatu	0.003265	Eritrea	0.001879
Samoa	0.002818	Netherlands Antilles	0.001839
St. Lucia	0.002586	Antigua/Barbuda	0.001838
Guam	0.002561	St. Lucia	0.001831
Channel Islands	0.002470	Seychelles	0.001682
Sao Tome/Principe	0.002453	Maldives	0.001578
Mayotte	0.002403	American Samoa	0.001505
Virgin Islands (U.S.)	0.002005	Djibouti	0.001464
Micronesia, Fed. Sts.	0.001957	Bermuda	0.001449
St. Vincent-Grenadines	0.001906	Gambia, The	0.001428
Aruba	0.001674	Bhutan	0.001267
Tonga	0.001661	Suriname	0.001225

Table 2.A.2 concluded—

Population Basis		Material Basis	
Nation	% of Total	Nation	% of Total
Grenada	0.001624	Grenada	0.001111
Kiribati	0.001503	Faeroe Islands	0.001035
Seychelles	0.001346	St. Vincent-Grenadines	0.000942
Isle of Man	0.001243	Solomon Islands	0.000850
Dominica	0.001210	St. Kitts and Nevis	0.000828
Northern Mariana Is.	0.001193	Cayman Islands	0.000805
Antigua/Barbuda	0.001127	Guinea-Bissau	0.000744
Andorra	0.001110	Dominica	0.000728
American Samoa	0.001085	Samoa	0.000724
Bermuda	0.001044	Comoros	0.000719
Greenland	0.000931	Vanuatu	0.000685
Marshall Islands	0.000862	Northern Mariana Is.	0.000616
Faeroe Islands	0.000746	Micronesia, Fed. Sts.	0.000606
St. Kitts and Nevis	0.000680	Mayotte	0.000527
Cayman Islands	0.000580	Tonga	0.000524
Liechtenstein	0.000530	Palau	0.000378
Monaco	0.000530	Marshall Islands	0.000246
San Marino	0.000447	Kiribati	0.000150
Palau	0.000315	Sao Tome/Principe	0.000149

3

SOME HISTORICAL BACKGROUND
ON WORLD GOVERNMENT

Even highly critical and dismissive discussions of world government are likely to concede that there is a deep-seated longing in human psychology for a universal political organization that would forever safeguard all of its citizens from the vicissitudes of foreign conquest. If all of humanity were politically united, then there would be no foreign lands in which invading armies could be mustered and sent forth to kill, rape, loot and pillage. Only in a world union could there be a reliable guarantee of world peace. Such a notion, say the critics of world government, is quite natural and perfectly understandable. At the same time, they say, this notion is unrealizable and quite possibly dangerous. Desire for world government is like a desire for the ability to fly like a bird. No doubt there have been many cases of mentally unbalanced people who, in their hopeless aspiration toward personal flight, have jumped to their deaths off cliffs or the rooftops of buildings. Mentally stable people recognize that, despite their aspiration to the contrary, they are physically unable to fly like birds, and hence they instantly suppress any temptations to jump off cliffs or the rooftops of buildings. Similarly, humanity as a whole should suppress any temptations it might experience to establish a world government, lest all of us be plunged—if not to our deaths—at least down into a form of totalitarian tyranny so horrific that we would be better off dead.

This book presents a plan for a specific form of world government, the Federal Union of Democratic Nations, that would indeed realize in a very complete and tangible manner the longstanding human aspiration toward a universal political state. At least the *long-run* objective would be universality, although in the short run, owing to the necessarily tolerant policy with respect to membership needed to make the foundation of the Federal Union possible, there might well be a significant number of non-member nations in the world. But there is a good chance that, owing to the tolerant membership policy as well as other key characteristics of the proposal, the founding nations of the world union, as a group, would be so large and powerful as to virtually preclude the possibility of future aggression by non-member nations against member nations. This would mark a close approach to realizing the ancient desire within individual human beings to be completely free of fears and apprehensions about foreign depredation, conquest and despoliation. At the same time, owing to certain key limitations and restrictions on its authority, it is very unlikely that the Federal Union of Democratic Nations would degenerate into the sort of oppressive totalitarian regime typically imagined by critics of world government.

This chapter will endeavor to provide the reader with some background information on the development of the world government concept in the history of ideas. My purpose in reviewing this development is, only to a minor extent, to try to gain a certain amount of sympathy and support for the notion by showing that it has a long history in human thinking. Although the very antiquity of the concept provides a certain amount of support for its validity and legitimacy, it need not be belabored that it is also true that a great many historically ancient ideas are in fact empirically false and seriously pernicious (e.g., the idea that some races are superior or inferior to others). I hope to persuade the reader, however, that the idea of world government does *not* fall into the category of false and pernicious. My principal purpose in presenting some background on world government, therefore, is simply to elucidate and clarify the critical differences between the concept and plan of world government being put forward in this book (embodied in the proposal for a Federal Union of Democratic Nations), and both the concept of world government associated with the imperial form, and the plan of world government associated with all or most prior world government proposals. A review of the development of the world government idea in human thinking will, it is hoped, instill a better understanding and a firmer grasp on the central innovative aspects of the present proposal.

EMPIRES IN HISTORY

To a significant extent, the difficulties experienced by the typical person today in properly understanding and evaluating world government stem from the conscious or unconscious identification of a world government with an all-powerful, all-encompassing, universal world empire. Such an identification is fully understandable in view of the paramount role of the imperial political form in the history of human civilization. But it is a false and misleading identification that unfairly diminishes and prejudices the case to be made for world government. It would be literally impossible today to construct a world government by the same means that were utilized to construct the great empires of history. Moreover, if by some magical means a world government were to come into existence in the contemporary world that endeavored to implement the principles of political organization applied by the great empires of history, it would instantly dissolve into bloody chaos.

The standard dictionary definition of an "empire" specifies a single political unit, under strong centralized authority, having an extensive territory and comprising a large number of subsidiary districts and diverse populations. Not ordinarily included in the basic definition are two additional salient characteristics: (1)

an empire is almost always founded upon military conquest rather than contract, and (2) an empire relies principally, following the era of conquest, upon military force and threat of military force rather than the consent of the governed to maintain its stability and control over the incorporated peoples and regions. A world government would share with the basic definition of empire that it would be "a single political unit, under strong centralized authority, having an extensive territory and comprising a large number of subsidiary districts and diverse populations"—with the possible exception of "strong" (in the short run) as a descriptor of "centralized authority." But an effort to construct an empire by the classical method of military conquest in the contemporary nuclear-armed world would almost certainly result in nuclear holocaust. And even if, for the sake of argument, we imagined a global empire in the contemporary world based on force and the threat of force, rather than upon the voluntary consent of the governed, it would be extremely unstable. In all probability, the world emperor would quickly be assassinated, and the world empire would thereupon immediately crumble into pieces.

Although virtually unimaginable in the contemporary world, empires and their reigning emperors figure prominently in the history of human civilization. A few examples include the Persian empire in Southwest Asia founded by Cyrus II after 546 BC and developed by Darius I and Xerxes; the short-lived Greek empire constructed from the conquests of Alexander the Great (356-323 BC); the famous Roman Empire that incorporated much of what is today Western Europe and extended far into the Middle East and North Africa, and that persisted, if counted from the pre-imperial republic (founded in 510 BC) to the final collapse of the Byzantine empire in 1453, for almost two millennia; the great Muslim empire from Spain to India, constructed from various holy wars following the death of Mohammed in 632; the Mongolian empire created by Genghis Khan (d. 1227) that at its height stretched from Eastern Europe to the East coast of Asia; as well as numerous great Far Eastern empires in China, India, and elsewhere. The "age of exploration" in early modern history witnessed the foundation and development of the great colonial empires of the Western European nations: those of Spain, Portugal, France, Britain, and the Netherlands. These empires brought under the political and economic control of the "metropolitan" nations vast territories in the Americas, Africa and Asia. At its height in the late 19th and early 20th centuries, the British colonial empire encompassed territories on all the inhabitable continents, comprising about one quarter of the world's land area and population. The imperial colonial territories were separated from their respective metropolitan owners by the oceans of the world; therefore—in contrast to the empires of ancient and medieval times—sea power was just as important to their control as land power.

Very little of the many notorious empires of human history remains discernible today. Their component regions and territories have mostly if not entirely devolved into the independent nation-states we know today. The American Revolutionary War (1775-1783) took what is today the United States out of the

British colonial empire, and the various Latin American wars of independence of the early 19th century ended the colonial dominion of Spain and Portugal in the Americas. The end of World War I saw the demise of the remnants of two ancient land empires which had survived into modern times: the Ottoman Empire and the Austro-Hungarian Empire. The two decades following the end of World War II saw the complete disintegration of the last remnants of the great Western European colonial empires. Clearly, the Age of Empire in human civilization is now finished. But there remains a compelling fascination in the saga of any great historical empire, even more in its fall than in its rise. One of the great works of world literature is Edward Gibbon's magisterial, multi-volume *The Decline and Fall of the Roman Empire*. Poets, moralists and historians alike agree that great imperial dominions, no less than the men who build them, are fated ultimately to crumble into dust. No doubt there is a valuable lesson in humility to be derived from the fate of empires. But does the fate of empires suggest that a world government, established at the present moment in the history of human civilization, would be nothing more than an exercise in futility—in that it also would inevitably be doomed to decline, fall, and eventual extinction?

The short answer to this question is "No," since the conditions which led to the decline and fall of historical empires need not, and probably would not, apply to a world government established at the present moment in human history. But before proceeding onward to justify this answer, it might be beneficial to pause briefly to make two especially important points regarding the role of empires in human civilization. The first point is that while the great empires of the past may have ultimately dissolved and disappeared, many of them lasted for prodigious periods of time, relative to the time frame of modern history. A conventional starting point for modern history is circa 1500, because of that year's proximity to two epochal events: the discovery of the American continent, and the start of the Protestant Reformation. By this reckoning, some 500 years separate the beginning of modern history from the present time. Many of the great empires persisted over far longer periods than 500 years. A world government, established at the present time and then persisting over a time span of 500 years, would be a very notable accomplishment.

The second point is that while the empires of history exhibited many serious shortcomings and liabilities by modern standards, they were nevertheless on the whole beneficial both to their citizens and to the cause of human civilization in general. In the circuses of Rome, for example, there took place gladiatorial contests and grotesque executions of early Christians which would be disgusting and horrible to modern eyes. How could those people, we ask ourselves, have been so insensitive, callous and brutal? The sobering fact is that the Romans were highly refined and civilized by the prevailing standards of their time. Of course, we do not have to go back into ancient history to find many shocking examples of mankind's capacity for cruelty and brutality. There is clearly a dark side to human nature which it is imperative to keep under a reasonable amount of control. The need for continued control, in fact, is a major part of the case to be made for world government. If individual human beings could always be relied upon to behave like gentle and benevolent saints, then there would be no need for world government—or for any other kind of government. But to return to the point, we must remember that the same civilization that mounted, for purposes of general entertainment, gladiatorial contests and public executions of Christians, also generated monumental achievements in art, science, literature, architecture, engineering and law. There can be little doubt that over the several centuries during which the Roman empire was at its height, the life of the typical individual living in a Roman town, even a remote provincial town, was longer, richer, better, fuller and indeed more civilized, than was the life of a comparable individual living in a barbarian village. There are few historians familiar with the civilization and culture of imperial Rome, in the perspective of the other civilizations and cultures of the time, who would sneer at the Roman accomplishment—despite such unfortunate lapses as gladiatorial contests and public executions.

Let us now consider the more important issue of the reasons why historical empires declined, and the related question of whether these reasons would necessarily apply to a potential future world government. In examining possible reasons for the decline of empires, there are really two separate questions involved: (1) why individual empires of the pre-modern past declined, and (2) why empires, as a whole, have declined in the modern era. Looking at question (1), what immediately comes to our attention, in examining the historical record, is military aggression against the empire from outside its boundaries, and military rebellion against the empire from inside its boundaries. Historical empires were created by the sword, and they were also destroyed by the sword. In their era of decline, chunks of the imperial territories would be torn off by invading armies from outside the empire. Also—and often simultaneously—chunks of the imperial territories would remove themselves from the imperial domain with the assistance of rebellious local armies.

Of course, it is not particularly enlightening to observe that the decline and fall of any given historical empire is attended by the defeat of its armed forces by enemies from outside and/or inside the empire. The deeper question concerns why the defeat occurred. The empire would not have arisen in the first place if it had not been able, at one point in its existence, to successfully counter both external and internal challenges to its authority. Why, at some point in its history, was the empire no longer able to fend off these challenges? We can speculate on human factors, and on non-human factors. With respect to non-human factors, our attention is called to exhaustion of natural resources, depletion of the fertility of the soil, possible overwhelming physical catastrophes such as the eruption of volcanoes and devastating storms, climatic changes leading to famine, or epidemics of disease. With respect to human factors, our attention is called to various character flaws and consequent judgmental errors among the imperial leadership: most commonly that personal hubris that results in over-expansion of the empire's boundaries and/or the mistreatment of its subjects. The relative importance of non-human versus human factors is an inherently intriguing, but probably unanswerable question, at least as far as the long-lasting empires are concerned.

Although a certain amount of speculation is to be found, in political literature written during the most successful and enthusiastic periods of imperial expansion, about extending the borders of the empire to encompass the "entire world," or in more modest cases, the "entire known world," no empire in human history has even remotely approached this goal. No empire has possessed either the human and material resources, or the military and communications technology, to accomplish this. Even the greatest of the ancient empires encompassed only a small proportion of the earth's total land area and population. They all had powerful, hostile civilizations, many of them also of the imperial form, lurking just beyond their borders. In the event that any one empire experienced serious internal difficulties and disruptions, its external enemies were always ready to pounce. Some of the less appealing characteristics of historical empires—the very attenuated democratic accountability of the political leadership, the glorification of military virtues, the brutalization of the entire population from the highest patricians to the lowest plebeians—these are plausibly attributed largely to the fact that these empires were in effect huge armed camps, in which both the citizens and their leaders lived in perpetual fear and apprehension of death, dishonor and despoliation at the hands of foreign invaders.

In this we perceive an important difference between the empires of past history and a potential world federation of the future. Even if the membership of the world federation envisioned herein is not universal, in all likelihood a sufficiently large number of the major world powers would join the federation at its inception that the possibility of invasion of a Federal Union member nation by a non-member nation would be minimal. It has been emphasized in the foregoing chapter that the formation of a world government under the presently prevailing international situation would not lead instantly, nor even very quickly, to sweeping nuclear and non-nuclear disarmament. However, the formation of a world government would very quickly and significantly reduce the probability that heavy armaments, including nuclear weapons, will be utilized by nations within the foreseeable future in warfare among one another. A world federation, in short, would not have to put up with the same everlasting, acute threat of foreign invasion that was such a major factor in the institutions, policies and behavior of the historical empires. Therefore, it would almost certainly be a far more benign and benevolent political organization than were any of the historical empires.

Historical empires were not only continuously subject to the threat of foreign invasion but also continuously subject to the threat of domestic rebellion. An important connotation of the term "empire" in the common understanding is that of continuous oppression and exploitation of vassal states and subject peoples. Thus, in George Lucas' renowned series of "Star Wars" movies, the principal villains (Darth Vadar and company) are in the service of "the Empire." Shortly after the release of the first Star Wars movie in 1977, and probably not coincidentally, President Ronald Reagan, in a hawkish mood toward the Soviet

Union, described that nation as "an Evil Empire." In contemplating the concept of "empire," therefore, an image comes readily to mind of a Simon Legree type character (the sadistic overseer in Harriet Beecher Stowe's famous 1851 antislavery novel *Uncle Tom's Cabin*), armed with a bullwhip, wandering around in a crowded marketplace lashing out randomly at helpless, unresisting, innocent women and children. Of course, Stowe's powerful depiction of cruelty and injustice was based on the evil realities of slavery in the pre-Civil War American South—which transpired not within an empire but within a nation that deemed itself at the time a democratic republic supposedly based on such noble principles as "all men are created equal." Clearly, many if not most of the worst instances in human history of harsh oppression based squarely and unapologetically on brute force had to do with the institution of slavery, an institution that was neither invented nor especially favored under imperial governments.

The great empires of the past were founded upon military conquest—of that there is no question. It is also true that in the first flush of victory, conquering imperial armies normally committed terrible atrocities, both to revenge earlier outrages committed against imperial citizens by armies emanating from the now-conquered territories, and also to cow the defeated populations into unresisting submission in the future to the imperial authority. But once the conquest had been completed, the role of force and violence in the ongoing daily maintenance of peace and order was probably very much the same as it had been prior to the conquest. Very likely the independent local government dislodged by the conquest had been just as oppressive and tyrannical as the new imperial government. Certainly in the case of the long-lasting empires, archetypical of which was the Roman empire, a very serious effort was made by the majority of the emperors to maintain the loyalty of the imperial subjects by means of wise and benevolent governance, as opposed to maintaining their resentful and involuntary submission based on fear and terror. The Roman empire could never have been as successful as it was if most of its officials had shared the same dysfunctional personality characteristics exhibited by Simon Legree.

On the other hand, judging from the regularity of armed insurrections against imperial authority within empires, efforts at wise and benevolent governance were frequently insufficient to maintain compliance. Imperial governments, of their nature, inevitably suffered from some major disadvantages relative to the local governments they supplanted. To begin with, there was a constant tension between the desirability of providing wise and benevolent governance over subject peoples in distant territories, and at the same time the necessity of maintaining a privileged status for those peoples closer to the imperial seat of power, especially those in the capital city itself. Of course, the most successful empires were those that were generous in awarding the privileges of citizenship to conquered peoples, that endeavored to assimilate and co-opt these peoples, that were relatively modest in the imposition of taxes and tributes, and that were extremely tolerant in matters of religion and culture. But at the same time, there was a permanent and unavoidable conflict between these commendably tolerant tendencies and the arrogant pride and egotistical self-esteem naturally inspired by the military conquest of other human beings.

In addition to the attitude problem, there was the possibly even more important communications problem. Assuming roughly equivalent attitudes among the political leadership, a local government would obviously have a more accurate and complete understanding of local conditions than a remote imperial government, and it would therefore be in a better position to implement specific legislation and policies most favorable to public welfare under local conditions. Finally, there was the fact that despite their best efforts to "blend in" with the local population, many officials of the imperial government would look, dress or sound different from those they governed. It is a natural human instinct to be suspicious of and hostile toward those who are different from one's accustomed colleagues and companions. And there is also a natural human instinct to resent authority. Aspirants to unconstrained local government power were often able to put this natural "us versus them" attitude among human beings to good use in raising rebellions against the imperial authority. A home-grown tyrant, they argued, is better than a foreign tyrant.

Opponents of world government today argue that such a government would almost certainly subject the national populations to a remote and oppressive authority in no way more wise and benevolent than the remote and oppressive imperial governments of the past—governments that were continuously inspiring armed insurrections because of their ignorant and malevolent governance. This argument fails to appreciate the salient and significant differences between the circumstances that surrounded the empires of history, and the circumstances that would surround the establishment of a world government today. Perhaps the most key and critical differences pertain to: (1) the greatly improved communications capabilities of the present time, relative to all past eras in human history, and (2) the tremendous advance of the democratic principle in the modern world, relative to all previous historical times. The imperial governments of past history had very sketchy and imprecise information on both material and psychological conditions in their remote territories. Thanks to modern data collection methods and communications technology, a world government in the modern era would have an immense informational advantage over any past imperial government. Policy determination would incorporate extensive and accurate information concerning local conditions and local opinions, and this would substantially reduce the possibility that local discontent and disaffection would become so prevalent as to cause the secession of nations from the world federation.

Possibly even more important than improved knowledge would be that the world government would be far more democratically accountable to its constituents than any imperial government of the past. Democracy, of course, is not a modern invention. The ancient Greeks of Athens are generally credited with devising and implementing a recognizably modern form of democracy. But there was considerable use of the concept long before—and after—the Athenian heyday. Even in political organizations that, according to modern standards, would be deemed highly undemocratic, the democratic principle continued to play some role. For example, during the height of the Roman empire, if there was a break in the hereditary imperial succession, the new emperor was to be elected by the Senate, the same legislative assembly that had been dominant during the earlier Roman republic. On the other hand, there is obviously a huge gap between the contemporary concept of democracy, and democracy as it was intermittently practiced in the pre-modern and early modern historical eras. There are at least three central criteria of genuine democracy as currently perceived: (1) high government officials are subject to election; (2) elections are authentically competitive; (3) the electorate comprises a very substantial proportion of the entire population. It is in terms of the third criterion of democracy—the extent of the franchise—that disqualifies political organizations in pre-modern and early modern times from being considered genuine democracies. For example, even though the Athenian democracy and early Roman republic supposedly empowered "all adult citizens" with the right to vote, all women and slaves were excluded, as well as many others resident in the area who would be deemed "citizens" by modern standards.

A distinction was drawn in the foregoing between two separate questions: (1) why individual empires of the pre-modern past declined, and (2) why empires, as a whole, have declined. The answer to the first question involves various weaknesses specific to the declining empire. In the case of the Roman empire, for example, declining fertility of the soil in Italy is often mentioned. But there were no fundamental developments in human thinking, during the centuries in which the Roman empire was declining, that implied less faith and confidence in the imperial principle itself. To a large extent, what was once the Roman empire was absorbed into newer, rising empires. For example, the North African territories of the old Roman empire were absorbed into the Islamic empire that arose in the centuries following the death of Mohammed. If we look, however, at human civilization as it has developed in the recent modern era, say from 1750 to the present, this era has seen two fundamental developments: (1) the final decline and fall of empires in general; and (2) the rise of the contemporary concept of democracy. Quite likely, these developments are closely interrelated.

During the nineteenth century, as the modern democratic principle advanced in the United States, Canada, several Western European nations, Australia and New Zealand in the South Pacific, and at a few other isolated locations around the world, people living in subsidiary regions of the remaining empires, especially the great Western European colonial empires, began to find a new and powerful focus for their previously generalized resentment against remote and oppressive governance. This focus was their lack of any sort of democratic control over those who governed them. A possible solution would have been to admit the peoples of the colonial territories into the electorates of the metropolitan nations. But this was impractical for two reasons. First, the slow communications between distant territories and the imperial capital would have drastically deteriorated the responsiveness and effectiveness of governance. Secondly, and still more important, it would have been inconceivable to the electorates of the metropolitan powers to share their control over domestic national governance with the "backward and uncivilized" native peoples of the colonial territories. But these "backward and uncivilized" peoples, more and more, wanted to have direct electoral control over those who governed them. Since the metropolitan electorate was unwilling to allow this, there remained only one sensible solution: that the remote colonial territories should become independent nations.

As is frequently the case in human affairs, this "sensible solution" required a considerable period of time and highly disruptive events before it was finally implemented. The last remnants of the great land empires of the past still existing at the beginning of the twentieth century were the Austro-Hungarian empire, headquartered in Austria, and the Ottoman empire, headquartered in Turkey. Austria and Turkey were among the defeated nations in World War I, and the Treaty of Versailles completed in 1919 stripped them of their imperial territories, from which several independent nations were created: Czechoslovakia, Romania, Yugoslavia and so on from the Austro-Hungarian empire, and Syria, Iran, Iraq and so on from the Ottoman empire. The great Western European colonial empires, foremost among which was the British empire, persisted until after World War II. Most of the component territories of these empires were granted national independence peacefully and relatively amicably, although there was one major exception: the Indochinese war between French army and the national liberation forces in Vietnam.

Centuries in the making, these colonial empires were dissolved within two decades of the end of World War II. Several factors may be cited to explain this remarkable transition. To begin with, the Western European nations had been greatly weakened, both militarily and economically, by the vicissitudes of two great wars within the three decades separating 1914 from 1945. In addition, these wars made fully apparent the dangerous envy aroused in those nations *not* in possession of great colonial empires. World War II was a natural progression from World War I, and if one factor may be cited as the single most important cause of World War I, it would be the determination of Germany to acquire a colonial empire comparable to those of its perceived national rivals, Britain and France. But if Britain and France had no colonial empires, Germany would no longer have cause to be envious and resentful on this score.

Another important factor may have been the emergence of the international communist menace. As the Cold War geared up in the years following World War II, the Soviet Union, followed shortly by the People's Republic of China, was making a concerted effort to win over the huge population of the Third World to its side of the ideological struggle between communism and capitalism. The theory of economic imperialism was developed by several socialist theoreticians in the late nineteenth and early twentieth centuries. In its post-World War II reincarnation in the hands of communist propagandists, this theory was "sharpened up" in the sense that primary emphasis was put on the proposition that economic relations between rich nations and poor nations adversely affected the economic welfare of the great majority of the populations of the latter nations. Clearly, this proposition would be far more plausible if the poor nations were being directly governed, as colonial territories, by the rich nations. But if the poor nations were sovereign and independent nations, with full and equal input into determining the institutions and conditions of trade and investment between themselves and the rich nations, then the proposition of harsh economic exploitation of the populations of the poor nations would be far less plausible. Therefore, granting of independence to the former colonial territories strengthened the Western hand in the war of ideas with the communist East.

Last but not least, we might consider the ever-increasing desire among virtually the entire world population, throughout the nineteenth and twentieth centuries, for democratic forms of governance. There is obviously a tremendous appeal in the notion that each and every citizen in good standing within a certain polity should possess that degree of personal control over his/her political leadership which is incorporated in the right to vote in free and contested elections for high office. Of course, the native populations of the colonial territories of the great Western European empires were not allowed to freely elect voting representatives to the legislatures of the metropolitan nations. As mentioned previously, this was precluded not only by communication lags but also by the fact that the populations of the Western European nations were fully unprepared to allow what would have effectively amounted to political unifications of the colonial territories with the metropolitan nations. But at the same time, the native colonial populations, owing to the ever-rising democratic spirit throughout the world, were increasingly unwilling to submit peacefully to a government over which they had no meaningful electoral control.

Accordingly, national liberation movements flourished in all of the colonial territories, and the metropolitan nations recognized that in order to maintain their empires, continuous violent suppression of these movements would be necessary. The expected costs of empire were soon perceived to be well in excess of the expected benefits. And thus, for the most part, the colonial territories were released peacefully from the imperial authority. One of the many ironies of history, oft commented upon, is that for many of the newly independent nations, authentically democratic political institutions—the urgent desire for which inspired and drove the independence movements—have not in fact been achieved. Nor has a high level of economic prosperity been achieved in most of these nations. But to some extent they are masters of their own fate, and none of the ex-colonial nations seems interested in returning to the imperial fold under the old terms. After all, better home-grown mismanagement and oppression than foreign mismanagement and oppression.

Mention has been made in the foregoing of the unwillingness of the populations of the metropolitan Western European nations, toward the end of the imperial era, to undertake political unification with their own colonies. One reason for this unwillingness was apprehension over the possibility that the relatively poor populations of the colonial territories would endeavor to improve their own living standards by establishing welfare systems the support of which would require heavy taxation of the more affluent metropolitan populations. This potential problem, of course, would also apply to a world federation composed of rich nations and poor nations. The proposed solution to this problem consists of the dual voting system in the world government legislature (the Union Chamber of Representatives), plus the reserved national rights of secession and armament. The dual voting system would allow the less populous richer nations to veto (in the material vote) any proposed legislation which they find unacceptable (as a primary example, because it would implement a global welfare state). At the same time, this system would allow the more populous poor nations to veto (in the population vote) any proposed legislation which they would find unacceptable (as a primary example, because it might tend to re-establish conditions of colonial economic exploitation). If despite the dual voting system, the world government legislature passes legislation regarded as unacceptable to any member nation, that nation would possess the formal, constitutionally guaranteed right to withdraw from the world federation. This right, moreover, would be supported by the parallel national right to maintain whatever military force and armaments (including nuclear weapons) the member nation deems necessary for purposes of national security.

The potential world government of the future would be qualitatively distinct from any imperial government in the past history of human civilization. Not even the most tolerant and liberal of these imperial governments would have allowed component regions to maintain military forces, or to depart unopposed from the imperial dominion. No imperial government of the past was democratically accountable, via free, open and contested elections, to any substantial proportion of its population. Rejecting the world government possibility on grounds that such a government would inevitably assume the characteristics of imperial governments of the past, would therefore be quite unreasonable. There is indeed a serious case to be made against world government—but that case does not rest on the imperial analogy.

CONTRACT-BASED UNIVERSAL GOVERNMENT

In his book *World Citizenship and Government: Cosmopolitan Ideas in the History of Western Political Thought* (1996), Derek Heater traces the roots of the world government concept back to the ancient Greeks. But note that we are referring here to the *roots*. Professor Heater is quite clear and explicit that the contemporary concept of a world government did not begin to develop until the modern era, commencing approximately around 1500. In ancient and medieval times, the philosophical notion of the "oneness of man," the political implications of which were ambiguous at best, coexisted with the notion of a universal empire, initially established by conquest, but thereafter governed with such wisdom and benevolence as to command the voluntary support and allegiance of its citizens. As for the ancient Greeks, much of their political history is the story of jealously sovereign and independent city-states, some of them democratically governed and some less so, often at war with one another. In the *Nicomachean Ethics*, Aristotle ventured the opinion that the optimal population of a single political organization could not exceed 100,000, lest there be inadequate social cohesion and political stability. On the other hand, a large number of small political units, each one of which might be desirable in terms of minimal internal strife, multiplies the opportunities for external strife, as dramatically witnessed in the Peloponnesian wars that devastated the Greek peninsula starting in 432 BC. Historical events of this sort may have prompted Aristotle's isolated remark, in the *Politics*, that the Greek people possess the intelligence that would enable them "to attain the highest political development, and to show a capacity for governing every other people—if only they could once achieve political unity." This statement suggests the optimal political organization, all things considered (external security as well as internal tranquillity), might well comprise more than 100,000 inhabitants, but the statement hardly prefigures a universal state based on contract. Rather it suggests the Greeks conquering and then ruling the world for their own security and benefit—albeit in a wise and tolerant manner that would command the peaceful consent of the various non-Greek populations.

The Greek city-states were eventually united in the kingdom created by the conquests of Philip II of Macedonia, whose son, Alexander the Great (356-323 BC), went on to establish by conquest a huge (by the standards of the time) but extremely ephemeral empire. Professor Heater describes the controversy among modern historians concerning how much, or how little, overlap exists between the ambitious dreams of Alexander the Great in his ascendancy, and the modern concept of a world state. One piece of relevant evidence consists of a lengthy epistle on prudent imperial policy, possibly written by Aristotle to his former pupil Alexander, that contains the following passage:

> I know that if mankind in general is destined to true felicity within the duration of this world, there will come about that concord and order which I shall describe. Happy is he who sees the resplendence of that day when men will agree to constitute one rule and one kingdom. They will cease from wars and strife, and will devote themselves to that which promotes their welfare and the welfare of their cities and countries.

The epistle survives only in Arabic translations dating from the medieval period, and its authenticity as an actual work of Aristotle is subject to considerable doubt. Despite doubt as to its origin, the passage eloquently expresses a vision which clearly *might* have inspired Alexander as he pursued his route of conquest across much of the known world of his day.

As a proponent of world government, I myself would very much prefer that the modern concept of a world state possessed an ancient lineage, and was entertained by various renowned historical personages such as Alexander the Great, especially since he was not, as conquerors go, exceptionally brutal and bloodthirsty in his conquests. However, unless "concept" is defined extremely loosely, this is most probably not the case. The putative epistle of Aristotle quoted above uses the critical phrasing: "men *will agree* to constitute one rule and one kingdom." But will this "agreeing" take place before or after most of them have been conquered by some dominant subgroup of the human population (the Greeks, the Romans, or whoever)? A contract is an agreement freely and voluntarily entered, without coercion or the threat of coercion. In our own day, the great majority believes that the nations of today will never freely agree (i.e., voluntarily contract) to establish a world government with significant authority over them. Most probably, the majority who believed that the independent political entities in Alexander's time (city-states, principalities, kingdoms, and empires) would never freely agree to establish a universal government encompassing them all, was even more overwhelming. But at the same time, it is not a serious argument against a world state based on contract that this basic concept has crystallized in the relatively recent historical past. There are many things which have become realities in the modern world (e.g., mass democracy, air travel, television, computers) which would have been deemed, by any educated person in earlier times, pure fantasy.

An important document in the post-World War II world government boom was a 532-page compilation by Edith Wynner and Georgia Lloyd titled *Searchlight on Peace Plans: Choose Your Road to World Government* (1944). Wynner and Lloyd undertook to enumerate and briefly describe a large proportion of existing "chartable" theoretical plans for supranational political entities. By "chartable" is meant that the plan provides specific, concrete details in all or most of the following categories: type (alliance, league, etc.); membership (universal, regional, etc.); organs of government (legislative, executive, and judicial); transfers of jurisdiction (supranational versus national rights and responsibilities); methods of enforcement (individuals versus nations); immediate steps (scenarios toward foundation); territorial changes (revisions in boundaries); ratification (process of formal approval). In actual fact, however, the process of charting each plan was only applied to world government proposals since 1914. In Part II of *Searchlight*, which catalogues theoretical plans to unite nations dating up to 1914, Wynner and Lloyd provide only "brief descriptions," as opposed to charts, of the plans. Part II catalogues some 74 plans, from the 1306 proposal of Pierre Dubois to the 1905 proposal of Richard Bartholdt. Apparently Wynner and Lloyd could not find anything earlier than 1306 that constituted a reasonable facsimile to the modern concept of a world state.

Moreover, if one reads through their list of brief descriptions, it becomes apparent that the earlier proposals, starting with that of Dubois, encompassed only the Christian nations of Western Europe, and were largely motivated by a warlike, crusading spirit: a tight political union of the Christian nations would enable a more effective military resistance to and subsequent conquest of the infidel territories, especially those of the Islamic Turks. However, several of the plans provided considerable detail on the mechanisms of political unification among the Western European nations, and these mechanisms, at least in principle, could be extended to encompass other regions of the world.

The first plan listed by Wynner and Lloyd that explicitly incorporates the entire world is attributed to the French monk Emeric Crucé, author of *The New Cyneas*, published in 1623. Wynner and Lloyd describe the proposal as follows:

> Suggested a permanent Council of Ambassadors, meeting in a neutral city to settle all differences between Princes by majority vote of the whole Council. Those refusing to accept the decisions of the Council to be disgraced. Member Princes to defend the Council against resistance by force of arms. Membership to be universal including the Pope, the Emperor of the Turks, the Jews, the Kings of Persia and China, the Grand Duke of Muscovy, and monarchs from India and Africa. A universal police, "useful equally to all nations and acceptable to those which have some light of reason and sentiment of humanity." The Council to exercise legislative power in order "to meet discontents half-way...and appease them by gentle means, if it could be done, or in case of necessity by force." Crucé urged religious toleration, encouragement of scientific discoveries, and of commerce by safeguarding communication and transportation against pirates. Suggested Venice as the place of meeting.

Except for the fact that the term "ambassadors" is used rather than the more appropriate "representatives" (given that the Council is to exercise "legislative power"), this is a recognizably modern proposal, particularly in the fact that all known territories of the world are included. It is perhaps symptomatic that Crucé's work was "ahead of its time" (as the phrase goes) from the fact that it was very little noticed, following its publication, prior to being "rediscovered" in the twentieth century. At least two other factors may also be relevant: (1) unlike several better known proponents of schemes for supranational political unity, at the time he published *The New Cyneas*, Crucé was not a well-known politician, statesman or intellectual; (2) the notion of extension of political unity beyond European borders may have seemed totally preposterous in the seventeenth century, owing to transport and communications problems, if nothing else.

On the transport and communications issue, however, Crucé may have been operating on the basis of a more clear-sighted appreciation of the true nature of the situation than his contemporaries. By the early 1600s, Africa had been circumnavigated, the world had been circumnavigated, trade with the Far East was well established, the Spanish and Portuguese empires in Latin America were well established, and the British, French and Dutch colonization of North America was gearing up. There may have been large "unknown" areas on maps of North America and Africa, but at least the general location of these areas was known. It may have required a sea voyage of several months to travel from Europe to anywhere else in the world, and this is certainly an appreciable period of time— but it is not the same as several years or several decades. As of the early 1600s, the process of global integration—a process that is continuing apace even today—was well underway. Crucé was exceptional in having a very early vision of the potential global political implications of global economic and social integration. But this vision was not in the same apparent fantasy realm as were accounts in the seventeenth century of voyages to the moon. (Another erstwhile "fantasy," be it noted, that has recently come true.)

What is perhaps even more remarkable about Crucé is that despite his clerical vocation, he was insistent upon the necessity and desirability of religious toleration. Religion was the reigning ideology of Crucé's time, and religious conflicts were the contemporary equivalent of the ideological conflicts of later times. As a Catholic priest, Crucé was capable of analyzing doctrinal differences with a professional's eye, and he devoted much of his book to arguing that most if not all doctrinal differences between the major religions of the world pertained to minor issues. With respect to major issues, such as the existence of a supreme being with a benevolent interest in humanity, the main principles of ethical behavior by human individuals, the existence of some kind of supernatural sanctions against unethical behavior, and so on and so forth, there was a large amount of overlap between the major religions. There was no sensible basis, therefore, for violent conflict between adherents to different religions. Another factor influencing Crucé's judgment in this matter was the abundance of violent conflict among adherents to each of the major world religions, including the Christian. Crucé published *The New Cyneas* in 1623, near the beginning of the Thirty Years' War (1618-1648), the last and perhaps the most devastating of the many religious wars inspired by the Protestant Reformation. He had absorbed the lesson that as far as the maintenance of peace was concerned, it would not be of much help to have the entire world population subscribing to any one religion, whether it be a form of Christianity, or a form of any other religion.

Although *The New Cyneas* is a remarkable work considering the date when it was published, it prefigures the modern notion of a world state chiefly in scope, rather than in its institutional features. As befits a work published during the rising age of absolute monarchy, it envisions that the subsidiary political units would all be hereditary monarchies of one sort or another. There would be no trace of democracy either at the national level or at the supranational level. The sole purpose of the Council would be to suppress armed conflicts among and within nations by the adjudication of controversies. The "legislation" referred to in the description of the proposal would not be the passage and promulgation of general legal rules and prescriptions, but rather specific resolutions of specific problems. The Council would not have a permanent executive arm nor armed forces at its immediate disposition. Rather it would marshal the forces of loyal monarchs against those of upstart monarchs (i.e., monarchs refusing to abide by the decisions of the Council). The concept is really that of a universal mutual assistance alliance, later realized in the form of the League of Nations and the United Nations—neither of which were particularly successful in discouraging aggressive war, and neither of which constitutes a genuine world state in the modern sense. Moreover, Crucé's Council of Ambassadors would not be concerned in any way—aside from the suppression of war—with improving the socioeconomic status of the population. Crucé probably assumed that economic living standards were roughly equivalent all around the world—which may not have been far from the truth in the early 1600s. *The New Cyneas* was thus oblivious to what is today a major impediment to world government.

In the three centuries of modern Western European history between 1700 and the present time, there were two veritably catastrophic periods of warfare: the "French wars" between 1792 and 1815, and the "German wars" between 1914 and 1945. In both cases, ideological as well as nationalistic factors played a major role in initiating and perpetuating the conflict. The German wars (i.e., World War I and World War II) will be discussed later. The earlier French wars were generated by the French Revolution, a cataclysmic political and social upheaval extending from the convening of the Estates-General at Versailles in May 1789 to the coup d'état in November 1799 that toppled the Directory and made Napoleon Bonaparte the dictatorial ruler of France.

A very serious and sustained effort was made in France, both before and after the advent of Napoleon, to put into practice the revolutionary principles of "liberty, equality and fraternity." During the tumultuous decade of the 1790s, both the hereditary aristocracy and the Roman Catholic clergy in France were stripped of most of their traditional entitlements and privileges, the monarchy was abolished and a republic established (albeit a short-lived republic), and the natural rights of the common man were exalted. Such sudden and prodigious legal, social and political transformation quite naturally aroused both intense enthusiasm and intense opposition inside France, as well as intense interest and considerable apprehension outside France. Some felt that the French example should be emulated either wholly or in part, while others looked upon developments in France with shock and horror. Austrian forces invaded France in the summer of 1792, and from then onward until the defeat of Napoleon on the battlefield of Waterloo in June 1815, all of Europe became convulsed in warfare. France itself became an armed camp, ruled from 1799 onward by a military dictator in the form of Napoleon Bonaparte—who proclaimed himself emperor in 1804. While Napoleonic France in the early 1800s was politically quite similar to the absolute monarchy of the Bourbon kings, the vast legal and social transformations of the Revolution were mostly continued and consolidated.

The French wars from 1792 through 1815 were the most comprehensive and destructive wars Europe had known since the chaos attending the fall of the Roman empire to barbarian invaders in the fifth century. The armies were larger and the weapons were more potent than anything witnessed in previous history. In addition, the extravagant fervor elicited by the ideological conflict between the principles of equality and democracy on the one hand, and aristocracy and stability on the other, was equal to anything that had attended the intense religious wars generated by the Protestant Reformation. To many Europeans, the French armies were glorious liberators who might finally release all of humanity from centuries of bondage to an arrogant aristocratic and religious elite. To many others, they were perfidious bearers of strife, leveling, anarchy and brutality. The combination of ideological controversy, mass armies, and increasingly powerful weaponry caused an unprecedented amount of death and destruction.

Napoleonic France was finally brought down by a coalition of major powers including Prussia, Austria, Britain and Russia. At the Congress of Vienna, convened from September 1814 to June 1815, the great powers restored the Bourbon monarchy in France, and redrew national boundaries in Europe in such a manner as to hopefully achieve a stable balance of power. However, restoring the Bourbon monarchy did not entirely undo the revolutionary transformation of French politics and society, and the French monarchy's final demise occurred in the disturbances of 1830. Most historians are complimentary toward the work of Metternich and other diplomats at the Congress of Vienna, in that the territorial boundaries devised there, in addition to the Concert of Europe (periodic meetings of national representatives to discuss and resolve emerging conflicts of interest), is generally thought to be responsible for a century of relative peace in Western Europe between the end of the French wars in 1815 and the beginning of the German wars in 1914. Estimates of the long-term stability of the nineteenth century balance of power, however, had to be revised downward in light of the unprecedented carnage of World War I (1914-1918).

It is often observed that proposals for supranational political organizations, up to and including literal world states, flourish most abundantly in periods beset by large-scale warfare. A numerical indication of this phenomenon is contained in the Wynner and Lloyd catalogue (Part II) of theoretical plans to unite nations from 1306 to 1905. Of the 74 plans from this 600-year interval enumerated and briefly described in the catalogue, some 28 date from 1792 through 1821, a period of 30 years. Thus approximately 38 percent of the plans date from an interval covering only 5 percent of the total time span. Some notable historical figures are to be found among the proposers of the 74 plans put forward between 1306 and 1905: in addition to those already mentioned, Dante Alighieri, Desiderius Erasmus, Pope Leo X, Hugo Grotius, William Penn, Jeremy Bentham, Johann Fichte, Immanuel Kant, Thomas Paine, Czar Alexander I, Count Henri de Saint-Simon, Napoleon Bonaparte, Simon Bolivar, Charles Sumner, Baroness Bertha von Suttner, and William T. Stead. No implication is intended that these individuals envisioned a world state as presently conceived. To begin with, most of the plans are extremely vague as to organization and procedure. In many if not most cases, the plans merely call for political unification of the Western European nations, i.e., for something along the lines of the European Union of today. Moreover, many of these regional plans, especially those earlier in the period, are inspired by a dubious vision of a politically united Europe conquering, or at least dominating, the rest of the world. Relatively few of the plans explicitly extended beyond the boundaries of Europe. Finally, in many if not most cases, the plans conceive "political unification" in terms merely of a formally recognized super-alliance, i.e., for something along the lines of the League of Nations of the interwar years and the United Nations of the postwar years. Few plans extended qualitatively beyond the alliance concept to the state concept.

For example, perhaps the best-known today of the plans from this period is that of Immanuel Kant, the renowned philosopher of the late Enlightenment period. His influential essay, *Perpetual Peace*, was published in 1795, when the European wars generated by the French Revolution were in full swing. Inspired by the American and French examples, Kant recommended that all nations should become some form of democratic republic. But he was explicit that these nations should not be organized into a federation, but rather the much looser form of a confederation. The confederation would function through a Congress of States attended by ministers and ambassadors, a body very similar to Crucé's Council of Ambassadors, except that the nations represented were to be republics rather than monarchies. As was the case with Crucé's Council, the principal function of Kant's Congress would be to mobilize military containment of aggressive nations (such as France was when Kant produced *Perpetual Peace*). The basic idea was to achieve a more timely and reliable means of dealing with aggressive nations than the slow and haphazard formation of coalitions.

Despite their wide diversity and serious limitations, there is one key and critical element that unites practically all of these plans: the idea that the supranational political entity is to be founded upon contract rather than upon conquest. Almost all of the plans specify that the adherence of the nations to the supranational political entity is to come about owing to free and voluntary decision on the part of each one of the member nations. This is fundamentally in opposition to the imperial concept, according to which nations (or other subsidiary regions) are initially brought into the imperial domain by means of military conquest. The imperial concept can itself be subdivided into the "liberal empire" concept, according to which, following conquest, the loyalty of the component regions is to be assured mainly by wise and benevolent governance, and the "authoritarian empire" concept, according to which, following conquest, the loyalty of the component regions is to be assured mainly by military force. The proposals for supranational political organization from modern history, illustrated by the 74 plans from 1306-1905 enumerated by Wynner and Lloyd, are qualitatively different from both the liberal empire concept and the authoritarian empire concept. They mark a definite forward progression in the evolution of human thinking on the potential role of formal organization in the realm of international relations.

Another very important point to be made is that while it was customary for critics of supranational political organization from 1306-1905 (and by extension, of the specific type of supranational political organization known today as a "world state") to lambaste and ridicule each and every one of the 74 proposals enumerated by Wynner and Lloyd, immediately upon its respective date of issuance, as thoroughly utopian and patently preposterous, in actual fact the substance of many of these proposals was in fact eventually realized in the real world in the form of the League of Nations, established in 1919 by the Treaty of Versailles. Clearly, the proposers of these schemes for international unity were not such deluded cranks and fuzzy-minded dreamers as their critics maintained. They may have been "ahead of their time," to use the standard cliché, but they were not wrong. There is clearly a very important distinction between a "vision" and a "delusion." Of course, the unfortunate subsequent history of the League of Nations established beyond a reasonable doubt that this particular form of supra-national political organization is not sufficient to guarantee peace and stability. More is needed. But the fact remains that mankind did in fact eventually imple-ment the basic recommendation of those who are today recognized as fore-runners of the contemporary notion of a world state. This suggests that there is a basic receptivity in mankind toward the notion of a universal political organi-zation. That receptivity may ultimately facilitate the inauguration of a world state along the lines of the proposed Federal Union of Democratic Nations.

FROM THE HAGUE TO HIROSHIMA

The Netherlands city of the Hague was the location of two "peace conferences," in 1899 and 1907, the major purpose of which was the reduction of the heavy armaments of the major European nations. Proposed by Czar Nicholas II of Russia and attended by delegates from many nations, the conferences attained a few agreements but made no significant progress in the area of disarmament. A planned third conference, scheduled for 1915, was cancelled because many of the participants were embroiled in World War I. Although it has never been seriously argued that the Hague conferences helped to bring on the First World War, the conferences apparently did little to forestall or mitigate that devastating conflict. The Hague conferences are therefore regarded today as commendably motivated but basically meaningless gestures. Clearly, not enough was done.

The Japanese city of Hiroshima was the location of the first military use of nuclear weapons. To date, that use was one of only two such uses, the other being on the city of Nagasaki three days afterward. At 8:15 on the morning of August 6, 1945, in the waning days of World War II, Hiroshima was devastated by the explosion of an atomic bomb code-named "Little Boy." The total number killed by the bomb, including those who died later of injuries, is estimated to have been around 200,000. This represents 57 percent of the 1940 Hiroshima population of approximately 350,000. According to a contemporary damage assessment report from the Supreme Allied Headquarters, 68 percent of Hiro-shima's buildings were completely destroyed, while another 24 percent were damaged. The report calculated that apart from casualties, almost 177,000 people were made homeless by the bombing. In terms of casualties and destruc-tiveness, the Hiroshima bombing was not the most costly of the war, but the fact that so much damage had been done in such a short space of time by a single bomb dropped from a single aircraft, together with the widespread dissemination throughout the world of photographs of the devastation, had—and continues to have—a profound effect on humanity's perception of the potential costs of unrestricted warfare in the nuclear age.

The tumultuous years between the Hague peace conferences at the turn of the twentieth century, and the atomic bombing of Hiroshima in 1945, witnessed what have been termed the "German wars." Although German people today are apt to argue that the responsibility for World War I and World War II must be shared by many nations, in that these wars were the outcome of a dysfunctional "overall world system," the fact remains that in an immediate sense, German efforts to revise the existing international status quo were the critical catalytic inputs into the origins of both world wars. It is also true that once the wars had started, German armies fanned out both to the east and to the west to invade and conquer adjoining nations.

Both wars provided an instructive lesson on the hazards of "miscalculated brinkmanship." In the case of both World War I and World War II, neither side "wanted war," in the sense that neither side made a deliberate decision to initiate war in full confidence that it would win the war. In both cases, the German government of the time engaged in a series of incremental provocations in the belief that these provocations would not be sufficient to cause its opponents to declare war—or, that if war was in fact declared, to prosecute the war vigorously. Eventually, this belief was contradicted by events. This unmistakable indication of the fallibility of human judgment carries profound implications for us who today live in a world in which several nations deem it essential to their national security that they possess large stockpiles of operational nuclear weapons. The fact that every reasonable person knows nuclear war would be disastrous will not necessarily permanently deter nuclear war. It does not require a deliberate decision to start a nuclear war, but rather merely one single instance of "miscalculated brinkmanship." If we continue to disregard this simple, uncongenial truth, the long-term prospects for global human civilization are not reassuring.

Germany's major allies in World War I, which commenced in August 1914 and persisted to the Armistice of November 1918, were the Austro-Hungarian empire and the Ottoman empire, while it was opposed by an alliance of several nations, the major powers of which were France, Britain, Italy and Russia. Russia underwent revolution in 1917 and by early 1918 had removed itself from the war. However, by that time the allied powers had been joined by the United States. Much of the war was fought along relatively static trench lines, and the combination of the conventional military wisdom of the time that victory could most reliably be attained through audacious offense, with the natural advantages given to the defense by machine guns and improved artillery, generated prodigious carnage. Upon their defeat at the end of the war, both the Austro-Hungarian empire and the Ottoman empire suffered dissolution. In contrast, Germany itself was not subdivided into the independent political units which it had incorporated upon unification in 1871 (Prussia, Saxony, Hanover, Bavaria, etc.); rather it retained its national identity. In addition, there was no military occupation of Germany after the war by the victorious allies. Its defeat, in a word, was not absolute. One of the major themes of Adolf Hitler, in his decade-long struggle to gain power in Germany after the war, was that the German people had been "stabbed in the back" in November 1918 by their pusillanimous military and political leaders. It was a theme which played well to the wounded pride of the German people.

Hitler's mission was to toughen up the German nation, get a rematch (so to speak) with its opponents in World War I, and this time prosecute the war with such commitment and zeal that Germany would emerge victorious and triumphant. Revenge was the central motivation, and the extremely powerful hold that this particular motivation has on human psychology cannot be doubted. During the relatively prosperous 1920s, the continuing attempts to gain power of Hitler's Nazi party were democratically rebuffed by the German people, but the vicissitudes visited upon them by the worldwide Great Depression of the 1930s sufficiently undermined rationality and moderation as to give the Nazi party the opportunity it needed. Consequently Hitler was eventually successful in bringing about a replay of World War I—and it turned out to be an even more widely encompassing and violently fought conflict than its predecessor. Unfortunately for Hitler and the German people, but fortunately for most of the rest of the human population, Germany and its allies in World War II (principally Italy and Japan) did not emerge victorious and triumphant. Rather they were defeated most decisively, and Germany, Italy and Japan all experienced several years of military occupation commencing in 1945.

The Nazi regime in Germany, initiated by Hitler's assumption of dictatorial powers in 1933, aroused intense revulsion and apprehension throughout the world. From the beginning, Hitler was recognized as a dire threat to peace. He almost immediately repudiated the arms limitations on Germany imposed by the 1919 Treaty of Versailles. In 1936, he sent military forces into the Rhineland, an area of Germany required by the Versailles Treaty to be demilitarized. In addition, the Nazi regime was ideologically repugnant to both the democratic Western powers and the communist Soviet Union to the East. In the early 1920s, a fascist regime, openly scornful of democratic principles, had been established in Italy by Benito Mussolini. The chauvinistically nationalistic, anti-democratic, anti-socialist ideology of fascism was pushed to even greater extremes in Germany in the 1930s under Adolf Hitler, who added a violently anti-Semitic ingredient to the brew. Following a failed putsch attempt in 1923, Hitler had spent a year in prison, during which he wrote a political tract entitled *Mein Kampf*. In the book Hitler argued the natural racial superiority of the Aryan people of Germany, and laid out a vision of a Germany purified of "Jewish pollution," liberated from the shackles of timidity and indecision imposed by political democracy, and pursuing a course of military conquest in the East. In Hitler's view, German conquest of the Soviet Union would not only make available to German colonists an abundance of much-needed lebensraum (living space) in the vast Russian hinterland, but it would also be a favor both to the Russian people (by liberating them from communist oppression), and to the rest of world population (by eliminating the communist menace once and for all).

Hitler's dreams of Germanic glory, of course, represented a veritably nightmarish prospect to many people outside of Germany. Jewish people around the world were fearful of a worldwide anti-Semitic pogrom. The Soviet government and most of the Soviet people were fearful of the abolition of socialism and the restoration of capitalism at the hands of a conquering foreign army. The major democratic nations, especially France, Britain and the United States, were fearful that if Germany were to gain control over the vast natural and human resources of the Soviet Union, it might eventually develop sufficient industrial and military resources to conquer the entire world. The entire world population could be reduced to the status of chattels, brutally mistreated and sadistically oppressed by a ruling class of arrogant Germans. Only a little over six years separated Hitler's accession to power in Germany and the September 1939 general declaration of war upon Germany's attack on Poland. Although this was a very quick march to war, in some ways it is surprising that it was not even quicker, considering the nature of the Nazi regime.

In those critical six years, Nazi Germany rearmed at a breakneck pace, and sought political and military allies elsewhere in the world, finding them in Italy and Japan, both of which also suffered from the fascist political disease— although not to such a level of intensity as Germany. (Recall that of the three principal Axis powers of the Second World War, only one, Germany, had suffered the humiliation of defeat in the First World War.) Hitler's basic strategy, in domestic politics, international diplomacy, and military warfare alike, was the time-tested and often successful formula: "divide and conquer." His basic error was in overreaching himself, of setting objectives which he did not have the resources to achieve. Not that this error was quickly manifested, once war had commenced. Almost two years elapsed between the declaration of war of Britain and France on Germany occasioned by the German invasion of Poland (September 1939), and the German invasion of Russia in June 1941. According to Hitler's personal analysis of World War I, Germany had been defeated in that conflict primarily owing to the mistake of waging a "two-front war," with France and Britain to the West and Russia to the East. With the 1940 defeat of France, and the ejection of British military forces from the Continent, Hitler deemed the Western front closed down, and turned eastward toward what had been his paramount objective from the beginning: the Soviet Union.

Later in 1941, the Japanese bombing of Pearl Harbor ended U.S. neutrality, and commenced a chain of military developments that culminated in the Allied invasion of Normandy in 1944. Apparently the Western front had not been closed down after all. At the same time, the Soviet Union, previously widely assumed throughout the world to be a "house of cards" (owing to two decades of "socialist blundering") proved to be a far more formidable opponent than expected. From June 1941 onwards, the Eastern front consumed a tremendous quantity of German resources, both human and material. The German onslaught on Russia reached its high tide at the battle of Stalingrad in the winter of 1942-43. The German army at Stalingrad was defeated, and after that it was all retreat. In May 1945, the last vestiges of Nazi resistance in Germany were crushed by Allied armies invading from the West and Soviet armies invading from the East. Once again, as in World War I, it had been demonstrated that Germany, even supported by powerful allies, did not possess the resources to win a "two-front war." Three months later, Japan surrendered after the atomic bombings of Hiroshima and Nagasaki. And so ended the most costly war in human history. Not counting the 6 million European Jews murdered in the Holocaust, military dead are estimated at 25 million and civilian dead at 30 million. The Soviet Union alone is estimated to have lost 20 million dead.

During the horrific carnage of World War I, three decades previously, an inspirational slogan had emerged that this was going to be "the war to end wars." At the end of the war, a supranational political organization was established known as the League of Nations, whose purpose it was to make a reality of this slogan. The League of Nations was in fact a real-world implementation of the typical pre-1914 proposal for supranational political union: a super-alliance of such power and resources that no non-member nation would dare attack a member nation. The League, obviously, was unsuccessful not only in preventing World War II, but also in either shortening the duration or moderating the ferocity of that conflict. The League was hobbled from the beginning by the fact that two of the major participants in World War I, Russia and the United States, did not join it upon its foundation in 1919. Russia was wracked by revolutionary turmoil and its government was calling stridently for worldwide proletarian revolution—obviously, therefore, it was not fit company in a supranational organization dedicated to peace, stability, and the preservation of the status quo. The United States succumbed, after the war, to an isolationist mentality according to which America should not allow itself to become entangled in periodic foreign bloodlettings—and especially in those on the politically devious and morally corrupted Western European continent.

But even if Russia and the United States had been charter members of the League of Nations, it is far from certain that this would have deterred Hitler and the German people from their revanchist policies and objectives. Throughout the period of German rearmament and expansionist maneuvers (the remilitarization of the Rhineland in 1936, the absorption of Austria and the partition of Czechoslovakia in 1938), Russia was in fact a member of the League of Nations, and it was also clear that the main sympathies of the United States lay with the democratic nations of Britain and France. The League issued quantities of warnings and resolutions, decrying not only German policies but those of Italy and Japan as well. The three aggressive fascist nations simply withdrew from the League so that their representatives would not be discomfited by the complaints of other nations. The League had no military forces of its own which could have been immediately dispatched to contain aggression. It is now generally agreed that even as late as the German military reoccupation of the Rhineland in 1936 (which could have been interpreted as a form of aggression), a relatively modest military force could have invaded Germany and overthrown the Nazi government. But the League did not command even a modest military force. Moreover, the member nations of the League of Nations did not trust each other to provide mutual support—all were afraid that if they militarily opposed Hitler's Germany they would be left alone to confront German military might. As a consequence of indecision and timidity, Nazi Germany was given time to equip itself with formidable military forces, the defeat of which entailed millions of casualties.

The League of Nations, established at the conclusion of World War I, did not possess the characteristics of a state entity. Representatives to it were appointed by the national governments of the member nations rather than being elected by their people. It possessed extremely little authority—beyond moral authority. It had no military forces of its own but had to rely on member nations to provide these. It had no effective means to collect levies on member nations, and these levies were very modest in any event. Although the League possessed a general assembly, a smaller-membership council, and a court, the general assembly was not a true legislative branch because it was merely advisory to the council, the council was not a true executive branch because it was merely advisory to the national governments, and the court was not a true judicial branch because its function was confined to the arbitration of disputes between two nations, both of which were willing to voluntarily submit to the arbitration process.

The United Nations of today, established at the conclusion of World War II, is institutionally a veritable carbon copy of the League of Nations. The only important difference between the two is that in 1919 the United States abstained from the League and Russia was not invited to join, whereas in 1945 both the United States and the Soviet Union became charter members of the United Nations. Considering their nature, it is not surprising that the League of Nations was unsuccessful in preventing a devastating Second World War, and that the United Nations was unsuccessful in suppressing the strategic confrontation and nuclear arms competition that might easily—had humanity been less fortunate— have led to an even more devastating Third World War. Even referring to the League of Nations and the United Nations as "supranational political organizations" is probably misleading. What they really are is "international political associations." They did not and do not have sufficient practical authority over the nations to use "supranational" in place of "international"; and they did not and do not possess sufficient purposeful institutional structure to merit the designation "organization" in place of "association."

Now, it is clearly apparent that the Federal Union of Democratic Nations proposed in this book would in fact, unlike the League of Nations and the United Nations, possess essential qualities and characteristics of a state entity. It would look like a state and act like a state. Adapting the well-known expression: "If it *looks* like a state and *acts* like a state, then it *is* a state." But at the same time it would encompass some key restrictions and limitations that are not commonly associated with the conception of a "state": most importantly, the right of member nations to withdraw from the Federal Union at their own unilateral discretion, and the right of member nations to maintain whatever military forces and armaments, up to and including nuclear weapons, they desire. Therefore, it should be understood that my argument is not that the Federal Union of Democratic Nations would *necessarily* have been more effective than the League of Nations was in averting World War II, or the United Nations was in averting the threat of World War III. If a Federal Union of Democratic Nations, exactly as described herein, had been established in 1919 in place of the League of Nations, quite possibly the course of events leading up to World War II would have been essentially the same. After all, it is obvious that if the United States was unwilling to join the League of Nations in 1919, it would have been equally unwilling to join a Federal Union. If Hitler had come to power in the 1930s and commenced the rearmament of Germany, in all probability Germany would have seceded from the Federal Union, and quite possibly the other member nations of the Union would have stood by quietly—as they did in reality—hoping against hope that events would somehow not lead to war. Similarly, if a Federal Union of Democratic Nations, exactly as described herein, had been established in 1945 in place of the United Nations, quite possibly the course of the Cold War, with its persistent threat of nuclear holocaust, would have been essentially the same.

What I am arguing, however, is that there would have been a *greater likelihood* of a favorable outcome had an authentic, genuine, legitimate supernational state entity been established at the appropriate moment. The state apparatus would have engendered, in the population of many if not most participating nations, an appreciable spirit of enthusiasm, solidarity and shared purpose, thus making it more likely that, in the 1930s, the Federal Union would have quickly stood up to and deterred the emerging threat represented by Nazi Germany. For the same reason, it is more likely that the Federal Union would have had more success, in the 1950s and 1960s, than the United Nations did in moderating the virulent ideological conflict between East and West that, at the height of the Cold War, had human civilization perched precariously on the edge of global nuclear destruction.

The years between the first Hague peace conference of 1899 and the atomic bombing of Hiroshima in 1945, were rich in the production of proposals for supranational political unification. The largest section (Part III) of Wynner and Lloyd's 522-page compilation of theoretical plans and practical attempts to unite nations pertains to theoretical plans advanced between 1914 and 1944 (the latter being the year of publication of their book). Excluding documents pertaining to international court plans, and also those pertaining to the actual United Nations organization founded in 1945, some 59 proposals are "charted." That is to say, specific details are provided in all or most of several categories: type (alliance, league, etc.); membership (universal, regional, etc.); organs of government (legislative, executive, and judicial); transfers of jurisdiction (supranational versus national rights and responsibilities); methods of enforcement (individuals versus nations); immediate steps (scenarios toward foundation); territorial changes (revisions in boundaries and jurisdictions); ratification (process of formal approval). If, as was usually the case, the plan was put forward during wartime, an additional category was included: liquidation of the war. The plans were grouped by Wynner and Lloyd according to whether they were universal (subcategories here including federal and confederal), regional, or ideological. By "ideological" is meant that the envisioned union would admit only democratic

TABLE 3.1

Categorization of Theoretical Plans to Unite Nations, 1914-1944, by Three Time Periods

Period	Universal		Regional	Ideological	Total
	Federal	Confederate			
1914-1918	4	0	3	0	7
1919-1938	3	2	1	1	7
1939-1944	18	7	15	5	45
Total	25	9	19	6	59

Source: Edith Wynner and Georgia Lloyd, *Searchlight on Peace Plans: Choose Your Road to World Government*, New York: E. P. Dutton, 1944.

nations. Table 3.1 shows the distribution of the plans over these categories, by three time periods: 1914-1918 were World War I years, 1919-1938 were interwar years, and 1939-1944 were World War II years. As can be seen from the table, most of the proposals (52 out of 59) were published in war years. This is testimony to the unfortunate reality that in the past most serious thinking about world government has been done when the bullets were already flying—conditions obviously not conducive to the formation of such a government.

As mentioned previously, the great majority of plans to unite nations prior to World War I went only as far as a permanent, institutionalized grand alliance whose main—if not sole—purpose would be the preservation of peace and the protection of the international status quo. There was very little consideration given to possible political, economic and social purposes beyond this. There was very little concern with achieving the *appearance* of a state, of creating a supernational government with many of the same characteristics as a typical national government. Rather what was envisioned was merely a council of ambassadors, each one of whom would be, at all times, under the direct control of his or her respective national government. The primary objective was simply to have a quick and reliable means of mustering an overwhelming alliance against any one nation contemplating or engaging in aggression against other nations.

This "collective security" system was thought to constitute an advance over the earlier "balance of power" system by which a single nation would seek bilateral alliances with one or more other nations to protect itself against aggression. The inherent weakness of the balance of power system was demonstrated by World War I. After World War I the League of Nations was established, which effectively implemented the notion of collective security. The inherent weakness of the collective security system was then clearly demonstrated by World War II. Although the 59 proposals collected by Wynner and Lloyd are extremely heterogeneous and diverse, most of them go qualitatively beyond the notion of collective security attained through a permanent, institutionalized alliance, to the notion of a full-fledged world government exhibiting the essential

characteristics of a state entity, and concerned with political, economic and
social purposes beyond the preservation of peace and security. This is not to say
that peace and security were not principal goals, but rather to say that peace and
security were not the only goals. And the political entities envisioned were far
more than assemblages of ambassadors: they were rather full-fledged governments, composed of legislative, executive and judicial branches, in permanent
and continuous operation, headed by elected officials, staffed by permanent
professional employees, with the power to tax, and with the power to raise and
maintain substantial armed forces.

Obviously it would be impractical to try to review even a small subset of 59
proposals, or even a small subset of the 25 proposals for universal federal world
government, which is the concept of present concern. Later in this chapter, a
more thorough discussion will be provided of a small number of illustrative
federal world government proposals from the post-World War II period. A few
comments will have to suffice on the 1914-1944 proposals. To begin with, the
numerical abundance of proposals might create a false impression of the degree
of interest in world government among the general population, the intelligentsia
and the political leadership. Many of the proposals are contained in thin
pamphlets, some of them self-published by the author, which are only preserved
as archival material in the dusty stacks of the largest public and university libra-
ries. Of the relatively small subset of proposals that enjoyed publication in book
form by trade, academic or university presses, only a very few attracted more
than vestigial attention, either at the time of publication or afterwards. The great
majority of the population was either ignorant of, indifferent to, or opposed to
plans for world government. In other words, the conventional attitude toward
world government then was much as it remains today.

Interestingly, some of the earliest proposals of the period, published during
World War I, utilize as the name of the proposed world federation the name later
given to the successor organization to the League of Nations: i.e., the United
Nations. The United States federal government structure was a major inspiration
for many proposers of world government schemes, especially for proposers of
U.S. citizenship. Theodore Harris's proposal for a "United Nations of the
World" is exceptionally parallel to the U.S.: this supernational government
would be composed of a bicameral legislature designated the United Nations
Congress, composed of a House in which representation of nations would be
proportional to population and a Senate in which each nation would be equally
represented, an executive branch headed by a President and a Vice-President,
and a judicial branch designated the Supreme Court. Some of the proposals
incorporate more sophisticated features than the standard proposal. For example,
Oskar Newfang's 1942 proposal to transform the League of Nations into an
authentic federal world government envisions a unicameral legislature which
would use a dual voting system to achieve more efficiently the same objective as
the bicameral legislature proposal of Theodore Harris and several others. The
dual voting system in Newfang's proposal would include a national basis in

which each nation would have equal voting weight, and a population basis in which relative voting weights would be proportional to relative national populations. To be approved, decisions would have to be passed by a majority on both bases. A dual voting system is of course a central element in the present proposal for a Federal Union of Democratic Nations, but the two bases would be population and material (i.e., based on revenue), as opposed to population and national. Some of the proposals contain elements that would clearly be unacceptable in today's world. For example, the 1918 proposal of Raleigh Minor, published by Oxford University Press, includes a bicameral legislature in which the voting weights of representatives to the House of Delegates would be proportional to national populations—but in enumerating populations, each white person would count as one, while each non-white person (i.e., black or Asian) would count as one third. An exception was graciously made for the Japanese: in their case each person would count as one, just as if that person were white. Obviously, this is not a viable way of getting around the perceived problem.

Of all the proposals enumerated from the 1914-1944 period by Wynner and Lloyd, certainly the most famous in its time was that of Clarence K. Streit, an American journalist and writer. Streit's proposal is categorized by Wynner and Lloyd as an "ideological" plan because it specifies that membership in the union would be available only to democratic nations. The envisioned federation would eventually encompass all nations—but each prospective member of the union would have to become internally democratic prior to joining. Streit's best-selling book *Union Now: A Proposal for a Federal Union of the Leading Democracies* (1939) envisioned a "Union of the Free" encompassing all the major democracies regardless of language, while his equally successful book *Union Now with Britain* (1941) envisioned the union restricted to the English-speaking democracies. The remarkable success of Streit's proposals—in terms of widespread public familiarity if not in terms of actual implementation—was obviously a function of the war jitters of the period. *Union Now* was published in 1939, the year that Hitler finally crossed over (by invading Poland) the line drawn by Britain and France. *Union Now with Britain* was published in 1941, the year that Germany invaded Russia and the United States was drawn into the war by the Japanese attack on Pearl Harbor. Although widely known, Streit's proposal for a world government to be called the "Union of the Free" was not actually implemented. By then it was too late—the impetus toward world war was inexorable.

There is an important lesson here for us of today's world, as we consider (or fail to consider) world government. Especially now that the Cold War has receded into insignificance, a dubious attitude of smug complacency is gaining ground. Added to all the old arguments against world government is a new argument: the argument that in the present age of peace and tranquillity world government is unnecessary and superfluous. The corollary to this argument is that we should sit back and wait until serious conflicts between nations emerge before reconsidering the possibility of world government. The operational essence of the corresponding policy might be described as "let's drift and see what happens." But if we do this, once it has become clear even to the most obtusely complacent that we are drifting into serious danger, it may be too late to do anything before disaster strikes. Back in the 1930s, the world had exactly six years—a split second in historical perspective—between the time Adolf Hitler took power in Germany and the commencement of the Second World War. If we now wait for one of Hitler's re-incarnations to stride forth onto the world stage, we will have waited too long.

Streit's proposal was creditable and commendable, but that did not alter the fact that by the time it was put forward, the disaster of world war had already befallen humanity. In a way, the last-second interest by a large number of people in Streit's proposal for world government was ludicrously futile. An even more ludicrous example of this too-little-too-late phenomenon was the June 1940 proposal of the British government (under Winston Churchill) to the French government for political unification of Britain and France. At that moment, German armies were completing their blitzkrieg conquest of France, and the long-term military prospects of Britain were extremely bleak. Even Winston Churchill, ever prior to that moment a relentless and unflinching champion of national sovereignty, could at last perceive—if only for a brief moment—the downside of national sovereignty. On June 16, 1940, the French Council of Ministers, meeting in the town of Bordeaux and on the verge of making a separate peace with Germany, rejected the proposal summarily as nothing more than a cynical ploy designed to sacrifice more French lives for British interests. Over the ensuing five years, both the British and the French reaped bitter fruit from their prior pompous and self-righteous insistence on national sovereignty.

THE POSTWAR WORLD GOVERNMENT BOOM

Public receptiveness toward the general concept of world government attained a sharply delineated pinnacle in the half-decade that separated the end of World War II in the summer of 1945 from the beginning of the Korean War in the summer of 1950. Unfortunately, the sudden and dramatic ascent in public receptiveness toward world government was almost immediately followed by an equally sudden and dramatic descent. No doubt a decisive factor in the rapid deflation of world government hopes and aspirations was the obstructionist, confrontational and uncooperative attitude of the Soviet Union in the years following the close of the Second World War. But it is by no means certain that if the Soviet Union had been a capitalist nation—even a democratic capitalist nation—that a genuine world government would have been possible at that time. Quite possibly the highly ephemeral post-World War II world government boom was largely a shock reaction to the first use of nuclear weapons in warfare—the atomic bombings of Hiroshima and Nagasaki in August 1945. But human beings are remarkably resilient and adaptive, mentally and emotionally as well as physically. Within a remarkably short space of time, most people had filed away the threat of dying in a worldwide nuclear holocaust in the same compartment as the threat of dying in an automobile accident. It was a regrettable but inevitable hazard, therefore there was nothing to be done about it. Therefore life went on as before, and the nuclear arms race between the superpowers steadily continued.

If one had to select the single most dramatic indicator of the postwar world government boom, it would probably be the remarkable commercial success enjoyed by a book entitled *The Anatomy of Peace* by Emery Reves, published by Harper and Brothers in 1945, shortly prior to the conclusion of the war. The thesis of the book was simply that collective security, as pursued by the League of Nations and the United Nations, was a dangerous delusion, and that the only way to stop, once and for all, an endless succession of devastating wars, was for the nations of the world to establish a strong and effective world government. The thesis was presented in a lively, passionate and highly readable (if somewhat breathless) style, as illustrated by the following representative passage:

> Violent conflicts between nations are the inevitable consequence of an in-effective and inadequate organization of relations between the nations, and we shall never be able to escape another and another world war so long as we do not recognize the elementary principles and mechanics of *any* society.
>
> It is a strange paradox that at any suggestion of a world-wide legal order which could guarantee mankind freedom from war for many generations to come, and consequently individual liberty, the worshipers of the present nation-states snipe: "Super-state!"
>
> *The reality is that the present nation-state has become a super-state.*
>
> It is this nation-state which today is making serfs of its citizens. It is this state which, to protect its particular vested interests, takes away the earnings of the people and wastes them on munitions in the constant fear of being attacked and destroyed by some other nation-state. It is this state which, by forcing passports and visas upon us, does not allow us to move freely. It is this state, wherever it exists, which by keeping prices high through artificial regulations and tariffs, believing that every state must be economically self-supporting, does not permit its citizens to enjoy the fruits of modern science and technology. It is this state which interferes more and more with our everyday life and tends to prescribe every minute of our existence. *This* is the "super-state"!
>
> It is not a future nightmare or a proposal we can freely accept or reject. We are living within it, in the middle of the twentieth century. We are entirely within its orbit, whether in America, in England, in Russia or Argentina, in Portugal or Turkey. And we shall become more and more subject to this all-powerful super-state if our supreme goal is to maintain the nation-state structure of the world.
>
> Democratic sovereignty of the people can be correctly expressed and effectively instituted only if local affairs are handled by local government, national affairs by national government, and international, world affairs, by international, world government.

In a *New York Times* book review, Orville Prescott wrote: "The logic of *The Anatomy of Peace* is simple and eloquent. It might be a good thing for the world if ten or twenty million persons read and discovered it." The Associated Press review, distributed to 1600 newspapers, declared: "Few books about the causes of war are as stirring as this one about the causes of peace." On October 10,

1945, the following statement, signed by such major luminaries as Mortimer Adler, Thomas Mann and Senator William Fulbright, appeared in the *New York Times* and 50 other leading U.S. newspapers: "At this anxious moment in our history a book has been published which expresses clearly and simply what so many of us have been thinking. That book is *The Anatomy of Peace* by Emery Reves. We urge American men and women to read this book, to think about its conclusions, to discuss it with neighbors and friends, privately and publicly." Albert Einstein, whose genius fathered the nuclear age, called *The Anatomy of Peace* "*the* political answer to the atomic bomb." *Reader's Digest* serialized a condensation of the book over three issues, and arranged 23,000 discussion groups across the United States to study it. The book was translated into 25 languages and distributed in 30 countries. Pocket Books published a paperback edition for a mass market. Total sales of *The Anatomy of Peace*, over its eight editions, approached half a million copies.

Despite the remarkable success of the book (or perhaps partly because of it), some writers on world government have been inclined to dismiss it as empty rhetoric which merely generated interest in world government—but did not sustain that interest. The fundamental complaint was (and remains) that there is little or nothing in *The Anatomy of Peace* that sensibly addresses the organizational specifics necessary to make world government viable in the real world. For example, Fremont Rider, a contemporary of Reves and author of *The Great Dilemma of World Organization* (1946), had this to say:

> Now, every would-be planner of world organization is well aware of the existence of this Dilemma [note: the fact that relatively poor people, over the world as a whole, greatly outnumber relatively rich people]. Also he knows in his heart that it is the crux of the practicality of his plan. But, just because it has always seemed an almost insoluble problem, each planner has either ignored it entirely, or has "solved" it only in terms of more or less vague generalities. Take, for example, Mr. Emery Reves' *The Anatomy of Peace*, which has received much comment lately. Perhaps it is unfair to call this book a "plan" at all, for it is rather an appeal for a world-state than a definite proposal for one, an appeal making up in apostolic fervor what it lacks in definiteness. What is its solution for the Great Dilemma? So far as its author gives one it appears in the following sentences in his two concluding paragraphs: "We shall have to organize peace independently of the Unholy Alliance stillborn in San Francisco or else we shall delude ourselves until the inevitable march of events into another and greater holocaust teaches us that equal and sovereign power units can never co-exist peacefully... After a disastrous half a century of antirationalism, we must return to rationalism... The task is by no means easy. There is no other fate for us than to climb the long, hard, steep, and stony road guided by reason."
>
> The trouble with this sort of thing is that it doesn't get us anywhere. Little appeal needs to be made for the world-state as a theory: in the abstract almost every one is already in favor of it. It is the world-state in whatever concrete form it has so far been put that has failed to win adherents. Yet, until it has been put into concrete form, has been made a definite proposal, all argument in favor of it is bound to be more or less *words*. The peoples of the world are demanding, not

vague generalities, but an extremely definite, and profoundly reasonable, answer to this question: "What exactly is to be the voting power of each of the nations in your world organization, and by what formula is this voting power arrived at?" Until they get such an answer they are not going to give up their national powers to any new order whatsoever, no matter how persuasive the arguments in favor of their doing so may seem to be.

Rider himself presented a carefully considered, highly specific proposal for world government (albeit in a rather short book)—and perhaps as a consequence of this specificity his book received little attention. More recently (1996), Derek Heater had this to say about *The Anatomy of Peace* (*World Citizenship and Government*, pp. 158-159):

> It is the extraordinary success of the book which commends it to our attention, rather than the quality of the thought. The text contains nothing original— the ideas were commonplace in the world federalist literature of the inter-war and wartime years. The text contains no advice about how a world state might be created—except for a few brief paragraphs in the Postscript to the 1947 edition. Here the author identifies five steps from "the conception of the idea" through the election of representatives to the ad hoc solution of the world's problems. There seems little doubt that Reves' success lay in the mood of the time, a splendid publicity campaign, a robust denunciatory style, passionate optimism and vagueness in detail in order to avoid criticism.

Although Reves himself eschewed specifics, in the few postwar years during which *The Anatomy of Peace* remained a widely discussed and highly inspirational appeal for world government, numerous groups and individuals did indeed endeavor to provide specific, concrete blueprints for a viable world government. Fremont Rider was only one of many—although he was among the relatively small minority whose proposals were actually published. Probably the best-known of these blueprints was the "Preliminary Draft of a World Constitution," the product of a group of distinguished citizens styling itself the "Committee to Frame a World Constitution." Not only did the committee include a number of well-known academics, writers and public figures, it was chaired by one of the most illustrious names in American higher education during the twentieth century: Robert Maynard Hutchins.

Although his overall reputation was somewhat on the flaky side, in the immediate post-World War II years, Robert M. Hutchins was quite widely recognized as a very solid citizen (presumably the Chancellor of the University of Chicago could not be anything but), and moreover one of the "great minds of America." In the immediate aftermath of the atomic bombing of Hiroshima and Nagasaki, along with many other great minds, he expressed the opinion that if mankind failed to establish a world government within the very near future, there was a very high probability that human civilization would be destroyed in a global nuclear holocaust. Soon after he made this opinion known, Hutchins was approached by two senior members of the University of Chicago humanities faculty, Richard McKeon and Giuseppe Borgese, with a proposal to form a study

group to write a draft constitution for an actual world government. Hutchins enthusiastically agreed to help form the study group. The Committee to Frame a
World Constitution, composed of about a dozen "blue ribbon" individuals, most
of them senior University of Chicago faculty members and administrators, with
Hutchins as chair and Borgese as secretary, commenced regular meetings in the
fall of 1945. From the approximately 4,000 pages of discussion papers and
minutes produced by the Committee over the next two years, there eventually
emerged the "Preliminary Draft of a World Constitution," published as a booklet
by the University of Chicago Press in 1948. The principal architect of the
finished product was Giuseppe Borgese, who included it as an appendix to his
1953 book *Foundations of the World Republic* (also published by the University
of Chicago Press).

By the time the Preliminary Draft was published, however, relations between
the Western democracies and the Soviet Union had deteriorated to the point
where serious questions were being asked about the loyalty and/or common
sense of those interested in world government. When the *Chicago Tribune*, a
traditional stronghold of America-first patriotism and isolationism, obtained an
early version of the Draft Constitution, its editor quickly alerted the *Tribune*'s
readership to the ominous news that a "super-secret constitution" was being
produced by "one of a rash of militant globalist organizations which have sprung
up in the United States and England since the United Nations has demonstrated
its uselessness." Meanwhile, Moscow Radio harshly condemned the Draft as an
effort "to justify the American Empire plan for world supremacy," and maintained that "the program of the Chicago world government embodies the
ambitions of the American warmongers." Nevertheless, the Draft Constitution
was translated into 40 different languages, and an estimated million copies were
circulated around the world. Reactions, pro and con, were so abundant that the
University of Chicago Press for two years published a special monthly journal,
entitled *Common Cause*, as a venue where proponents of world government
could respond to and debate their numerous critics.

In his highly influential critical study of world government, published in
1953, Gerard J. Mangone, possibly out of respect for its origins in one of the
leading U.S. universities, was gentle with the Preliminary Draft, describing it as
follows (*The Idea and Practice of World Government*, p. 167): "One of the most
commendable efforts of recent years, especially among a spate of nonsensical
diagrams, has been the document produced by several savants of Chicago and
elsewhere entitled 'Preliminary Draft for a World Constitution.'" However, in
the same paragraph, Mangone refers to the "inescapable omnipotence" of the
proposed world government, and dismisses it as manifestly unworkable: "Unfortunately, the peoples of the world do not have the remotest prospect of such a
de novo creation, but at the moment are still fumbling along with the shambles of
traditional international law." The world government scheme of the Committee
to Frame a World Constitution is sufficiently important in the history of world
government thinking to be worth careful description and comparison with the

present proposal for a Federal Union of Democratic Nations. This description and comparison will be undertaken later in this chapter.

While the best-selling author Emery Reves drummed up support for the general concept of world government, and academics such as Robert Hutchins and Giuseppe Borgese worked busily on trying to develop a practical plan for world government, still others applied themselves to the practical organizational work of building mass support for world government. Henry Usborne, a member of the British Parliament, and Harold S. Bidmead were instrumental in establishing a parent association to coordinate the activities of the "rash of militant globalist organizations" described by the editor of the *Chicago Tribune*: the association was designated the World Movement for World Federal Government (WMWFG). It held its first World Congress in Montreux, Switzerland, in 1947, and issued a Declaration describing in considerable detail what the delegates deemed the necessary characteristics of a world state. Most adherents at that time to the WMWFG expected that the world state would be formally established and ratified by actions of the various national governments.

Henry Usborne, for example, tried to enlist his colleagues in the British Parliament in the world government movement. In the United States, Fyke Farmer, a member of the Tennessee state legislature, secured a resolution to send delegates to a world constituent assembly which would endeavor to draft a constitution for a world government. The high tide of this endeavor was an assembly designated the People's World Convention, held in the Palais Electoral in Geneva, Switzerland, commencing on December 30, 1950. Although there were more than 500 representatives in attendance from more than 47 nations, only four delegates had been properly appointed by duly authorized government bodies—three from the state of Tennessee, and one from Nigeria. The convention continued on for seven days while the delegates argued themselves to a standstill on all substantive matters. The World People's Convention not only did not adopt a world government constitution, it could not even agree on when and where to hold future conventions, and on how delegates should be elected or appointed to them.

Although numerous luminaries at the dawn of the nuclear age in 1945, including Emery Reves, Albert Einstein, Robert Hutchins, and many, many others, immediately proclaimed the urgent need for world government in light of what had happened to Hiroshima and Nagasaki, it soon became apparent that government officials—especially national government officials—were not going to be very helpful toward this end. The United Nations, established at San Francisco on October 24, 1945—and little more than a renamed League of Nations with the added membership of the United States and the Soviet Union— was as far as they were willing to go. In the eyes of world federalists, this was not far enough. There developed among many world federalists a strong suspicion that national government officials would tend to be especially skeptical and obstructionist toward world government because such a government could and probably would reduce their own personal power and prestige. The "common people," it was hypothesized, would be more receptive toward world government because it would not be so threatening to their private interests. It might even be necessary, in the extreme version of this viewpoint, for the people to circumvent the national governments entirely—to hold a world constitutional convention and establish a world government without any participation of representatives of national governments. In a less extreme version, the national governments could eventually be brought into line—but only by virtue of massive pressure toward world government exerted by the general population.

One of the best-known and most colorful exponents of the direct-to-the-people approach was Garry W. Davis. Davis had been a bomber pilot in the World War II and had experience as a Broadway actor. His flair for the dramatic attracted a considerable amount of attention to the world government cause in both the U.S. and the international press. With all the fanfare he could muster, Davis appeared at the American embassy in Paris on May 25, 1948, turned in his U.S. passport (contrary to some reports, he did not burn it or tear it up), declared that he was renouncing his U.S. citizenship, and proclaimed that he was henceforth a "citizen of the world." As intended, this led to numerous quasi-comedic encounters with border guards and customs officials nonplussed by his inability to produce anything beyond a "world passport." In his 1961 autobiography (*The World Is My Country*), Davis describes his normal predicament in the following terms: "I had no papers which would permit me to enter any other country... Here I called myself a citizen of the world, but I was being told by national bureaucrats either to seek asylum on another planet, die, become a perpetual mariner living in international waters, or go to jail permanently."

His most successful stunts took place in the fall of 1948. At that time, the United Nations General Assembly was meeting in the Palais de Chaillot in Paris. The grounds of the Palais had been declared "international territory" by the French government, and Garry Davis—in his mind quite legally as a "citizen of the world"—pitched a tent on those grounds. Unfortunately for Davis, he attracted less sympathy from the U.N. delegates than attention from the Parisian press: he was declared by U.N. officials to be a trespasser, and the Paris police were called in to haul him back to "French territory." Soon released from jail, on November 19, with the connivance and assistance of Robert Sarrazac and Albert Camus, Davis appeared in the gallery of the General Assembly meeting hall and commenced a speech of admonition to the delegates for neglecting the true interests of the "people of the world." Immediately hustled away by the Paris police, Davis' speech was completed for him by Robert Sarrazac, a former leader of the French resistance during the Nazi occupation.

The following summer, Davis, as "World Citizen Number 1," was the featured speaker at a world government rally, attended by 15,000 people, in the Vélodrome d'Hiver in Paris. This was followed by his address to a standing-room-only meeting at the Salle Pleyel. Written and telegraphed greetings were read from Albert Einstein, Albert Schweitzer, Sir John Boyd-Orr and many British MPs. Davis was supported on the speaker's platform by Albert Camus,

André Breton, and several other prominent Frenchmen. This event marked the high point of his success. Afterwards, he settled down to more conventional methods of publicity and proselytization. In 1953, he founded the World Service Authority to issue "world passports" (not recognized as valid by any nation) to those who want them—an organization that carries on to this day.

As suggested by the above brief account, the French (some of them anyway) were especially receptive to Garry Davis's message during the ephemeral post-war world government boom in the latter 1940s. Perhaps this receptivity was partially a function of the fact that France had been occupied by German military forces from the French surrender in June 1940 to the liberation of France in late 1944. The French people were therefore especially conscious of the fact that totalitarian oppression of a nation is more likely to come about as a consequence of its being defeated by another nation, than it is to come about as a consequence of that nation's participation in a world government.

It will never be known with certainty whether a genuine world government would have been founded in 1945 if it had not been for the ideological conflict between the Soviet Union and the Western capitalist nations. We will be much preoccupied, later in this book, with the economic impediment to world government, and that particular impediment was almost as important in 1945 as it is today. The economic impediment alone might well have precluded genuine world government in 1945, even if the Soviet Union had been a democratic capitalist nation similar to the United States, Britain, France and others. And even aside from the economic impediment, there is the basic issue of nationalism which, according to some, would be virtually as important as it is now even if all the nations of the world were extremely homogeneous in terms of economics, politics, religion, culture, language, etc. Be that as it may, certainly the most dramatic and obvious impediment to genuine world government in the postwar years was the increasingly hostile confrontation between the Soviet Union and the Western democracies—the rapidly developing Cold War.

While a virulent ideological controversy over the respective virtues and vices of democratic capitalism versus communistic socialism set the stage, the immediate impetus to the rapid degeneration of international relations after World War II was the status of the Eastern European nations which had been overrun by Soviet military forces during the final phase of the War: the Baltic nations, Poland, Czechoslovakia, Hungary, Rumania, and Bulgaria. In the calmer hindsight of today, it is widely accepted that the communization of the Eastern European nations was not in fact part of a detailed plan whose objective was the attainment of Russian global hegemony within a brief period of time. It is now seen as more of a defensive maneuver than an offensive maneuver: Russia had just suffered a devastating invasion by Nazi Germany (only the most recent of a long series of invasions from the West throughout Russian history), and Stalin wanted communist governments in the Eastern European nations to provide a "buffer zone" against possible future repetitions. Be that as it may, the distinction between military offense and military defense is often rather subtle.

Nor was the communist threat confined to the Soviet Union and the Eastern European nations. The Soviet Union also took control of a substantial part of defeated Germany (East Germany) through its militarily enforced establishment of the German Democratic Republic. In Asia, several nations were communized in the latter 1940s: North Vietnam, North Korea, and most importantly China. These communizations were carried out by indigenous movements without direct support of Soviet troops, but with the assistance of arms and other war material provided by the Soviet Union. It all looked very much like what had gone on in Western Europe during the rapid ascent of Nazi Germany in the latter 1930s. An effective response to those inclined to argue in the postwar years that Stalin, Mao and the other leaders of the communist nations were not *really* serious about communizing the entire world was: "That's what they said about Hitler!"

In 1947, U.S. President Harry Truman proposed that the world communist movement be "contained" until such time as it desists from its perverse, misguided, and extremely hazardous global messianic mission. The containment policy, also known as the Truman Doctrine, remained a cornerstone of Western foreign policy throughout the long and perilous decades of the Cold War. In its early years, containment involved military assistance to the eventually victorious noncommunist forces in Greece and Turkey, the Berlin airlift, the Korean War, worldwide stationing of American military forces, and the nuclear arms race. World War III seemed just around the corner, and it would be generated by the same sort of geopolitical-ideological conflict that had generated World War II—only this time the villain would be communism instead of fascism.

The tensions introduced into international relations by the strategic maneuverings of the two superpowers, the United States and the Soviet Union, each espousing radically different and diametrically opposed ideologies, were drastically exacerbated by the rapid escalation of the nuclear peril. The Soviet Union exploded its first atomic bomb in 1949, thus terminating the short-lived U.S. monopoly in nuclear weapons. Hardly had atomic bombs been perfected when they were superceded by hydrogen bombs of far greater destructive power. Both the United States and the Soviet Union soon accumulated thousands of nuclear devices. In the latter 1950s and early 1960s, the competition between the superpowers turned to so-called "delivery systems"—especially to the development of nuclear-tipped long-range missiles equipped with very accurate inertial guidance systems. Prior to the development of these missiles, nuclear weapons could have been delivered by conventional bombers of the type that had been used in World War II. World War II had clearly demonstrated that even with highly effective air defense, it was impossible to completely avert bombing attacks by a determined enemy. Therefore, by the early 1950s, the possibility of mass destruction of the major cities of the world by airborne nuclear bombing was no longer a nightmare of the distant future—it was rather an existent reality. People everywhere in the world took a deep breath, reassured themselves with the thought (hope?) that no one would be stupid enough to start a nuclear war, and carried on as before. But the added psychic strain took its toll.

Among the casualties was any sort of rational thinking about world government. Fear and anxiety ruled out any degree of mental flexibility and imagination with respect to the concept. Both the opponents of world government (the vast majority) and the proponents of world government (the tiny majority) could imagine no world government other than an all-powerful state entity that would assume a complete and total monopoly over any and all nuclear weapons, as well as any and all "conventional" heavy weaponry. Opponents of world government were convinced that such an all all-powerful entity would very quickly produce a global totalitarian condition as bad as anything recently witnessed in the Nazi Germany of Adolf Hitler and the Soviet Union of Joseph Stalin. If the proponents of world government had any qualms on this score, they kept them to themselves. In their view, the basic survival of humanity took precedence over the possibility of tyranny. Not to mention the fact that as bad as global tyranny might be, the only thing worse would be the proliferation of local tyrannies over the entire face of the globe in the aftermath of a nuclear holocaust. No blueprint for a limited world government was ever considered, as the Cold War grew and matured, either by the opponents or the proponents of world government. The oppressive tensions of the period effectively shut down the reasoning and judgmental faculties of the human race—at least insofar as these faculties applied to international relations. Even highly sophisticated academic writers could not rise above either-or, black-or-white, night-versus-day thinking.

Gerard Mangone's influential book, *The Idea and Practice of World Government* (Columbia University Press, 1951), distilled the final postwar verdict on world government: a fine and noble idea in principle, but (alas) thoroughly impractical in the real world owing to the great strength of ideological preconceptions and nationalistic prejudices. The negative verdict on world government enunciated by Mangone rapidly achieved consensus status among the vast majority of professional academics, political leaders, and rank-and-file citizens. The basic problem, according to Mangone, is the absence of sufficient consensus within humanity on what constitutes a just and legitimate social order:

> If a structure of world government is to be imagined, then its size, strength and shape will be conditioned by the social order it intends to establish. Should there be a genuine consensus among the members on the hierarchy of values within such a community, the coercive element will be minimized; if but little consensus exists, an autocratic leadership would be the obvious recourse for universal conformity.

But from whence would come the most urgent pressures for "universal conformity," pressures sufficiently urgent to require "autocratic leadership"? From a variety of sources, answers Mangone, not least of which is the communist leadership of the Soviet Union and its allied nations:

> Racists, for example, who rant of "naturally" inferior people, demand every means to compel such a status; the Crusaders, on capturing Jerusalem in 1099, to attest the superior morality of the Christian faith, massacred all the Moslems and

burned the Jews alive; and Marxists, certain of the inevitable "victory of the proletariat," are painstaking in their efforts to assure the fall of the bourgeoisie.

This sentence lumps together the likes of Adolf Hitler, a racist who instigated (among other things) the genocide of the European Jews, a genocide involving approximately six million murders, on grounds of racial purity, the Christian Crusaders who in 1099 engaged in mass slaughter on grounds of religious purity, and the mid-century communist leadership who would, given the opportunity, happily engineer a massive extermination throughout the world of opponents of communism, on grounds of ideological purity. Of the three, obviously it was the communist leadership who represented for Mangone the most immediate threat. The Nazi regime in Germany had just been dislodged by the massive bloodbath of World War II, Adolf Hitler and his chief henchmen had been physically eliminated, and the German people, under military occupation, were highly receptive to re-education on the matter of racial toleration. The crusading spirit of militant European Christianity had been pretty much extinct for well over 500 years. As of 1951, only the communist leadership constituted a real and present danger.

I do not dispute Mangone's judgment that the mid-twentieth-century communist leadership, owing to its ideological fanaticism, was capable of prodigious slaughter in pursuit of what they imagined would be a socialist quasi-utopia. There is no question that individuals such as Joseph Stalin and Mao Tse-tung had been sufficiently brutalized by their respective struggles for power that they would have outdone Adolf Hitler in the area of mass murder—had they been given the opportunity. What Mangone does not explain is precisely how the formation of a world state would have presented the likes of Joseph Stalin and Mao Tse-tung with the opportunity to fulfill their dreams of mass extermination of all the bourgeoisie and their allies. It would depend on the nature of the world state. As argued herein, there is nothing inherently impossible about the concept of a limited world government in which member nations would maintain their own military forces as safeguards against externally imposed totalitarianism and mass exterminations. Mangone simply assumes that any world state would be sufficiently powerful to impose its will on every member nation. Indeed, the same was assumed by communist ideologues on the other side, who viewed themselves as the likely target of extermination programs (such as that implemented in Nazi-occupied Russia during World War II) should a world state be established.

THE SOVIET DESIGN FOR A WORLD STATE

This section takes its title from the title of a book by Elliot R. Goodman, published in 1960 by Columbia University Press, at a time when the Cold War between East and West had fully matured. Although the title of Goodman's book would have served well as the title of a paperback or pamphlet expressing rabidly anticommunist viewpoints, it was in fact a very sedate and polished academic work based on Goodman's Ph.D. dissertation at Columbia University.

Goodman marshaled a prodigious quantity of documentary evidence to demonstrate that the Soviet leadership had always, from the beginning of its control over Russia and the USSR in 1918, envisioned a worldwide socialist republic as the final destination of human civilization. This material was presented in a calm, lucid and intelligent manner. Still, the basic message of the book was the same as in any rabidly anticommunist pamphlet of the period: It is absolutely essential that the West be fully aware of, and take adequate precautions against, the dire menace represented by Soviet-led international communism.

Although Goodman's book adhered generally to prevailing standards of dispassionate scholarly discourse, the extreme fear and loathing of the communist social system which underlay it was occasionally apparent—and nowhere more so than in the book's title. Specifically, the word "design," in this context, is a seriously misleading misnomer. This word implies a comprehensive, consistent, and carefully thought out objective, together with a comprehensive, consistent, and carefully thought out plan for achieving the objective. But as Goodman's book makes abundantly clear, the Soviet leadership, even at its most dictatorial and aggressive level during the ascendancy of Joseph Stalin, never had anything more than a very fuzzy and imprecise notion of what the socialist world state would consist of, and never had anything more than a very fuzzy and imprecise notion about how this socialist world state would come into being. A more accurate title for Goodman's book would have been *The Soviet Notion of a World State*. Of course, as a title, *The Soviet Design for a World State* has a much more ominous feeling about it. Perhaps this title was selected to enhance sales of the book, which were no doubt more abundant than is normally the case for an academic book published by a university press.

As of 1960, and for many long years afterward, the typical image in the mind of the average noncommunist of a Soviet-dominated world state would have been horrific in the extreme. The empirical basis of the image was the nightmarish condition within the Soviet Union during the worst years of Stalin's dictatorship in the late 1930s, at which time the veritably psychotic dictator sent literally millions of people to their deaths either by execution or debilitation in the slave labor camps of the gulag archipelago. Take this terrifying image of a single dictator, armed with immense personal power and awash in rampant paranoia—and apply it to the entire world. Nowhere in the entire world would one be safe from nocturnal visits from the secret police, separation from one's family, mental and physical torture, condemnation at drumhead trials, and unjustifiable and unreasonable imprisonment or execution. This chilling vision of unparalleled and unbridled tyranny was realistically depicted in George Orwell's famous novel *1984*, which gave the Western noncommunist world a grim glimpse at its probable condition under a Soviet-style regime.

There was a kernel of validity in this concept, and it was this: Joseph Stalin had been sufficiently brutalized by his long struggle to achieve absolute personal power within the Soviet Union that, during the few years that separated the end of World War II in 1945 from his death in 1953, had Soviet military control of every nation in the world been achieved similar to the control exercised over the Eastern European nations overrun by the Soviet army in the wake of Nazi retreat, then a situation of utter horror would have been the inevitable result. Stalin would have sent tens of millions, perhaps hundreds of millions, to their doom in an insane effort to safeguard his personal power against all conceivable threats. Stalin would have outdone Adolf Hitler, not to mention all the despots and tyrants of ancient and medieval times, from Caligula to Genghis Khan, in the matter of mass murder. Not just the bourgeoisie and all their allies, sympathizers and supporters would have gone into the flames, but great chunks of the Soviet political and military elite—the ruling class—would have gone as well. There is no doubt that in his later years Joseph Stalin became a monster, and had such a monster ruled the world, the consequences would have been horrific.

Most students of the political and military situation immediately following World War II would agree that there was extremely little chance that Stalin could have achieved absolute personal power throughout the world within what was left of his lifetime. In those years, direct Soviet military control was taken over some Eastern European nations, and the Soviet Union provided some military assistance to communist movements in other nations, most notably in China. But the expansion of Soviet power during that period was still a long, long way from a Soviet-ruled world state. Aside from the fact that four years of desperate warfare with Nazi Germany had left the Soviet Union greatly weakened, there was less chance of support from outside the Soviet Union. The most fluid situations prevailed in Western European nations that had experienced Nazi occupation. But the internal communist movements in those nations were much weaker than they might have been, since Stalin's personal orchestration of the purges in the USSR in the latter 1930s had drastically discredited communism throughout the noncommunist world. For all his faults, Stalin was not stupid: he could certainly perceive this reality in the years following World War II, and therefore it is very doubtful that he wasted any appreciable amount of time daydreaming about personally ruling the world and slaughtering with impunity hundreds of millions of his actual and potential enemies. The image of a world state under the dictatorship of Joseph Stalin was taken far more seriously outside the USSR than it was within the USSR.

Now, it is certainly true that the Soviet leadership, particularly in the early years of the USSR, issued numerous appeals for a "World Socialist Republic." In the minds of noncommunists around the world, this phrase conjured up images of the entire world under the brutal dominion of a socialistic Russian empire. Upon the descent of the USSR into the nightmare of Stalinist totalitarianism in the 1930s, these images became even more horrific and terrifying. They reached a peak in the 1945-1955 decade during which Stalin as a world dictator seemed fully possible—a dictator who would have been as bad as, if not worse than, Adolf Hitler. But the fact is that in the minds of the Soviet leadership—before, during and after Stalin's era—the term "World Socialist Republic" did not signify or imply a world of nations subservient to Russia. The Soviet leadership never entertained a vision of Russian world hegemony comparable to Hitler's vision of German world hegemony. In any event, Russian or German world hegemony, had it become a fact, need not and probably would not have involved a world state. It would rather have involved the Russian or German leadership appointing the high officials of all other nations, even though these nations would have remained formally independent.

Soviet interest in a world state stemmed from the fact that the great master himself, Karl Marx, had prophesied a *worldwide* proletarian revolution within the fairly proximate future. The revolution might start in one of the metropolitan European nations, or perhaps in a nation on the European periphery such as Russia, or perhaps even in one of the colonial nations such as India. But wherever and however it started, Marx imagined that the proletarian revolution would quickly spread, like an uncontrollable wildfire, throughout the entire world. Within a few years, according to the prophecy, the entire world would have experienced the proletarian revolution, the central objective of which would be the abolition of capitalism and the institution of socialism.

Karl Marx devoted rather little attention to nations, as such. The only interesting questions involving nations, to his mind, were: (1) in which nation would the worldwide proletarian revolution commence? (2) once commenced, how would it spread out among other nations? He was highly impatient with and unsympathetic toward any sort of nationalistic thinking, because he viewed it as needlessly complicating the real issue of capitalist exploitation of the proletariat, and thereby delaying the revolutionary abrogation of this exploitation. Nationalism was regarded by Marx as an artificial allegiance and loyalty hypocritically fostered by capitalists as a means of increasing their own wealth through economic exploitation of colonies and/or the sale of armaments, munitions and other military supplies to national governments. Nationalism and militarism were seen as derivative side-effects of capitalism. Abolishing capitalism would cut the fuel supply to nationalism and militarism, leading to their rapid extinction as well.

The founder of communism had no special interest in a world state for its own sake. He would have regarded a world state as especially unlikely in a capitalist world owing to capitalism's natural propensity toward nationalism and militarism—the equivalent in the political sphere to competition among business enterprises in the economic sphere. But the world state was not an end in itself; rather it would merely be a side-effect of the worldwide abolition of capitalism. Marx and Engels concluded the *Communist Manifesto* with the appeal: "Workers of the world, unite—you have nothing to lose but your chains!" The "chains" referred to were those of economic exploitation by the capitalist class, not those imposed by the continuing propensity of the independent nation-state system to waste economic resources on armaments, and to generate wars which massacred millions of proletarians while destroying masses of economic resources.

Marx's predicted demise ("withering away") of the state following the worldwide proletarian revolution's successful substitution of a planned socialist economy for the anarchic market capitalist economy is today widely viewed among noncommunists as a prime example of his unrealistic and naive attitude. Had Marx been correct that a worldwide proletarian revolution would establish a worldwide socialist economy and a worldwide state structure, then he might well also have been correct that the state structure would have simply disintegrated and faded away. "World state" would have been followed by "no state." But today the idea of human civilization advancing and progressing without any sort of operating central authority, either at the regional, national or international level, seems totally fantastic and utopian. Elliot Goodman also points out the apparent inconsistency in the Marx forecast that the state would wither away and there would be no political authority with the power to compel obedience to the social will, and yet at the same time the global economy would somehow be guided by comprehensive economic planning. This is represented as still another clearcut demonstration of Marx's habitual fuzzy-mindedness.

In his lifetime, Marx thought that the Paris Commune, a revolutionary movement in the city of Paris occasioned by the hardships attendant upon France's defeat in the Franco-Prussian War of 1870-1871, might be the starting point of a global proletarian revolution. He thought briefly that the example of the Commune might ignite socialist revolution throughout the entire world. The Paris Commune, however, was quickly suppressed by French military forces from outside Paris, and it soon became apparent that the revolutionary opportunity had passed. Once again, Marx had to accept the unpalatable fact (to him) that the coming global proletarian revolution might be a very long time in coming.

Marx was long dead when Lenin, Trotsky and other Bolsheviks, taking advantage of revolutionary turmoil in war-ravaged Russia, gained control of the Russian government in November 1917. During the early years of the revolutionary transformation of Russia, the Bolshevik leadership imagined that worldwide proletarian revolution was imminent. Unfortunately for them, no such revolution occurred. However, these leaders were certainly more successful than the leaders of the Paris Commune had been. While the latter had mostly been executed or imprisoned following the collapse of the Commune, the Bolsheviks—albeit after a long and bitter struggle against both internal opponents and a certain amount of foreign intervention—eventually gained secure and permanent control of a major nation with a very substantial population and by far the largest land area of any nation in the world. The Bolsheviks became the Communist Party of the USSR, the de facto leaders of the newly established Union of Soviet Socialist Republics.

The various non-Russian components of that empire, including the Ukraine, Kazakhstan, etc., were designated "Soviet Socialist Republics." The first USSR constitution envisioned other nations (England, France, Germany, etc.) joining the USSR as Soviet Socialist Republics, upon successful completion of their respective proletarian revolutions. In those early years, the Soviet leadership did not expect that these other revolutions would be assisted by Soviet military power. It was imagined that these revolutions would be completed successfully by internal means alone. Had that scenario actually occurred, the English SSR, the French SSR, the German SSR, etc., would clearly not have been dominated by the Russian SSR in the same way that the Ukrainian SSR, the Kazakh SSR, etc., were dominated by the Russian SSR. The domination of the latter was based on the same military occupation that had characterized the tsarist era. Had the English SSR, the French SSR, the German SSR, etc., come about through domestic revolutions, they would have been at least as powerful as the Russian SSR and in no way under the domination of the Russian SSR. Nevertheless, it would have been preferable for the Russian SSR to have English, French and German SSRs in the West, as opposed to their existing capitalist-dominated states, because then there would have been less danger of invasion to suppress the burgeoning socialist threat. This perceived danger was not in fact entirely chimerical. After all, there had been a certain amount of foreign intervention on the side of anti-revolutionary forces during the Civil War of 1918-1921, although the Western nations were too exhausted after World War I to undertake a sufficient amount of intervention to affect the outcome. Goodman (pp. 34-35) quotes from a manifesto issued in 1920 by the Second Comintern Congress: "The Communist International has proclaimed the cause of Soviet Russia as its own. The international proletariat will not sheath its sword until Soviet Russia is incorporated as a link in the World Federation of Soviet Republics." Use of the phrase "incorporated as a link" suggests that the Soviet leadership in the early 1920s wanted a world federation not so much as a means of establishing Russian hegemony throughout the world, but rather merely as a means of ensuring the continued existence of socialism in Russia and the USSR.

Goodman's book explores in considerable documentary detail, from the foundation of the USSR to the latter 1950s, the persistent tension between the universalist aspiration of Soviet communism, and the Soviet leadership's recognition that national distinctions would inevitably play an important role in the success or failure of this aspiration. Certainly it is true that the Soviet leadership took the attitude that "all is fair in love and (class) war" and that "the ends justify the means." By customary moral standards, they were highly deficient in thought and deed. However, in fairness, it must be conceded that there were some important extenuating circumstances. First, they sincerely believed—at least at first—that socialism was hugely preferable to capitalism in terms of overall, long-term human welfare. Second, they were genuinely apprehensive that the huge capitalist outside world would one day mount an invasion to crush out the dangerous sparks of socialist revolution being harbored by the USSR. They were in a quasi-desperate frame of mind, and this frame of mind explains some of their behavior even if it does not justify it.

There were tensions inside the USSR as the Soviet leadership attempted to co-opt the non-Russian peoples into the communist world mission, while at the same time maintaining tight control by the Russian majority within the Union. Their success in this was smaller than many outsiders realized during the heyday of the Soviet national buildup in the 1920s and 1930s. Goodman's section on "Tsarist and Soviet Russian Nationalism Compared" makes the point that there was an ideological ideal incorporated into Soviet Russian nationalism, but aside from this it was pretty much the same as pre-Soviet Russian nationalism. There were also tensions outside the USSR as the Soviet leadership attempted to enlist nationalistic motivations, especially desires of native populations for liberation from the colonial empires established by several Western European nations, in support of both the Soviet Union and the goal of worldwide proletarian revolution. Once again, their success in this was less than it appeared to many during the heyday of Soviet expansionism in the 1940s through the 1960s.

Hitler's long-term objective, which even he probably realized could not be attained during his own lifetime, was strong German hegemony over the entire world. As mentioned earlier, had this objective been attained, a world state need not and probably would not have been involved. The other nations of the world would have been formally independent, but German military power would have been deployed to make these formally independent nations puppets in the same manner as the Nazi-occupied nations during World War II had been puppets. Although this is admittedly a somewhat speculative point, it is probably true that even at the height of his power Stalin probably never lusted after Russian world hegemony in the same way that Hitler had lusted after German world hegemony. More likely, in his final years Stalin desired only a relative power situation which would have made the USSR almost completely immune against foreign invasion and conquest. It is significant that when the Eastern European nations went under Soviet military occupation at the end of World War II, they were not made SSRs and incorporated into the USSR, although they might well have been had Stalin been genuinely interested in establishing a Russian-dominated world state. This point is perhaps worthy of some elaboration.

Stalin himself, it is clear, eventually degenerated into a monster, as abundantly demonstrated by the Great Terror during the 1930s. But in the early going of Stalin's rise to absolute power, during the 1920s and into the early 1930s, he defeated his rivals by means of open argumentative competition within the small circle of high Soviet leaders (the Central Committee of the Communist Party of the USSR), and the rivals defeated in the voting of the Central Committee were removed from power and consigned to "early retirement." At this point, Stalin probably did not think explicitly about the possible need to have tens of thousands of people executed in order to achieve impregnable personal control over the Soviet government. But later on, as Stalin's power gradually grew, the Central Committee more and more approved his decisions not so much on the basis of having been persuaded as on the basis of fear. In order to ensure the continuation of his own personal dominance within the Soviet leadership, Stalin eventually (from the mid-1930s onwards) found it both possible and "necessary" to physically eliminate, by execution or exile to concentration camps, more and more rivals and potential rivals. Eventually the direct and indirect victims of his lust for unchallenged personal power numbered in the millions.

After World War II, Soviet military forces overran a number of Eastern European nations. Stalin's power at that point in the international arena was somewhat comparable to his power in the mid-1920s in the Soviet Union. Had Stalin achieved power over the entire world comparable to the power which he achieved over the Soviet Union in the latter 1930s, clearly a nightmarish condition would have ensued as he attempted to physically eliminate any and every actual and potential threat to his continued absolute power. But Stalin never got to that point in the world arena. That he did not was not due to any scruples, squeamishness or timidity on Stalin's part. It was rather due to external forces over which Stalin had no personal control, and over which he never gained personal control. It was unlikely that Stalin in the 1920s was in conscious pursuit of the tremendous power he later acquired within the Soviet Union—the power to unilaterally and without consultation order the imprisonment, enslavement, or execution of virtually any and every person resident in the Soviet Union. That power evolved gradually, one step at a time, without a conscious long-term plan. When it finally got to the level it eventually did, Stalin was probably somewhat amazed and horrified. But by that time he had the tiger by the tail. If he let go, i.e., if he displayed any weakness or lack of resolution, then those formerly terrified of him would quickly have risen up to kill him, for fear of what he might do in the future if allowed to continue in power.

In the same way, in the late 1940s with several Eastern European nations governed by communist regimes installed by the Soviet occupying forces, it is unlikely that Stalin seriously entertained the notion that one day, within his own lifetime, Soviet military forces would be occupying all or most of the nations of the world. After all, he had just seen to what ignominious fate blind ambition had led Hitler. Hitler had failed to recognize that German military strength was insufficient to attain direct power even within the nations of Western Europe, let alone over the entire world. He had gambled that he could divide and conquer in the classic imperial manner, and complete the conquest of a large area one nation at a time. The gamble worked for a while, but eventually the odds caught up with Hitler, and he became enmeshed in a gigantic war which Germany did not have the numerical resources to win. Stalin did not want to make the same mistake. When the communist insurrection in Greece was put down, and when the communist parties in France and Italy failed to win majorities in the respective national governments, Stalin (and his successors) desisted from any short-term tactics aimed at the quick establishment of worldwide Russian hegemony.

In the years prior to and during World War I, pacifists discussed notions such as a "United States of Europe" or a "United States of the World." Revisionist socialists such as Karl Kautsky considered such federations possible and possibly desirable. Lenin, Trotsky and other Bolshevik leaders generally derided such ideas as utopian nonsense (because capitalist nations are obliged to compete with one another in much the same way that individual capitalists are obliged to compete with one another) and/or as reactionary (because a federation of capitalist nations might be a way to forestall the international wars the suffering from which would eventually generate proletarian revolution—in the same way that the Franco-Prussian War led to the Paris Commune). The motivations behind such notions were regarded as reactionary—but the objective was unachievable. From the beginning of the Soviet era, any and all world state proposals emanating from the noncommunist world were viewed with deep suspicion and distrust by the Soviet leadership. These proposals were invariably perceived as disingenuous efforts to form a super-alliance of capitalist nations for purposes of eliminating the potential threat to world capitalism represented by the existence of socialist nations and/or socialist revolutionary movements in capitalist nations. At the same time, the Soviet leadership always remained quite complacent that nothing would ever come of these efforts, because the capitalistic elite of the world was too short-sighted, stupid and disunited to accomplish something that might well save them from ultimate disaster. This attitude was adopted very early in the history of the USSR. For example, Goodman quotes an appraisal of the recently established League of Nations contained in a 1919 "elementary textbook of Communist knowledge" by N. I. Bukharin and E. Preobrazhenskii entitled *The ABC of Communism*:

> The League of Nations is something in the nature of an attempt to create a monstrous world-wide trust, that would embrace our entire globe and exploit the whole world and which, on the other hand, would everywhere crush the working-class movement and its revolution with utmost ferocity. All talk to the effect that the League was established to insure peace is so much trash... However, the League of Nations will not be able to fulfill its two aims: the organization of the whole world economy into a single trust and the universal suppression of revolution. The great powers do not have sufficient unity to accomplish this.

As we have seen in the previous section of this chapter, interest in world government reached a short-lived peak in the years just following the end of World War II. In the noncommunist West, conservatives warned that the establishment of a world government could and probably would lead to the final triumph of international communism. Meanwhile, communist ideologues in the Soviet Union pronounced an equally negative warning to the effect that the establishment of a world government could and probably would lead to the final triumph of international capitalism. For example, Goodman quotes the following from a postwar Soviet essay on international law by E. A. Korovin:

> The dreams of Eden and Bevin [regarding the establishment of world government to reduce the peril of nuclear war] are quite removed from reality; they bring to mind the talk at the end of the First World War about "super-imperialism" and "superstate," about the gradual development of the League of Nations into a "world parliament" and so on—these were the arguments with which journalists and publicists, predominantly of the social reformist type, used to console both themselves and others. The chief fault of these theories lies in their authors' inability, either willingly or unwillingly, to understand the simple truth that the roots of aggressive nationalism which the "world parliament" would supposedly check, lie in the very nature of capitalist society... It is scarcely possible that the contemporary gravediggers of sovereignty are so naive as to believe in earnest that peace and harmony on earth can be obtained by the creation of a world parliament... Is it not true that at the bottom of these political

fantasies lies an extremely shrewd calculation—in the realm of political arithmetic and voting games? The eager troubadours of a world parliament are inspired by the thought of the voting majority in this new organ through which they can dictate their will to the rest of mankind.

What Korovin has in mind here is that even with the postwar accessions to the communist camp (the Eastern European nations, China, and so on), the noncommunist nations still considerably outnumbered the communist nations. Thus if a vote were taken on the question of capitalism versus socialism in a world parliament operating under the one-nation-one-vote principle, the vote (it was assumed) would go against socialism. It never occurred to E. A. Korovin, just as it never occurred to the multitude of other world government critics both in the noncommunist West and the communist East, that a world government might be established which would remain completely neutral toward the issue of capitalism versus socialism, just as most national governments remain completely neutral on the issue of one religion against another religion. It also never occurred to him, or to the others, that a world federation might be established which allowed member nations to peacefully depart the federation if it attempted to impose capitalism (or socialism) on all member nations, against the will of the populations of those nations. Finally, it never occurred to him, or to the others, that a world federation might be established which allowed member nations to retain their own military forces, as a guarantee of independence should it be desired at some future time. The mind of E. A. Korovin was just as impenetrably closed as were the minds of his fellow critics of world government in both the communist East and the noncommunist West.

Soviet opposition to, and derisive criticism of, extended to all proposals for either worldwide or regional or cultural federations of nations which would retain their capitalistic economies. Examples include the post-World War I League of Nations, the pan-Europe movement of 1920s and early 1930s calling for a European Union, Clarence Streit's proposal for a Federation of the Western Democracies, the post-World War II United Nations, any and all subsequent proposals for a strengthened United Nations, as well as any and all proposals for world government outside of or beyond the United Nations. All of these were seen as malevolent strategic maneuvers intended to envelop and destroy the socialist threat in the Soviet Union and elsewhere. The threat of international war, according to the orthodox Party line, comes from the capitalist economic system, not from the sovereign nation-state system. Throughout its history, the Soviet Union never endeavored nor attempted to create a world state; it never developed a "design" for a world state. It did, however, consistently pursue the objective, by direct and indirect means, of worldwide communization. If worldwide communization had led to a world state, that would have been merely incidental. The Soviet Union's motivations in pursuing this objective were a combination of messianic concern for worldwide human welfare (which would have been quite commendable if it had not been so dangerously misguided), and paranoiac apprehension that if this objective were not achieved, the Soviet Union would perpetually remain a potential target for invasion by hostile capitalist nations. In the latter motivation, the Soviet leadership was heeding the principle urged by Macbeth's wife on her reluctant husband: "It has become necessary for you to kill the king—otherwise he will kill you!"

POSTWAR WESTERN DESIGNS FOR A WORLD STATE

In a very general sense, there have been only two fundamental technological advances in the history of weaponry. The first was the application of chemical reactions such as the ignition of gunpowder. Very soon thereafter the principal weapon of the typical foot soldier was some sort of a firearm, as opposed to a sword, spear, club, or bow and arrow. At the same time, cannons replaced catapults as a means of inflicting damage from a distance. The second fundamental advance in the history of weaponry occurred in 1945 with the application of nuclear reactions. This advance was manifested in the atomic bombings of Hiroshima and Nagasaki. The earlier application of chemical reactions led to a quantum jump in the destructiveness of weaponry, relative to what had been managed by applying inertial forces and sharpened instruments. The more recent application of nuclear reactions also led to a quantum jump in the destructiveness of weaponry, relative to what may be managed by applying chemical reactions. The power of contemporary nuclear weapons is measured in megatons: one megaton being the explosive force of 1,000,000 tons of TNT. It is difficult to imagine what the detonation of one or more hydrogen bombs over a large city would accomplish, but some clue may be derived from the thousands of photographs of the devastation wrought by the relatively puny nuclear devices detonated over Hiroshima and Nagasaki. The difficulty of imagining the potential destructiveness of nuclear war lies not merely in the gigantic scale of the disaster, but in humanity's natural psychological aversion to contemplating such a terrifying possibility.

Nevertheless, in the grim light of what had happened to Hiroshima and Nagasaki, enough people forced themselves to think long enough about nuclear war for a significant forward surge in the pacifist belief that the hazards of warfare—at this point in history if not at earlier points—were now greater than the hazards of tyranny. This in turn created a surge of interest in and plans for world government. Unfortunately for the long-term prospects of humanity, the surge soon dissipated, a victim primarily of the emerging Cold War confrontation between the communist and noncommunist blocs of nations. However, even after the Cold War had eliminated any practical possibility of a world government being established in the immediate future, a very small minority of the population retained their faith in the concept, and continued their work on it and toward it. There does not exist a compilation of post-World War II world government proposals comparable to that of Wynner and Lloyd's compilation of pre-World War II proposals. However, it seems safe to say that the accumulation of proposals in the postwar period was at least as great as it had been in the interwar period (1918-1939). There are probably dozens of such proposals—although many of them are either entirely unpublished or else published in very obscure sources. The recent development of the World Wide Web has provided a new means of dissemination of such proposals—although the sheer volume of material available on the Web probably precludes these proposals from having any appreciable impact unless they are also available in traditional print media.

Obviously a comprehensive survey of post-World War II world government proposals is far beyond the time and patience of both this author and the reader. My purpose, therefore, will be limited to trying to show that the common conception of the "typical" world government proposal of the postwar era, among both proponents and opponents of world government, was (and remains) substantially different from the proposal being put forward in this book for a Federal Union of Democratic Nations. The "typical" proposal envisions a far more centralized and powerful world government than the Federal Union proposal. It has been demonstrated by postwar history that the fear of nuclear war—however terrible that war would be if it were to occur—is *not* sufficient to impel humanity to establish a world government along the lines of the "typical" proposal. World federalists bemoan this fact, and take it as evidence of the sadly limited judgmental faculties of humanity. But it remains, nevertheless, a fact. To those with a strong, genuine and realistic aspiration toward world government, it should at this point be quite clear and obvious that the thing to do is to scale back the concept of world government to a *limited* world government. Such a government would not be able to eliminate the threat of nuclear war in the short run. However, it *would* alter the international situation in such a way that the long-term threat of nuclear war would be appreciably less than it would be if the sovereign nation-state system of today persists unchanged into the indefinite future.

Although post-World War II world government proposals are highly diverse, most of them adhere in general terms to the Declaration of the first World Congress of the World Movement for World Federal Government (WMWFG), held in 1947 at Montreux, Switzerland. The Declaration puts forward six essential characteristics of an effective world government, as follows:

1.   Universal membership: The world federal government must be open to all peoples and nations.
2.   Limitations of national sovereignty, and the transfer to the world federal government of such legislative, executive and judicial powers as relate to world affairs.
3.   Enforcement of world law directly on the individual whoever or wherever he may be, within the jurisdiction of the world federal government: guarantee of the rights of man and suppression of all attempts against the security of the federation.
4.   Creation of supranational armed forces capable of guaranteeing the security of the world federal government and of its member states. Disarmament of member nations to the level of their internal policing requirements.

5. Ownership and control by the world federal government of atomic devel-
    opment and of other scientific discoveries capable of mass destruction.
6. Power to raise adequate revenues directly and independently of state taxes.

Interestingly, it is not specified that the world government be subject to democratic control. It is specified, in point 1, that there be "universal membership" in
the sense that membership would be "open" to all the nations of the world.
Nothing is specified, however, with respect to nations that join the world federation and then decide at a later date to withdraw. However, a phrase included in
point 3 ("suppression of all attempts against the security of the federation") may
well be directed against such nations. This would be in line with the well-
remembered fact (in 1947) that one of the first indications of the aggressive
intentions of Nazi Germany and the other fascist nations was their withdrawal
from the League of Nations in the 1930s. At any rate, a "right of withdrawal"
would be essentially meaningless if nations had no armed forces with which to
back up their decision to withdraw from the world federation. And in points 4
and 5, it is clearly specified that the member nations of the world federation
would be deprived of all heavy weaponry (i.e., weaponry beyond the requirements of "internal policing"), both nuclear and conventional. Obviously, the
present proposal for a Federal Union of Democratic Nations would not constitute
a "world government" as defined in the 1947 Montreux Declaration, because of
the proposal's allowance both for member nations retaining as much in the way
of armaments as they desire, and for member nations being able to freely withdraw from the Federal Union at their own unilateral discretion.

The Declaration set forth very general principles for a world government, but
was unspecific with respect to details. A substantial number of individuals subsequently came forward with more detailed plans. Since it would be impractical to
consider any significant number of these, I will describe only three of the best-
known proposals, which may be taken as "typical" of the entire body of postwar
world government proposals: (1) the proposal of Giuseppe Borgese for a Federal
Republic of the World; (2) the proposal of Grenville Clark and Louis Sohn for a
strengthened United Nations; and (3) the proposal of Philip Isely et al for a
Federation of Earth. These proposals will be compared and contrasted with this
author's proposal for a Federal Union of Democratic Nations. Table 3.2 below
provides a schematic comparison of four world government proposals: the three
"typical" proposals of Borgese, Clark-Sohn, and Isely, and the fourth "atypical"
proposal of the present author. The table sets forth the basic source and nomenclature of each proposal, together with selected information concerning each of
four areas: the legislative branch, the executive branch, the judicial branch, and
enforcement and security.

TABLE 3.2
A Schematic Comparison of Four
Postwar World Government Proposals

1. Giuseppe Borgese

Source	Giuseppe A. Borgese, *Foundations of the World Republic*, Chicago: University of Chicago Press, 1953.
Name	Federal Republic of the World (World Republic) based on a World Constitution.
Legislature	World Council (unicameral) of 99 Councilors, 9 each from 9 Electoral Colleges, plus 18 more from any Electoral College. Councilors elected for 3-year terms from a Federal Convention meeting triannually for one month.
Executive	President elected by majority of two thirds for a term of 6 years by every other Federal Convention. President serves one term only since "no two successive presidents shall originate from the same Region." President appoints Chancellor, who appoints the Cabinet (with President's approval).
Judicial	Grand Tribunal of 60 Justices appointed by President (subject to Council approval) for terms of 15 years with no reappointment: 12 Justices assigned to each of 5 benches.
Enforcement and Security	Control of the armed forces of the Federal Republic of the World is assigned exclusively to a Chamber of Guardians consisting of the President, one ex-President and six Councilmen elected by the Council and Grand Tribunal.

2. Grenville Clark and Louis Sohn

Source	Grenville Clark and Louis B. Sohn, *World Peace through World Law*, third enlarged edition, Cambridge, MA: Harvard University Press, 1966.
Name	United Nations based on a revised, amended and expanded Charter.
Legislature	General Assembly (unicameral) of approximately 600 elected members serving 4-year terms. Larger nations in terms of population have larger number of representatives. Authority confined solely to matters pertaining to disarmament and the maintenance of peace.
Executive	Executive Council (replacing Security Council) as executive arm of strengthened United Nations, consisting of 17 Representatives elected by the General Assembly. Larger nations guaranteed reps in the Executive Council. The 4 largest nations in terms of population each guaranteed 1; 4 of the next 8 largest would have 1 each in rotation. Important issues need a majority of 12 out of 17 for passage.
Judicial	International Court of Justice (existing but with enlarged powers). New U.N. Courts: World Equity Tribunal (elected by the General Assembly); World Conciliation Board.
Enforcement and Security	United Nations Peace Force (World Police Force) with standing component of between 200,000 and 400,000 full-time soldiers.

3. Philip Isely et al

Source	Philip Isely at al, "A Constitution for the Federation of Earth," Lakewood, CO: World Constitution and Parliament Association, last revised 1991.
Name	Federation of Earth based on the Constitution for the Federation of Earth.
Legislature	World Parliament (tricameral): House of Peoples: directly elected by populations for terms of 5 years. House of Nations: between 1 and 3 representatives from each nation appointed by national governments for terms of 5 years. House of Counselors: 200 counselors elected by the other two houses.
Executive	World Executive to consist of a Presidium of five members elected from the membership of the World Parliament for five-year terms, one each from the five Continental Divisions. Each member of the Presidium to rotate into the Presidency of the Presidium for a one-year term. Decisions of the Presidium to be taken by majority vote.
Judicial	World Supreme Court to consist of at least 8 Benches (Human Rights, Criminal Cases, Civil Cases, etc.) staffed by members of the Collegium of World Judges, a group of between 20 to 60 member judges elected by the World Parliament.
Enforcement and Security	Enforcement of world law to be the responsibility of the Office of World Attorneys General and the Commission of Regional World Attorneys. These groups will direct a World Police organization for enforcement of world law on individuals.

4. James Yunker (the author)

Source	James A. Yunker, this volume.
Name	Federal Union of Democratic Nations based on the Federal Union Constitution.
Legislature	Union Chamber of Representatives (unicameral): Union Representatives to be directly elected by the populations of between 100 and 200 electoral districts for terms of 5 years. Legislation must be approved by 60 percent majority on two voting bases: population base and material base.
Executive	Union Chief Executive elected by majority vote of population of entire Federal Union for a ten-year term. Executive branch to consist of nine agencies: Ministry of the Interior, Ministry of Finance, Ministry of Justice, Ministry of Science, Education and Culture, Ministry of Planning, Ministry of External Development, Ministry of Security, Ministry of Non-Union Affairs, World Development Authority.
Judicial	Union High Court composed of 25 Union Justices elected for terms of 25 years by the entire Federal Union population. Terms would be staggered: 5 Union Justices would be elected in each quinquennial Union election.
Enforcement and Security	Ministry of Security to direct a Union Security Force consisting of both units directly maintained by the Federal Union, and units maintained by member nation-states.

All three of the "typical" proposals schematically outlined in the above table had their roots in the heady years just following World War II, when best-selling books and world-renowned scientists, statesmen and humanitarians were proclaiming the need for world government. As described in the earlier section on "The Postwar World Government Boom," Giuseppe Borgese was the secretary of a committee of influential concerned citizens (the Committee to Frame a World Constitution, active from 1946 through 1948) chaired by Robert M. Hutchins, at that time Chancellor of the University of Chicago. Borgese's book *Foundations of the World Republic*, published by the University of Chicago Press in 1953, reflected the committee's deliberations on the urgent need for world government, and contained as an appendix the "Preliminary Draft of a World Constitution" developed by the committee. Grenville Clark and Louis B. Sohn were well-known international lawyers who took upon themselves the task of proposing a revised United Nations charter which would have effectively transformed the organization into a legitimate world government. All three editions of their magisterial tome, *World Peace through World Law* (1958, 1960 and 1966), were published by Harvard University Press. By the later 1960s, the idea of world government had become sufficiently disreputable that there were no further publications of full-fledged advocacies by major university presses.

The Isely proposal is unique among world government proposals in that a serious effort has been made by its originator to implement it in the real world. Philip Isely, a disciple of Gerry Krause (one of the prime movers behind the abortive 1950 "People's World Convention" held in Geneva, Switzerland), has for many years been Secretary-General of the World Constitution and Parliament Association (with headquarters in Lakewood, Colorado). The Association has organized a considerable number of international conferences from the 1960s onwards. One of these conferences, called the second session of the World Constituent Assembly, held at Innsbruck, Austria, in June 1977, ratified the initial version of the Constitution for the Federation of Earth. The document carries the signatures of approximately 150 individuals from many different nations. An amended version was later ratified at the fourth session of the World Constituent Assembly, held at Troia, Portugal, in May 1991, and carries the signatures of well over 200 individuals. Some of the signatories to these versions, such as Linus Pauling of the United States, Tony Benn of the United Kingdom, and Desmond Tutu of South Africa, are well-known figures. However, none of them were authorized representatives of a national government at the time.

Under the terms of the Constitution, a Provisional World Parliament has met on several occasions during the 1980s and 1990s, and has passed a number of legislative bills. World Legislative Bill Number One (Sept. 11, 1982), for example, carries the title: "To Outlaw Nuclear Weapons and Other Weapons of Mass Destruction." The bill specifies the establishment of a World Disarmament Agency (WDA), but enforcement of the WDA's decisions is to be left to political units (cities, counties, provinces, states, etc.) within nations whose national governments have ratified the bill. To date, no national governments have in fact ratified World Legislative Bill Number One. Indeed, it is probably fair to say that despite prodigious effort by Philip Isely over several decades, only a tiny handful of people throughout the contemporary world are even aware of the existence of the World Constitution and Parliament Association and its various affiliates, and of those few, many would categorize the participants in these organizations as lunatic fringe political enthusiasts.

The world government possibility has, to date, been rejected by the overwhelming majority of humanity on grounds that such a government would create such a severe risk of tyranny as to outweigh the countervailing advantage of that it would reduce the probability of disastrous nuclear war. Obviously, the proponents of the three "typical" world government blueprints under consideration here were not completely oblivious to the threat of tyranny, nor did they rely solely upon the proposition that tyranny would be the lesser of two evils, compared to the carnage and destruction of a nuclear world war. All of them endeavored to install various barriers and impediments to tyranny within their plans. For example, they all have in common that the world government would be federal in nature, that the existing structure of national governments would be preserved, that the member nation-states would reserve a certain amount of autonomy and independence, and that their populations would retain certain natural rights not to be infringed by higher levels of government.

They also have in common that there would be a division of power within the supernational government itself, that its authority would be spread over separate legislative, executive, and judicial branches, and that it would be subject to democratic control by the citizens through free, contested elections. In addition, they all incorporate provisions designed to safeguard against any one nation, or small group of nations, becoming dominant within any of the three branches of government. Of course, one extremely important lesson provided by the history of the USSR, especially during the worst period of Stalin's tyrannical dominion, is that there can be a vast gap between formal constitutional provisions of governance, and the reality of governance. Had the formal provisions of the Soviet Union's various constitutions been implemented and observed, the Soviet Union would have been a model of free and open democracy, with commendably strict observance of human rights. As is well known, however, the provisions of the constitutions did not prevent the Soviet Union from being, in reality, an extravagantly totalitarian dictatorship based predominantly upon brute force.

Within any totalitarian regime, there is a separation between one group whose interests are favored and another group whose interests are disfavored. For example, throughout the history of the Soviet Union, the favored group consisted of the high Communist Party elite, and the disfavored group consisted of the rest of the population. A totalitarian regime is worse to the extent that the favored group is small relative to the disfavored group, and to the extent of the gap that separates the welfare of the favored group from that of the disfavored group. We can imagine numerous ways in which a world government might be transformed into a totalitarian regime which favors some particular group (using as a guide all the numerous ways in which various national governments in the past have been transformed into totalitarian regimes). The world government might be "taken over" by the United States, so that the citizens of the United States would be the favored group, and all the rest of the world population would be the disfavored group. Or the world government might be "taken over" by the Russian Federation, to an analogous effect. We might imagine the world government taken over by all members of the white race, or by those of the black race, or by those of the Asiatic race. We might imagine the world government taken over by adherents to any of the Christian religions, or by those to any of the Islamic religions. Of course, none of these scenarios seems particularly plausible, because of the substantial diversity of interests and purposes which exists within any of the above-mentioned groups. For example, Christianity has been subdivided, especially since the Protestant Reformation of the 1500s, into a plethora of jealously independent sects.

But we can also envision the world government being "taken over," through a coup d'etat, by a single megalomaniac individual in the mold of Adolf Hitler or Joseph Stalin. When it comes to a single individual, "diversity of interests and purposes" is not an issue. On the other hand, in order to become securely and permanently established in power, a potential dictator has to enjoy an appreciable measure of support, not just among his small coterie of cronies, but among the general population, even including the "disfavored group." At the height of the Stalin dictatorship, for example, Stalin was insulated from opposition and assassination attempts, not merely through liberal application of terror, but also through the belief of most Soviet citizens of the time that despite his liabilities, Stalin was guiding the nation forward toward a great and glorious future. Of course, Stalin had a cause, of general appeal, which enabled him to gain and maintain a personal stranglehold on the Soviet government: the vision of a socialist quasi-utopia. Equally so, Adolf Hitler had a generally appealing cause (to the German people of his time) which enabled him to gain and maintain a personal stranglehold on the German government during the Third Reich era: the vision of a Germany restored to the dignity and respect it had enjoyed prior to its defeat in World War I.

In pondering the possibility that a potential world government of the future might become an instrument of a megalomaniac dictator along the lines of Adolf Hitler or Joseph Stalin, we might ask whether there is a generally appealing cause which might facilitate such a dictator gaining and maintaining a personal stranglehold on the world government. The advancement of the interests of any particular national population is not such a cause: outside of Germany, Hitler's appeal to German patriotism carried no weight. The advancement of one particular religion is not such a cause: there is too much awareness in the modern world of the multiplicity of religious beliefs for reasonable adherents to any one religious group to seriously believe that they are "God's chosen people." The advancement of the interests of any one racial group is not such a cause: since the abolition of black slavery in the nineteenth century, followed by the defeat of

Nazism in World War II, ideologies revolving around alleged racial superiorities and inferiorities have been very much in abeyance. However, there does exist one fairly plausible candidate for such a cause: significant reduction of global economic inequality.

If we imagine a moral philosopher imported from the planet Mars, he might well deem it highly unsatisfactory that at the same time that billions of people around the world can barely feed themselves and have very little in the way of material possessions beyond the clothes on their backs, there exists a small fraction of the world's population, mostly resident in the United States and the nations of Western Europe, which enjoys veritably astronomical living standards. What might be an obvious solution to the problem, to our hypothetical moral philosopher from Mars, is drastic redistribution of world income by means of a highly progressive global income tax in conjunction with a relatively generous global guaranteed minimum income. Such a policy, if maintained for any length of time, might well entail such transitions as a U.S. family which is currently living in a 3000 square foot home with four bedrooms and driving a $45,000 sport utility vehicle, having to move into a 1500 square foot home with two bedrooms and having to downgrade the family vehicle to an $18,000 Ford Escort. Even worse transitions may easily be imagined. However intolerable these transitions might seem to U.S. families, they might well be outweighed (in the mind of the Martian moral philosopher) by the beneficial transitions of billions of poor people in the world to a more comfortable standard of living. Moral philosophers (and others) in the United States and Western Europe are apt to dissent from this judgment of our hypothetical disinterested moral philosopher from Mars. But moral philosophers (and others) in the Less Developed Nations (LDCs) are apt to concur with it. If the matter is put to democratic determination at the global level, given that the populations of the LDCs greatly outnumber the populations of the rich nations, the decision might well be to implement such a policy of global income redistribution.

Note that a scenario of drastic global income redistribution, entailing the relative impoverishment of the populations of the rich nations to benefit the populations of the poor nations, does not necessarily require a megalomaniac dictator "taking over" the world government by means of a coup d'etat. Quite possibly the enabling legislation would be passed by the large majority of a democratically elected legislature, would be implemented and enforced by a democratically elected executive authority, and would be duly reviewed and approved by a democratically accountable judiciary. The effective implementation of the policy in the rich nations could and probably would require considerable force, but this force might well be deployed by a world government enjoying the high degree of legitimacy conferred by democratic accountability. Of course, rioting and armed resistance throughout the rich nations would generate "emergency conditions" that would greatly facilitate the advent of a dictator. We ask, therefore, what (if any) aspects of the three "typical" world government proposals would be especially useful toward forestalling the possibility that the world government would embark on a policy of drastic global income redistribution despite intense opposition by the populations of the rich nations? We will look first at the issue of voting weights in the world government legislature, and then more briefly at the issue of military forces of the supernational government relative to the national governments.

Looking first at the Giuseppe Borgese proposal, the legislative arm is a unicameral World Council consisting of 99 councilors, 9 each from 9 different Electoral Colleges, plus 18 more from any Electoral College. The "Electoral Colleges" are defined as geographically contiguous regions (for the most part) encompassing "kindred nations and cultures." They are as follows (somewhat simplifying and updating from Borgese, pp. 307-308): (1) Western Europe; (2) U.S., U.K., Canada, Australia and New Zealand; (3) Russia and neighboring; (4) North Africa, Near and Middle East; (5) Sub-Saharan Africa; (6) India, Pakistan, Bangladesh and neighboring; (7) China, Korea, Japan and neighboring; (8) Indonesia, Vietnam and neighboring; (9) Western hemisphere south of the U.S. These are merely suggestions, and Borgese proposes that individual nations be allowed to associate with whatever Electoral College they desire, regardless of geography. By economic criteria, for example, Japan is today far more similar to Western Europe and the United States than to China. Also it is doubtful that predominantly Muslim Pakistan would want to associate with predominantly Hindu India. And so on and so forth. Through the Electoral College system, Borgese, Hutchins and the other members of the "Committee to Frame a World Constitution" meant to guarantee that no one nation would gain excessive power within the world government, nor would any one bloc of nations encompassing "kindred nations and cultures" do so. Each of the nine regional/cultural Electoral Colleges would be assured of an approximately equal voice.

One might quibble with various details of the proposal. For example, there might be less than nine Electoral Colleges, or there might be more. Whatever the number and nature of the Electoral Colleges eventually determined, some nations might want to join an Electoral College other than that with which they are "most logically" associated. Some nations, moreover, might not be happy with any of the proposed Electoral Colleges. But quite possibly a far more important issue is that unless the Electoral Colleges are specified in a very artificial manner, most of them will be composed largely of nations which are either poorer, much poorer, or very much poorer than the nations in the wealthiest Electoral Colleges. In the World Council, therefore, representatives of poor Electoral Colleges would greatly outnumber representatives of rich Electoral Colleges. In the original Borgese proposal, to illustrate, only Electoral Colleges 1 (Western Europe) and 2 (U.S., etc.) would be composed of the richest nations; the other seven Electoral Colleges would mostly be composed of much poorer nations. The only way to circumvent this situation would be to spread the rich nations over a much greater number of Electoral Colleges, while at the same time keeping a high level of aggregation in the Electoral Colleges composed of poor nations. But this would mean that the populations of the rich Electoral Colleges would be a very small fraction of the populations of the poor Electoral Colleges, and it is doubtful whether this would be acceptable to the poor nations.

The proposal of Grenville Clark and Louis Sohn for a strengthened United Nations would transform the General Assembly into an elected unicameral legislature with the power to make laws and specify policies with respect to general disarmament and the maintenance of world peace. The voting weight of each nation in the General Assembly would be an increasing function of its population, but the rate of increase in voting weight would be a declining function of population. Specifically, Clark-Sohn set forth the following formula (amended here to include the larger number of "smallest nations" today relative to the time of writing):

The 4 largest nations …	30 representatives each …	120
The 8 next largest nations …	15 representatives each …	120
The 20 next largest nations …	6 representatives each …	120
The 30 next largest nations …	4 representatives each …	120
The 34 next largest nations …	2 representatives each …	68
The 112 smallest nations …	1 representative each …	112
All 208 nations …	Total representatives …	662

Of course, one of the most striking features of this schema is its totally arbitrary nature. It is also an inelegant way to make voting weight a concave upward-sloping function of population. One could far more elegantly specify a mathematical formula similar to the one proposed in the previous chapter for the Federal Union Chamber of Representatives to compute the number of representatives from any nation as a function of its population. Use of a formula would have the important advantage of making the determination of number of representatives seem more fair and objective. Far more serious than the clumsiness and arbitrariness of the formula, however, is the fact that whatever range of population size is specified, most of the nations in that range are likely to be poor. What this means is that the General Assembly will inevitably be dominated by representatives from poorer nations. For example, by actual computation using the Clark-Sohn formula, representatives from nations with per capita income less than $5,000 would account for approximately 74 percent of the total number of representatives. There is no way around this situation as long as the basic approach of making voting weights of nations a positive function of the national populations is utilized. It does not matter which specific positive function is applied, whether it be a continuous function expressed through a mathematical equation or a discrete numerical formula such as represented by the Clark-Sohn schema shown above.

With respect to the executive branch of the revamped United Nations, Clark and Sohn propose that the Security Council be replaced by an Executive Council, consisting of 17 councilors elected by the General Assembly from among its Representatives, and responsible for implementation and enforcement of legislation and policy directives of the General Assembly. Executive decisions on "important matters" would require a majority of 12 out of the 17 councilors. The four largest nations in the world (China, India, the USA and the USSR at the time of writing, and China, India, the USA and Indonesia at the present time) would be entitled to one councilor each on the Executive Council, while four out of the next eight largest nations would in rotation have one councilor each. The remaining 9 councilors could be selected from any nation. The Executive Council would be subject to the same problem observed for the General Assembly: the large majority of its members at any point in time are likely to be from the poorer nations.

Clark and Sohn are very explicit that the first order of business of the United Nations world government would be the near-total disarming of the nations, and that very shortly after the revised Charter has been approved and implemented, the only substantial military force in the world, equipped with nuclear weapons as well as heavy conventional armament, would be the United Nations Peace Force (the World Police). They specify some fairly complicated provisions with respect to this military force to render it "tyranny-proof." The basic concept is to draw both the enlisted personnel and the officers of the U.N. Peace Force from a relatively large number of relatively small nations. Their primary apprehension is that if the military force is staffed mostly by individuals from a small number of relatively large nations, it would be more likely to subjugate itself to the will of a dictator representing the interests of those nations. However, they seem much less aware of the possibility that the military force might be utilized to enforce drastic global income redistribution. The fact is that the majority of nations of any particular size in terms of population will mostly be poor nations. Even if the U.N. Peace Force is drawn mostly from the small nations, its personnel will mostly be from poorer nations, and these personnel could well be sympathetic toward redistributive projects.

Philip Isely's general approach to forestalling totalitarian conditions within the proposed Federation of Earth is to complicate the structure of world government with numerous divisions of authority and numerous high level officials. The purpose of these structural conditions is to minimize the possibility that a single individual, or a small group of individuals, could gain control over the world government by means of a coup d'etat. Isely's proposal contains two particularly important separations within branches: (1) the legislature is composed of three houses (the House of Peoples, the House of Nations, and the House of Counselors, the major function of the third House being to break deadlocks between the first two); and (2) the executive authority is exercised by a five-person committee (termed the Presidium—one member from each major continent) whose chairmanship would revolve among its membership. Another important division of power is that pertaining to authority over the World Police: this would be divided between the Office of World Attorneys General and the Commission of Regional World Attorneys. However, as already suggested, repressive conditions do not necessarily require a dictatorial or even oligarchic government. Potentially, there can come to pass a tyranny of the majority over a minority. Or, at least, what the minority would regard as a form of tyranny—as in the case of the potential policy of drastic redistribution of global income under consideration here.

As we know, the number of nations in the world today with very high living standards constitutes a small minority of the total number of nations. In the Federation of Earth's House of Nations, therefore, representatives of relatively poor nations would greatly outnumber representatives of rich nations. Similarly, the number of people in the world today enjoying very high living standards constitutes a small minority of the total world population. In the Federation of Earth's House of Peoples, therefore, representatives of relatively poor people would also greatly outnumber representatives of rich people. Therefore, quite possibly a substantial majority of both the House of Nations and the House of Peoples would favor a proposed legislative bill mandating a drastic redistribution of world income from the rich to the poor. So let us imagine that both Houses pass the bill.

One of the well-known checks and balances from the U.S. Constitution *not* included in Isely's Constitution for the Federation of Earth is the executive veto. Article VI, Section F.2, specifies: "The World Executive shall not have veto power over any legislation passed by the World Parliament." Even if the Executive did possess veto power, it might not be used to overcome a legislative act mandating radical redistribution of world income. Article VI, Section C.3, specifies that "The decisions of the Presidium shall be taken collectively, on the basis of majority decisions." The Presidium would be composed of one representative from each major continental division: Europe, North America, South America, Asia and Africa. If the representatives from the latter three divisions vote to uphold radical world income redistribution against the dissenting votes of the representatives from the first two divisions, the legislation would be supported by majority vote within the executive branch. Thus, by fully democratic means, the populations of the rich nations would find themselves subjected to what they would no doubt consider exorbitant and well-nigh confiscatory rates of taxation. No doubt the rich populations would appeal these high tax rates to the World Supreme Court on the basis that they constitute violations of human rights. But there are no mechanisms for ensuring that the World Supreme Court would represent the interests of the rich populations, since the World Judges would be nominated and elected by the World Parliament. Quite likely the World Supreme Court would reject arguments that radical redistribution constitutes a significant violation of the human rights of the rich populations.

Table 3.3 is provided to enable some numerical insight into the voting weight problem in the world legislature as set forth in the three "typical" world government proposals, along with the tentative solution of this particular problem embodied in the "dual voting system" aspect of the present proposal for a Federal Union of Democratic Nations. The table is based on 2000 data on population and per capita income for 207 nations in the World Bank's CD-ROM *World Development Indicators 2002*, as displayed in Table 2.A.1 above.

TABLE 3.3
Distribution of Voting Weights by Per Capita Income
Brackets for Four World Government Proposals

1. Borgese: Electoral Colleges of the Federal Republic of the World

Per Capita Income	less than 500	500 to 1,000	1,000 to 2,500	2,500 to 5,000	5,000 to 10,000	10,000 to 20,000	20,000 and over
Percent of Electoral College Population:							
Elec Col 1	0.00	0.00	0.00	0.00	0.00	18.26	81.74
Elec Col 2	0.00	0.00	0.00	0.00	0.00	0.97	99.03
Elec Col 3	19.00	15.98	46.34	12.92	5.33	0.43	0.00
Elec Col 4	20.71	3.78	45.21	20.87	6.54	2.24	0.65
Elec Col 5	68.81	21.73	1.22	8.23	0.00	0.00	0.00
Elec Col 6	99.93	0.07	0.00	0.00	0.00	0.00	0.00
Elec Col 7	0.00	86.14	1.52	0.00	0.00	3.23	9.12
Elec Col 8	13.95	54.44	18.63	12.24	0.04	0.07	0.63
Elec Col 9	2.58	5.70	23.67	57.07	10.83	0.14	0.00
Cumulative Percent of Electoral College Population:							
Elec Col 1	0.00	0.00	0.00	0.00	0.00	18.26	100.00
Elec Col 2	0.00	0.00	0.00	0.00	0.00	0.97	100.00
Elec Col 3	19.00	34.97	81.32	94.24	99.57	100.00	100.00
Elec Col 4	20.71	24.49	69.70	90.57	97.11	99.35	100.00
Elec Col 5	68.81	90.55	91.77	100.00	100.00	100.00	100.00
Elec Col 6	99.93	100.00	100.00	100.00	100.00	100.00	100.00
Elec Col 7	0.00	86.14	87.65	87.65	87.65	90.88	100.00
Elec Col 8	13.95	68.39	87.02	99.27	99.30	99.37	100.00
Elec Col 9	2.58	8.28	31.95	89.03	99.86	100.00	100.00

2. Clark-Sohn: Representatives to United Nations General Assembly

Per Capita Income	less than 500	500 to 1,000	1,000 to 2,500	2,500 to 5,000	5,000 to 10,000	10,000 to 20,000	20,000 and over
Representatives by Population Level:							
Pop Lev 1	30	60	0	0	0	0	30
Pop Lev 2	30	15	15	30	0	0	30
Pop Lev 3	30	12	36	24	6	12	24
Pop Lev 4	40	24	32	12	8	0	8
Pop Lev 5	20	12	10	2	4	6	10
Pop Lev 6	13	13	20	18	18	11	15
Total Representatives over All Population Levels							
Number	163	136	113	86	36	29	117
Percent	23.97	20.00	16.62	12.65	5.29	4.26	17.21
Cum Pct	23.97	43.97	60.59	73.24	78.53	82.79	100.00

Table 3.3 concluded —

3. Isely: Representatives to World Parliament of the Federation of Earth

Per Capita Income	less than 500	500 to 1,000	1,000 to 2,500	2,500 to 5,000	5,000 to 10,000	10,000 to 20,000	20,000 and over
House of Nations:							
Percent	23.91	15.58	20.29	13.04	7.25	6.88	13.04
Cum Pct	23.91	39.49	59.78	72.83	80.07	86.96	100.00
House of Peoples:							
Percent	30.30	31.19	11.58	9.74	1.85	2.06	13.28
Cum Pct	30.30	61.49	73.07	82.81	84.66	86.72	100.00

4. Yunker: Voting Weights of Union Representatives in the Chamber of Representatives of the Federal Union of Democratic Nations

Per Capita Income	less than 500	500 to 1,000	1,000 to 2,500	2,500 to 5,000	5,000 to 10,000	10,000 to 20,000	20,000 and over
Population Basis:							
Percent	30.30	31.19	11.58	9.74	1.85	2.06	13.28
Cum Pct	30.30	61.49	73.07	82.81	84.66	86.72	100.00
Material Basis (GDP-based tax receipts):							
Percent	2.09	4.52	3.58	6.69	2.21	5.48	75.43
Cum Pct	2.09	6.62	10.19	16.88	19.09	24.57	100.00

The four sections of the table show the respective distributions of voting weights in the world legislature for the three "typical" world government proposals and the author's fourth "atypical" proposal. Section 1 of Table 3.3, pertaining to the Borgese proposal, shows the distribution of the populations of the nine Electoral Colleges by per capita income bracket. Looking at the lower part of this section of the table, we see, for example, that six of the nine Electoral Colleges have large majorities in nations with per capita income of $2,500 or below. (For comparison, the per capita income for the United States for 2000 was $31,996.) Section 2 of the table shows that using the Clark-Sohn formula, representatives from nations with per capita income less than $5,000 would account for approximately 73 percent of the total number of representatives. Section 3 of the table shows that using the Isely formula, representatives from nations with per capita income less than $5,000 would account for over 72 percent of the total number of representatives in the House of Nations and for over 82 percent of the total number of representatives in the House of Peoples.

It is fully apparent from sections 1 through 3 of Table 3.3 that implementation of any one of these three world government proposals would result in a world legislature in which representatives from rich nations would exercise very much less voting power than representatives from poor nations. The Borgese,

Clark-Sohn and Isely proposals are typical of postwar world government proposals in failing to deal realistically with this issue. To my knowledge, the only world government advocate prior to myself to have responded, in the form of an institutional proposal, to the difficulty presented by global economic inequality was Fremont Rider. In his 1946 book (mentioned earlier) *The Great Dilemma of World Organization*, Rider expressed the problem in terms of the gap between the "civilized" and the "uncivilized" nations. The "civilized" nations of North America, Western Europe and so on (i.e., the rich nations) would never consider participating in a world government with genuine power and authority that was subject to majority rule—and that would therefore be controlled by the vast, impoverished populations of the "uncivilized" nations.

Rider's proposed solution was to make the respective voting weights of the nations in the world government legislature proportional to their "educational attainments," in terms of total number of years of education completed by their populations. Since the average educational attainment in the "civilized" nations was high, they would enjoy dominant voting weight in the world legislature. But this would be acceptable to the poor nations as well, since it makes good sense to give more voting weight to individuals with more education. Such individuals would presumably utilize their greater voting weight more wisely and intelligently. Rider envisioned arms races being replaced by "education races" as nations enthusiastically threw their resources into educating their respective populations. Their immediate motivation would be to increase their influence in the world government, but this strategy would also increase their economic prosperity, which is largely determined by the productivity of the citizens, which in turn is largely determined by educational attainment.

A goofy idea, to be sure, but at least it constituted a sincere effort to deal with a serious problem mostly ignored by other, better known formulators of world government schemes. This problem is addressed, in my own proposal for a Federal Union of Democratic Nations, via the dual voting system in the Union Chamber of Representatives. This will hopefully be perceived by most readers as a more plausible, direct and effective way of dealing with the problem than Fremont Rider's proposal. According to the dual voting system, any proposed measure would have to be passed by a 60 percent majority on two bases: the population basis and the material basis. In the population vote, a particular Union Representative's voting weight would be equal to the proportion of the population of the entire Union represented by the population of his or her own Union District. In the material vote, that same Union Representative's voting weight would be equal to the proportion of the overall revenue of the entire Union represented by the revenue raised in that Representative's Union District.

Thus, the richer nations, as providers of most of the Union's revenues, would retain more power in the legislature than would be the case if voting weight were based exclusively on population represented. Section 4 of Table 3.3 indicates, for example, that approximately 75 percent of voting weight in the material vote would be disposed by representatives from nations with per capita income in excess of $20,000. It also indicates that about 73 percent of voting weight in the population vote would be disposed by representatives from nations with per capita income of $2,500 or less. Thus the populous poorer nations would dominate the population vote, while the less populous richer nations would dominate the material vote. Only measures on which both the richer nations and the poorer nations could achieve a degree of consensus would be capable of passing on both votes. Note that the practical relevance of the distinction between the population vote and the material vote would be obviated were all nations of the world to have approximately equal per capita income. This condition, of course, would be the long-term objective of the World Economic Equalization Program (WEEP). The dual voting system is regarded as a short-term expedient to give the WEEP a fair chance of success by supporting it with an existent world government structure. This system is most emphatically not intended as a permanent solution to the problem of global economic inequality.

The dual voting scheme is important because it would prevent a program of radical, short-term redistribution of world income (or any other policy unacceptable either to the rich nations as a whole or the poor nations as a whole) to achieve the legitimacy of being democratically approved by the world federation legislature. But in light of "Mao's law" that "all power grows out of the barrel of a gun," we need to be sensitive to the possibility that if the executive branch of the world government succumbs to dictatorial temptations, and simply dissolves what it deems an uncooperative legislative branch, and at the same time maintains the loyalty of the military, then radical world income distribution would be a definite possibility. Of course, if the member nations of the world state were allowed to maintain their own military forces and armaments, up to and including nuclear weapons (as in the present proposal for a Federal Union of Democratic Nations), then there would not be such a clear danger that the military forces and armaments of the world state might be utilized to enforce radical redistribution of world income despite the legislature's failure to authorize such a program. But the authors of the three typical world state proposals under consideration here are quite explicit on the point that the overwhelming preponderance of military power must be concentrated under the direct control of the world state.

Giuseppe Borgese puts it as follows:

> If the World Republic is defective in power, it will disintegrate as did the Roman unity when it grew weak. Or it will be an empty name from the beginning, as were, more or less, the Christian empire in the Middle Ages and the League or United Nations in our years. Against this danger the World Republic as we see it claims the monopoly of weapons, wields all the sanctions and forces that are needed to repress insurrection and separation.

Grenville Clark and Louis Sohn state (1966, p. xv):

> The complete disarmament of all the nations (rather than the mere "reduction" or "limitation" of armaments) is essential for any solid and lasting peace,

this disarmament to be accomplished in a simultaneous and proportionate manner by carefully verified stages and subject to a well-organized system of inspection. It is now generally accepted that disarmament must be universal and enforceable. That it must also be complete is no less necessary, since: (a) in the nuclear age no mere reduction in the new means of mass destruction could be effective to remove fear and tension; and (b) if any substantial national armaments were to remain, even if only ten per cent of the armaments of 1960, it would be impracticable to maintain a sufficiently strong world police force to deal with any possible aggression or revolt against the authority of the world organization. We should face the fact that until there is *complete* disarmament of every nation without exception there can be no assurance of genuine peace.

Finally, in the course of his critique of the 1995 Report of the Commission on Global Governance (*Our Global Neighborhood*), Philip Isely writes:

> The Commission also recommends a "mandatory Arms Register, and prohibition of the financing or subsidy of arms exports by governments," but seems to forget that under its own nebulous proposal for "global governance," there is no way to make anything mandatory—short of war. We cannot help but observe that having rejected, as "leading to less democracy," any proposal for world government (such as the Constitution for the Federation of Earth, which would require total disarmament to proceed upon ratification), the Commission prefers the obviously more democratic procedure of wasting $500 billion or more per year on the entrenched benefits of the autocratic military-industrial system under national sovereignty.

These are typical expressions of the conventional viewpoint among world state traditionalists that there can be no sharing of military power between the world government and the national governments—not even in the short run. This rigid and unimaginative stance, more than any other single factor, accounts for the impotence, to date, of the world federalist movement.

Borgese and Clark-Sohn are quite explicit that the world government will control very substantial military forces, possibly armed with nuclear weapons as well as potent conventional weapons, while at the same time the nations would be confined to light weaponry suitable for purposes of internal policing. Isely's proposal is somewhat different from the other two in that the world government is also envisioned as being confined to light weaponry suitable for policing purposes. Applying a popular dictum among many world federalists, world law is not to be enforced upon nations but rather upon individuals. It might be argued by an advocate of Isely's proposal that the Federation of Earth would not itself possess the military means of enforcing measures which of their nature would be extremely unpopular in some nations (such as drastic income redistribution). Article II, Section 2, of the Federation Constitution specifies, among other things, that the Federation of Earth shall be "non-military." This implies that it would not maintain an army, navy and air force comparable to the armed forces which are today considered by most nations to be indispensable to the preservation and protection of their essential national interests. Rather it would utilize non-violent means of coercion in the (presumably unlikely) event that it becomes necessary to enforce world law upon nations as opposed to individuals (e.g., trade restrictions and boycotts).

But Isely is in fact sufficiently realistic to include, in Article X of the draft Constitution, provision for a "World Police." It is specified that the World Police would be "armed only with weapons appropriate for the apprehension of individuals responsible for violation of world law." The idea is that strife between nations, and/or serious human rights abuses, normally arise from the activities of misguided and/or malevolent individuals such as Adolf Hitler or Saddam Hussein. Therefore, all that is necessary to the suppression of international strife and/or human rights abuses is the removal of a handful of individuals. The problem is, of course, that many trouble-making national leaders enjoy a very high level of support among their own national populations. Often that high level of support is based upon fear rather than popularity—but that does not alter the fact that the support exists. In order to be effective in such situations, the World Police of the Federation of Earth would have to be a very large and heavily armed organization. Such an organization could make short work of national leaders in the United States and other rich nations who might be resisting the redistributive project under consideration here—assuming the U.S. and the other rich nations were unarmed. In other words, the formula that world law is "to be enforced upon individuals rather than nations" does not satisfactorily address the problem that an extreme imbalance in the relative military power of the supernational government vis-à-vis the national governments could set the stage for a militarily supported totalitarian world government. However, allowing the nations to retain whatever they desire in the way of armaments, as in the Federal Union proposal, does in fact address this problem in a satisfactory manner. It is not a "perfect" solution, but it may be the only "feasible" solution.

Of the three "conventional" proposals for world government, that of Grenville Clark and Louis Sohn exhibits the maximum careful thinking about institutional safeguards against the possibility that the world government would degenerate into a military dictatorship. The Clark-Sohn proposals relating to this issue are worthy of careful consideration, and they are presented here verbatim as they appear in *World Peace through World Law*:

> Another distinct set of provisions would provide strict safeguards to prevent subversion of the Peace Force either by external or internal influences. These safeguards would include the following provisions:
>
> 1. Units of the Peace Force shall be composed to the greatest possible extent of nationals of different nations and no unit exceeding fifty in number shall be composed of nationals of a single nation.
>
> 2. Units of the Peace Force shall be stationed in military bases leased and controlled by the United Nations itself; these bases to be located in easily defensible places (such as islands and peninsulas), and all to be located in the territories of the smaller nations, i.e., the nearly ninety nations which would be entitled to less than fifteen Representatives in the General Assembly.
>
> 3. The standing component of the Peace Force shall be distributed in such a way that not less than five per cent or more than ten per cent of its total strength

would be stationed in any one of the eleven to twenty regions of the world to be delineated for that purpose by the General Assembly.

4. The immediate direction of the Peace Force would not be in the hands of a single person, but would be entrusted to a committee of five persons all of whom would be nationals of the smaller nations—the Military Staff Committee. Only if action by the Peace Force had been ordered by the General Assembly, or in case of an emergency by the Executive Council, could commanders for its land, sea and air components and regional commanders, or in exceptional circumstances a temporary Commander-in-Chief, be appointed by the Executive Council; and their terms would expire at the end of the particular operation.

5. The Military Staff Committee would be under the general control of the Executive Council; and the General Assembly, through its Standing Committee on the Peace Enforcement Agencies, would exercise a close watch over the carrying out by the Military Staff Committee and the Executive Council of their responsibilities.

With regard to authority to order action by the Peace Force, such authority would be limited solely to the civilian authorities of the United Nations, i.e., the General Assembly itself or the Executive Council. Action by the Council would, however, be authorized only if the Assembly is not in session and special circumstances require immediate action, and there would be the additional safeguard that if the Council orders any such action, it must forthwith summon the Assembly in special session. These strict requirements should not, of course, prejudice the right of the Peace Force to defend itself in case of a possible direct attack.

The solution proposed for the equipment of the Peace Force with nuclear weapons and their possible use is that the Force shall not be normally equipped with nuclear weapons at all, but that such weapons shall be held in reserve in the custody of the Nuclear Energy Authority, never to be used save by the order of the General Assembly itself and then only if such weapons have actually been used against the United Nations or such use is imminently threatened. While it would be possible to equip a world police force with these weapons of mass destruction so that it could crush forthwith any aggression by ruthless action, this is deemed no more consistent with the purpose of the Peace Force than it would be to equip a city police force with weapons which might tempt it to suppress a riot by the slaughter of thousands of citizens.

The Peace Force would, therefore, be so organized and equipped as to operate with the absolute minimum of force and destruction. On the other hand, while the possibility remains, as it would remain under the most effective inspection system, that somewhere or somehow nuclear weapons could be secretly concealed or manufactured, it seems necessary to make such counter-weapons available to the Peace Force in case of absolute need. The proposed precautions whereby these nuclear weapons would not ordinarily be in the possession of the Peace Force at all, but would be in charge of the Nuclear Energy Authority, subject only to release by order of the General Assembly itself, are intended to provide the maximum possible assurance against the misuse of these weapons.

From these provisions, and from other discussions elsewhere in *World Peace through World Law*, the basic strategy of Clark and Sohn, to reduce the threat of a militarily imposed tyranny, is simply to distribute the world government's military forces widely around the world, and to draw both the rank-and-file soldiers and the high military officers from a substantial number of small nations. This is certainly a prescription for a weak military force. But a weak military force may be highly effective if it confronts no opposition whatever. Clark and Sohn are quite unambiguous and insistent that all heavy military armament, including nuclear weapons, be under the direct control of the empowered United Nations, and that all member nations be strictly reduced to minor armed forces suitable only for internal policing. But in making provisions that would hinder a small number of large nations from taking effective control over the world state's military force, Clark and Sohn do not address the equally serious possibility that the poor nations, as a group, would take control of this force, and use it as an instrument with which to compel radical redistribution of world income.

The great majority of small nations, no less than the great majority of all nations, are relatively poor. This means that under the Clark-Sohn provisions for the U.N. Peace Force, the majority of the rank-and-file soldiers and the majority of the high military officers, would be drawn from the poorer nations of the world. All of these nations have a common interest in greater economic equality throughout the world. Thus, under conditions of internal crisis brought about by armed resistance in the rich nations to confiscatory taxation to support a world-wide welfare state, the majority elements in the military in favor of this policy might well take it upon themselves to neutralize the minority elements not in favor of it. This is not to altogether discount the possibility that the force could be used against the poor nations. It could be that personnel from small but rich nations such as Switzerland and Sweden would gain effective control over the force in a crisis situation. At one point in their book, Clark and Sohn state: "These careful and interrelated safeguards embody, it is believed, every reasonable precaution against abuse of power by the armed forces of the United Nations, and should provide strong assurance that the world police force would be tyranny-proof." Unfortunately, I cannot agree.

Quite possibly, the Clark-Sohn provisions would indeed be adequate if the nations of the world were far more homogeneous—especially in the economic sense. But given the condition of the world today, and the condition of the world as it is most likely to evolve over the next several decades, the only truly effective way to make the world government militarily "tyranny-proof" is to allow the member nation-states to maintain whatever military forces they feel it necessary to maintain, armed with whatever weaponry with which they feel it necessary to arm them. This is not a happy situation, to be sure. This situation is very dangerous now, and it would continue to be dangerous even if we do move forward to establish a limited world government such as the proposed Federal Union of Democratic Nations. But if we do establish the Federal Union, and we do authorize the Federal Union to undertake a massive, determined World Economic Equalization Program to eradicate the economic gap over the next several decades, then there will be a considerably higher likelihood that the world political system, and all its subsidiary components, will indeed ultimately be rendered "tyranny-proof."

PART II

OVERCOMING THE
ECONOMIC IMPEDIMENT

4

WORLD ECONOMIC INEQUALITY

At the present time in world history, the large majority of humanity is experiencing economic living standards a small fraction of those experienced by a small minority of humanity mostly resident in the wealthy nations of North America and Western Europe. By the standards of the wealthiest nations, most of humanity subsists under conditions of unimaginably abysmal poverty. Nevertheless, the current consensus viewpoint among the small minority of the human population enjoying very high living standards is that very little should be done by the wealthy nations to directly assist the economic development of the poor nations. The standard perception is that large-scale foreign development assistance programs would impose heavy economic burdens on the wealthy populations—their living standards would be very appreciably reduced, possibly to the point of poverty. Therefore, the policy of *not* engaging in large-scale foreign development assistance programs is perceived by the populations of the wealthy nations to be in their own self-interest. But at the same time these populations have been instructed since earliest childhood in the moral obligation to provide help and assistance to those in need, that charity is a cardinal virtue of great nobility, that "it is better to give than to receive," and so on and so forth. The inconsistency between these basic moral principles, and the typical disinclination to support foreign development assistance at anything beyond a token level, creates a moral dilemma which demands a solution. Otherwise, a person's conscience might become troublesome. Thus the natural emergence of the standard rationalizations with which we are familiar.

According to these rationalizations, the impact of large-scale foreign development assistance programs on the billions of poor people living in the world would range from insignificant to highly adverse. It is alleged that the size of the gap is so huge that only by impoverishing themselves could the rich populations make an appreciable dent on the poverty of the poor nations. It is alleged that even if foreign development assistance were provided in vast amounts, most of it would be siphoned off into the private Swiss bank accounts of corrupt bureaucrats and dishonest businessmen. It is alleged that the provision of large amounts of foreign development assistance would breed a spirit of helpless dependency in the recipient nations, undermine the self-reliance of their populations, and deter the internal saving and investment necessary for them to raise their economic condition and prospects. Finally, at the extreme end of the rationalization spectrum is the allegation that economic development—even if it could be brought about without placing undue strains on the rich populations—would be contrary to the psychological, social and spiritual wellbeing of the poor populations. Economic wealth would bring with it (according to this extreme rationalization) materialism, alienation, greed, selfishness, crime, pollution, and a host of ancillary and related problems. After all, the simple, wholesome life of the rural peasant in the Third World is actually far preferable to the harried, harassed and unrewarding existence of the typical urbanite of the First World. So-called "poverty" is actually good for the body, good for the mind, and good for the soul.

The remarkable thing is that the great majority of those who recite these kinds of viewpoints seem totally and blissfully unaware of their rationalizing motivations. It is apparently not a matter of conscious hypocrisy at all, but rather of unconscious self-delusion. Most people easily perceive the self-serving motivations in the positions taken by others with whom they are in disagreement, and most people thereupon frequently accuse those others of being "hypocrites." But in actual fact conscious hypocrisy probably plays a very minor role in ordinary human psychology. Hypocrisy requires a person not only to be aware of the self-serving nature of a certain proposition, but also to believe that the proposition is itself invalid. Most people have consciences that are far too strong and active for conscious hypocrisy to be a tolerable option. Therefore conscious hypocrisy is not a viable means of coping with the problem that what is in the interest of the person with the conscience is at the same time *not* in the interest of other persons. What *is* a viable means of coping with this problem, however, is the development of reasons (however dubious from an objective standpoint) why what is in the interest of the person with the conscience is *also* in the interests of other persons—or at least not significantly *against* the interests of other persons.

The proposition that world poverty constitutes a "threat to peace" has been widely accepted for at least the last half-century, though opinions differ widely with respect to how great is the threat, and what is the basis and mechanism of the threat. Very few people, therefore, think that it would be a bad thing, as far as world peace is concerned, if the poorer nations became richer. On the other hand, very few people believe that the rich nations should undertake a massive foreign development assistance effort to spur the economic growth of the poor nations. The vast majority in the middle thinks that economic growth in the poor nations would be a good thing, but that this growth should come about mostly on the basis of the internal efforts of the poor nations themselves, with minimal assistance by the rich nations. This dominant mainstream consensus is based on the self-serving rationalization that the provision of large quantities of foreign aid would: (1) impose very heavy economic burdens on the rich nations; (2) mostly be wasted so that it would have little improving effect on the living standards of the great majority of the populations of the poor nations; or (3) both of the above. It will be argued here that this self-serving rationalization is especially perverse because it is, in all likelihood, empirically false. It will be argued here that the provision of large quantities of foreign aid by the rich nations, in all likelihood, would: (1) impose very minor economic burdens on the rich nations; and (2) have a dramatic improving effect on the living standards of the great majority of the populations of the poor nations. The currently operative benefit-cost calculations on foreign aid are in very serious error. The benefits are being seriously underestimated and the costs are being seriously overestimated. By the same token, the initiation of a massive, worldwide economic development assistance program, with the objective of drastically reducing the gap between economic living standards in the richest and the poorest nations within a relatively abbreviated period of historical time, is fully merited on the basis of an accurate assessment of the probable costs and benefits. Such a program ought to be started as soon as possible.

Discussion of world government, in both the professional literature and the popular media, is extremely limited at the present time. This appears to be an excellent example of a self-fulfilling prophecy. Authors, editors and publishers believe that there is little general interest in world government, with the result that very little appears on the subject, with the result that there is very little general interest in world government. Be that as it may, discussion of world government has not as yet been totally expunged from the professional and popular literature. Most discussion of world government is quite cursory and incidental to the main purposes of the author. It is normally brusquely dismissive of the idea, sometimes on the basis that there is no strong political movement toward world government, sometimes on the basis that such a government would be undesirable for one reason or another (too undemocratic, too bureaucratic, etc.), and sometimes on the basis of both.

In dealing with world government, authors from the rich countries rarely if ever voice apprehensions that such a government would be likely to engage in excessive taxation of the rich nations for purposes of financing either immediate welfare programs or economic development programs in the poor nations. The emphasis is rather on the "undemocratic conditions" likely to be fostered by a world government. It is very rarely admitted that these undemocratic conditions are a likely outcome of irreconcilable differences over whether and to what extent the world government should endeavor to equalize world income. Perhaps these authors are reluctant to appear selfish, to appear to be favoring the interests of the minority of rich people in the world over those of the entire human population, most of which is quite poor. If economic issues are mentioned at all, the point more likely to be raised is that the poor populations are apprehensive that a world government would become a tool for the economic exploitation of the Third World by the First World. I am not denying that this apprehension exists. What I am asserting, however, is that this particular apprehension is far less important, as a practical impediment to world government, than is the apprehension of the rich populations that a world government would become a tool for the drastic redistribution of income from the First World to the Third World. This is because it is sufficiently clear that a world government subject to democratic control by the majority (according to the currently prevailing definitions of "democratic control"—and considering that without exception world government proposals specify democratic control of that government), will be more likely to favor the interests of the Third World populations rather than those of the First World nations simply because the Third World population is much larger than the First World population. Why is it, then, that the economic apprehensions of the populations of the poor nations regarding world government get more attention than do the economic apprehensions of the populations of the rich nations?

The answer, as suggested above, is not conscious hypocrisy—although a truly impartial and objective observer (if one existed) might be strongly inclined to suspect conscious hypocrisy. The answer is rather, almost certainly, unconscious self-delusion. Authors from the rich nations, in thinking about and commenting on world government, simply cannot admit to themselves that their viewpoints are largely determined by their perceptions of personal self-interest. They are strongly impelled toward the belief that what is good for the rich nations (i.e., the absence of a world government that might engage in confiscatory taxation of the rich nations to support a lavish worldwide welfare state benefiting principally the poor nations) is also good for the poor nations (i.e., the absence of a world government that might engage in colonial-style economic exploitation of the poor nations for the benefit of the rich nations).

But in the end, it is immaterial whether such beliefs and attitudes are the product of conscious hypocrisy or unconscious self-delusion. What is important is that these beliefs and attitudes are extremely prevalent. And what is even more important is that these beliefs and attitudes are very likely to be incorrect and invalid. As shown in the previous part of this book, it would be possible to establish a fully functional, albeit limited, federal world government that would not be able to engage in either massive income redistribution that would be unacceptable to the rich nations, nor to establish a global economic exploitation system favoring the "have" nations that would be unacceptable to the poor nations. Owing to the limitations built into the proposal for a Federal Union of Democratic Nations, this federation could no more favor the poor nations at the expense of the rich nations than it could favor the rich nations at the expense of the poor nations. By its nature, it would have to take the interests of both types of nation fully into account in formulating policies. But the existence of a federal world government, albeit of a very limited nature in its early decades, would make it more likely that the rich nations and the poor nations would cooperate in a determined program of worldwide economic equalization.

It might be suggested that global economic equalization should precede the formation of a global government. This is actually a formula for the *prevention* of both global economic equalization and global government. Unless there is planned and coordinated intervention on a gigantic scale, the economic gap is likely to persist indefinitely, and the economic gap will continue to be utilized indefinitely as a pretext for disregarding the world government option. As continually stressed herein, however, it is indeed impractical to think in terms of an extremely powerful and centralized world government. Few if any of the nations of the world, whether they be rich or poor, will give any consideration to an extremely powerful and centralized world government. What is needed, rather, is a *limited* world government *as an instrument* toward gradual global economic equalization. During its early history, by far the single most important item on the world government's agenda would be coordination of a massive program of global economic development. As gradual global economic equalization proceeds, the limitations on the global government could gradually be removed without this leading to a dire threat of global tyranny. The global government would gradually become more efficient and less coercive, because of the gradual subsidence of those economic inequalities which impede efficient regulatory policy as well as free and voluntary cooperation and coordination of effort.

In this second part of *Political Globalization* ("Overcoming the Economic Impediment") consisting of three chapters ("World Economic Inequality," "Foreign Development Assistance," and "The World Economic Equalization Program"), we will examine the nature of this impediment and possible means for overcoming it. Now that the ideological conflict between communism and its alternatives is fading, and the Cold War is greatly in decline (if not completely extinct), the economic impediment to world government has displaced the political impediment as the single most important obstacle to human civilization taking the logical next step in its long-term political evolution. Although there is a tremendous economic literature on global economic inequality and the prospects for economic development, consideration of this inequality plays a limited role in political discussions of world government—despite the critical bearing of the former upon the latter. I wish to rectify this unfortunate situation by means of a relatively comprehensive consideration of economic factors as they impinge on the desirability and practicality of federal world government.

THE GLOBAL ECONOMIC GAP

It is difficult for any human being, whether a resident of a rich nation or a poor nation, and whatever his or her socioeconomic status, to gain a full comprehension and appreciation of the human significance of economic inequality. Most of us spend most of our lives within a relatively narrow geographical and socioeconomic range. Most of our friends and acquaintances are very much like ourselves. Our interactions with those from distant territories and/or different social strata tend to be limited and ephemeral. An affluent citizen of New York, London or Paris may travel to Egypt or India to see such wonders as the pyramids or the Taj Mahal, but he or she is unlikely to want to wander around in the slums of Cairo or Mumbai. Not only would the opportunities for meaningful communication be limited owing to language and other problems, but it might be physically dangerous.

Those of us who, for whatever professional or personal reason, try to educate ourselves regarding the extent and significance of economic inequality among nations, rely only to a very minor extent on personal familiarity with daily life and living standards at various points along the socioeconomic spectrum in a variety of nations. Evidence obtained from personal observation is likely to be so partial and incomplete as to be seriously misleading. For the most part, therefore, we are dependent on published information from a variety of sources. It need not be unduly emphasized that this information also has severe deficiencies as a basis for understanding. One problem is simply the overwhelming abundance of available statistical and empirical information pertaining to global economic inequality. Trying to assimilate this information might be compared to trying to drink from a fire hose. Another problem is that even with the best available measurement techniques, there is a substantial margin of error in the published data. We are never certain of how accurate or inaccurate a given published estimate might be. Still another problem is the difficulty of translating an array of impersonal numbers into a valid and legitimate appreciation of the practical significance of the existence of economic inequality. Does a high degree of economic inequality translate into a large amount of subjective misery and dissatisfaction? And does a large amount of subjective misery and dissatisfaction, even granting its existence, translate into a high degree of international instability?

We shall return to these questions shortly, but it is obviously incumbent upon us, at this point, to examine some numerical data on the issue of world economic inequality. I have selected some illustrative data provided by the International Bank for Reconstruction and Development, more commonly known as the World Bank. As a leading symbol of international financial authority, the World Bank does not lack for adamant critics. Many of its critics view it as an instrument of the conservative establishment, as a pillar of the international status quo, as a major roadblock against a more equitable world order, as part of the problem rather than part of the solution. If this is true, it would seem to follow that the statistical department of the Bank would be under standing orders to collect and report data in such a way as to minimize the material gap between rich nations and poor nations. After all, to the extent that the existing gap is smaller, there is less incentive to dissatisfaction with the contemporary international status quo. But if the material gap is in fact being significantly underreported by the World Bank, then the gap must be almost inconceivably huge. Table 4.1 shows some data from a recent issue of the Bank's *World Development Indicators* (*WDI*). This source is issued annually in print and CD-ROM form, and contains data on somewhat over 200 different nations. Variables range from population and GDP (Gross Domestic Product) to life expectancy and exports.

For present purposes, it will suffice to provide recent information for eight nations on eight variables, taken from the 2002 *WDI*. The selected nations cover a wide range from richest to poorest, and the selected variables are representative of the large number of available variables. The eight nations include the United States, France, Italy, Spain, Algeria, Ecuador, Ghana and India. The first four of these are representative of the rich nations of the world, while the latter four are representative of the poor nations of the world. The eight variables in-

TABLE 4.1
Selected Indicators for Eight Nations

Nation	GDP per capita in 1995 U.S. $ (2000)	Under-5 mortality rate per 1,000 (2000)	Male life expectancy in years, at birth (2000)	Total fertility rate, births per woman (2000)
U.S.	31,996	8.65	74.27	2.13
France	29,811	5.88	75.20	1.89
Italy	20,885	6.94	75.53	1.23
Spain	17,798	6.16	74.68	1.23
Algeria	1,606	39.00	69.46	3.24
Ecuador	1,425	34.26	68.18	3.03
Ghana	413	112.10	55.78	4.20
India	459	87.74	62.20	3.06
World	5,631	77.79	64.54	2.68

Nation	Electric power consumption per capita, kilowatt-hrs (1999)	Television sets per 1,000 people (2000)	Pupil-teacher ratio, primary education (1996-98)	Public expenditure on health, % of GDP (1997-98)
U.S.	11,994	854	15.41	12.89
France	6,392	628	18.91	9.35
Italy	4,535	494	11.33	8.19
Spain	4,497	591	15.04	7.01
Algeria	581	110	28.19	3.60
Ecuador	620	218	26.90	3.63
Ghana	204	118	32.71	4.71
India	379	78	71.94	5.41
World	2,107	254	25.27	9.22

Source: World Bank, *World Development Indicators*, 2002 edition.

clude GDP per capita (per capita income), under-5 mortality rate, male life expectancy, total fertility rate (births per woman), per capita electric power consumption, television sets per 1000 persons, public expenditure on health as a percent of GDP (Gross Domestic Product), and pupil-teacher ratio in primary education. Of these variables, the most widely utilized measure of economic living standards within nations is per capita income. According to the World Bank, as of 2000 the ratio between per capita income in the United States to per capita income in India was 69.71 ($31,996 divided by $459). This means that the average person in the U.S. had purchasing power almost 70 times the purchasing power of the average person in India. Another way of looking at this is that per capita income in India was 1.43 percent of per capita income in the U.S.

One way for a person in the United States to try to get a feel for the significance of this differential is to take 1.43 percent of his or her current income, and then try to imagine what it would be like to live on that amount. For example, if one were part of a household with $100,000 annual family income, what would it be like to try to live on $1,430 in annual family income? The reduction in living standards is virtually impossible to imagine. Survival itself would be in question. Now it is true that standard measures of per capita income exaggerate differences in actual living standards because they do not take adequate account of non-market income. But alternative measures that do attempt to take account of this factor still show extreme differences. For example, according to the World Bank statistics, per capita income in 2000 in PPP terms (purchasing power parity) was $34,100 for the U.S. and $2,340 for India. Thus in PPP terms U.S. per capita income was still 14.57 times that of India, and Indian per capita income was only 6.86 percent of U.S.

The correlations between per capita income and the various other indicators in Table 4.1 are not perfect but they are strong. As a rule, the positive indicators are higher for higher levels of per capita income, and the negative indicators are lower for higher levels of per capita income. The positive indicators include male life expectancy, electric power consumption, television sets per 1,000, public expenditure on health, and public expenditure on education. The negative indicators include the under-5 mortality rate and the total fertility rate. It is intuitively evident that any kind of a death rate, such as the under-5 mortality rate, will tend to be higher the poorer the nation. But categorizing the total fertility rate as a "negative indicator" perhaps needs a word of explanation. High living standards, of course, enable the *possibility* of high fertility rates. On the other hand, there has long been observed a strong *negative* association between national per capita income and national fertility rates: the richer nations with high per capita income tend to have lower fertility rates and the poorer nations with low per capita income tend to have higher fertility rates. Apparently the economic incentives to fertility diminish with household income, so that even though higher-income households would be physically capable of producing more children, they actually produce less children.

With respect to the positive indicators, the level of inequality is generally less than that with respect to per capita income. For example, while we noted above that the per capita income of the United States is about 70 times that of India, we can also see from Table 4.1 that per capita electric power consumption in the United States is only about 31 times that in India, and that the number of television sets per 1,000 persons in the United States is not quite 11 times that in India. Of all the positive indicators, the least unequal pertains to male life expectancy: it stands at 74.27 years for the United States and only somewhat under that—62.20 years—in India. This is the sort of indication which leads some to argue that emphasis on per capita income tends to greatly exaggerate differentials in economic living standards, and that the actual level of economic inequality in the world is much less than is suggested by comparisons of per capita income. Clearly this is a very comforting notion, but it may not be very

TABLE 4.2
Growth in Real GDP per Capita
Eight Nations, 1960-2000

Year	U.S.	France	Italy	Spain	Algeria	Ecuador	Ghana	India
1960	13,227	10,611	6,606	4,620	1,139	777	450	183
1965	15,363	13,156	8,199	6,618	1,080	822	453	194
1970	16,985	16,412	10,734	8,506	1,277	879	475	211
1975	18,378	18,759	12,035	10,480	1,452	1,301	411	217
1980	21,001	21,418	14,592	10,973	1,681	1,547	394	226
1985	23,384	22,742	15,808	11,423	1,814	1,504	328	264
1990	26,141	25,967	18,161	14,073	1,648	1,475	346	323
1995	27,713	26,850	19,181	14,899	1,488	1,565	373	380
2000	31,996	29,811	20,885	17,798	1,606	1,425	413	459

Source: World Bank, *World Development Indicators 2002* (CD-ROM).

realistic. Life expectancy measures quantity of life—not quality of life.

Table 4.2, drawn from the same World Bank source, provides some insight into changes in per capita income among nations over the latter half of the twentieth century. Per capita income figures are shown for the same eight nations included in Table 4.1, in terms of annual data from 1960 through 2000. These figures have been adjusted for inflation: they are in terms of constant 1995 U.S. dollars. Thus they represent "real per capita income" as opposed to "nominal per capita income." The data are plotted in the corresponding Figures 4.1 and 4.2.

We can see in these numbers manifestations of both the "good news" and the "bad news" concerning the global economic situation. The good news is displayed in Figure 4.1, which contains plots of real GDP per capita for the four poorer nations among the selected eight: Algeria, Ecuador, Ghana and India. This figure illustrates the fact that most of the Less Developed Nations (the Third World nations) are in fact making substantial economic progress as measured by real GDP per capita. In fact, some LDCs have done considerably better over the recent past than the four representative nations utilized here. For example, China's economic progress has accelerated dramatically since the economic reforms of the 1980s which moved the Chinese economy away from the central planning associated with the planned socialism developed in the Soviet Union during the 1930s, and toward greater reliance on individual financial incentives and free market mechanisms. On the other hand, some LDCs have done quite poorly in terms of economic growth over the last few decades. This is especially true of many of the sub-Saharan African nations, such as Ghana.

The bad news concerning the current global economic gap is displayed in Figure 4.2. This figure contains plots of real GNP per capita for all eight nations included in Table 4.1. Figures 4.1 and 4.2 were drawn by a graphing program that automatically adjusts the axis range according to the data to be plotted. The

FIGURE 4.1
Per Capita Income Growth, 1960-2000
Algeria, Ecuador, Ghana, India

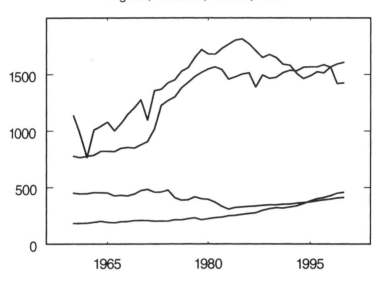

FIGURE 4.2
Per Capita Income Growth, 1960-2000
United States, France, Italy, Spain, Algeria, Ecuador, Ghana, India

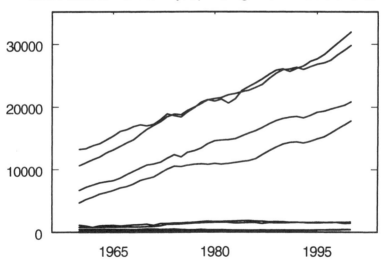

vertical axis range on Figure 4.1, based on data pertaining to the four poorer nations Algeria, Ecuador, Ghana and India, is from a minimum of 0 to a maximum of 1800. The vertical axis range on Figure 4.2, based on data for these four nations, plus the four rich nations U.S., France, Italy and Spain, is from a minimum of 0 to a maximum of 35000. As can be seen, the plots for the poor nations are barely perceptible and hardly distinguishable when included in a diagram which also shows plots for the rich nations. The economic progress of the poor nations, which may look quite respectable when these nations are compared only to each other (as in Figure 4.1), looks quite insignificant when these nations are compared with the rich nations of the world (as in Figure 4.2). Despite some progress among the poor nations, the economic gap is getting larger. Economic inequality may be measured in a variety of ways, no one of which is generally accepted as being significantly superior to all others. However, it is not particularly important which measure of inequality is utilized, because all commonly utilized measures, if applied to the nations of the world over the last few decades, indicate increasing inequality.

Table 4.3 and the corresponding Figure 4.3 provide further insight into the numerical dimensions of the contemporary economic gap. This table and figure are derived from Table 2.A.1, included in the tabular appendix to Chapter 2, which shows per capita income (in 1995 U.S. dollars), population, and Gross Domestic Product for 207 nations as of 2000. In 2000, Ethiopia had the lowest per capita income of $116, Luxembourg had the highest per capita income of $56,372, the United States had a per capita income of $31,996, and the mean per capita income over all 207 nations was $5,604.

Table 4.3 shows for each per capita income range: the percent of nations or population with a per capita income above the lower limit of the corresponding per capita income range and less than or equal to the upper limit of the range, and also two versions of the cumulative percent of nations or population. The first version is ascending: cumulation proceeds from the poorest to the richest. The second version is descending: cumulation proceeds from the richest to the poorest. The descending cumulative percents are simply the ascending cumulative percents subtracted from 100. By way of explanation, consider the 3000-4000 bracket. Some 5.797 percent of the 207 nations had per capita income in this range, and some 4.027 percent of the total population of the 207 nations lived in these nations. The ascending cumulative percentages tell us that 63.768 percent of nations had per capita income of $4,000 or less and 78.808 percent of the total population lives in those nations. The descending cumulative percentages tell us that 36.232 percent of nations have per capita income above $4,000 and 21.192 percent of the total population lives in those nations.

The table makes clear that the large majority of the world, whether considered in terms of nations or population, is relatively poor, and what is the other side of the same coin, that the small minority of the world, whether considered in terms of nations or population, is relatively rich. For example, if we were to take $10,000 as the per capita income differentiating relatively poor from relatively

TABLE 4.3
Distribution of Nations and Population
by Per Capita Income

Per Capita Income Range	Nations			Population		
	Percent	Cumulative Percent		Percent	Cumulative Percent	
		ascend.	descend.		ascend.	descend.
0-250	6.280	6.280	93.720	3.459	3.459	96.541
250-500	13.527	19.807	80.193	26.837	30.297	69.703
500-750	7.246	27.053	72.947	4.020	34.317	65.683
750-1000	7.246	34.300	65.700	27.170	61.487	38.513
1000-1500	7.246	41.546	58.454	4.920	66.407	33.593
1500-2000	8.213	49.758	50.242	2.725	69.131	30.869
2000-2500	3.865	53.623	46.377	3.940	73.071	26.929
2500-3000	4.348	57.971	42.029	1.709	74.780	25.220
3000-4000	5.797	63.768	36.232	4.027	78.808	21.192
4000-6000	6.280	70.048	29.952	4.725	83.533	16.467
6000-8000	6.280	76.329	23.671	1.025	84.557	15.443
8000-10000	1.932	78.261	21.739	0.105	84.662	15.338
10000-15000	4.348	82.609	17.391	1.224	85.886	14.114
15000-20000	3.382	85.990	14.010	0.837	86.723	13.277
20000-25000	4.831	90.821	9.179	2.939	89.662	10.338
25000-40000	7.729	98.551	1.449	8.109	97.771	2.229
40000-	1.449	100.000	0.000	2.229	100.000	0.000

Note:
"Percent" refers to the percentage of nations or population with a per capita income above the lower limit of the corresponding per capita income range and less than or equal to the upper limit of this range.
"Cumulative Percent—ascending" refers to the percentage of nations or population with a per capita income equal to or lower than the upper limit of the corresponding per capita income range. "Cumulative Percent—descending" refers to the percentage of nations or population with a per capita income higher than the upper limit of the corresponding per capita income range.

rich, some 78.261 percent of nations and 84.662 percent of population have this level of per capita income or less, while only 21.739 percent of nations and 15.338 percent of population have above this level of per capita income. The descending cumulative percent figures in Table 4.3 clearly demonstrate that whether we consider nations or population, the percent having more than a given per capita income is a rapidly declining function of the level of per capita income.

This indication is conveyed in graphical terms by Figure 4.3, which shows the two percentages (of nations and of population) plotted against per capita income. These plots are based on information on all 207 nations in ascending order of per capita income. Thus Figure 4.3 is more accurate than if it had been

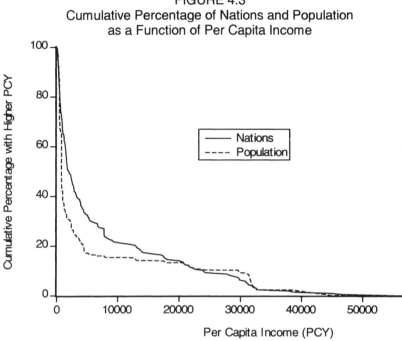

FIGURE 4.3
Cumulative Percentage of Nations and Population
as a Function of Per Capita Income

Per Capita Income (PCY)

based on the numbers shown in Table 4.3. One can see clearly in this figure the precipitous declines in the respective percentages up to approximately $10,000 in per capita income. This is a graphical depiction of the disturbing fact that the relatively poor people of the world greatly outnumber the relatively rich people. In the previous paragraph we considered the possibility of using $10,000 in per capita income as the cutoff separating "relatively poor" from "relatively rich." Another possibility would be to define "relatively poor" as having less than the mean income over 207 nations of $5,604 and "relatively rich" as having a per capita income above this level. Using this criterion and the nation-specific data displayed in Table 2.A.1, we ascertain that 83.533 percent of the world population is relatively poor and 16.467 percent is relatively rich.

SELF-SUSTAINED GROWTH: AN ILLUSORY PANACEA

The basic argument of this book is that the time has come for humanity to undertake a significant advance on two separate but closely interrelated fronts: the economic and the political. On the economic front we should attempt to overcome the problem of world poverty by means of a worldwide economic development effort designated the World Economic Equalization Program. On the political front we should attempt to overcome the problem of international anarchy by means of a limited world government designated the Federal Union of Democratic Nations. Success on either front is likely to hinge critically on success on the other front. A concerted international economic development effort on the necessary scale is unlikely to be undertaken and vigorously pursued if not supported by a supernational political organization qualitatively beyond the United Nations of today. And unless we eventually achieve a high degree of economic equality across all the nations of the world, the prospects for benign and effective world government in the long term would be precarious.

At the present time, there does in fact exist a significant, ongoing international economic development effort involving the transfer of investment resources from the rich nations to the poor nations. Some of these transfers are in the form of profit-seeking investment by transnational corporations, and some are in the form of government sponsored development assistance programs. The organizational infrastructure is indeed in place. It is simply a question of scale. The present transfers are far short of what is needed to attain a reasonable degree of economic equalization within a reasonable period of historical time. A very large-scale expansion of government sponsored economic development assistance programs is well merited and ought to be implemented as soon as possible.

The opposed argument—that the rich nations should either reduce their foreign aid contributions or maintain the status quo on foreign aid—may be supported by either the "pessimistic scenario" or the "optimistic scenario." According to the pessimistic scenario, the economic gap of today cannot and will not be closed within any foreseeable period of time. The gap will persist for centuries, possibly for millennia. During these centuries and even millennia, any impulses in the poor nations toward forcible redistribution of world income will have to be deterred by the powerful military establishments of the rich nations. This situation, according to the pessimists, is absolutely unavoidable—therefore it is a waste of energy to bemoan it or try to change it.

According to the optimistic scenario, the economic gap can and will be closed within a foreseeable period of time—in the absence of any major expansion in the overseas development assistance contributions of the rich nations. The dramatic economic progress of Japan over the second half of the twentieth century—progress which has made Japan into one of the richest nations in the contemporary world—will eventually be repeated by all the nations of the world, even those that are currently among the poorest. Rapid growth, in this view, is the "natural" condition of the economy. Transition from economic stagnation or slow economic growth to rapid economic growth is veritably inevitable in the modern world, with its pervasive trade and technological connections among the national economies. The "upward path" will eventually be found by all nations—for each nation it is merely a question of when. Finding that upward path does not depend significantly on foreign aid contributions; rather it depends on opening the national economy to the world economy by eliminating trade and investment barriers, and on reducing to a minimum governmental regulation of business enterprise and taxation of private households. There is no need to expand foreign aid, since the desired objective will be achieved without any such expansion. This cheerful scenario is no doubt captivating, but it most probably represents mere wishful thinking.

In the 1950s and 1960s, the term "self-sustained growth" (or "self-sustaining growth") achieved the status of a mantra among the optimists. If the Less Developed Countries (LDCs) of the Third World could only be set on the path of self-sustained growth, then the huge economic gap separating the rich nations from the poor nations would soon be eliminated. The general presumption was (and remains) that a very modest amount of economic development assistance— if any at all—would be required to get the LDCs on the path of self-sustained growth. More recently, in response to growing environmental concerns, the term "sustainable growth" has become popular. Sustainable growth is economic growth of such a nature and rate as not to put too great a strain on natural resources and the natural environment. Growth at greater than the sustainable rate would lead eventually to resource exhaustion and environmental breakdown, which in turn would precipitate economic stagnation or decline.

The problem is that self-sustained growth, in and of itself, whether at a sustainable rate or a non-sustainable rate, is not a sufficient condition for economic convergence between the rich nations and the poor nations within a foreseeable period of historical time. If we are to have a significant hope of such convergence, we need to go qualitatively beyond self-sustained growth. It would greatly improve the prospects for the long-term success of worldwide human civilization if we would put aside such notions as "self-sustained growth" and "sustainable growth," and replace them with "economic equalization" as the central economic objective to be sought and attained. In all likelihood, economic equalization within a reasonable period of historical time will not happen easily and automatically. In all likelihood, it will not happen in the absence of a tremendous, coordinated program of hugely expanded economic development assistance from the rich nations to the poor nations.

The ultimate objective of such a program would indeed be self-sustained growth and sustainable growth for each and every nation in the world. That is, once the program has been successfully completed, no nation will be dependent on foreign aid contributions from other nations to assist its growth (growth will be self-sustained), and also no nation will be growing at a rate that puts undue stress on natural resources and the environment (growth will be sustainable). But it will *also* be true that there will be no extravagant variations in average living standards among the nations. The idea is to have both self-sustained growth and sustainable growth for all nations in the long term, but in the short term to concentrate on economic equalization between rich nations and poor nations.

The achievement of self-sustained growth (and sustainable growth) in the poor nations will not, in and of itself, lead to economic convergence between the rich nations and the poor nations. To begin with, it is obvious that if the rate of self-sustained growth in a poor nation is lower than the rate of self-sustained growth in a rich nation, then the economic gap between the two nations will perpetually widen as long as this situation persists. The only way it will be possible for the poor nation to catch up with the rich nation is for the poor nation to be growing more rapidly than the rich nation. But there is no significant evidence at the present time that the poor nations as a whole are in fact growing faster than the rich nations as a whole.

In absolute terms, they are clearly growing more slowly, as shown by the widening gap over the 1960-2000 period depicted in Figure 4.2. It might be thought that if the absolute gap between rich nations and poor nations is getting wider, then it *must* be true that the rich nations are growing faster than the poor nations. But it is a technical fact that this is not the case—as far as *percentage* growth is concerned. A commonplace simplification in the analysis of economic growth is that of percentage growth at a constant geometric rate. Although the real-world economic growth of nations is subject to a great deal of short-term variability, in many cases constant-rate geometric increase provides a reasonable approximation to actual growth over a lengthy interval of time. Let us imagine two nations, a poor nation and a rich nation, both of which are growing at a constant rate of geometric growth. Of course, if the geometric growth rate of the rich nation remains higher than the geometric growth rate of the poor nation for an indefinite period, then it is clear that the absolute gap between the rich nation and the poor nation will continue to become larger for an indefinite period.

But let us now imagine that in fact the geometric growth rate of the poor nation is higher than the geometric growth rate of the rich nation. Clearly, the poor nation will eventually catch up with the rich nation. But there are two points that must be emphasized even if we envision this optimistic case. First, even if the poor nation is indeed experiencing a significantly higher rate of geometric growth than the rich nation, if the current difference in living standards is very large then it may require many decades—even centuries—for the difference to be overcome. Second, if the initial gap in living standards is very large then the absolute gap between the rich nation and the poor nation might continue to increase for a long period of time, even though the poor nation is growing at a significantly higher rate of geometric growth than the rich nation. Thus it is *not* the case (contrary to intuition) that a widening absolute gap necessarily means that the rich nation is growing faster than the poor nation in percentage terms.

Without going into the analytical details, if we assume that nation 2 (the poor nation) is growing at a faster annual rate of geometric growth than nation 1 (the rich nation), we may then ascertain both the number of years it will take for nation 2 to catch up to nation 1 ("convergence years"), and also the number of years until the maximum absolute difference between the two nations is reached ("maximum difference years"). Table 4.4 shows convergence years and maximum difference years as a function of: (1) the initial year ratio between nation 1 and nation 2 per capita income, and (2) the growth rate in nation 2, for a case in which the annual growth rate in nation 1 is .010 (1 percent). For example, if the initial year ratio is 50, and nation 2 grows at a rate of .020 per annum (2 percent), which is twice as high as the nation 1 rate of growth, it will require 398 years for nation 2 to catch up with nation 1, and some 327 years will elapse

TABLE 4.4
Convergence Years and
Maximum Difference Years

A. Years required for nation 2 per capita income to catch up to nation 1
   per capita income

g_2	initial year ratio of PCY_1 to PCY_2				
	10	20	30	40	50
.015	466	607	689	747	792
.020	234	304	345	374	398
.025	156	203	231	250	265
.030	117	153	173	188	199

B. Years required for the maximum absolute difference to occur between
   nation 2 per capita income and nation 1 per capita income

g_2	initial year ratio of PCY_1 to PCY_2				
	10	20	30	40	50
.015	385	525	607	665	711
.020	164	234	275	305	327
.025	95	141	169	189	204
.030	62	97	118	133	144

before the absolute difference in the per capita incomes of the two nations starts to decline. The numbers in Table 4.4 are probably higher than most people would have guessed. The initial ratios of per capita income along the top of the two parts of the table are representative of existing ratios of GNP per capita between contemporary real-world nations at various points along the income spectrum. The poor nation growth rates along the sides of the table are probably rather optimistic. And yet decades at a minimum and centuries at a maximum are required to start lowering the absolute gap (the maximum difference years) and to eliminate the absolute gap (the convergence years).

There is nothing magical, therefore, in the condition of self-sustained growth at a constant geometric growth rate. It is certainly not the case that once this condition has been achieved in all of the LDCs, the problem of radical differences in living standards across nations will melt away in short order. The real-world economic gap is sufficiently huge that even under very optimistic assumptions about future growth rates as between rich nations and poor nations, the gap promises to remain very persistent.

Of course, the biggest single problem with the idea that the achievement of self-sustained growth by all of the poor nations of today will lead to the elimination of the economic gap in a reasonable period of time is not that unless the poor nations commence growing at ridiculously unrealistic rates, it will take a very long period of time for them to catch up with the rich nations. Rather the biggest single problem is that there is no good reason to expect the poor nations—in the absence of a tremendous expansion of foreign development assistance from the rich nations—to achieve rates of self-sustained economic growth higher than the rates currently being maintained by the rich nations. Among those with limited knowledge of the evolution of global economic conditions over the past few decades, a certain rosy optimism is commonplace, which might be summed up as follows: "The rich nations of today—the United States, the Western European nations, Japan and so on—have shown the way to a high level of economic prosperity. They have shown the kind of science and technology that is necessary, and also the legal institutions and cultural attitudes that are necessary. All the poor nations of today have to do is to imitate exactly the science, technology, law and culture that prevails in the rich nations—and then they too will be rich nations." In this sanguine view, now that it is clear what is needed for economic prosperity, economic prosperity is the natural order of things, and soon—by means of comprehensive and careful emulation of the rich nations—the poor nations will also achieve economic prosperity.

The central problem here is that in order to imitate the "science and technology" of economic production as it exists in the rich nations, the poor nations need to accumulate a tremendous amount of capital of all types: physical capital (plant and equipment) for use in business enterprise, human capital (education and training), and social infrastructure capital (roads, schools, hospitals, etc.). Modern production techniques are intensive in the use of capital—if you do not possess the capital you cannot use the modern production techniques. There are at least two major impediments to the poor nations accumulating the large amount of required capital on their own. First, there is a tendency for poorer nations with lower per capita income to have lower rates of saving, and saving is necessary as a basis for capital investment. Second, there is a tendency for poorer nations with lower per capita income to have higher population growth rates, which retards progress with respect to per capita income, and thereby with respect to saving.

If we even briefly contemplate the long-term economic history of human civilization over the approximately 5000 years of recorded history, we immediately recognize that strong growth in the economic living standards of the general human population has been a rare and ephemeral phenomenon, and that the dramatic economic progress that has been made over the last 250 years in the richest nations of today has been utterly unprecedented in the history of humanity. Consideration of the hundreds and thousands of years in which the technology of production and general living standards remained more or less static, brings home the fact that the general rule throughout human history has not been economic growth but rather economic stagnation. In this light, the prevailing economic condition in the great majority of poor nations today is "typical"— what is "atypical" is the prevailing economic condition in the handful of very rich nations. It is probably quite unrealistic, therefore, to expect the poor nations, in the absence of very substantial assistance from the rich nations, to bootstrap themselves up to the economic level currently enjoyed by the rich nations.

As to the economic success of the rich nations of today, there is at least one critical determinant of their rise that is clearly non-reproducible in today's world. As of the early 1600s, Western Europe's population was perhaps 50 million, certainly not more than 100 million. This was the era that saw the first important steps taken toward the intensive development of the North American continent, a continent which contained at least five to ten times the resource endowment of Europe, and which up to that time had been, for practical purposes, untouched by modern civilization. Now consider the present-day nation of India, a nation of approximately one billion persons with a natural resource base thinner than that of Europe now, let alone the Europe of 1600. Where is India's North American continent? Where is a virgin wilderness containing five to ten times India's resource endowment, into which India can advance with a confidence born of "manifest destiny"? India cannot advance into China, a densely populated nation of 1.25 billion, nor can it advance into the equally densely populated nations of Southeast Asia or the Middle East. Nor are there lightly populated, resource-rich regions overseas over which India has established firm political control. The fact of the matter is that there is not now—nor will there ever be—the equivalent to India of what the North American continent represented to the Western Europe of the early 1600s. The same thing is true of all the other less developed nations of the world. Therefore, it is obnoxiously patronizing and self-serving for the rich nations today to say to the poor nations: "Just follow our example, and you too will achieve the economic prosperity that we have achieved." The poor nations could very legitimately—if undiplomatically—respond to such an admonition along these lines: "We are certainly endeavoring very hard to follow your example. But you could make it easier for us by magically conjuring up for our use millions of square miles of resource-rich virgin wilderness equivalent to what was available to you in the form of the North American continent as of the early 1600s."

POVERTY AS A THREAT TO HARMONY

In some ways, "poverty" is more sensibly understood as a relative concept rather than as an absolute concept. Let us imagine a population that had a sufficient amount to eat and drink to avoid death from hunger or thirst, a sufficient amount of clothing and shelter to avoid death from exposure, and a sufficiently balanced birth rate and death rate to maintain a constant level of population. Now imagine that everyone in this population consumes exactly the same amount of each and every consumption good, so that perfect equality prevails. Finally, imagine that this population is entirely isolated, and is aware of no other population in the world with either higher living standards or lower living standards. No one in such a population would be considered, either by himself/herself or anyone else in the population, to be either "poor" or "rich." No one in such a population would have less than any other individual, within either the same or any other population, and so no one would be "poor." Similarly, no one in such a population would have more than any other individual, within either the same or any other population, and so no one would be "rich." There would be no stresses on the social fabric generated by emotional reactions to economic inequality.

This is not to say that there would be no stresses and strains at all. Human nature being what it is, it seems likely that it would occur to at least a few individuals that they could increase their own living standards by stealing, or otherwise appropriating, some consumption goods from other individuals, and that some such schemes might actually be carried out. Also, it is not to say that a condition of perfect economic equality is either possible or even desirable. It is obvious to most people that there are many differences between individual human beings, that some of these differences impact significantly on relative earning capabilities, and that over-zealous endeavors to equalize consumption could and probably would have an adverse effect on effort incentives and economic production. But while most people believe that a certain amount of economic inequality is necessary for a high overall level of economic prosperity, they recognize in that same inequality a definite problem as far as internal harmony and political stability within a nation are concerned. Just as economic inequality within their borders creates internal problems for nations, so too economic inequality among nations intensifies frictions and conflicts among these nations.

Although world federalists in the post-World War II era have viewed a world government primarily as an instrument for the reduction of the risk of a nuclear war among the superpowers, they have also viewed such a government as an instrument through which to overcome the long-term threat to international harmony and permanent peace represented by the economic gap between rich nations and poor nations. One of the earliest expressions of this particular vision was contributed by the historian Stringfellow Barr, a member of the "Committee to Frame a World Constitution" formed by Robert Hutchins and Giuseppe Borgese of the University of Chicago in the immediate aftermath of the Second World War. In 1950, following completion of the Committee's work and the publication of their "Preliminary Draft of a World Constitution," the University of Chicago Press published a 30-page pamphlet by Barr entitled "Let's Join the Human Race." The themes and ideas in this short tract were later amplified in his book *Citizens of the World* (Doubleday, 1952), which boasted a preface by Justice William O. Douglas of the U.S. Supreme Court. Barr asserted that the highly interdependent goals of world government and worldwide economic equalization should be pursued simultaneously, and that neither one was likely to be a success in the absence of the other. This, of course, is exactly the thesis being argued herein. The following passage from "Let's Join the Human Race" contains Barr's explanation of what we refer to herein as the "economic impediment to world government":

> No human community has ever lived in peace for long without a government. The new world community will prove no exception to this rule. It is unrealistic to expect it to. Those who have discovered why a "world government" is necessary are accused of being "idealistic"; but only the most starry-eyed "idealist" can

expect the new world-wide community which science and invention have created to be unlike all previous human communities and to get along without common government. In any case, the chances are overwhelming that it will get a common government, either by mutual agreement or by conquest. That is why so many human beings in the world fear and distrust both Russia and America. Both of them look like strong candidates for world empire. On the one hand, they seem to believe more and more in the use of force—in "getting tough," as we Americans love to say. The rest of the world is not surprised that each claims to be a peace-loving nation. The ancient Romans loved peace too—and imposed it by force on others.

But there is a frightful obstacle to getting a common government by mutual consent. I am not speaking of the world community's many races or its many languages or its national jealousies or its different religions. Racism seems either silly or vicious to more and more men today—even white men, who have had a vested economic interest in racism. Language barriers are awkward, but they can be surmounted. Nationalism is violent today in countries that are fighting for national independence, particularly in Asia and Africa. But in the independent countries, nationalist feeling is beginning to look to more and more people like comic opera, and this for two simple reasons. First, economic nationalism squeezes hard on a great many people. Second, national governments can no longer offer their peoples even reasonable military security, not even by taxing them half to death and conscripting their strongest young men to boot. As to religion, there are not many parts of the planet where people are determined to force their religion on their neighbors or to refuse to live under a common government with neighbors of a different creed.

None of these obstacles to a common government is decisive. There is a much more serious obstacle. It is an obstacle that the philosopher Plato was speaking of when he said that most cities were not really one city but two—the city of the rich and the city of the poor. In the last century a Conservative prime minister of Britain wrote a novel under the subtitle, "The Two Nations"—the rich and the poor. History suggests that wherever a community is too sharply divided between rich and poor, one of two things happens: either the "city of the poor" rises and overthrows the other "city" or this other city imposes order by force on the city of the poor. If our generation were to set up a common government for the world community, before it moved aggressively to revive the world's economy, one of these two fates would sorely threaten it. In contemporary terms, the world government would be under heavy pressure to go Communist or to go Fascist.

The City of the Rich, based largely on the economy of the United States, sees this problem less clearly than does the City of the Poor—the hungry, half-naked, diseased, and mostly colored millions. If Americans propose to them a common government "to keep law and order" in the world-wide City of Man, to control "the bomb," and let us all enjoy life in peace, then those who are not enjoying life and who fear the bomb much less than they fear famine may well be unmoved. There is a lot of ease and abundance in America for a bomb to destroy, so we go to bed at night asking, "How can we sleep?" But they ask, "When do we eat?" Those questions measure a yawning gulf between the Two Cities—cities that really do need one government. It is true that man shall not live by bread alone, but should this particular statement by Jesus Christ be quoted between meals to those who have had no meal at all?

Another way to state the problem of the Two Cities is to say that though law and order have to be *enforced* in human communities by means of government, no government enforces them for long that does not bother about justice. Today the City of the Poor might well wish to know whether the City of the Rich really cares, before setting up political housekeeping with it. Nothing would reassure it more quickly or surely than a frontal assault by the whole City on the unspeakable misery of most of its inhabitants. That is why President Truman's "Point Four" remarks, even though timid and vague, briefly stirred not only the consciences of Americans but the hopes of men throughout the planet. The discussion which followed those remarks has now bogged down, because the false assumptions on which it was based could not sustain its weight. So "Point Four" has become a gimmick in the cold war against Russia; and the problem back of the cold war, back of the Korean catastrophe, and even back of World War III, if that should break out before these words are in print—that problem has not been tackled.

Barr refers here to the inaugural address of Harry S. Truman on January 20, 1949. Truman proposed that United States foreign policy be guided by four points. Point one was to continue "unfaltering support for the United Nations and related agencies." Point two was to continue support for "world economic recovery" from the ravages of World War II, with special emphasis on the European Recovery Program, commonly known as the Marshall Plan. Point three was to "strengthen freedom-loving nations against the dangers of aggression" from the communist bloc, specifically by means of founding an organization later designated the North Atlantic Treaty Organization (NATO). Finally, point four was to "embark on a bold new program for making the benefits of our scientific advances and industrial progress available for the improvement and growth of underdeveloped areas."

Strictly interpreted, the amplification of this fourth point provided by Truman in his inaugural address did not amount to a design for real-world foreign development assistance programs as they later evolved, still less for a World Economic Equalization Program along the lines advocated herein. In 1949, the United States economy was laboring under the burden of Cold War rearmament, as well as the Marshall Plan aid program to Western Europe. Truman states that "the material resources [i.e., overseas capital investment] which we can afford to use for the assistance of other peoples are limited," and proposes that development assistance be primarily in terms of encouraging private investment and providing relatively inexpensive technical assistance. Later experience strongly suggested that technical assistance is of modest value if the financial capital is not available to adequately implement the technologies with which the technical specialists are most familiar. It also strongly suggested that profit-seeking private investment becomes important only after nations are well into the economic development process—that by itself it is unlikely to initiate this process. But this is not to denigrate the historic importance of Truman's proposal that the rich nations make a serious effort to assist the poor nations to raise their living standards. By way of justification of the effort, Truman states: "Their poverty [that of the un-

derdeveloped nations] is a handicap and a threat both to them and to more prosperous areas."

Let us focus here on Truman's statement that the poverty of the Third World
is a "threat" to the rich nations. The acknowledgement of a "threat," in and of
itself, is not particularly meaningful, since it says nothing about the *magnitude* of
the threat. The appropriate amount of resources to devote to either controlling, or
permanently eliminating, a certain threat is directly proportional to the magnitude of the threat. If the threat is major, it makes sense to devote a large amount
of resources to dealing with it. On the other hand, if the threat is minor, it makes
sense to devote a small amount of resources to dealing with it. Whether the
threat is major or minor, determination of the appropriate amount of resources to
devote to it involves a benefit-cost calculation: i.e., the benefits of controlling or
eliminating the threat must be weighed against the costs of the resources necessary to do so.

The prevailing, mainstream assumption of the present day is that the threat
posed by the poor nations to the rich nations is relatively minor, hence relatively
minor resources should be devoted to foreign development assistance for purposes of dealing with this threat. The calculus underlying this prevailing judgment is muddled in two separate ways. First, the long-term threat posed by the
existence of global economic inequality is being underestimated, and second, the
costs of permanently eliminating (as opposed to "controlling") this particular
long-term threat are being overestimated. Of these two errors, the second (the
error of overestimating the costs of eliminating the threat) is probably more important than the first (the error of underestimating the threat). In Chapter 6
below, I will present important evidence that the problem of global economic
equality could be overcome at the veritably negligible cost to the rich nations of
a very slight reduction—not in their existing living standards—but rather in the
rate of growth of their living standards. In other words, world economic equalization is achievable on the basis of what I call "Common Progress." The failure
of the populations of the rich nations in the past to grasp this is responsible for
the overestimation of the costs of eliminating global poverty—such elimination
is erroneously assumed to be possible only on the basis of what I term "Crude
Redistribution." But for the remainder of the present chapter, I will concentrate
on the first error: the underestimation by the populations of the rich nations of
the magnitude of the long-term threat to their own welfare posed by the existence
of the global economic gap.

The threat to international stability inherent in the economic gap proceeds
from the natural propensity within all human beings toward the emotion of envy.
Envy is deemed by all human cultures past and present to be one of the cardinal
vices. An important part of the socialization of young children by their parents
and teachers is to instill in children respect for the property rights of others and
control over their inherent impulses toward furtive or forcible appropriation of
the property of others. Individuals who were inadequately socialized in this
regard as children, tend to end up in prison for the crime of theft. As adults, we

are all under constant pressure—some of it provided by the law enforcement system and some of it provided by the exhortations of others—to suppress within ourselves any and all tendencies toward "childish envy," lest these tendencies precipitate unacceptable behavior that will be punished either here or in the here-after. But the vice of envy, as is the case with all other vices, is inherent in human nature. It cannot be completely eradicated but merely imperfectly con-trolled. And very often the primeval tendency toward envy is rationalized as "legitimate resentment." Legitimate resentment is the emotion of hostility one feels against others who have violated one's own property rights. If one is robbed at gunpoint, legitimate resentment is the emotion one feels against the robber. Whether any given emotion of hostility generated by issues of property ownership constitutes "childish envy" or "legitimate resentment" is often a very subjective judgment. Similarly, whether any given action pertaining to property ownership represents "justice" or "injustice" is also, in many cases, a very sub-jective judgment. As are many related questions of "morality" and "immorality."

Consider, for example, person A who robs at gunpoint another person B. Normally we would say that prior to the robbery, person A entertained the unworthy emotion of "childish envy" toward person B, while after the robbery person B harbored the understandable emotion of "legitimate resentment" toward person A. But we can certainly imagine circumstances in which the usual moral perspective would be reversed. Perhaps person B is both very wealthy and very nasty, and has accumulated his current wealth by various deplorable means such as cheating elderly people out of their life savings, or trafficking in such devastating drugs as heroin or cocaine. And perhaps person A is a very pleasant and conscientious person who has been driven to desperation by events beyond his control, and who utilizes the proceeds from the robbery to feed his helpless young children. We can go even further than this in our imaginings. We can imagine that at some time in the past, person B, by means of trickery and deceit, appropriated a large amount of person A's financial resources, and that the robbery is for the purpose of restoring to A his rightful property. In this case, clearly, A's emotion toward B would not be "childish envy" but rather "legi-timate resentment," and the robbery itself, while probably illegal, would defin-itely not be immoral.

To the extent that the populations of the poor nations today are aware of the much higher living standards of the populations of the rich nations, they must inevitably conceive a desire for these higher living standards. This is merely human nature, and as everyone knows, it is impossible to change human nature. The populations of the rich nations want the populations of the poor nations to suppress the emotions naturally aroused by desires for higher living standards on the basis that they are "childish envy." But there is a natural tendency in the populations of the poor nations to interpret these same emotions as "legitimate resentment." Everyone wants to feel justified in his or her emotions, and this is no less true of the populations of the poor nations as of the populations of the rich nations. The tendency toward rationalization of one's natural emotions goes hand in hand with a tendency toward blaming other human beings for one's own misfortunes. It is very difficult for any normal human being to accept that his/her misfortunes are the result of either random fate or his/her own failings. It is so much more satisfying to place the blame on other human beings. Sorrow is easily transformed into hostility, because sorrow is immutable, while hostility can be assuaged by punishing the object(s) of hostility.

This brings us to the concept of "economic imperialism," according to which the rich nations of today owe a considerable proportion of their high living standards to their past and present economic relationships with the poor nations. Whether these relationships manifested (and still manifest) unethical exploitation or voluntary interchange, is a highly subjective question, as is the question of whether and to what extent these relationships should be altered in the future. At one extreme is the viewpoint that a very great deal of the present-day economic gap between the rich nations and the poor nations is owing to past and present exploitation of the latter by the former, and that in consequence the former have a moral obligation to provide to the latter the amount of economic resources required to bring about dramatic economic progress. At the other extreme is the viewpoint that the poor nations owe whatever economic progress they have achieved over the last two centuries to their interaction with the rich nations, and that the reasons why the poor nations have not achieved greater economic progress are entirely their own responsibility: a combination of excessive fertility with dysfunctional political institutions and cultural attitudes. Somewhere between these two is the mainstream viewpoint (more dominant in the rich nations than in the poor nations) that it was an unfortunate accident that past economic progress has been uneven, that the responsibility for this accident lies neither with the rich nations nor with the poor nations, and that satisfactory economic progress in the poor nations can be achieved by means of a combination of limited development assistance from the rich nations with significant changes in the political institutions and cultural attitudes within the poor nations.

It is unquestionable that trade and investment with the poor nations has been economically beneficial to the rich nations. The benefits that have accrued to the advanced nations from economic interchange with the less developed world fall into two general categories. First, trade has given the advanced nations access to natural resources and primary agricultural commodities. No doubt the most dramatic single example of this is petroleum from the Middle East and Latin America. A lengthy list could be compiled of important commodities supplied exclusively, mostly, or in large part by the underdeveloped nations. Second, there is the fact that the underdeveloped world provides profitable opportunities for capital in two ways: by providing markets for manufactured goods, and by providing opportunities for direct capital investment. But although these benefits are obviously important, any estimations of exactly *how important* they are, in a precise numerical sense, would be extremely problematical. And just as it is impossible to determine exactly how important economic interaction between rich nations and poor nations has been for the rich nations, the same holds true for the poor nations. For example, several oil-rich Middle Eastern nations have achieved high per capita income on the basis of oil exports. On the other hand, many nations primarily dependent on agricultural exports remain among the poorest in the world. Foreign private investment has been very important to the progress of some nations such as South Korea and Taiwan, but it has left many other poor nations laboring under a tremendous burden of external debt. It would be difficult if not impossible to extract from these diverse indications a reliable and accurate estimate of the overall effect on the poor nations of their economic relations with the rich nations.

In a political sense, it is not necessarily very reassuring that no very compelling case can be made, in a strictly scientific or rigorously academic sense, in support of the basic proposition from the economic imperialism concept that economic relations between the rich nations and the poor nations have benefited the former more than the latter. Given the tremendous size of the economic gap between rich nations and poor nations, this proposition has tremendous intuitive appeal to the populations of the poor nations, regardless of its status in terms of a purely objective evaluation. No one, whether an inhabitant of a rich nation or of a poor nation, is in a position to make a purely objective evaluation of this particular proposition. From a psychological point of view, the proposition offers a compelling rationalization for the discomfort naturally engendered in the relatively poor by the awareness that they coexist in the world with the relatively rich. It strengthens the subjective case that the emotion associated with this discomfort is to be deemed "legitimate resentment" rather than "childish envy." To the extent that the poor harbor what they consider to be legitimate resentment against the rich, their propensity to live in peaceful cooperation and harmony with the rich is diminished.

Let us now envision that humanity does *not* move forward toward a world government along the lines of the herein proposed Federal Union of Democratic Nations, and does *not* initiate a massive international economic development effort along the lines of the proposed World Economic Equalization Program. Instead of these progressive initiatives, imagine that we continue with the sovereign nation-state system and minimalist foreign aid, and consequently the economic gap between the rich nations and the poor nations continues to widen, as it has done for the last several decades. What, then, may we look forward to?

To begin with, it will be necessary for the rich nations to maintain very substantial military forces in order to deter the poor nations from armed aggression. History is full of plundering expeditions by poorer peoples desirous of appropriating the material possessions of richer peoples. At the present time, it is conventional for military authorities in the rich nations to dismiss the military capabilities of the poor nations as negligible and insignificant. They point confidently to the Persian Gulf War of January-February 1991—in which the technically superior and better trained forces of the U.S.-led coalition slaughtered Iraqi forces with impunity—as an example of what would almost certainly happen if a poor nation were ever so imprudent as to take up arms against a rich nation. Even assuming this is true, and without commenting on the morality (or lack thereof) of this rather arrogant attitude, we should consider the matter of cost—financial cost. Citizens of the rich nations at the present time are reluctant to undertake significant expansion of foreign aid because "it would cost too much." But they are neglecting to take account of the costs of supporting a military establishment sufficiently strong to deter aggression by poor nations for a prolonged period stretching into the indefinite future. During the several decades of the Cold War, the rich nations became accustomed to a heavy military burden because it was considered indispensable owing to the aggressive tendencies of communism. Now that the Cold War is winding down and communist aggression is a declining threat, the need to finance a large military establishment is also declining. Military expenditures by the rich nations have indeed declined significantly over the last decade, but they have not declined as much as would have been possible in the absence of the large economic gap. If all or most nations had roughly equivalent per capita income, and thus the tendency toward economically-inspired aggression were much lower, it might become possible for the rich nations to reduce military expenditure to perhaps one or two percent of Gross National Product.

What I am proposing in this book is that the rich nations undertake a massive foreign development assistance program, that would cost them between four and seven percent of GNP—for a relatively brief period of time. If the program were to be a failure, i.e., if living standards in the recipient poor nations were not to rise quickly and dramatically, then the program would be discontinued after only one to two decades. On the other hand, if the initial indications were favorable, it might have to be continued for several decades before sufficient success is achieved for the program to be terminated. If such a program is not undertaken, then the economic gap is likely to persist for centuries—and throughout those centuries it will be necessary for the rich nations to continuously maintain powerful military forces. From the perspective of the populations of the rich nations, it will be very much cheaper in the long run to abrogate the economic underpinnings of international hostility and aggression.

Nor can it be assumed that the costs of deterring the poor nations will be confined to supporting military forces. So long as tensions remain, there is always the possibility that war will occur despite generous expenditures by all sides on military forces whose purpose it is to deter other nations from initiating warfare. Basic predispositions toward hostility generate arms competitions, and arms competitions further increase the probability of warfare. Arms competitions preceded both World War I and World War II. The nuclear arms competition associated with the Cold War has not generated World War III—yet. It is true that the probability of World War III within the immediate future has diminished greatly in the recent past, owing to the collapse and dissolution of the Soviet Union. But in light of all prior human history, complacency would be ill-advised. The United States and the Russian Federation are still armed with thousands of thermonuclear warheads, and their newfound "friendship" is somewhat strained and precarious. Of course, living standards in the Russian Federation, despite several years of assiduous effort to emulate the democratic market capitalist system of the United States, remain quite low in relation to those in the United States. This does not assist the cause of amity and common purpose between these two superpowers. Living standards in the Russian Federation are astronomical relative to those in China, India and Pakistan—nations that have deemed a nuclear capability essential to their national interests. The past history of the Soviet Union suggests that a nation does not necessarily have to be very wealthy in order to field a very formidable military machine. The current history of the People's Republic of China, a nation that has not—unlike the Soviet Union—abandoned Marxism, may be leading toward the same suggestion. Other Third World nations may eventually choose to emulate the Chinese example.

Throughout the four decades of the Cold War, the wealthy capitalist nations kept the communist threat embodied in Moscow at bay, because if it became absolutely necessary in a last-resort, desperation situation, they possessed the capability and the determination to "nuke" Moscow. What made the situation so dangerous was that the Soviet leaders in Moscow possessed an equivalent capability and the determination to "nuke" Washington, New York, London, Paris, and so on and so forth—if it became absolutely necessary. At the present time, the nuclear capability of the PRC is roughly equivalent to what the USSR's was in the early to mid-1950s, at a time when American military leaders were confident that the U.S. could and would win a nuclear war with the Soviets.

Not too long after that the Soviet nuclear capability increased to a point where conventional wisdom held that an all-out nuclear war would result in "Mutual Assured Destruction." At the present time, American military leaders are equally confident that the West could and would win a nuclear war with the PRC. But China, as everyone knows, is rapidly building up economic muscle, and with economic muscle goes military capability. At the moment the West could "nuke" Peking without too serious a threat that Washington, New York, London, Paris, and so on and so forth, would be nuked in retaliation. But the situation would be quite different if there were indeed a significant probability that China could destroy the major cities of the West, either in retaliation or possibly preemptively—if the latter were ordained by history. Japan was an "up and coming" superpower when it decided to bomb Pearl Harbor on December 7, 1941. At the present time, China is an "up and coming" superpower. If we (humanity) persist too long with the present policy of aimless drift, history may repeat itself—and this time the consequences for human civilization could be fatal.

Of course, at the present time a "nuclear sneak attack" by the PRC against any of the major Western powers seems preposterously unlikely. Things would have to evolve a long way for that to happen, both in terms of China's nuclear capability, and in terms of antagonistic confrontation between China and other nations. But the point remains that if we look into the future—and not too long into the future at that—such things could indeed happen. Looking back at history, we see that Japan had been developing for well over half a century prior to the fateful attack on Pearl Harbor. As of 1941, Japan felt that her economic power entitled her to an economic empire (the "Greater East-Asia Co-Prosperity Sphere"), that such an empire would benefit many peoples in the area just as much as it would benefit the Japanese people, and thus she was righteously incensed that the United States was opposing this objective. The military situation at the time of the attack was highly complicated, with much U.S. attention focused on the European war. The attack itself was on a military objective rather than on a civilian objective. Japan's leaders in 1941 believed that this "warning shot," as it were, would induce the United States to desist from its opposition to Japanese imperialism in the Far East. History records that the Japanese leaders were in error. Once again, as so often in the past, miscalculation by the leadership embroiled a nation in a devastating war. Is it reasonable to expect that never again will such miscalculations occur—even though the current international situation is fundamentally similar to what it was in the past?

In current discussions of the threat to worldwide security and equity represented by the relative poverty of such a large proportion of the world population, the possibility of armed aggression by the poorest nations against the richest nations is rarely considered, owing to the fact that the implicit time horizons of these discussions are very short, and do not allow for significant changes in current conditions. To the extent that all-out nuclear world war is envisioned, it is in the context of the poorer regions of the world generating localized wars in which the superpowers might become embroiled. There is a long tradition in modern history of geopolitical confrontations between the major powers. Each nation endeavors, by means of formal and informal alliances, to maintain an appropriate balance of power under which it will be secure against attack from other nations. The basic problem is that what one nation regards as an appropriate balance of power tends to be regarded by other nations as an "imbalance of power"—this leads to constant destabilizing adjustments and maneuvers. In some cases, the outbreak of warfare between the smaller members of opposing alliances leads to warfare between the major members. This happened in the case of World War I, when Austria's declaration of war on Serbia quickly escalated into total warfare between the alliance of Germany, Austria-Hungary and Turkey on the one side, and the alliance of Britain, France, Italy and Russia on the other side.

An example of what might eventually happen in the future is provided by the more recent Persian Gulf War. Iraq, under the onerous dictatorship of Saddam Hussein, lusted for the lucrative oil wells of Kuwait. Less generously endowed with oil resources than Kuwait, Iraq's 1990 per capita income in current U.S. dollars (according to World Bank data) was $2,170, relative to Kuwait's per capita income of $12,590. On the pretext of a long-defunct historical claim, Iraq invaded Kuwait in the modern equivalent to a plundering expedition. Clearly the motivation in this case was entirely economic. Saddam Hussein would have had no interest in Kuwait if it had not been for its oil wells. Quite possibly the United

States and its allies would have been equally uninterested in Iraq's conquest of Kuwait if it had not been for those same oil wells. But in the actual event, the United States and its allies came to the rescue of Kuwait, and expelled the Iraqi forces in a "short, victorious war" of the sort that is always desired but rarely achieved.

But let us imagine that in 1991 Iraq had had a military alliance with the Soviet Union analogous to the military alliance that Serbia had with Russia in 1914. Let us further imagine that in 1991 the Soviet Union was not on the verge of dissolution, but was still very much the same as it had been in 1970 or 1980. In that case, the Soviet Union might well have accepted the Iraqi historic claim to Kuwait, have taken the position that the Iraqi invasion of Kuwait was an "internal matter," and have demanded that the United States and its allies desist from their intervention. Ultimatums may well have ensued. After that, nuclear war may well have ensued. It would not have been that the USSR regarded an attack on Iraq literally as an attack on itself, but rather that Iraq's defeat and humiliation at the hands of the United States and its allies would have had intolerable consequences on the geopolitical balance of power. In the minds of the Soviet leadership, allowing the United States and its allies such a success would embolden them to further actions in the future that would more directly threaten Soviet security. Therefore, the line must be drawn here and now (i.e., in this hypothetical scenario—in 1991 in the sands of the Middle East).

Call it stupid if you will, but the fact remains that this is exactly the sort of reasoning that has generated war after war after war in the past. This example shows how the existence of economic inequality sets up tendencies toward aggression and warfare. And it also shows how a "little war" might, under adverse circumstances, escalate into a "big war." Are such situations indeed preposterously unlikely in the future? Is it wise to gamble the destiny of human civilization on this assumption?

But let us put aside, for the moment, apocalyptic visions of nuclear Armageddon. I have repeatedly emphasized the point that there are other good reasons for world government aside from reducing the threat of nuclear disaster. The impotence of the world federalist movement over the last several decades, a period of time during most of which there was a far more acute threat of nuclear disaster than there is presently, has sufficiently established that prophecies of nuclear doom, no matter how vivid and urgent, will not be sufficient to stampede the nations into forming a world government. In order to have a reasonable chance of formation, the proposed world government must be far more limited than the classic vision within the world federalist movement up to this point in time, and also the case for world government must emphasize the positive incentives to world government as well as the negative incentives.

Humanity confronts very serious threats aside from nuclear disaster. The population explosion throughout the world over the last century is putting ever-greater pressure on both the natural resource base and the purity of the physical environment. The AIDS crisis has reminded us of our potential vulnerability to catastrophic epidemics of contagious diseases. Drug abuse has become a major contributor to crime and a major threat to the social fabric. These are global problems in that they have important ramifications in almost every nation on earth. The extent to which humanity will be able to cope effectively with these problems is critically affected by the predisposition among nations toward mutual respect, trust and cooperation.

The economic gap is seriously reducing this predisposition. The wide gulf between living standards in the rich nations and those in the poor nations naturally generates a certain amount of hostility and resentment in the latter against the former. This in turn creates a reluctance in the poor nations to do "favors" for the rich nations. The United States wants Mexico to exert more effort to stem the flow of illegal migration from Mexico to the U.S., but to Mexico this migration reduces its own unemployment problems, and brings into Mexico a considerable amount of U.S. currency from illegal aliens in the U.S. to their families in Mexico. It might seem to the Mexicans rather selfish of the U.S. to want to keep out Mexican migrants, when U.S. per capita income is more than eight times that of Mexico ($31,996 in 2000 relative to $3,819). The United States also wants Columbia to exert more effort to stem the flow of illegal drugs from Columbia to the U.S., but to Columbia this traffic provides a lot of both domestic employment and foreign exchange. It might seem to the Columbians rather selfish of the U.S. to be so insistent on Columbian assistance in fighting the U.S. drug war, when U.S. per capita income is almost fourteen times that of Columbia ($31,996 in 2000 relative to $2,290). Many rich nations throughout the world want Indonesia to exert more effort to suppress slash and burn methods among its subsistence farmers, because these methods result in atmospheric pollution. One major constraint on the Indonesians in acceding willingly to this desire, however, is the low per capita income of Indonesia ($994 in 2000).

To some extent it is a problem of lack of resources. It requires police resources for Mexico to impede the flow of its migrants into the U.S., for Columbia to suppress drug production and marketing, for Indonesia to deter its subsistence farmers from engaging in slash and burn agriculture. But also to some extent it is a problem of lack of will. Is it unreasonable for a poor population, with a standard of living that would be considered grinding poverty in the rich nations, to be reluctant to commit significant resources to policies the major benefits of which accrue to the populations of the rich nations, who are enjoying living standards almost beyond imagination? Is it unreasonable that these populations, and their political leaders, experience a strong temptation to simply say "Go to hell!" to representatives from the rich nations who come to them with transparently self-serving advice and recommendations on what they should be doing? The rich countries are generally uninterested in various proposals put forward by the poor nations toward reducing the economic gap. Is it fair, therefore, to expect the poor countries to happily embrace policies that are more obviously beneficial to the rich nations than they are to the poor nations?

In conclusion, world economic inequality constitutes a serious threat to the future success of human civilization on this planet. World economic inequality increases the threat that human civilization will be devastated, and perhaps anni- hilated, by nuclear war. It also increases the threat that human civilization will be slowly, gradually, almost imperceptibly destroyed by the interrelated problems of explosive population growth and environmental deterioration. But there is no need for us to sit idly by while these threats increase to the point where they can no longer be controlled. By means of concerted and coordinated human action, on a global scale, it is more than likely that we can overcome the problem of world economic inequality within a reasonable period of historical time, perhaps within one or two generations. We owe it both to ourselves and all human pos- terity to at least make a serious effort to accomplish this. The World Economic Equalization Program to be described below, as complemented and assisted by the Federal Union of Democratic Nations earlier described, should and could be the instrument through which the problem of world economic inequality is eradicated once and for all.

5

FOREIGN DEVELOPMENT ASSISTANCE

A massive "global Marshall Plan" has been periodically bruited about ever since the original Marshall Plan was completed in 1952. But to date, nothing has come of these grandiose speculations. Among citizens of the richer nations, it is a conventional assumption that such a massive international economic development effort would almost certainly be no more than an exercise in futility: despite heavy burdens on the rich nations, the poor nations—owing mostly to graft, corruption and incompetence—would fail to experience significant economic progress. This assumption is somewhat less conventional among the citizens of the poor nations, but the latter tend to assume that such a massive international effort is impossible simply because it would be far beyond the bounds of generosity that can reasonably be expected of the citizens of the rich nations.

Although the current prospects for a World Economic Equalization Program along the lines proposed in this book would be described as "very bleak" by most informed people, there is at least one important ray of hope. The fact is that there exists at the present moment in time an ongoing international economic development effort. The majority of the populations of the rich nations recognize that they have an economic, political and moral interest in the economic development of the poor nations, and they have accepted that the pursuit of this interest requires the expenditure of significant resources. At the same time, the majority of the populations of the poor nations recognize their own natural interest in economic development, and have accepted that receipt of development resources from abroad, while not fully consistent with such virtues as self-reliance and independence, is nevertheless useful and desirable.

Not only are the appropriate attitudes already well-established, but the institutional structures and procedures are similarly well-established. The United States established the Agency for International Development (AID) in 1961, and analogous agencies have been long established in most if not all of the other member nations of the Development Assistance Committee (DAC) of the Organization for Economic Cooperation and Development (OECD). The International Bank for Reconstruction and Development, established in 1945 and commonly known as the World Bank, has for many decades operated as a major conduit for multilateral aid flows from the wealthy industrialized nations to the poorer developing nations. For their part, the developing nations possess various government agencies, financial institutions, private business enterprises, and non-governmental organizations (NGOs) for channeling investment resources received from abroad into various productive applications.

The attitudes are there and the institutions are there. It is simply a matter of scale. The less developed countries are growing, and in all likelihood aid receipts have been an important factor in their growth. But they are not growing fast enough and as a consequence the economic gap between the rich nations and the poor nations is getting wider. This widening gap is strong prima facie evidence that the scale of the present-day international economic development effort is simply too small for dramatic success to be achieved within the foreseeable future. This effort must be scaled up very considerably in order to have a reasonable hope of dramatic success within the lifetimes of people now living. The requisite scaling-up will not be an easy matter. It will require a major attitude shift on the part of millions of people around the world. But at least it is not a matter of starting from scratch. The program we want has already been commenced and is presently rolling along. All that is needed at this point is to increase its size and velocity. Once it achieves the necessary momentum, then we will begin to see unmistakable evidences of eventual success.

Of course, if today's conservative critics of foreign aid are correct, no such evidences will in fact be witnessed, but instead only the spectacle of waste and corruption on a gigantic scale. If that were to happen, then the World Economic Equalization Program would soon be scaled down and perhaps discontinued altogether. That would be a very depressing outcome, and would bode ill for the future of human civilization on this planet. But at least we would have made a fair and sincere effort to overcome the problem of global economic inequality. We would have determined by a meaningful and legitimate scientific experiment, and to a high level of assurance, that this problem cannot be overcome by a sufficiently large increase in the scale of the foreign aid donations of the rich nations to the economic development of the poor nations.

The position of this book is not that a World Economic Equalization Program *would definitely* be a success, but merely that *there is a sufficiently substantial probability* that it would be a success to merit its initiation on a tentative and provisional basis for a reasonable trial period. The position taken here is that any predictions at the present time of the future failure of such a program can be based on nothing more solid and substantive than speculation. It would be a great tragedy for humanity if unreasonably pessimistic speculation continues to deter a massive global economic development effort whose potential for success would quickly be demonstrated if it were given a fair chance to prove itself.

This chapter provides a selective review of diverse statistical information and professional commentary that bears on the potential success or failure of a World Economic Equalization Program along the lines proposed in this book. The program itself will be described in the following chapter, and evidence from computer simulations will be presented there in support of its potentially high level of effectiveness. We are concerned in this chapter with insights to be gained from the past history of foreign aid. But two disclaimers must be provided at the outset concerning the contribution of the present chapter. First, the review provided here is far from being a comprehensive and exhaustive survey of the economic and political literature on foreign aid. Even in this specialized area within the broader field of economic development, the theoretical and empirical literature has become very substantial, and anything beyond a bare introduction would be excessively lengthy and elaborate. Second, the relevancy of the reviewed material to the central question of present interest is somewhat indirect and tangential. The central question of present interest is as follows: "How likely is it that a worldwide economic development assistance program, on a sufficiently massive scale, would achieve a relatively high level of equalization in living standards across all or most nations within a relatively brief period of historical time?" Owing to the fact that the great majority of economists and other social scientists at the present time assume that such a program would be very unlikely to succeed, this question is rarely if ever addressed in the professional literature, at least in a systematic manner.

Instead, the central concern at the present time of development specialists is with the more limited question: "How likely is it that the existing foreign assistance contributions of the rich nations are making a significant and appreciable contribution to the goal of achieving self-sustained growth in the poor nations?" Not only is this a more limited question, but no definitive and widely accepted answer to the question seems to be emerging from the research. It would certainly assist the argument of this book concerning the potential effectiveness of a World Economic Equalization Program if strong empirical evidence existed that foreign aid was indeed having a significant and appreciable effect on the economic growth of the poor nations. Unfortunately, this is not the case. Statistical evidence supportive of this proposition is rather fragile, to say the least. The position argued here is that the reason for this is that in the past foreign aid has not been provided in sufficient abundance for a strong and obvious effect to be observed. Relative to the need, foreign aid has been minimal, and as a consequence its effect has been minimal—and thus difficult to measure.

FOREIGN AID: BASIC FACTS AND CONTROVERSIES

The great majority of resource transfers from the rich nations to the poor nations fall into one of four basic categories: (1) export earnings; (2) private investment; (3) private charity; and (4) development assistance. The first two of these are "commercial" in the sense that they are driven by the profit incentive, and consequently they operate under an economic quid pro quo situation. Importers in the rich nations purchase goods and services from exporters in the poor nations in the expectation that they can either be resold at a profit or utilized as inputs into profitable production operations. The poor nations get financial payments for their exports but in exchange they must give up the exported goods and services. Investors in the rich nations undertake physical and financial investments in poor nations in the expectation that such investments will yield a satisfactory rate of financial return. Although there is a certain amount of direct overseas investing by individual investors (as when a private capitalist purchases interest-bearing bonds issued by a Third World government or common stocks issued by a Third World business enterprise), the preponderance of international investing transpires through the operations of multinational corporations (MNCs), otherwise known as transnational corporations (TNCs). Majority ownership of most if not all MNCs resides with investors who are citizens of the wealthy nations. These companies, some of them quite huge, undertake various extractive and productive operations in Third World nations, and a substantial proportion of the profits from these operations are returned to the owners in the rich nations. The poor nations get the value of the investment resources but in exchange they are subjected to explicit or implicit repayment obligations—which can become quite heavy if the profitability of the investments is less than expected.

The third and fourth categories, respectively private charity and development assistance, are not driven by the profit motive and do not involve commercial exchange as understood in the economic marketplace. Examples of private charity include monetary transfers from immigrant workers in the rich nations to relatives in the poor nations, and schools and hospitals in poor nations constructed and operated by religious or philanthropic organizations supported mostly by individuals in the rich nations. These kinds of transfers are difficult to measure accurately, but in any event it is believed by most development economists that they account for a fairly small proportion of overall transfers. Development assistance, often designated "ODA" (official development assistance), includes all financial and material resource transfers initiated by the governments of the rich nations, as opposed to their business enterprises, non-governmental organizations, or private citizens. The transfers may be in the form of grants or of loans, but in the event that they are loans, there must be a significant "concessional" component: i.e., the amount of specified repayment must be less than would be customary if the loan had been made by a private financial institution. The transfers may be "multilateral," as when (for example) the government of the United Kingdom increases its subscription with (i.e., bond purchases from) the World Bank, or they may be "bilateral," as when (for example), the government of the Netherlands supports a road-building project in Indonesia. Recipients of the transfers in the poor nations include government agencies, non-governmental organizations, and business enterprises. Important aid categories include project assistance (resources for the building of roads, dams, factories, etc.), technical assistance (provision of technical experts), food aid, debt relief, and emergency assistance. In the very early history of foreign aid, military assistance was lumped together with economic assistance, but this confusing and misleading practice was fairly quickly revised. Emergency assistance shares with military assistance the characteristic that it does not directly contribute to the productive capacities of the poor nations; however, emergency assistance is a small fraction of the overall flow of official development assistance.

TABLE 5.1
OECD Foreign Aid Statistics, 2000

Nation	ODA millions U.S. $	% of Total DAC ODA 1999/00	Multi-lateral Aid % of ODA	ODA % of GNI	Total Resource Flows % of GNI
Australia	987	1.8	23.2	0.27	0.40
Austria	423	0.9	39.3	0.23	0.57
Belgium	820	1.4	41.8	0.36	1.00
Canada	1,744	3.1	33.5	0.25	0.95
Denmark	1,664	3.1	38.5	1.06	1.39
Finland	371	0.7	41.5	0.31	0.88
France	4,105	8.8	31.1	0.32	0.43
Germany	5,030	9.6	46.6	0.27	0.67
Greece	226	0.4	56.2	0.20	0.20
Ireland	235	0.4	34.1	0.30	0.93
Italy	1376	2.9	72.6	0.13	1.01
Japan	13,508	26.2	27.7	0.28	0.23
Luxembourg	127	0.2	26.3	0.71	0.80
Netherlands	3,135	5.7	28.5	0.84	0.95
New Zealand	113	0.2	25.0	0.25	0.32
Norway	1,264	2.4	26.1	0.80	0.91
Portugal	271	0.5	34.0	0.26	0.89
Spain	1,195	2.3	39.7	0.22	0.74
Sweden	1,799	3.1	31.0	0.80	1.76
Switzerland	890	1.7	29.5	0.34	0.80
United Kingdom	4,501	7.2	39.8	0.32	0.50
United States	9,955	17.3	25.6	0.10	0.26
Total DAC	53,737	100.0	32.9	0.22	0.53

Source: Based on Aid section Table 1 from *OECD in Figures 2002*, available from the OECD Website (URL: *http://www.oecd.org*). This table is derived in turn from *Development Cooperation: 2001 Report*, Paris: Organization for Economic Cooperation and Development. Note: ODA = Official Development Assistance; GNI = Gross National Income.

Table 5.1 presents some recent statistics on foreign aid disbursements by the member nations of the Development Assistance Committee (DAC) of the Organization for Economic Cooperation and Development (OECD). Total official development assistance expended by the DAC member nations during the year 2000 amounted to nearly 54 billion dollars. Clearly this is a great deal of money in an absolute sense. But from the last row in Table 2.A.1 above, we see that in 2000 the total Gross Domestic Product of the 207 nations included in the table was 33,813,336,367,597 dollars. In words, this is 33 trillion, 813 billion, 336 million, 367 thousand and 597 dollars. When dealing with the world economy, the figures are indeed truly astronomical and veritably mind-boggling. Relative to world GDP, the 54 billion in ODA was approximately 0.159 percent, about halfway between one tenth of one percent and one fifth of one percent. In the larger context, therefore, 54 billion in ODA might legitimately be described as "a drop in the bucket."

Table 5.1 indicates that in 2000 the largest single provider of ODA was Japan, accounting for 26.2 percent of the total, followed by the United States with 17.3 percent of the total. It can be seen that only a few of the DAC donor nations in 2000 met the long-established United Nations goal for industrialized nations of devoting 0.7 percent of their GNPs to foreign development assistance. The short honor roll of nations meeting this goal included Denmark, Luxembourg, Netherlands, Norway and Sweden. On the other hand, several more DAC nations met the 0.7 standard on the basis of *total* resource flows. Total resource flows, shown in the last column of the table, include private capital investment flows in addition to government-sponsored aid.

Motivations of donor nations, in the provision of foreign aid, may be generally classified (with some inevitable degree of overlap) as political, economic, and humanitarian. Politically, foreign aid is intended to keep populations and governments of poorer nations friendly toward donor nations: to keep radical political parties that preach hostility toward rich nations out of power in poorer nations, and to dispose the poorer nations to cooperation with donor nations in the preservation of strategic security. The political motivation, obviously, has declined substantially in the wake of the decline of the Cold War in the years since the collapse and dissolution of the Soviet Union. However, it is by no means entirely extinct, particularly if "strategic security" is interpreted in much broader terms than merely avoiding total nuclear war. For example, strategic security may also include reducing the frequency and intensity of terrorist activity throughout the world. Economically, foreign aid is intended (in the short run) to induce poorer nations to follow trading and investment policies (i.e., relatively free trade with minimal tariff and quota restrictions, together with a high level of receptivity to outside investment by foreign individuals and firms) that tend to foster prosperity in the donor nations, and (in the long run) to enable poorer nations to themselves achieve a higher level of prosperity and become stronger trading/investment partners with the donor nations. This in turn would further reinforce prosperity in the latter nations. The humanitarian motivation derives from humanity's innate tendencies toward cooperation and mutual assistance, the result of millennia of Darwinian natural selection (total egotists have difficulty reproducing), as reinforced by intensive socialization of the young by their parents and educators. As to the relative importance of these three motivations, any estimation of this would obviously be highly speculative.

Throughout the second half of the twentieth century, a substantial quantity of economic resources have been transferred via foreign aid from a relatively small number of rich donor nations to a relatively large number of poor recipient nations. In the same period, most of the poor recipient nations have made substantial economic gains. The most important exception to the rule of appreciable economic progress within the poorer nations has been the sub-Saharan African nations. Although most of the poorer nations of the world have registered substantial economic gains over the last few decades, the progress has not been as dramatic as had been hoped. On the whole, as we saw in the previous chapter, economic progress in the rich nations has been greater than that in the poor nations, with the result that the absolute gap in living standards has been growing. No doubt a significant drag on individual living standards in the poorer nations has been the relatively high rate of population growth in most of these nations. But population growth is not the only factor, nor even necessarily the most important factor, in the stubborn persistence of the economic gap.

Opinions on the role and effectiveness of foreign aid cover a wide range. At one extreme are adamant critics of foreign aid, who argue that foreign aid in the past has obviously not achieved either its political or its economic goals—and moreover, it will not achieve these goals in the future, no matter what the scale on which it is provided. Foreign aid, according to this point of view, not only places a heavy burden on the tax-paying citizens of the rich donor nations, but it is incapable of improving the productive capacity of the poor nations. Within the latter nations, the only parties to benefit from foreign aid are pre-existing wealthy elites and corrupt government bureaucrats entrusted with the management of foreign aid funds. Adherents to this viewpoint urge that foreign aid be terminated quickly and completely. At the other extreme, enthusiastic supporters of foreign aid maintain that it has been a vital component in whatever economic progress has been achieved by the poor nations. Without the foreign aid of the past, they say, the present situation would be much worse than it is. The disappointing degree of economic progress in the poor nations they attribute to two factors: (1) foreign aid has not been provided in sufficient abundance to have a dramatic impact on economic progress in these nations; (2) what foreign aid has been provided has included too high a component of relatively unproductive aid forms (e.g., military assistance and food aid rather than project assistance). They argue that foreign aid contributions to the economic development of the poor nations of the Third World should be significantly expanded—not reduced.

In most of the wealthy nations, including the United States, foreign aid has become institutionally entrenched as a recurrent component of the national government budget. But relative to other recurrent components of the national government budget, such as defense and domestic welfare, its entrenchment is not deep. In the United States, for example, few if any calls are heard for the abolition of the U.S. Department of Defense or the Social Security Administration, and the "zeroing out" of their annual appropriations. The same cannot be said for the U.S. Agency for International Development (AID), through which most United States foreign aid disbursements are channeled. In a policy paper by Doug Bandow entitled "A New Aid Policy for a New World," posted on the World Wide Web by the Cato Institute, Bandow summarizes the anti-aid viewpoint and policy proposal as follows:

Since 1945, Washington has disbursed generous amounts of foreign aid in attempts to achieve a variety of foreign policy goals ranging from political influence to economic development. Today, the poor record of foreign assistance programs is widely recognized. Many countries receiving the aid are more impoverished now than when U.S. assistance began; the few that are making progress are
doing so in spite of, not because of, foreign aid... Some Republican proposals to
reform foreign aid are more encouraging [than Clinton's proposals] because they
envision cutting programs that have clearly failed or serve no national interest.
But the Republican proposals should be viewed only as a starting point. In the
post-Cold War world, developing countries are moving away from the type of
central economic planning that U.S. aid has financed in the past. The United
States should encourage that trend by zeroing out foreign aid. That includes foreign aid programs intended to promote free-market reform; even that type of assistance tends to delay, rather than accelerate liberalization... Washington can do
much to help poor nations by abolishing the U.S. Agency for International Development and most of its functions. Instead of disbursing foreign aid, the United
States should open its market to the developing world's goods.

This so-called "new aid policy" proposed by Doug Bandow amounts basically to
a "no aid policy."

The extreme right-wing case against foreign aid usually endeavors to evade
inferences that the case is based squarely upon crude selfishness by alleging that
the termination of foreign aid would be "for their own good"—referring to the
general populations of the LDCs. Rarely is the case put forward as a calm balancing of the marginal costs versus the marginal benefits to the populations of
the rich nations, with the former being estimated as greater than the latter. Nor is
the case expressed in terms of the costs to the populations of the rich nations
being numerically greater than the benefits to the poor nations. Rather, the fairly
implausible argument is routinely put forward that foreign aid not only reduces
the welfare of the populations of the rich nations *but it also* reduces the welfare
of the populations of the poor nations. Another indication of insincerity with
respect to concern for the welfare of the populations of the poor nations is the
fact that many of the complaints about foreign aid have to do with potentially
correctable errors and deficiencies. If food aid is bankrupting local farmers, this
problem could potentially be avoided by providing aid in different forms. If foreign aid is being provided to oppressive regimes with an excessive penchant for
military hardware and presidential palaces, this problem could potentially be
avoided by redirecting aid to nations whose leaders are democratically accountable and who content themselves with reasonable armed forces and living standards. If foreign aid is being extended to LDC governments that are pursuing
obviously dysfunctional economic policies such as protectionism or centralization, this problem could potentially be avoided by making aid conditional upon
more sensible economic policies. Such potential solutions are ignored amid strident calls for the complete termination of foreign aid. Open hostility and contempt are frequently expressed toward allegedly corrupt and greedy politicians
and government bureaucrats in the LDCs; just beneath the surface one senses an

equally virulent hostility and contempt toward the general populations of these nations, who are presumably, for whatever reason, either unwilling or unable to require their authorities to adhere to reasonable standards of civilized behavior. After all, presumably governments reflect peoples: corrupt peoples tend to generate corrupt governments. The possibility that poverty itself may aggravate natural human tendencies toward greed and corruption is generally disregarded.

Most of the evidence cited in support of the ineffectiveness or perversity of foreign aid is anecdotal in nature and dubiously representative of the overall picture. For example, while much is made of specific failed projects, more balanced appraisals indicate that the rate of return is high on most projects, especially those funded by multilateral agencies such as the World Bank. Inconsistent evidence, such as the fact that South Korea and Taiwan were major aid recipients during the initial phases of their extraordinary growth eras, is either ignored or dismissed with unsupportable statements to the effect that aid "had nothing to do" with growth acceleration. Equally unsupportable are dogmatic statements that foreign aid depresses economic growth by sapping incentives, encouraging waste, distorting relative prices, and so on. To most thoughtful observers, a more reasonable explanation for the disappointing growth rates in many if not most of the LDCs is simply that foreign aid has not been provided in sufficient abundance to make a significant difference.

The pro-aid response centers around the argument that although the strategic political purposes of foreign aid have been greatly downgraded by the decline of the Cold War, these purposes have certainly not disappeared altogether, and the economic and humanitarian purposes of foreign aid are just as relevant now as they were during the Cold War. Increasing prosperity among the LDCs would create a more favorable international economic environment for the rich nations. Many individuals in the rich nations continue to perceive a strong moral obligation to provide a reasonable amount of economic assistance to those in need. Although not as dramatic as the Cold War threat of instantaneous nuclear holocaust, the continuing interrelated threats of global environmental degradation and overpopulation could be just as dangerous to the long-run welfare of the populations of the rich nations. The following excerpts from testimony of Donald F. Gordon, of the Overseas Development Council, given before the House International Relations Committee on February 26, 1997, suggest the flavor of the current pro-aid case:

> Under Brian Atwood's energetic and creative leadership, USAID has gone a significant way toward streamlining its bureaucracy and redirecting its operations. Despite these efforts, however, the U.S. foreign aid program remains politically adrift, having lost its Cold War anchor as a tool for containing communist expansion. Foreign assistance has lost its core political constituency and much of its support, and foreign aid levels are in decline. Forced continually to defend its eroding mandate, USAID finds it ever more difficult to undertake effective development work. What is called for is not the end to aid, nor the continued nibbling away of USAID's capacity to undertake its mandate, which will

make aid failure a self-fulfilling prophecy. Rather, we need an even more substantial revision of our assistance policies and practices in ways consistent with
changing foreign policy purposes and changed realities in the developing world.
To do so necessitates better integrating our aid efforts into our foreign policy
process.

During the Cold War, the main purpose of aid was to support strategically
important regimes regardless of whether the recipient government was following
effective development policies or used aid resources efficiently. Some argue that,
after the Cold War, there is no longer a foreign policy role for foreign aid. According to this view, eliminating most aid is an appropriate "peace dividend"
from the end of the Cold War. While containing a kernel of truth—some types of
aid have become passe and some longtime recipients are no longer attractive—this view ignores the emerging foreign policy interests of the United States.
Today, it is advancing global problem-solving, promoting crucial transitions, and
development itself, not the buying of allies, that serve our contemporary foreign
policy interests.

In a world no longer dominated by major power conflict, an array of serious
global problems (some new, others unattended to in the past) that no nation can
handle on its own call for new forms of international cooperation. Among the
most important of these are global environmental degradation, international drug
trafficking and the spread of infectious diseases. These problems directly affect
our quality of life at home and can only be addressed through effective cooperation with developing countries. Absent aid, we would be totally dependent upon
persuasion and treaty negotiations for tackling these problems, especially in poor
countries that may want to respond but lack the financial and technical where-
withal to do so.

Although the collapse of the Soviet Union and the end of Cold War has
greatly reduced the apparent need for foreign aid as an instrument for the containment of communism, at the same time this development has improved the
prospects for effective utilization of foreign aid resources. During the height of
the Cold War, a disproportionate amount of foreign aid was directed to nations
in immediate danger of communist takeovers, to nations ruled by overbearing
dictators whose only virtue was their opposition to communism, to "socialist-
leaning" nations of geopolitical significance whose governments threatened to
become more friendly with the Soviet Union or the People's Republic of China.
The bargaining power of recipient LDC nations in foreign aid negotiations was
in a long-term state of decline for a prolonged period prior to the termination of
the Cold War, but no doubt the termination accelerated the decline. This suggests that in the future, it will be easier for donor nations to induce recipient nations to abide more closely to the various precepts of what has become known as
the "Washington consensus."

The "Washington consensus" is that the prospects for a given nation's economic growth and development are greater to the extent that that nation: (1) par-
ticipates more in the world economy by reducing import restrictions and encouraging export growth; (2) reduces direct government participation and intervention in the economy by privatizing public enterprises, minimizing bureaucratic

regulation of private enterprise, abolishing institutions and curbing policies that involve any sort of economic planning, and generally increasing the scope of laissez faire in the domestic economic realm; (3) maintains redistributive taxation and social welfare programs at a modest and reasonable level; (4) welcomes foreign private investment and strictly respects the private property rights of foreign investors. Of course, not all of the precepts of the Washington consensus, some of which are directly contrary to propositions described as being part of the conventional wisdom of the 1940s and 1950s, are universally applauded. Evidence is far from compelling that LDCs which enthusiastically embrace all or most of the Washington consensus thereupon experience rapid growth. When even professional economists cannot agree on specific policy issues, it is no wonder that ordinary citizens and political authorities cannot agree. In addition, the factor of national pride inevitably enters into economic policy discussions between officials of different national governments. Predictably enough, officials of recipient nations don't relish "being dictated to" by officials of donor nations. No opinions will be offered herein on the validity of the Washington consensus. But what does seem obvious is that in the future, donor nations will have more clout in determining actual internal economic policies of recipient nations than they had during the Cold War, when LDC governments were able to "play off" the noncommunist and communist superpowers against one another.

Of course, another major factor in determining the amount of clout possessed by representatives of the donor nations, aside from the presence or absence of superpower confrontations in the global arena, is the amount of foreign aid that is at stake. Officials of recipient nations who are dubious concerning policy changes proposed by officials of donor nations will be more inclined to acquiesce the larger are the aid donations under consideration. The end of the Cold War in the early 1990s initiated a major downsizing of military expenditures, especially among the wealthy donor nations. In the United States, defense expenditures fell from 6.5 percent of GDP in 1986 to a little over 3 percent in 2000. It is hardly implausible that this major reduction in the military burden on the economy was a major factor in the highly successful economic record of the 1990s. The donor nations of the world are richer than they have been at any time in their histories, in terms of both total income and "disposable" income (income left after the "military obligation" has been met). Being richer, they are able to afford more of all goods—and one such good consists of a politically stable, ecologically sound, and morally equitable global environment. Foreign aid remains a sound investment in the future. It will be argued that this particular form of investing in the future ought to be greatly expanded.

FROM THE MARSHALL PLAN TO THE NINETIES

A half-century ago, the United States, in cooperation with the Western European nations, planned and implemented what still stands as the largest and most successful single philanthropic endeavor in the history of humanity: the European

TABLE 5.2
Marshall Plan Statistics

Year	(1) Marshall Plan Aid (billions of current U.S. $)	(2) U.S. GNP (billions of current $)	(3) Marshall Plan Aid as % of U.S. GNP	(4) Western European GNP (billions of current U.S. $)	(5) Marshall Plan Aid as % of Western European GNP
1948	5.953	257.6	2.31	131.6	4.50
1949	3.523	256.5	1.37	140.8	2.50
1950	2.406	284.8	0.84	151.4	1.59
1951	1.486	328.4	0.45	158.5	0.94
all	13.368	1127.3	1.18	582.3	2.29

Sources: (1) Herbert Carleton Mayer, *German Recovery and the Marshall Plan: 1948-1952*, Bonn, Brussels and New York: Edition Atlantic Forum, 1969, unnumbered table (page 73): "ECA/MSA—Allotments to All Member Countries between 3 April 1948–31 December 1952"; (2) *Historical Statistics of the United States: Colonial Times to 1970*, Washington D.C.: U.S. Department of Commerce, Bureau of the Census, 1975, Series F 1-5 (page 224): "Gross National Product, Total and Per Capita, in Current and 1958 Prices: 1869 to 1970"; (3) computed from (1) and (2); (4) Imanuel Wexler, *The Marshall Plan Revisited: The European Recovery Program in Economic Perspective*, Westport, CT: Greenwood Press, 1983, Table 26 (page 251): "Western Europe's Gross National Product, 1947-51"; (5) Computed from (1) and (4).

Recovery Program, commonly known as the Marshall Plan (after George C. Marshall, Secretary of State at the time, and formerly overall U.S. military commander during World War II). Between 1948 and 1952, the United States provided over $13 billion in economic assistance to help the Western European nations recover from the devastating destruction brought about by World War II. The large-scale resources provided by the Marshall Plan dramatically accelerated the rate of Western European economic recovery, and set these nations firmly on the path to the high level of prosperity they enjoy today.

Table 5.2 provides some basic statistics on the Marshall Plan. The large scale of the economic assistance provided under the Plan is evident both in terms of the donor nation (the United States) and the recipient nations (the Western European nations). Over the four-year period of the Plan's operation, well over 1 percent of U.S. GNP went into Marshall Plan transfers, while these transfers represented well over 2 percent of the combined GNPs of the Western European nations. The largest annual amount was transferred in the first year of the Plan period, with the annual amounts being gradually reduced over the remaining three years.

The profound impact of the Marshall Plan on the human imagination is still felt today. It still provides a source of legitimate national pride to Americans, and residual gratitude among Europeans helps to maintain generally friendly and cooperative international relations between the United States and the European nations even to the present day. Still, it would be naive to interpret the Marshall Plan as an exercise in pure and unadulterated altruism. Pure and unadulterated altruism involves significant self-sacrifice with no consideration of either present or future recompense. But the American people during the period of the Marshall Plan had at least two vital motivations of self-interest: economic and political. The economic recovery of Western Europe after World War II would help to assure continued prosperity for the United States by restoring its important pre-war trading partners to economic health.

The political motivation was probably even more important. The economic recovery of Western Europe was vital to containing postwar Soviet expansionism, that if left unchecked might well have ultimately constituted a direct threat to the two central institutions of the U.S. socioeconomic system: capitalism and democracy. In the absence of these self-interested political and economic motivations, it is very doubtful that the United States would have supported anything approaching the scale of the Marshall Plan. No doubt some purely humanitarian aid would have been extended to the suffering people of postwar Europe, but it would have been a small fraction of the actual economic assistance provided under the Marshall Plan. Primarily the Marshall Plan was a manifestation of enlightened self-interest rather than pure altruism, and its planning and implementation were more testimony to the intelligence and vision of the American people than to its benevolence. That said, it is also true that benevolence was an important factor that helped to swing public opinion in favor of the Plan, thereby reducing political opposition against it to a manageable level.

World attention during the 1930s and 1940s was largely focused on the emergent fascist threat, a threat that led up to the cataclysm of World War II from 1939 through 1945. Political and economic recovery from the ravages of World War II was greatly complicated by the emergence of the communist threat. The "grand alliance" between the Soviet Union and the Western allies broke down almost immediately after the war. To most Western observers, the totalitarian dictatorship of Joseph Stalin appeared almost as socially dysfunctional as the totalitarian dictatorship of Adolf Hitler, and the hegemonic ambitions of the Soviet Union as hardly less hazardous as those of Nazi Germany. Prior to World War II, the Soviet Union was alone in the world in its espousal of worldwide socialist revolution. Within a few years of the end of World War II, communist governments espousing worldwide socialist revolution were in control of many other nations: East Germany, Poland, Hungary, Czechoslovakia, Rumania, Bulgaria, Albania, Yugoslavia, North Korea, North Vietnam and above all, China, with its large land territory and huge population. Communist parties were active in many noncommunist nations, seeking to gain power through democratic elections if possible, but by revolutionary violence if necessary. It was a time of acute anxiety, as evidenced by the excesses of the House Un-American Activities Committee (HUAC) and the demagogic Senator Joe McCarthy.

The main elements of the international confrontation between the noncommunist nations and the communist nations were well-established by the mid-1950s. The central military aspect of containment was the "balance of terror" created by the nuclear arms competition between the United States and the Soviet Union, in which the initial emphasis on sheer destructiveness (megatonnage) of individual bombs was gradually replaced by emphasis on reliable delivery via ballistic missiles. In addition to this central aspect, the Western powers had also given notice of their intention to resist localized communist expansion by military means short of nuclear war: weaponry delivered to the noncommunist Greek government in the latter 1940s had been used to defeat the communist guerillas, and Western armed forces, chiefly American, had been used to oust North Korean and Chinese forces from South Korea in the early 1950s.

The central economic aspect of containment consisted of the effort to raise living standards within the noncommunist less-developed nations (LDCs—the "Third World") of Africa, Asia, and South America, in order to make them more resistant to communist infiltration and takeover. This anti-communist strategic motivation was certainly an important factor—and quite possibly the dominant factor—in the foreign aid programs of the richer Western nations as they developed during the 1950s, 1960s, and beyond. Of its nature, communist ideology seeks support among the poor and oppressed, since they are presumably to be the chief beneficiaries of socialist revolution. The teeming masses of the LDCs apparently provided fertile ground for communist ideology. The rich Western nations reasoned that the less abundant were poor and oppressed people throughout the world, the less dangerous would be the international communist movement.

By the mid-1950s, earlier concerns about communist parties gaining power within the wealthy capitalist nations, either by democratic processes or revolutionary means, were rapidly fading. First and foremost, the social and political liabilities of the communist nations, especially the lack of free speech and genuine democracy, greatly reduced the credibility and appeal of communist ideology. But while communism was a fading threat as far as the populations of the rich nations were concerned, the huge populations of the poor nations were another question. Presumably it is easier for prosperous and well-educated people to perceive the various deficiencies of the communist social system, than it is for impoverished and poorly-educated people to do so. Economists in the wealthy capitalist nations did their part to meet the threat by focusing on the determinants of economic progress, and by considering possible policies by which the rate of economic progress might be accelerated. When the noted economic historian Walt Whitman Rostow published his influential *Stages of Economic Growth* in 1960, the work's subtitle (*A Non-Communist Manifesto*) clearly evidenced the fact that a major motivation for concern over the economic development of the LDCs was the perception that poverty in these nations strengthened the communist side in the Cold War confrontation.

Central to Rostow's theory was the notion of a "take-off into self-sustaining growth." This refers to the critical period during which a national economy raises its level of saving and investment to a point where long-term economic growth becomes permanent. According to Rostow, all of the rich nations of the current period underwent this transition at some point in the past, and presumably (hopefully?) all of the currently poor nations will also undergo it at some point in the future. When all or most of the currently poor nations have finally achieved self-sustaining growth, then the communist strategic threat will presumably (hopefully?) wither away. An obvious mechanism for achieving "take-off" conditions within a poor nation would be the provision of generous but temporary foreign aid contributions by wealthy nations, analogous to the Marshall Plan aid contributions that had been instrumental in the postwar recovery of Western Europe. Such was the prevailing vision at the time of the "institutionalization" of foreign aid in the early 1960s, as manifested by the establishment of the U.S. Agency for International Development (AID) and various other national foreign aid bureaus, as well as by the formation of the multilateral Organization for Economic Cooperation and Development (OECD), headquartered in Paris.

As the years and decades have passed since the early 1960s, the relative optimism of that period regarding the prospects for rapid, world-wide economic progress, has gradually faded. Although almost all of the poor nations have witnessed some economic progress, and a few of them have indeed experienced dramatic "take-off" transitions, an extremely high level of economic inequality persists, and a large percentage of the total human population continues to live in conditions of extreme poverty. At the same time, throughout the 1960s, 1970s, and 1980s, concerns about communist expansionism gradually declined. For the most part, the populations of the poor nations remained resistant to communist ideology. Almost all of these nations have small but influential wealthy elites with a strong interest in preserving the capitalist status quo. An important development was the empirical falsification of the "domino theory" in the years following the communist takeover of South Vietnam in 1975, a nation whose abortive defense had cost the United States 60,000 dead and tens of billions of dollars. During the 1990s, the collapse of the Soviet Union and ensuing events still further reduced concerns over communist expansionism among the populations of the rich nations. In short, both the perceived effectiveness of foreign aid, and the perceived necessity for foreign aid, have declined dramatically since the early 1960s.

Tables 5.3 and 5.4 provide some basic numerical information on the history of foreign aid from the 1960s through the 1990s. Table 5.3 shows the total amount of Official Development Assistance (ODA) expended by the member nations of the Development Assistance Committee (DAC) of the OECD between 1960 and 2000, at 5-year intervals. The table shows a very substantial increase in Official Development Assistance between 1960 and 2000, from 4.676 billion U.S. dollars at the beginning of the period to 53.737 billion U.S. dollars at the

TABLE 5.3
Total DAC ODA, 1960-2000
Adjusted for Inflation and Population Growth

year	total DAC ODA		Total Population	per capita DAC ODA	
	millions of current U.S. $	millions of 1996 U.S. $	of Low-Income Countries	current U.S. $	1996 U.S. $
1960	4,676	21,063	1,005,379,904	4.65	20.95
1965	6,489	27,265	1,127,655,680	5.75	24.18
1970	6,713	23,069	1,269,404,544	5.29	18.17
1975	13,254	33,135	1,428,696,064	9.28	23.19
1980	26,195	45,956	1,609,527,296	16.27	28.55
1985	28,756	39,018	1,801,598,336	15.96	21.66
1990	52,961	61,227	2,016,593,664	26.26	30.36
1995	58,926	60,067	2,231,427,328	26.41	26.92
2000	53,737	50,269	2,459,787,008	21.85	20.44

Data Sources: Official Development Assistance (ODA) of member nations of the Development Assistance Committee (DAC) downloaded from the Website of the Organization for Economic Cooperation and Development (OECD); current $ figures translated into 1996 $ figures using the Implicit Price Deflator index (1996 = 1) downloaded from the Website of the Federal Reserve Economic Database (FRED) sponsored by the Federal Reserve Bank of St. Louis; Total Population of Low-Income Nations obtained from the World Bank's *World Development Indicators 2002* CD-ROM.

end of the period. This is more than a tenfold increase. Specifically, the increase factor (ODA in 2000 divided by ODA in 1960) is 11.492. However, these raw figures do not take into account either inflation or the increase in the recipient population. To convert the current-dollar figures into constant-dollar figures (1996 dollars), we multiply the current-dollar figures by the U.S. Implicit Price Deflator (IPD) index, which is currently set in terms of 1996 dollars. In 1996 dollars, ODA expenditures rose from 21.063 billion in 1960 to 50.269 billion in 2000. The increase factor here is 2.386—far less than 11.492. The recipient population may be approximated by the population of low-income nations, as reported by the World Bank. The final two columns of Table 5.3, which show ODA per capita, are obtained by dividing current-dollar ODA and constant-dollar ODA, respectively, by this population. As can be seen, in constant-dollar terms, ODA per capita has remained fairly constant over the entire period.

At the present time, the nations of Japan and the U.S. are the two largest providers of foreign development assistance. Table 5.4 presents some historical statistics on the ODA expenditures of these two nations in constant 1996 dollar terms. As can be seen, during the 1990s Japan supplanted the United States as the largest single provider of foreign development assistance. This table also shows the Gross National Income (GNI) of the two nations, and ODA expendi-

TABLE 5.4
ODA as a Percent of GNI, 1960-2000
Japan and the United States

year	Official Development Assistance (ODA), millions of 1996 U.S. $		Gross National Income (GNI), millions of 1996 U.S. $		ODA Percent (%) of GNI		Mil. % of GNI
	Japan	U.S.	Japan	U.S.	Japan	U.S.	U.S.
1960	105	2,760	45,023	517,945	0.233	0.533	8.302
1965	244	4,023	92,234	710,503	0.265	0.566	7.389
1970	458	3,153	205,975	1,021,510	0.222	0.309	7.714
1975	1,148	4,161	505,812	1,613,400	0.227	0.258	5.808
1980	3,353	7,138	1,072,840	2,772,800	0.313	0.257	5.269
1985	3,797	9,403	1,370,890	4,188,500	0.277	0.224	6.119
1990	9,069	11,394	3,071,202	5,749,200	0.295	0.198	5.413
1995	14,489	7,367	5,332,526	7,332,200	0.272	0.100	4.089
2000	13,508	9,955	4,901,157	9,825,305	0.276	0.101	3.300

Data Sources: Official Development Assistance (ODA) of member nations of the Development Assistance Committee (DAC) downloaded from the Website of the Organization for Economic Cooperation and Development (OECD); U.S. military (defense) expenditure downloaded from the Website of the Federal Reserve Economic Database (FRED) sponsored by the Federal Reserve Bank of St. Louis; GNI of Japan and the United States obtained from the World Bank's *World Development Indicators 2002* CD-ROM.

tures as a percent of GNI. During the 1960s, the United States contributed somewhat over one half of one percent of its national income to foreign development assistance, but this declined over the next three decades as the perceived threat of communist expansionism declined, so that currently the United States is contributing about one tenth of one percent of its national income to foreign development assistance. In percentage terms, Japan is more generous with its percentage approaching three tenths of one percent. To provide perspective on these percentages, the final column in Table 5.4 shows U.S. military (defense) spending as a percentage of national income. In 1960, the United States expended 22.60 times more national income on the military as it did on foreign aid (8.302 percent versus 0.533 percent). In 2000, the United States expended 32.67 times more national income on the military as it did on foreign aid (3.300 percent versus 0.101 percent). Both military spending and foreign aid spending can be regarded as investments in national security. But the for the United States—and the other advanced industrialized nations as well—the former investment has always dwarfed the latter investment.

ASSESSING THE EFFECTIVENESS OF FOREIGN AID

Has foreign aid had a positive effect on the economic development of the recipient nations? It is generally accepted among development economists that this question cannot be reliably answered on the basis of evidence from individual projects, even if results from a great many individual projects are examined. When foreign aid is utilized to build a factory, for example, that factory might become highly profitable, or it might become bankrupted. If it is highly profitable, that does not necessarily show that foreign aid is effective, because that factory might have been constructed more economically by private investors, either foreign or local. Moreover, the success of the factory might be at the cost of bankrupting other, previously established factories. On the other hand, if the factory built with foreign aid is soon bankrupted, that does not necessarily show that foreign aid is ineffective. Even in the most prosperous of the wealthy capitalist nations, numerous business enterprises established by profit-seeking private investors encounter unanticipated difficulties and end up bankrupted. It is also true that although the factory eventually failed, while it operated it may have pumped into the economy a large quantity of physical and financial resources which benefited other sectors. When we turn to projects for the expansion or deepening of social overhead capital, it becomes much more difficult to evaluate relative success or failure, because this cannot simply be estimated on the basis of the bottom line of a profit-loss statement. When a road or a school is built, the benefits are widely dispersed and estimates of their financial equivalent are necessarily subject to a very high degree of uncertainty and error.

Owing to these problems, therefore, the great majority of serious professional work on aid effectiveness utilizes aggregate statistics rather than enumeration of project results. One could try to estimate the effect of foreign aid on economic growth for one nation over an extended period of time (time series analysis), or the effect of foreign aid on economic growth for a large group of nations at one period of time (cross section analysis), or the effect of foreign aid on economic growth for a large group of nations over an extended period of time (pooled analysis). A large quantity of statistical data has accumulated over time, some issued directly by the national governments, and some collected from the national governments and issued by international agencies such as the United Nations, the Organization for Economic Cooperation and Development, and the World Bank. The single most comprehensive and widely utilized economic statistics today are those published by the World Bank. Although the statistical methodology utilized to examine the data is varied, it also seems safe to say that the multiple regression methodology is dominant. This technique produces the "best-fitting" estimate of a linear relationship between a given dependent variable and a set of independent variables, along with a test statistic for each of the independent variables for determining whether the respective independent variable has a statistically significant effect on the dependent variable, holding the other independent variables constant.

Over the last several decades, numerous economists have made numerous attempts to determine the effect of aid on growth. These attempts normally utilize some variant of multiple regression to estimate the effect on some specific growth variable of some specific aid variable, holding other determinants of growth constant. Emphasis is normally focused on whether or not there is a positive and statistically significant effect of the aid variable on the growth variable. Less attention has been paid to the issue of the *numerical* effect of aid. Conceivably there could be a statistically significant positive effect of aid on growth, but the effect would be of such small magnitude as to be numerically immaterial. On the other hand, it is also conceivable that there could be a numerically material positive effect that is not statistically significant by classical hypothesis testing standards.

On the basis of a large quantity of completed research to date, there is (I am personally sorry to say) no compelling statistical evidence to support the hypothesis that foreign aid has a statistically significant and numerically material positive effect on the economic development of the recipient nations. A very considerable number of statistical investigations have indicated no statistically significant effect at all of aid on growth. These studies are counter-balanced by a very considerable number of statistical investigations that do find a statistically significant positive effect of aid on growth. The "great success stories" of foreign aid, such as South Korea and Taiwan, were mostly completed by the end of the 1960s. Using more recent data, it appears that normally a fairly sophisticated approach to the data is required to obtain the result that aid has a positive effect on growth. Simple inspection of the raw data does not suggest much if any effect. Although statistical specialists are not unduly influenced by the absence of strong indications in the raw data, most people are not statistical specialists.

The great abundance of literature on this matter precludes anything more than a cursory review. I will confine myself, therefore, to brief summaries of a few representative studies. Perhaps the best-known of the earlier studies supportive of aid effectiveness is that of Gustav F. Papanek (1973). Papanek's dataset consisted of 85 observations on nations, 34 from the 1950s and 51 from the 1960s. Variables included the dependent variable of average annual growth rate of GDP, and four independent variables: domestic savings, aid receipts, foreign private investment, and other foreign inflows, all taken as percentages of GDP. Equations were estimated using ordinary least squares. In the equation for all observations, using all four independent variables as explanatory variables, the estimated coefficient of the aid variable was 0.39 with a corresponding t-statistic of 5.8 (Papanek, 1973, Table 1). This highly significant result indicates that an increase in 1 percent in the foreign aid percentage of GDP will, other things being equal, lead to a .39 percent increase in the growth rate of GDP. All four explanatory variables in the main equation had the expected positive coefficients, and were significant at the 5 percent level. The numerical value of the estimated coefficient of the aid variable was higher than that of any of the others. Papanek also reported results for Asian countries only ($n = 31$) and countries in the

Americas only ($n = 37$): the indication of these latter regression equations being that aid effectiveness had been much greater for Asian countries than for countries in the Americas.

Although fairly strong as econometric evidence goes, Papanek's results did not persuade the growing number of foreign aid skeptics. One of the more plausible arguments put forward by the skeptics has been that foreign aid receipts permit LDC governments to ease up on their own internal development effort, to reduce domestic saving and investment, and to allocate more public expenditure to wasteful purposes (the "fungibility" hypothesis). To the extent that this is true, and foreign aid merely substitutes external resources for the internal resources that would otherwise have been mustered to achieve the goal level of growth, there should be no relationship between foreign aid and growth. Or if any relationship is found to exist, it would be of an "accidental" rather than a causal nature. Therefore, the question remained as to whether the results obtained by Papanek would hold up using different samples of nations, different time periods, and different equation specifications and/or estimation methods.

Of the various studies that have offered a negative answer to this question, one of the most ambitious and influential was that of Paul Mosley, John Hudson, and Sara Horrell (M-H-H), published in 1987. The M-H-H Table 3 reports a number of regression equations similar to those of Papanek, except that two additional control variables are added: growth rate of export values and growth in the adult literacy rate, and national output growth is measured in GNP terms rather than GDP terms. In addition, the raw data on aid are adjusted to incorporate a lagging process designed to simulate the actual time of impact of aid flows: this lagging process is based on World Bank estimates of the average distribution across years of benefits from aid-financed projects. Separate results are reported for the 1960-1970, 1970-1980, and 1980-1983 time frames, and for all developing countries, poorest countries, middle income countries, African countries only, Asian countries only, and Latin American countries only. There are a total of 18 estimated equations, and the aid variable is statistically insignificant in all but three. In the three cases of significance, aid is found to be positively related to growth for the Asian countries only in the 1970-1980 and 1980-1983 periods, while it is found to be *negatively* related to growth for all developing countries in the 1960-1970 period. In their Table 4, M-H-H compare ordinary least squares estimates with three-stage least squares estimates (a theoretically appropriate method) for the case of all developing countries, for 1970-1980. Both the OLS and 3SLS estimates indicate an insignificant effect of aid on GNP growth. M-H-H conclude that the main qualitative conclusion from the OLS estimates of Table 3—that there is no robust statistical evidence for a positive effect of foreign aid on growth—is unaffected by a switch to 3SLS estimation.

The M-H-H study is representative of the several more recent studies that contradict Papanek's 1973 findings in favor of aid effectiveness. However, there have also been a number of more recent studies which do find a positive effect of foreign aid on growth. One of these was done by Craig Burnside and David Dollar. First issued as a working paper by the World Bank Policy Research Department in June 1997, the study was then summarized in the 1998 World Bank monograph *Assessing Aid: What Works, What Doesn't, and Why*. More recently, it appeared as an article in the *American Economic Review* (September 2000). Given the sponsorship of the study, it is perhaps not overly surprising that its findings are fully consistent with the "party line" of the World Bank, which is that foreign development assistance is indeed effective in promoting the economic growth of the recipient nations—but only if the governments of the recipient nations are implementing "good policy." By "good policy" is meant policy consistent with the above-described "Washington consensus": fiscal discipline to avoid budget deficits and inflation, modest welfare programs, limited business regulation, minimal economic planning, trade liberalization, and openness to foreign investment.

Burnside and Dollar's dataset includes information for six four-year time periods (1970-1973 to 1990-1993) on 56 developing countries. In addition to the usual economic variables, it includes a "political instability" variable based on ethnic fractionalization and assassinations, and an "economic management" or "policy" variable based on four subsidiary indicators: an index of trade openness, the rate of inflation, government surplus or deficit, and an index of "institutional quality." The variable of main interest is foreign aid as a proportion of Gross Domestic Product (GDP). The foreign aid variable is adjusted to include the concessional component of loans as well as grants. In the regression equations, the aid variable is not the observed value of aid (as a proportion of GDP) but rather its "instrumented" value. "Instrumented aid" is the estimated value of aid from a subsidiary regression of aid on such exogenous variables as initial GNP per capita, population, policy, region, and arms imports. Use of instrumented as opposed to observed aid is an effort to evade the statistical problem of feedback causation (normally described by the term "simultaneous equations bias" in the econometric literature). In this context, the problem is as follows: Foreign aid receipts might have a positive effect on economic growth performance—but economic growth performance might have a negative feedback impact on foreign aid receipts. That is to say, foreign aid to countries with strong growth might be reduced because the "need" for aid is smaller. This feedback effect tends to make it difficult to estimate the causative impact of foreign aid on economic growth. In other words, if there are two causative relationships operating simultaneously, the first a positive causative relation between foreign aid as the independent variable and economic growth as the dependent variable, and the second a negative relation between economic growth as the independent variable and foreign aid as the dependent variable—it is difficult for statistical analysis to separate the first from the second. Econometric theory has produced a standard methodology for dealing with the problem that will be successful in disentangling the two relations—if certain preconditions are met. But it is frequently uncertain whether these preconditions are actually met in any given practical application. Thus there is an additional element of uncertainty regarding the reliability and validity of statistical estimations under "feedback causation" conditions.

Using the standard econometric methodology for dealing with feedback causation, Burnside and Dollar find that the aid variable (the ratio of foreign aid to GDP) has a significant positive effect on the growth rate of per capita GNP—but only when it is combined in a multiplicative fashion with the policy variable (economic management). To be more precise, their variable "aid/GDP" is statistically insignificant in the determination of per capita GNP growth, but their variable "Management x aid/GDP" (the product of the policy variable times the aid variable) does in fact have a positive and statistically significant effect on per capita GNP growth. This result seems fairly robust over a variety of specifications that include or exclude middle-income countries, include or exclude outliers ("unusual" observations), and treat the policy variable as endogenous or exogenous. They define "mediocre policy" as a value of the policy variable of 1.1 and "good policy" as a value of the policy variable of 2.7. With good policy, the mean marginal effect of aid on growth over several specifications is computed as 0.5. This indicates that a unit increase in the aid/GNP percentage—given that policy is "good"—will increase the growth rate of per capita income by 0.5 percent. On the other hand, if policy is "mediocre," the mean marginal effect of aid on growth is computed to be zero. The clear implication of this finding, as expounded thoroughly in *Assessing Aid* (written by David Dollar and Lance Pritchett of the World Bank's Development Research Group), is that if more developing countries would simply follow "good policy," then there would be a substantial and easily verified positive effect of foreign aid on economic growth. There is also an implicit warning to governments of developing countries tempted to persist with "bad policy": "If you do so, your foreign aid may well be curtailed because it is a burden on us and it is not doing you any good."

This result is almost "too good" in the sense of being so precisely in line with the ideological preconceptions of the World Bank. One cannot help but wonder how much data manipulation and specification experimentation were required in order to reach these conclusions. One cannot help but wonder, accordingly, whether similar results would be obtained with different datasets and/or specifications. It is not that I personally find the result ideologically disagreeable or intuitively implausible—quite the opposite. The proposal contained in this book for a World Economic Equalization Program is obviously based on the belief that foreign aid is—or could be if provided in sufficient quantity—very beneficial to the recipient nations. But at the same time, I am fully conscious of the fragility of this particular evidence. I cannot imagine that the Burnside-Dollar research will have any perceptible impact on the preconceptions of critics of foreign aid in the mold of Doug Bandow, who was quoted earlier in this chapter. For one thing, it is too subtle and sophisticated in a statistical sense. Only professional economists are likely to be able to fully appreciate the methodology. As far as the rest of the world is concerned, only far more basic statistical indications are likely to have any impact. And the fact is that if we look directly at the "raw data," so to speak, there is no obvious impact of foreign aid on economic growth. The raw data tells us that despite a significant amount of foreign aid spending over the last several decades, most of the nations of the world are still relatively poor, and the economic gap between the rich nations and the poor nations is getting wider. To those not familiar with statistical issues (i.e., the great majority of the human population), this simple fact is strong prima facie evidence that foreign aid is not doing any good.

As we have seen, however, using sophisticated statistical methodology one *can* find in the data indications that foreign aid has a positive effect on economic growth. Unfortunately, it is not an easy matter to do so. And thus far the statistical indications that foreign aid has a significant positive effect on the economic growth of the recipient nations has been quite fragile. In the foregoing, I alluded briefly to the basic problem. This problem bedevils all efforts to confirm or refute social scientific hypotheses by means of statistical investigation. The problem is that the data utilized in social scientific statistical investigations—with rare exceptions—is what scientists call "non-experimental." That is to say, the data is not obtained by means of controlled laboratory experiments of the sort routinely conducted to substantiate hypotheses in the physical sciences. Rather the empirical data is generated by complex real-world phenomena involving a great many diverse variables and a great many diverse relationships. Some important variables may not be measured at all. For example, most social scientists would agree that the "perceptions" or "state of mind" of the human population regarding certain issues could have a strong impact on behavior. Although there is an increasing effort at the present time to obtain information on perceptions and states of mind by means of surveys, we obviously have a long way to go before we will have a large fund of reliable information on these kinds of variables. This also holds with respect to various political and social conditions, such as the level of democracy or the amount of religious diversity, that interact with economic conditions.

Aside from absent or inaccurate data, there is the more theoretically fundamental issue of confused causation owing to the simultaneous interaction of multiple relationships. In contemporary econometric thinking, there are two essential preconditions for the accurate estimation of any particular relationship out of the host of interacting relationships that produce the observed data: specification and identification. First, the relationship must be properly specified: the investigator must incorporate as independent explanatory variables for the dependent variable all of the variables that substantially affect it. If one or two important independent variables are omitted, the estimation will be biased and unreliable. Second, the relationship must be properly identified: there must be important exogenous variables that *do* affect the overall system in which the relationship of interest is incorporated, but that are *not* included among the major explanatory variables in the relationship of interest. These exogenous variables are necessary for the proper estimation of the relationship of interest. If they are either unmeasured, measured inaccurately, or not incorporated into the statistical analysis, then the estimation will be biased and unreliable. Needless to say, despite the best efforts of statistical investigators, there is no absolute guarantee that the statistical estimates they obtain are based on properly specified and identified relationships.

There are some economic propositions that enjoy a high level of plausibility because there exists a very large body of statistical evidence consistent with them. Into this category we could probably put the neoclassical production function (that the amounts of capital and labor have a positive effect on output), and the Keynesian consumption function (that the level of national income has a positive effect on the level of national consumption). Unfortunately for proponents of foreign aid as an instrument toward global economic equalization, we *cannot* put into this category the proposition that foreign aid has a statistically significant and numerically appreciable positive effect on the economic growth of the recipient nations. There is simply too much statistical evidence that fails to uncover such an effect.

However, this unfortunate fact should not cause us to despair and to embrace the conventional pessimism of the present day with respect to the prospects for achieving a high level of worldwide economic prosperity within a relatively brief period of historical time by means of a massive global foreign development assistance program along the lines of the World Economic Equalization Program being put forward here. In the first place, the available statistical evidence is by no means uniformly and strongly inconsistent with a positive effect of foreign aid on economic growth. The findings discussed earlier of Gustav Papanek and of Burnside and Dollar indicate such an effect. These are examples of the substantial number of studies that do find that aid benefits growth. These indications may well be the accurate indications; other statistical studies (such as the Mosley-Hudson-Horrell study) showing no effect might be invalid for one reason or another. The consensus feeling among econometric researchers is that owing to the difficulty of extracting statistically significant relationships from the non-experimental data produced by the real world, positive findings, on the whole, are more probative than are negative findings. By "positive" findings we mean findings that do indicate that X has an effect on Y, whether the effect be positive or negative. By "negative" findings we mean findings that do *not* indicate that X has an effect on Y, either positive or negative. By "probative" we mean the extent to which the evidence has an impact on judgment. The complexity of the real world tends to obscure true relationships to a much greater extent than it tends to manufacture false relationships. False relationships may be defined as statistical associations that have nothing to do with causation but are rather generated by underlying variables impacting on both X and Y. Common sense and basic economic theory both suggest strongly that if rich nations provide economic resources to poor nations, this will assist the economic growth of the poor nations—presumably not *all* of the transferred resources will find their way into the luxury cars, country villas and Swiss bank accounts of crooked bureaucrats. There is an *expectation* of a positive relationship between aid and growth, and if a particular statistical study fails to show this relationship, there should be (assuming one is not a close-minded critic of foreign aid) strong suspicion that this finding is the result of statistical problems.

But even if, for the sake of argument, it was in fact *true* that over the last 50 years, the foreign development assistance provided by the rich nations to the poor nations has not had a statistically significant and numerically appreciable positive effect on the economic growth of the latter nations, this does not mean that *in the future* foreign development assistance will have no such effect. As human beings, we tend to learn from our mistakes. A large fund of information concerning foreign aid, accumulated over the last 50 years, is helping us to determine (as the title of the World Bank monograph puts it) "what works, what doesn't, and why." Obviously, there is some optimal allocation of an existing quantity of foreign aid investment resources over social infrastructure capital, business capital and human capital (education and training). By means of trial and error, we are gradually getting closer to this optimal allocation. Similarly, there is obviously some optimal policy mix in the areas of planning versus market, protectionism versus trade, the social safety net, fertility and family planning, and so on. Once again, by means of trial and error, we are gradually gaining insights into the nature of this optimal policy mix. Whatever the level of achieved effectiveness of foreign aid in the past, that level is likely to increase in the future.

But there is another issue that has not attracted so much attention as have the issues of allocation and policy, but that may be far more important in a practical sense. This is the issue of the *amount* of foreign aid being provided by the rich nations to the poor nations. Investigators tend to assume that the amount of aid is fixed, and concern themselves with questions concerning how it should be allocated, and what is the best policy environment for its effective allocation. Rarely if ever do they ask serious questions about what amount of foreign aid is indicated. The fundamental proposition motivating the World Economic Equalization Program described and evaluated in the following chapter is that the amount of foreign aid currently being provided by the rich countries to the poor countries is thoroughly inadequate to the huge task.

The Marshall Plan of 1948-1952 was indeed the greatest single example of enlightened self-interest combined with humanitarian altruism ever seen in the history of human civilization. As such, it stands as a permanent and highly inspirational example of what might be accomplished in the future. But in one important sense, the experience of the Marshall Plan may have been fundamentally misleading, insofar as expanding the basic concept to the global arena. Specifically, the numerical magnitudes that were involved in the Marshall Plan are not correctly indicative of the numerical magnitudes that would be involved in a global Marshall Plan to eliminate the problem of world economic inequality. The original Marshall Plan was completed in the four-year interval between 1948 and 1951. As can be seen from Table 5.2, it involved the transfer of slightly over 1 percent of U.S. GNP to the Western European nations, to whom it represented something over 2 percent of their combined GNP. It is virtually self-evident, to anyone acquainted with the numerical dimensions of the contemporary world economic inequality problem, that this problem cannot be solved by means of the rich nations transferring to the poor nations 1 percent of their combined GNP over a 4-year period. A more realistic estimate would have the rich nations transferring to the poor nations around 3-5 percent of their combined GNP over a 50-year period. The reason for this is simply that the economic gap between the rich nations and the poor nations today is far, far larger than was the economic gap in 1948 between the United States and Western Europe. Prior to World War II, the nations of Western Europe enjoyed a living standard only slightly below that in the United States. Although the war caused a tremendous amount of physical and human damage in an absolute sense, relative to the total available pre-war physical and human resources, the losses were not overwhelmingly catastrophic. Quite possibly the recovery process from the war would have been fairly rapid even if the Marshall Plan had not been undertaken.

These observations are not intended to deprecate the contribution of the Marshall Plan. It was—and it remains—a shining example of what could and should be done today to overcome the world poverty problem. But the World Economic Equalization Program will have to be much more ambitious, financially and geographically, than was the original Marshall Plan. That is to say—if the program is to successfully achieve its objective. Over the last half of the twentieth century, the rich nations, as a whole, transferred considerably less than 1 percent of their combined GNP to the poor nations as foreign development assistance. This aid probably amounted to between 1 and 3 percent of the combined GNP of the recipient nations. That this is not enough to get the job done has been strongly suggested by 50 years of experience to date. What has been given to date has indeed been enough to somewhat improve the economic condition of most of the recipient nations—but it has not been enough to boost and propel them into an era of dramatic economic progress. Under the World Economic Equalization Program described in the following chapter, the equivalent of ODA would be a dramatically larger proportion of GNP than is ODA today, especially for the poorest nations. These much larger proportions are what is needed to get the job done.

6

A WORLD ECONOMIC
EQUALIZATION PROGRAM

Now that the intense ideological conflict of the Cold War is a rapidly fading memory, the drastic inequality in economic living standards among the nations of the contemporary world has become the single most important impediment to international harmony and world peace. Among visionaries, the notion of a massive, coordinated, worldwide effort to ameliorate the economic gap—along the lines of the post-World War II Marshall Plan but far more ambitious both financially and geographically—has a long history. One of these visionaries was George J. Church. Some representative excerpts from Church's editorial "The Case for a Global Marshall Plan" in the June 12, 1978, issue of *Time Magazine* are as follows:

> The advanced countries have an urgent self-interest in improving a situation [world economic inequality] that in a few years may well overshadow any other international issue. The self-interest is partly political: poverty in the LDCs provides fertile soil for demagogues... These strains have bred North-South tensions that easily match in bitterness the East-West ideological clashes. At conference after conference, LDCs have demanded a "new international economic order" involving vaguely defined transfers of wealth from North to South. Northern statesmen, with much justice, have regarded this rhetoric as a kind of impractical Robin Hoodism. But with no discernible justice, the industrial countries have kept a tight lid on their assistance to LDCs. The Northern attitude is myopically stingy... Says West German Economics Minister Count Otto Lambsdorff: "I do not believe that a kind of Marshall Plan for the Third World—which today would have to be shouldered jointly by the U.S., Europe and Japan—is a feasible solution." Yet a new version of the Marshall Plan that rebuilt Europe after World War II may well be the most workable solution. Only such a plan could overcome the widespread feeling among voters that much aid to LDCs is wasted because it consists of piecemeal efforts by the givers to finance uncoordinated projects... Any Marshall Plan for the developing nations would admittedly be imperfect. But consider the alternatives: for the LDCs, continued poverty; for the industrial nations, endless political threats and damage to their own economies. Rich and poor countries do not have to like each other to realize they have a common interest they cannot escape.

The passing of a quarter century has not diminished the potential importance of this idea. The World Economic Equalization Program (WEEP) proposed in this book—as a companion to the main proposal for the Federal Union of Democratic Nations—would constitute a practical implementation of the global Marshall Plan envisioned by George J. Church and several other visionary social thinkers over the last half-century.

But among the several objections that could be lodged against the present proposal for a World Economic Equalization Program, one of the most important is that "there is not a shred of worthwhile evidence" that such a program would achieve significant success. One possible response to this objection is that "there is not a shred of worthwhile evidence" that it would *not* achieve significant success. The WEEP envisioned here would involve transfers of investment resources from the rich nations to the poor nations at least ten times larger than the current transfers. Thus far in modern human history, a WEEP on this scale has not been attempted. Thus, in a very strict sense, no "worthwhile evidence" of any sort at all exists—evidence supporting either the program's success or its failure. If a WEEP on the scale proposed here is undertaken and pursued for one or two decades, and little or no progress is made toward reducing the economic gap between the rich nations and the poor nations, then that would constitute worthwhile evidence that the program was doomed to failure. By the same token, if a WEEP is undertaken and pursued for one or two decades, and significant progress *is* made toward reducing the economic gap between the rich nations and the poor nations, then that would constitute worthwhile evidence that the program was destined for success. "Worthwhile evidence," in this strict sense, can only be achieved by means of actual experiment.

Of course, if we loosen up to an extent on how we define "worthwhile evidence," then it can certainly be said that worthwhile evidence exists concerning the potential performance of a real-world WEEP. This chapter will be devoted to description and discussion of some relevant economic research conducted by the present author (an economist by profession) on the potential success or failure of a hypothetical World Economic Equalization Program. The question is whether or not a sufficiently ambitious international economic development effort, involving all nations large and small, rich and poor, would be likely to achieve a significantly higher level of economic equality throughout the world, within a relatively abbreviated period of historical time, and without imposing excessive costs on the rich nations. To my mind, this is an extremely important question that deserves far more attention than it has received to date from the economics profession. No doubt a large part of the reason for this inattention is that at the present time almost all economists assume that the answer to this particular question is self-evidently in the negative. Economists are often chided, criticized and even ridiculed for the dubious assumptions they habitually make. Although not presently recognized as such, this happens to be a particularly glaring example of this unfortunate tendency. To abstain from research on an important economic issue because the outcome of any such research is *assumed*, is hardly consistent with that spirit of high-minded scientific inquiry that economists self-righteously proclaim as their guiding motivation and inspiration. But as the saying goes: "It is never too late to change." I earnestly hope that my own research on this issue will inspire other economists to become seriously interested in it, and to develop models explicitly designed to provide tentative answers to what is without doubt the most important economic policy question of the modern age.

In the meantime, my own research, described in this chapter, provides a starting point. That starting point is decidedly optimistic. The research clearly indicates a non-negligible possibility that a real-world WEEP could be a spectacular success, with a high degree of convergence being achieved in the living standards of all nations—without this causing a serious decline in the rate of increase of living standards in the rich nations. In other words, the research shows the possibility that a high level of worldwide economic equality can be achieved on the basis of Common Progress. The poor nations of today can be brought to a high level of prosperity without this causing any diminishment in the high level of prosperity currently being enjoyed by the rich nations.

It must be emphasized at the outset, however, that I am certainly not operating under the misconception that the research discussed here constitutes "proof," in either the scientific sense or the legal sense, that a real-world WEEP would in fact be a success. "Proof" of *any* proposition, whether positive or negative, about the outcome of an untried public policy measure is beyond the power of social science, even at its most methodologically sophisticated. Contemporary social science makes considerable use of mathematics, and mathematical manipulations, if they are performed correctly according to established mathematical principles, are impervious to error. Unfortunately, this does not imply the infallibility of analysis based on mathematical models. If the assumptions which provide the starting point of the analysis are invalid, then the conclusions will be invalid despite flawless mathematical manipulations.

Similarly, there is no guarantee of the infallibility of conclusions based on arithmetical calculations performed by a computer. Use of computers is certainly a strong guarantee against serious arithmetical errors. But according to the well-known maxim enunciated at the dawn of modern computing—"garbage in, garbage out." Aside from questions concerning the conceptual foundations ("assumptions") of the research, there is the fact that the research indicates not only that a real-world WEEP *could be* a spectacular success—but also that it *could be* a spectacular failure. The outcome of success or failure depends on the numerical values of certain model parameters. Even if we were prepared to assume that the model was a reasonable approximation of reality, we have no way of knowing the exact numerical values of its parameters. Indications of success are achieved with what I consider to be a reasonable set of numerical parameter values. But I also show that with numerical parameter values that I consider to be much less plausible—but that others might deem more plausible—the outcome is complete failure. In a way, this situation reinforces the plausibility of the WEEP model as a conceptual construct. If the conceptual construct indicated that a real-world WEEP would necessarily be a success, regardless of the numerical values of the model's parameters, then we would be legitimately skeptical of the conceptual construct. There is such a thing, in social scientific work as well as in the ordinary business of life, of results that are "too good." That is, they are too good to be believable. But this is not the case with respect to the research reported here. Paradoxically, the fact that the model results admit the possibility of failure lends more credence, rather than less, to the model's indication of the possibility of success.

THE WEEP MODEL

The WEEP model (so designated because it pertains to the potential performance of a World Economic Equalization Program—WEEP) is a model of the world economy with nations as economic units and years as time periods. Intended for computer simulation, the model's purpose is to develop formal scientific evidence on the potential performance of the very large-scale worldwide economic development assistance program herein termed the World Economic Equalization Program (WEEP). The model represents an effort to achieve a reasonable compromise between the diverse objectives of realistic economic content, tight focus on the main questions of interest, analytical simplicity, and computational convenience. Key elements of the model are the production function, the consumption function, the transfer allocation function determining each nation's foreign aid contribution, and the share function determining each nation's foreign aid receipts. Owing to the model's tight focus on foreign aid, the single model link between the national economies consists of transfers of generalized capital investment resources through the WEEP. The model does not encompass various other links between national economies such as foreign trade, private foreign investment, and private voluntary transfers.

Although the WEEP model is mathematically implemented, I will not provide here the various mathematical details on the structure of the model and its setup for the simulations. This book is intended for the general reader, and many if not most general readers are either unfamiliar with higher mathematics in general, or at least unfamiliar with the usage of higher mathematics in the field of economics. I could have provided mathematical details either in the text or in an appendix, with reassurances to the general reader that the technical material could be ignored without appreciable diminishment of one's comprehension of the "practical significance" of the research. However, the appearance of a significant amount of mathematics anywhere in this book might be distracting and misleading to the general reader. Therefore, with apologies to those readers with an interest in the technical details, I will refer them to my book *Common Progress: The Case for a World Economic Equalization Program* (Praeger, 2000). As far as the present discussion of the model is concerned, I will utilize symbolic notation for variables and parameters, but I will describe relationships involving these variables and parameters in informal terms only, and will not undertake to supplement these informal descriptions with the corresponding mathematical equations.

The WEEP model production function is a Cobb-Douglas form in generalized capital and labor. The descriptor "Cobb-Douglas" is a reference to the function's originators in the 1920s: Paul H. Douglas (an economist—later a U.S. Senator from the state of Illinois) and Charles W. Cobb (a professor of mathematics). Owing to its mathematical form, the function is also referred to as the "power function" or "log-linear form." It was designed to embody various fundamental principles normally assumed in economics of both production functions and utility functions: it has positive first derivatives, negative second derivatives, and its isoquants are convex downward-sloping. This function has been extensively utilized within economics ever since its introduction in an article entitled "A Theory of Production," published in the March 1928 issue of the *American Economic Review*.

Raw labor is proxied in the model by population P. It is an abstraction from reality, of course, to utilize population for productive labor, because the ratio of productive labor to total population is not the same over all nations. However, usage of labor force participation rates to infer productive labor from total population would be problematical, even if such rates were reliably available for all nations, because in the poorer agrarian nations a considerable amount of productive labor is actually provided within the household by children or other dependents who are not considered to be labor force participants. Generalized capital (symbolized by K), for which no empirical measures are currently available, is the value of all physical capital (plant and equipment) utilized in production, plus the value of all education and training inputs into the population, plus the value of all social infrastructure physical capital such as roads and schools. To summarize, for any nation at any point in time, output Y is a Cobb-Douglas function of population P (a proxy for productive labor), generalized capital K, the total factor productivity coefficient A, and the parameters α and β, representing respectively the output elasticity of generalized capital K and the output elasticity of population (labor) P.

Statistical data are utilized for Y and P in the numerical implementation of the model, but K, *generalized* capital, represents a hypothetical construct for which existing statistical proxies such as "plant and equipment," even if they were reliably available for all nations, would not be appropriate. "Generalized capital" is the value of all reproducible inputs *other than* physical labor power. In addition to the usual "plant and equipment," to reiterate, it would definitely include the value of educational and training inputs into the labor force (human capital components) as well as the value of various publicly provided productive resources such as roads, bridges, dams, and schools (social capital components). Generalized capital plays a pivotal role in the WEEP model. It is presumed: (1) that the extreme differentials in per capita output between nations in the contemporary world may be all or mostly attributed to extreme differentials in current endowments of generalized capital between nations; and (2) that generalized capital is transferable between nations, in the sense that a given investment in generalized capital may be installed in any nation and it will have the same impact on production. The proposed WEEP is based on the hypothesis that most of the observed differences in output per capita ($y = Y/P$) across nations are the result of K differentials rather than A differentials. The program aims at influencing the future development of national K stocks: the K stocks of rich nations will grow at a slower rate in order that the K stocks of poor nations grow at a faster rate.

Needless to emphasize, both of the above assumptions are highly controversial. As to the first, it has long been proposed by politically conservative economists that the bulk of the productivity differentials in the world today may be attributed to imbedded political, cultural and institutional factors that are virtually impervious to human control. In other words, the main reason for observed differences in per capita output are total factor productivity differentials: these tend to be low for poor nations because of imbedded political, cultural and institutional conditions. To the extent that the conservative hypothesis is valid, and per capita income differentials are in fact principally a result of A differentials rather than K differentials, it is intuitively evident that a WEEP would have limited impact on the world inequality problem. If the observed productivity differentials in the world today are the result of A differentials rather than K differentials, then a program such as the WEEP proposed herein—that would alter the future allocation of world investment in K as between nations—would have a very small impact on the distribution of production over nations. Quite simply, the program would be ineffective. This possibility is encompassed in the WEEP model by a parameter designated ξ (the "productivity differential source coefficient"), which represents the proportion of the initial per capita income differentials that may be attributed to differentials in total factor productivity coefficients, as opposed to differentials in generalized capital stocks. The numerical range of ξ is between 0 (zero) and 1 (one). If $\xi = 0$, then all the A are equal and all differentials in per capita income are owing to differentials in generalized capital K. If $\xi = 1$, then every nation has the same amount of K in proportion to output Y as every other nation, and all differentials in per capita income are owing to differentials in the total factor productivity coefficient A. If ξ is between 0 and 1, then differentials in per capita income are partially owing to differentials in generalized capital stock and partially owing to differentials in total factor productivity coefficients. Simulation experimentation verifies that if the ξ parameter becomes too high, a WEEP would not be effective.

As to the second assumption (that generalized capital is transferable between nations), according to conservative critics of foreign aid, only a small proportion of foreign aid is actually put to productive use, owing to high administrative costs and/or to the diversion of significant resources to private uses through the machinations of dishonest businessmen and corrupt bureaucrats. Graft, corruption, dishonesty and malfeasance consumes the bulk of foreign aid (according to the critics), leaving very little left over for the intended purposes. This possibility is encompassed in the WEEP model by a parameter designated χ (the "conversion effectiveness coefficient"), which represents the proportion of each nation's net share of the total transfer fund that is actually transformed effectively into generalized capital. The numerical range of χ is also between 0 (zero) and 1 (one). If $\chi = 1$, then all transfer shares are converted into generalized capital. If $\chi = 0$, then no transfer shares are converted into generalized capital. If χ is between 0 and 1, then the proportion χ of a recipient's transfer shares is converted into generalized capital, while the remainder $(1 - \chi)$ goes to waste. Once again, simulation experimentation verifies that if the χ parameter becomes sufficiently adverse (this time taking on too low a value rather than too high a value), a WEEP would not be effective.

An informal description of the basic workings of the WEEP model is as follows. At the start of each time period (i.e., year), there is determined for each nation (via the Cobb-Douglas production function) a certain output level Y on the basis of population P, generalized capital K, and total factor productivity A. Once output Y in a certain nation at a certain time period is produced, it is then allocated among four uses: military expenditure M, consumption C, gross transfer T, and domestic investment I. Military expenditure is assumed to be a fixed proportion of total output. Consumption is derived from a linear function of "disposable income," defined as total output less military expenditure. The gross transfer T is a proportion λ of the nation's "residual," defined as total output less military expenditure and consumption. The remainder $(1 - \lambda)$ of the nation's residual goes to domestic investment I. The proportion λ for a particular nation is determined by that nation's "ratio," defined as the ratio of that nation's per capita consumption to maximum per capita consumption (i.e., per capita consumption of the richest nation in the world). The "transfer allocation function" is designed so that richer nations have larger proportions of their residuals going into the total transfer fund. Another formula is derived to determine the share of each nation in the total transfer fund. The share of each particular nation is determined by two factors: its population and its "difference," the latter defined as the difference between the per capita consumption of the richest nation in the world and the per capita consumption of that particular nation. Transfer amounts and share amounts of each nation are computed separately. The net transfer is the difference between the transfer amount and the share amount. This amount will be positive for rich nations and negative for poor nations. Positive net transfers are foreign aid donations; negative net transfers are foreign aid receipts. The model is completed by a set of equations representing transition from period t to period $t + 1$. These latter equations introduce a number of additional parameters, one of which is χ (the "conversion effectiveness coefficient"), discussed above.

The empirical basis for the model is the "World Bank dataset": the 140 nations in the dataset include all nations that (according to the World Bank) had populations over one million people as of 1970. Even with this restriction to "larger" nations, the set of nations accounts for somewhat over 98 percent of the world population. The principal motivation for eliminating the smaller nations is to reduce the amount of random error introduced by making various ad hoc estimations of missing data (missing data in the World Bank statistical source is more frequent for smaller nations). The two variables in the dataset include population and real per capita income of the 140 nations annually from 1970 through 2000. Data from the 31-year period 1970 through 2000 are used to calibrate the model: that is, to set the numerical parameters of the model to values that create a reasonably close fit between the observed data and results from the WEEP model validation simulation. The WEEP model policy simulations, as opposed to the validation simulation, cover the 51-year period from 2000 through 2050. Since the initial year of this interval has already passed into history, the policy simulation results should be thought of as "what if" results. That is to say, these are potential results if a WEEP had (or had not—in the case of without-WEEP simulations) been initiated in 2000.

Although the structure of the WEEP model used to obtain the results reported in this book is exactly the same as that of the WEEP model used to obtain the results reported in *Common Progress*, there are a few numerical differences. The empirical data underlying the *Common Progress* results were obtained from the World Bank 1997 *World Development Indicators* CD-ROM, while the empirical data underlying the present results were obtained from the 2002 *World Development Indicators* CD-ROM. Even though only five years separate the issuance dates of these two sources, there are some fairly substantial differences. Owing to these differences, it was found that a considerably better fit to the actual per capita income data over the validation interval was obtained with a slightly different set of benchmark parameter values from those utilized for the *Common Progress* simulations.

Owing to various data and estimation problems, it would be unrealistic to aspire to a high level of numerical precision and accuracy in specifying model parameters. However, the benchmark parameter values utilized to produce the various tables and figures below do in fact satisfy the following criteria: (1) they are consistent with basic *a priori* economic theory; (2) they lie within the wide boundaries of plausibility established by an impressionistic appreciation of related empirical literature; (3) they produce a reasonably satisfactory fit between the empirical data and the model results over the validation interval extending from 1970 through 2000. Of course, it goes without saying that the uncertainty that inevitably exists with respect to model parameter values means that an important part of the research is "sensitivity analysis": the determination of how various model simulations are affected by changes in numerical parameter values. Qualitative model results are more weighty to the extent that they are "robust": that is, to the extent that they continue to hold true under alternative parameter values. As a particularly important example of this pertains to the two especially controversial parameters, ξ and χ. In the benchmark case, both of these are set to the most "optimistic" values: respectively $\xi = 0$ (indicating that all initial per capita income differentials are owing to differences in generalized capital endowments and none to total factor productivity differentials), and $\chi = 1$ (indicating that all net transfer fund shares of recipient nations are successfully translated into increases in general capital stocks). Later on, we will examine the consequences of setting these parameters to less optimistic values.

The validation simulation uses the WEEP model to generate estimated values of per capita income for each nation over the 1970-2000 interval, using as initial values the actual population and per capita income figures for each nation in 1970, and also using the average annual rate of population growth in each nation between 1970 and 2000 to generate population increase for that nation during the interval, under the assumption that there is no World Economic Equalization Program in effect. This is done by setting the parameters of the transfer allocation function to values such that no nation pays any proportion of its residual into the foreign development assistance transfer fund. As we saw in the last chapter, there was in fact over the 1970-1995 interval a certain amount of foreign development assistance resources transferred from rich donor nations to poor recipient nations. It perhaps tells us something about the inadequacy of these transfers that a model which completely ignores them (as well as ignoring foreign trade and foreign investment) still manages to produce a reasonable fit to the actual data.

The validation simulation of the WEEP model estimates the 2000 per capita income of most nations with a reasonable degree of accuracy. A regression of actual PCY (per capita income) for 2000 on model estimate PCY for 2000 has an R-Square (coefficient of determination) of 0.9025. This is a quite a good fit, in view of the fact that the numerical range of the coefficient of determination is from 0 (zero), indicating no association at all between the independent and dependent variables, to 1 (one), indicating a perfect linear association between the two. Further insight into the degree of goodness-of-fit is provided by Figures 6.1 and 6.2, which show actual PCY growth (solid lines) and model estimate PCY growth (dashed lines) for a group of eight representative nations ranging from rich to poor.

The eight representative nations are those selected for Tables 4.1 and 4.2 in Chapter 4. In order of 1970 per capita income (according to the 2002 *World Development Indicators* CD-ROM), they are the United States, France, Italy, Spain, Algeria, Ecuador, Ghana and India. The first four are representative of high-income nations (using the World Bank classification), and the latter four are representative of low-income nations. From visual inspection of Figures 6.1 and 6.2, it is apparent that while the WEEP model certainly does not provide perfect tracking of real-world growth of the per capita income of nations, it does a reasonably good job of tracking long-term trends, taking due account of the relative simplicity of the model. Note that the growth estimated by the WEEP model is "smoothed out"—that is, it does not track the short-term fluctuations in actual growth. A model of such a high level of abstraction and simplicity as that embodied in the WEEP model obviously cannot encompass the myriad factors affecting short-term growth patterns. But this is not a matter of consequence, because the WEEP model is not designed for short-term forecasting and policy analysis. Rather it is designed for long-term forecasting and policy analysis, i.e., to evaluate the potential performance of a WEEP.

FIGURE 6.1
Actual and Estimated Per Capita Income Growth, 1970-2000
Four High-Income Nations (U.S., France, Italy, Spain)

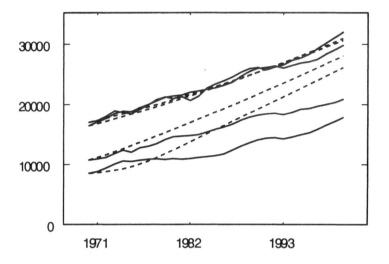

FIGURE 6.2
Actual and Estimated Per Capita Income Growth, 1970-2000
Four Low-Income Nations (Algeria, Ecuador, Ghana, India)

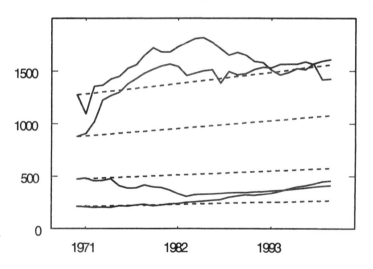

WEEP MODEL POLICY SIMULATIONS

The WEEP model policy simulations reported in *Common Progress* cover the 51-year period commencing in 1970 and concluding in 2020. They represent "what-if" experiments: they estimate what would have happened had a real-world WEEP (World Economic Equalization Program) been started (or not started) in 1970. The WEEP model policy simulations reported here cover the 51-year period commencing in 2000 and concluding in 2050. Once again these results represent "what-if" experiments: they estimate would have happened if a real-world WEEP had been started (or not started) in 2000. There have been some fairly important changes in the economic status of nations as between 1970 and 2000, among both the rich nations and the poor nations. These changes affect both the relative size of the rich nation donations and the relative size of the poor nation receipts. For example, in the 1997 World Bank dataset utilized as a basis for the *Common Progress* simulations, in 1970 the United States was the richest nation in the world (in terms of per capita income), and accordingly would have paid the largest percentage of its GNP (somewhat over 7 percent) into the foreign economic development assistance transfer fund. In contrast, in the 2002 World Bank dataset utilized as a basis for the simulations reported here, in 2000 the United States was the ninth richest nation in the world (after Luxembourg, Switzerland, Japan, Denmark, Norway, Austria, Germany and Finland), and accordingly would have paid (if a WEEP had been initiated) into the foreign economic development assistance transfer fund a considerably smaller percentage of its GNP (slightly over 2 percent).

The two benchmark WEEP model simulations comprise the without-WEEP simulation and the with-WEEP simulation. In the without-WEEP simulation, the parameters of the transfer allocation function are set so that no nation pays any part of its GNP into the transfer fund. Figures 6.3 and 6.4 show per capita income growth results for the eight representative nations previously utilized: United States, France, Italy and Spain (the high-income nations), and Algeria, Ecuador, Ghana and India (the low-income nations). Figure 6.3 pertains to the without-WEEP case: it shows a projection of the likely evolution of per capita income in the absence of a World Economic Equalization Program. It would appear that we may expect "more of the same." The economic gap continues to widen: the rich nations get richer, while the low-income nations continue the same slow-growth pattern they have exhibited for the last several decades. There is no evidence whatsoever of any sort of economic convergence of the relatively poor nations on the relatively rich nations.

On the other hand, if a World Economic Equalization Program were set into motion, there could, according to the with-WEEP simulation illustrated by Figure 6.4, occur a truly remarkable amount of progress toward overcoming the economic gap within a 51-year time span. The contrast between the without-WEEP simulation (illustrated by Figure 6.3) and the with-WEEP simulation (illustrated by Figure 6.4) can only be described as remarkable. True, we do not

FIGURE 6.3
Estimated Per Capita Income Growth without a WEEP, 2000-2050
United States, France, Italy, Spain, Algeria, Ecuador, Ghana, India

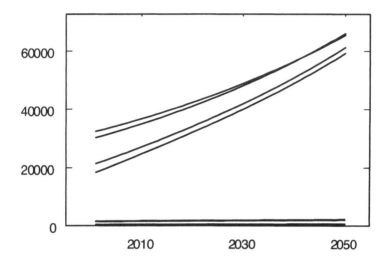

FIGURE 6.4
Estimated Per Capita Income Growth with a WEEP, 2000-2050
United States, France, Italy, Spain, Algeria, Ecuador, Ghana, India

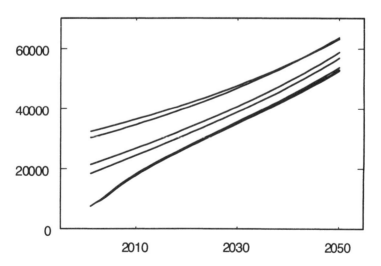

see absolute convergence in the sense that the poorest nations, at the end of the 51-year period, would have living standards as high as those in the richest nations at that time. However, these results suggest that the living standards of what are the poorest nations of today would have improved sufficiently, by the end of the period, to be comparable to those of the richest nations today. They also suggest that all nations, from the relatively rich to the relatively poor, would be growing at comparable rates.

Of course, the WEEP model does not encompass all those factors affecting growth. Clearly it does not encompass short-term factors affecting growth. If humanity were to undertake a real-world WEEP, the actual growth patterns of various nations would be highly variable: growth would not be according to the smooth, neat curves shown in Figure 6.4. In addition to that, there are several long-term factors that influence the long-term rates of economic growth of the various nations. It seems unlikely, for example, that Japan will continue the high-growth pattern it has exhibited over the last 50 years through the next 50 years. As for the poor nations of today, under a WEEP some would no doubt be benefited more than others. As a result, there could well be some substantial alterations in the relative economic positions of nations. The possibility exists, even, that some of the poorest nations of today may end up overtaking the richest nations of today. For example, India could conceivably overtake the United States within a 50-year period. If that were to happen, however, India would soon change from a recipient nation to a donor nation within the WEEP. Recall that a nation's receipts from the foreign aid transfer fund depend on its relative economic prosperity. The more prosperous a nation becomes, the less it would receive in foreign aid. As a nation becomes steadily richer, at some point it would shift from being a recipient nation to being a donor nation.

The strongest indication from the with-WEEP simulation is not what it projects for individual nations, but rather what it suggests about the entire family of nations. What it suggests is a leveling of the "global economic playing field," as it were: that is to say, the development of a global economy in which there are not two qualitatively different types of nations: those that have been very rich for a long period of time and those that have been relatively poor for a long period of time. Instead, we would see a world in which all nations are characterized by living standards that are high by our present standards, but in which the finer degrees of prosperity would fluctuate over time. The relative economic status of the nations would vary, so that at one point in time nation A would be richer (in terms of PCY) than nation B, while at a later time their relative positions would be reversed. But the differentials in PCY would not be so large and so persistent for these differentials to be a source of hostility and conflict among nations. For example, in 2000 Switzerland had a PCY in 1995 U.S. dollars of $46,737 while the United States had a PCY of $31,996. This is a substantial differential, but it is not enough to cause the people of the United States to feel relatively poor, and to experience unhealthy impulses toward envious resentment against the people of Switzerland. What we should actually be pursuing—and what a real-world

WEEP would give us a fair and reasonable opportunity of achieving—is not a world of perfect equality, but rather a world in which all per capita income differentials between pairs of nations would be in the general order of magnitude of that between Switzerland and the United States at the present time. Unlike perfect equality, this would be a feasible objective.

Table 6.1 supplements Figures 6.1 and 6.2 by showing the development of some numerical measures of aggregate inequality over the 2000-2050 interval with and without a WEEP in operation. *WMRatio* is the "weighted mean ratio," defined as the weighted mean ratio of each nation's per capita income to the richest nation's per capita income. For example, out of the 140 nations in the dataset, the richest in 2000 was Switzerland, with a PCY of $46,737. In the same year India's PCY was $459, therefore India's ratio in that year was 0.00982. *WMRatio* is the weighted mean of this measure over all nations, using relative population as the weights. *MinRatio* is the lowest over all nations of each nation's ratio of PCY to richest nation PCY. For example, in 2000 the poorest nation in PCY was Ethiopia, with a PCY of $116. Thus *MinRatio* for 2000 was 0.00248, which is rounded off in Table 6.1 to 0.0025. Finally, *RangePCY* is the absolute difference between PCY in the richest nation and PCY in the poorest nation. In 2000, this value was 46621, the difference between Swiss PCY of $46,737 and Ethiopian PCY of $116. *WMRatio* and *MinRatio* are negative measures of inequality: the higher their values, the lower the level of inequality. *RangePCY* is a positive measure of inequality: the higher its value, the higher the level of inequality.

As can be seen from the table, without a WEEP in operation, the expectation would be that of a gradual but steady worsening of the economic gap. Without a WEEP, *WMRatio* declines, *MinRatio* declines, and *RangePCY* increases. There would be a continuation of the empirical trend toward increasing inequality witnessed throughout the 1970-2000 validation interval. This is consistent with Figure 6.3, which shows a steadily widening gap, in the absence of a WEEP, between the four representative high-income nations and the four representative low-income nations. As to the contention that this is implausibly pessimistic, this contention is put to rest simply by means of a comparison of Figure 6.3, which shows probable growth in PCY from 2000 through 2050 in the absence of a WEEP, for all eight representative nations on the same vertical axis, with Figure 4.2 in Chapter 4 above, which shows actual growth in PCY from 1970 through 2000 for the same eight representative nations on the same vertical axis. It is visually inescapable that Figure 6.3 is merely a continuation of the same pattern of increasing inequality clearly manifested by Figure 4.2. It is not implausibly pessimistic that the 1970-2000 trend will continue (in the absence of a WEEP) well into the 21st century—rather it is implausibly optimistic that without a WEEP this trend will *not* continue well into the 21st century. On the other hand, Figure 6.2 and the with-WEEP results shown in Table 6.1 indicate that this need not be the case. With a WEEP in operation, the expectation is that there would be quite dramatic increases in *WMRatio* and *MinRatio*, and a corresponding de-

TABLE 6.1
Projected Aggregate Inequality Measures 2000-2050,
with and without a World Economic Equalization Program

Year	WMRatio		MinRatio		RangePCY	
	with	without	with	without	with	without
2000	0.1195	0.1195	0.0025	0.0025	46621	46621
2005	0.3030	0.1169	0.2150	0.0024	38894	49511
2010	0.3891	0.1140	0.2744	0.0024	38120	52600
2015	0.4465	0.1115	0.3454	0.0023	36478	55902
2020	0.4894	0.1086	0.4024	0.0022	35330	59433
2025	0.5242	0.1055	0.4484	0.0022	34608	63213
2030	0.5538	0.1021	0.4856	0.0021	34259	67260
2035	0.5796	0.0987	0.5121	0.0020	34511	71596
2040	0.6027	0.0953	0.5352	0.0020	34924	76244
2045	0.6233	0.0921	0.5558	0.0019	35467	81228
2050	0.6416	0.0887	0.5745	0.0019	36122	86575

crease in *RangePCY*, albeit the change in the latter would not be so dramatic.

The results illustrated in Figure 6.4 are representative of the entire range of nations in the 140-nation dataset. That is to say, over all nations the losses in terms of a slightly lower growth rate for the small number of rich nations would be minuscule relative to the tremendous gains of the large number of poor nations. This, of course, raises the question of believability. Are not these results simply too good to be true? Would not the actual situation under a hypothetical future gigantic real-world economic development assistance program have little or nothing in common with the benchmark WEEP model simulations under consideration here? Obviously, the only way to answer questions such as these definitively would be to initiate a gigantic real-world economic development assistance program and observe the outcome. Short of that, discussion of these questions must necessarily remain highly speculative and inconclusive. However, the chances that a real-world WEEP will actually be initiated (on a provisional and experimental basis to determine its likelihood of long-term success) will be enhanced to the extent to which a case may be made—even though a highly speculative and inconclusive case—that these benchmark WEEP model results are *not*, despite understandable initial impressions to the contrary, wholly implausible.

A first step toward the development of this case is simply to point out that the results shown above in Figure 6.4 are a consequence of one of the oldest and most universally accepted economic principles of all: the law of diminishing returns to a factor of production. The factor of production in this case is generalized capital, comprising not only the value of physical plant and machinery, but also the value of human capital resources (knowledge and skills achieved via education and training) and the value of social capital resources (roads, bridges, dams, schools, and so on). According to the law of diminishing returns, as the absolute amount of a particular input to the productive process increases, the marginal product of that input decreases. That is to say, fixed increases in the amount of the input utilized will generate steadily decreasing amounts of additional output as the total amount of the input utilized increases. In graphical terms, the relationship between input and output is concave upward-sloping ("bowed over").

The rich nations are utilizing large amounts of generalized capital, therefore the marginal product of generalized capital in these nations is low. The poor nations are utilizing small amounts of generalized capital, therefore the marginal product of generalized capital in these nations is high. Consequently, if a certain increment of generalized capital that would have been installed in a rich nation, is instead installed in a poor nation, the reduction in potential output of the rich nation will be small, while the increase in actual output of the poor nation will be large. This proposition, in and of itself, is hardly a matter for debate. But according to the benchmark WEEP model simulations with and without a World Economic Equalization Program in operation, the numerical implications of this proposition, in the context of the world economic inequality problem, are far more dramatic than have ever been imagined by the great majority of contemporary mainstream economists.

Without doubt most contemporary mainstream economists will be inclined to resist the numerical indications of the benchmark simulations since they pose such a direct challenge to the wisdom of current policy in this area, which confines economic development assistance to inconsequential amounts. But the important thing to recognize and appreciate is that there is nothing in these simulation results contrary to received economic theory. In fact, the *qualitative* proposition that poor nations gain more from economic development transfers than these transfers cost the rich nations, is fully consistent with the virtually axiomatic law of diminishing returns to a factor of production, and would in fact be accepted by a large majority of economists. It is simply the *quantitative significance* of this qualitative proposition with which economists (and others) would tend to have difficulty. But the difficulty stems from the conflict with an established policy—not from a conflict with economic principles. There is nothing in received economic theory that opposes these numerical results.

According to the Cobb-Douglas form used in the WEEP model for the production function of each nation, the marginal productivity of generalized capital K is positively affected by the A coefficient (total factor productivity) and by the population (i.e., labor) level P, but is negatively affected by the level of generalized capital K. The benchmark WEEP model simulations assume that the entire difference between the per capita income of any one nation and that of any other nation is the result of a difference in generalized capital stocks, and that none of the difference is attributable to a difference in the total factor productivity coefficients between the two nations (i.e., the A coefficient is the same for all nations). This presumption leads to very large differences in initial generalized capital stocks K, and consequently very large differentials in the initial marginal productivity of generalized capital, as between various nations. For example, the huge differential in the initial marginal productivity of generalized capital in China relative to the United States is partly a result of the substantial difference between the two nations in population P—but is mostly a result of the tremendous difference in initial generalized capital K. Thus if a certain increment in generalized capital is installed in China rather than in the United States, the "clout" of that certain increment, in terms of increased output, is much, much greater. Of course, as China accumulates more generalized capital as the WEEP proceeds, the marginal productivity of its generalized capital would decrease, and therefore the marginal productivity gap for this factor of production between the two nations would narrow. Eventually the marginal productivity of generalized capital in China would become comparable to that in the United States.

Thus it is the principle of diminishing returns to a factor of production, in conjunction with the very large disparities currently existing in generalized capital stocks across nations, that accounts for the remarkable difference between the without-WEEP simulation result and the with-WEEP simulation result. There is nothing magical or mystical about it. This does not make the results any less remarkable, but it does make them more understandable—we can at least see a sensible, logical, plausible reason why these results might indeed be valid, despite initial impressions to the contrary. This is a large first step on the road to fully accepting these results, and acting accordingly.

From the standpoint of professional economic logic, the most sensible and meaningful cost imposed on the rich nations by their contributions into the transfer fund of a World Economic Equalization Program would be in terms of foregone growth: the difference between their per capita incomes at the end of the 51-year period 2000-2050 if no WEEP takes place and no contributions are made into the transfer fund, and their per capita incomes at the end of this period if a WEEP does take place and they do make contributions into the transfer fund. The estimated differences between the benchmark without-WEEP simulation and with-WEEP simulation, in percentage terms, are shown in Table 6.2 for the 20 richest nations in per capita income (PCY) in the year 2000. The five columns of the table show respectively the name of the nation, its actual PCY in 2000, its projected PCY in 2050 without a WEEP, its projected PCY in 2050 with a WEEP, and the percentage difference between the two. For all nations the percentage differences are well under 4 percent. The foregone growth of the rich nations, according to the benchmark WEEP model simulations, could reasonably be described as inconsequential.

The information shown in Table 6.2 suggests that the costs to the rich nations, in terms of slower economic growth, would be quite modest. But there is an alternative way to look at the cost of the program, an alternative with a long tradition in the real-world history of foreign development assistance programs over the last half-century. This alternative would look at the proportion of a nation's total current output that would go to the global transfer fund. It should be noted that from the structure of the WEEP model, the actual amount of the trans-

TABLE 6.2
Burden of the WEEP
Foregone Growth for the 20 Richest Nations

Nation	PCY 2000	PCY 2050 without WEEP	PCY 2050 with WEEP	percentage difference
Switzerland	46737	86736	84883	-2.136
Japan	44830	82658	80715	-2.350
Denmark	38521	76866	74685	-2.838
Norway	37954	74774	72589	-2.922
Austria	32763	70173	67794	-3.391
Germany	32623	70482	68108	-3.368
Finland	32024	68871	66499	-3.443
United States	31996	65591	63308	-3.481
Sweden	31206	68301	65922	-3.483
Netherlands	30966	66593	64231	-3.547
Belgium	30830	68594	66183	-3.515
France	29811	66179	63810	-3.580
Singapore	28230	58412	56262	-3.682
Ireland	27741	63407	61026	-3.755
Hong Kong	24218	58146	55920	-3.829
Australia	23838	58953	56700	-3.823
Canada	22541	59083	56809	-3.849
United Kingdom	21667	61508	59137	-3.855
Italy	20885	61284	58910	-3.874
Spain	17798	59289	57010	-3.844

fer fund contribution would be a *net* amount: it would be the difference between a certain nation's gross transfer fund contribution and that same nation's share of the transfer fund. Both the contribution and the share are determined by the nation's position relative to the richest nation in the world (Switzerland in the case of the benchmark WEEP simulation from 2000 through 2050). Every nation in the world, with the exception of the richest nation, would—for accounting purposes—receive a share of the global transfer fund. This would be true even of quite rich nations. But if the share amount is less than the gross transfer fund contribution (as it would be for rich nations), then the nation would pay the difference into the fund. In this case, the nation would be a donor nation. On the other hand, if the share amount is greater than the gross transfer fund contribution, then the nation would receive the difference as a disbursement from the fund. In this case, the nation would be a recipient nation. The net transfer ratio is the ratio of the net transfer (contribution less share) to total national output.

Table 6.3 presents data on the net transfer ratio, derived from the benchmark with-WEEP simulation, for the 20 richest nations in per capita income as of 2000, at 10-year intervals from 2000 through 2050. The highest proportion of GNP contributed into the global transfer fund for 2000 would have been from

TABLE 6.3
WEEP Contributions as Percentages of
National Income for the 20 Richest Nations

Nation	Net Transfer Ratio (%)					
	2000	2010	2020	2030	2040	2050
Switzerland	4.241	4.345	4.438	4.521	4.595	4.662
Japan	3.981	4.054	4.098	4.125	4.139	4.141
Denmark	3.028	3.139	3.179	3.210	3.244	3.288
Norway	2.924	3.007	3.008	2.994	2.977	2.967
Austria	2.220	2.327	2.311	2.291	2.288	2.313
Germany	2.176	2.292	2.285	2.278	2.289	2.332
Finland	2.089	2.185	2.148	2.105	2.079	2.084
United States	2.033	2.060	1.934	1.787	1.641	1.516
Sweden	1.953	2.055	2.017	1.977	1.957	1.972
Netherlands	1.931	2.003	1.924	1.835	1.762	1.718
Belgium	1.921	2.038	2.014	1.994	1.998	2.040
France	1.736	1.823	1.752	1.679	1.627	1.612
Singapore	1.467	1.411	1.139	0.835	0.534	0.263
Ireland	1.486	1.564	1.455	1.346	1.260	1.214
Hong Kong	0.981	1.029	0.829	0.627	0.447	0.306
Australia	0.906	0.982	0.813	0.649	0.513	0.419
Canada	0.734	0.854	0.718	0.595	0.505	0.458
United Kingdom	0.590	0.783	0.731	0.714	0.747	0.835
Italy	0.493	0.711	0.672	0.670	0.717	0.820
Spain	0.069	0.366	0.344	0.352	0.401	0.497

Switzerland: 4.231 percent. The second highest would have been from Japan: 3.981 percent. These high contributions reflect the high 2000 PCY of Switzerland and Japan: respectively $46,737 and $44,830. The United States, with a 2000 PCY of $31,996, would have contributed 2.033 percent of its GNP. Because of its relatively large population and high GNP, the United States would have made the largest single contribution in terms of percentage of the total transfer fund. Some other examples include Germany (2000 PCY = $32,623; 2000 net transfer percent = 2.176), France (2000 PCY = $29,811; 2000 net transfer percent = 1.736), United Kingdom (2000 PCY = $21,667; 2000 net transfer percent = 0.590), Sweden (2000 PCY = $31,206; 2000 net transfer percent = 1.953). And so on for the other nations in the table.

The important indication from Table 6.3 is not the precise numerical information on contributions of specific richer nations. For one thing, these numbers pertain to 2000. A WEEP was not initiated in 2000. If a real-world WEEP is initiated, it will be in some future year, and the relative economic positions of the nations will obviously be somewhat different—in some cases quite a bit different—from what they were in 2000. In addition, it must be emphasized that the specific "transfer allocation function" utilized in the WEEP model is merely a suggestion. Upon future deliberation, another formula might be adopted. The important thing is not what specific formula is utilized to determine contributions by the rich nations, but merely that the formula be such that the richer the nation is, the larger its contribution as a percentage of national output.

Consequently the important indication from Table 6.3 is not the specific numbers shown therein—but rather the fact that the indicated net transfer ratios are not excessively high. For the richest nations the ratios are *high*, to be sure, but they are not *excessively* high. During the Cold War era, many of the rich nations allocated more than these percentages to military expenditure. If the benchmark with-WEEP model simulation were to tell us that the richest nations would have to allocate 20, 30 or 40 percent of their GNPs in order for a World Economic Equalization Program to be a success, then we could more legitimately conclude that the entire concept was wholly impractical. But the actual percentages are mostly in the order of 1, 2 or 3 percent. These numbers are within the realm of feasibility.

Up to this point we have looked at the benchmark WEEP model simulations: the benchmark simulation without a World Economic Equalization Program in operation, and the benchmark simulation with such a program in operation. The without-WEEP simulation indicates continuation of the present situation: increasing inequality owing to the fact that the living standards (as measured by per capita income PCY) of the rich nations are growing faster than those of the poor nations. The with-WEEP simulation suggests that a very large-scale economic development assistance program might generate a large amount of economic equalization across all nations of the world without imposing a serious cost on the rich nations. The cost to the rich nations would be in the form of a slightly lower *rate of growth* in living standards, but by no means in terms of a *decline* in living standards. Presuming that the benchmark simulation results represent a reasonable approximation to potential reality, the desirability of a real-world World Economic Equalization Program is manifest.

The conventional viewpoint in the world today, particularly within the richer nations, is that a very large-scale economic development assistance program along the lines of the envisioned WEEP would almost certainly be a very expensive failure. Such a program would substantially reduce economic growth in the rich nations. At the same time, improvement in the poor nations would be at best modest and at worst negligible. The natural reaction to the benchmark WEEP model results described above stemming from this conventional viewpoint is that these results are simply too good to be true. Either the WEEP model itself is in error (does not represent an adequate approximation to real-world variables and relationships), or the benchmark parameter values are in error (do not represent adequate approximations to the real-world numerical parameter values). At this point the model itself will not be defended other than to say that it is based on conventional and widely accepted economic principles (a Cobb-Douglas production function, a linear consumption function, and so on). But the numerical values of the model's parameters are another story—it cannot be reasonably maintained that these values are "very conventional and widely accepted." The actual parameter values utilized for purposes of policy simulations of economic models are normally subject to a considerable amount of uncertainty and error.

Therefore, in assessing the policy implications of any particular economic model, considerable weight is normally placed on sensitivity analysis: on the investigation of how changes in the numerical input into the model simulation affect the numerical output. The question to be addressed is how robust are particular qualitative policy indications against changes in parameter values. Do these qualitative policy indications change dramatically if the parameter values are changed slightly? If so, we deem the initial policy indications to be non-robust. On the other hand, do these qualitative policy indications remain basically intact despite substantial variation in the numerical values of the parameters? If so, we deem the initial policy indications to be robust. In the case of the present research, the initial policy indication is that a World Economic Equalization Program would be highly beneficial. To what extent is this indication robust?

In the section entitled "Selected Sensitivity Analyses" of Chapter 4 of *Common Progress*, I presented results from a large number of WEEP model simulations with parameters set to different values from the benchmark values. Something over ten pages of tabular data were provided. Replicating this information here would constitute overkill, in view of the fact that a more general readership is envisioned. Suffice it to say that the initial policy indication that a World Economic Equalization Program would be highly beneficial is indeed highly robust over a considerable range of numerical variation in *most* of the parameters of the WEEP model. These include the parameters of the production function, the parameters of the consumption function, and various other parameters governing technological progress, population growth and military spending.

However, it must conceded that there are indeed two very important exceptions to this rule. Our attention in the remainder of this section will be focused on these two exceptions. The exceptions pertain, respectively, to the "productivity differential source coefficient" (ξ) and to the "conversion effectiveness coefficient" (χ). It must be frankly acknowledged that with sufficiently adverse numerical values for either of these two parameters, the WEEP model simulation results are fully consistent with the pessimistic preconceptions, so widespread at the present time, regarding the futility of very large-scale economic development assistance efforts. The fact that WEEP simulations run using adverse values for these parameters show little or no progress at overcoming the economic gap was not unanticipated, because these parameters were incorporated into the model precisely in order to encompass the pessimistic beliefs of foreign aid skeptics.

Let us consider first the ξ parameter, the productivity differential source coefficient. This is the parameter that determines the extent to which observed differentials in initial-period per capita income y among the 140 nations of the World Bank dataset may be attributed to differentials in generalized capital stock endowments K, as opposed to differentials in total factor productivity coeffi-

TABLE 6.4

Comparative Statics Analysis

Effect of Parameter ξ on Economic Equalization

ξ	WMRatio ($t = 50$)	MinRatio ($t = 50$)	RangePCY ($t = 50$)	U.S. PCY ($t = 50$)	India PCY ($t = 50$)
0.00	0.6248	0.5533	38602	65196	53037
0.05	0.5859	0.5213	41374	64534	49354
0.10	0.5472	0.4852	44489	63896	45709
0.15	0.5087	0.4444	48014	63281	42080
0.20	0.4702	0.4015	51726	62686	38363
0.25	0.4319	0.3598	55329	62113	34703
0.30	0.3935	0.3177	58962	61560	31096
0.35	0.3549	0.2736	62777	61028	27381
0.40	0.3159	0.2292	66614	60515	23725
0.45	0.2762	0.1837	70548	60022	19961
0.50	0.2355	0.1394	74375	59549	16011
0.55	0.1948	0.1140	76573	59095	12044
0.60	0.1624	0.0977	77982	58660	9109
0.65	0.1454	0.0859	79000	58243	7914
0.70	0.1327	0.0736	80062	57844	6828
0.75	0.1213	0.0619	81075	57463	5761
0.80	0.1103	0.0499	82107	57099	4718
0.85	0.0996	0.0381	83131	56753	3672
0.90	0.0893	0.0260	84172	56424	2624
0.95	0.0795	0.0140	85211	56112	1582
1.00	0.0723	0.0022	86229	55816	714

cients A. An alternative descriptive designation of this parameter would be the "K differential vs. A differential coefficient." The benchmark value of this parameter is 0 (zero), which indicates that *all* differentials in per capita income are the result of differentials in generalized capital stocks (i.e., the total factor productivity coefficients A are the same over all nations). At the other end of the spectrum would be $\xi = 1$, according to which *all* differentials in per capita income are the result of differentials in total factor productivity coefficients (i.e., the ratios of initial generalized capital K to initial total output Y are the same over all nations). If the value of $\xi = .5$, this would indicate that one half of the differentials in per capita income y could be attributed to differentials in generalized capital K, and the other one half of the differentials could be attributed to differentials in the total factor productivity coefficients A.

Table 6.4 shows the consequences for the benchmark with-WEEP simulation of different values of the ξ parameter: ξ is varied from its minimum possible value of 0 (the most optimistic value) to its maximum possible value of 1 (the most pessimistic value) by increments of 0.05. For each value of ξ the table reports the period-50 *WMRatio*, *MinRatio* and *RangePCY*. It is observed that the equalizing effect of a WEEP is steadily degraded as the value of ξ increases. It should also be noted, however, that unless the ξ value becomes quite large, a substantial amount of economic equalization still takes place. For example, if ξ is at its midpoint value of 0.50, the terminal-period *WMRatio* is 0.2355, which is a great improvement over the expected without-WEEP *WMRatio* in 2050 of 0.0887.

Far more important, however, is the indication in the final two columns of Table 6.4, which report respectively the period-50 per capita income (PCY) of the United States and the period-50 per capita income of India. The United States is representative of the rich donor nations while India is representative of the poor recipient nations. We observe that while terminal-period U.S. PCY and Indian PCY are both adversely affected by increasing ξ, the effect is far stronger for India than it is for the United States. This suggests that if a real-world WEEP were unsuccessful, it would be unsuccessful in terms of not achieving much acceleration in the economic growth of the recipient nations. But it would not be unsuccessful in terms of having a substantial adverse effect on the economic growth of the rich nations. That is to say, if the rich nations are investing heavily in a real-world WEEP and the program is not having the desired effect, this would be bad news far more to the populations of the recipient nations than to the populations of the donor nations. The rich nations would continue to grow at a brisk rate even if the WEEP is a near-total failure as far as the poor nations are concerned. If the program is inevitably destined for failure, whether because the real-world ξ is close to 1 or some other reason, then soon enough the rich nations would give up on the effort.

But the very significant indication of the last two columns of Table 6.4 is that such an experiment would not be especially costly to the rich nations. Clearly this indication—if valid—supports the sensibility of inaugurating a real-world WEEP on a tentative and experimental basis in the hope that it will succeed. There are two conceptually distinct issues in deciding whether humanity should undertake a real-world WEEP: (1) benefits; (2) costs. What the results shown in Table 6.4 suggest is that while the benefits to the poor nations of such a program are uncertain, the costs to the rich nations are very likely to be modest in any case. It would of course be terribly unfortunate if the benefits to the poor nations of a real-world WEEP turned out to be minor. Such an outcome would bode ill for the future destiny of human civilization. But at least this outcome would not entail a direct, immediate and substantial material penalty on the rich nations.

The other highly sensitive WEEP model parameter is χ, the conversion effectiveness coefficient. A familiar and quite fundamental objection to the notion of a World Economic Equalization Program is that the "resources would not get through." Owing partly to legitimate administrative expenses, and partly to illegitimate graft, a large part of the transferred resources would be diverted away from productive uses. Those of a particularly pessimistic and cynical nature would no doubt be tempted to assert that the "vast majority" of large-scale economic development assistance resources would end up in the pockets of corrupt bureaucrats and/or dishonest businessmen. But even if considerably less than the "vast majority" of these resources were wasted, it could seriously debilitate the effectiveness of a potential future World Economic Equalization Program. This possibility is encompassed in the WEEP model by means of the χ parameter, representing the proportion of the poor nations' shares in the global transfer fund that are successfully converted into productive generalized capital resources.

Results for the χ parameter exactly parallel those for the ξ parameter, so I will very briefly summarize them. The benchmark value for the χ parameter is 1, indicating that the entire amount of the shares of the poorer nations in the global transfer fund are successfully converted into generalized capital. From simulation results for χ values less than the benchmark value, it would appear that the losses from administrative costs and theft would have to be extremely large for the effectiveness of a WEEP to be seriously impaired. Even if χ is as low as .1, indicating that only 10 percent of transfer fund resources "get through," the impact on world poverty remains very high—while the same time the costs of the program to the rich nations remain very low. Only if the value of χ is actually 0, indicating that nothing gets through, does the WEEP become totally ineffective. And even then, the cost of the WEEP to the rich nations continues to be minor. The results for the conversion effectiveness coefficient are thus fully analogous to those already described for the productivity source differential coefficient. In both cases, these results are basically supportive of the desirability of a real-world WEEP.

EVALUATION OF THE EVIDENCE

Pessimism regarding the economic prospects of the poorer nations of the world has a long—if not honored—tradition among the populations of the wealthy nations. The Vietnam entanglement may have been the critical turning point. Over the 15-year period between 1960 and 1975, the United States suffered military casualties of 57,685 killed and 153,303 wounded while expending tens of billions of dollars on military operations and another 5.6 billion dollars on economic development assistance to South Vietnam in an ultimately futile effort to prevent the communization of that nation. In 1973, the year that witnessed the withdrawal of the last U.S. combatant troops from South Vietnam, the Overseas Development Council, a pro-aid pressure group, published the results of a survey of the United States population on economic development and foreign aid under the authorship of Paul Laudicina. According to the survey, the U.S. population had pretty well resigned itself to the poverty of the Third World, as manifested by the fact that only 15 percent of the U.S. population believed that "poverty could be eliminated in the world within 50 years" (p. 8). Moreover, the U.S. population did not perceive any moral responsibility to help the Third World overcome poverty, as manifested by the fact that only 17 percent of the U.S. population felt that the U.S. government was "doing too little to fight world poverty" (p. 21). To my knowledge, the Overseas Development Council has not been inspired to sponsor any further surveys on U.S. public opinion toward foreign aid during the more than three decades since its publication of the Laudicina survey. It is not difficult to see why. The Overseas Development Council has waged a noble struggle to educate the U.S. public on the benefits of foreign aid, but it has been a rearguard effort. In practice the objective has been more to retard the decline of public support for foreign aid, rather than to actually increase the level of support.

Given the reigning pessimism with respect to the near-term economic prospects for the Less Developed Countries (LDCs), the immediate reaction of most people to the WEEP model policy simulation results described in the previous section will be that they are "too good to be true," that they fall beyond the remotest bounds of plausibility, that they are simply not believable. I would hope that most readers of this book will resist the understandably strong impulse to reject these results categorically and peremptorily. Given what may be at stake, the WEEP simulation results are deserving of calm and deliberate contemplation. In the end, of course, it may indeed be reasonable to ignore or reject them, but before that they deserve what might be termed a "fair trial." Let us consider, therefore, some of the more important objections that might be raised against the fundamental conclusion of the WEEP model research that a tremendously expanded, worldwide economic development assistance effort might well be highly successful in terms of dramatically raising living standards in poor nations while costing the rich nations only a modest retardation in the rate of growth of their own living standards.

Over-Optimistic Parameter Values. The argument here is that the encouraging results shown by the benchmark with-WEEP simulation are an invalid artifact stemming from over-optimistic parameter values. This argument would stipulate that the theoretical structure of the WEEP model is reasonable, but maintains that the numerical parameter values used in the benchmark simulation are unrealistic. Perhaps the single most fundamentally unrealistic benchmark parameter value (continuing with the argument) is $\xi = 0$, which says that all observed differences in per capita income between nations are the result of differentials in generalized capital stocks K, and that none are the result of differentials in total factor productivity A. But a plausible hypothesis is that owing to deeply entrenched political and cultural factors, total factor productivity varies widely across nations: it is low for poor nations and high for rich nations. Probably the second most fundamentally unrealistic benchmark parameter value is $\chi = 1$, which says that all foreign aid receipts of recipient nations will be successfully converted into generalized capital. But a plausible hypothesis here is that owing to substantial administrative costs and substantial losses to graft and corruption, only a fraction of foreign aid receipts will in fact be successfully converted into generalized capital. In addition to these obviously unrealistic parameter values, there may be other cases of inaccurate parameter values, for example in the production and/or consumption function, which combine to generate invalid results.

Of all the objections to the results, this is the only one capable of being explored within the context of the WEEP model itself. This was done by means of the "selected sensitivity analyses" reported in the concluding section of Chapter 4 of my book *Common Progress*. Results are shown there for variations in the numerical values of some 14 model parameters. Of the 14 parameters, variation in 12 of them within reasonable numerical ranges does not affect the qualitative conclusion that a very large amount of progress in the living standards of the poor nations may be achieved at the cost of a very minor retardation in the growth rates of living standards in the rich nations. However, it must be conceded that the impact of the two parameters representing the two objections described above, ξ and χ, is just as predicted by skeptics. If either of these parameters departs sufficiently from its benchmark value, then the WEEP model simulations demonstrate that the World Economic Equalization Program would indeed be a complete failure. On the other hand, the model simulations run with less optimistic values of these parameters do bring to light two very important offsetting indications: (1) the departures from the benchmark value would have to be very large for the program to be fully ineffective; (2) even with these parameters at their extreme pessimistic values, showing little economic progress among the poor nations despite the WEEP, the retarding effect on the rates of growth of per capita income in the rich nations would not be significantly increased. In other words, the worst-case scenario is that a WEEP would simply not benefit the poor nations—not that a WEEP would not benefit the poor nations *and* impose heavy costs on the rich nations.

Results Inconsistent with Past Experience. The argument here is that if it were true that extreme differentials in per capita income were the result of extreme differentials in generalized capital stocks, then the foreign aid programs of the past would have achieved a much higher level of success. After all, according to the underlying hypothesis being put forward in support of the proposed World Economic Equalization Program, the generalized capital stocks of the poor nations are tiny and virtually microscopic relative to the generalized capital stocks of the rich nations. This explains the tremendously accelerated growth of the poor nations at the same time that the rich nations experience only a minor retardation of growth: the marginal products of the extremely small generalized capital stocks of the poor nations are huge in relation to the marginal products of the extremely large generalized capital stocks of the rich nations. But if this were actually the case, would we not have witnessed a much greater payoff to the foreign aid receipts of the poor nations during the last half-century? True, the amounts of foreign aid provided to the poor nations were small in relation to those envisioned by the proposed World Economic Equalization Program, but they were still fairly substantial in an absolute sense. For example, many LDCs at certain points in time have received amounts comparable to the amounts that were received by the Western European nations during the operation of the Marshall Plan from 1948 through 1952—but these LDCs did not emulate the explosive growth of the Western European recipient nations during that period.

The answer to this objection is that the foreign aid flows of the past, while they have been large in an absolute sense, were small in relation to the need, and for most of the LDCs did not constitute the necessary "critical mass" to initiate rapid economic progress. In nuclear physics, as everyone has learned since the appearance of operational nuclear weapons in 1945, the critical mass is that quantity of uranium that when compacted will initiate a nuclear explosion. If one were to compact a quantity of uranium even slightly below the critical mass, nothing would happen. This basic concept has applications outside of nuclear physics. For example, in behavioral psychology, the "threshold of perception" refers to that minimum level of sensory stimulation required for the individual to become consciously aware of the stimulation. "Threshold of perception" could equally be termed the "critical mass" of sensory stimulation that will initiate conscious awareness of the stimulation.

I submit that the notion of a "critical mass" is fully relevant to the real-world success or failure of economic development assistance programs, and that the principal reason for the poor performance of the recipient nations in the past has been the fact that the resources provided fell short of the necessary critical mass. The argument that the resources provided actually exceeded what should have been a critical mass because they involved "billions and billions of dollars" may well represent faulty accounting—because the sums are not properly deflated. "Billions and billions of dollars" continues to be a lot of money to one individual or one household, but it may not be particularly impressive in terms of billions of individuals or billions of households.

For example, in 2000 the member nations of the Development Assistance Committee of the OECD provided almost 54 billion current U.S. dollars in foreign aid (Table 5.1). But in the same year, the total population of nations categorized by the World Bank as low-income stood at about 2.5 billion persons (Table 5.3). The foreign aid amount in 2000 therefore worked out to approximately $22 per capita. This is probably not enough to get the job done. The global economic inequality problem is a massive, deeply entrenched problem. As such, it will probably require a massive, coordinated effort to overcome it. It will probably require a much larger effort, indeed, than that of the Marshall Plan of 1948-1952. The Western European nations at that time were already economically advanced, industrialized nations—the purpose of the Marshall Plan was merely to assist them in recovering from the destruction of World War II, not to enable them to attain a qualitatively higher level of economic development.

Deficiencies of the WEEP Model. The argument here is that the WEEP model is too simplistic and unrealistic for the results derived from it to be taken seriously. For example, it ignores international trade and investment, it utilizes very simple mathematical forms for the production and consumption functions, and it takes no account of complicating factors within the national economies, such as different levels of domestic income inequality within different nations. There is at least one clear indication that these various deficiencies generate results that are not to be trusted: the fact that the benchmark with-WEEP simulation, illustrated for the eight representative nations by Figure 6.4, indicates drastic improvements occurring in the very first year of initiation of the WEEP. A model that is clearly invalid in this one important respect may well be invalid in other respects as well.

To begin with, it must be frankly admitted that the extremely rapid improvement in the global economic inequality situation shown by the benchmark with-WEEP simulation (Figure 6.4) is not to be believed. Clearly, the model does not incorporate the lags that would surely apply in the real world. It would be a simple enough matter to add a lag structure in the application of the total transfer fund to generalized capital accumulation in the LDCs. Such a structure would evade the problem of an excessively rapid improvement in the first year of program operation. I did not do so for two reasons. First, specifying a precise structure of the lag would involve pure guesswork. Second and more importantly, I want to be honest and forthcoming in presenting this research, and not withhold important evidence from the reader, even if that evidence is not supportive of the WEEP model's realism. My response to the problem is simply that the WEEP model is designed to represent long-term development rather than short-term development. The long-term focus is manifested by the fact that in validation simulations (illustrated by Figures 6.1 and 6.2), the WEEP model does not allow for short-term fluctuations in economic variables but merely tracks their smoothed long-term evolution. The WEEP model is clearly unrealistic in its failure to account for short-term fluctuations, but this particular unrealism is not a serious problem in view of the long-term focus of the model. I would argue that the same is true of the WEEP model's failure to incorporate lags, which are a short-term phenomenon rather than a long-term phenomenon.

As for the "simplicity" of the WEEP model, this in itself is not a serious criticism of the research. Simplicity is relative. While the WEEP model does not attain the scale and complexity of some of the largest general equilibrium models and macroeconometric models in usage today, it is certainly not below the average scale and complexity of economic models routinely utilized in the analysis of economic policy issues. As all practitioners of economic policy analysis realize, there is a steep tradeoff between realism and practicality. Non-economists often sneer at economic models on grounds that they "assume away" many obviously important aspects of economic decision-making and interaction—while at the same time, somewhat inconsistently, they complain about the mathematical complexity of these same models. The fact remains, however, that only by "assuming away" many aspects of the problem is the analysis able to proceed, and to reach meaningful conclusions. True, the absence of complete realism means that the evidence derived from formal policy analysis is never conclusive, and is merely circumstantial evidence that has to be evaluated along with other evidence of a less formal nature, in arriving at a final judgment on a specific policy issue. But this does not mean that the evidence is worthless and should be disregarded.

Another important point in this regard is that the "simplicity of the model," in and of itself, does not necessarily bias the results in one direction or the other. In our case specifically, the simplicity of the WEEP model does not necessarily predispose it to showing that a real-world WEEP would be highly successful. Or if it does in fact do this, it is not apparent how. To the contrary, one obvious counter-example might be proposed to suggest that the simplicity of the WEEP model might bias it *against* showing successful results from the proposed World Economic Equalization Program. The WEEP model does not incorporate trade among nations, and a strong consensus exists among contemporary economists that international trade is highly beneficial to all participants, and moreover, that increased participation in international trade is the chief remaining hope to those LDCs wishing to initiate rapid economic progress. Presumably, therefore, a model that incorporated the various "expansionary feedback effects" of international trade might display an even higher level of success for a massive, worldwide economic development assistance effort. Be this as it may, the level of success displayed by the benchmark with-WEEP simulation of the actual WEEP model is surely sufficient. As it is, these results are in grave danger of being dismissed out of hand because they are simply "too good to be true." It would not necessarily be advantageous to show results even more highly successful.

Ignores Implementation Questions. The argument here is that the research presented has nothing at all to say on the numerous applied policy questions in the area of foreign aid, questions that have intrigued and puzzled a generation of economists. But unless clear and cogent answers are provided to these questions, and these answers are duly incorporated into the actual operation of the World Economic Equalization Program, the program would just be "throwing money at the problem" on a massive scale—the overwhelmingly probable consequence of which would be profligacy and waste on an equally massive scale. These questions include, but are not confined to, the following: What would be the appropriate proportions, of the total amount of foreign aid provided to each recipient nation under the WEEP, to be allocated to plant and equipment, education and training, and social infrastructure? How should specific projects be chosen? What proportion of assistance should be provided in the form of grants, and what proportion in the form of interest-bearing loans? To what extent should assistance be tied, that is, required to be spent by the specific recipient nation in the specific donor nation? What should be the role of the OPEC nations, most of which are oil-rich but otherwise poor? What, if any, requirements should be placed on the recipient nations as a precondition for receiving aid? For example, should they be required to abolish certain tariffs or quotas, to privatize publicly-owned enterprises or to operate publicly-owned enterprises on a commercial basis, to curtail welfare entitlements or to restrict regulation of privately owned businesses, to implement population control policies and/or environmental safeguards, to institute and enforce anti-corruption measures, to maintain authentically democratic political conditions? And so on and so forth.

It is quite true that the WEEP model, in and of itself, has nothing to add to the discussion of these kinds of questions. But it is necessary to proceed one step at a time. The purpose of the research described above is simply to *demonstrate the possibility*—as opposed to establish the fact—that a sufficiently massive economic development assistance program might be dramatically successful, raising the living standards of poorer nations by a tremendous amount while at the same time only slightly reducing the growth rate of living standards in the richer nations. Once this possibility has been established and accepted, then would be the time to get into the details of program functioning. It is not necessary to resolve all the myriad implementation issues in advance of deciding whether or not to undertake the proposed World Economic Equalization Program. Indeed, if resolution of all these issues were made a precondition for deciding the basic question of whether or not to initiate a WEEP, then this latter decision would probably never be made. Specifics of foreign aid implementation have been debated for decades in the past, are being debated at the present time, and will no doubt continue to be debated into the indefinite future. Even if a real-world WEEP were initiated and were soon in full swing, these issues would still be controversial. It is far beyond my own abilities, just as it would be far beyond the abilities of any economist endowed with less than godlike intellectual and persuasive powers, to decisively resolve these controversial issues.

The only fundamental implementation principle suggested by the WEEP research described above is that as much as humanly possible of the transfer fund contributions of the rich donor nations should find its way into augmenting the generalized capital stocks of the poor recipient nations. This suggests that the overwhelming emphasis of WEEP expenditures ought to be on education and training in the human sphere, and in the capital sphere on what is generally known as "project assistance"—as opposed to alternative aid forms such as technical assistance, food aid, debt relief, humanitarian aid, and so on. The core objective would be to get as much physical capital as possible into place (social capital and commercial capital), and to provide the labor force with the knowledge and skills necessary to make effective use of that physical capital. Obviously, there must be administrators in both the donor nations and the recipient nations, but equally obviously the purely administrative expenses of the program should be kept to a reasonable minimum. As to the diversion and loss of resources through graft and corruption, I believe that it would be reasonable, in view of the overwhelming importance of the program to the future of humanity, to attempt to deter this by means of a draconian enforcement system.

Beyond these obvious points I would not be prepared to go at this point. The specifics of program operation are certainly important, and would have a significant effect on program performance. But they would not have a decisive and determinative effect. That is to say, whether or not the program would be successful depends critically on whether sufficiently large transfers take place. It seems safe to say, in the light of 50 years of past experience with foreign aid, that egregious errors would be avoided. We have certainly learned a great deal from the experiences of the past. Assuming that sufficient resources are committed to the program by the rich nations to reach the desired goal, the degree of operational efficiency attained by the program might affect the time taken to achieve the goal by a factor of plus or minus 20 percent. But the degree of operational efficiency, in and of itself, is not likely to determine the qualitative outcome, i.e., to determine whether or not success is achieved within a reasonably abbreviated period of historical time.

Consider an analogy. Imagine a hunter being charged by a huge, enraged rhinoceros. The huge, enraged rhinoceros is a metaphor for the world poverty problem (we would not want any harm to come to actual, real-world members of this endangered species), and the hunter is a metaphor for humanity. The rhino is approaching quickly, and the hunter will have time for only one shot. If the hunter were armed with only a BB-gun, he would obviously be doomed. Not even the most well-aimed shot from a BB-gun would be capable of bringing down a huge, enraged, charging rhinoceros. On the other hand, if the hunter were armed with a heavy-caliber rifle (an "elephant gun"), he would have a reasonable chance at survival. Accuracy of aim is comparable to the efficiency of the global economic development program, while the caliber of the weapon is comparable to the resources devoted to the program. Just as the accuracy of the hunter's aim will be irrelevant to the outcome if the caliber of his weapon is sufficiently puny, so too an admirably efficient global economic development program will accomplish little if the resources allocated to it are sufficiently meager. If, on the other hand, the hunter's weapon is sufficiently powerful, it will most likely get the job done even if the hunter's aim is not perfect. In the same way, if sufficiently massive resources are devoted to the global economic development program, the program will likely be successful even if it is not optimally efficient. And it must be kept in mind that owing to the limitations of human knowledge, it is very unlikely that a real-world global economic development program would in fact be optimally efficient.

In summary, it must be acknowledged—as I have already done several times in the foregoing—that the WEEP model simulation results described above most certainly do not constitute "proof" that a World Economic Equalization Program would be successful in achieving a substantial degree of economic equalization across the world within a reasonably abbreviated period of historical time. They do, however, constitute "proof" that a World Economic Equalization Program *could* be successful in achieving a substantial degree of economic equalization across the world within a reasonably abbreviated period of historical time. Replacing "would" by "could," in the minds of some, relegates the results described above to oblivion. The results are, to these same minds, academic, irrelevant, meaningless, useless, deserving of no consideration whatsoever.

But these people possess a sadly deficient understanding of the nature and purposes of scientific inquiry. Rarely does any particular piece of evidence, whether based on empirical investigation, mathematical analysis or syllogistic reasoning, absolutely confirm or refute any given proposition. Rather it merely has the power—among those capable of grasping the evidence—of affecting the subjective probability that the proposition is true or false. There are heated controversies in the physical sciences over propositions (for example, concerning the origin and evolution of the universe) that have absolutely no bearing on the controversial social policy issues of our time. It is no wonder, therefore, that there continues to be a high level of disagreement on propositions that do bear directly on these issues. In these more sensitive areas, any one piece of evidence, no matter how substantive it might appear to a disinterested observer, is unlikely to have a pronounced impact on peoples' judgment. The fact is that very few observers are truly disinterested—most have already arrived at tentative judgments on various social policy issues and believe that their personal self-interest is, or could be, affected by social decisions on these issues. Thus evidence that would probably have a substantial effect on judgment with respect to less sensitive matters (e.g., the origin and evolution of the universe) is routinely shrugged off as "weak and inconclusive." This is particularly true of evidence that supports substantial alterations in well-established social policies—such as the policy of minimal allocations to foreign development assistance.

But this is not as it should be. The great strength of humanity is that of openness to change, of rational adaptation to evolving conditions. Humanity would not have come as far as we have if thoughtless inertial conservatism forever ruled out substantial changes in social policy. But thoughtless inertial conservatism has certainly delayed the progress of human civilization, and in the future, thoughtless inertial conservatism may yet—if humanity is sufficiently unlucky—be responsible for the downfall of human civilization. This thought should be borne in mind when pondering what the WEEP model policy simulations may be telling us about the potential success of the proposed World Economic Equalization Program. Another important point to bear in mind is that it is not being proposed that humanity continue indefinitely with a real-world WEEP even if little progress is being made in the poor nations. The proposal is rather than a WEEP be initiated on a tentative and provisional basis, and only continued beyond a trial period of 10 to 15 years if there are strong indications of long-term success. Only an actual experiment with a WEEP will give us compelling evidence regarding its effectiveness. The proof of the pudding will be in the eating. The necessary "eating" experiment should be commenced soon.

IT IS WORTH TRYING

Although the most direct and obvious benefit of a World Economic Equalization Program would be to the huge populations of the poorer nations lifted once and for all out of poverty, the populations of the richer nations would garner significant benefits as well. To begin with, there is basic human compassion. It has always been a fundamental strength of the human species, throughout the evolutionary struggle, that we take care of our own, that if we are able to, we provide help and assistance to those in need, that we do not readily turn our backs on our fellow human beings. It is hard to imagine the pride and relief that would be felt throughout the world if by human action we were able to finally overcome the problem of world poverty. Aside from that, economic prosperity among those nations today termed "LDCs" would impact favorably on the future economic prosperity of today's "advanced nations." International trade and investment would be strengthened, there would be further exploitation of economies of scale in the production of many commodities, the interrelated problems of excessive population growth and environmental degradation would be made subject to better control. Finally, there is the key political dimension. Worldwide prosperity would provide a more secure foundation for civil harmony and democratic institutions within nations, would reduce the economic motivations toward conflict that have historically been a major factor in the generation of international warfare. If, as proposed in this book, a World Economic Equalization Program is commenced in conjunction with the foundation of a world federation to be known as the Federal Union of Democratic Nations, the economic program would greatly augment the probability that the world federation would persist and prosper. The world federation, at the same time, would have a positive feedback effect on the WEEP, and greatly augment the probability that the economic program would persevere until it had reached a successful conclusion. But whether a world federation is involved or is not involved, a World Economic Equalization Program would be a solid investment in the future for all humanity—not just for the populations of the Less Developed Countries.

A start has already been made. Foreign development assistance programs have been an integral part of international relations for well over half a century. These programs have shifted a certain quantity of investment resources from the rich nations to the poor nations, and have quite likely been instrumental to the observed economic progress of the poor nations. But the rate of observed economic progress in most of the poor nations has been unsatisfactory, as manifested by the widening economic gap between the richest and poorest nations. Foreign aid programs should be dramatically increased and expanded. Policy changes (e.g., trade liberalization, privatization of public enterprises) might be desirable because they improve the efficiency with which any given amount of foreign aid is invested—but they are unlikely to be decisive in and of themselves. Without a major increase in the *quantity* of foreign aid, improvements in quality will probably have only a minor effect. As far as quality by itself is concerned, we are now well into the range of diminishing returns. Roughly what is needed is an expansion of the foreign aid contributions of the richest nations from well under 1 percent of GNP to somewhere between 2 and 4 percent of GNP. This increase could be easily afforded by most of the richest nations. An important reason for supplementing a real-world WEEP with a world federation along the lines of the Federal Union of Democratic Nations is that the rich nations would probably be encouraged to a higher level of generosity if there existed meaningful political unification between their citizen bodies and those of the developing nations. The existence of a functioning world government would facilitate those psychological attitudes of common interest and shared purpose under which a real-world WEEP is more likely to be pursued with sufficient intensity to achieve success.

In all likelihood, the success probability of a real-world WEEP is being seriously underestimated at the present time. As discussed earlier in this chapter, computer simulations of a model of the proposed World Economic Equalization Program show the possibility of a tremendous rise in the living standards of the poor nations, while at the same time the living standards of the rich nations continue to rise at rates comparable to the rates observed throughout the last few decades. A diminution of the growth rates of living standards in the rich nations does in fact occur, but it is a very minor diminution—arguably a virtually unnoticeable diminution. The program is therefore based on the concept of Common Progress: that the living standards in all nations of the world will continue to advance (progress would be common to all nations), but the living standards in the rich nations will rise at a very slightly diminished rate in order that the living standards in the poor nations rise at a tremendously accelerated rate. The results of these simulations pose a direct challenge to the commonly expressed opinion that "there exists no meaningful evidence" that any foreign aid program within reasonable limits could overcome the world inequality problem within a reasonable period of time.

But what guarantees, it might be asked, are there that results obtained from computer simulations of a theoretical model of a World Economic Equalization Program will have any bearing whatsoever on real-world outcomes? Are these results not merely wishful thinking? Would not the more likely outcome of a real-world WEEP on the scale proposed be the generation of waste, graft, and corruption on an unimaginable scale, of the enrichment of a handful of bureaucrats and administrators while the economic status of the great masses of poor people in the LDCs is only marginally improved, if at all?

It must be conceded, of course, that there are *no* guarantees that a real-world WEEP would not be a colossal failure. Even in terms of the WEEP model developed in this research, not all of the computer simulations show good results. Good results—in fact, spectacularly good results—are obtained for the benchmark numerical values of the model parameters. A case may be made that the benchmark parameter values are inherently plausible, but the case is hardly conclusive. Furthermore, the model is developed in such a way as to encompass the viewpoints of those who maintain that foreign aid is of little or no value in promoting the economic growth of recipient nations. One familiar allegation is that differences in economic productivity between nations are based mostly on different political circumstances or cultural conditions, and that differences in capital stocks, however "capital" is defined, have little or nothing to do with economic productivity differences. This allegation is encompassed by the WEEP model parameter ξ. Another familiar allegation is that foreign aid resources are mostly consumed by administrative costs and graft, and that very few of these resources are actually put to the intended purposes. This allegation is encompassed by the WEEP model parameter χ. It is shown, by means of running WEEP computer simulations with these parameters set to sufficiently adverse values, that the program might well have little or no reducing effect on world economic inequality.

The fact of the matter is, however, that *no* social policy decision (even if that social policy decision be that there be *no* active social policy to ameliorate a particular problem) can ever be based on fully conclusive evidence. Despite our best efforts at prognostication and forecasting, the future remains obscure, and the consequences that any particular policy will bring about in the future remain equally obscure. Decision-making under uncertainty—that is, making decisions now that will impact on future outcomes in unpredictable ways—is an inevitable feature of all human existence, whether it be at the individual level, the organizational level, or the social level. Although there is no guarantee that a real-world WEEP would be a success, there is equally no compelling or conclusive evidence that it would be a failure. What I want to put forward here is simply the proposition that it would be most unreasonable to reject a World Economic Equalization Program out of hand, on the basis of the mere *possibility* that it would be a failure.

The benchmark with-WEEP policy simulation described earlier clearly establishes the alternative possibility that a real-world World Economic Equalization Program might well be dramatically successful. The benchmark simulation also indicates that the cost to the rich nations of financing the program would not be excessive either in terms of foregone growth or of foreign aid contributions as a percentage of national output. And it is worth noting that these results are obtained from a benchmark simulation which in some ways is biased against progress. This simulation does not allow for positive effects from increased international trade, nor for positive effects from further exploitation of economies of large-scale production. It does not presume that population increase will slow down, nor that military spending will diminish. Also, the World Bank dataset which provides the basis for the WEEP policy simulations clearly exaggerates the economic differences among nations. The standard GNP estimates of the World Bank take inadequate account of non-monetary production and exchange. Thus the poor nations are not actually so far below the rich nations in terms of living standards as these figures indicate. Therefore, the gap to be closed is actually quite a bit smaller than the initial gap utilized in the WEEP model simulations.

There is a traditional proverb that is most apt: "The proof of the pudding is in the eating." You cannot resolve the question of whether a certain pudding tastes good by lengthy theoretical disputations about the human sense of taste and the relative proportions of ingredients in the pudding. Rather you have to eat the pudding—or at least taste it. In the same way, you cannot resolve the question of the potential performance of a World Economic Equalization Program by lengthy theoretical disputations based on the inconclusive evidence of our past experiences with economic development assistance. Rather you must initiate such a program and observe the results. There is simply no meaningful substitute for experiment.

Another fundamental point deserves reiteration here: Owing to the unavoidable fact that there is a non-negligible probability that an actual World Economic

Equalization Program would be extremely *in*effective in attaining its goals, the proposal of this book is that such a program be initiated *on a tentative and experimental basis*. This does not mean that it would be initiated on a small basis. For a worthwhile test, it must be initiated on a very large basis. What it means, rather, is that the program should be initiated with a clear understanding on the part of all participants, including both rich donor nations and poor recipient nations, that continuation of the program beyond an experimental period of 10 to 15 years will depend on the achievement of tangible, dramatic progress in terms of rising living standards within all parts of the populations of the poorer nations. If tangible, dramatic progress is *not* being made after a reasonable interval has elapsed, then the program would be very quickly either scaled down or phased out altogether. The proposal is most definitely *not* that a World Economic Equalization Program be pursued indefinitely, for decade after decade, even if results continue to be disappointing.

Predictably, skeptics will complain that if a WEEP were actually undertaken in the real world, it would constitute nothing more that a "giant pork barrel" for the personal enrichment of venal and corrupt bureaucrats. Sad to say, they may be right. But should the possibility of failure—a possibility which is of course inevitable where any important undertaking is concerned—be allowed to forestall even an attempt at success? It is to be hoped that most readers will agree that the answer to this question ought to be a firm and resolute "No!" The answer should rather be that we should most certainly *try*—we should make the effort. A World Economic Equalization Program holds the promise of a dazzling success, of an epochal advance. It offers humanity the possibility that the next generation will witness monumental progress in human wellbeing, progress on a gigantic scale never before witnessed in human history. It is worth trying! If we are doomed to disappointment, then so be it—we will soon be made aware of the futility of the effort. But surely we ought not be deterred by those cynical skeptics and petty-minded pessimists who callously disparage even the mere aspiration toward a better world.

PART III

OVERCOMING THE
POLITICAL IMPEDIMENT

7

THE ISSUE OF NATIONALISM

Note that the title of this chapter is not—as some might have expected—"The Problem of Nationalism." The title is rather "The Issue of Nationalism." This is because nationalism, in and of itself, is not necessarily a major and unavoidable impediment to stable and benign federal world government in the long term. The widespread belief that nationalism constitutes an important barrier to federal world government is based on misconceptions on both the nature of nationalism and the nature of federal world government. Once these misconceptions have been corrected, it becomes apparent that nationalism is more accurately described as an "issue" than as a "problem." Nationalism is not like world economic inequality, with which we were concerned in the previous part of this book, comprising Chapters 4 through 6. World economic inequality, in contrast to nationalism, is indeed a major and unavoidable impediment to world government at the present point in time, and it will remain so until such time as it has been greatly reduced by an international economic development effort along the lines of the proposed World Economic Equalization Program (WEEP). World economic inequality is therefore properly described as more than an "issue"—it is a legitimate "problem." The economic impediment to world government is based on hard, existent realities which cannot be quickly and easily eliminated.

When compared to economic inequality, the force of nationalism in the modern world is a relatively minor and easily overcome impediment to world government. I am not claiming, of course, that nationalism does not constitute an impediment to world government. It is in fact a political impediment, and in this final part of the book, we will be looking at ways and means to overcome this impediment. But overcoming this particular impediment will not involve a tremendous development program involving many trillions of dollars expended over several decades. The problem of nationalism can be effectively dealt with merely by making a sufficient number of people around the world sufficiently aware of—and properly appreciative of—the institutional details of the proposal for limited world government advanced herein. Once it has been adequately absorbed by people that we can establish a world government that will most certainly not constitute a serious threat of global tyranny or overwhelming bureaucracy, then such a world government will become fully possible. A "campaign of enlightenment" is needed, the financial cost of which will be a tiny fraction of the financial cost of the World Economic Equalization Program.

Twenty-five years ago, at a time when the Cold War and the nuclear arms competition between the United States and the Soviet Union constituted a dire and immediate threat to human civilization, a convenient and reasonably comprehensive categorization of the most significant impediments to world government would have included the following three factors: (1) ideological conflict; (2) economic inequality; (3) nationalism. There were certainly other impediments, of which the three that come most readily to mind are race, religion and language. But these others were far less important then and they remain far less important today. There are quite a few nations in the modern world that have achieved a high level of internal stability notwithstanding the fact that there is considerable racial, religious and linguistic diversity within their populations.

While ideological conflict, economic inequality and nationalism are conceptually distinct in a logical sense, they are very closely interrelated in a practical sense. Specifically, the nationalistic fervor of any particular national population is positively related to the degree it feels ideologically threatened by other nations and/or economically threatened by other nations. Throughout the Cold War, nationalism in the capitalist nations was heightened by the fact that the communist nations were working actively to overthrow capitalism throughout the world and replace it by socialism. The nation-state was regarded as the main line of defense against the intolerable impositions of an alien and malignant socioeconomic system. Now that the Cold War has faded, nationalism in the advanced capitalist nations (the First World nations) continues to be heightened beyond what it would otherwise be by the fact that a large majority of the world population lives in relatively poor Third World nations. The nation-state is regarded as the main line of defense against a forcible redistribution of world income in favor of the Third World nations, a redistribution that would impoverish the populations of the rich nations.

Owing to the highly fortuitous collapse of communism in the ex-USSR and its Eastern European satellites, ideological conflict in the world today is a small fraction of what it was at the height of the Cold War a quarter century ago. Obviously the ideological impediment to world government has been greatly mitigated—although it would definitely be an exaggeration to say that it has been abrogated. Unfortunately, the economic impediment is still very much alive and well, and in fact, since the economic gap has been widening, it would be fair to say that this impediment is even worse now than it was a quarter-century ago. But by means of a dual voting system in the world government legislature and the retention of critical national rights (the right to maintain armaments and the right to withdraw peacefully from the federation), a limited world government such as the proposed Federal Union of Democratic Nations would have a sufficient amount of breathing space to undertake a World Economic Equalization Program (WEEP) for the purpose of reducing economic inequality among nations to a tolerable level sufficient to guarantee the long-term stability of the federation. Now if we envision a world in which ideological disagreements between nations are modest, and moreover in which economic differences among nations are relatively modest, surely most people would agree that the obstacles to a viable and effective world government would be substantially less.

Even so, those who have an exaggerated estimate of the independent importance of nationalism would be likely to argue that even under hypothetical conditions of very high ideological agreement and economic equality, a world state would still be impossible. They would maintain that the force of nationalism, in and of itself and without regard to ideological conflict and economic inequality (not to mention racial distinctions, religious distinctions, linguistic distinctions, and various other distinctions), would be sufficient to render impossible any sort of a meaningful, legitimate, functioning federal world government. I would have to agree with the typical, conventional-minded world government skeptic that a world government is indeed impossible in today's world—with the qualification that this is true of the *conventional understanding* of "world government" as a veritably omnipotent state entity that would monopolize all heavy armaments including nuclear weapons, would absolutely forbid the defection of any member nation, and would utilize some sort of perverse voting system that would guarantee either the domination of the poor Third World nations or the domination of the rich First World nations. But this conventional understanding of world government has nothing in common with the limited and carefully designed world government under consideration in this book. What nationalism in fact rules out is *omnipotent* federal world government—it does not rule out *limited* federal world government.

THE NATURE OF NATIONALISM

Nationalism may be—and has been—defined in any number of ways. While almost all authorities on the subject, past and present, are agreed that no single brief definition is capable of adequately encompassing and clearly describing the full significance of the phenomenon, most of them are unable to resist the temptation (or perhaps avoid the obligation) to provide such a definition. Thus, in his *The Historical Evolution of Modern Nationalism* (1931), Carlton J. H. Hayes defines nationalism as "the paramount devotion of human beings to fairly large nationalities and the conscious founding of a political 'nation' on linguistic and cultural nationality." In *The Idea of Nationalism: A Study of Its Origins and Background* (1944), Hans Kohn describes nationalism as "a state of mind," "an act of consciousness" of a "large majority of a people," which acknowledges "the nation-state as the ideal form of political organization and the nationality as the source of all creative cultural energy and of economic well-being." In *The Meaning of Nationalism* (1954), Louis Snyder defines nationalism as "a condition of mind, feeling, or sentiment of a group of people living in a well-defined geographical area, speaking a common language, possessing a literature in which the aspirations of the nation have been expressed, attached to common traditions and common customs, venerating its own heroes, and, in some cases, having a common religion." In *Faces of Nationalism: New Realities and Old Myths* (1972), Boyd C. Shafer specifies no less than ten attributes commonly associated with nationalism: "(1) a certain defined territory of land; (2) a people who share or hope to share a common culture; (3) some dominant social, religious or ideological institutions; (4) a common independent or sovereign state or the desire for one; (5) a shared belief in common history or ethnic origin; (6) preference and esteem for fellow nationals; (7) a shared, common pride; (8) a shared indifference or hostility toward some (not all) other peoples similarly organized in nations; (9) a devotion to the entity called the nation; and (10) a shared hope that the nation will have a secure and happy future." In *Nationalism and the State* (1985), John Breuilly writes: "The term 'nationalism' is used to refer to political movements seeking or exercising state power and justifying such actions with nationalist arguments... A nationalist argument is a political doctrine built upon three basic assertions: (a) there exists a nation with an explicit and peculiar character; (b) the interests and values of this nation take priority over all other interests and values; (c) the nation must be as independent as possible." The foregoing represent merely a few illustrative examples.

If I myself were required to produce an original, one-sentence definition of nationalism, I would say that it is the belief or perception in a citizen of a certain actual or potential nation—a belief or perception sufficiently strong to significantly affect the person's behavior—that there exists a close correlation between his/her personal interests and the interests of the national population as a whole. By way of explication, I would go on to say that the nationalistic belief or perception is fundamentally opposed to that egotistical individualism, to which all human beings are subject, that resists recognizing and honoring the social involvement of the individual. Nationalism is a manifestation of adherence to such positive principles as "no man is an island," "we are all in this together," and "all for one—one for all." Within nations, nationalism is a great cementing force binding thousands and millions of citizens into a relatively harmonious whole. In and of itself—in moderation and within the nation—it may certainly be described as a positive phenomenon, as facilitating the interests both of society as a whole and of the individual members of it. If there is a problem with it domestically, it is that it might lead to inadequate toleration for intellectual and cultural diversity, inadequate respect for the human rights of minorities, and over-zealous suppression of dissent. But the principal problem with nationalism is not internal but external, i.e., at the international level. The admirably strong sense of community interest and common purpose instilled by nationalism in any given person tends to be strictly confined and restricted to the citizens of that person's own nation. It follows that any respect shown by that person for the rights and interests of peoples of other nations is derived only to a very slight extent from a psychological sense of overall human unity and solidarity; rather it mostly derives from fear that the rest of the world might retaliate forcibly if the interests of the rest of the world are sufficiently disregarded. Nationalism therefore degrades the underpinnings of peaceful international cooperation.

As a means of gaining insights into the nature of any particular phenomenon, social or otherwise, it is customary to draw analogies between it and other phenomena. Thus nationalism has been compared to religion on the basis that they are both "non-rational." For example, just as the belief in a person that his/her religion offers salvation whereas other religions do not cannot be supported by objectively compelling argumentation, so too the belief in a person that his/her nation is superior to others cannot be so supported. For another example, just as a moderate religious faith is consistent with an attitude of religious toleration under which many different religions can coexist peacefully in the world, so too a moderate nationalistic persuasion is consistent with sufficient cosmopolitanism to enable peaceful coexistence among the nations—and possibly their participation in a functional supernational federation. Humanity has had much experience in the past with religiously inspired—or perhaps, more accurately, religiously aggravated—conflict, violence and warfare. One thinks immediately of the Islamic wars of expansion, of the Crusades, of the wars of the Protestant Reformation, of the remaining tensions between India and Pakistan, Israel and the Arab states, and so on at the international level, as well as domestic tensions between Protestants and Catholics in Northern Ireland, to cite one well publicized example. Clearly, religious differences can make peaceful accommodation, compromise and cooperation more difficult to achieve. But despite all the tragic setbacks and reversals, there has been a gradual, general, global trend throughout history in the direction of religious toleration, to the point where very few people today believe that religious differences need necessarily provoke violent conflict either within or among nations. It follows that religious differences need not be a serious impediment to political unity at the global level. And what is true of religious differences is also true of national differences.

A possibly even more informative analogy is that between the political concept of nationalism and the psychological concept of self-esteem. Self-esteem may be defined as taking a positive attitude toward oneself, while nationalism may be defined as taking a positive attitude toward one's nation. They are alike in that they imply taking a positive attitude. They are also alike in that the "happy medium" notion applies to both. If a person suffers from pathologically low self-esteem, he or she will tend to be trampled upon by others. On the other hand, if self-esteem becomes pathologically high, it could lead to inconsiderate, immoral and even criminal behavior by the individual—behavior that is also quite likely to lead ultimately to the individual's destruction. Since it is a fairly standard piece of conventional wisdom that "criminals have low self-esteem," it is worthwhile to emphasize that the assertion that "pathologically high self-esteem might precipitate criminal behavior" implies an ex ante, operational understanding of self-esteem. If an individual is arrested, convicted and imprisoned for the commission of a crime, this is likely to cause either actual low self-esteem because the crime was detected and punished, or feigned low self-esteem as the prisoner endeavors to convince psychologists and officials that he or she has genuinely reformed and is now deserving of release. But this was not the attitude that led to commission of the crime in the first place. Prior to the commission of the crime, the individual believed that his/her personal interests took precedence over the personal interests of the victim(s) of the crime, and that competent performance of the crime would keep the probability of punishment to a low level. These latter attitudes are ex ante in the sense that they were held prior to the commission of the crime, and they are operational in the sense that they motivated the commission of the crime.

Proceeding with this specialized understanding of "self-esteem," it is more or less obvious that the optimal amount of self-esteem in a person lies somewhere between a pathologically low level and a pathologically high level. Similarly with nationalism, if there is too little of it, a nation's people will occupy themselves with internal squabbling and dissension, enabling other nations to take advantage of them—possibly even to invade and conquer them. On the other hand, if there is too much of it, the nation might become greedy and bellicose, thus setting the stage for warfare. Germany during the Third Reich period (1933-1945) exemplifies what most would deem pathologically overdeveloped nationalism, the consequences of which were ultimately disastrous for the German population of that time. Given a condition of pathological nationalism in a nation, such as that prevailing in Nazi Germany from 1933 through 1945, certainly that nation would be very unlikely to take membership in even a very limited and constrained supernational federation. But pathological nationalism is not the normal state of affairs. Normally nationalism is closer to the "happy medium" level, and therefore reluctance to join a relatively limited and constrained supernational federation (such as we are considering here) would be far less. But would it be sufficiently less to permit the nation to actually join the federation? That is the key question—and I am proposing to answer that key question in the affirmative.

Historians, political scientists, and other professionals who have closely studied the phenomenon of nationalism are prone to argue with one another over subtle issues of emphasis and interpretation that have little apparent bearing on such practical questions as the one with which we are concerned herein: namely, the question of how serious an impediment to world government is the force of nationalism in the contemporary world. For example, is nationalism merely a modern version, linked by gradual historical evolution, of the tribal ethnocentrism of primitive mankind that provided the initial basis for political organization? Or is it a fundamentally new and different phenomenon dating back, at the earliest, to the Renaissance and the Reformation? For another example, is nationalism merely a tool by which social elites manipulate the masses into providing muscle for political transformations that benefit mainly the elites? Or do all strata of society, even the lowest, have a legitimate self-interest in various nationalistic objectives? Another question of considerable interest throughout most of the twentieth century, but of fading importance in the wake of the Soviet Union's abandonment of communism, involves the Marxist accusation that the contemporary capitalist socioeconomic system exacerbates such dysfunctional aspects of nationalism as imperialism, militarism and bellicosity. Still other questions concern the relative importance of various psychological, political, religious, and functional aspects of nationalism.

Consider the question, for example, whether nationalism in modern history is a qualitatively different phenomenon from the tribal ethnocentrism of primitive times, or is rather merely a smooth evolutionary development from tribal ethnocentrism different only in a "quantitative" sense rather than a "qualitative" sense. This question is roughly equivalent to the question of whether the species Hyracotherium, which has probably been extinct for more than 30 million years, is "qualitatively" or "quantitatively" different from the modern horse (Equus caballus). Among paleontologists, the species Hyracotherium (otherwise known as Eohippus—"dawn horse"), the earliest fossils of which date back more than 50 million years, is taken as the first identifiable ancestor of the modern horse. But one does not have to be an enthusiastic creationist to find this identification somewhat farfetched, at least at first glance. Among numerous other dissimilarities, Hyracotherium was about the size of a medium-size dog, had an arched back and raised hindquarters, and had relatively short legs ending in padded toes rather than hooves. One reasonable way to define "a qualitative difference" between two species of animals is that they are not able to interbreed, and there is no question that a Hyracotherium, if one could be magically recreated, would not be able to produce offspring with a modern horse. On the other hand, if one were to see a recreated Hyracotherium walking around its paddock, it would look more like a small, strange horse than anything else—it definitely would not be taken for a dog, a cat, a rodent of any sort, of any other living creature aside from a horse. In addition, there are innumerable species in the fossil record showing clear progression between Hyracotherium and Equus caballus: Orohippus, Epihippus, Mesohippus, Miohippus, Parahippus, Merychippus, Pliohippus, to name a few of the more important. Not that the progression is absolutely smooth and linear (various evolutionary retrogressions and dead-ends provide ammunition for creationists intent upon "refuting evolution," both in general and with respect to the horse), but the links are certainly striking and, taken as a whole, they represent one of the most detailed examples of evolutionary development known to paleontology. In light of these latter considerations, it seems more reasonable to say that there is only a "quantitative," as opposed to a more substantial "qualitative" difference, between Hyracotherium and the modern horse. At least it would be far easier to say that there is a qualitative difference between a horse and, say, a marine iguana, than that there is a qualitative difference between a horse and a Hyracotherium. But whether or not there is a "qualitative difference" between the two species is actually a rather trivial and pointless question. This is simply a semantic issue depending on how one chooses to define the term "qualitative difference" in an operational sense.

It is the same thing with the question of whether modern nationalism is quantitatively different or qualitatively different from primitive tribal ethnocentrism. Just as there are important similarities between Hyracotherium and the modern horse, so too there are important similarities between modern nationalism and tribal ethnocentrism. For example, Hyracotherium and the modern horse have in common that that they are browsing mammals that look roughly similar. Analogously, tribal ethnocentrism and modern nationalism have in common a preference for one's own group over other groups, and that this preference is not based upon an objective evaluation but rather simply on the person's membership in one group and not in the other. On the basis of such striking similarities, one is inclined to say that tribal ethnocentrism and modern nationalism are two versions of the same fundamental social-psychological phenomenon. On the other hand, Hyracotherium and the modern horse are obviously quite different in terms of both size and anatomy (toes versus hooves, etc.), and also they would certainly not be capable of interbreeding. Analogously, tribal ethnocentrism and modern nationalism are obviously quite different in terms of the relevant groups: relatively small, invariably homogeneous, weakly organized tribal peoples, on the one hand, versus, on the other hand, the large, often quite diverse, strongly organized national populations of the present day. In addition, modern nationalism, in contrast to tribal ethnocentrism, is normally supported by a rich written literature, contributed by poets, historians, journalists and others, laying out in great detail the fine qualities and noble history of the nation. On the basis of such striking dissimilarities, one is inclined to say that tribal ethnocentrism and modern nationalism are fundamentally different social-psychological phenomena. One could debate the relative importance of various similarities and dissimilarities at great length. Such debates tend to be diverting, and arguably they provide good practice in rhetoric. But they are unlikely to get anywhere, either in terms of the generation of new knowledge, or of changing anyone's mind.

It is also difficult to see how this question has any significant bearing on the question with which we are presently concerned: the extent to which nationalism, as it is known in the contemporary world, constitutes an impediment to world government. One could certainly imagine various strained arguments, but their relevance would be tenuous at best. For example, let us assume that contemporary nationalism "is fundamentally" the same force that it was millennia ago, in the form of tribal ethnocentrism. Under this assumption, a world government skeptic might point to the apparently inexorable and impermeable nature of this divisive force, drawing forth the implication that it can never be altered or modified in such a way as to permit the foundation of a federal world government. In response to this line of thought, a world government advocate could easily respond that despite the continual presence of this divisive force in human affairs, there has been throughout history a steady progression from the small tribal groupings in pre-historic times to the great nation-states of today, showing that the force has not been strong enough to forestall that political progress that has extended the influence of specific governments over ever more extensive areas and ever larger populations. On the other hand, if it is assumed that contemporary nationalism is indeed a "fundamentally new" force, the world government skeptic might endeavor to use this perspective against the feasibility of world government by arguing that contemporary nationalism is so much stronger than anything that went before, that it will never be overcome as a barrier to world government. But if contemporary nationalism is indeed something fundamentally new, this would suggest the inherent adaptability of political institutions and attitudes, and that in due course the various national patriotisms could someday be supplanted by what might be termed "world patriotism."

The nebulous relevancy, for our present purposes, of various issues pertaining to the nature and characteristics of nationalism is also illustrated by the "political action" view of nationalism in modern history. Perhaps the most influential, at the present time, of the newer "theories of nationalism" is that of John Breuilly, as explicated in *Nationalism and the State* (1985). Breuilly argues that nationalism does not arise in a vacuum out of the communal will of the common people. Rather nationalism is a concept that is nurtured (if not invented), disseminated and exploited as a tool by organized political groups interested in gaining or retaining control over government power. It is impossible, in Breuilly's view, to gain an adequate understanding of nationalism without clearly recognizing the fact that it is an instrument by which various elites endeavor to manipulate the general population into doing their (the elites') will. This is certainly a highly non-idealistic view of nationalism, but conceivably it draws too strong a distinction between the elites and the general population. Obviously in any real-world society past or present, whether ostensibly democratic or otherwise, the distribution of political power, no less than the distribution of economic wealth, is highly unequal. But there are definite limits to the practical power of "elites," however defined. These elites cannot misinform and manipulate the general population into supporting institutions and policies that are *strongly* contrary to the true interests of the general population. In the case of nationalism, there must be pre-existing tendencies in the population toward this emotion for appeals to it to be effective in generating support for specific political organizations desirous of securing government authority. Conservatively stated, there is undoubtedly a considerable degree of validity in Breuilly's theory of nationalistic enthusiasm stoked by power-seeking activities of organized elites. But if the theory is pushed too far, it becomes equivalent to Karl Marx's vision of the worthy and uncorrupted "masses" of proletarians dominated and ruled by a small minority of plutocratic capitalists.

Does the issue of whether nationalism mostly comes from deep within the psyches of the general population, or alternatively mostly comes from the crass self-interest of manipulative elites, have anything much to do with the question of how much of an impediment to world government is represented by contemporary nationalism? I rather doubt that it does. At one time it was a fairly prevalent speculation among world federalists that "the people" very much wanted world government, but that their desires were being thwarted by the nasty "power elite" that regarded world government as a threat to its own personal, entrenched special interests. But when certain world federalist activists attempted to "go directly to the people," their efforts were no more successful than those of world federalists trying to work "through channels," i.e., through the officials, personnel and organizations of established national governments. It has always been my personal belief that generalized opposition to world government is no weaker among the general population than it is among the socioeconomic upper crust and government personnel. In any event, it does not really matter what the distribution of power is among the elite and the general population: if world government is to become a reality within our lifetimes, it is necessary that both groups be persuaded that world government would be to their own particular advantage. In view of inevitable uncertainties concerning the "real" or "actual" distribution of political power in society, it would probably be unproductive to spend any appreciable amount of time deliberating the question: should the elite be "converted" to world government first, in the expectation that the general population will then fall into line—or vice versa? Another unproductive question, most probably, is whether the socioeconomic elite or the general population is more susceptible to the vision of world government, is more likely to view world government favorably as facilitating its own interests.

The "origins of modern nationalism" are variously traced to the rise of absolute monarchy on the European continent, to the religious wars of the Protestant Reformation in Germany, to the Puritan Revolution in England, to the Enlightenment, and to the European wars associated with the French Revolution. It is generally agreed, however, that by the early nineteenth century, nationalistic patriotism toward one's own nation was a powerful force in Western Europe and several other areas of the world. As to what, precisely, was responsible for the transformation, this is not a question easily answered. It seems obvious that underlying social, political, demographic and economic transitions were driving forces behind the rise of nationalism: population increase, the decline of agriculture, the growth of industry, the expansion of education, the development of international trade, the rise of political democracy, urbanization and so on. But the interactions and feedback effects between these factors and the nationalism factor were many, varied and complex. It is unlikely that we will ever understand a social phenomenon such as nationalism to the extent and clarity that we understand such physical phenomena as the conductivity of electricity or the propagation of radio waves. But if a very brief speculation is desired on why nationalism has become so important in the modern world, it would probably best focus on the interaction between nationalism and various fundamental political and economic realities. The essence of nationalism, it would seem, is that it promotes political stability and cooperative behavior over large expanses of territory. It also seems self-evident that political stability and cooperative behavior promote economic growth and development. Therefore, nationalism can be seen as both a cause and a consequence of economic progress. It became a dominant force because, in its time, it fostered and furthered the progress of global human civilization. It was good for humanity.

Of course, what was good for humanity at one stage in the development of civilization might not be good at a later stage. To the extent that the influence of nationalism in the contemporary world is making it difficult for people to perceive and comprehend the advantages of federal world government, to this extent nationalism is no longer a healthy force. Consider an historical analogy. As the Western European nations moved forward from the medieval period into the modern period, more and more effective political power migrated from a multitude of princes, dukes and barons to the kings. This centralization of political power eventually resulted in the era of "absolute monarchy," as manifested dramatically in France, Spain, Russia and elsewhere during the 17th and 18th centuries. In its era, the principle of absolute monarchy was beneficial because it greatly reduced the costs inflicted on society by conflicts and warfare among the multitude of princes, dukes and barons. Eventually the evolution of society reached a point where some form of constitutional democracy was more effective than absolute monarchy. But the transition between absolute monarchy and constitutional democracy was much delayed and complicated by residual faith, among both the intelligentsia and the general population, in a political principle whose time had come and gone. Just as absolute monarchy made a contribution to human civilization at one point in time but later became an impediment to the further development of human civilization, the same is true of nationalism. Nationalism is both a unifying force (within nations), and a divisive force (between nations). At one time—between 200 and 300 years ago—its unifying characteristic was dominant, and it could be regarded, on the whole, as a positive factor in human affairs. But this is no longer the case. To the extent that nationalism today is delaying and complicating the foundation of a federal world government, it is a negative factor in human affairs.

Several historical events and episodes are customarily cited as landmarks in the evolution of the modern concept of nationalism. Among these are certainly the American Revolution (commenced in 1775) which violently separated the United States from the British Empire, and the French Revolution (commenced in 1789) which violently terminated the Bourbon dynasty of absolute monarchs. Both the American Revolution and the French Revolution brought forth into the modern world democratic republics consciously modeled on the rationalistic and utilitarian principles of the Enlightenment, the subsequent consequences of which were quite profound. A major development of the latter half of the nineteenth century was the rise of German and Italian nationalism to a point adequate to the establishment of the modern nations of Germany and Italy. The Kingdom of Italy was proclaimed in 1861 under King Victor Emmanuel II, and the nation of Italy was completed in its contemporary form by the addition of Venice (1866) and Rome (1870). The contemporary nation of Germany was established with the declaration of the German Empire under Wilhelm I at Versailles in 1871. In order to achieve the political unification of Germany, Prussia (under Minister-President Otto von Bismarck) had defeated Austria in 1866 and France in 1870. Both the Austrians and the French had been adverse to the development of a strong German nation, and their objections had to be overcome by military force. The unification of Germany soon created problems because the newly fledged German nation was resentful of the fact that it did not possess a colonial empire comparable to that of Britain and France. The ultimate consequences of this resentment were disastrous, in that it was instrumental in generating circumstances that ultimately eventuated in World War I. During the interwar period, Germany succumbed to a fascist dictatorship under Adolf Hitler, allied itself with two other fascist nations, also relatively new and imperially inclined, namely Italy and Japan, and thus came about World War II.

By the time World War II was concluded, historians and others were very much conscious of the fact that the rise of nationalism in any particular area of the world is not necessarily something to be joyfully welcomed. Nevertheless, at that very time the vast populations of the Third World regions, many of them incorporated into the colonial empires of European nations, were becoming increasingly familiar with the joys and allure of nationalism. Exhausted by war and beset by self-doubt, the European nations liberated their colonies with relatively little fuss, releasing into the modern world dozens of new independent nations very seriously determined to pursue their national interests. These nations were uniformly poor and economically underdeveloped at the time of their respective liberations, and despite some progress, most of them can still be described as such today. Another significant proliferation of nations occurred in the aftermath of the dissolutions of the USSR and Yugoslavia in the early 1990s. Although the present count of sovereign and independent nations in the world stands well above 200, separatist movements still abound: Quebec in Canada, Chechnya in Russia, the Basque region in Spain, the Kurd region in Turkey and Iraq, the Tamil region of Sri Lanka, to name but a few. If they were all successful, it would create dozens more sovereign and independent nations in the world.

PERSONAL FREEDOM AND NATIONAL SOVEREIGNTY

The argument that the nationalistic impediment to world government is virtually insuperable might be expressed along the lines that any kind of world government would necessitate severe and unacceptable constraints on national sovereignty. The term "sovereignty" has an appropriately sonorous tone: it tends to evoke deep and abiding emotions, to elicit intimations of fundamental issues of survival and wellbeing, to generate what might even be termed a "mystical" frame of mind in the individual. Once in this frame of mind, it is relatively easy to imagine that the concept of national sovereignty does indeed constitute an impermeable and insuperable obstacle to supernational federation. Such a federation would necessarily constitute an abridgement of and an infringement upon the national sovereignty of its member nation-states. But nation-states cannot permit such a "competitor" for their traditional authority to exist and yet remain nation-states. They simply could not and would not permit such significant restrictions on their authority. But by the same token, a world state—in order to constitute a proper state entity—could not tolerate the limitations upon its own sovereignty represented by the sovereignty of its component nation-states.

Therefore, one or the other would have to go: either the concept of national sovereignty or the concept of supernational sovereignty. Since it is inconceivable that the nation-states of today will ever surrender any significant part of their national sovereignty, we are forced to conclude that a world state is impossible.

Such thinking is muddled and fallacious. It manifests an excessively rigid mentality that perceives only black and white rather than shades of gray, that focuses only on the extreme endpoints of the spectrum of possibilities rather than looking for the happy medium. The formation of a world state would not necessarily manifest the abrogation of national sovereignty, nor would the continuation of national sovereignty necessarily imply an absence of sovereignty on the part of the world state. The world state and the component nation-states would each have their respective areas of sovereignty: areas in which they would indeed exercise absolute and undisputed authority. In some areas the world state would possess sovereign authority, and in other areas the individual nation-states would possess sovereign authority. In the United States today, for example, individual states such as Texas and New York are frequently described as "the sovereign state of Texas" and "the sovereign state of New York." Such phrases are not contradictory to Texas and New York being components of the "sovereign United States of America." At first it may seem paradoxical to think about "areas" of sovereignty and "limitations" on sovereignty—such restrictive notions may seem basically contradictory to the essential concept of sovereignty. But we must take a more sophisticated view of reality. It would be intellectually crippling to think of the notion of sovereignty as an absolute rather than a relative concept. No valid conclusions could be reached on the basis of such a faulty and inadequate notion.

In actual fact, the notion of "sovereignty" with respect to a state is closely analogous to the notion of "freedom" with respect to an individual. "Freedom" is of course a marvelous abstraction: it expresses the deepest and most sublime human aspirations toward individual autonomy, discretion, and self-determination. Every rational human being desires to have as much freedom for himself or herself as is conceivably possible. But at the same time, every rational human being also recognizes the many practical and unavoidable constraints which must restrain autonomy, discretion, and self-determination. Some of these constraints are imposed by nature: human beings cannot fly like birds, they cannot breathe water like fish, they require food, drink, and shelter to survive, and despite their best personal efforts to implement the instinct of self-preservation indefinitely, they are all eventually subject to the physical dissolution of death. Some of these constraints are imposed by economic realities: the person of average means, even in the most prosperous nations, is not able to live in a large mansion on an extensive estate, is not able to eat steak and lobster every day, is not able to take six-month tours around the world. Some constraints are imposed by the social enforcement system: theft, rape, murder, and many other actions that may appeal to certain persons at certain times, will normally eventuate in confinement and the spartan living conditions of prisons. Some constraints are imposed by the political system: even in the most democratic polities, no individual citizen can autonomously specify who shall be the head of state—such as himself/herself or some close friend or relative.

Such constraints, however, do not constitute flat contradictions to a sensible understanding of freedom. It is fully sensible to interpret "freedom" as involving simply *a substantial amount* of personal autonomy, discretion, and self-determination—even if that amount is indeed far short of what could be imagined. We may certainly think of ourselves as free, even though we may be subject to physical limitations and mortality, even though we may be able to afford only a relatively modest standard of living, even though we must avoid criminal behavior or suffer the consequences, even though our own personal influence in determining the political leadership may be minimal. It is the same thing with national sovereignty. Just as it is possible to legitimately describe a person as free even though there may be many practical constraints operative upon his or her individual autonomy, discretion, and self-determination, so too it is possible to legitimately describe a state as sovereign even though there may be many practical constraints on the power and authority of that state, and even though that state must share the loyalty of its citizens with other state entities.

A realistic appreciation of history and contemporary civilization clearly manifests that "state sovereignty," whether that state is a nation-state or some other form, is in fact significantly limited both internally and externally. Internally, the government cannot ignore the interests and desires of its citizens, or it runs the risk of being ousted by election or overturned by revolution. Even if elections are not on the social agenda, there are still limits on the degree of control exercised over the citizen body by even the most brutally despotic regimes. A completely coerced obedience obtained solely through brute force is highly dangerous and unreliable. If disaffection becomes too widespread among the population, then that disaffection will tend to percolate upward into the highest corridors of power. And when that happens, the despot loses his personal security, regardless of how unassailable he may appear to be from the outside. The externally imposed limitations on the sovereign power of a state—including a nation-state—are no less important than the internally imposed limitations. Throughout human history, the exercise of sovereign power has frequently brought states into armed conflict, and the possibility of armed conflict constitutes a major constraint on the autonomy, discretion, and self-determination of state entities. This major constraint is just as operative upon the modern nation-state as it was upon earlier state entities. No national government can afford to entirely ignore or disregard the strong national interests of other national governments—sovereignty or no sovereignty. All this is not to deny the existence and significance of the concept of sovereignty. It is rather merely to point out that in practice, sovereignty does not imply absolute and unlimited power.

This is neither a subtle proposition nor a new one. The practical limitations on sovereignty have been recognized for as long the concept has been extant. The French jurist and political philosopher Jean Bodin (1530-1596) is generally considered to be the seminal authority on the concept of sovereignty. In his *Six Books on the Commonwealth*, published in 1576, Bodin examined a wide range of issues in the political governance of human society, one of the most important of which is the nature and characteristics of sovereignty. Bodin's contribution is a major milestone in the intellectual development of the case for absolute monarchy as the simplest and most effective bulwark against civil strife and anarchy. Of course, appreciation for the virtues and benefits of "law and order" tends to crest during periods of civil disorder and war. Bodin's *Six Books on the Commonwealth* was produced in the midst of a lengthy period of civil strife in France between Roman Catholics and Protestants known as Huguenots, lasting from the Massacre at Vassy in 1562 to the Edict of Nantes in 1598, and encompassing the infamous St. Bartholomew's Day Massacre in 1572. Perhaps the single most topical element of Bodin's *Commonwealth* treatise was its adamant insistence on the need for complete religious toleration. The wars were indeed brought to a conclusion with the issuance of the Edict of Nantes during the reign of Henry IV. The Edict granted French Protestants civil rights and freedom to worship according to conscience. In the longer run, however, Catholicism reasserted its dominance in France, as evidenced by the revocation of the Edict of Nantes by Louis XIV (the "Sun King") in 1685.

The immediate purpose of Jean Bodin, in writing his *Commonwealth* treatise, was simply to make as convincing a case as possible for a strong central government to counteract the divisive tendencies exerted by such inescapable factors as religious differences. In this respect, Bodin's work is quite comparable to the more famous *Leviathan* by Thomas Hobbes (1588-1679), published in 1651 and written during the English Civil War that had culminated in the beheading of King Charles I in 1649. Bodin and Hobbes were both adamant that strong government was necessary that civilization rise above anarchic chaos. In France, the principle of absolute monarchy reached its apogee under Louis XIV. Whether the theoretical arguments of political analysts have much to do with the outcome is of course debatable, but it is not impossible that the triumph of absolute monarchy in France was facilitated by Bodin's treatise. In Book Four, Chapter IV of *Commonwealth*, Bodin considered whether the objective of strong and legitimate government is best served by a popular government (in which a popularly elected body is dominant), an aristocratic government (in which the dominant body is composed exclusively of members of the hereditary nobility), or a monarchial government (in which a hereditary absolute monarch is dominant). The weight of the controversy, in Bodin's opinion, came down in favor of absolute monarchy. To most political analysts of our own time, of course, the various arguments Bodin advanced against popular government (that honor and virtue are inadequately rewarded, that most of the common people are stupid and/or wicked, that the property of the great families is not respected, that such governments tend to degenerate quickly into despotism owing to the gullible public's susceptibility to evil demagogues, etc.) are not taken too seriously.

In urging the advantages of strong central government Bodin waxed lyrical on the subject of "sovereignty" and its wondrously beneficial nature. But what is particularly important for our present purposes is that even this most adamant advocate of strong central government clearly recognized some critical limitations on sovereignty. Bodin was quite explicit and emphatic that, properly interpreted, the sovereign is most definitely *not* legally and morally entitled to do anything at all that he might consider doing. Sovereignty is limited, in Bodin's view, in at least three fundamental ways: (1) by the precepts of divine law, natural law and constitutional law (e.g., the Ten Commandments of the Old Testament); (2) by the obligation to honor faithfully all promises, agreements, contracts, conventions, and so on; (3) by the absolute requirement to respect the private property of the citizens of the commonwealth. This last limitation meant that even a completely sovereign absolute monarch could not, in Bodin's judgment, levy taxes without first obtaining the assent of those taxed. Bodin was realistic enough to admit that a sovereign might become despotic, in which case he would commence to ignore the proper limits on his sovereignty. In such a case, Bodin reluctantly conceded, legitimate sovereignty was forfeit and the ruler could be removed by whatever means required, up to and including violent revolution.

Bodin's famous discussion of the sovereignty principle is contained in Book One: Chapter VIII ("Concerning Sovereignty") of *Six Books on the Commonwealth*. In this chapter are to be found a large number of portentous proclamations concerning the tremendous extent and profound depth of the authority implied by the term "sovereignty," some of which are as follows (the page references are to the translation and abridgement by M. J. Tooley):

> Sovereignty is that absolute and perpetual power vested in a commonwealth which in Latin is termed *majestas*... The true sovereign remains always seized of his power. Just as a feudal lord who grants lands to another retains his eminent domain over them, so the ruler who delegates authority to judge and command, whether it be for a short period, or during pleasure, remains seized of those rights of jurisdiction actually exercised by another in the form of a revocable grant, or precarious tenancy. [p. 25] A perpetual authority therefore must be understood to mean one that lasts for the lifetime of him who exercises it. [p. 26] On the other hand it is the distinguishing mark of the sovereign that he cannot in any way be subject to the commands of another, for it is he who makes law for the subject, abrogates law already made, and amends obsolete law. No one who is subject either to the law or to some other person can do this. This is why it is laid down in the civil law that the prince is above the law, for the word *law* in Latin implies the command of him who is invested with sovereign power. [p. 28] A law proceeds from him who has sovereign power, and by it he binds the subject to obedience, but cannot bind himself. [p. 30] From all this it is clear that the principal mark of sovereign majesty and absolute power is the right to impose laws generally on all subjects regardless of their consent. [p. 32]

These statements seem most unambiguous and impressively weighty. But interspersed among these statements are many others intended to correct the possible misunderstanding that the sovereign's authority knows no bounds in heaven or earth, of which the following are a sampling:

> If we insist however that absolute power means exemption from all law whatsoever, there is no prince in the world who can be regarded as sovereign, since all the princes of the earth are subject to the laws of God and of nature, and even to certain human laws common to all nations. [p. 28] It is far otherwise with divine and natural laws. All the princes of the earth are subject to them and cannot contravene them without treason and rebellion against God. His yoke is upon them and they must bow their heads in fear and reverence before His divine majesty... The same holds good of promises made by the sovereign to the subject, even if the promises were made prior to his election (for this does not make the difference that many suppose). It is not that the prince is bound either by his own laws or those of his predecessors. But he is bound by the just covenants and promises he has made, whether under oath to do so or not, to exactly the same extent that a private individual is bound in like case. [p. 29] The constitutional laws of the realm, especially those that concern the king's estate being, like the salic law, annexed and united to the Crown, cannot be infringed by the prince. Should he do so, his successor can always annul any act prejudicial to the traditional form of the monarchy, since on this is founded and sustained his very claim to sovereign majesty. [p. 31] It may be objected that no extraordinary taxes or subsidies can be imposed without the agreement and consent of the [English] Parliament. King Edward I agreed to this principle in the Great Charter, which is always appealed to by the people against the claims of the crown. But I hold that in this matter no other king has any more right than has the King of England, since it is not within the competence of any prince to level taxes at will on his people, or seize the goods of another arbitrarily, as Philippe de Comines very wisely argued at the Estate at Tours, as we may read in his *Memoirs*. [p. 32] But may it not be objected that if the prince forbids a sin, such as homicide, on pain of death, he is in this case bound to keep his own law? The answer is that this is not properly the prince's own law, but a law of God and nature, to which he is more strictly bound than any of his subjects. [p. 33] From this principle we can deduce that other rule, that the sovereign prince is bound by the covenants he makes either with his subjects, or with some other prince. Just because he enforces the covenants and mutual engagements entered into by his subjects among themselves, he must be the mirror of justice in all his own acts. He has a double obligation in this case. He is bound in the first place by the principles of natural equity, which require that conventions and solemn promises should be kept, and in the second place in the interests of his own good faith, which he ought to preserve even to his own disadvantage, because he is the formal guarantor to all his subjects of the mutual faith they owe one another. [p. 34] Neither Pope nor Emperor is exempt from this [divine or natural] law, though certain flatterers say that they can take the goods of their subjects at will. But both civilians and canonists have repudiated this opinion as contrary to the law of God. They err who assert that in virtue of their sovereign power princes can do this. It is rather the law of the jungle, an act of force and violence. For as we have shown above, absolute power only implies freedom in relation to positive laws, and not in relation to the law of God. God has declared explicitly in His Law that it is not just to take, or even to covet, the goods of another. [p. 35]

The chapter of *Commonwealth* from which the above quotations were taken pertains mostly to limitations on the domestic authority of the sovereign. But of course our main concern in this book is with the international sphere. Specifically, we want to know whether participation in a supernational federation would so limit the discretion of a member nation as to effectively nullify that nation's sovereignty in any sense whatever. My argument is that this is *not* true: that participation in a federal world government of the future would no more blot out any particular member nation's sovereignty than that same nation's previous participation in various international treaties, alliances and organizations blotted out its sovereignty in the past. The argument asserts that participation in a limited world government such as the Federal Union of Democratic Nations under consideration herein merely represents another step—albeit a very substantial and significant step—on a long path of political evolution, from pre-history to the current age, leading to unified state organizations covering ever more extensive territories. Skeptics of world government might be tempted to speculate that Jean Bodin, the "prophet of sovereignty" himself, would have been generally opposed to "foreign entanglements," and would have advised that any such entanglements previously entered into be renounced and abrogated as soon as their adverse effect on short-term national interests becomes apparent. Such an expectation, however, would be disappointed. Not surprisingly in view of France's preeminent position on the continent of Europe in the sixteenth century, Bodin believed that active participation in international affairs was very much to the nation's interest, and he was insistent that any and all international agreements be honored even if this was to the immediate disadvantage of the nation. The following are some typical quotations from Book Five: Chapter VI ("The Keeping of Treaties and Alliances between Princes"):

> Many think that it is safest for a prince to adopt a policy of neutrality, and so keep out of other people's wars. The principal argument in support of this view is that whereas loss and expense is shared in common, the fruits of victory all accrue to the ruler on whose behalf the quarrel is sustained, added to which one must declare oneself the enemy of princes who have in no way offended one's interests... But the arguments on the other side appear stronger. First of all, in matters of state one ought always to be either the stronger, or of the stronger party. There are few exceptions to this rule, whether one is considering a single commonwealth, or a number of princes. Otherwise one falls a prey to the whim of the victor... Without looking further afield, we have the example of the Florentines. Having abandoned their alliance with the French royal house, but at the same time refusing to join the league of the Pope, the Emperor, the Kings of England and of Spain, they almost immediately felt the evil effects of their neutrality. [pp. 175-176] Good faith is little regarded by many princes in the alliances which they make with one another. What is more, there are those so perfidious that they only enter into solemn engagements with the intention of deceiving, in this emulating the captain Lysander, who boasted that he cheated adults by his sworn assurances, and children by his conjuring. But God punished his perfidy according to his merits. [p. 177] Since faith is the sole foundation and prop of that justice on which all commonwealths, alliances, and associations of men whatsoever, is founded, it should be preserved sacred and inviolable in all cases where no injus-

tice is contemplated. This applies most particularly to the relations between princes, for seeing that they are the guarantors of good faith and sworn engagements, what assurance will those subject to them have of their own mutual undertakings if the rulers themselves are the principal breakers and violators of good faith? [pp. 177-178] The Emperor Charles V himself pledged his word to Martin Luther, though he had been denounced as an enemy to the faith in a Papal bull, that he might safely attend the Imperial Diet at Worms in 1519. There van Eyck, seeing that Luther would not renounce his opinions, cited the decree of Constance as grounds for proceeding against him regardless of the pledged word of the Emperor. But there was not a prince present that did not express horror at van Eyck's petition, and in fact the Emperor dismissed Luther with a safe-conduct, and under armed protection. I do not wish to discuss the merits of the decree, but the opinion of Bartolus, and those who maintain that one need not keep faith with the enemy is not worthy of formal refutation, so contrary is it to ordinary common sense. [p. 179]

Jean Bodin, of course, was not an advocate of the universal state, as "world government" would have been known in his time. No doubt he shared the conventional opinion of his day (and ours) that any effort to establish such a state would be very impractical and dangerous. Quite probably Bodin was correct that world government was not possible as of the second half of the sixteenth century. But much has changed since that time and our own time, and arguments against world government that may have been quite legitimate in the sixteenth century are most definitely no longer legitimate in the twenty-first century. But the point I wish to make here is merely that Jean Bodin, the original "guru of sovereignty," was certainly no isolationist. He saw no contradiction whatever between the principle of national sovereignty and active participation in international affairs. Although it is not widely understood at the present time, there is equally no contradiction whatever between the principle of national sovereignty and taking an active membership in a limited world government such as the Federal Union of Democratic Nations herein proposed.

The international relations literature of our own age is filled to overflowing not only with statements to the effect that there have always been definite limitations on national sovereignty, but also statements to the effect that these limitations are steadily increasing. That is to say, national sovereignty has been on the decline for a long time, and will probably go on declining in the future. But this trend, in the judgment of most observers, should not be regarded as perverse or threatening. It is rather regarded by most of them as a natural concomitant of increasing international trade, migration and communication as the technical and social evolution of worldwide human civilization continues. One derives the overall impression from these many statements that the "decline of sovereignty," so far from being disparaged and resisted, should be encouraged and assisted, because this is now, as it has ever been in the past, the path of progress.

The foundation of a properly limited federal world government such as the proposed Federal Union of Democratic Nations would not abrogate the national sovereignty of its member nations any more than being a citizen of a particular nation abrogates the personal freedom of a certain individual. It is certainly true that an active and functioning world government might pass laws and implement policies not completely to the taste of certain national populations. But these burdens and restrictions would not be dramatically more onerous than those to which we are currently accustomed. These burdens and restrictions would not necessarily be worse, on the whole, than the burdens and restrictions currently being placed on nations by their incorporation within an essentially anarchic international situation. One obvious example is that almost every nation today, large and small, feels it necessary to support a significant military establishment—in some cases, a huge military establishment. These establishments impose heavy financial burdens on the taxpaying citizens. Having less discretionary income, the citizens possess less freedom in the sense of ability to purchase desired commodities. In addition to this, even a heavy burden of military expenditure does not result in complete freedom from fear, because other nations are also supporting large military establishments, and humanity has accumulated a great deal of experience in the past with armaments competitions culminating in warfare. Now it certainly cannot be promised that the establishment of the Federal Union of Democratic Nations would instantly and completely absolve the nations, especially the military superpowers, from the need to maintain large military establishments. However, it would almost certainly lay a firmer basis for the evolutionary development of material and psychological conditions at the global level under which the military establishments of the nations could be considerably smaller without a proportionate reduction in security of their respective populations.

No doubt there is an optimal distribution of sovereign power over the world government, the national governments, and lower-level governments. But it is doubtful whether we will ever be able to ascertain this optimal distribution in a precise and scientific manner. This means that if a world government is established in the real world, there would be perpetual debate and controversy over the appropriate distribution of authority over the supernational state and the member nation-states, just as there has always been perpetual debate and controversy in the past over the appropriate distribution of authority over the national governments and the various regional and local governments. The fact that this debate and controversy has continued in the past does not mean that it is not a good idea to supplement local and regional governments with formally superior national governments.

And the fact that analogous debate and controversy would continue in the future if a supernational state were to be established, does not mean that it is not a good idea to supplement national governments with a formally superior supernational government. If we consider the distribution of effective sovereign authority beyond that exercised by regional and local governments, at the present time about 99 percent of it is exercised by the national governments and about 1 percent by the United Nations. The situation at the international level may reasonably be described by the term "anarchy." Whatever international cooperation and mutual respect exists is based almost exclusively on bargaining and negotiation backed up by the potential use of military power. The situation is basically the same as the situation that generated two devastating world wars during the first half in the twentieth century and came perilously close to generating a nuclear World War III during the second half. Therefore, the present distribution of higher-level sovereign authority is extremely unlikely to be the optimal distribution. Humanity ought to establish a world government entrusted with perhaps 20 to 30 percent of sovereign authority exercised at higher than the regional and local levels. Just as national governments are indispensable political tools for dealing with national problems and exploiting national opportunities, so too a global government would quickly become an indispensable political tool for dealing with global problems and exploiting global opportunities. The longer we deprive ourselves of this tool, the more harm is being done to the future prospects of human civilization.

WHY FEDERATIONS FAIL

As its name indicates, the Federal Union of Democratic Nations would be a federal rather than a unitary state organization. According to the formal distinction, a unitary state is one in which the regional offices of government are strictly subordinate to the central government office, while a federal state is one in which the regional offices of government are to some extent independent of the central government. In a unitary state, the executive powers of the regional offices of government are exercised by individuals appointed by the central government office. In a federal state, the executive powers of regional offices of government are exercised by those elected, appointed or approved in some manner by the local population of the region. The effective distribution of power may be quite different from the formal distribution according to the written constitution. For example, the defunct Union of Soviet Socialist Republics, while formally a federation according to the Soviet Constitution, was in reality a unitary state because effective power throughout the nation was exercised by the Communist Party, a highly centralized, oligarchic political organization. Still, the distinction between a federal state and a unitary state is quite clear in principle, and there are numerous examples of federal states in the world today (for example, the United States, Canada, Australia, Germany, Italy, Switzerland, Russia, Mexico, Brazil, Venezuela, India, Pakistan, South Africa) that are certainly federal in practice as well as in principle. The fact that federalism can be successful at the national level suggests the possibility that it could also be successful at the international level.

Human civilization has not yet had much experience with federations consisting of established nation-states. In some cases, as with the United States and Canada, the federations were established at or around the time of achieving independence from a colonial power in which the component states had previously been administrative sub-divisions within a colonial empire. In other cases, as with Switzerland, Italy and Germany, the component states had previously been fully independent, but they fit the image of a city-state or a principality rather than the image of a modern nation. The European Union of today, which started out as a simple customs union, is beginning to take on some of the characteristics of a federation, but it still has far to go before it would be comparable to full-scale, legitimate federations such as the United States or Canada.

Of course, there has been no experience with a federation of nations on the scale and comprehensiveness of the envisioned Federal Union of Democratic Nations. World government skeptics see the force of nationalism, in and of itself and without reference to such aggravating factors as ideological conflict and economic inequality, as a tremendous obstacle to a supernational federation encompassing all or a large majority of the nations of the world. They would point to the fact that the contemporary federal nations are not constituted of what were, prior to their joining their respective federations, political entities that fit the modern concept of a nation-state. Therefore these federations were not ruled out by what we now know as "nationalism." But a world federal government, in this view, is in fact ruled out by nationalism. This argument can be, and is, supported by simply pointing to the fact that no world federation presently exists in the world. But to say that something is impossible simply because it does not currently exist is clearly a very flimsy argument in and of itself. For example, an argument in 1950 that a spaceship that could carry human beings to the moon was impossible because it did not exist would have been falsified in 1969, when human beings first landed on the moon. For another example, an argument in 1500 that a representative democracy with near-universal suffrage was impossible because it did not exist would have been falsified by the establishment and success of the United States of America.

For the argument that world government is impossible owing to the force of nationalism to carry much weight, it must be supported by some sort of coherent reasoning involving empirical evidence—beyond the "evidence" that world government does not currently exist in the real world. One possible source of such evidence would be actual real-world historical experiences with federations of nations that ultimately dissolved, whether owing to the "power of nationalism" or some other reason or reasons. In 1968, Thomas M. Franck published (as editor and contributor) a volume of articles on recently defunct federations of nations entitled *Why Federations Fail: An Inquiry into the Requisites for Successful Federalism*. Four failed federations were examined in the book: (1) the East African Federation incorporating Tanganyika, Zanzibar, Kenya and Uganda; (2) the Federation of Rhodesia and Nyasaland (now Malawi); (3) the West Indian Federation incorporating Jamaica, Trinidad, Barbados and the Windward and Leeward Islands; (4) the Federation of Malaysia incorporating Malaya, Singapore, North Borneo and Sarawak. Actually, the characterization of all these as "failed federations" may be too strong. In the case of the East African Federation, two of the four nations involved did afterwards amalgamate into the single nation of Tanzania. And in the case of the Federation of Malaysia, of the four principal components only Singapore withdrew following its formation. Although the book was not explicitly intended as an assault upon the feasibility of federal world government, it was no doubt taken as such by many of its readers. It appeared, after all, at the height of the Cold War, at a time when the possibility of world government was routinely disparaged as little more than a utopian pipe dream by virtually all reputable mainstream international relations authorities. And although the book's sub-title makes reference to the requisites for *successful* federations of nations, all of the cases actually examined pertained to *unsuccessful* federations of nations, perhaps suggesting that the requisites for successful federations of nations were nowhere to be found in the real world, dominated as it is by the power of nationalism.

A close examination of *Why Federations Fail*, however, does not bring to light serious and substantive evidence against the feasibility of a *world* federation in the image of the proposed Federal Union of Democratic Nations. To begin with, all of the federations examined in Franck's book were *regional* federations consisting of a very small number of nations, none of which was very large in terms of population. None of these federations, had they persisted, would have constituted a major nation on the international scene in terms of population or Gross National Product. They were not of sufficient scale and comprehensiveness to excite the imaginations of either the leaders or the rank-and-file citizens of the nations involved. From the point of view of their populations, the difference between entering the federation versus remaining independent, was simply the difference between being a citizen of a very small, very poor nation, and being a citizen of a slightly larger—but still very small, very poor nation. The probable benefits to be derived from each of these federations were in each case simply too minor and problematical to be worth the administrative and political problems involved in forming them and making them operational. The possibility of being invaded by hostile foreign nations would not have been appreciably reduced, nor would the prospects for economic growth been appreciably augmented. In a word, they simply were not worth the trouble. They fell victim to the "why bother" syndrome.

Of course, the evaluation of whether or not a certain project is "worth the trouble" is often a highly subjective matter largely determined by general assumptions and preconceptions derived from real-world history and intellectual history. There were no such general assumptions and preconceptions supporting the desirability of federation among the specific nations involved in the federal projects examined in *Why Federations Fail*. In each case, the idea of federation arose because the nations involved had all recently gained their independence from European colonial empires. In fact, one of the reasons they foundered was simply the perception within these newly independent nations that the proposed federations were being advocated by the European nations so that they could maintain a higher level of effective control over their erstwhile colonies. But there had been no long-term indigenous movements toward these particular federations. As Franck himself says in reference to the leaders of the four nations involved in the projected East African Federation: "The case of East African unity suffered from bad timing, but also from the singular failure to develop an ideology of unity. Kuanda, Nyerere, Mboya, and Obote are men of intellect, imagination and vision. Yet, while they attracted to their cause many skillful political pragmatists, they produced no ideologists to develop and enunciate a systematic blueprint for East African unity, a grand design to fire the imagination and quicken the pulse."

On the other hand, the idea of a federal *world* government, most definitely "a grand design to fire the imagination and quicken the pulse," has been under development literally for centuries, and the development process greatly intensified throughout the twentieth century. There are blueprints aplenty and exhortations aplenty. There is an existent and substantial "ideology of unity," and both the League of Nations and the United Nations—while failures in a strict sense—give testimony to the latent power of this ideology. Aside from the fact that a universal world federation is inherently a far more potently inspirational concept than that of any possible regional federation, there are other factors, perhaps less important but still significant, why the failure of the federations examined in *Why Federations Fail* does not necessarily bode ill for the prospects of a supranational federation such as the proposed Federal Union of Democratic Nations. One of these factors was the weakness of democracy in the nations involved in these regional federal projects. On the other hand, as we look forward to a possible Federal Union of Democratic Nations with long-term aspirations toward universal membership by all nations of the world, it is apparent that many very important potential member nations are highly democratic in both principle and practice: the United States, Japan, the nations of Europe including the Russian Federation, most of the nations of Central America and South America, and an increasing number of nations in Africa, the Middle East, and Asia. Democratic nations, I would argue, are more likely to contemplate joining a supranational federation than non-democratic nations. In a democratic nation, the general population has greater influence over the high political leadership than in non-democratic nations. The high political leadership of any given nation, at the same time, is more likely to perceive a supranational federation as a threat to their personal authority, power and prestige, than is the general population who are more or less destitute of personal authority, power and prestige whether the nation is or is not part of a larger federation. On the whole, I am reluctant to put too much emphasis on alleged divergences in self-interest between "the people" and their political leaders, but in this case the possibility may be worth at least some degree of consideration.

Of course, if a new book were to be published today on the topic of "why federations fail," far more dramatic examples could be examined than were examined in Franck's 1968 book on the handful of unsuccessful federations in the wake of the dissolution of the great European colonial empires in Africa and Asia. By far the most dramatic would be the 1991 dissolution of the USSR into 15 independent nations in the wake of the collapse of communism. One of the most remarkable aspects of this transformation was the fact that it was, on the whole, peaceful. Not so fortunate was the nation of Yugoslavia, which fragmented in the early 1990s into five independent nations: the republics of Serbia and Montenegro carry on as the Federal Republic of Yugoslavia, but the other four republics, Bosnia-Herzegovina, Croatia, Macedonia and Slovenia, have all become independent nations. The breakup was marked by warfare between Serbia and Croatia, also between Serbia and Slovenia, and not least by the bitter civil war in Bosnia-Herzegovina between ethnic Serbs and ethnic Muslims—a war that added the term "ethnic cleansing" to the dictionary of man's inhumanity to man. Nor are the difficulties in the former Yugoslavia entirely in the past. Serbia's brutal repression of a separatist uprising in its southern province of Kosovo (much of the population of which is ethnically Albanian) resulted in prolonged and intensive bombing of the Serbian capital city of Belgrade, as well as many other targets, by NATO air power. Serbian military forces were finally withdrawn from Kosovo and the Serbian leader Slobodan Milosevic was later removed from power owing to domestic opposition. At this point, the outlook is unclear, but a partition seems likely, with the Serb-dominated northern region of Kosovo remaining in Serbia and the Albanian-dominated southern region going to Albania. This outcome might be preferable to making Kosovo into yet another small-scale yet fully sovereign and independent nation.

The question is whether the dissolutions of the Soviet federation and the Yugoslavian federation constitute serious evidence against the potential long-term viability and stability of a federal world government along the lines of the proposed Federal Union of Democratic Nations. It could be argued that these dissolutions constitute extremely potent evidence of the remarkable resilience of nationalistic impulses against the most prolonged and vigorous efforts to suppress these impulses and replace them with a cosmopolitan attitude under which people would be completely blind to nationalistic distinctions. Prior to their dissolutions, both the USSR and Yugoslavia had been totally dominated by their respective communist parties. The Communist Party in the USSR had exercised complete domestic authority since the early 1920s, while the Communist Party of Yugoslavia had exercised complete domestic authority since the mid 1940s. These parties did everything within their power, which extended to full control over both the educational system and the communications media, to instill in their populations unqualified adherence to the Marxist ideology and worldview, according to which nationalism is merely a tool cynically exploited by iniquitous capitalists to further their own selfish interests. The communist elite obviously failed to get this message across. As soon as communist control over the state apparatus weakened and ultimately failed, nationalism came roaring back, causing the dissolution of both the USSR and Yugoslavia. Is it not likely, therefore, that the same persistence of nationalism would quickly lead to the dissolution of the Federal Union of Democratic Nations, were it to be established in the first place?

It cannot be denied that this scenario is a possibility. Built into the constitution for the Federal Union of Democratic Nations would be a formal mechanism for the peaceful dissolution of the federation should that be desired by its member nations. This mechanism would be the constitutionally guaranteed right of member nations to withdraw from the Federal Union at any time at their own unilateral discretion. This right, as has frequently been reiterated, would be supported by the constitutionally guaranteed right of member nations to maintain whatever independent military forces they desire, armed with whatever weaponry they desire, including nuclear weaponry. But owing to these very rights, the possibility of dissolution would be small, because it is very unlikely, in light of these constitutionally guaranteed rights, that the world federal government would pass legislation or undertake policies that would impel a substantial number of member nations to withdraw from the Union.

The lack of long-term stability of both the Soviet federation and the Yugoslavian federation may be attributed largely to two factors, neither of which would likely be applicable to a potential future Federal Union of Democratic Nations. First, there was the unpopularity, among a large percentage of their respective populations, of the communist social system. In the case of both the Soviet Union and Yugoslavia, communism was not established by means of open debate and free elections—rather it was established by means of strident propaganda and armed force. Not only was the institution of private property swept away, but overly centralized economic planning was imposed, religion was discouraged, any aspirations toward genuine political democracy were suppressed, and owing to what was perceived by the communist leadership as a moral obligation and a practical necessity (for national security purposes) to spread communism throughout the world, both the Soviet Union and Yugoslavia became enmeshed, after 1950, in a perilous Cold War confrontation with the capitalist nations that threatened human civilization with nuclear holocaust. In response to this dire threat, Marshal Tito did his best to distance Yugoslavia from the Soviet Union—just as General de Gaulle did his best to distance France from the NATO allies. But there was little doubt that Yugoslavia was part of the communist camp just as France was part of the capitalist camp. Thus it is hardly surprising that a large part of the populations of the USSR and Yugoslavia remained in a resentful and resistant frame of mind toward their respective communist-controlled national governments. It goes without saying, on the other hand, that the Federal Union of Democratic Nations would have no ideological predisposition in favor of the various aspects of Marxist ideology. It would make no effort whatever to impose or encourage communism in any of its member nations. Nor would it make any effort to impose capitalism on nations that prefer to maintain a socialist economy, such as the People's Republic of China. (Pressure would, however, be placed on the PRC to implement genuinely democratic domestic governance—but this pressure would be gentle and unhurried.) The main problem with the ideological controversy that raged throughout most of the twentieth century between communists and anticommunists, was that it was so virulent and intense. The two sides not only took diametrically opposed views on good social institutions and policy, but they also believed that the consequences of these differences on overall human welfare were profound. The emotions thus aroused were easily the equal of the emotions aroused by the religious disagreements that bedeviled the earlier part of the modern era. But just as the intensity of religious beliefs declined and the attitude of religious toleration became dominant in earlier times, so too the intensity of ideological beliefs is declining and the attitude of ideological toleration is rapidly gaining ground in our own time. This is especially true with respect to the economic issue of capitalism versus socialism—although not so much with respect to the political issue of democracy versus oligarchy. Since the Federal Union of Democratic Nations would not pursue an ideologically controversial mission, it would not inculcate in its citizens the degree of opposition that contributed to the eventual downfall of the Soviet and Yugoslavian federations.

The second principal factor that contributed to this downfall was the domination of both of these federations by one territorial component in which a certain ethnic group was predominant: specifically, the USSR was dominated by the Russian SSR, and Yugoslavia was dominated by the Serbian republic. It might be argued, with a certain degree of plausibility, that the "domination" involved was more a matter of perception than of reality. After all, the most dominant figure in Soviet history was Joseph Stalin, of Georgian national origin, while the most dominant figure in Yugoslavian history was Marshal Tito, of Croatian national origin. The fact that Stalin was not a Russian and Tito was not a Serb argues against the hypothesis that the Soviet Union was in fact dominated by Russia and that the Yugoslavian federation was dominated by Serbia. On the other hand, most experts on these federations would agree that, despite the specific national origins of the dictators at the very top, there was in fact, over their entire history, a high degree of Russian domination of the Soviet Union and of Serbian domination of the Yugoslavian federation. It is difficult to see how such a situation of perceived domination by a specific ethnic group could come about in the Federal Union of Democratic Nations. Probably the leading candidate for the role of "domination" would be the United States of America. That is to say, the people of other nations will naturally tend to be apprehensive that the United States would be excessively influential in the world government. It is helpful, in this respect, that the U.S. population is not excessively dominated by one specific ethnic or national group. During the great era of immigration, several Western European nations contributed substantial components to the present-day population of the United States: Britain, France, Ireland, Germany, Russia, Poland, the Scandinavian countries, Greece and the Balkan nations. In addition, substantial components of the present-day population of the United States originated in Asia, Africa and Latin America. Perhaps more than any other nation in the world, the United States has been a melting pot of different nations and cultures. The fact that despite this diversity of origins, the U.S. population has achieved a high level of internal cohesion and solidarity is strong evidence that the same condition, in due course, may indeed be achieved at the global level.

But leaving aside the issue of possible ethnic domination, it could be argued that the United States would become "nationally dominant" (as opposed to "ethnically dominant"), owing to its large population. This would depend on the membership of the Federal Union. If the United States joined the Federation and only a small number of other nations, then there might be a problem with U.S. domination. But if many other nations were to join, the U.S. population would not form an unduly large percentage of the overall population. Currently the United States population accounts for well under five percent of the total world population. If we envision the Federal Union being joined by a substantial majority—but not all—of the nations of the world, this would mean that the United States population would account for only around five to six percent of the entire population of the Union. Even given the high relative importance of the United States in the finances of the Federal Union (U.S. GNP is approximately 25 percent of total world GNP), its population would not be large enough, in a relative sense, to achieve domination. U.S. population as a percentage of total Federal Union population would almost certainly be far less than the Russian population was as a percentage of the total Soviet population, or than the Serbian population was as a percentage of the total Yugoslavian population.

But regardless of whatever the percentage of population or of GNP the United States—or any other large nation—may account for within the Federal Union of Democratic Nations, there are critical aspects of the organization of the Federal Union that would militate against the rise of either the reality or the perception of domination of the Union's policies by one nation or one ethnic group. The highest officials of all three branches of the Federal Union government, legislative, executive and judicial, would be democratically elected in free and open elections. Of course there was no such thing as genuinely democratic election of high officials either in the Soviet Union or in Yugoslavia. In addition, all member nations of the Federal Union of Democratic Nations would enjoy constitutionally guaranteed rights of armaments and secession. Needless to emphasize, these rights were not enjoyed by any of the components of the former Soviet Union or the former Yugoslavia. And so, if despite the best plans and intentions, one nation or ethnic group were to become dominant within the Federal Union, and were to commence to exercise this domination to benefit itself at the expense of other member nations, this would soon result in the peaceful dissolution of the world federation. If such a nation as the USSR was capable of dissolving itself peacefully in 1991, then the Federal Union of Democratic nations could surely accomplish the same thing. The risks involved in this type of federal world government would not be large, and once this has been recognized by a sufficient number of the human population throughout the world, then nationalism will no longer constitute a serious impediment to federal world government. The problem is a problem of perception—not a problem of reality.

Owing to the unpopularity of the ideological and social systems promoted by their central governments, and owing to the fact that that there was a degree of real or perceived ethnic domination in their operations, the dissolutions of the former Soviet Union and the former Yugoslavia are not so much examples of "why federations fail" as they are examples of "why empires fail." This is not to say that the communist leadership of the Soviet Union and Yugoslavia had the same beliefs and attitudes as the leadership, say, of the ancient Roman empire. The ancient Romans had no doubt that the strong had a natural right and responsibility to control and rule the weak relying mainly on brute force. There is a commendable emphasis in communist ideology, on the other hand, on the natural equality of mankind and the paramount need for social consciousness and solidarity. If it were not for its dubious assumption that the capitalist economic system is the root of all evil and must therefore be destroyed by any means, communism would have to be acknowledged as a highly moral and progressive ideological system. But because of this flaw, in the final analysis the communist leadership shared with the Roman leadership one central attitude that makes long-term political stability problematical: the attitude that "might makes right." It was this imperial aspect that finally brought down the Soviet and Yugoslavian federations. Of course, as has been thoroughly emphasized in the foregoing, if the Federal Union of Democratic Nations were to be perceived by any substantial number of its citizens as the equivalent of an empire, then it would be doomed. But I have also very thoroughly emphasized in the foregoing the critical distinctions, in terms of communications, democracy, constitutional guarantees, attitudes and so on, between the imperial form and the proposed supernational federation.

Separatist motivations and activities have always been an important part of human history, but it should be understood that despite this there has been a gradual, long-term trend toward more and more amalgamation. At the present time there are not 2,000 or 10,000 sovereign and independent governments in the world, but only something over 200 national governments. If all of the separatist movements in the world today were to succeed in establishing sovereign and independent nations, it might mean another 50 to 100 nations would be created. Separatist movements are typically regarded as evidence that a world government is impractical. But there exists one significant possibility according to which separatism and world government might actually be complementary to one another. If it is possible for the proposed supernational federation to encompass around 200 nations, then most probably it could also encompass 250 to 300 nations. (Somewhat fewer in fact since quite likely there would be some nations declining membership at the outset.) Now if we consider various separatist movements of the present day, such as that in Chechnya against Russia, in Quebec against Canada and in East Timor against Indonesia, there are two particularly important reasons why these movements are deemed adverse and threatening by the populations and governments of the larger nations. First, a decrease in the size of a particular nation decreases its economic and military strength, leaving it more at risk within an anarchic international condition in which each nation regards every other nation as a potential enemy. Second, the departure of a certain region might leave those residents of the region who are members of the

dominant ethnic or cultural group in the nation as a whole vulnerable to persecution and oppression by whatever ethnic or cultural group is dominant within the
departing region. The proposed Federal Union of Democratic Nations would be
a stabilizing force and a progressive force at the international level. That is to
say, it would be an instrument toward the amelioration of the anarchic international system, and it would also be an instrument toward the protection and preservation of fundamental human rights. Its effectiveness toward these objectives
might not be dramatic in the short run, but its existence would establish a firm
foundation for evolutionary development toward a higher level of effectiveness
in the long run. Ultimately—if things go well—it might virtually eliminate both
international and civil war, and ultimately it might virtually eliminate significant
human rights abuses within any particular region of the world. Thus the people
and the government of a particular nation within the Federal Union might not be
so adverse to specific regions becoming independent nations, especially if these
newly independent nations would also become members of the Federal Union. If
there were an operative world government in existence, there would be far less
of a risk that the departure of any specific region would significantly reduce the
nation's security, and/or that it would lead to significant persecution and oppression of whatever cultural or ethnic group is dominant within the nation as a
whole. Therefore, the creation of a federal world government might actually encourage and assist the peaceful sub-division of certain nations into two or more
independent nations. Clearly, a somewhat larger number of nations is not a problem, so long as most nations participate in the world government.

   To summarize, the fact that certain federations of nations have failed in the
past is not a good argument against establishing a world federation open to all
nations of the world. Close consideration of these failed federations reveals important differences relative to the proposed world federation. The small-scale
federations examined in Thomas Franck's 1968 book, *Why Federations Fail*,
were too limited to arouse enthusiasm, especially as none of them was supported
by a pre-existing ideology of unity. The communist federations which splintered
in the early 1990s, the USSR and Yugoslavia, had too much in common with the
imperial form, owing both to ideological complications and ethnic complications. Between the four federations examined in Franck's book and the two
communist federations, we have a total of six failed federations, and in the case
of only one of them, Yugoslavia, was the dissolution process accompanied by
violence. Thus these cases suggest the possibility—if need be—of peaceful dissolution, and this is yet another good argument for undertaking a world federation.

8

THE PROGRESS OF
INTERNATIONALISM

A large proportion of the skeptical and dismissive comments on world government that are heard or read today may be classified as rhetorical rather than intellectual. That is to say, they represent what is known as "arm waving" rather than serious, logical, reasoned, substantive argument based on virtually universal perceptions of empirical reality. They are thin and superficial and rely mainly for their effect on dubious preconceptions and unwarranted assumptions. I am trying to show, in this book, that in addition to that they are also erroneous and invalid. But I recognize that an unsupported belief is not necessarily wrong, and that the fact that the presently existing case against world government is very fragile in a strictly intellectual sense does not necessarily mean that world government would in fact be desirable. Therefore I am endeavoring to keep my own dependence on arm-waving, in developing the case for world government, to a minimum. Despite these good intentions, no doubt the exposition herein sometimes degenerates into arm-waving. However, I am hopeful that most fair-minded readers will agree that I am far less dependent on arm-waving than is the typical world government critic. But in any event, amidst the arm-waving tirades of world government critics, one sometimes encounters statements along the following lines: "History demonstrates, and current events verify, that sovereign nations never countenance even the most vestigial restrictions on their freedom of action. Their behavior is solely and completely guided by their own self-interest. They are oblivious to the interests of other nations, and never submit to the interests of other nations unless they have suffered decisive military defeat on the field of battle. This self-evident, factual reality demonstrates the utter impossibility of world government to all reasonable persons."

I would respond to this kind of statement that by saying that upon a little reflection, the statement will be recognized as a preposterous exaggeration by all reasonable persons. Any nation that completely ignored the interests of other nations in determining its policy would be as swiftly and completely doomed as would be any person who completely ignored the interests of other persons in determining his/her behavior. It has already been argued, in the earlier examination of personal freedom and national sovereignty, that neither of these concepts implies the maximum conceivable discretionary self-determination. Personal freedom does not mean that the individual "can do anything he or she might desire to do," and national sovereignty does not mean that the nation "can do anything its people and government might desire that it do." In practice, nations are obliged to take into account the interests of other nations, no less than individuals are obliged to take into account the interests of other individuals. Individuals who fail to take adequate account of the interests of other individuals will quite likely become subject to the gross indignity and inconvenience of being arrested, convicted and consigned to prison. Or if their transgressions have not been as severe as that, they will at least be shunned and ostracized by their fellow human beings. Analogously, nations that fail to take adequate account of the interests of other nations are likely to become involved in warfare, the human and material costs of which will be even greater if they are militarily defeated. Or if the nation's transgressions have not been severe enough to provoke war, it will be shunned and ostracized by other nations—its citizens will not be welcome when they travel abroad, its capital investment will be declined, its exports will be subjected to restrictions—in extreme cases the nation may find itself subjected to economic sanctions imposed by a large number of other nations.

Among the more self-righteously patriotic citizens of any particular nation, it is taken as a sign of weakness that the nation undertakes cooperative behavior with other nations in which its immediate interests are sacrificed. But such behavior is more legitimately attributed to intelligence than to weakness. As the fictional Detective Harry Callahan once put it, "A wise man knows his limitations." Equally so, the wise nation knows its limitations. Knowing one's limitations, whether at the individual level or the national level, and behaving accordingly, should not be regarded as abandoning the pursuit of one's own self-interest. There is an obvious distinction between short-run self-interest and long-run self-interest. Behavior which may be desirable in terms of short-run self-interest may be highly undesirable in terms of long-run self-interest. Therefore, the intelligent pursuit of one's long-run self-interest may well entail the sacrifice of one's short-term self-interest. This is not a manifestation of moral weakness but of intellectual strength.

The forward thrust of human civilization up to the present time has been the effort to substitute peaceful negotiation and bargaining for violent confrontation and warfare (i.e., to adopt cooperative behavior in place of uncooperative behavior) in determining the policies of political organizations, from the simple tribal associations of pre-history to the nation-states of today. This chapter briefly reviews the progress that has been made in this regard throughout modern history. We look at some of the major treaties and alliances concluded throughout modern history, at the League of Nations and the United Nations, and at the currently evolving European Union. What this review indicates is that in the past, nations have in fact quite frequently engaged in behavior that sacrifices their short-term, narrowly defined self-interest in favor of their long-term, broadly defined self-interest. A limited world government such as the proposed Federal Union of

Democratic Nations would simply be a further development along this well-established evolutionary track. It would not represent a renunciation of the past or any sort of a radical, qualitative discontinuity with the ongoing political growth of human civilization. Perceptions to the contrary are based on invalid prejudices and inadequate imagination, on the failure to grasp the possibility of an alternative to the standard, conventional world government blueprint. The standard proposal envisions a far more centralized, authoritarian and militarily dominant world state than can be safely established at the present time. A feasible world state must allow the member nations the right to withdraw from the federation, and it must allow the member nations to retain whatever military forces and armaments, including nuclear weapons, that they believe are necessary for their national security.

But if these constitutional limitations are placed on the authority of the world government, it could be established and could commence operating. Clearly, the very first item on its historical agenda should be the elimination of the drastic differential that presently exists between economic living standards in the richest nations and the poorest nations. This could be done by means of the initiation of the World Economic Equalization Program (WEEP) discussed in Chapter 6 above. As these economic differentials fade, and as the world federation gradually furthers the amount and degree of cooperative behavior among its member nations, the perceived need among these nations for independent military forces will gradually decline. Disarmament will come about not through formal negotiations and treaties, but rather through the voluntary and unilateral choice of the member nations. The nations will come to see that owing to favorable evolution in the economic and political characteristics of the international community, they will be safe and secure even if they maintain only a minimal military force under their direct control. The objective is to achieve a world in which the economic, political and psychological differences among nations such as, for example, the United States and Mexico, or Russia and Germany, would be of the same order of magnitude as are the differences today between the American states of New York, Massachusetts, California and Nevada.

Just as the American states today do not believe it necessary to maintain large military forces armed with heavy weaponry in order to protect themselves against other states, so too in the future the nations of the world will not believe that it is necessary to maintain large military forces armed with heavy weaponry in order to protect themselves against other nations. I am not arguing that this situation will come about quickly. It may require 50 years, 100 years, or even more. What I am arguing, however, is that we are more likely to achieve this condition more quickly if we do establish a limited world government along the lines of the Federal Union of Democratic Nations, than if we do not do so. Nothing that we do, or fail to do, is capable of absolutely assuring the future safety, security and prosperity of the world's population. But we most assuredly are capable of taking action that will improve the odds on a favorable outcome.

TREATIES AND ALLIANCES

The proposed Federal Union of Democratic Nations would be an exercise in international cooperation—a very innovative, fundamental and important exercise to be sure—but different only in degree, rather than in substance, from the myriad of past exercises in international cooperation. Throughout all recorded history and into the modern era, there has been a plethora of treaties and alliances among sovereign and independent governments. In the modern era, most of these sovereign and independent governments have been governments of nation-states as we know them today. Each one of these treaties and alliances may be regarded, to a greater or lesser extent, as an exercise in international cooperation. As such, each one of them provides a precedent for the proposed Federal Union of Democratic Nations.

Treaties and alliances are closely connected, especially in the sense that most alliances are formalized by means of a treaty. But the distinction is that a treaty is a formal agreement among nations regarding some specific issue, signed and ratified at some specific point in time, while an alliance is a formal association among nations for the purpose of jointly pursuing the common interests of the member nations over some more or less prolonged period of time. In analytical jargon, treaties are "discrete" while "alliances" are continuous. A treaty may set up an alliance, or it may not. Probably the single most important type of treaty in modern history has been the peace treaty concluded after a period of warfare. The defeated nations formally agree to whatever penalties are imposed by the victorious nations, and the victorious nations agree on the disposition of the spoils of war. The victorious nations may or may not formally reaffirm, by means of a separate treaty, the alliance born of war, but even if they do they are unlikely to ask the defeated nations to join the alliance—at least until a decent interval of time has transpired.

For example, the Congress of Vienna, from September 1814 to June 1815, reestablished the territorial divisions of Europe at the end of the Napoleonic Wars. As a result of the various treaties produced by the Congress, France was deprived of all territories conquered by Napoleon, the Dutch Republic was united with the Austrian Netherlands to form a single Kingdom of the Netherlands, Norway and Sweden were joined under a single ruler, Swiss independence and neutrality were guaranteed, and Russia, Prussia, Hanover, Austria, Great Britain, and Sardinia all gained new territory. The Congress also condemned the slave trade and proclaimed freedom of navigation on rivers that crossed several states or formed boundaries between states. Historians tend to be complimentary toward the diplomats involved in the Congress of Vienna, especially its chief architect, Prince Klemens von Metternich (1773-1859), on grounds that following the Congress, the balance of power was so finely calculated that there were no major wars involving the European nations for almost 100 years. (The Russo-Turkish War of 1828-1829, the Crimean War of 1853-1856, the Austro-Prussian War of 1866, the Franco-Prussian War of 1870-1871, the Russo-Turkish War of

1877-1878, the Russo-Japanese War of 1904-1905, the First Balkan War of 1912-1913, and the Second Balkan War of 1913 were not "major wars.") Unfortunately for the reputation of Metternich and his colleagues at the Congress of Vienna, the balance of power eventually became decidedly unbalanced, resulting in the commencement of World War I (1914-1918). Combined battle deaths for the eight wars included in the parenthesized sentence above are estimated at about 1.2 million, while battle deaths in World War I are estimated at about 10 million. This last, historians allow, was indeed a "major war."

Another important example of a peace treaty was the Treaty of Versailles, signed on June 28, 1919, in the wake of World War I, which among other things imposed financial reparations on Germany, transferred ownership of the territory of Alsace-Lorraine back to France, and divided Germany's African colonies between Britain and France. In light of subsequent history, the Treaty of Versailles is generally regarded as an essential part of the groundwork for World War II which commenced only a little over 20 years following its signing, and which resulted in approximately 16 million battle deaths. The complexus of treaties signed in the wake of World War II established what the historians John Wheeler-Bennett and Anthony Nichols termed "the semblance of peace" in the post-World War II world.

Aside from peace treaties, there are many other types of treaties. General agreements on the conduct of war include the Declaration of Paris (1856), the First Geneva Convention (1864), the second Geneva Convention (1906), the Third Geneva Convention (1929), the 1930 protocol on submarine warfare, the 1948 expanded Geneva conventions on protection of civilians, treatment of prisoners of war, relief of wounded and sick in field armies, and extension to maritime warfare, and the supplementary protocols of 1977 extending the Geneva conventions to wars of national liberation and civil wars. General agreements on the protection of intellectual property include the Paris Convention for the Protection of Industrial Property (1883, with subsequent revisions in 1925, 1958, and 1967), the European Patent Convention (1973), the Berne Copyright Convention (1886, with subsequent revisions in 1896, 1908, 1928, 1948, 1967 and 1971), and the Universal Copyright Convention (1952, revised 1971). General agreements on nuclear and other weapons of mass destruction include the Nuclear Test-Ban Treaty (1963), the Nuclear Non-Proliferation Treaty (1968), the Treaty on Control of Arms on the Seabed (1971), the Convention on the Prohibition and Destruction of Bacteriological Weapons (1971), and the Convention on the Prohibition of Military or Any Other Hostile Use of Environmental Modification Techniques (1976). Agreements on scientific, space and environmental cooperation include the Antarctic Treaty (1959, expanded in 1972 and 1978), the International Telecommunications Satellite Agreement (1964), the Outer Space Treaty (1966), the European Space Agency Agreement (1975), the Bilateral U.S.-Soviet Space Cooperation Agreement (1977), the Convention against Marine Pollution (1972), the Convention for the Prevention of Marine Pollution from Land-Based Sources (1974), the various IMCO (Intergovernmental Maritime Consultative Organization) conventions on marine pollution (1954, 1969, 1972, and 1973), the various agreements developed by the International Whaling Commission established by the International Convention on the Regulation of Whaling (1946), and agreements among several international fisheries organizations such as the North-East Atlantic Fisheries Commission. All of these illustrative treaties and agreements remain in effect today, although in some cases a significant number of nations have not subscribed to them.

Treaties represent an effort to create among nations the equivalent of a legal contract among individuals or organizations within nations. They differ from domestic contracts mainly in that the enforcement mechanism is relatively vague, indirect and weak. If a domestic contract is breached, the aggrieved party may bring suit in a civil court, and if the judgment of the court is in favor of the plaintiff, there exists a strong enforcement system. A defendant who ignores a court judgment indefinitely will eventually be arrested and imprisoned. The court decision can thus be imposed effectively on individual culprits. In the case of a treaty entered into by a nation, on the other hand, the treaty may be disregarded or repudiated by that nation at almost any time, and it is most unlikely that the national government officials responsible for this will soon be imprisoned, fined, or otherwise personally punished for what amounts to breach of contract. One of the most dramatic treaty repudiations of the twentieth century was the repudiation of the Treaty of Versailles by the Nazi-controlled German national government in the 1930s. Several high officials of the German national government of the 1930s were eventually hanged in the aftermath of World War II, but this was not for the transgression of treaty repudiation, but rather for crimes against humanity committed during the war. Had Germany and its allies not lost the war, no penalty at all would have been imposed on these high government officials.

In a word, treaties among nations, unlike domestic contracts within nations, are non-binding agreements which may be cancelled at any time by any participant. It would be a gross exaggeration, however, to say that international treaties are therefore "meaningless." Any national government that flagrantly disregards a treaty obligation puts itself at a certain amount of risk—albeit that risk is not as strong and direct as the risk incurred by an individual or organization within a nation that flagrantly disregards a formal legal contract. Other parties to the treaty may retaliate in some way against the errant nation; in the extreme case, war may result. The fact that a given nation enters into any treaties at all is evidence of the core reality that it cannot heedlessly pursue its own interests but must rather take into some account the interests of other nations. If a given nation were truly all-powerful, it would not have to enter any treaties at all—it would merely "rule the world" by military force. Of course, ruling an unwilling and uncooperative world by military force would not be a cost-free proposition. Even if it were possible to achieve global military domination temporarily, the costs of the military forces necessary to maintain such control would quite likely outweigh the material benefits forthcoming from the control.

In contrast to a treaty, an alliance may be defined as a formal association be-

tween two or more nations to maintain a relatively protracted cooperative relationship among themselves, from which relationship other nations are excluded.
The cooperative relationship may be confined to a very specific objective (such
as deterring a war or winning a war), or it may be over a wide range of current
and future issues. Certainly the most important single function of most alliances
in modern history has been military: to achieve an amalgamated military force
for purposes of preserving and enhancing the national interests of the participating nations. Just as military alliances were frequent in pre-modern history, they
have been frequent in modern history.

Modern history is often dated from 1517, when Martin Luther posted his 95
theses on the church door at Wittenberg, and thereby initiated what history
knows as the Protestant Reformation. The principalities of Germany rapidly became polarized on the validity of the new Lutheran version of Christianity. In
1531 Philip of Hesse and John Frederick of Saxony organized the pro-Luther
principalities and city-states into an alliance termed the Schmalkaldic League
(owing to its formation in the town of Schmalkalden) for the purpose of opposing Charles V, then Holy Roman Emperor, who was preparing to quash Luther-
anism by force. The League was eventually destroyed in 1547, but by that time
numerous Protestant sects had put down firm roots across much of northern
Europe. Religious warfare between Protestants and Catholics continued throughout Europe, climaxing in the Thirty Years' War (1618-1648), a complex event
that was commenced when two alliances came to blows: the Evangelical Union
(formed of Protestant principalities and cities) and the Catholic League (as its
name suggests, formed of Catholic principalities and cities). Fast forwarding
through history, the Seven Years' War (1756-1763) was fought between an alliance of Great Britain, Prussia and Hanover on one side, versus Austria, Saxony,
France, Russia, Sweden and Spain on the other side (in North American history,
the conflict is known as the French and Indian War).

Continuing onward into the early nineteenth century, Napoleonic France was
finally brought down, after a series of wars dating from 1792, at the battle of
Waterloo in 1815 by an alliance of Great Britain, Russia, Prussia and Austria.
Later in the nineteenth century, Russian aspirations toward annexing Balkan re-
gions within the Ottoman Empire were opposed by an alliance of Great Britain,
France and Sardinia in the Crimean War (1853-1856). Moving on to the twentieth century, World War I (1914-1918) was fought between two alliances: the
Allies and Associated Powers comprising 28 nations the most important of
which were Great Britain, France, Russia, Italy and the United States, and the
Central Powers consisting of Germany, Austria-Hungary, Turkey and Bulgaria.
The alliances involved in World War II (1939-1945) were the Axis Powers on
one side (Germany, Italy, Japan, Finland, Romania, Hungary and Bulgaria) and
the Allied Powers on the other side (Britain, France, Poland, Belgium, Holland,
Norway, Yugoslavia, Greece, Russia, the United States, Canada, Australia, New
Zealand, South Africa, China, Thailand, Mexico, Brazil and Ethiopia).

Military alliances may be relatively informal and temporary, as was the "grand alliance" of Britain, the United States and the Soviet Union during World War II. Or they may be relatively formal and permanent, as has been the North Atlantic Treaty Organization (NATO) of the post-World War II era. Because the interests of the participating nations in the typical military alliance are not completely complementary, its nature and membership tends to be highly transitory. The virtually immediate breakdown of the grand alliance in the aftermath of the Second World War set the stage for the perilous Cold War confrontation between the communist and capitalist blocs of nations. NATO has lasted a long time, as alliances go, but perhaps that is because it was never tested. It was originally established to deter a Soviet land invasion of Western Europe, and the strength of this deterrence was directly proportional to the probability that the United States would have responded to such an invasion by a nuclear attack on the USSR. By the 1970s, by which time the Soviet Union had an offensive nuclear capacity comparable to that of the United States, it is problematic whether the U.S. would have carried out this threat in the event of a Soviet land invasion of Western Europe. In the mid-1960s, France withdrew from NATO on the calculation that its own national interests were better served by non-participation. Quite possibly the United States would have made an analogous calculation had the Soviet Union invaded Western Europe in the mid-1970s. Fortunately for NATO and human civilization, the Soviet Union in the 1970s was more inclined toward defense rather than offense. Certainly if the USSR had invaded Western Europe in the 1970s, there would have been a very serious threat that this would precipitate unrestricted nuclear warfare.

Just as there is no well-defined and clearly effective enforcement system in support of treaties, so too none exists for alliances. But this does not imply that alliances are "meaningless" any more than it means that treaties are "meaningless." When a nation enters an alliance, no less than when it signs a treaty, it is signaling that it is not omnipotent but rather that it relies and depends on cooperation with other nations in pursuit of joint interests and goals. Treaties and alliances are implicit admissions that there are indeed natural, unavoidable restrictions on the autonomy and sovereignty of individual nations, that nations have a wide range of complementary interests, and that the peaceful pursuit of these interests involves a significant amount of formal, written quasi-contracts among nations.

The proposed Federal Union of Democratic Nations can be sensibly viewed merely as the continued evolution of the principles of international cooperation embodied in the past history of treaties and alliances in the international sphere. Clearly the existence and functioning of a supranational government such as the Federal Union would to some extent increase the effective pressure on nations to enter into international agreements, and to abide by these agreements faithfully. But given the intended restrictions and limitations on the supranational government, especially the fact that it would not hold a monopoly on either nuclear or conventional weapons, the pressure would hardly be irresistible. Just as nations today may break treaties and withdraw from alliances without incurring instantaneous disaster, the same basic situation would hold if there were an operating Federal Union in existence. If a given member nation came to the conclusion that its long-term national interests were better served by removing itself from the Federal Union, that option would be available by explicit constitutional provision. Joining the Federal Union of Democratic Nations would thus be similar to joining an alliance today, except that this alliance will hopefully be far more inclusive, successful and permanent than any past alliance in the history of humanity. And participation in the drafting, passage and implementation of Union legislation would be similar to developing and signing a multilateral treaty. Thus every alliance formed throughout the history of humanity provides a precedent for nations forming a federal world government, and every treaty signed in the history of humanity provides a precedent for supernational legislation.

A world government, therefore, need not actually be such a radical departure from the past that it is often imagined to be—always presuming that it is a limited world government and not an "omnipotent" world government. Of course, one must remain cognizant of the distinction between the short-term realities of world government and the long-term aspirations of world government. The long-term aspiration is to evolve an international situation in which individual nations, whether members or non-members of the Federal Union, could not simply ignore important legislation passed by the Union. The long-term aspiration is to achieve a situation under which national government officials could indeed be arrested and prosecuted as individuals for ignoring or violating international law without sufficient reason—just as individuals within nations make themselves subject to arrest and prosecution by ignoring or violating the law of the land. But this kind of very strict and uniform enforcement of supernational law within nations depends on a reasonable degree of economic and ideological homogeneity among nations, so that there is a high degree of willing, voluntary compliance with the law. That level of homogeneity does not yet exist at the international level. Thus enforcement of Federal Union law will, in the short term, necessarily be less strict and uniform than it will hopefully become in the long term.

THE LEAGUE OF NATIONS

The League of Nations commenced its short, unhappy career on January 16, 1920, with a brief Council meeting in Paris to appoint a commission to ascertain the boundaries of the Saar. Established by a Covenant of the 1919 Treaty of Versailles, the League convened its first Assembly meeting at its permanent headquarters in Geneva, Switzerland, in November 1920. By this time it was clear that the United States would not be taking membership. Although the League had been the special enthusiasm of President Woodrow Wilson, a resurgence of American isolationism following the nation's brief but costly involvement in World War I, induced the U.S. Senate to reject the Treaty, and with it United States membership in the League. This was by no means the only inauspicious note as the League commenced its activities. Many if not most of the leading nations of the world harbored serious reservations about both the Treaty and the League. France felt betrayed because in the Treaty negotiations she had given up her claim on territory on the east bank of the Rhine on the presumption that American participation in the League would guarantee her security against future German aggression. The Japanese were aggrieved that the Covenant did not include a declaration on racial equality. The Italians were disappointed that they were not awarded African mandates. Germany and Austria, initially excluded from the League, regarded the Versailles peace terms as intolerably harsh, as veritably sadistic. The Russians remained uninvolved owing to internal revolution and civil war. And so on and so forth. Little confidence existed that the League would provide effective security against a recurrence of major warfare. The member nations continued to play the time-honored balance of power game, and regarded the League as merely a minor adjunct to their traditional foreign policy. Possibly this was a case of a self-fulfilling prophecy, but within a very brief period of historical time the League did indeed prove its ineffectiveness beyond a reasonable doubt.

The League of Nations was comprised of four component bodies: (1) an Assembly in which all member nations were equally represented; (2) a much smaller Council in which the major powers had permanent seats, with additional seats allocated to smaller nations on a rotating basis; (3) an administrative Secretariat guided by a Secretary-General; and (4) a Permanent Court of International Justice intended as a supplementary body to the Permanent Court of Arbitration established in 1899 by the first Hague peace conference. The Assembly fielded a supporting network of committees and subcommittees in six general areas: legal and constitutional matters, technical organization of the League, reduction of armaments, budgetary and financial matters, social and general matters, and political matters. The Assembly met once a year for a month at a time, and passed a series of resolutions concerning matters it wanted addressed by the Council and the Secretariat. The Council was obligated to meet once a year but normally it met more or less continuously. According to Article 5 of the League Covenant, decisions and directives of the Council had to be approved unanimously by all members in attendance at the meeting—in the light of subsequent history, this provision is now generally considered to have been fatal to the League's effectiveness as a guarantor of peace. The Secretariat consisted of thirteen sections staffed by about 700 "international civil servants" drawn from a wide range of member nations. Sir Eric Drummond, formerly an official in the British Foreign Office, served as the League's first Secretary-General from 1919 to 1933. Within its first few years, the League created several functional institutions: the Economic and Financial Organizations, the Health Organization, the Permanent Mandates Commission, the Advisory Committee on Traffic in Opium and Other Dangerous Drugs, and the Advisory Committee of Experts on Slavery. While the League failed miserably in the essential matter of preserving peace, it did achieve a substantial measure of success in these functional areas. Although the League certainly did not invent the concept of multilateral functional cooperation among nations, it significantly fostered and facilitated it during the 1920s and 1930s.

The League had a superficial resemblance to a typical national government since the Assembly might be considered analogous to the lower house of a legislature, the Council analogous to the upper house of a legislature, the Secretariat as the executive branch, and the Permanent Court of International Justice as the judicial branch. But it lacked three essential characteristics of a national government: (1) it possessed no military forces under its direct control; (2) it did not possess the authority to levy taxes; and (3) it was separated from any direct connection with the populations of the member nations because delegates to both the Assembly and the Council were appointed by the national governments of the member nations rather than being elected by the populations of the member nations. Thus in practice the League was merely an assemblage of ambassadors, the creature of the national governments. Citizens of the member nations did not have the sense of being citizens of a higher political authority than that of their respective national governments, of participating in a qualitatively higher form of international cooperation. Very little effective power and authority was delegated by the member nations to the League. The Assembly of the League of Nations was merely an advisory body to the Council, just as the Council was merely an advisory body to the national governments of the member nations. Member nations were torn between their visions of being protected against foreign aggression by the overwhelming combined military force of the League membership, and their apprehensions that the League would become either an instrument through which many other nations would "gang up" on them and hinder the reasonable pursuit of their legitimate national interests, or an instrument through which they would be "dragged into" devastating warfare unrelated to their legitimate national interests. Rather more weight came down on the side of apprehension than came down on the side of vision, with the result that the League never possessed the moral authority and practical clout associated with direct control of military power and the authority to levy taxes.

The fragile and insubstantial nature of the League's authority was reflected in its judicial arm, the Permanent Court of International Justice. The Permanent Court of International Justice (popularly known as the World Court) did not re-place but rather supplemented the Permanent Court of Arbitration (popularly known as the Hague Tribunal), established earlier (1899) by the first Hague peace conference. Except to international lawyers, the distinction between the World Court and the Hague Tribunal is rather vague, and it is further blurred by the fact that both were (and remain) located in the city of The Hague in the Netherlands. After World War II, the League of Nations was replaced by the United Nations and the Permanent Court of International Justice was replaced by the International Court of Justice (ICJ). Just as the United Nations was very close to being a carbon copy of the League of Nations in terms of basic organiza-tion and functions, so too the International Court of Justice was similarly very close to being a carbon copy of the Permanent Court of International Justice. A minor difference between the two tribunals is that the World Court (now the ICJ) hears only cases in which the disputants are both national governments, whereas the Hague Tribunal hears cases in which one or both of the parties is a private individual or organization. But the principal distinction between the World Court and the Hague Tribunal is roughly the distinction between adjudication and arbitration. In arbitration, the two parties to a dispute submit it to a panel of impartial arbitrators and agree to abide by the arbitrators' decision. The arbitrators may be jurists versed in law, or possibly just laypersons since it is more a matter of finding a practical compromise than of implementing principles of formal law. In adjudication, on the other hand, formal legal principles are invoked by one or both parties to a dispute, and the panel consists of judges with appropriate educational and professional credentials. Within nations, adjudication is further distinguished from arbitration by the fact that the court may call upon the criminal justice system to enforce its decision. Any party to a dispute who ignores the adjudicated decision of a court becomes subject to arrest and imprisonment for contempt of court. In arbitration, on the other hand, there is no direct enforcement of the arbitrators' decision. However, if one party ignores the arbitrated decision, the injured party may bring suit in a judicial court over the same dispute, and if the judicial panel then affirms the arbitration panel's decision, compulsory enforcement could then be brought to bear. Therefore, in principle, adjudication is a large step beyond arbitration.

Thus at the time of its foundation in 1920, it was hoped that the World Court would represent a significant advance over the Hague Tribunal, since it would go beyond the realm of arbitration into the realm of adjudication. However, there was one critical element missing: a means of compulsory enforcement. Although called a "court," the Permanent Court of International Justice associated with the League of Nations lacked those critical powers of enforcement wielded by courts within nations. Theoretically, if a nation ignored its ruling, the Permanent Court could have appealed to its parent organization, the League of Nations, to impose sanctions against the errant nation—possibly even to launch military operations against it. But this was never done. For one thing, the issues involved were too minor. For another, the League of Nations did not have the necessary solidarity and determination even to entertain such a notion. After all, even when it was a case of outright military invasion of one nation by another, the League either looked the other way altogether, or merely issued statements of mild remonstrance. It never mustered military action against errant nations. Therefore the Permanent Court of International Justice was not really a substantive advance beyond the Permanent Court of Arbitration (the same is true of the former's direct successor, the International Court of Justice).

Both courts provided (and still provide) rulings on controversies voluntarily submitted by nations (or, in the case of the PCA—Permanent Court of Arbitration—private individuals or organizations as well). But since they have no power to enforce their rulings, the rulings may be, and often are, rejected or ignored by one or both of the parties to the dispute. As a result, there is not a great deal of incentive to bring cases before these courts. According to the 1999 annual report of the Hague Tribunal, over its 100-year history, it has rendered decisions in only 33 cases. One of the first of these was the "Venezuela claims" case, decided in 1904. Germany, Britain and Italy, following a precedent that had been firmly established by the "dollar diplomacy" of the United States in Latin America, sent a naval force to Venezuela in 1902 to seek redress for unpaid loans. This was objectionable to the United States because it constituted a violation of the Monroe Doctrine, according to which European nations should not intervene forcibly against Latin American nations (only the United States was permitted to do that). A repayment agreement was reached in Caracas in 1903, but Germany, Britain and Italy felt that they should receive preferential treatment in the repayment process since it had been their blockading naval forces that had persuaded the Venezuelans to come to their senses and pay their debts to foreign investors. They presented their case to the PCA and the PCA agreed that those nations that use muscle to obtain repayment of debts are entitled to preferential treatment in the repayment of those debts. At the time, this case was regarded as very encouraging evidence that nations could now live in perpetual peace, assisted as they were by the Hague Tribunal. Undue optimism in that regard, however, was shattered by World War I. In the crisis that followed the assassination of Archduke Francis Ferdinand and his wife, the Hague Tribunal was not consulted by any party. Through the four years during which World War I raged, the Hague Tribunal rendered no decisions. The reality that became clear at that time was that if there were serious issues of national interest involved in specific international disagreements and confrontations, about which the nations involved felt strongly, the Hague Tribunal would not be consulted. It could only cope successfully with very minor issues that the parties could probably have resolved themselves by the conventional bargaining and negotiation processes.

Seriously sobered by what had occurred between 1914 and 1918, the nations of the world attempted to move beyond the old balance of power politics of alliances and counter-alliances, by means of establishing, in the form of the League of Nations, a super-alliance composed of the majority of the nations of the world, the combined military strength of which would supposedly be sufficient to deter any aggressively-minded upstart nation in the future. The League was hobbled from the start, however, by the non-adherence of the United States, the unanimity rule in the Council, and pervasive doubt among its member nations that it could actually accomplish its mission. As a result, the same old balance of power game that had brought on World War I continued to be played after World War I, and (predictably enough in hindsight) it duly brought on World War II. Just as the designers of the League of Nations sought to go from the small-scale, limited alliances of the "old diplomacy" to a large-scale, quasi-universal alliance (the League) of the "new diplomacy," so too they sought to move beyond the arbitration concept embodied in the Permanent Court of Arbitration to the adjudication concept embodied in the Permanent Court of International Justice. But just as the League of Nations was not a sufficiently universal and cohesive alliance to achieve its objective of perpetual peace, so too the Permanent Court of International Justice, owing to the parent League's weakness, was deprived of a meaningful enforcement power for its decisions. As a result, appeals to it by disputant nations were rather infrequent, and invariably involved relatively minor issues. During the 25 years of its existence, it rendered only 32 judgments and 27 advisory opinions. A typical example of its accomplishments was its 1933 decision affirming Danish sovereignty over the north coast of Greenland and disallowing Norway's claim. Greenland, although the largest island in the world, lies mostly within the Arctic circle and is a remote, frozen and desolate area devoid of resources and habitability. It was and remains economically unimportant to every nation in the world, including Norway and Denmark. On the whole, the Permanent Court of International Justice was a negligible element in the international politics of the interwar period. And what was true of this Court during this period, continued to hold true of its direct successor, the International Court of Justice in the post-World War II period. Just as the name change from the "League of Nations" to the "United Nations" failed to effect significant improvement, so too the name change from the "Permanent Court of International Justice" to the "International Court of Justice" likewise failed to effect significant improvement.

The League of Nations operated during an interval of time that in the longer historical perspective is perceived as little more than an uneasy truce separating the two "German wars": World War I (1914-1918) and World War II (1939-1945). The basic problem was that the peace terms imposed on Germany and her allies by France, Britain, Italy and the United States after World War I were excessively harsh given that the German defeat had not been sufficiently decisive. Unlike the situation after World War II, the entire German nation was not placed under military occupation. Most of the First World War had been fought on French soil and Russian soil, and that in conjunction with the fact that aerial bombing was in its infancy, meant that the German people had been spared the worst horrors of modern warfare. In the immediate aftermath of the Versailles Treaty, demagogues such as Adolf Hitler put forward the theory that if Germany had persisted she would have won the war, but instead the nation had been done in by "a stab in the back" administered by cowardly civilian government officials in the capital city of Berlin. The theory appealed greatly to the wounded pride of many Germans.

The economic suffering and social dislocation generated by the Great Depression of the 1930s gave the German Nazi party of Adolf Hitler the chance it had been waiting for throughout the 1920s. Hitler gained dictatorial powers over the German government early in 1933, and immediately launched into a vigorous program of "national regeneration." The main key to German national regeneration, in the minds of the Nazis, was the rectification of the terrible injustice done to Germany by the 1919 Treaty of Versailles. Therefore, one of Hitler's first actions, upon gaining power, was to repudiate the arms limitations imposed by the Treaty of Versailles and commence a crash program of rearmament. At that

time, the League of Nations was promoting multilateral disarmament negotiations, but these broke down soon after Hitler withdrew Germany from the
League in October 1933. Germany enlisted as allies certain other non-democratic
nations that were dissatisfied with the post-World War I international status quo,
principally Italy and Japan. Japan concentrated on extending its influence in Asia
by invading the Chinese province of Manchuria (September 1931) and eventually establishing there a puppet regime known as "Manchukuo." The League sent
an investigative commission to Manchuria (by slow boat), but by the time the
League Assembly adopted the commission's report condemning the Japanese
invasion, the conquest had been completed. Although no action was taken by the
League beyond verbal condemnation, Japan announced its withdrawal from the
League in March, 1933. Subsequently, Japan assiduously furthered what it
termed the "Greater East-Asia Co-Prosperity Sphere," the pursuit of which entailed a full-scale invasion of China in 1937. In 1935, Italy invaded and conquered Abyssinia (now known as Ethiopia), a member in good standing of the
League of Nations and one of the few independent nations in Africa at that time.
At the time of the invasion, the League imposed economic sanctions on Italy, but
they were ineffective in preventing the conquest, and as soon as the conquest had
been completed the sanctions were lifted on grounds that since the conquest of
Ethiopia was now a fait accompli, no further useful purpose was served by the
sanctions. (At that time, Britain and France were still hoping to enlist Italy in a
united front against Nazi Germany.)

Meanwhile, Hitler had not been idle. Under Hitler's complete control, and
emboldened by its rapidly growing military power, Nazi Germany remilitarized
the Rhineland (1936), absorbed Austria (spring 1938), annexed part of Czechoslovakia (fall 1938) and then conquered the rest (spring 1939). Protestations
against these aggressive actions in the League of Nations were ineffective. When
Britain and France finally declared war on Germany in September 1939, after the
latter had invaded Poland, it was on the basis of their mutual defense treaties
with Poland and not on the basis of resistance to aggression organized by the
League of Nations. There then followed the so-called "sitzkrieg" along France's
Maginot Line from the fall of 1939 to the late spring of 1940. Although they had
declared war on Germany, Britain and France were reluctant to have matters
escalate into a shooting war. Their restraint was not rewarded. Too impatient to
wait for a negotiated peace, Hitler invaded and conquered France in May 1940,
and drove the remnants of the British military forces from continental Europe.
Flushed with success, Hitler followed this up with the miscalculation that eventually doomed him: the invasion of the USSR in June 1941. The Second World
War, which lasted almost six years from September 1939 to August 1945, re-
wrote the record books established by the First World War: it was far worse in
terms of scale, extent, cost, destruction, injury and death.

In view of its inability to forestall World War II, it is easy to be contemp-
tuous of the League of Nations. But contempt ought to be tempered with a certain amount of respect for this pioneering effort to establish an institutional un-

derpinning for the principle of collective security and active cooperation among the nations. What doomed the League of Nations in general was the fact that it did not represent an adequate advance beyond the sovereign nation-state system that had preceded it, and what doomed it in particular was the dissatisfaction of several large and powerful nations with the international status quo, especially Germany, Italy and Japan. Of the three, Germany was clearly the principal catalyst. Had Germany been treated more generously following World War I so that repudiation of the Versailles Treaty had not been an issue, conceivably the League of Nations would have compiled a record comparable to that of the United Nations in the post-World War II era.

The League of Nations did register a few successes during the more temperate 1920s, prior to the arrival of the Great Depression. Probably the most notable of these was the League's intervention in and resolution of the Greek-Bulgarian crisis in October, 1925. This involved a border incident in a remote region which had long been troubled by raids into Greek territory by gangs of Bulgarian bandits composed largely of ex-military personnel. These raids elicited suspicion in Greece that the Bulgarians had designs on Greek territory—perhaps they wanted a southern outlet to the Aegean Sea. To this day it is not clear what exactly happened to commence the shooting. One story has it that Greek and Bulgarian border guards were playing cards in a Bulgarian border post when an argument erupted during which a Greek soldier was shot and killed. Accounts of the incident then converge on the point that a Greek officer advancing under a white flag of truce, ostensibly to retrieve the body of the dead soldier and resolve the difficulty, was shot down. Bulgarian accounts put forward the possibility that the officer was killed by "friendly fire" from the Greek side, but most impartial authorities believe it more likely that the fatal shot had indeed come from the Bulgarian side, though possibly it was accidental or otherwise unauthorized. In any event, a substantial Greek military force then made a substantial penetration, as much as several kilometers in depth, into Bulgarian territory. This was not a planned invasion, however, and the Greek forces soon halted and contented themselves with burning some villages suspected of being bandit refuges. Acting with uncharacteristic rapidity and decisiveness, the League of Nations interceded on Bulgaria's behalf. A firm demand was issued that Greece withdraw its troops from Bulgaria, a demand quickly acceded to by Greece. Shortly thereafter, a League investigation came to the conclusion that Greece should be made to pay an indemnity to Bulgaria to compensate for damage done to the property of Bulgarian citizens during the incursion. After a certain amount of stalling on the part of Greece, the fairly modest indemnity was in fact paid over to Bulgaria.

In the euphoria that followed this demonstration of the League's potential effectiveness as an enforcer of peace, certain salient facts tended to be overlooked. Neither Greece nor Bulgaria had been either determined or prepared to go to war with one another. The Greeks and the Bulgarians did not especially like each other, of course—but they were not, at that particular moment in time, in the grip of any sort of nationalistic frenzy aimed at each other. The whole incident was merely a common-garden-variety border skirmish that had gotten out of hand. None of the Great Powers, as of 1925, had any special interest in either Greece or Bulgaria. The area in which the incident occurred was not rich in petroleum, diamonds, or any other natural resource worthy of notice. In light of subsequent history, it seems rather doubtful that if Greece and Bulgaria had both been determined to fight a full-scale war, the League of Nations would have mustered military forces from among its membership to quash the fighting. What would probably have happened is what happened in the case of the "Chaco war" between Bolivia and Paraguay (so-called for the Bolivian region under dispute, in which the U.S. Standard Oil company happened to have extractive operations). This extremely costly conflict (to the two nations directly involved) persisted from 1928 through 1935. The League eventually bestirred itself to organize an arms embargo, but it is quite possible that what finally brought the fighting to an end was not so much the embargo as the exhaustion of the combatants. Had Greece and Bulgaria persisted in their conflict, the outcome would likely have been comparable to the outcome in the case of the Chaco war.

Even so, the League's handling of the Greek-Bulgarian incident of 1925 is legitimately regarded as the most unalloyed success ever achieved by the League of Nations. True, the kind of judicious common sense and moral authority that was applied in that case was inadequate to resolve major disagreements among major powers. But it may have reduced the burden of "minor wars" on the nations that would have been affected, and it also clearly demonstrated what might eventually be accomplished on a larger scale. As previously noted, the League also accomplished some functional purposes, such as the suppression of trade in narcotics and the collection of comparable international statistics. In fact, one leading authority on the League of Nations, the historian James Barros, has speculated that the League might have achieved a great deal more than it actually did, if it had concentrated solely on the advancement of functional cooperation among the nations. It simply did not have adequate support among its member nations to be an effective instrument for the preservation of peace, and its inadequacy in this regard may have undermined its overall credibility and hampered its achievements in terms of functional cooperation.

Be this as it may, and whatever opinion we may have about the League's effectiveness in whatever dimension, there is no denying its historic symbolic significance. The foundation and operation of the League of Nations clearly manifested the fact that among a substantial proportion of the human race, there existed a strong desire for and aspiration toward greater stability and harmony among nations through the mechanism of a formal and universal political organization of nations. This desire and aspiration still exists today, and it is stronger now than it was at the time of the League's birth in 1920. It is said that "where there is a will, there is a way." The League of Nations, no less than the United Nations that succeeded it, demonstrated the will. All that humanity needs is a "way": a practical, realistic plan for world government as an evolutionary development from the ongoing processes of globalization and internationalism. This book, of course, is putting forward the proposed Federal Union of Democratic Nations as a candidate for the needed plan. If this plan, or some comparable plan, is someday achieved in the real world, it must be allowed that the League of Nations, whatever its limitations and deficiencies, was indeed an important landmark on the road to ultimate success.

THE UNITED NATIONS

Somewhere around the middle of the terrible years between 1939 and 1945, as inconceivable economic resources where being devoted on both sides to destroying enemy property and lives, resulting in the maiming and killing of millions, but at a point where the Allied powers were starting, slowly and painfully, to get the upper hand over the Axis powers, an idea commenced to gain support: the idea of a new and greatly improved League of Nations to be known as the United Nations. The name "United Nations" is generally attributed to U.S. President Franklin D. Roosevelt, although as far back as 1918, one Theodore Harris had put forward a detailed blueprint for a world government to be known as the "United Nations of the World." The first official use of the term "United Nations" was in the Declaration of the United Nations of January 1, 1942, in which 26 nations pledged themselves to continue the war effort against the Axis powers until final victory was attained, and not to make peace separately under any circumstances. The first official statement of the need for a new international organization to replace the League of Nations was the Moscow Declaration of October 30, 1943, issued by China, Great Britain, the United States and the USSR. Specific proposals for the new organization were drafted by representatives of these four nations at the Dumbarton Oaks Conference of August-October 1944 (named for the mansion in Washington D.C. at which it was held). These proposals were refined at the Yalta Conference in February 1945. The founding conference, attended by all 50 nations that had subscribed to the Declaration of the United Nations and had declared war on Germany or Japan by March 1, 1945, was held at San Francisco from April 25 through June 26, 1945. The final United Nations Charter, having been approved unanimously by all national delegations to the San Francisco Conference at a ceremony in the San Francisco Opera House on June 25, 1945, was then ratified by the required number of nations on October 24, 1945. October 24 has thus been declared "United Nations Day," but it is symptomatic of the disappointed hopes aroused by the United Nations that October 24 is an official holiday in few of its member nations. The charter members of the U.N. included the majority of independent nations of the time, one of the few important exceptions being Switzerland. The first meetings of the General Assembly and the Security Council took place in London, respectively on January 10 and January 17, 1946. The U.N.'s first Secretary-General, Trygve Lie of Norway, was designated by the Security Council on February 1, 1946.

In the minds of those who designed and implemented it, the first and foremost distinction between the United Nations and its little lamented predecessor, the League of Nations, would be that no major power would be missing from membership in the former organization. Specifically, the United States would not only be a founding member, but it would be a driving force in this new attempt to achieve collective security by means of a permanent, well-organized and generously staffed super-alliance. The extent of its commitment to the United Nations may be gauged from the fact that the United States agreed to meet no less than one-third of the U.N.'s operating expenses. The aspiration toward near-universality implied that the defeated Axis nations would be admitted fairly soon after the war, once the remnants of fascism within them had been eradicated—or at least adequately suppressed. Italy was admitted in 1955 and Japan in 1956, although owing to Cold War complications, specifically the partition of Germany into the noncommunist West Germany (the Federal Republic of Germany) and the communist East Germany (the German Democratic Republic), the two parts were not admitted to separate U.N. membership until 1973 (effective with the accession of the German Democratic Republic to the Federal Republic of Germany in 1990, Germany has had one seat in the United Nations). In addition to virtually universal membership, the United Nations, in contrast to the League of Nations, would make a far more systematic and determined attempt to eradicate the roots of warfare by fostering economic, political and social progress throughout the world. In other words, the United Nations would undertake a "peace-building" mission as well as a "peacekeeping" mission. The theme of "a new beginning" was reinforced by abandoning the somewhat stodgy League of Nations headquarters in Geneva and opening a shiny new glass-and-steel sky-scraper, built on a parcel of high-priced real estate (donated by John D. Rocke-feller Jr.) on the East River in New York City, to serve as U.N. headquarters. Consisting as it does of large quantities of uplifting prose ("We the peoples of the United Nations, determined to save succeeding generations from the scourge of war, which twice in our lifetime has brought untold sorrow to mankind..."), the U.N. Charter is a far more elaborate document than was the old League Covenant. The Charter was soon supplemented by the Universal Declaration of Human Rights, adopted by the General Assembly on December 10, 1948. While this document has been described by some as a "pious wish list," it nevertheless clearly delineates the kind of human condition within world society to which any and all rational persons aspire.

But although its membership was larger and its goals more ambitious, the United Nations was virtually a carbon copy of the defunct League of Nations in terms of institutional structure. The "Assembly" of the League of Nations became the "General Assembly" of the United Nations. The "Council" of the League of Nations became the "Security Council" of the United Nations. The distinction between the permanent seats on the Security Council of the major powers and the rotating seats of the smaller powers was continued, as was the requirement that decisions of the Security Council be unanimously approved by the permanent members (i.e., any major power could veto a decision of the Secu-rity Council). The "Secretariat" of the League of Nations became the "Secretariat" of the United Nations. The "Secretary-General" of the League of Nations became the "Secretary-General" of the United Nations. The "Permanent Court of International Justice" of the League of Nations became the "International Court of Justice" of the United Nations. The United Nations did, however, add two new councils to supplement the Security Council: the Trusteeship Council and the Economic and Social Council. The purpose of the former was mainly to oversee the devolution of the colonial empires, a purpose largely completed by the 1960s. The purpose of the latter has been, and continues to be, fostering material, institutional and cultural progress throughout the world. But despite various superficial efforts to differentiate the United Nations from its toothless and ineffective predecessor, from the moment of its origin in 1945 there was not a great deal more confidence in the U.N. as a guarantor of peace than there was in the League of Nations at the time of its origin in 1919. The two organizations were too much alike in structure and mission. And the various pressures toward antagonism and conflict among nations were, if anything, far worse in 1945 than they had been in 1919.

First and foremost, the one nation in the world incapable of abiding the capitalist economic system and determined to overthrow that system all over the world, namely the USSR, had progressed from being a wobbly infant in 1919 to being a military colossus in 1945. The hopes and intentions underlying the United Nations almost immediately foundered on the deadly reef represented by the polarization of the world's nations into two hostile camps: the camp of communism and the camp of capitalism. Among the optimists at the time of the U.N.'s formation, it was intended that the new international organization would have substantial, permanent military forces under its direct control, and Article 47 directed the formation of a Military Staff Committee, composed of the Chiefs of Staff of the five permanent members of the Security Council, to develop formal agreements that would have put specific military units of member nations under the direct command of the Security Council. But unfortunately, owing to the inability of the representative of the USSR in the Military Staff Committee to reach agreement with the representatives of the other four major powers on the Security Council, nothing came of this idea. The same split nullified the efforts of two other special bodies established by the Security Council, the Atomic Energy Commission and the Commission on Conventional Armaments.

Given the virtually immediate polarization of the world along ideological lines in the aftermath of the Second World War, the fundamental defects of the United Nations were obvious almost from the very beginning to both the "realist" majority and the "visionary" (not to use the term "utopian") minority. The realist majority viewed the U.N. mainly as just another tool for the pursuance of national interests, but far less important as such than foreign ministries and war departments. The visionary minority—those people responsible for the ephemeral "world government boom" in the immediate aftermath of World War II— saw the U.N. as a hollow shadow of the federal world government that it ought to be. The realists envisioned the indefinite continuation of time-honored balance of power politics, U.N. or no U.N. They also saw no reason why the advent of nuclear weapons should fundamentally alter this game. True, nuclear weapons were far more destructive than anything witnessed in the past—but in a way this was good because the threat of nuclear holocaust would reduce the incentives in nations toward provocative and belligerent behavior. So the increase in the destructiveness of weapons was counter-balanced by a decrease in the probability that they would be utilized. Since humanity was presumably no more threatened by warfare than it had been before the invention and dissemination of nuclear weapons, there was thus no compelling reason for a substantive departure from the familiar balance of power politics of the pre-nuclear age. The visionaries were far less optimistic on this point: according to them, the development of nuclear weapons immeasurably increased the overall threat to human civilization embodied in warfare. While the prospect of nuclear destruction might somewhat reduce the propensity toward provocative and belligerent behavior among nations, it would by no means eliminate it, and sooner or later some nation would stray over the line separating peace from unimaginably devastating warfare. What was obviously needed, in the view of the visionaries, was a world government with direct control over a large and dominant military force, with the power of taxation, and guided by officials subject to direct democratic accountability to the people through free and open elections. For a brief period, this idea gained an appreciable amount of currency, and it was seriously entertained far more widely than had ever been the case in the past. But as described earlier, the world government boom quickly deflated, a victim of the intractable Cold War conflict among the communist and noncommunist blocs of nations. In very short order, the realist viewpoint was completely dominant that whatever might be the attractions of world government "in theory," it was completely infeasible "in practice" owing to the irreconcilable ideological gulf between communists and noncommunists.

Even if ideological disagreement had not been a factor in the postwar world, there were various weaknesses in the design of the United Nations that militated against its becoming a highly effective participant in international politics. To begin with, any involvement of the U.N. in military resistance to aggression depended on (and still depends on) a unanimous vote by the permanent members of the Security Council. The possibility that the United Nations, in and of itself, would become an important deterrent to aggression was (and remains) considerably reduced by the veto rule within the Security Council. It is a truism that in collective decision-making, true unanimity is very difficult to achieve. Collective security becomes rather nebulous if a single major member of the super-alliance can block joint action by the super-alliance. Not that this *necessarily* makes much difference. Those members of the alliance who believe that military action is advisable could go ahead without those who do not. Alternatively, those members of the alliance who believe that military action is *not* advisable can simply depart from the alliance when called upon to provide assistance. After all, this has been the way of alliances throughout human history, pre-modern and modern.

At the time the United Nations was established, in the eyes of its charter members the principal function of the organization was the preservation of international peace, i.e., to strengthen deterrence against the sort of very obvious and straightforward military aggression practiced by the Axis nations prior to World War II. It was hoped that the existence of the United Nations would make it easier to quickly muster an overwhelming military coalition against any nation that launched a full-scale military invasion of a member nation. In the judgment of the principal noncommunist nations, the most likely candidate for launching such invasions was the USSR, and their most likely target would be the Western European nations still wobbly from the vicissitudes of the War. The intention was to deter Stalin from trying to follow in the footsteps of Hitler. In fact, neither Stalin nor his successors did try to follow in Hitler's footsteps, although the reason for this was not so much the existence of the United Nations as it was the NATO alliance, the possession of nuclear weapons by the United States, Britain and France, and a substantial U.S. military presence in Western Europe (the "tripwire" force). But in any event, there was little or no intention at that time of having the United Nations intervene in civil wars within nations, especially if the foreign involvement was limited and confined mainly to the provision of arms and material, as opposed to combat personnel, to one side or the other. There is no specific provision in the U.N. Charter under which intervention in domestic conflicts is authorized. Nevertheless, the great majority of actual U.N. peacekeeping missions have in fact involved predominantly domestic conflicts. For the most part, however, the U.N. forces involved have been fairly small, especially when compared to the military capabilities of the major powers. And when conflicts arose in which important interests of the major powers were involved, the United Nations kept out of it, as for example in the case of the Soviet suppression of the Hungarian uprising of 1956 and the Czechoslovakian independence movement of 1968, in the Falkland Islands war between Britain and Argentina in 1982, and in the chronic violence in Northern Ireland. The United Nations was also excluded from a number of conflict situations in Asia, such as the Chinese occupation of Tibet, the Sino-Indian and Sino-Soviet border conflicts, the war in Indochina and Vietnam, the Vietnamese action in Kampuchea and the Chinese action against Vietnam. The United Nations also stayed out of the Iran-Iraq War of 1980-1988, a border war that is estimated to have cost the combatants 1 million dead and 1.7 million wounded. Neither side appealed to the U.N. for assistance during the course of the conflict, but given the magnitude of the conflict and the fact that it was confined to border regions, together with the fact that both combatants were significant military powers, it is questionable that the United Nations would have been willing to take sides.

There have only been two occasions in the history of the United Nations in which the vision that initially inspired the organization was actually realized: the rapid mustering of large-scale military forces to oppose a conventional invasion. The first was the Korean War of 1950-1953, and the second was the Persian

Gulf War of January-February 1991. In both of these cases, the invading nation argued that the conflict was an internal affair outside the jurisdiction of the United Nations. In 1950, the dictator of North Korea, Kim Il-sung, maintained that the purpose of the conflict was to achieve national unification in the face of intolerable provocations from hostile separatist elements in South Korea. In 1990, the dictator of Iraq, Saddam Hussein, maintained that the purpose of the conflict was to achieve national unification in the face of intolerable provocations from hostile separatist elements in Kuwait. The allegation that Iraq's invasion and conquest of Kuwait in August, 1990, constituted an exercise in national unification rested on political circumstances prevailing under the Ottoman Empire, a state organization defunct since 1918. The allegation was considered highly dubious, not to say specious, by most people outside of Iraq. The real reason for the invasion of Kuwait was Iraq's financial problems incurred during the prolonged border war with Iran (1980-1988), which Saddam Hussein hoped to ameliorate by taking over Kuwait's enormous income from petroleum exports. Hussein's reputation as one of the most brutal and repellent dictators in the contemporary world did not help the cause of Iraq. The invasion of Kuwait greatly alarmed Iraq's neighbors in the Middle East, especially the equally oil-rich Saudi Arabia, whose government proposed military action to the United States and other nations for the purpose of ousting the Iraqis from Kuwait.

On August 2, 1990, the day following the Iraqi invasion of Kuwait, the United Nations Security Council called for Iraq to withdraw from Kuwait, and on August 6 it imposed a worldwide ban on trade with Iraq. Hussein responded on August 8 by formally annexing Kuwait. On November 29 the Security Council authorized the use of force against Iraq unless it withdrew its forces from Kuwait by January 15, 1991. Ten or twenty years previously, such resolutions would almost certainly have been impossible owing to opposition by the communist permanent members of the Security Council, Russia and China. But by 1990, the Cold War was in rapid decline, and the superpowers were no longer always being forced into opposition against one another on general ideological principles. Hussein ignored the U.N. demands, continued to build up the Iraqi commitment in Kuwait, and warned that if there was foreign intervention, Iraq's enemies would be annihilated in the "mother of all battles." By January 1991, an Allied coalition of 32 nations, including the United States, Britain, France, Saudi Arabia, Egypt and Syria, had fielded a force of 700,000 combat troops and supporting personnel, of which the U.S. contribution was 540,000. On the night of January 16-17, 1991, Operation Desert Storm launched a massive air offensive against Iraqi military, production and infrastructure targets. After more than a month of intensive bombardment, Operation Desert Saber was commenced on February 24, unleashing an overwhelming ground offensive into Kuwait and southern Iraq. The ground war lasted only four days, within which time the Iraqi presence in Kuwait was completely eliminated. In the wake of the defeat, there were popular uprisings against Saddam Hussein in Iraq, which the dictator put down with considerable difficulty. At this time, there was discussion among the

Allies about pushing onward to a military occupation of Iraq and the removal of the Hussein regime, but the idea was discarded on grounds that it would have exceeded the official U.N. mandate, and in any event, in the face of such disastrous eventualities Hussein would probably soon be overthrown by internal opposition forces. But internal opposition forces had been greatly weakened by Hussein's longstanding policy of physically eliminating anyone who uttered one word of doubt or dissension (a policy previously employed by such notorious twentieth century dictators as Adolf Hitler and Joseph Stalin). Hussein therefore weathered the storm, and remained in control of Iraq until 2003.

Whatever the shortcomings and limitations of the United Nations in terms of lowering the probability of nuclear holocaust and/or of reducing the incidence of localized civil war, on the basis of the Gulf War episode, it could certainly be argued that the U.N.'s existence operates as an effective deterrent against one specific type of conflict: aggression against smaller nations by somewhat larger nations that are still well short of superpower status. The 1991 U.N. intervention against the Iraqi invasion of Kuwait may have provided a cautionary example of what the U.N. is increasingly capable of accomplishing, especially now that the Cold War is fading. If the Iraqi invasion of Kuwait had occurred in 1970 at the height of the Cold War, quite possibly the Soviet Union would have vetoed intervention simply because it was favorable to almost any kind of disruption and destruction in the capitalist world. Of course, it is fully possible that the United States and its NATO allies in Western Europe would have dealt firmly with a hypothetical Iraqi invasion of Kuwait back in 1970 even in the absence of U.N. endorsement—ostensibly to maintain stability in the region for humanitarian reasons, but principally to keep the price of crude oil lower than it would otherwise likely have been. But on the other hand, U.N. endorsement of military intervention endows it with far greater legitimacy than it would otherwise possess. The greater the likelihood of obtaining U.N. endorsement against aggressive actions such as the Iraqi invasion of Kuwait, the more likely it is that military intervention will take place, and consequently the greater will be the level of deterrence against this particular type of aggression. To the people of small nations such as Kuwait, this is definite progress.

Clearly the Gulf War might be held up as a shining example of the progress made possible by the decline of the Cold War and the creation of a "New World Order" under which regional dictators and warlords will no longer be able to operate with impunity, attacking their neighbors under the implicit shield of protection created by the nuclear standoff among the communist and noncommunist superpowers. But there are some discordant elements that must inevitably dim the luster of this achievement. The Gulf War did not get rid of Saddam Hussein, who continued to pose a threat to peace and security both in the Mideast and throughout the rest of the world. There is also the uncongenial fact that although the Hussein regime in Iraq was clearly undemocratic, other regimes in the area, such as that in Kuwait, Saudi Arabia and elsewhere, are essentially quasi-feudal monarchies equally devoid of democratic traditions, institutions and attitudes. A persistent and understandable suspicion exists that the United States and its NATO allies would not have come to the assistance of Kuwait if it had not been for their concern to maintain a high level of competition among Mideast OPEC members in the interest of keeping the price of crude oil supplies relatively low. Beyond this possible venality of the United States and its major European allies, there is unease in many quarters that the world may be on the verge of an oppressive hegemony imposed by the large and powerful nations over the smaller and weaker nations of the world. This unease is made all the greater by the almost incredible ease with which the coalition forces decisively defeated the Iraqi army. Estimates of Iraqi battle deaths range from 8,000 to 100,000, while coalition losses are estimated at around 300. The Gulf War demonstrated the tremendous effectiveness, at least under some circumstances, of the high-tech weaponry possessed in large quantities only by the military superpowers of the world.

During the 1990s, in the wake of the Gulf War, there occurred something approaching a proliferation of U.N. peacekeeping missions. Up to and including 1990, some 17 peacekeeping missions had been mandated by the United Nations. From 1991 through 1999, some 39 additional missions were mandated: 5 in 1991, 4 in 1992, 8 in 1993, 2 in 1994, 4 in 1995, 3 in 1996, 6 in 1997, 3 in 1998 and 4 in 1999. A few of these missions have been unmitigated disasters and very high-profile failures. Although the 1992 mission to war-torn Yugoslavia had an authorized strength of 45,000, that turned out to be completely inadequate to the control of a desperate civil war fueled by ethnic hostilities nurtured over centuries. The outnumbered and outgunned U.N. peacekeepers only managed to survive by staying out of the way of the warring forces; in some cases they were literally held hostage. The humanitarian purposes of the mission went unfulfilled, to say the least. A 1993 mission to Somalia, with an authorized strength of 28,000, was even more disastrous in a public relations sense. World public opinion had been outraged by extensive media coverage, prominently featuring photographs of starving children, of the man-made famine in Somalia caused by worsening civil strife. Once again the strength of the United Nations forces was completely inadequate to the task of disarming the combatants and restoring order. On October 3, 1993, a gun battle in the streets of Mogadishu between a U.S. unit and adherents to Mohammed Farah Aideed, whom the unit was attempting to apprehend, left 18 American soldiers dead and their bodies abused by being dragged through the streets by hostile mobs. Photographic coverage of that tragedy provoked outrage throughout the United States against presumably callous U.N. commanders employing U.S. soldiers as cannon fodder against hopeless odds. According to some authorities, however, the United States unit involved was in fact acting independently and not in accordance with orders issued by the U.N. commander in Mogadishu. Indeed, one of the chronic weaknesses of U.N. peacekeeping missions is that frequently their various national components are inadequately cohesive owing to competing centers of authority. In any event, anyone capable of accepting hard military realities knows that the "zero casualties" principle is completely unrealistic in a hostile environment. Be that as it may, the U.N. mission to Somalia was quickly reduced to immediate humanitarian objectives (as opposed to the restoration of peace), and was fully withdrawn in 1995. World public opinion had created the mission to begin with, and world public opinion also pulled the plug on it when it became apparent that it was going to entail significant losses. Somalia was left to its fate, which predictably enough has been bleak. If Somalia serves any useful purpose at the present time, it is simply as an example of the likely consequences of anarchy.

While it is now generally agreed that United Nations intervention, at force and casualty levels that are politically acceptable, is unlikely to be adequate to quell severe civil strife such as occurred in the former Yugoslavia in 1992, in Somalia in 1993, and in Rwanda in 1995, it is also fairly well accepted that U.N. peacekeeping missions can be a positive factor in less severe cases by placing on the scene an "impartial" military force not pre-committed to one side or the other. Such forces can sometimes appreciably facilitate the achievement of ceasefires and/or political settlements. Among the several "U.N. success stories" are the missions to West New Guinea in 1962, to the Indian-Pakistani border in 1965, to the Sinai Peninsula in 1973, to the Afghanistan-Pakistan border in 1988, to Namibia in 1989, to El Salvador in 1991, to the Iraq-Kuwait border in 1991, and to Cambodia and Mozambique in 1992. So in some specialized cases a U.N. peacekeeping mission can be an effective instrument of peace.

It would be possible go on at great length pondering and debating the question of how much of a contribution, on the whole, the United Nations has made to preserving peace and fostering cooperation in the international sphere. At one extreme are those who assert that the U.N. has been a completely negligible factor in world politics, while at the other extreme are those who assert that it has made a major positive contribution. Obviously the truth lies somewhere in between. It is probably safe to say that the United Nations has made an "appreciable" contribution to peace, although it would probably be excessive to say that it has made an "important" or an "extraordinary" contribution. This level of assessment of the peacekeeping effort of the United Nations is probably applicable also to its "peace-building" effort.

That is to say, the United Nations has made an "appreciable" contribution to the economic and social progress of nations, but it has not made an "important" or "extraordinary" contribution. The economic status of the world, and especially the existence of a large gulf between living standards in the richest and the poorest nations, has already been discussed at some length in Chapters 4-6 above. Just as the U.N. has made a limited contribution to peace and security throughout the world owing to the unwillingness of the member nations to entrust substantial military forces to it, so too it has made a limited contribution to global economic development because of the unwillingness of the member nations to entrust substantial foreign development assistance resources to it. According to the World Bank, official development assistance and official aid made available to developing countries in 1999 was approximately 130 billion current U.S. dollars. The World Bank, through which a substantial part of the current foreign aid flow to the LDCs is channeled, is considered a "specialized agency" of the United Nations, but this is more in the nature of a courtesy gesture than a practical reality. Neither the General Assembly nor the Security Council nor the Secretary-General have any directive control over the World Bank, and the World Bank budget is not included in the United Nations budget. The entire United Nations budget for 1999, including assessed amounts and voluntary contributions, was approximately 10 billion current U.S. dollars. Even if the U.N. were spending its entire budget on economic development (in actual fact it spends only a small fraction of its budget for purposes that have anything to do with economic development), it would not account for a substantial share of the total foreign aid flow—which, according to the argument of Part II above, has clearly been inadequate to get the job done. Another way of putting the U.N. budget into perspective is to compare it with the government budgets of the larger member nations. For example, in 1999, United States federal government outlays were 1,700 billion current dollars, of which 275 billion went to national defense. The total United Nations budget in the latter 1990s was therefore about 0.58 percent of the total U.S. federal government budget (a little over one half of one percent), and was 3.6 percent of the U.S. national defense budget. If the United Nations has not yet "solved world problems," including the problem of global economic inequality, it is not difficult to see why. One cannot construct mansions with the resources appropriate for the construction of shacks.

Not that I wish to be too hard on the United Nations. Questions about the practical effect of the U.N. can be debated endlessly without approaching a meaningful resolution. But there is an important distinction to be drawn between the practical impact of the United Nations and the psychological impact, as well as between the short-term impact and the long-term impact. The fact that the U.N.'s short-term practical impact has not been dramatic does not necessarily mean that it has not been effective in a psychological sense as a symbol of human unity, and that it will not ultimately prove to have been, in the long run, extremely important in a practical sense as well. It could be quite important simply that the United Nations is an existent organization, that it has an impressive headquarters on the East River, that it has a flag, that its "blue helmets" have appeared at many times and in many places over the past half-century, that it represents a foreshadowing of the federal world government that humanity ought to establish, and possibly will establish in the not-distant future. The cumulative psychological impact of this symbol could be decisive. Taking the League of Nations and the United Nations together, their history covers four fifths of the twentieth century. For four fifths of the twentieth century, these organizations have stood as clear indications of humanity's desire for a benign, global political unity that will effectively eliminate the human tragedy and material waste associated with warfare and will raise human civilization to new and commanding heights. In due course, it may be clearly seen that both the League of Nations and the United Nations were instrumental in paving the way toward a genuine, effective world government—the Federal Union of Democratic Nations.

THE EUROPEAN UNION

From its humble beginnings in 1951 as a limited customs union designated the European Coal and Steel Community, at which time it contained only six member nations (Belgium, Germany, France, Italy, Luxembourg, and the Netherlands), the European Union has developed into an extremely important quasi-state political organization encompassing 15 European nations (the original six plus Britain, Spain, Portugal, Sweden, Austria, Denmark, Finland and Ireland). Only Switzerland and Norway, of the Western European nations, are not yet included. Several Eastern European and Balkan nations may eventually join the Union, including the Russian Federation. Of all the regional organizations in the world, it is clearly the most fully advanced, and indeed, it is beginning to strongly resemble the old "United States of Europe" concept long prevalent in the visionary literature on international organization.

Since the origin of the European Union lay in a mere customs union, and a limited one at that, it is tempting to interpret its development as functional cooperation evolving into political unity. There is some truth in this, and certainly the history of the European Union in some respects strengthens the case for world government, as well as providing lessons on how that government should be organized and what it should attempt to accomplish. But it is important not to exaggerate either the degree of support or the usefulness of the lessons. Obviously the European continent during the latter half of the twentieth century has not been an accurate microcosm of the world as a whole as it exists at the present time. As far as the attainment of political unity is concerned, Europe had certain key advantages, including relatively homogeneous economic development and culture. On the other hand, it is important to recognize that Europe also had some significant disadvantages, most prominently the psychological residue from centuries of internal conflict and warfare. It is said that you can only truly hate those whom you know well, and the vicissitudes of history have seen to it that the peoples of the European nations know each other very well. Physical proximity may increase the practical need for cooperation, but it also lays a firmer basis for confrontation and conflict. Especially when viewed in light of what happened in Europe during the first half of the twentieth century, what has been accomplished there during the second half of the twentieth century seems truly remarkable.

The objectives of the European statesmen who founded the European Coal and Steel Community (ECSC) were hardly confined to reaping whatever relatively modest economic benefits may be derived from a customs union for coal and steel products. In actual fact, these economic benefits were quite secondary and incidental. The main purpose was to initiate a process that would eventually lead to a much higher level of political unity within the European continent, for purposes of erecting both practical and psychological barriers against the resumption of the perpetual internecine conflict and warfare that had plagued Europe throughout its history. Those responsible for the concept and design of the ECSC, Jean Monnet and Robert Schuman of France, and the many European statesmen who thereupon implemented it, such as Paul-Henri Spaak of Belgium, Konrad Adenauer of Germany, and many others, had lived through the horrors of both World War I and World War II. On the basis of this personal experience, they were determined to exert every effort toward preventing a recurrence of these catastrophes. Fifty years following the establishment of the ECSC, that intention has been realized to some extent, but certainly not completely. There are a great many people in Europe, as well as throughout the rest of the world, who well remember the past—but have not learned much from it. Consequently the European Union of today can be described only as a "quasi-state" rather than a "full-fledged state." Its peoples think of themselves primarily as French or German or British, and only secondarily, if at all, as "Europeans." They think of themselves far more as citizens of France or Germany or Great Britain rather than as citizens of the European Union. Still, if a Federal Union of Democratic Nations were to be established today, the sense of loyalty to it felt by the people of its various member nations would probably be on a par with the sense of loyalty that Europeans today feel toward the European Union. That would be enough. It would be enough to provide a firm foundation on which to build.

The current form of the European Union was established upon the full implementation on November 1, 1993, of the Treaty on European Union (the Maastricht Treaty). The European Union is composed of a number of separate entities, of which the most important are the European Commission, the Council of Ministers, the European Parliament, and the Court of Justice. The major force within the Union is the European Commission, consisting of 20 commissioners (two from each of the five larger members—Germany, France, Italy, Britain and Spain—and one each from the remaining ten members) and supported by a staff numbering approximately 15,000 (according to the Commission's publicity, this is about the same number of civil servants as employed by a single medium-size European city). It has both legislative and executive responsibilities. Not only does it conceive and draft legislation for submission to the Council of Ministers and the European Parliament, but it also oversees the enforcement of approved EU legislation. The Council of Ministers consists of the ministers of each of the member nations broken down by functional area: for example, one sub-group consists of the finance ministers, another of the education ministers, and so on. The European Parliament consists of 626 delegates, with the distribution of delegates over the member nations in proportion to population. Neither the Council of Ministers nor the European Parliament has the formal authority to revise or veto legislation proposed by the European Commission. However, the Commission is normally responsive to input received from these bodies on proposed legislation. It is responsive to the Parliament since the Parliament possesses the formal authority to dismiss the Commission as a whole (although so far this has never happened), and it must also approve the President of the Commission who, once approved, selects the other 19 commissioners. As for the Council of Ministers, if opposition to legislation among this group is sufficiently intense, the implementation of the legislation could conceivably lead to the departure of some nations from the Union (this also has not happened so far). Assuming legislation is approved by all three bodies (the Commission, the Council and the Parliament) it can still be challenged by member nations, organizations or individuals before the Court of Justice. Although called a "treaty," the Treaty on European Union is in some respects the equivalent of a constitution. Among other things, it upholds the principle of subsidiarity (any function that can be successfully handled at a lower level of government should be handled by that lower level), and it is emphatic about human rights. "Constitutional" challenges to Union legislation, as well as other disputes, are decided by the Court of Justice.

Considering the extremely ambitious nature of the EU agenda, it is not surprising that the Court of Justice is quite a busy place. Although the customs union and the efforts toward homogenization and unification of the entire internal market have had an extremely beneficial effect on the material prosperity of most Europeans, not every European has benefited from the transformations. To begin with, whenever and wherever customs duties and other trade restrictions are lowered, at least a few of the industries exposed to greater foreign competition go into serious decline. Large numbers of European workers working in the declining industries have lost their employment over the years that the Common Market has functioned, and by no means all of them have been re-hired by the rising industries. Agriculture has been a particularly difficult problem area because practically every advanced industrialized nation, for fear of becoming unduly dependent on foreign food sources, subsidizes or otherwise protects its farmers. As the traditional protections and guarantees are phased out, many farmers are financially injured, often to the point of bankruptcy. In the process of homogenizing innumerable commercial rules and regulations, as well as a multitude of social, educational and other institutions and legislation, a great many Europeans have been at the least inconvenienced and at the most completely ruined.

All this leads periodically to ugly street protests and demonstrations. The intensity of the opposition is all the greater because in the view of those who have lost out in the process, all these intolerable aggravations and impositions are owing to the misguided and malevolent machinations of nasty foreigners. Even among the large majority of the population that has been materially benefited by the European Union's policies, there are vague anxieties and apprehensions, no less acute for being hazy and indistinct, that somehow one's own national identity and sovereignty will be completely submerged and lost, and that at some point in the future, by gradual, almost unnoticeable stages, the European Union will take on the form of a malignant tyranny, enforced not so much by police truncheons as by the sheer weight of its own vast bureaucracy. To the rest of the world unfamiliar with the details of its history and current status, the European Union sometimes appears to be a blandly monolithic expression of a unified public will. But the fact is that the development of the European Union has been accompanied by problems and controversies every step of the way.

Not too much confidence should be placed, therefore, in the predictions of some to the effect that the European Union will soon be a United States of Europe in no fundamental respect different from its cousin across the North Atlantic Ocean, the United States of America. This could eventually happen, of course, but there is still a long distance between the EU and a potential USE (United States of Europe) of the future. Our interest in the future direction of the European Union, however, is only incidental to our interest in international organization at the global level. What bearing, if any, does the European Union have on the prospects for a Federal Union of Democratic Nations? What are the positive indications from the EU experience, and what are the negative indications?

Looking first at the positive side, the European Union has clearly established that even very large and powerful nations with long, proud traditions of absolute independence may be induced to surrender a substantial proportion of their autonomy and sovereignty when there exist compelling economic and political reasons for doing so. Many of the nations composing today's European Union have long histories of bitter enmity, punctuated at regular intervals by desperate and devastating warfare. This tortured history extends up to the recent past. Many living Europeans have vivid and painful memories of the Second World War. If we were to consider all the pairwise combinations of nations in a potential world state of the future, few of these pairs would have the same difficult past history as, say, France and Germany or Britain and Ireland. It requires geographical proximity to engender the worst extremes of hatred and enmity, and each particular nation in the world is sufficiently remote from most other nations that these extremes have not been realized. Another positive consideration is that the economic success of nations within a customs union operates as a powerful incentive to nations outside the union to join it. By virtue of the English Channel and its overseas Commonwealth, Britain has traditionally thought of itself as quite separate and distinct from "continental Europe." But this traditional detachment was eventually overcome (in 1973) simply because it was costing too much in terms of foregone economic prosperity. One of the most urgent projects of the Federal Union of Democratic Nations in its early decades, second only to the World Economic Equalization Program, would be the development of a very large, open and unimpeded free trade area among the member nations. Just as Britain was eventually persuaded to join the European Union for economic reasons, hopefully those nations initially declining to join the Federal Union will eventually be persuaded to join for the same reasons.

Turning to the negative side, we first take note of the fact that from the beginnings of the European Union, the economic status of its component nations has been relatively homogeneous. The difference in per capita income between the richest member nations of the European Union and the poorest member nations has always been a small fraction of the difference between the richest nations of the First World and the poorest nations of the Third World. In a word, the European Union never confronted the very difficult economic impediment to political union that federal world government on a global basis has always confronted, and continues to confront. In addition, throughout the development era of the European Union its member nations have been relatively homogeneous ideologically, politically and culturally. Its membership has included no communist nations, although several ex-communist nations may join it in the future. Also its membership included no anti-democratic fascist nations (the Franco regime in Spain was defunct as of Spain's entry into the European Union in 1986). Apart from several different languages, Western Europe has been extremely homogeneous in terms of culture: in literature, art, and music. The proposed Federal Union of Democratic Nations, in contrast, would have to cope with a great deal more diversity. To cite one very important example, the Federal Union would have to be flexible enough to include the People's Republic of China even though this nation still formally subscribes to communism and is largely controlled by its communist party elite.

Owing to the high level of economic development and homogeneity among its member nations, the European Union has been very active—not to say intrusive—in certain areas that should not even be contemplated by the Federal Union of Democratic Nations until it has also achieved, after many decades, a high level of economic development and homogeneity among its member nations. Much of the European Union's effort has been focused on establishing a completely uniform regulatory and socioeconomic environment for business enterprise. This has gone well beyond simply establishing a free trade area by eliminating tariffs, import quotas and the like. It has also involved a great deal of paternalistic consumer protection and worker rights legislation, among many other things. This has generated a considerable amount of resentment and opposition, as evidenced by the narrow margin by which the 1992 Maastricht Treaty was approved. The Federal Union of Democratic Nations, assuming it is established, would be ill-advised to pursue the same kind of policies that the European Union has pursued. The main thing is the development of psychological unity, followed by the development of basic comparability in material living standards. Any effort to achieve a high level of regulatory and socioeconomic uniformity among all the nations of the Federal Union would probably lead to so many withdrawals that the Union would collapse. As inspiring as has been the example set by the European Union, one must recognize that far more would be at stake in the Federal Union. The European Union, as its name indicates, is only a regional association. Even if it achieves the same level of internal unity as that presently existing within the United States of America, so that it would be a legitimate "United States of Europe," this would just mean that there would be one more superpower in the world. Europeans would be spared any further "European wars" among themselves—which is certainly progress. But if nothing else in the world changes, there would still be a significant threat of "world wars" in which the members of the European Union might suffer as much—or more—as they did in their internecine wars of the past. A high level of security against world war will only be attained through worldwide political unity. This is the primary goal, and matters involving regulatory and socioeconomic uniformity among the member nations can wait until later.

On the negative side also is that despite several decades of development, the European Union is still far short of the authentic, legitimate statehood envisioned for the Federal Union of Democratic Nations. The EU has gone a remarkable way toward a unified economy, but meaningful political unification is still quite a long way off. The Union's equivalent to the legislative branch of government, i.e., the European Parliament, although directly elected since 1979, still cannot promulgate legislation. Effective power in the European Union is exercised by a 20-member Commission which makes legislation and determines policies. The Commission's legislation and policies do not require approval by the Parliament, although presumably if there were strong opposition in the Parliament they would be modified. The Parliament has the power to dismiss the entire Commission, although this power has never been exercised. The European Union, as such, cannot levy mandatory taxes on member states or their populations, nor does it directly control either a military force or a police force of its own. Although many of the Western European nations comprising the European Union are members of the NATO alliance, their military forces are still very much under the independent control of the various national governments. Considering the amount of dissension and protest that certain of the Union's policies have evoked in some of its member nations, it is rather remarkable how much effective power the Union apparently exercises, despite its lack of any military or police power. There is no military or police deterrent to member nations simply ignoring Union policies. The sole deterrent to such behavior is the threat that the recalcitrant nation will be expelled from the Union and will no longer partake of the economic benefits membership entails. Apparently this can be a very strong deterrent.

In contrast to the European Union, the proposed Federal Union of Democratic Nations would constitute a genuine state organization with a clearly defined legislative branch, executive branch and judicial branch, all three branches being directly elected by the population of the Federal Union. It would have well-defined state powers—albeit of a limited nature. That is, it would possess the power of taxation, although this power would be confined to a relatively small percentage of the national income of the member nations. It would also exercise direct control over an appreciable military force armed with both conventional and nuclear weapons—although this power would be counterbalanced by the right of member nations to maintain independent military forces of their own, armed with nuclear as well as conventional weapons. The idea would be to make the Federal Union, from the moment of its foundation, a force to be reckoned with in international politics—a "power" but not a "superpower." If the path of development is smooth, and trust, faith and confidence in the benign nature of this political organization grows, the "superpowers" of today (in a military sense) will evolve toward mere "powers" as they gradually disarm. The very long-term goal would be such a high degree of trust, faith and confidence in the world government that each national government would be satisfied with a minimal military capacity under its direct control.

In the eyes of some international relations analysts, the European Union is an archetypical example of functional cooperation evolving into political unity. Functional cooperation is embodied in a wide range of international agreements and organizations ranging from regional groupings such as the Organization of American States (OAS) and the Organization of African Unity (OAU) to special purpose associations such as the Universal Postal Union (UPU), the International Telecommunications Union (ITU), the International Standardization Organization (ISO), the International Civil Aviation Organization (ICAO), and many others. In contrast to alliances, these agreements and organizations have important purposes other than military security, and in contrast to treaties, they are ongoing operations (albeit usually founded on a charter known as a "treaty") intended to deal with a succession of issues as they arise. Largely oriented to the facilitation of international interchange (communications, transportation, investment, trade and migration), a great many functional cooperation organizations are deemed specialized agencies within the United Nations. But most of these specialized agencies are highly autonomous in practice. In fact, many of them long predated the establishment of the United Nations.

As the processes of globalization proceed, more and more international interchange is taking place, and functional cooperation among nations is increasing. No doubt there is some advance in mutual toleration and respect whenever people from different nations work together on a common project with a common aim. In this sense, the advance of functional cooperation is creating conditions favorable to the foundation of a world government. But too often the relationship between functional cooperation and political unity is exaggerated. It is often speculated that functional cooperation might proceed to a point where world government would become automatic—even "inevitable." This is a dubious speculation. There was a great deal of functional cooperation in the world back in the nineteenth century, prior to the disastrous warfare of the first half of the twentieth century. For example, the Universal Postal Union was established by the Treaty of Berne in 1874. The UPU did not prevent World War I, it did not prevent World War II, and it did not prevent the Cold War that might easily have escalated into World War III. One must recall that functional cooperation is "forced" upon nations: there simply *must* be standardized procedures for dealing with the postal mail, telecommunications, air travel, merchant shipping and so on. In the negotiations leading to these standardized procedures, there is much room for friction and disagreement. Often agreement on technical matters cannot be reached despite protracted and laborious deliberations. Despite the efforts of the International Standardization Organization, for example, the United States and several other nations have not yet adopted the metric system. Despite the efforts of the International Telecommunications Union, there are still three different color television standards in use throughout the world (the American

NTSC, the German PAL, and the French SECAM): the adoption of multiple color television standards was necessitated by the fact that consensus was made impossible by the conflicting economic interests of the major negotiating parties. There are numerous other instances of no agreements being reached at all, or of certain nations declining to participate in certain agreements. But even after they have approved them, many nations participating in functional cooperation agreements feel aggrieved and oppressed by them—feel that the agreements have been "forced" upon them by the more powerful nations. At the same time, these "more powerful" nations quite likely are not entirely happy with the agreements either. Human beings possess endless propensities toward disagreement and disputation, even on relatively abstract and trivial issues. The situation is that much worse when the issues are both relevant and important. The fact that many functional cooperation agreements have been reached under the auspices of international organizations does not necessarily mean that the agreements were reached amicably and that they are being implemented cheerfully by all nations subscribing to them.

Of all the factors impeding the full flowering of functional cooperation in the contemporary world, probably the single most important has always been, and continues to be, the economic gap. If there is a large gap in the material living standards between two nations, what is optimal policy and procedure in one nation is likely to be quite a bit different from optimal policy and procedure in the other nation. This holds true both of completely domestic issues and of issues relating to international interchange. But a single set of policies and procedures relating to international interchange must be determined by all nations. To some extent, working together on a common project fosters mutual toleration and respect, but at the same time working on a common project can foster considerable mutual irritation and hostility—especially when the attitudes and preferences of the participants vary substantially. The net effect, balancing together the tendency toward mutual toleration and respect and the countervailing tendency toward mutual irritation and hostility, might be fairly negligible. Therefore, the advance of functional cooperation does not necessarily mean that a firm foundation is being laid for world government.

The existence of a large and increasing amount of functional cooperation in the contemporary world most likely, on the whole, augments the case that world government is both feasible and desirable. But the principal support probably does not lie in the dubious proposition that functional cooperation will tend gradually to evolve into political unity. Rather the main support is to be found in the likelihood that a functioning world government would enhance the efficiency and effectiveness of functional cooperation at the global level. If such existing organizations as the International Telecommunications Union, the International Maritime Organization, the World Meteorological Organization and the World Intellectual Property Organization, and so on and so forth, were divisions within the executive branch of a supernational federation among whose members were counted the large majority of the nations of the world, then quite likely they would be able to pursue their respective missions more comprehensively and successfully than they are at present. Existing functional cooperation agreements could quite possibly be broadened and deepened, and given the force of law, so that member nations could not disregard these agreements with impunity whenever it suited them. On the other hand, one must not become overly enthusiastic about the prospect of better functional cooperation owing to more effective enforcement of the majority will. One must always keep in mind that during its first few decades especially, the Federal Union of Democratic Nations would be a fairly fragile political organization. Quite likely many important nations will be observing the experiment dubiously, in a state of mind that would facilitate "jumping ship," so to speak, upon what might be deemed, by an impartial observer, rather modest provocation.

The issue of functional cooperation versus political unity is similar to the issue of social homogeneity versus political unity in having a "chicken or the egg" dimension. It was argued early in this book that the familiar argument that social homogeneity among the nations must precede the formation of a world government is logically equivalent to the argument (in response to the query: "Which came first—the chicken or the egg?") that since chickens come out of eggs, the egg came first. The problem with the argument is that it is also true that eggs come out of chickens. In actual fact, the chicken-egg-chicken progression has proceeded in a certain evolutionary direction over a prolonged period of time. Such a process may also hold true of social homogeneity (or functional cooperation) versus political unity. Functional cooperation is closely correlated with social homogeneity: the more there is of one, the more there will be of the other. A rise in functional cooperation at the international level increases political unity at the international level (in terms of the effectiveness of the existing United Nations or the potential Federal Union of Democratic Nations), and a rise in political unity at the international level increases functional cooperation at the international level. The causative process here is simultaneous and interactive, and the question "Which came first?" is ludicrously illogical. If the United Nations of today is succeeded in the future by a Federal Union of Democratic Nations (especially if the Federal Union is supplemented by the recommended World Economic Equalization Program), this beneficial process would be faster, more reliable, and far less likely to be derailed—perhaps disastrously derailed—by disruptive unforeseen eventualities.

9

TAKING THE NEXT STEP

Almost all of us agree that government, as a general concept, is a good thing. But if government is a good thing at the local level, and government is also a good thing at the regional level, and government is also a good thing at the national level, the question arises: Why is government *not* also a good thing at the international level? The answer typically given to this query is that the nations of the contemporary world are far too diverse and heterogeneous to form a stable supernational government, i.e., a world government. Were they ever to join forces in a single political entity, the differences between the nations would soon generate devastating civil war and the dissolution of the union. The only way by which this outcome could be avoided would be through endowing the world government with such overwhelming military and police power that it would quickly degenerate into an horrific totalitarian tyranny. Humanity is sufficiently sensible to perceive these inescapable hazards of world government, and therefore refuses to establish one. Albeit this answer is widely accepted at the present time, it is an unsatisfactory and inadequate answer.

To begin with, if the differences among the nations are indeed such as to generate irresistible pressures toward violent conflict if the nations are united in a world government, then how is it that these same differences will *not* generate irresistible pressures toward violent conflict in the absence of a world government? If it is proposed that the common sense and good judgment of humanity will keep violent conflict to an acceptable minimum under the sovereign nation-state system, than why cannot this same common sense and good judgment of humanity also keep violent conflict to an acceptable minimum if the nation-state system is supplemented by a supernational federation? The answer is that the common sense and good judgment of humanity *can* keep violent conflict to an acceptable minimum within a world in which both a world government and the national governments are active participants in the political life of humanity—*if* that world government possesses the appropriate amount of power and authority: not too much and not too little. The conventional dismissal of the world government possibility on grounds of excessive differences among the nations is based on a misperception that the supernational government must necessarily be an extremely strong and unified political entity. But a supernational federation does not have to be this strong and unified in order to make a meaningful and valuable contribution to the further progress of human civilization.

The Federal Union of Democratic Nations proposed in this book represents a practical, viable, workable blueprint for world government. This political organization would have the "look and feel" of a genuine state: a legislative branch, an executive branch, a judicial branch, an administrative bureaucracy, powers of taxation, an armed force under its direct control, a flag, an anthem, a capital city, and offices in the capital cities of all the member nations. Owing to direct democratic election of the highest officials of all three branches of government, it would possess a high level of prima facie legitimacy and would be both conceptually and practically very much distinct from the national governments of the member nations.

At the same time, there would be appropriate limitations on the Federal Union to prevent it from evolving into a totalitarian regime. There would be strict limitations on its taxation authority, and these limitations would guarantee that neither its military establishment nor its bureaucratic apparatus becomes excessively large. Member nations would retain the right to peacefully withdraw from the Union at any time and at their own unilateral discretion. The right to secession would be supported by each nation's right to maintain whatever military forces under its direct control that it deems necessary. The national governments would most definitely *not* be disarmed as a result of the foundation of this type of limited world government. Above all else as a psychologically based political impediment to world government is the image harbored by so many among the various national populations that if a world government were established, their nations would be disarmed and helpless to defend themselves against the intolerable impositions of the rest of the world. But it is perfectly possible to set up a meaningful world government that is nevertheless sufficiently limited that there would be no serious possibility of this nightmarish outcome.

Human history, of course, has by no means been smoothly linear, a succession of tiny, imperceptible evolutionary changes no one of which stands out and commands attention. If this had been the case, the history books would either be empty or so boring that no one would care to read them. In actual fact, the forward progress of humanity has been composed of a series of discretely large, observable events ("steps"), each one of sufficient importance for contemporary chroniclers to record and later historians to study. It goes without saying that much of human history is a bleak recitation of folly, misfortune, tragedy and disaster. Two steps forward seem normally to have been immediately followed by one step backward—and in some cases the "one step backward" was so large as to virtually eliminate the progress made by the two steps forward. But at the same time it seems obvious that on the whole there has been much progress: most of humanity today is appreciably better off than most of humanity was in ancient times. True, there have been myriad wars—but these wars have ended and peace resumed. True, many violent revolutions have led to disappointing outcomes in the short term, but their long-term effects have been positive. For example, the French Revolution of 1789 was followed by the Jacobin Terror, that was followed by the Napoleonic dictatorship, and that was followed by the Bourbon restoration. Nevertheless, most would agree that the French Revolution, by putting to rest the notion of hereditary privilege and absolute monarchy, and by exalting the rights and dignity of mankind, had a very positive effect in the long term for both France and the rest of the world.

My point is not that the setting up of a world government will necessarily involve violence, and that in this case the ends justify the means. Even the most adamant skeptics of world government are likely to speculate that if an unlimited nuclear world war were to occur, the survivors might well be sympathetic to world government. I myself put no stock whatsoever in this chilling scenario. If an unlimited nuclear world war were to occur, I think it far more likely that the desperate and embittered survivors, having little left to lose, would go on squabbling and battling and killing one another unto the extinction of the species. My point is rather that we cannot expect world government to "evolve" into existence in such a gradual and unnoticeable manner that we will wake up one morning and suddenly realize that it does indeed exist. Some sort of a discretely large, observable event will have to occur: a "step" will have to be taken. The argument of this book is that the appropriate next step in the political evolution of human civilization would be the foundation of a world state along the lines of the Federal Union of Democratic Nations—and that the appropriate time to take this step is now.

In this final chapter, I will endeavor to draw together various strands of the case that some form of limited world government along the lines of the Federal Union of Democratic Nations, but possibly using some other name and possibly differing in various minor institutional and organizational details, is in fact the appropriate next step in the political evolution of human civilization. But I will endeavor to avoid simply reviewing and/or summarizing what has gone before. A certain amount of repetition has been unavoidable in this book for the same reason that it is necessary to use a jackhammer to break through thick concrete: faulty preconceptions and misconceptions concerning the necessary characteristics of world government are so widespread and so deeply entrenched throughout the world today that they can only be successfully challenged by means of frequent reiteration of the key point that there would be considerable value in a *limited* world government. Just as a jackhammer eventually breaks through concrete by means of administering numerous repeated strikes, so too I am hoping to eventually break through the encrusted prejudice against world government by means of numerous reiterations of the fundamental point that a properly designed limited world government can make an appreciable contribution to the evolutionary development of global governance without being either a militarily omnipotent police state or a giant, suffocating bureaucracy. But while a considerable amount of repetition of this fundamental point has been necessary, I do not want to go over the same ground any more than is necessary. I will endeavor, therefore, to keep to a minimum the amount of straightforward review and summarization contained in this final chapter.

Instead of review and summarization, I want to deepen and extend the case for world government by means of a thorough analysis and critical evaluation of three skeptical questions often put to advocates of world government. Of course, these three specific questions by no means constitute an exhaustive list of skeptical questions concerning world government. But they provide a convenient starting point for addressing several fundamental dimensions of the overall question of whether or not world government would be desirable at the present point in the historical development of global human civilization. These questions are today normally posed as rhetorical questions: that is to say, the poser is not interested in the answers because he or she believes that there is in fact no effective answer to be made to any of these questions, and that this situation is so well known and widely accepted among intelligent and informed people that there is no point in listening to and thinking about whatever the world government advocate might offer as a response. Hopefully in the future the responses to be made to these questions will not simply be ignored but will be seriously pondered by many people. This remains to be seen. The three questions are as follows:

- First, is it not obvious that the concept of world government is a utopian delusion fully analogous to the innumerable impractical and borderline preposterous schemes for social improvement put forward by hordes of naive enthusiasts throughout the ages?
- Second, is it not obvious that the risks of establishing a world government are far larger than the risks of maintaining the status quo, especially now that the possibilities for benign global governance—without incurring the costs of an oppressive, bureaucratic global government—are manifestly increasing by leaps and bounds?
- Third, is it not obvious that whatever might be put forward as the logical and rational case for world government, that world government is nevertheless impossible because there is simply no conceivable way that we can go from the world as it is today to a world government within the foreseeable future?

My answer is that *none* of these three propositions is "obvious." Each of these questions will be considered respectively in the following three sections of this chapter. First, I will argue that the "utopian" charge can be characterized as nothing less than a despicable smear, and that a world government of the limited nature under consideration in this book is no more utopian at the present time than was the notion of establishing a democratic republic on the North American continent at the time of the foundation of the United States of America in 1788. Second, I will argue that the risks of establishing a world government at this time are considerably less than the risks of not establishing a world government. Third, I will argue that the belief that world government is simply impossible regardless of the rational pros and cons is tantamount to the psychoneurotic condition of hysterical paralysis, under which a person is convinced that he or she is incapable of walking even though no physical condition exists that would make it impossible for him or her to walk.

The basis of the responses provided to these questions, however, will not be the concept of world government "in general," but rather the specific proposal under consideration herein for a limited world government according to the specifications of the Federal Union of Democratic Nations. I do *not* claim that persuasive responses to these questions are possible if it is a question of the conventional world government proposal according to which the world government would be militarily omnipotent and otherwise unlimited and unrestricted in its operations. However, I *do* most certainly claim that persuasive responses to these questions are indeed possible if the frame of reference is a *limited* world government such as the Federal Union of Democratic Nations.

THE UTOPIAN SMEAR

In the past, the world government concept has routinely been dismissed as a "utopian" proposal since it supposedly proposes an ideal condition of perfect stability, serenity and bliss—a condition that is, to every reasonable person, manifestly impossible owing to unavoidable constraints imposed by the limitless desires and aspirations of human nature in conjunction with the limited resources provided by the natural environment. Such trite, banal and hackneyed dismissals have continued on to the present time, and are so familiar to all of us as to constitute a recognizable cliché. But no reasonable proponent of world government has ever said that such a government would produce "an ideal condition of perfect stability, serenity and bliss." This is because all reasonable proponents of world government are quite well aware of these "unavoidable constraints." All that they say is that the world with a world government would be *better* than the world without a world government: it would be more secure and more prosperous. They are not saying that the world with a world government would attain such Olympian heights of security and prosperity as are only possible in the human imagination.

To dismiss the world government concept on the basis that it is allegedly a "utopian" concept constitutes an example of tendentious terminology. "Tendentious terminology" may be defined as application of a loaded word or phrase to a certain concept or proposal in an effort to derail and terminate serious, focused consideration of it. Illuminating examples of the tendentious terminology strategy might occur in the context of ideological disputations over the relative merits of capitalism versus socialism. A proponent of the capitalist economic system might habitually employ the term "entrepreneur" (or even more obviously, "self-made entrepreneur") as a synonym for "capitalist," while a proponent of the socialist economic system might habitually employ the term "rentier" (or even more obviously, "parasitical rentier") as a synonym for "capitalist." Obviously the employment of such loaded terms for "capitalist" would be unacceptable in a serious professional discussion of the relative merits of capitalism versus socialism. Professional discussions are in fact often polemical in nature, but even if they are polemical, ideally they rely far more on coherent argumentation based on factual evidence and sound logic than they do on propagandistic appeals to prejudice and preconception. Given that the objective is to put forward an objectively, intellectually persuasive argument either to the effect that the typical capitalist under capitalism earns his income by means of productive contributions (enterprise management, establishment of new enterprises, innovation, discovery, risk-taking, saving, etc.) or to the effect that the typical capitalist under capitalism receives unearned income (equivalent to "Ricardian rent" in classical economics), use of either one of these terms—"entrepreneur" by a proponent of capitalism or "rentier" by a proponent of socialism—would constitute a case of assuming that which is to be proved. However successful they might be as propaganda, these terms are intellectually disreputable.

Tendentious terminology would enter the debate between a proponent of world government and an opponent of world government as soon as words such as "utopian" or "anarchic" are employed. The opponent might say: "Your proposal for a world government is a utopian fantasy. Its establishment and operation would require the peoples of the nations to act contrary to their own personal self-interest and their national interest. Any sensible person can see that this will never happen." To this the proponent might reply: "So you are advocating the continuation of the anarchic system currently operative at the international level? But history has proven time and time again that unless there exists some higher authority over private individuals and nations, they will continue to do bloody battle with each other indefinitely. What is utopian is not in fact world government, but the notion that humanity will forever avoid the catastrophe of nuclear war in the absence of world government. In actual fact, world government is desirable in terms of both the personal self-interest of private individuals and the national interest of all the nations of the world. Any sensible person can see the truth of this—assuming he or she can for a moment rise above the nationalistic misconceptions purveyed by the media and the educational system." It should be apparent that neither of these quotations manifests serious, legitimate argumentation. The opponent of world government does not offer any substantive evidence that world government is undesirable, and the proponent does not offer any substantive evidence that world government is desirable. Both sides are merely begging the question by employing loaded, propagandistic terms that, so to speak, "assume that which is to be proved."

In coining the word "Utopia" as the title of his speculative work on the ideal society, published in 1516, Thomas More called upon his classical education in the Greek language. The word is derived from the Greek words *ou*, meaning "not" or "no," and *topos*, meaning "place": thus "utopia" is "no place." It can also mean "good place" since the Greek word *eu*, meaning "good," is pronounced the same as *ou*. More's *Utopia* was published at the height of the era of European expansion, just following the discovery of the Americas, during which travelers' accounts of faraway lands and peoples in the tradition of *The Travels of Marco Polo* were extremely popular. Even those accounts of the period based on fact tended to be somewhat fanciful and inaccurate, but many were purely fictional, intended only as entertainment and/or instruction. In this latter category belongs More's work. Students of utopian thought are still divided on the question whether More personally approved of all or most of the various laws, processes and customs of the people living on the remote island Utopia, or whether he was ridiculing all or most of them as patently preposterous and impracticable. The ambiguous tone of the work, and its presentation as a work of fiction rather than a serious treatise on social improvement, may have been intentional. One must recall that in More's time, the "wrong" kind of thinking might easily lead to execution for heresy, treason, or both.

More's *Utopia* is often perceived as a modern outgrowth of and variation on the ancient myth of a "millennial era" of perfect peace, justice, harmony and happiness: the "earthly paradise" as described (in its Christian incarnation) in John the Divine's Revelations 20, and in St. Augustine's *The City of God*. But there is an important distinction between the "utopian society" and the "earthly paradise," just as there is between the "earthly paradise" and the "heavenly paradise." In the "heavenly paradise"—to which the souls of the just will allegedly ascend following the deaths of their material bodies—there is no suffering or death whatsoever, and each individual soul lives eternally in perfect happiness. In the "earthly paradise," on the other hand, death remains as the terminal point of each individual's earthly existence, but any suffering would be very minor and confined only to the inevitable infirmities of old age. Moreover, the individual would be fortified in coping with these infirmities by the assured knowledge that once the gate of death has been passed through, he or she will resume, in the heavenly paradise, a very pleasant existence that will *not* ultimately be terminated by death. The inhabitants of the utopian societies imagined by More and numerous other contributors to this literature are far from achieving the continual beatific euphoria and unadulterated bliss experienced by the lucky inhabitants of either the earthly paradise or the heavenly paradise. Relative to what could be imagined of a truly perfect world free from every conceivable problem and care, the utopian societies fall far short. In the theoretical and applied literature on mathematical optimization, a distinction is made between "unconstrained optimization" and "constrained optimization." In constrained optimization, the decision variables must satisfy certain constraints, while in unconstrained optimization there are no constraints. Of course, the value achieved by the criterion variable will be lower under constrained optimization than it would be under an equivalent unconstrained optimization problem. The writers of the utopian literature, from Thomas More on down, are proposing solutions to the *constrained* optimization problem. Their principles of social organization are intended to maximize social welfare subject to various constraints imposed by the innate and unavoidable physical, intellectual and moral limitations of individual human beings. Or, perhaps, some of them are ridiculing proposed solutions of others that they themselves believe to be more or less sub-optimal—perhaps drastically sub-optimal.

Certain characteristics distinguish utopian literature from the broader category of social improvement literature. Utopian literature is set within an explicitly fictional framework, it envisions a society very different from, and very superior to, the real-world society familiar to the authors and their readers, and it
sets forth a very wide range of proposed improvements across the board of social
organization, encompassing economic production and distribution, political institutions and practices, and social customs and traditions. Amidst this welter of
ideas, set in the context of a fictional fantasy, there are at least some that will no
doubt seem silly and preposterous to any given reader—as distinctly unpromising avenues of improvement. This may be what is responsible for the primary
denotation of the term "utopian" today: as any completely impractical, idealistic
scheme for social and political reform. But it should be recognized and appreciated that a great many of the proposed reforms in the works of utopian authors,
reforms that seemed absurd when first proposed, have indeed become firmly
established in modern societies. Amidst a great deal of chaff in utopian writings,
there has been quite a lot of what turned out to be wheat.

Illustrations of these points may be found in the original utopian work: Thomas More's *Utopia*. That the lives of the inhabitants of the imaginary island of
Utopia are far from the imaginable ideal may be deduced from the following
(among many other things): (1) serious offenses against the law are dealt with by
capital punishment or enslavement; (2) slaves are essential to the operation of
the economy because they do all the menial, unpleasant work that citizens in
good standing abhor, and a steady supply of slaves is assured by means of convictions for crimes, purchases from abroad, and prisoners of war; (3) although
themselves inclined toward peace, the citizens of Utopia are often forced to wage
war with foreign nations—but if possible they hire armies of mercenaries to fight
these wars for them. As an example of a somewhat zany-seeming social custom
supported by law, on More's island of Utopia a prospective bride and bride-
groom are required to inspect each other in the nude prior to marriage. (Considering the prevalence of pre-marital sex in contemporary society, perhaps this
proposal was not as off-target as it might at first seem.) That there is a good deal
of sensible thought ("wheat") in utopian writing amidst the dubious thought
("chaff") is illustrated in More's *Utopia* by the following. Among the numerous
minor details (such as nude pre-marital inspections), there are three especially
important characteristics of the proposed utopian society: (1) a very high level of
diversity in religious beliefs, and a very high level of religious toleration; (2)
democratic election of public officials instead of their appointment by hereditary
monarchs; (3) the absence of an economic market and a high level of economic
egalitarianism (workshops would deliver their products to central warehouses
from which citizens would take reasonable and appropriate amounts for their
own use). Of these three ideas, only the last would be confidently dismissed by
most people today as clearly impractical. In the modern world, religious toleration is preached loudly and widely, although its actual practice often leaves
something to be desired. Many nations in the world today have implemented

highly democratic election of key public officials, and the ideology of democracy has become so dominant throughout the world that the less-democratic nations are defensive rather than offensive. That is, instead of denouncing democracy they claim their current political practices achieve the "essence" or the "essential aim" of political democracy, which is governance "in the interests" of the general public—if not always "according to their desires."

Even with respect to More's specification of socialist egalitarianism on the island of Utopia, this is not so much at variance with present-day preferences as it might at first seem. At the present time, the concepts of socialism and egalitarianism are in a bad odor with a large proportion of the world's population owing to certain disastrous experiences of the twentieth century such as the Great Terror of the 1930s in the Soviet Union under Joseph Stalin and the Cultural Revolution of the 1960s in the People's Republic of China under Mao Tsetung. But few historians familiar with these experiences would argue that they were solely, or even mainly, the outgrowths of the fundamental concept of socialism (that capital property used in production, such as plant and machinery, should be publicly owned) or of the fundamental concept of egalitarianism (that there should be a certain amount of public intervention in socioeconomic processes to reduce the degree of economic inequality). Historians might agree that the concepts of socialism and egalitarianism might be taken to extremes and thereby cause harm; but this does not necessarily mean that the concepts themselves, if interpreted and implemented properly (i.e., according to the "happy medium" principle), cannot be socially beneficial. If we compare Britain today with Britain as it was in the time of Thomas More, there is a great deal more government ownership of capital (in the form of roads, schools, hospitals, as well as some types of business enterprise) and there is also a great deal more economic equality brought about by public intervention in socioeconomic processes. Clearly, much of what More proposed of an ideal society as manifested by conditions in his fictional Utopia, has indeed been realized—and the world is a better place for it.

One way to look at utopian writing is that it is equivalent to "brainstorming": it sets out a wide array of possible reforms and improvements without subjecting each and every one of them to careful, critical consideration. The purpose of brainstorming is to get a lot of ideas quickly "on the table," so to speak, with the intention of examining each one of them more carefully later on. It is not unusual for many of the ideas produced during brainstorming sessions to be unsound, but this does not preclude others from being sound and valuable. It is also a misconception that utopian speculations are produced solely by ivory-tower academics with little or no experience of the practical business of life. Thomas More, for example, pursued a successful career as an English court official during the reign of Henry VIII, and rose to the exalted position of Lord Chancellor of England, somewhat akin to King Henry's second-in-command. He did, however, demonstrate a somewhat impractical side by refusing to comply, on grounds of conscience, with the Act of Supremacy by which English subjects were enjoined to recognize Henry VIII's authority over the Pope—an error in judgment with which More paid with his life. He was beheaded in the Tower of London in 1535. (Conceivably this was *not* an error in judgment on More's part. It would not have been an error in judgment, certainly, if refusal to accept the Act of Supremacy gained More's soul entry into the heavenly paradise—as More himself clearly hoped that it would.)

Another good example of a "utopian concept" that was later realized in the real world is provided by the thinking of Robert Owen. In Karl Marx and Friedrich Engels's 1848 "pamphlet that changed the world," *The Communist Manifesto*, Owen was lumped together with Charles Fourier and the Comte de Saint-Simon (Claude Henri de Rouvroy) as a dreamy "utopian socialist." The impractical dreaming of these three was sharply contrasted to the supposedly down-to-earth "scientific socialism" that Marx and Engels were promulgating. The designation "utopian socialist" shows clearly that by the middle of the 19th century, the term "utopian" was well established as a pejorative epithet indicating extreme impracticality. Most contemporary scholars of socialist thought and practice would indeed categorize the reform proposals of Fourier and Saint-Simon (as well as those of Marx and Engels) as thoroughly impractical. But Owen is quite different. It is true that later in his career he dabbled in small-scale, supposedly self-sufficient communities intended to put utopian principles into practice. Unless supported by powerful religious faith, these little communities tended to have short, unhappy life expectancies. One of their key problems was simply the inefficiency of handicraft production in the machine age. Another key problem was their persistent tendency to implement extreme equality in distribution despite considerable inequality in productivity and industry among the members of the commune. Owen's communes did little better than other such communes. But where Robert Owen made his reputation was in his management of the cotton mills at New Lanark, Scotland, during the first two decades of the 19th century. This was during the early industrialization period in which the condition of factory workers was horrible by modern standards: long hours, low pay, and a complete absence of security against the infirmities of injury and old age. Owen believed that it would be commercially sound to treat workers better—to shorten their hours, increase their pay, and provide them with insurance and other amenities—because the greatly increased productivity of a happy, healthy and well-motivated labor force would more than pay for these benefits. This, of course, is the basic notion underlying the "enlightened capitalism" or "reformed capitalism" of modern times, as practiced in the advanced industrial nations, and the profound success of this idea in modern history is indeed generally believed to be responsible for the falsification of the confident prediction of Marx and Engels in *The Communist Manifesto* that the capitalist economic system would eventually be abolished consequent upon a violent socialist revolution. That is to say, this prediction was falsified for the Western European nations, the United States, and most of the rest of the world. Russia, China and the other communist nations were a very different story—although that story departed radically from the scenario envisioned by Karl Marx and Friedrich Engels.

Of all the twentieth century writers who contributed to utopian fiction, no doubt the most prominent is Herbert George Wells (1866-1946), better known as H.G. Wells. Immensely popular as a story-teller, technological analyst and social critic, Wells was passionately interested in all aspects of the future of humanity: scientific, social and political. By the turn of the twentieth century, Wells's reputation as a prophet was such that *The Fortnightly Review*, a leading English magazine, asked him to write a series of serious, non-fiction articles on the potential future of human civilization. The resulting articles, published in 1901, were collected into a book entitled *Anticipations of the Reactions of Mechanical and Scientific Progress upon Human Life and Thought*, usually cited merely as *Anticipations*. Much of the work was concerned with technological forecasts: labor-saving devices in the household such as vacuum cleaners and dishwashers, communications breakthroughs such as radio and television, transportation advances such as automobiles, trucks and airplanes. But the later articles dealt with economic, social and political issues. Wells came out firmly in favor of planned socialism and world government. Market capitalism would have to go because of its intolerable inefficiency and instability. Or at least capitalism in the nineteenth century form excoriated by Karl Marx would have to go. Moreover, the international system of national sovereignty, also as known in the nineteenth century, would have to go owing to its inexorable and intolerable propensity toward perpetual warfare—warfare that could and would become steadily more destructive owing to continuing scientific and technological progress.

Wells did not anticipate that the necessary transformations would come about smoothly and peacefully. He predicted ominously that terrible wars would be fought at some point during the twentieth century. Of course, following the First World War (1914-1918), Wells's reputation as a seer was assured. When the idea of a League of Nations was broached during the war by U.S. President Woodrow Wilson, Wells was almost ecstatically enthusiastic. But once the details of the organization had become clear, specifically the fact that it would be a mere super-alliance as opposed to a genuine world government, his earlier enthusiasm was replaced by bitter disappointment. He experienced that same bitter disappointment in 1945, near the end of his life, when it became clear that the much-vaunted United Nations born of the Second World War was simply a replication of the League of Nations. In a bleakly pessimistic book published in 1945, *Mind at the End of Its Tether*, Wells concluded that humanity was apparently not capable of learning from our mistakes after all, and despite all our scientific achievements, we are most likely doomed to extinction within the near future.

A persistent theme throughout the body of Wells's writing is that of the ultimate redemption of human civilization through the purifying crucible of devastating warfare. First enunciated in the non-fiction *Anticipations*, this theme was elaborated in several works of fiction, most notably in *The Shape of Things to*

Come, a novel published in 1933. Once again Wells's reputation as a prophet was well served by *Things to Come*: in it he forecast that World War II would commence in 1940 and that it would be precipitated by a conflict between Germany and Poland. The actual World War II was started in September 1939, by means of the German invasion of Poland. But while he foresaw the near future of humanity as filled with death and destruction, Wells was optimistic about our long-term future. Wells foresaw that humanity would be chastened and enlightened by its vicissitudes, that it would repudiate leadership by lawyers, politicians, generals, and others of that mode of thinking, and instead entrust the future of the race to the progressive, broad-minded, tolerant and intelligent elements within humanity, as represented most ideally by scientists, engineers and technologists. Greedy, short-sighted and paranoiac competition would be replaced by generous, long-sighted and benign cooperation. Unshackled from the needless, egregious suffering and loss imposed by warfare, human civilization would rise to new peaks of happiness, serenity and accomplishment. *Things to Come*, for example, concludes with a stirring vision of a revived and regenerated human civilization preparing for the launching of giant spaceships to explore and colonize not merely the solar system, but the galaxy—perhaps the universe. The overall scenario might be described as a dystopia of rampant warfare followed by a utopia of boundless progress.

Wells did produce at least three books that could be described as "conventional" utopian works in that the major emphasis was on the characteristics of the much-improved future world society, rather than on the bumpy path by which this much-improved future was to be achieved: *A Modern Utopia* (1905), *Men Like Gods* (1923) and *World Brain* (1938). These works imply that it just might be possible to attain a better world without running the gauntlet of more war. Of the three, only the first is explicit about the need for world government to ensure a better human condition. Wells envisions a well-ordered, peaceful, and progressive society guided by a class of totally rational, impartial and incorruptible "Samurai." Accession to this class would not be through the crass political maneuverings of today, but rather through highly selective mental testing and psychological screening. The society described in *A Modern Utopia* is similar to the typical happy, healthy and hearty society of utopian speculation, with the exception that Wells is at pains to paint a dynamic rather than a static picture. In other words, there is much emphasis on continuous scientific progress and technological advance leading to ever-higher living standards and ever larger and more impressive buildings and machines. In *Men Like Gods*, there is less emphasis on tight organization and discipline in achieving an improved society, and more on the spreading of high-quality education out among the entire population. In *World Brain*, the means of human salvation is to be a huge encyclopedia, published in all languages and continuously updated, that encompasses and codifies "all human knowledge." (Quite possibly Wells would have perceived the World Wide Web of today as the first small step toward the "world brain.")

The world government skeptic will assert, of course, that H.G. Wells's favorable assessment of world government is no more to be taken seriously than that of any other world government enthusiast. Certainly Wells's fame as a literary story-teller does not entitle his opinions regarding international organization to any special consideration. A gift for story-telling does not necessarily imply any special gift with respect to economic, political and sociological prognostication and prescription. After all, as a story-teller Wells achieved fame through the creation of fantasies involving such things as time travel and invisibility (respectively in *The Time Machine* of 1895 and *The Invisible Man* of 1897). Any competent scientist will attest that neither time travel nor invisibility, at least as literally described in Wells's stories, is within the realm of possibility. Quite possibly, therefore, world government is also not within the realm of possibility. I would have to agree with the world government skeptic that it will most probably be forever impossible to send a person forward or backward in time, notwithstanding the numerous depictions of this phenomenon in literary and cinematic fiction. The same holds true of invisibility. But the same does *not* hold true of world government. In the case of world government, we are not concerned with violations of the basic principles of the natural universe. We are concerned, rather, with the principles of political organization. That it is possible to establish effective governmental authority over huge masses of people, most of whom are completely unknown to each other, has been clearly established by the existing, functioning national governments in the world today. If it is possible for the People's Republic of China to effectively encompass a population of one billion persons, then it would also be possible for the proposed Federal Union of Democratic Nations to encompass the six billion persons presently resident on this planet.

In only one of his books, *A Modern Utopia* (1905), did Wells utilize the term "utopia" to describe the better and brighter future that might await humanity. As a rather relentlessly prolix, didactic and undramatic work, it was not one of the author's more successful productions. The narrative framework is that of two ordinary, turn-of the-century professional men (a writer in the image of H.G. Wells, and a professor of biology) who by some quasi-mystical means end up on a planet called Utopia, that may be in a "parallel universe" relationship to Earth, may be an altered reflection of Earth on the other side of the galaxy, or may simply be a dream. There they observe the people, customs and institutions of a world far more peaceful and prosperous than that from which they have come. Much of the contents of *A Modern Utopia* consists of fairly abstract ruminations on the intellectual history of utopianism, and on the practical questions of which utopian ideas are probably invalid (most of them, in Wells's judgment) and which may be valid. The ratio of substantive concepts and conclusions to word count is quite low, even by the standards of discursive fiction. One has to search long and hard for such nuggets of prescription/prognostication that inheritances would be heavily taxed as a means of equalizing the distribution of wealth, and that slow and smoky steam trains have been replaced by fast and clean electric monorails. There is a world state in existence, staffed by a class of superlatively competent and completely incorruptible "Samurai"—but very little hard information is imparted on either the world government or the Samurai.

Wells is typical of utopian writers in depicting the general population of the planet "Utopia" as noticeably healthier, happier and heartier than their counterparts on Earth. But they are by no means ecstatic, and their world, while better than Earth, certainly does not approach the imaginable ideal of the heavenly or earthly paradise. The same limitations of human nature and scarce natural resources apply as apply on Earth. Although hardier and more resistant, the people of Utopia are still subject to pain, injury, disease and death. Although there is no threat of international warfare or violent civil disturbances, society is still subject to serious problems such as crime, unemployment and disability. Although he was a tireless worker himself, Wells rejected any notions that labor was inherently pleasurable and need not be financially rewarded. In fact he was quite insistent that labor would be considered the solemn responsibility of every able-bodied adult citizen, man or woman, and that any person shirking this responsibility would be treated in the same way as a common criminal. In Wells's view, if common criminals and shirkers did not respond to efforts at re-education, they would be removed permanently from society—not by means of capital punishment (not utilized even for the crime of homicide), nor by confinement to jails or prisons. It would be simpler and cheaper, according to Wells, to ship them off to remote islands, provide them with the basic supplies needed for existence, and then leave them to their own devices. Some of this should surely appeal to the "hard-headed" political conservatives of today.

Wells depicts a world that is far from perfect, but that copes with problems somewhat more successfully than did his own world of 1905. To be sure, some of his notions for improvement seem daffy (e.g., the elimination of the legal profession for "lack of need"), but others seem quite reasonable by today's standards. For example, he is insistent that every vestige of racial prejudice be removed, that racial toleration be no less sincere and universal than religious toleration. He sees as the ultimate "salvation of women" from overbearing and abusive husbands not police protection so much as their economic independence through full-time participation in the labor force. During the working day, society would provide day care centers and schools to take care of the children. All this is to say that H.G. Wells cannot be classified as a totally unrealistic and impractical dreamer, as being the equivalent to a fanatic or an imbecile best confined to an asylum. All of Wells's ideas about possible means toward a better and brighter future for humanity are worthy of consideration, and this is certainly true of his advice that a world government be made part of the future political history of human civilization.

Understandably enough considering the trials and tribulations that the twentieth century inflicted on mankind, throughout the century dystopian writing was far more prevalent than utopian writing. As the word suggests, "dystopia" is the antonym of "utopia." A "utopia" defines a condition of life dramatically superior to life as we know it today, while a "dystopia" defines a condition of life dramatically inferior to life as we know it today. Often, the road to dystopia is perceived to pass through utopia: a misguided effort among humanity to achieve utopian conditions actually results in the exact opposite through the "law of unintended consequences."

The single most famous dystopian novel to come out of the twentieth century was George Orwell's *1984*. Written in the immediate aftermath of World War II, before the economic and psychological recovery process from the war had fairly begun, *1984* lays out a terrifyingly bleak image of the human condition in 1984, some 35 years following the book's publication in 1949. According to the image, all of the nations of the world will have been incorporated into three great empires: Oceania, Eastasia and Eurasia. All three empires are governed by brutal dictatorships, supported by blizzards of propaganda, in the direct line and image of Adolf Hitler's Nazi Germany and Joseph Stalin's Soviet Russia. All three empires are engaged in perpetual warfare among one another. The alliances continually shift: first Oceania and Eastasia battle against Eurasia, then when Eurasia weakens it joins with Oceania to battle Eastasia, and so on and so forth. However, all three sides refrain from the use of nuclear weapons for fear of the consequences, a restraint which preserves the basic existence of human civilization but has the disadvantage of perpetuating warfare indefinitely. The living standards of the populations of these empires have been reduced to bare subsistence: there is no health, joy or culture. Order is maintained by a brutal secret police in conjunction with a massive propaganda apparatus that cranks out "Newspeak" slogans such as "War Is Peace," "Freedom Is Slavery," and "Ignorance Is Strength." Everywhere in Oceania there are posters of the supreme dictator, known euphemistically as "Big Brother," in the eyes of whom are concealed surveillance cameras. There is an underground resistance, of course, but it is easily kept under control by the state apparatus. The story concerns one Winston Smith, a minor Party operative in the "Ministry of Truth," whose job it is to "correct" news items so that they conform to the Party line. Winston is unhappy in his work, and drawn toward dissidence and resistance, but soon after making contact with the rebels, he is arrested and subjected to brainwashing prior to execution, according to the pattern established by the infamous Great Terror in the USSR of the latter 1930s.

Orwell was not a well man when he wrote *1984*, either physically or psychologically. Although a brilliant writer since early youth, he had not had a successful career. In his 1933 book *Down and Out in Paris and London*, Orwell described a period in his life (1928-1929) when he had been reduced to living as a tramp and a beggar. In 1936 he was commissioned by the publisher Victor Gollancz to write a documentary account of unemployment in the North of England for the Left Book Club. The result, published in 1937 as *The Road to Wigan Pier*, was a literary success but a commercial failure. From 1936 to 1940 Orwell worked as a shopkeeper in Wallingford, Hertfordshire, and during World War II, he was a journalist and editor for various newspapers and the BBC. Motivated by concern for others, both Orwell and his wife sacrificed some of their ration coupons during the war to help local children. It was to the physical weakening entailed by this generosity that Orwell attributed the death of his wife in 1945 following a minor surgery. No doubt it also aggravated the health problems that led to his own death from tuberculosis five years later. Always left-leaning in his basic political viewpoint, he became fairly enthusiastic about Soviet communism following his visit to the front lines of the Spanish Civil War described in *Homage to Catalonia* (1938). But when the enormity of the Stalinist tyranny became evident with the proliferating purges of the latter 1930s, he turned against communism, and authored a savage assault on it in the satirical fantasy *Animal Farm* (1945), later realized in an animated film of the same name (1955). Orwell only attained a measure of personal prosperity with *Animal Farm* and *1984*, the latter published only one year prior to his death in 1950 at the age of 47.

To anyone who has read this harrowing novel, it will come as no surprise that the author of *1984* was an unhappy, unhealthy and embittered individual at the time he wrote it. Be that as it may, *1984* is not only a literary masterpiece, but the importance of its message is such that it should be required reading in the educational system, along with detailed historical accounts of the fascist and communist regimes that inspired it. The novel presents a vivid picture of a potential future that we should all make it our solemn duty to avoid. But as a proponent of world government, I must strenuously object to any and all assertions or innuendoes that the condition of human life and civilization depicted in *1984* would be the likely consequence of world government. The basic mechanism underlying the abject poverty and corrupt political system of *1984* is continuous international warfare. So vast are the economic resources being committed to the war effort that the material condition of the general population has necessarily been reduced to bare survival. So strong are the tendencies toward political instability generated by these low living standards, that they must necessarily be kept under control by a combination of brutal repression and cynical propaganda. But if there were no international warfare, then the living standards of the general population would not have to be so low, and the political system would not have to be so repressive and manipulative. A central purpose of a world government, obviously, is to reduce the threat of international warfare. Therefore a world government, if successful, would reduce the propensities within human civilization toward the miserable conditions depicted in *1984*.

I am not saying that George Orwell himself would have recognized in world government a feasible means of escaping the bleak destiny conjured up by *1984*. Toward the end of his life, Orwell was disgusted with any and all ideologies, and no doubt he would have classified proponents of world government as ideological enthusiasts. No doubt as an intelligent and well-bred, if somewhat unsuccessful and disreputable Englishman, Orwell would have held out some hope that humanity might be able to "muddle through" to a better future—but even if so, any and all ideologies certainly would be of no help. I would hope that if Orwell were alive today to read this book, he would recognize in it a "non-ideological" advocacy of world government. But of course it is impossible to ascertain what

Orwell's attitude would have been toward this book. Given his state of mind in his final years, quite likely he could not have been bothered to read such a fundamentally optimistic book as this.

I am also not saying that if humanity established just *any* kind of a world government, this would improve humanity's prospects for evading the fate so vividly and effectively portrayed in George Orwell's *1984*. If the world government were to be excessively powerful in a military sense, and the member nations completely disarmed, then even if the government were democratically controlled by majority will, there would be a very considerable danger, to the populations of the richer member nations, of the policy described in this book as Crude Redistribution. Although it is hard to imagine Crude Redistribution leading to living standards among the populations of the rich nations quite so low as those depicted in *1984*, there would certainly be a very considerable reduction in these standards. While a man such as George Orwell, who was capable of sacrificing his own household's ration coupons during World War II for the sake of others, might not see a problem with this, I cannot expect that the average person (in the rich nations) would not see a problem with it. Thus it has often been reiterated throughout this book that Crude Redistribution is politically impossible, and that the only feasible means by which global living standards can be equalized is through the mechanism of Common Progress. To ensure that Common Progress is implemented, and not Crude Redistribution, the world government has to be restrained and limited both financially and militarily. Thus the provisions for dual voting in the world government legislature, for limitations on the world government's taxing authority, for the retention by member nations of the right to withdraw peacefully from the world federation, and finally and probably most importantly, the retention by member nations of the right to maintain whatever military forces and armaments they desire under their direct control.

If we interpret the word "utopian" as an "impossible dream," then there is nothing at all utopian about the plan presented herein for a limited world government to be known as the Federal Union of Democratic Nations. On the other hand, if we interpret "utopian" simply as a "better world" than the world we know today, then one would have to describe the present plan of world government as utopian in that specific sense. Clearly, at the present time, the dominant implication of "utopian" is that of an "impossible dream" and not simply a "better world." Thus it is incumbent upon me to deny most strenuously that this plan of world government is utopian in this dominant and generally accepted sense. Far from being utopian, this proposal is absolutely and positively practical, possible, pragmatic, viable and workable. But to say that something *can* be done is not necessarily to say that it *should* be done. Even if we grant that world government is not utopian in the sense of impossible, impractical, etc., that does not establish that it is advisable and desirable. This central question will be addressed in the following section, which compares the possible outcome for human civilization under two circumstances: (1) a world government is established; (2) a world government is not established.

RISKS OF ACTION VERSUS RISKS OF INACTION

Human existence, at the personal, organizational and social levels, is filled with the need to make choices. For an individual person, a critical choice might be whether to take an attractive-looking new job or to remain with one's present job. For a business enterprise, a critical choice might be whether or not to introduce a new product line. For a democratically elected government, a critical choice might be whether to maintain taxation and spending at the current level, or to increase or decrease them. Whatever decision is taken, there are risks. If the person in question stays with his/her current job, and that job happens to be a unpleasant, low-paying, low-prestige, no-future type of a job, then that person will spend the better part of his/her life in a dissatisfied, unhappy state. But if the person takes the attractive-looking new job and shortly thereafter becomes unemployed for one reason or another (perhaps the company went bankrupt, or the individual encountered an incompatible supervisor), then that person is likely to spend the better part of his/her life regretting the job change. If the business enterprise introduces a new product line and the line is unsuccessful, then it may be bankrupted. On the other hand, if the market for the firm's current product lines is declining and it does not introduce the new product line, then it also may well be bankrupted. If the democratically elected government keeps taxation and spending at the current level, it might be swept out of office by a tide of public dissatisfaction. But if it increases (or decreases) taxation and spending, it might still be swept out of office by a tide of public dissatisfaction. Whatever choice is taken, whether it be the active choice (trying something new) or the passive choice (staying with the existing status quo), risk is inevitable. Whatever choice is taken, if "things go wrong," the outcome will be adverse—perhaps *very* adverse.

In the formal theory of decision-making under uncertainty, there are three basic types of variable: the criterion variable, the control variable and the state variable. The criterion variable is that which is to be maximized. For example, for a business enterprise considering whether or not to introduce a new product line, the criterion variable might be the expected value of profits. Control variables are those variables the decision-maker has control over: that the decision-maker sets to levels intended to maximize the criterion variable. For example, the business enterprise decides how much of its productive capacity will be devoted to existing product lines and how much to the new product line under consideration. The amounts of productive capacity devoted to each of the product lines are the control variables. State variables are random variables: these are variables whose values cannot be accurately predicted at the time the decision must be taken (i.e., the control variables must be set). For example, these would be the future market conditions for the various product lines of the firm. The actual, realized level of the criterion variable depends on both the control variables and the state variables. If the business enterprise of our example introduces the new product line and the market for it turns out to be limited, realized profits may become negative and the firm bankrupted. On the other hand, if the firm does not introduce the new product line and the market for its existing product lines declines, then realized profits may also become negative and the firm bankrupted.

This book is concerned with one especially important choice out of the multitude of choices confronting humanity at the present juncture in our history: the choice between maintaining the status quo situation under which the United Nations remains the highest level of international organization in the world, or to proceed beyond the United Nations to establish a genuine and legitimate—albeit limited—world government along the lines of the proposed Federal Union of Democratic Nations. There is no escaping the fact that whatever we do, whether we establish a world government or do not establish a world government, we will confront very serious risks. If we establish a world government, there is a risk that forcing the nations together into a single political organization will exacerbate the frictions and antagonisms among them, inciting civil disturbances, riotous mobs, and eventual civil war. Or there is the risk that this particular threat will be met and overcome by means of a totalitarian regime propped up by a draconian police apparatus—a bleak fate possibly even worse than warfare. On the other hand, if we do not establish a world government, it is possible that the future course of history will generate the same kind of hostile confrontations among competing blocs of nations with which all past history of humanity has been replete, and that some of these confrontations will escalate over into the same kind of fearful and devastating warfare that has plagued humanity since earliest recorded history. What divides the future from the past is the quantum jump in the potential destructiveness of warfare consequent upon the invention of nuclear weapons. Has this factor been taken into adequate account in weighing the relative risks of proceeding into the future without a world government in operation, versus proceeding into the future with a world government in operation?

The argument of this book is that this entire question hinges on *what kind* of a world government is intended. Among most of that tiny minority of the population that favors world government, the world government would be so powerful that no single nation, nor any group of nations, would be able to challenge its power. The world government would directly control all or most heavy weaponry in the world, including all nuclear weapons. Personally, I concur with the majority that such a world government, established in the contemporary world, would be excessively risky. It would be far too likely to abuse its power. For this reason, such a world government cannot be peacefully formed, by social contract, among the nations of the contemporary world. This kind of a world government is indeed—if not impossible—at least so improbable as to justify its complete disregard. For most people at the present time, consideration of world government terminates at this point.

But to terminate consideration of world government on grounds that an extremely powerful world government would most likely be undesirable is a profound and terrible error. Conceivably, in due course, this error could be fatal not only to human civilization but to the human species itself. It is an error because there is *no need* for the world government to be "extremely powerful," so that its power would be comparable to the power currently exercised by the national governments over their component parts. There is nothing in the laws of nature, logic or mankind preventing an appropriate *sharing* of power and authority between the national governments and the world government, so that there would be adequate guarantees for the legitimate rights of nations and adequate safeguards against the world government evolving into a monolithic tyranny and/or a crushing bureaucracy. The Federal Union of Democratic Nations set forth in this book would definitely fit the definition of a "state" or a "government," while at the same time obviously being far short of an "omnipotent state" or an "all-powerful government."

In terms of the formal theory of decision-making under uncertainty, the *nature* of the world government represents the *value* of a decision variable. There is a wide range of values at which this variable might be set—reflecting the wide range of possible specific distributions of effective power between the world government and the national governments. It is a misconception that world government is an either-or, black-or-white, yes-or-no choice—that it is what, in analytical reasoning, is called a "dichotomous variable." Rather it is a "continuous variable" that may take on any of a wide range of different values. True, the choice between "some world government" and "no world government" is a dichotomous choice, but once this particular choice has been made in the affirmative, the more interesting and challenging question emerges: what *type* of a world government do we want? As a matter of fact, if we were to broaden the definition of "world government" to signify merely "a large-scale political organization encompassing all or most nations of the world," the decision to have a world government was made back in 1920 when the League of Nations was established. The United Nations of 1945 then slightly ratcheted up the power and authority of the existent world government. I am arguing here that the time has come to further ratchet up the power and authority of the existent world government by replacing the United Nations with the Federal Union of Democratic Nations. Of course, to describe the United Nations of today as a "world government" definitely would not be consistent with most people's understanding of "government." On the other hand, the proposed Federal Union of Democratic Nations is certainly consistent with the usual conception of a government. So there are actually two questions rather than one to be answered. The first question, whether we should have *any* sort of supernational government, should almost certainly be answered in the affirmative. The second question, given an affirmative answer to the first, is what *type* of a world government should we have? The proposed Federal Union of Democratic Nations described herein is, I believe, a very plausible candidate for the appropriate *type* of world government. If not this exact plan, then something very close to it.

If we envision a relatively limited form of world government instead of a virtually omnipotent form of world government, the evaluation of the relative risk question is greatly altered. The risks of continuing with the sovereign nation-state system of the present day are not changed, but the risks of establishing a world government are greatly reduced. If we continue with the sovereign nation-state system of today, we continue to run the risk that this system will go on generating large-scale warfare in the future just as it has generated large-scale warfare in the past, despite the fact that the introduction of nuclear weapons has made warfare far more costly than ever before. Those who argue that nuclear weapons will "frighten" humanity into maintaining the peace indefinitely would seem to possess a very deficient appreciation of history, which has demonstrated time and time again, in numerous diverse ways, that the storms of warfare can blow up very suddenly and unexpectedly out of what appeared to be calm, clear, blue skies. As just one of numerous examples of this, consider the international condition as of 1900—shortly prior to World War I. There was no conflict at that time between nations espousing capitalism and nations espousing socialism. There was some awareness of differences in economic status and culture, but much of the Third World was incorporated into the colonial empires of the major First World nations, and in any event the poorer regions represented no military threat to the advanced nations. Great advances had recently been made in terms of machine guns, long-range artillery and high explosives, and there was an acute awareness of how destructive warfare would be if fought with these new weapons. The nations of Western Europe had achieved the highest living standards in history, and they were still advancing. Many of the heads of state of the European powers were related by marriage. What could possibly go wrong?

History showed what could go wrong. The German Kaiser Wilhelm II believed that his nation was greatly disadvantaged by not possessing an overseas colonial empire. Disgruntled by this situation, and also fond of military pomp and circumstance, Wilhelm gradually built up a huge military establishment so that other nations would be properly deferential toward German national interests, and this increased deference would somehow, someway, lead to German acquisition of a nice colonial empire. Therefore the other European nations found it necessary also to maintain huge military establishments for the usual "defensive purposes." The arms competition percolated along happily. Then, on June 28, 1914, the Archduke Francis Ferdinand, heir to the throne of the Austro-Hungarian empire, and his wife were assassinated in Sarajevo by a Serbian nationalist, one Gavrilo Princip. At first, few expected that the agitated negotiations that followed this outrage would lead to war. Nevertheless, as history duly recorded, they did lead to war.

Can nothing analogous to this occur in the future? Are we so much superior to the people of 1900 that we can disregard the repeated lessons of history? Has the invention of nuclear weapons so much altered the calculus of warfare that never again will provocation and miscalculated brinkmanship generate a world-wide conflict? Clearly, these questions cannot be answered in the affirmative. There is clearly some degree of risk. There are many national leaders in the world today whose thought processes are very similar to the thought processes of Kaiser Wilhelm II as of 1900. They certainly do not intend war, but they are quite bound and determined that the national interests of their respective nations be honored and respected by the rest of the world—or else. Many large nations in the world today, although "peace-loving" in the sense that they are basically satisfied with the international status quo, find it necessary to maintain powerful military forces. They are ready to disarm at any time—presuming all the other nations do so first. Therefore a gigantic powder keg sits amidst human civilization, with its fuse dangling down, just waiting to be lit.

At the same time there are many other fanatic mentalities in the world today whose thought processes are very close to the thought processes of Gavrilo Princip, the Serbian nationalist responsible for the assassination of the Archduke and his wife in 1914. In fact, the continued existence and formidable capabilities of these kind of people was recently dramatically demonstrated by the terrible events of September 11, 2001. On that fateful day, to the horror and consternation of much of the world population, hijacked civilian airliners were deliberately crashed into both towers of the World Trade Center, and also into one side of the Pentagon in Washington D.C. Thousands of people were killed, most of them in the collapse of the World Trade Center towers. The results of the attack were so overwhelming that no individual, group, or national government took credit for it, possibly for fear of nuclear retaliation by the United States. The suicidal hijackers were quickly identified as Islamic extremists with ties to the shadowy al-Qaeda terrorist organization guided and supported by the renegade Saudi Arabian millionaire Osama bin Laden. At the time of the attack, bin Laden was the "guest" of the Taliban government of Afghanistan, which publicly averred that the attack could not have been the responsibility of bin Laden because he had been "forbidden" to engage in terrorist operations. This suspicious disavowal did not satisfy the United States government, which immediately initiated a large-scale diplomatic and military campaign to bring bin Laden, as well as his associates and protectors, to justice. The kind of people who conceived, planned, financed and carried out the 9/11 action are not troubled by the fact that their activities might be regarded by others as intolerably provocative, and that these activities might eventually light the fuse on the gigantic powder keg sitting amidst human civilization. They are so warped and distorted with unreasoning hatred that they quite likely experience a warm, happy glow from the thought that their activities might set in motion a chain of events leading to catastrophic world war.

Realistically, it will probably be no more feasible to "eradicate" terrorist attacks than it has been proven feasible to eradicate crime generally. Despite heavy investments in law enforcement systems, every national society in the world continues to be afflicted by non-negligible crime incidence. Therefore it is not a question of "eradicating" crime so much as it is a question of keeping the costs of crime to an acceptably low level. Even in a world that was veritably utopian by present standards, there would almost certainly be individuals sufficiently disaffected and fanatical to launch terrorist attacks, suicidal or otherwise. But such attacks would be less frequent and less deadly if there were fewer individuals motivated to engage in them. And there would be fewer individuals motivated to engage in them if there were less economic inequality among the nations of the world (which might be brought about through a vigorous World Economic Equalization Program), and if all or most of the nations of the world were participants in a supernational federation (such as the Federal Union of Democratic Nations) dedicated to the long-term interests of the entire human race.

Terrorist attacks are directly harmful to their victims and their victims' families and friends. But they are unlikely, in and of themselves, to inflict a serious amount of death and damage on worldwide human civilization as a whole. From a larger perspective, the real danger of terrorist attacks is that they will lead to confrontations between powerful nations, and that these confrontations, in turn, will lead to general warfare. Such was the outcome of the 1914 assassination of the Archduke Francis Ferdinand and his wife by Gavrilo Princip. From the larger human perspective, this murder, in and of itself, was nothing more than a relatively minor crime. But this "relatively minor crime," occurring within the context of tensions generated by the sovereign nation-state system, was the catalyst to the terrific cycle of violence known as World Wars I and II.

Something similar to this might easily happen again. To be sure, the terrorist attacks of September 11, 2001, were horrific. But it is easy to imagine circumstances under which they would have been worse and their ultimate consequences would have been devastating to the entire human population. The attacks proved beyond a shadow of a doubt that there are individuals and organizations in the world today who are both technically competent and under no constraints of conscience. It is obvious, in the light of these attacks, that had the al-Qaeda organization possessed nuclear weapons on September 11, they would have been used on New York City. Instead of thousands killed, there would have been hundreds of thousands killed, perhaps millions. Now also consider the possibility that the Soviet Union had *not* capitulated back in the early 1990s, and that it still welcomed and supported almost any kind of misfortune and disruption in the West, on grounds that these misfortunes and disruptions weakened its sworn national enemy. Now suppose in the aftermath of September 11, that this unregenerate Soviet Union had proclaimed that there must be no military action against Afghanistan, by the United States or anyone else, because there was no incontrovertible proof that anyone in Afghanistan had had anything to do with the attacks. The stage would have then been set for that single incident of miscalculated brinkmanship that will unleash a nuclear holocaust upon the world. At the present moment the United States and the Russian Federation are "friends and allies"—to a limited extent. But throughout the history of human civilization there have been innumerable instances of the friends and allies of yesterday becoming the implacable enemies of today. If we wait long enough, serious confrontations and conflicts will inevitably emerge among powerful nations. It is merely a matter of time—unless the human race moves forward to a qualitatively higher form of international unity than we possess today.

At the present time, of course, humanity is still breathing a collective sigh of relief owing to the steep decline in Cold War anxieties over the past decade. It is almost universally assumed that the decline of the ideological struggle between communism and noncommunism has resulted in a much safer world, at least as far as the possibility of nuclear holocaust in the immediate future is concerned. However, more than a decade has elapsed since the East-West Cold War went into steep decline, and as yet there has been no perceptible movement even toward strengthening the United Nations, to say nothing of establishing a genuine world government. Therefore the *long-term* prospects of avoiding full-scale, nuclear world war may not be as favorable as most people today seem to assume. There is little evidence at the present time of a meaningful shift away from the present policy of drift in the international realm, and if the entire history of humanity offers any guidance and insight, it is that sooner or latter, if there are no fundamental revisions at the international level, humanity will drift into dangerously troubled waters.

Thus far the discussion has emphasized the possibility of disaster, particularly through the instrumentality of eventual nuclear world war, if we continue with the policy of inaction—that is, if we persevere with the sovereign nation-state system of today. Some may deem this possibility very serious, while some may deem it negligibly tiny. But any rational person must admit that the possibility *exists*. At this point, therefore, let us try to imagine an alternative future world in which the Federal Union of Democratic Nations is an active participant in the political governance of human civilization. How would such a world differ from the world without such a limited world government? Would serious hazards exist that would not exist without such a government? We have looked at the "risks of inaction" in the foregoing—but now what about the "risks of action"?

The "risks of action" are strongly affected by the specific nature of the world government under consideration, as well as by the circumstances under which it is founded and commences to operate. We assume here that the world government is federal in nature and appropriately limited, yet possesses the essential characteristics of a state entity. These essential characteristics include the authority to levy taxes, the authority to maintain military forces, the division of the government into separate legislative, executive and judicial branches, all three of which would be directly elected by the populations of the Union districts, and such trappings of state authority as a capital city, a flag, an anthem and emblems. On the other hand, the world government would not possess the same degree of authority and military dominance over the member nations of the supernational federation that is typical of the national governments in relation to their subsidiary political units. There would be two especially important limitations on its authority: (1) member nations would retain the right to leave the federation peacefully at any time at their own unilateral discretion; (2) member nations would retain the right to maintain whatever military forces and armaments they desire, including nuclear weapons, under their direct control. In addition, the unicameral legislature would utilize a dual voting system by which measures would have to be approved on both the population basis and the material basis. In the population vote, each representative's voting weight would be in proportion to the population represented, while in the material vote, each representative's voting weight would be proportional to the federation revenue derived from the representative's district. As the population vote would be dominated by the more populous poorer nations, and the material vote would be dominated by the less populous richer nations, both groups of nations would possess the effective power to veto measures that they find unacceptable. In addition, there would be specific restrictions on the federation's taxation authority, some of them contained in a transitional codicil to the constitution to remain in effect for the first few decades of the federation's existence. On the other hand, member nations may at their discretion make voluntary directed contributions—on which there would be no limitations—for the support of specific programs and activities of the federation. These are the essential characteristics of the Federal Union of Democratic Nations under consideration in this book. In light of these characteristics, the "risks of action" would be minimal, while at the same time the Federal Union would be sufficiently cohesive and authoritative to make a significant positive contribution to global governance. At first, the contribution might well not be dramatic, but in all likelihood the contribution would steadily strengthen over time.

As to the circumstances under which the Federal Union would be founded and would commence to operate, there are two essential features. First, the Federal Union political initiative would be accompanied by an economic initiative designated the World Economic Equalization Program (WEEP), designed to achieve approximately equal living standards over all nations within a relatively abbreviated period of historical time on the order of 50 years. Second, both the Federal Union political initiative and the WEEP economic initiative would be undertaken on a tentative and experimental basis, with the clear understanding of all parties involved that if after a reasonable trial period the initiatives are not making substantial progress toward their respective goals, they will be phased out and discontinued. If, despite the large-scale transfers of the WEEP, the economic living standards in the poorer nations are not improving dramatically, the WEEP will be shut down. And if the Federal Union finds itself immobilized by political deadlock, whether owing to North-South problems or any other problems, so that it proves itself ineffective and serves only as a forum for acrimonious, counter-productive controversy, then its member nations will withdraw from it, gradually or quickly as the case may be, until the few remaining members dissolve it completely.

An obvious—and also obviously invalid—argument against the dual initiatives of the Federal Union and the WEEP is that there are no guarantees that either initiative would be successful. The argument is invalid because it is a simple, hard fact that success can never be "guaranteed," no matter what we do or do not do. There is obviously no guarantee that if we do *not* make an effort to achieve greater stability and control at the international level, but merely let the international system drift on aimlessly, that the future of human civilization will be successful. Anyone who is capable of transcending the self-delusive wishful thinking that is so endangering the future prospects of our species, will be capable of perceiving clearly that if we continue to drift, quite possibly we will drift into ultimate disaster. A good metaphor for the intention of world government is that of attaching a rudder and installing an engine in a boat drifting down a broad, quiet river. The idea is to improve the degree of control over the boat, so that there is less likelihood that it will be destroyed if rapids or a waterfall are encountered. Of course, maybe there are no rapids or waterfalls ahead on the river, so that if we continue drifting down it indefinitely we will eventually emerge into a deep, blue, quiet sea. In this case, we would never need the engine and the rudder, and installing them would have been a waste of time and energy. Or, perhaps, the engine and rudder that we might install will be too weak to do any good should we be unlucky enough to encounter rapids and/or a waterfall. Once again, the installation of the engine and the rudder would have been a waste of time and energy. But even if either of these two cases happened to be true, these possibilities are not good arguments against installing the engine/rudder—unless it is assumed that the "wastage of time and energy" would be extreme. The only good argument *against* installing an engine and a rudder is that such action would *worsen* our overall prospects. Arguments to this effect can be put forward, but on an objective, common sense basis they are fairly unconvincing.

I can perceive only one quasi-plausible argument why setting up a world government along the lines of the Federal Union, and simultaneously launching a World Economic Equalization Program, would entail significant risk of eventually increasing the level of hostility and conflict in the world over what it would be in the absence of these initiatives. This is the argument that these initiatives would create unrealistic aspirations and expectations, especially among that very large proportion of the human race that lives in the poorer nations, and if and when these aspirations and expectations are eventually disappointed by the failure of both the WEEP and the Federal Union, the frustration of these people will boil over and cause a significant rise in hostility and war-risk. According to this scenario, while the populations of the poor nations of today are certainly not happy concerning their economic condition, they are in fact resigned to it. They have accepted the fact that they cannot expect large-scale aid and/or economic concessions from the richer nations, and that if they are to catch up with the rich nations, they are going to have to do it through a combination of their own domestic effort and openness to foreign direct investment. They may not like the attitude of the populations of the rich nations, but they respect it—among other things because they realize that if the roles were reversed they would be doing exactly the same thing. But if such grandiose schemes as a world government and a WEEP are broached and then implemented in the real world, the delicate emotional and attitudinal equilibrium of the last few decades will be drastically upset. Aspirations and expectations will be revised upwards—drastically upwards. If everything proceeds smoothly, and steady progress is made toward a high level of equalization without this causing appreciable slowing in the economic growth rates in the rich nations, then everything will be fine. But what if things do *not* proceed smoothly? What if the rich nations quickly become dissatisfied with the WEEP, on the basis that there is not enough progress in the poor nations, or there is too much retarding effect on the rich nations, or a combination of both? As the rich nations begin phasing out the WEEP, the poor nations will become outraged and incensed, and will commence accusing the rich nations of short-sighted selfishness, of callous indifference to their fellow human beings, and of shirking and reneging on their solemn commitments. In the end, North-South relations will be poisoned for generations, leading to even less cooperation and mutual forbearance than we see today.

As the saying goes, *anything* is possible. It must be conceded, therefore, that this scenario lies within the wide boundaries of the *possible*. But it is hardly probable. To begin with, it is thoroughly unrealistic that the populations of the poor nations today are philosophically resigned to and blissfully contented with their inferior economic status, and that they do not resent and blame the populations of the rich nations for this situation. Such a level of calm, rational objectivity truly is contrary to human nature. Any citizen of a rich nation who has had any sort of close personal interaction with a citizen of a poor nation will acknowledge the deep resentment and bitterness that lies just beneath the surface. As long as the conversation sticks to such neutral topics as the weather and the relative merits of pop singers, then there will be no hints of disharmony. But let the conversation turn to such things as foreign aid, or foreign investment, or multinational corporations, or possible reasons for the poverty of the Third World nations—and it will not be long before there are red faces and raised voices on both sides. The Third World citizen will attempt to lecture the First World citizen on the evils of colonial imperialism as well as its modern version, economic imperialism, the inevitable long-term result of which is the immiseration of the downtrodden but hard-working people of the Third World nations. Even if the First World is not responsible for the poverty of the Third World in a strict legal sense, so goes the lecture, it is certainly responsible in a general moral sense. The First World citizen will attempt to lecture the Third World citizen on the bad public policies, the entrenched local elites, and the perverse customs and attitudes of the masses. These are the factors that are truly holding the Third World down, according to the lecture—it has absolutely nothing to do with the past or present policies of the rich nations. But the fact is that neither party is interested in listening to the lecture of the other side. In fact, listening to the other side's lecture for any length of time is likely to generate emotions of virtually murderous rage. It is very much equivalent to the typical discussion about race relations between the typical white citizen of the United States and the typical black citizen. The typical white citizen can only listen so long to implicitly accusatory recitations of injustices done to blacks before reminding the black citizen that there has been a great deal of progress since the time of slavery and the present time. But the typical black citizen can only listen so long to accounts of black progress since the time of slavery before reminding the white citizen that there is still much racial prejudice and disharmony in the country. To one, the glass is half empty; to the other, the glass is half full. Both are prone to anger because the other party fails to see the glass as they see it. The outcome is raised voices and red faces on both sides.

Now if a full-scale World Economic Equalization Program were undertaken with the explicit intention of overcoming, once and for all, the persistent problem of world economic inequality, no doubt this would have a favorable immediate impact on relations between citizens of rich nations and citizens of poor nations. Quite likely it would inspire great enthusiasm, not just in the poor nations but in the rich nations as well. Quite likely there are today vast, untapped reservoirs throughout the world of hope, belief and faith in progress that would be opened up by such an initiative. In some psychological respects it will be like wartime: the great majority of the world's population would partake of an overwhelming sense of shared endeavor and great accomplishment. The old, traditional resentments and hatreds will not disappear, but they will go into a steep decline. Unprecedented pressures will be put on assorted pessimists, nay-sayers, shirkers, malcontents and curmudgeons to get with the program, to stop whining and complaining, to put their shoulders to the wheel, to do their part for the cause. During this period, we may anticipate a substantial decline in those suspicions and resentments which provide fertile breeding ground for terrorist activities. Fewer individuals would be drawn to these activities, and of those that are, they would find far less sympathy and support from others. The world would not only be a happier place, but a safer place as well.

The world government skeptic will likely concede that the creation of a world government, along with a massive global economic development program, would very likely be accompanied by a "honeymoon period" of great joy, pride and enthusiasm. But that very "honeymoon bliss," claims the skeptic, will lay the basis for future problems if the expected economic progress does not materialize. In marriage ceremonies, the partners pledge to eternal loyalty "for better or for worse." Especially severe strains are placed on this pledge when events bring about "the worse." Enthusiasm and joy will turn to indignation and rage. The poor nations will accuse the rich nations of sabotaging the effort by failing to provide adequate resources. The rich nations will accuse the poor nations of sabotaging the effort through the misdirection, mismanagement and wastage of those resources. In the end the WEEP will be shut down and the Federal Union of Democratic Nations dissolved amidst howls of anger and anguish from the poor nations. After the brief honeymoon period, the world will once again lapse into the usual strife and recriminations—except that now the strife and recriminations will be worse than ever. With the last fond hopes shattered and the last progressive idealism dissolved, a despairing world will be plunged into the maelstrom. Terrorist activity will mushroom, ominous threats and warnings will multiply, and war-risk will rise exponentially.

I say that this bleakly pessimistic scenario is so wildly far-fetched that it does not constitute a believable argument against the kind of limited world government envisioned in this book. The world population would not be undertaking the economic and political transformations detailed herein in an excessively optimistic spirit. The spirit would be optimistic, to be sure, but not *excessively* optimistic. The possibility of failure would not be minimized. These initiatives would be undertaken calmly and deliberately, in the spirit of a scientific experiment. Any scientific experiment admits the possibility that results will not be according to expectation and hope. If the outcome of an experiment were absolutely assured, were beyond any reasonable doubt—then there would be no need for the experiment in the first place. In a way, recognition of the possibility of failure would be healthy in terms of effort and commitment on the part of everyone. If it were assumed by everyone that success was assured, then many individuals would reason that they personally do not have to do much toward achieving success, that they could indulge in what economists call "free riding" and what the rest of the world calls "shirking," without this causing any significant social harm. If there were no fear of failure, this would cause complacency, and with complacency would in fact come an even greater danger of failure.

The other way in which recognition of the possibility of failure would be healthy is in the case that failure actually does come about. In this case, there would be greater readiness to accept failure with resignation and good grace. The emotions elicited by failure would not be so much acute indignation and rage as gentle sorrow and sadness. There would be less tendency to blame failure on others, and more readiness to accept that the problem lies with the shortcomings of humanity as a whole, of the flaws and weaknesses within each and every human being in the world. The ability to cope with an unfavorable outcome would also be augmented by the fact that a very determined and honorable effort had been made to advance the cause of human civilization. Humanity could comfort itself that it had given the problems of the world "its best shot," and that it had done so in a shoulder-to-shoulder manner embodying high standards of solidarity. Emotions would be equivalent to those among the members of a sports team that, despite exerting its highest effort, had just been defeated by overwhelming odds. In some ways, the bonding caused by defeat is greater than that caused by victory. Indeed, it is not too much to suggest that the positive impact of the Federal Union of Democratic Nations and the World Economic Equalization Program—even though they might be adjudged failures in the short run—would be decisive in the long run. Perhaps after another 10 years, or 20 years, or 50 years, using lessons learned from the endeavor, another effort would be made to achieve global economic equality and political unity—and perhaps this time the effort would be rewarded with success.

I certainly do not want to linger too long on the subject of possible failure. The possibility of failure must be acknowledged and it must be taken into proper account in planning the endeavor. We need to have an "exit strategy" if things do not go well. But we must also maintain a good level of confidence that things will indeed go well and we will not have to implement the exit strategy. In this context, it must be strongly emphasized that it would not constitute "failure" of these initiatives if there is not immediate and dramatic improvement. I have strongly emphasized that even with a massive WEEP in operation, at a minimum it will require several decades to equalize material living standards across nations. What is true of the economic initiative of the WEEP is also true of the political initiative of the Federal Union of Democratic Nations. It may take decades for the Federal Union to achieve its full potential in terms of global governance. The world government skeptic will argue that the dual voting mechanism in the Federal Union legislature would lead to total, permanent deadlock. There is no doubt that the dual voting mechanism, which essentially gives both the rich nations and the poor nations an effective veto power, will make it difficult to get approval for legislation, budgets and so on. That is indeed the intention of the mechanism; it is a guarantee that only measures which enjoy a high level of worldwide consensus will be undertaken. But the world government skeptic neglects two essential counterpoints. One is that the described "total, permanent deadlock" situation already exists currently under the sovereign nation-state system, which effectively gives each and every sovereign nation the ability to veto global measures. The second point is that the existence and functioning of a world government will tend to erode those forces inclining toward deadlock. Most likely there will indeed be a high degree of deadlock—at first. But it will not be "total" and it will not be "permanent." The world government will give the people and the nations a more effective tool for seeking common ground. The first piece of global legislation might pertain to something relatively non-controversial, perhaps the exploitation of resources under the seabed in international waters. But it would be followed by another, and another, and another. As the representatives to the world government become more comfortable with one another, more accustomed to working together toward the solution of common problems, the effectiveness of the world government would increase. Progress might be very gradual, almost imperceptible at times, but it would be *progress*. It may well take decades before it can be confidently judged that the Federal Union of Democratic Nations is indeed a success and ought to be continued indefinitely. But that day most likely *will* come—*if* the Federal Union is given a chance to prove itself by being established in the first place.

DELUSIONS OF IMPOTENCE

Two well-known objections to world government are: (1) that "it is impossible because it is simply a utopian delusion"; and (2) that "it is impossible because of the overwhelming strength of nationalistic prejudices in the contemporary world." Although these propositions are very closely related and they arrive at exactly the same conclusion (that world government is impossible), there is actually a subtle but significant distinction. To allege that world government is a utopian delusion implies that for it to work properly, human nature would have to be fundamentally different from what it actually is and will forever be: people would have to be innately less individualistic and more socially minded (that is, less competitively and more cooperatively oriented) than they actually are and will always continue to be. Because of this basic incompatibility between actual human nature and the hypothetical human nature that would be required to make world government a successful endeavor, world government would inevitably be unsuccessful, that it to say, it would be undesirable. To allege, on the other hand, that "the force of nationalism" precludes world government is not necessarily to say that world government—if established despite the force of nationalism— would be unsuccessful and undesirable. The common conception of nationalism is that it is a type of enthusiasm not solidly based on reason and self-interest. It might be going too far to call it irrational, but it certainly seems to be "non-rational." Invoking nationalism as the factor responsible for the purported "impossibility of world government" is not, therefore, logically inconsistent with world government actually being desirable on grounds of the rational self-interest of the vast majority of the human population. In fact, there are certainly some world government skeptics who, in unguarded moments, might be willing to stipulate that quite a solid and impressive case may indeed be made in favor of limited world government—but that this fact is nevertheless irrelevant because regardless of the objective pros and cons of limited world government, humanity will never, owing to the force of nationalism, look at these pros and cons in a sufficiently careful, objective and clear-sighted way to be able to perceive that they actually lean more toward the desirability of limited world government than the undesirability of limited world government.

I have argued elsewhere in this book that this particular judgment is a discredit to the person who makes it not only because it is unbearably negative and pessimistic but also because it manifests a virtually arrogant contempt for the perceptiveness and rationality of mankind. To maintain dogmatically that humanity is incapable of recognizing, appreciating and acting upon the simple truth of the matter (in this case, that there would be higher probability of a benign future for human civilization if we establish a properly designed, limited world government than if we do not do so) constitutes a virtual insult to all mankind. For a person to say that "*I* may be capable of understanding this simple truth, but very few others will be capable of doing so" suggests that the person thinks that he or she possesses far more in the way of perceptiveness and intelligence than does the great majority of humanity. But there may be a less invidious interpretation of this particular judgment: an interpretation less dependent on the person taking a consciously supercilious and condescending attitude toward others, and more dependent on a psychological state of mind over which the person has no conscious control. I refer to the possible analogue between this judgment and the condition known to psychiatry as "hysterical paralysis." This condition is brought about by some kind of psychological trauma to which the patient involuntarily responds by losing control over movement of the limbs. For example, the patient may be unable to walk, or to move his or her arms, or to move one side of his/her body. It is a protective reaction in that its unconscious purpose is to assist the patient to escape from or reduce some kind of extremely stressful environment or circumstance. But it is a dysfunctional reaction in that it creates new problems for the patient that may be as bad as, or worse than, the problems which induced the hysterical paralysis. For example, a prolonged condition of hysterical paralysis might so atrophy the muscles as to cause permanent physical damage.

Hysterical paralysis is a specific type of the general psychiatric disorder termed "hysteria," in which a wide variety of sensory, motor or psychic disturbances may occur. Until recently, hysteria was classified as a neurosis (i.e., involving exaggerated and unconstructive reactions to emotionally stressful stimuli) as opposed to a psychosis (i.e., involving drastic loss of contact with reality), and is not dependent upon any known organic or structural pathology. (In 1980 the American Psychiatric Association proclaimed the retirement of "neurosis" and "psychosis" as legitimate categories because the former was being used simplistically to indicate "mild" mental disorders while the latter was being used, equally simplistically, to indicate "severe" mental disorders.) The term hysteria is derived from the Greek word "hystera," meaning "uterus," and reflects the ancient belief that hysteria was a specifically female disorder stemming from problems in uterine functions. But in actual fact, while more common in women than in men, hysterical symptoms may develop in either sex, and may occur in children or elderly people, although they occur most commonly in early adult life. In the non-medical context, an hysterical condition is understood as a temporary reaction to a severe shock, involving agitation, crying, babbling, screaming, fear and trembling, and rushing about randomly like a frightened animal in a cage trying to escape some mortal peril. In such a state, the person may do physical harm to himself or to others, but assuming there is no injury the condition will eventually subside and the person will return to normalcy. Even in the non-medical context, hysteria is generally viewed as an unproductive, even a counter-productive, way of coping with a problem or threat. If the threat really is mortal, the hysterical person is less likely to survive it than the person who remains calm, alert and rational. In the medical context, hysteria is understood as a prolonged condition the symptoms of which may not be as dramatic as crying and screaming, but which are generally an unproductive or counter-productive means of coping with whatever stressful circumstances are responsible for the condition.

Hysterical reactions are subdivided into dissociative reactions and conversion reactions. In dissociative reactions, the subject endeavors to escape, as it were, from unpleasant reality by psychic means: the most common form is amnesia, but other forms include somnambulism and multiple personality disorder (MPD). In conversion reactions, the subject endeavors to escape unpleasant reality by physical means: sensory or motor manifestations. Sensory disturbances may range from "peculiar" sensations (paresthesia) to hypersensitivity (hyperesthesia) to loss of sensation (anesthesia). Motor symptoms vary from complete paralysis to tremors, tics, contractures or convulsions (hystero-epilepsy). In each case neurological examination of the affected body part indicates intact neuromuscular apparatus with normal reflexes and normal electrical activity and responses. Other motor disturbances that may be hysterical in origin include loss of speech (aphonia), coughing, hiccuping, nausea and vomiting. Clinical descriptions of conversion disorders date back almost 4000 years: the ancient Egyptians attributed the symptoms to a "wandering uterus." The term "conversion" was first used by Sigmund Freud in the nineteenth century to refer to the substitution of a somatic symptom (e.g., paralysis) for a repressed memory or idea. Most of Freud's hysterical patients were women, and this continues to be the case in contemporary psychotherapy, although the incidence of classic hysteria seems to have diminished greatly in more recent times, possibly because of developments in sexual knowledge and practices. Another major source of contemporary knowledge about conversion reactions comes from military medicine, because of the immense psychological stress placed on soldiers and sailors engaged in mortal combat. Debilitating conditions once described as "shellshock" or "battle fatigue" are now customarily described by military physicians as varieties of conversion disorder. There is far less tendency to dismiss those suffering from these conditions simply as weak-minded or cowardly. According to the authoritative *Diagnostic and Statistical Manual* (DSM) of the American Psychiatric Association, a conversion reaction is defined as a loss or alteration of physical functioning suggestive of physical disease but expressing a psychological conflict or need in a nonvoluntary fashion.

Consider the distinction between the condition of ordinary paralysis and the condition of hysterical paralysis. Ordinary paralysis is caused by a variety of verifiable physical problems: spinal cord damage, brain damage, or nerve damage. Hysterical paralysis, on the other hand, has no physical basis, and is caused by psychological problems brought on by traumatic stress and emotion. It is treated not by physical therapy but by psychotherapy. Of course, hysterical paralysis, or indeed any sort of conversion disorder, tends to be a difficult and controversial diagnosis in any particular case. There are always two alternative possibilities: that the condition is being feigned by the patient (most likely as a means of getting attention, sympathy, and/or dispensation from duties and responsibilities), or that the condition has a physical basis not yet known to medical science. But from the well-established fact that some cases of paralysis have been successfully treated by psychotherapeutic means alone, it is obvious that at least some cases of paralysis are indeed hysterical in nature. Hysterical paralysis can often be cured simply by talking with the patient, gradually deepening the patient's understanding of his or her circumstances and emotions, and in so doing strengthening the patient's coping mechanisms. At some point in the process, the patient regains control over his or her limbs and is able to carry on with life more successfully.

Now let us consider the proposition that it is impossible for humanity to establish a world government as analogous to a condition of paralysis in a person such that it is impossible for the person to move his or her limbs. There are two possibilities as far as the person is concerned: either the person is afflicted with a physical problem which does indeed make movement of the limbs physically impossible, or the person is afflicted with a psychological problem and in actual fact movement of the limbs is physically quite possible. Analogously, there are two possibilities as far as humanity is concerned. First, it might be impossible to establish a world government because world government manifestly *would* be highly undesirable. This would be "legitimate" paralysis—equivalent to ordinary paralysis in a person caused by physical problems. Second, it might be impossible to establish a world government because humanity merely *believes* (incorrectly) that world government would be highly undesirable. This would be "illegitimate" paralysis—equivalent to hysterical paralysis in a person caused by psychological problems. It is the firm belief of this author (obviously) that the currently widespread belief among humanity that formation of a world government is "impossible because of nationalism" is nothing more and nothing less than what might be described as "mass hysterical paralysis." It is a case of "mind over matter"—only in this case "mind" is preventing things from happening in the real world rather than causing them to happen. It is a mental disorder, and in standard medical thinking mental disorders are not communicable—except through heredity. But social psychology recognizes that ideas and beliefs can spread through a given population in much the same manner as epidemics of contagious diseases. A classic example is the witch hunting craze in early modern Europe, a craze that extended into colonial America in the notorious Salem witch trials in 1692.

What has been responsible for this condition in humanity? I attribute it to exactly the same thing that is responsible for hysterical paralysis in specific human individuals: psychological stress. For example, hysterical paralysis is often encountered in adolescent children from highly dysfunctional households characterized by deep hostilities and endless bickering, poverty, alcoholism, drug abuse, and so on. The child can see no possible means of escape from this depressing and debilitating environment, there is a collapse of psychological resilience and resistance, and thus the somatic symptoms emerge. In the same way, humanity as a whole is stressed by a social environment perpetually disrupted by either the reality of warfare or the threat of warfare. But there appears to be no escape from this environment. In particular, world government is ruled out by the perceived likelihood that it would immediately degenerate into a repressive global dictatorship—a fear closely equivalent to the adolescent girl's fear that if she runs away from home, she will be faced with destitution and starvation. The general threat posed by warfare to society as a whole and each individual within it has been greatly augmented in the post-World War II era owing to the advent of nuclear weapons. But still world government is ruled out—there can be no escape from the fearful possibility of nuclear holocaust. Under this level of stress, the minds of a great many people have cracked, and they have descended into an uncritical, unresponsive, dogmatic attitude that "world government is impossible because of nationalism," and thus it is no use talking or even thinking about world government. This attitude may not be an exact analogue to hysterical paralysis, but it is, to utilize the well-known expression, a "reasonable facsimile thereof."

As mentioned above, in clinical cases of hysterical paralysis, the condition can often be cured or alleviated simply by the therapist engaging in a calm, collected, supportive dialogue with the patient that gradually raises the patient's self-awareness and self-confidence. The patient is urged to fully acknowledge and recognize the adverse conditions under which he or she must live, and to express openly the pain, anger and dissatisfaction these conditions naturally elicit. But at the same time the therapist tries to help the patient perceive whatever positive and hopeful aspects may exist, and whatever sensible courses of action the patient might take to improve the situation. For example, adolescent children in dysfunctional homes are encouraged to dwell on the fact that they are getting older and will eventually be in a position to leave home without encountering destitution and starvation. In this way, the patient eventually comes to realize, perhaps consciously or perhaps unconsciously, that there are more effective ways of dealing with and overcoming personal problems than paralysis. And with this realization, the condition of hysterical paralysis diminishes and finally disappears. In an analogous sense, therefore, the purpose of this book is to initiate a kind of psychotherapeutic dialogue within humanity on the nature of the current unsatisfactory international situation, and on the potential positive contribution that a limited world government could make toward the improvement of the situation. The hope is that such a calm, collected dialogue will ultimately dissolve and dispel the perverse belief that "world government is impossible," whether owing to nationalism or anything else. Therefore, let us now look carefully and critically at the proposition that "nationalism makes world government impossible." What possible flaws and weaknesses are there in this proposition?

One highly influential current misconception, for example, is that establishing a world government would be a radical departure from the present course of development. But radical changes, as we all know, are very hazardous and ought to be avoided at all costs. "Evolution and not revolution" is the dominant catch phrase. But what is being proposed in this book is indeed "evolution and not revolution." No doubt to most people today, establishing a world government will seem to be a very dramatic and important transition. But one hundred or two hundred or three hundred years from today, people might well interpret the event as a natural and relatively minor step in the long-term political evolution of human civilization on earth. It looks more important to us who are alive today simply because it is so close to us. We don't have "perspective" on this transition. Contributing to this misconception is the mistaken belief that major historical transitions require highly stressful circumstances—that the tendencies toward "inertial conservatism" are so strong within people that they will only contemplate major changes when the status quo has generated unmitigated disaster. Certainly one can find historical episodes consistent with this theory: for example, the Russian Revolution occurred in 1917 after World War I had inflicted horrific death and devastation on the Russian nation. But there are many countercases of revolutions occurring amid relatively stable and prosperous conditions. This was true of the three other major revolutions in modern Western history: the English Revolution of the 1640s, the American Revolution of 1776, and the French Revolution of 1789. A thoughtful consideration of the historical record casts severe doubt on the commonplace assertion that humanity will only give serious consideration to world government when human civilization is engulfed in nuclear holocaust or environmental catastrophe. If anything, the historical record suggests that when conditions are literally disastrous, people are too preoccupied with and exhausted by the daily struggle for survival to take much interest in political or social reforms.

It is also a misconception that establishing a world state would be such a radical break from the status quo that it could never be accomplished peacefully. While it may be true that there are some possible reforms so drastic that their implementation would entail violence, the establishment of a limited world government, such as the Federal Union of Democratic Nations proposed here, does not fall into this category. And even granting that a world government would be a far more ambitious reform than the average reform, history records many instances of major reforms occurring without appreciable violence or bloodshed. For instance, the repeal of the Corn Laws in England in 1846 is regarded by historians as on a par with much of the social legislation passed during the French Revolution to curb the traditional privileges of the hereditary aristocracy. A more recent example, and far more dramatic, was the peaceful renunciation of communism by the ex-Soviet Union and its erstwhile Eastern European satellite nations. This abrupt and completely unexpected transition was veritably astounding to the political leaders of the world, to the intelligentsia and to the general public alike. While the economic condition of these nations was definitely deficient compared to that of the advanced capitalist nations of Western Europe, it was by no means disastrous, and in fact it was much better than that of many politically stable capitalist nations in the Third World. It was certainly not clear, as of 1985, that the Soviet Union was entering the final years of its history. Just as the Soviet Union in 1985 was closer than anyone realized to throwing off communist ideology and embracing democratic capitalism, so too the world today may be closer than anyone realizes to proceeding beyond the sovereign nation-state system and embracing a limited world government. And just as the transition of the Soviet Union to the Russian Federation and the other successor republics was accomplished peacefully, so too a world state may be formed peacefully.

Among world government skeptics, it is a tired cliché that there exists "no plausible scenario" by which world government could be peacefully inaugurated in the real world. The implicit challenge is that unless the proponents of world government can produce a detailed chronology of future events—a "plausible" chronology, no less—the case for world government can be disregarded. That this challenge is quite absurd and most unfair is, I hope, fairly obvious to the reader, even if the reader is not yet ready to categorize himself or herself as a "proponent of world government." Had anyone had an intuition in 1985 that the Soviet Union was in its final years, that person certainly could not have specified the exact course of events leading up to the USSR's dissolution in 1991. Quite clearly, therefore, it would be highly premature and most unwise to try to set forth any sort of a definite timetable for the achievement of world government, or to set forth precise details for the campaign of enlightenment necessary to establish the preconditions for this achievement. Obviously a great many people must become aware of the blueprint for world government advanced herein, and they must also consider this information sufficiently important to be worth sharing with others. Whether this process will commence this year, next year, or ten years from now, is impossible to predict. Whether the process, once commenced, will proceed to the level necessary for success, is also impossible to predict. What may be argued strongly, however, is that for the greater good of humanity, this process *should* commence, and the sooner it commences, the better.

As a matter of fact, the "how can it possibly come to pass?" challenge to world government is merely a slightly more sophisticated variation on the more obviously faulty position that "world government has not happened in the past, ergo it cannot happen in the future" But this is quite obtuse—it is like asking "how could it come to pass" that a group of hungry, thirsty people wandering in a desert and suddenly finding an oasis containing a pond of clear, cold water surrounded by fruit trees, would thereupon eat and drink. Does the asker of such a question want a detailed scientific account, using principles from such disciplines as physics, optics, biochemistry, physiology, etc., utilizing large blocks of text, many equations, numerous diagrams, and so on and so forth, on how sensory awareness of the presence of food and water in human beings who are hungry and thirsty results in various mental and physical phenomena culminating in the consumption of food and water? Does any rational person actually need such an account to acknowledge that hungry and thirsty people, suddenly finding food and water, will proceed to eat and drink? The real question is not "how will it happen?" but rather "should it happen?" That is to say, does the present proposal for a Federal Union of Democratic Nations represent an actual oasis (to continue with the metaphor) toward which our group of hungry, thirsty people in the desert should make haste to approach?

While it clearly impossible to specify a precise, detailed and compellingly plausible schedule running from the here and now to the establishment of a world government according to the specifications of the proposed Federal Union of Democratic Nations, I will conclude this section with some observations that provide the beginnings of a response to the challenge that there is "no plausible scenario" toward the foundation of a world government. First and foremost, this proposal did not suddenly drop down, completely unheralded and unanticipated, out of the clear blue sky. The vast majority of sane, sensible and informed people in the world today are fully aware of the ongoing processes of globalization, are cosmopolitan in their outlook and favorably disposed toward increasing international cooperation. A wide and diverse assortment of authorities, experts, intellectuals and politicians are continually preaching the cause of global understanding, and are constantly appealing for "fresh, new ideas" toward the furtherance of this cause. The basic idea of world government, of a universal political entity embracing—or at least open to—all of the peoples and nations of the world, has been under consideration and development literally for centuries. It is a concept that is fully accepted "in principle" and "in theory" by a very large proportion of those people who have ever thought seriously about it. The perceived obstacles are "practical" in nature: i.e., world government would be good *in theory* but not, alas, *in practice*. But the proposed Federal Union of Democratic Nations is in fact a thoroughly practical and sensible means of dealing with and overcoming the practical impediments to world government. In the light of this possibility, allegations that world government is impractical simply do not make sense. This plan is exactly the sort of "fresh, new idea" that people everywhere are calling for and looking for. It offers the population of the world an attractive, secure avenue toward a better, safer, and more rewarding future.

There is nothing at all preposterous and unrealizable about the Federal Union blueprint for a functional and functioning world government. It is not to be compared with lunatic fringe proposals toward world peace. The typical Christian televangelist, for example, has a very simple prescription for world peace: that everyone in the world "accept Christ into their heart." Should this vision be realized, it would no doubt vastly increase the financial revenues of these televangelists, but whether it would insure world peace is another question—there was a profusion of bloodshed and warfare in medieval Europe, at a time when virtually everyone, ostensibly at least, had accepted Christ into their hearts. Another example of arrant nonsense is provided by assorted lunatic fringe anarchists and pacifists whose merry prescription for world peace is that "the people" take matters into their own hand, dissolve the governments, disband the armies, and live happily ever after in a myriad of self-sufficient little communes scattered over the face of the globe. Should this vision be realized, the little communes would waste no time accumulating stocks of weapons with which to do battle with one another. The battles might be on a smaller scale, but there would be many more of them, and the death toll might well be on the same order of magnitude as the death toll that could be realized in one, big nuclear world war today. The proposal for a Federal Union of Democratic Nations put forward in this book has nothing in common with any and all schemes that envision drastic changes either in human nature or in the presently existing institutions of human civilization. No governments would be dissolved, no armies would be disbanded, and no one who had not already done so would be required to "accept Christ into his/her heart."

The world government skeptic might grant that *as individuals* a great many people might be favorably disposed toward world government if they were to become fully aware of such limited world government possibilities as the Federal Union of Democratic Nations, because they would see it as benefiting both their own personal interests and the interests of humanity as a whole—but the real problem lies not at the *individual* level but at the *organizational* level. According to the skeptic, organizations would naturally tend toward opposition to world government because they would see it as an organizational competitor to themselves, a competitor that would inevitably limit their own power and authority. But it does not make sense to attribute to organizations a higher degree of paranoia than exists at the individual level. Any organization is built on the principle of cooperation toward a common goal, and thus it stands to reason that the leaders of organizations would be generally predisposed in favor of cooperation with other organizations. This is not to deny that there are some organizations in the world today that would in all probability be opposed to world government: for example, the John Birch Society, America's Survival Inc., and the Ku Klux Klan. At the same time, there are numerous organizations that are definitely predisposed in favor of world government—assuming that a practical and effective scheme toward it can be devised. The World Federalist Association is perhaps the foremost among several similar groups. In addition, there are a great many interest organizations and think tanks that—although they have not yet gone on record in support of world government because they are not yet aware of a practical scheme toward it—are nevertheless in favor of progressive and outward-looking international policy. Some of the more important of these are the Carnegie Endowment for International Peace, the Council on Foreign Relations, the Institute for Policy Studies, and the Center for Strategic and International Studies. There are also many international organizations that might see in the Federal Union of Democratic Nations an effective instrument for the pursuit of their own goals: the many multinational corporations, the World Trade Organization, the International Monetary Fund, and the World Bank.

But then there are two other types of organizations of great importance in the contemporary world: the national governments, and the United Nations. Surely (according to the world government skeptic) both the national governments and the United Nations will perceive in a possible Federal Union of Democratic Nations a direct competitor against their own interests, power and authority—as an organization that could and probably would encroach on their own "turf." Once again, I would respond to this position that it places far too much reliance on paranoiac tendencies. The human personnel of both the United Nations and the national governments, whether primarily politicians or administrators or rank-and-file employees, are not only (by and large) sane, rational and intelligent people, but by virtue of the role of the organizations of which they are part, they are predisposed in favor of cooperation, authority and governance. As a group, they are not predisposed toward paranoia. Therefore, many if not most of these people will recognize in the Federal Union of Democratic Nations a potentially very positive force in the world. The personnel of the national governments might look toward a potential world government much as do the personnel of the various state governments in the United States toward the federal government—as a helpful partner toward the pursuit of their internal goals. And the personnel of the United Nations might look forward to a potential world government as a more effective means of pursuing their personal and professional goals.

Nor is it the case that the Federal Union of Democratic Nations would present a direct and immediate threat to the employment of the personnel of the national governments and the United Nations. What the long-term effect of the Federal Union on overall employment in governance organizations might be is difficult to predict. While world government skeptics invariably argue that world government would automatically increase the bureaucratic overload on human civilization, this is pure speculation. Certainly the overall objective would be to maintain aggregate administrative costs over all levels of government, including the supernational, the national, the regional and the local, at a reasonable level consistent with the central importance of good governance to human society. The existence of a world government would enable certain administrative functions of national governments to be handled more efficiently and effectively at the supernational level. Thus the world government could well lead to reductions in the total number of employees involved with those specific functions. On the other hand, there might be an increase in the total number of personnel involved in other types of administrative functions. What will happen in the long run is therefore quite uncertain. In the short run, however, over the first 10 to 20 years of the world government's operations, it is most likely that there will be a significant increase in the total number of personnel employed by governance organizations. To start with, the personnel of the Federal Union of Democratic Nations will likely be five to ten times more numerous than the personnel of the United Nations At the same time, there will likely be very little decrease in the personnel of the national governments. Thus the establishment of the world government would open up new employment opportunities for all types of governance personnel: politicians, administrators, and rank-and-file employees. And some of these new opportunities might seem very attractive indeed to those who would be qualified for them. Just as the governors of the states of the United States today may aspire to becoming the President of the United States, so too the national leaders of the future could aspire to becoming the Union Chief Executive of the Federal Union of Democratic Nations. It hardly seems unlikely that many of various national presidents and prime ministers would indeed, with considerable relish, imagine themselves rising to that honored and exalted position in human affairs.

All this may very well be true, says the world government skeptic, of a world in which a world government is an existent reality, or even of a world in which a substantial proportion of the population recognizes in world government a practical and immediate possibility. But this is not the world we know today. The human population of the world today, according to the skeptic, is virtually oblivious to the possibility of world government: the vast majority assumes that it would be undesirable, but that even if it *were* desirable, it would still be impossible because of the overwhelming strength of nationalistically based prejudice against it. How could one possibly overcome this immense inertial force against world government? How could one conceivably get people to depart from their preconceived notions and start seriously thinking about world government? My answer to this is that while there is indeed a great mass of encrusted prejudice against world government in today's world, this prejudice is not rooted solidly in a sensible interpretation of the facts as we know them today. Specifically, this great mass of encrusted prejudice is based on a false image of world government as *necessarily* a militarily omnipotent state organization possessing strong innate tendencies toward tyrannical governance. This image of world government has nothing in common with the proposed limited world government under consideration herein. Therefore the encrusted prejudice against world government, as monolithic and impervious as it may seem, is actually quite precarious and unstable. It may not take much to dissolve it.

A SUMMING UP

Although a century of progress on the whole, the twentieth century was troubled by three terrible world wars. World War I raged from 1914 to 1918; this was followed by World War II from 1939 to 1945; and this was followed by the Cold War between the communist and noncommunist superpowers from approximately 1950 through 1990. Fortunately, the Cold War did not ignite into the nuclear holocaust that would have been known to the survivors (if any) as World War III. Although the Cold War did not become hot, it nevertheless exacted a heavy cost from humanity in terms not only of a tremendous amount of economic resources devoted to military purposes, but also in the cultivation of a spirit of apprehension, pessimism and timidity—a further loss of faith in the idea of progress. The mentality of humanity during the Cold War might be compared to that of a man crossing Niagara Falls on a tightrope—"one false move and I am dead." Of course, a man crossing Niagara Falls on a tightrope needs to maintain a certain amount of physical adaptability to changing conditions (such as a sudden gust of wind), and this ability to cope with changing conditions is not helped by dwelling on the proposition "one false move and I am dead."

At the conclusion of the unprecedented carnage and destruction of World War I, humanity took an unprecedented step forward toward global political unity with the formation of the League of Nations. At the conclusion of the even more devastating carnage and destruction of World War II, humanity took another small but significant step forward by upgrading the League of Nations into the United Nations. Although very similar to the League of Nations, the United Nations was an improvement over the League in proposing that the community of nations undertake to ameliorate the underlying root causes of warfare, rather than simply dealing with the periodic emergence of war or the threat of war by means of mustering a super-alliance against the aggressor nations. In other words, from suppression of war itself, the emphasis was now to be placed on suppressing the conditions conducive to warfare, most especially the relative poverty of the Third World nations. It need not be emphasized that both the League of Nations and the United Nations have been deep disappointments in a practical sense. However, this is not to denigrate their importance as symbols of humanity's latent aspirations toward a truly effective global polity. In the long run, the League of Nations and the United Nations may yet prove to have been extremely important in laying the attitudinal foundations for genuine world government. As the conclusion of World War I saw the foundation of the League of Nations, and as the conclusion of World War II saw the foundation of the United Nations, it seems fitting and natural that the conclusion of the Cold War should see a further advance toward the goal of a world state. That advance could and should be through the foundation of the Federal Union of Democratic Nations, and the simultaneous initiation of the World Economic Equalization Program.

Humanity now confronts a puzzling and portentous dilemma. The course of history makes clear that there are deep and ineradicable inclinations in every human being toward hostility and violence toward other human beings. But it is also clear that there are deep and ineradicable inclinations in human beings toward friendship and cooperation with other human beings. Governments are established for the control of the former inclinations and the facilitation of the latter inclinations. They have been remarkably successful, as manifested by the fact that the larger nation-states of today maintain basically peaceful and harmonious conditions within populations numbering in the tens of millions, even hundreds of millions. But the impulses toward hostility and violence, pent-up within polities, tend to surface in relations between polities. Instead of the warfare between individuals that would be inevitable in the absence of governments, we have warfare between huge groups of individuals organized under governments. Modern history has witnessed a profusion of deadly and destructive violent conflicts among nations and blocs of nations. Although the technological advance of weaponry has made these conflicts steadily more terrible, they have continued to occur. Still another future conflict involving nuclear weapons—although it would be terrifically destructive—appears to be highly probable, over a sufficiently long period of future time. We should not be lulled into a false sense of security by the short-term decline in the nuclear threat owing to the end of the Cold War. In a world of burgeoning population, ever-increasing pressure on the natural environment, and slow and uncertain economic progress in the Third World, adverse developments are quite possible, and these adverse developments could greatly intensify the disruptive pressures that foster confrontation and warfare.

Common sense suggests a solution: form a supernational federal government composed of an overwhelming preponderance of nations. This government would suppress conflict among the nations in the same way that national governments suppress internal conflict among their citizens. But alas, there are severe obstacles to this common sense solution. The nations of the world are extremely heterogeneous in terms of economic status, ideological preferences, and cultural characteristics—not to mention race, religion and language. If one nation or a small group of nations gains control over the world government, and that government possesses a monopoly on heavy armament, then it would be likely to try to impose its own preferences on all nations—preferences that would be odious and intolerable to millions if not billions of its citizens. Either the world polity would degenerate into a horrific, totalitarian police state, or it would dissolve amid disastrous civil war. So while the risks of proceeding into the future without a world government are clear, so too are the risks of proceeding into the future with a world government. To date, the vast majority of humanity has assessed the latter risks to be even larger than the former risks.

The assessment of relative risk is fundamentally altered if instead of imagining an extremely powerful world government that would be essentially equivalent to a typical national government of the present day, we envision a limited world government that, although exhibiting all the essential characteristics of a state organization and being in fact a genuine state organization, would nevertheless share a considerable amount of effective power and authority with the member nations of the supernational federation. Specifically, the member nations would retain the right to maintain independent military forces under their direct control (armed, if desired, with nuclear weapons), would retain the right to withdraw peacefully from the federation at their own unilateral discretion, and would exercise a reasonable and appropriate amount of relative weight in the supernational legislature by means of the dual voting system. According to this system, legislation would have to be approved on both the material basis and population basis. The less populous richer nations would dominate the material vote while the more populous poorer nations would dominate the population vote. Thus neither type of nation would be able to enforce its preferences on the other type of nation against the will of the other type of nation. This type of limited world government, as proposed herein in the institutional form of the Federal Union of Democratic Nations, is a plan for world government that would acceptable to most of the nations of the world and the peoples of the world—if and when they become aware of it.

An essential component of the overall scenario proposed in this book is the World Economic Equalization Program (WEEP). Now that ideological conflict within humanity is in sharp decline consequent upon the collapse and dissolution of the USSR, the economic gap between the rich nations and the poor nations has taken over as the single most important impediment to the long-term viability and stability of world government. So long as there is a dramatic differential between average living standards in the richest nations and those in the poorest nations, then a democratically organized world government would be subjected to constant pressures toward what is termed herein Crude Redistribution. The short-term solution to this politico-economic problem is to incorporate such provisions into the structure of world government as to reduce pressures toward Crude Redistribution to a manageable level: thus the above-described provisions for dual voting, the national right to withdrawal from the federation, and the national right to maintain whatever military forces and armaments (up to and including nuclear weapons) desired under the independent control of the nation. The fundamental purpose behind these provisions is to make world government feasible in the short run, that it might assist in the initiation, operation and completion of the World Economic Equalization Program. The long-term solution to the problem is the WEEP, a program intended to bring about substantial equalization of living standards across the world, within a reasonably abbreviated period of historical time on the order of 50 years, on the basis of the Common Progress principle. That is to say, while the program would transfer huge amounts of generalized capital from the rich nations to the poor nations, these transfers would nevertheless be sufficiently limited as not to decrease living standards in the rich nations. The basic Common Progress concept is to very slightly reduce the rate of increase in the living standards of the rich nations, in order to greatly accelerate the rate of increase of the living standards of the poor nations. Therefore both types of nation would continue to experience increasing living standards—progress would be "common" to all types of nation. In the long term, after the WEEP has equalized living standards throughout the world, the above political provisions—while they would probably be formally retained—would have become dead letters, relics of an earlier age. Nations will be satisfied with very limited military forces under their direct control, and secession from the world federation will no longer be a serious option for any sane and sensible national official. It is said that sometimes the whole can be greater than the sum of the parts. That is true in this case: the Federal Union would make the WEEP possible, and the WEEP would make the Federal Union possible. Neither component would likely survive in the absence of the other; but together they would assure each other of survival and success.

It would be useless to deny that the hopes and dreams underlying the interrelated Federal Union and WEEP proposals might be disappointed. But the possibility of failure is not a good reason for never even trying. Until we actually establish a Federal Union and initiate a WEEP, predictions of failure are sheer speculation. Therefore, it is proposed that the entire enterprise be conducted on the same experimental lines that have been the basis of all progress in science and technology since time immemorial. It would be understood by all those enrolling in the Federal Union and in its economic associate, the World Economic Equalization Program, that both of these initiatives were being undertaken not necessarily in the complete confidence that they would be successful, but rather in the spirit of experimentation. That is to say, both the political initiative and the economic initiative are considered tentative and provisional, to be pursued for a reasonable trial period of perhaps 10 to 15 years. If the initial indications are sufficiently unpromising, then the World Economic Equalization Program would be drastically downsized or perhaps terminated altogether, and the Federal Union of Democratic Nations would be peacefully dissolved. Humanity would be back to where we are today, sadder but wiser, and otherwise none the worse for wear. Some lessons will have been learned that might be valuable in the future. In the past, much of human progress has been through trial and error, and this situation will no doubt continue in the future. If we envision world government in these terms, clearly the risks of proceeding into the future with a world government are very significantly less than they would be if the world government was to be necessarily a permanent and omnipotent polity.

The purpose of world government in this alternative vision is not to achieve in one fell swoop a millennial condition of perfect peace, prosperity and happiness throughout the world. It is evident to sensible people that millennial conditions are impossible now, and will probably forever remain so. An ineffable characteristic of humanity, which is simultaneously a great strength and a great weakness, is that whatever our current condition, we can always imagine a better condition. Be that as it may, it is not a sound argument against progress that no matter how much progress is achieved, humanity will always be able to imagine further progress. The condition of the world today is unsatisfactory in many ways—even very unimaginative people can perceive the possibility of improvement. The proposed Federal Union of Democratic Nations, even if we imagine it established with great panoply and high expectations, could not instantly abrogate all the problems of the world. The foundation of the Federal Union would not mark the "end of history" after which humanity would settle into a boring rut of perpetual peace and plenty. The Federal Union would rather be an "organic *part* of history"—as opposed to the "end of history." It has taken a thousand steps to get human civilization to its present condition, and if we now take the logical next step of establishing a world government, this step would merely be the first step of what might well be thousands of future steps into the unknown future.

The Federal Union of Democratic Nations, therefore, cannot be compared to the "happy ending" of the typical children's story, following which "everyone lives happily ever after." What the Federal Union would do, however, is to put into the hands of humanity a new political tool, a highly useful new tool that would significantly foster and facilitate gradual, evolutionary progress toward, perhaps not the abrogation, but at least the substantial abatement of the problems and threats confronting our global society. Establishing a world government may be likened to building a superhighway. Just as building a superhighway deepens the physical infrastructure available to society, so too establishing a world government would deepen the political infrastructure available to society. Just as it is impossible to predict in advance exactly how much traffic a new superhighway will carry, so too it is impossible to predict in advance exactly when and how a world government will be able to benefit global society. But if we establish a world government now, it will be there when we need it in the future. If problems or crises emerge, we will not have to waste time and energy getting organized politically in order to cope with and overcome these problems and crises. The time and energy thus saved could mean the difference between success and failure—conceivably it could mean the difference between survival and extinction. Therefore, the next step in the political evolution of human civilization upon earth could and should be the foundation of a supernational federation to be known as the Federal Union of Democratic Nations, an incipient world government through which eventually, in the fullness of time, humanity will be enabled to achieve dizzying new heights of personal and social development.

The time has come to cast off that conservative timidity that is unduly prevalent in contemporary culture—the mentality that keeps insisting "one false move and I am dead." The time has come to restore the idea of progress to its rightful place in the intellectual pantheon. The foundation of a Federal Union of Democratic Nations could well have a tremendously beneficial impact upon the future of human civilization. It could well be the instrumentality through which such potential disasters as nuclear Armageddon or environmental breakdown are avoided. It could be the instrumentality through which the misery of mass poverty throughout the Third World will be abolished. It could be the instrumentality through which mankind's powerful aspirations toward interstellar expansion are eventually realized. It could be the instrumentality through which individual human beings will achieve a higher level of moral existence—less vexed and distressed by resentment and hostility toward their fellow human beings, more receptive to attitudes of respect and friendship, and more disposed to actions of cooperation and support.

We cannot know whether a campaign to establish a world government will be crowned with success. It is certainly possible that even many decades of dedicated effort on the part of a great many people will fail to establish the appropriate mental and emotional attitudes in the general human population necessary to the foundation and successful operation of the Federal Union of Democratic Nations. But we should not let this possibility of failure stay us from the proper course. If our ancestors had refused to take risks, to venture beyond the familiar, to take positive action toward a better world, then we would still be living in caves and beating one another over the head with clubs. Now it is our turn—the precious destiny of human civilization, passed forward from generation to generation, has reached our hands. We must live up to the highest standards embodied in our species. From our present perspective, a federal world government would, in all probability, be a fine and glorious embodiment and manifestation of all the finest qualities of humanity. It would provide a firm foundation on which to base further progress toward our higher purposes, both individual and social. We already have the capability—we hold it in our hands. As soon as we muster the will and the resolution, we will be ready to take the next step.

BIBLIOGRAPHY

CHAPTER 1
A NEW APPROACH TO WORLD GOVERNMENT

Treatment of world government by mainstream international relations authorities:

Amstutz, Mark. *International Conflict and Cooperation: An Introduction to World Politics*, second edition. New York: McGraw-Hill College, 1999. Page 329.

Bull, Hedley. *The Anarchical Society: A Study of Order in World Politics*. New York: Columbia University Press, 1977. Page 261.

Claude, Inis L. *Swords into Plowshares: The Problems and Progress of International Organization*, fourth edition. New York: Random House, 1971. Page 430.

Claude, Inis. *Power and International Relations*. New York: Random House, 1962. Page 208.

Falk, Richard. *A Global Approach to National Policy*. Cambridge, Mass.: Harvard University Press, 1975. Page 245.

Goodspeed, Stephen. *The Nature and Function of International Organization*, second edition. New York: Oxford University Press, 1967. Page 662-663.

Hilsman, Roger. *The Crouching Future: International Politics and U.S. Foreign Policy, A Forecast*. Garden City, NY: Doubleday, 1975. Page 574.

Kegley, Charles and Eugene Wittkopf. *World Politics: Trend and Transformation*, seventh edition. New York: Worth Publishers, 1999. Pages 534-535.

von Weizsacker, Carl Friedrich. *The Politics of Peril: Economics, Society and the Prevention of War*. New York: Seabury Press, 1978. Page 110.

Waltz, Kenneth. *Man, the State and War: A Theoretical Analysis*. New York: Columbia University Press, 1959. Page 228.

Illustrative contributions on alcohol prohibition in the United States:

Clark, Norman H. *Deliver Us From Evil: An Interpretation of American Prohibition*. New York: Norton, 1976.

Kobler, John. *Ardent Spirits: The Rise and Fall of Prohibition*. New York: Putnam: 1973.

Krout, John A. *The Origins of Prohibition* New York: Russell and Russell, 1967.

Kyvig, David, *Repealing National Prohibition*. Chicago: University of Chicago Press, 1979.

Lee, Henry. *How Dry We Were: Prohibition Revisited*. Englewood Cliffs, NJ: Prentice-Hall, 1963.

Rorabaugh, William J. *The Alcoholic Republic: An American Tradition.* New York: Oxford University Press, 1979.

Rumbarger, John J. *Profits, Power and Prohibition: Alcohol Reform and the Industrializing of America 1800-1930.* Albany, NY: State University of New York Press, 1989.

Sinclair, Andrew. *Era of Excess: A Social History of Prohibition.* New York: Harper and Row, 1964.

CHAPTER 2
A PRAGMATIC BLUEPRINT FOR WORLD GOVERNMENT

Illustrative references on the federal form of government:

Burgess, Michael, and Alain G. Gagnon, editors. *Comparative Federalism and Federation: Competing Traditions and Future Directions.* Toronto: University of Toronto Press, 1993.

Forsyth, Murray. *Federalism and Nationalism.* New York: St. Martin's Press, 1987.

Franck, Thomas M. editor. *Why Federations Fail: An Inquiry into the Requisites for Successful Federalism.* New York: New York University Press, 1968.

Katz, Ellis, and G. Alan Tarr, editors. *Federalism and Rights.* Lanham, Md.: Rowman and Littlefield, 1996.

King, Preston. *Federalism and Federation.* London: Frank Cass, 2000.

Macmahon, Arthur W. *Federalism: Mature and Emergent.* New York: Russell and Russell, 1962.

McWhinney, Edward. *Comparative Federalism: States' Rights and National Power.* Toronto: University of Toronto Press, 1962.

Michelmann, Hans J., and Panayotis Soldatos, *Federalism and International Relations: The Role of Subnational Units.* Oxford: Oxford University Press, 1990.

Scheiber, Harry N., and Malcolm M. Feeley, editors. *Power Divided: Essays on the Theory and Practice of Federalism.* Berkeley, Cal. University of California Press, 1989.

Languages:

Crystal, David. *English as a Global Language.* Cambridge: Cambridge University Press, 1997.

Grimes, Barbara F., and Joseph E. Grimes *Ethnologue: Languages of the World*, 14th edition. Dallas, Texas: SIL International, 2000.

Ostler, Nicholas. *Empires of the Word: A Language History of the World.* New York: HarperCollins, 2006.

Separatism:

Dobratz, Betty, and Stephanie Shanks-Meile. *White Power, White Pride! The White Separatist Movement in the United States.* New York: Simon and Schuster, 1997.

Sanz, Timothy L. *Separatist Movements: Research Sources 1990-1995.* Fort Leavenworth, Ks.: Foreign Military Studies Office, 1995.

Roehner, Bertrand M., and Leonard J. Rahilly. *Separatism and Integration: A Study in Analytical History.* Lanham, Md.: Rowmand and Littlefield, 2002.

Spencer, Metta, editor. *Separatism: Democracy and Disintegration.* Lanham, Md.: Rowman and Littlefield, 1998.

The role of slavery in bringing on the United States Civil War:

Auer, J. Jeffrey editor. *Antislavery and Disunion, 1858-1861: Studies in the Rhetoric of Compromise and Conflict.* New York: Harper and Row, 1963.

Barney, William J. *The Road to Secession: A New Perspective on the Old South.* New York: Praeger, 1972.

Brandon, Mark E. *Free in the World: American Slavery and Constitutional Failure.* Princeton, NJ: Princeton University Press, 1998.

Faust, Drew, editor, *The Ideology of Slavery: Proslavery Thought in the Antebellum South, 1830-1860.* Baton Rouge: Louisiana State University Press, 1981.

Filler, Louis. *The Crusade against Slavery: 1830-1860.* New York: Harper and Bros., 1960.

Lane, Ann J. *The Debate over Slavery: Stanley Elkins and His Critics.* Urbana: University of Illinois Press, 1971.

Patterson, Patterson. *Slavery and Social Death: A Comparative Study.* Cambridge, Mass.: Harvard University Press, 1982.

Pease, William, and Jane Pease. *The Antislavery Argument.* Indianapolis: Bobbs-Merrill, 1965.

Potter, David M. *The Impending Crisis: 1848-1861.* New York: Harper and Row, 1976.

Stampp, Kenneth M. *The Imperiled Union: Essays on the Background of the Civil War.* New York: Oxford University Press, 1980.

Illustrative references on arms control and reduction during the Cold War:

Beres, Louis Rene. *Mimicking Sisyphus: America's Countervailing Nuclear Strategy.* Lexington, Mass.: D. C. Heath, 1983.

Bull, Hedley. *The Control of the Arms Race: Disarmament and Arms Control in the Missile Age,* second edition. New York: Frederick A. Praeger, 1965.

Clarke, Duncan. *Politics of Arms Control: The Role and Effectiveness of the U.S. Arms Control and Disarmament Agency.* New York: Free Press, 1979.

Newhouse, John. *Cold Dawn: The Story of SALT.* New York: Holt, Rinehart and Winston, 1973.

Russett, Bruce. *The Prisoners of Insecurity: Deterrence, Arms Races, and Arms Control.* San Francisco: Freeman, 1983.

Schelling, Thomas C. and Morton H. Halperin. *Strategy and Arms Control.* New York: Twentieth Century Fund, 1961.

Smith, Gerald. *Doubletalk: The Story of the First Strategic Arms Limitation Talks.* Garden City, New York: Doubleday, 1980.

Spanier, John W., and Joseph L. Noge, *The Politics of Disarmament: A Study in Soviet-American Gamesmanship.* New York: Frederick A. Praeger, 1962.

Humanitarian disasters of the recent past in Bosnia and elsewhere:

Adelman, Howard, and Astri Suhrke, editors. *The Path of a Genocide: The Rwanda Crisis from Uganda to Zaire.* New Brunswick, NJ: Transaction Publishers, 2000.

Brune, Lester H. *The United States and Post-Cold War Interventions: Bush and Clinton in Somalia, Haiti and Bosnia, 1992-1998.* Claremont, Cal.: Regina Books, 1999.

Campbell, David. *National Deconstruction: Violence, Identity, and Justice in Bosnia.* Minneapolis: University of Minnesota Press, 1998.

Clarke, Walter, and Jeffrey Herbst, editors. *Learning from Somalia: The Lessons of Armed Humanitarian Intervention.* Boulder, Col.: Westview Press, 1997.

Cushman, Thomas, and Stjepan G. Mestrovic, editors. *This Time We Knew: Western Responses to Genocide in Bosnia.* New York: New York University Press, 1996.

Destexhe, Alain, and Anthony Daley, editors. *Rwanda and Genocide in the Twentieth Century.* New York: New York University Press, 1996.

Gutman, Roy. *A Witness to Genocide.* London: Macmillan, 1993.

Haas, Michael. *Genocide by Proxy: Cambodian Pawn on a Superpower Chessboard.* Westport, Conn.: Greenwood Publishing Group, 1991.

Kamm, Henry. *Cambodia: Report from a Stricken Land.* New York: Arcade Publishing, 1998.

Keane, Fergal. *Season of Blood: A Rwanda Journey.* New York: Viking, 1995.

Kiernan, Ben. *The Pol Pot Regime: Race, Power and Genocide in Cambodia under the Khmer Rouge, 1975-79.* New Haven, Conn.: Yale University Press, 1998.

Kuperman, Alan J. *Limits of Humanitarian Intervention: Genocide in Rwanda.* Washington: Brookings Institution Press, 2001.

O'Ballance, Edgar. *Civil War in Bosnia, 1992-94.* New York: St. Martin's Press, 1995.

Prunier, Gerard. *The Rwanda Crisis: History of a Genocide.* New York: Columbia University Press, 1997.

Rieff, David. *Slaughterhouse: Bosnia and the Failure of the West.* New York: Simon and Schuster, 1995.

Rohde, David W. *Endgame: The Betrayal and Fall of Srebrenica, Europe's Worst Massacre Since World War II.* New York: Farrar, Straus and Giroux, 1997.

Simons, Anna. *Networks of Dissolution: Somalia Undone.* Boulder, Co.: Westview Press, 1996.

Vulliamy, Ed. *Seasons in Hell: Understanding Bosnia's War.* New York: St. Martin's Press, 1994.

CHAPTER 3
SOME HISTORICAL BACKGROUND
ON WORLD GOVERNMENT

Contributions related to world government cited in this chapter:

Borgese, Giuseppe. *Foundations of the World Republic.* Chicago: University of Chicago Press, 1953.

Clark, Grenville, and Louis B. Sohn. *World Peace through World Law,* third edition. Cambridge, Mass.: Harvard University Press, 1966.

Davis, Garry. *The World Is My Country.* New York: Putnam, 1961.

Davis, Garry. *World Government: Ready or Not!* Sorrento, Maine: Juniper Ledge, 1984.

Harris, Theodore. *A Proposed Constitution for the United Nations of the World.* New York: C. F. Ruckstuhl, 1918.

Heater, Derek. *World Citizenship and Government: Cosmopolitan Ideas in the History of Western Political Thought.* New York: St. Martin's Press, 1996.

Hutchins, Robert M. *Foundations for World Order.* Denver: University of Denver Press, 1949.

Hutchins, Robert M., et al. *Preliminary Draft of a World Constitution.* Chicago: University of Chicago Press, 1948.

Isely, Philip, et al. "A Constitution for the Federation of Earth." In Errol E. Harris, *One World or None: Prescription for Survival,* Atlantic Highlands, NJ: Humanities Press, 1993.

Isley, Philip. "A Critique of Our Global Neighborhood." In Errol E. Harris and James A. Yunker, editors, *Toward Genuine Global Governance: Critical Reactions to Our Global Neighborhood,* Westport, Conn.: Praeger Publishers, 1999.

Mangone, Gerald J. *The Idea and Practice of World Government.* New York: Columbia University Press, 1951.

Minor, Raleigh Colston. *A Republic of Nations: A Study of the Organization of a Federal League of Nations.* New York: Oxford University Press, 1918.

Newcombe, Hanna. *Design for a Better World.* Lanham, Md.: University Press of America, 1984.

Newfang, Oskar. *World Government.* New York: Barnes and Noble, 1942.

Reves, Emery. *The Anatomy of Peace,* second edition. New York: Harper and Brothers, 1945.

Rider, Fremont. *The Great Dilemma of World Organization.* New York: Reynal and Hitchcock, 1946.

Streit, Clarence K. *Union Now: A Proposal for a Federal Union of the Leading Democracies of the North Atlantic.* New York: Harper and Brothers, 1939.

Streit, Clarence K. *Union Now with Britain.* New York: Harper and Brothers, 1941.

Streit, Clarence K. *Union Now: A Proposal for an Atlantic Federal Union of the Free.* New York: Harper and Brothers, 1949.

Wynner, Edith, and Georgia Lloyd, *Searchlight on Peace Plans: Choose Your Road to World Government.* New York: Dutton, 1944.

Additional contributions related to world government:

Baratta, Joseph P. *The Politics of World Federation.* Vol. I: *United Nations, UN Reform, Atomic Control.* Vol. II: *From World Federalism to Global Governance.* Westport, Conn.: Praeger, 2004.

Bassett, Noble P. *Constitution of the United Nations of the World.* Boston: Christopher, 1944.

Bidmead, Harold S. *The Parliament of Man: The Federation of the World.* Barnstaple: Patton, 1992.

Corbett, Percy E. *World Government Proposals before Congress.* New Haven: Yale Institute of International Studies, 1950.

Curry, William B. in *The Case for Federal Union.* Harmondsworth, England: Penguin, 1939.

Curtis, Lionel. *Civitas Dei (World Order),* second revised edition. London: George Allen and Unwin, 1950.

de Vasconcellos, Henrique Pinheiro. *The World State, or, The New Order of Common Sense.* Rio de Janeiro: Grafica Olimpia, 1944.

Eaton, Howard O., et al. *The Coming Structure of World Government.* Norman: University of Oklahoma Press, 1944.

Glossop, Ronald J. *World Federation? A Critical Analysis of Federal World Government.* Jefferson, NC: McFarland, 1993.

Harris, Errol E. *One World or None: A Prescription for Survival.* Atlantic Highlands, NJ: Humanities Press, 1993.

Harris, Errol E. *Earth Federation Now! Tomorrow Is Too Late.* Radford, Va.: Institute for Economic Democracy, 2005.

Hemleben, Sylvester J. *Plans for World Peace through Six Centuries.* Chicago: University of Chicago Press, 1943.

Jessup, Philip C. *A Modern Law of Nations.* New York: Macmillan, 1952.

Johnson, Julia E., compiler. *Federal World Government*. New York: H. W. Wilson, 1948.

Kelsen, Hans. *Peace through Law*. Chapel Hill: University of North Carolina Press, 1944.

Lilienthal, Alfred M. *Which Way to World Government?* New York: Foreign Policy Association, 1950.

Mayne, Richard, and John Pinder. *Federal Union: The Pioneers— A History of Federal Union*. London: Macmillan, 1990.

Newfang, Oskar. *The Road to World Peace: A Federation of Nations*. New York: G. P. Putnam, 1924.

Newfang, Oskar. *World Federation*. New York: Barnes and Noble, 1939.

Roberts, John C. de V. *List of Works on World Federalism*. London: Association of World Federalists, 1990.

Roberts, John C. de V. *World Citizenship and Mundialism: A Guide to the Building of a World Community*. Westport, Conn.: Praeger, 1999.

Roberts, Owen J., and John F. Schmidt. *The New Federalist*. New York: Harper and Brothers, 1950.

Schuman, Frederick L. *The Commonwealth of Man: An Inquiry into Power Politics and World Government*. New York: Alfred A. Knopf, 1952.

Sprading, Charles T. *The World State Craze*. Los Angeles: Wetzel, 1954.

Suganami, Hidemi. *The Domestic Analogy and World Order Proposals*. New York: Cambridge University Press, 1989.

Wagar, Warren W. *The City of Man: Prophecies of a World Civilization in Twentieth Century Thought*. Boston: Houghton Mifflin, 1963.

Walker, Barbara, compiler. *Uniting the Peoples and the Nations: Readings in World Federalism*. Washington DC: World Federalist Association, 1993.

Wofford, Harris. *It's Up to Us: Federal World Government in Our Time*. New York: Harcourt Brace, 1946.

Wynner, Edith. *World Federal Government: Why? What? How?* Afton, NY: Fedonat Press, 1954.

Yunker, James A. *World Union on the Horizon*. Lanham, Md.: University Press of America, 1993.

Yunker, James A. *Rethinking World Government: A New App*roach. Lanham, Md.: University Press of America, 2005.

Yunker, James A., and Errol Harris, editors. *Toward Genuine Global Governance: Critical Reactions to Our Global Neighborhood*. Westport, Conn.: Praeger, 1999.

Zolo, Danilo. *Cosmopolis: Prospects for World Government*. Cambridge, UK: Polity Press, 1997.

Illustrative contributions on the history of empires:

Abernethy, David B. *The Dynamics of Global Dominance: European Overseas Empires, 1415-1980*. New Haven: Yale University Press, 2001.

Armitage, David. *The Ideological Origins of the British Empire*. Cambridge: Cambridge University Press, 2000.

Conklin, Alice L. *A Mission to Civilize: The Republican Idea of Empire in France and West Africa, 1895-1930*. Stanford, Cal.: Stanford University Press, 2000.

Curtin, Philip D. *The World and the West: European Challenge and the Overseas Response in the Age of Empire*. Cambridge: Cambridge University Press, 2000.

Elliott, John H. *Empires of the Atlantic World: Britain and Spain in America 1492-1830*. New Haven, Conn.: Yale University Press, 2006.

Goodwin, Jason. *Lords of the Horizon: A History of the Ottoman Empire*. New York: Picador USA, 2002.

Gould, Elisa H. *The Persistence of Empire: British Political Culture in the Age of the American Revolution*. Raleigh: University of North Carolina Press, 2000.

Heather, Peter. *The Fall of the Roman Empire: A New History of Rome and the Barbarians*. New York: Oxford University Press, 2005.

Holland, Tom. *Persian Fire: The First World Empire and the Battle for the West*. New York: Doubleday, 2006.

Laurence, Ray, and Joanne Berry. *Cultural Identity in the Roman Empire*. New York: Routledge, 2001.

McCarthy, Justin. *The Ottoman Peoples and the End of Empire*. Oxford: Oxford University Press, 2000.

Quinn, Frederick. *The French Overseas Empire*. Westport, Conn.: Greenwood Publishing Group, 2000.

Roshwald, Aviel. *Ethnic Nationalism and the Fall of Empires: Central Europe, the Middle East and Russia, 1914-1923*. New York: Routledge, 2001.

Russell-Woods, A. J. R. *Government and Governance of Empires, 1450-1800*. Aldershot, UK: Ashgate Publishing, 2000.

CHAPTER 4
WORLD ECONOMIC INEQUALITY

Illustrative references world economic inequality and economic development:

Alpert, Paul. *Partnership or Confrontation? Poor Lands and Rich*. New York: Free Press, 1973.

Angelopoulos, Angelos T., and Melvin Fagen. *The Third World and the Rich Countries: Proposals to Combat the Global Economic Crisis*. Lanham, Md.: University Press of America, 1993.

Bapna, Ashok, editor. *One World, One Future: New International Strategies for Development*. New York: Praeger, 1985.

Bello, Walden F., Shea Cunningham, and Bill Rau. *Dark Victory: The United States and Global Poverty*, second edition. Oakland, Cal.: Institute for Food and Development Policy, 1998.

Clague, Christopher, editor. *Institutions and Economic Development: Growth and Governance in Less-Developed and Post-Socialist Countries*. Baltimore: Johns Hopkins University Press, 1997.

Colmans, David, and Frederick Nixson. *Economics of Change in Less Developed Nations*. New York: John Wiley, 1978.

Cypher James M., and James L. Dietz. *The Process of Economic Development*. New York: Routledge, 1997.

Dammann, Erik. *The Future in Our Hands*. Oxford: Pergamon Press, 1979.

Dixon, John, and David MacArov, editors. *Poverty: A Persistent Global Reality*. New York: Routledge, 1998.

Fishlow Albert, et al. *Rich Nations and Poor Nations in the World Economy*. New York: McGraw-Hill, 1978.

Griffin, Keith B. *International Inequality and World Poverty.* New York: Holmes and Meier, 1978.

Harrison, Paul. *Inside the Third World: The Anatomy of Poverty*, third edition. New York: Viking Penguin, 1994.

Langdon, Steven. *Global Poverty, Democracy and North-South Change.* Aurora, Ontario: Garamond Press, 1998.

Loup, Jacques. *Can the Third World Survive?* Baltimore, Md.: Johns Hopkins University Press, 1983.

Murdock, William W. *The Poverty of Nations: The Political Economy of Hunger and Population.* Baltimore: Johns Hopkins University Press, 1980.

Mushkat, Mario'n. *The Third World and Peace: Some Aspects of the Interrelationship of Underdevelopment and International Security.* New York: St. Martin's Press, 1982.

Myrdal, Gunnar. *The Challenge of World Poverty: A World Anti-Poverty Program in Outline.* New York: Pantheon, 1970.

Nurnberger, Klaus. *Prosperity, Poverty and Pollution: The Emergence of a Global Economic Responsibility.* New York: St. Martin's Press, 1999.

Ranis, Gustav, editor. *The Gap between the Rich and Poor Nations.* New York: St. Martin's Press, 1972.

Rostow, Walt Whitman. *The Stages of Economic Growth: An Anti-Communist Manifesto.* New York: Cambridge University Press, 1960.

Ryrie, William. *First World, Third World.* New York: St. Martin's Press, 1995.

Vandersluis, Sarah Owen, editor. *Poverty in World Politics: Whose Global Era?* New York: St. Martin's Press, 1999.

Ward, Barbara, et al. *The Widening Gap: Development in the 1970s.* New York: Columbia University Press, 1971.

Illustrative references on imperialism:

Alam, M. S. "Colonialism, Decolonisation and Growth Rates: Theory and Empirical Evidence," *Cambridge Journal of Economics* 18(3): 235-257, June 1994.

Brewer, Anthony. *Marxist Theories of Imperialism: A Critical Survey*, second edition. New York: Routledge, 1990.

Chilcote, Ronald M., editor. *The Political Economy of Imperialism: Critical Appraisals.* Boston: Kluwer Academic, 1999.

Davis, Lance E., and Robert A. Huttenback. *Mammon and the Pursuit of Empire: The Political Economy of British Imperialism, 1860-1912.* Cambridge: Cambridge University Press, 1986.

Emmanuel, Arghiri. *Unequal Exchange: A Study of the Imperialism of Trade.* New York: Monthly Review Press, 1972.

Feuer, Lewis. *Imperialism and the Anti-Imperialist Mind.* Buffalo, NY: Prometheus Books, 1986.

Griffin, Keith B., and John Gurley. "Radical Analyses of Imperialism, the Third World, and the Transition to Socialism," *Journal of Economic Literature* 23(3): 1089-1143, September 1985.

Hobson, John A.. *Imperialism.* London: Allen and Unwin, 1948. Originally published in 1902.

Isaacman, Allan, and Richard Roberts, editors. *Cotton, Colonialism, and Social History in Sub-Saharan Africa.* London: Currey, 1995.

Jalee, Pierre. *The Pillage of the Third World.* New York: Monthly Review Press, 1968.

Korten, David C. *When Corporations Rule the World.* London: Earthscan, 1995.

Lenin, Vladimir I. *Imperialism: The Highest Stage of Capitalism.* Chicago: Pluto, 1996. Originally published in Russian in 1916.

Luxemburg, Rosa. *Accumulation of Capital.* New York: Monthly Review Press, 1968. Originally published in German in 1913.

Rhodes, Robert I., editor. *Imperialism and Underdevelopment: A Reader.* New York: Monthly Review Press, 1970.

Sau, Ranjit. *Unequal Exchange: Imperialism and Development.* Calcutta: Oxford University Press, 1978.

Waites, Bernard. *Europe and the Third World: From Colonization to Decolonization c. 1500-1998.* New York: St. Martin's Press, 1999.

CHAPTER 5
FOREIGN DEVELOPMENT ASSISTANCE

General references on the nature, purposes and potential effects of foreign aid:

Hayter, Teresa. *Aid as Imperialism.* New York: Penguin, 1971.

Parkinson, John R., editor. *Poverty and Aid.* Oxford: Basil Blackwell, 1983.

Mikesell, Raymond F. *The Economics of Foreign Aid and Self-Sustaining Development.* Boulder, Col.: Westview, 1983.

Riddell, Roger C. *Foreign Aid Reconsidered.* Baltimore: Johns Hopkins University Press, 1987.

Mosley, Paul. *Overseas Aid: Its Defense and Reform.* Lexington, Ky.: University Press of Kentucky, 1987.

Browne, Stephen. *Foreign Aid in Practice.* New York: New York University Press, 1990.

Mosley, Paul, Jane Harrigan, and John Toye. *Aid and Power: The World Bank and Policy-Based Lending, Vol. 1: Analysis and Policy Proposals, Vol. 2: Case Studies.* New York: Routledge, 1991.

Cassen, Robert H. *Does Aid Work? Report to An Intergovernmental Task Force,* second edition. New York: Oxford University Press, 1994.

Kemp, Murray C. *The Gains from Trade and the Gains from Aid.* New York: Routledge, 1995.

Boone, Peter. "Politics and the Effectiveness of Foreign Aid," *European Economic Review* 40(2): 289-329, February 1996.

Rebien, Claus C. *Evaluating Development Assistance in Theory and Practice.* Brookfield, Vt.: Ashgate, 1996.

Opeskin, Brian R. "The Moral Foundations of Foreign Aid," *World Development* 24(1): 21-44, January 1996.

Dollar, David, and Lant Pritchett. *Assessing Aid: What Works, What Doesn't, and Why.* New York: Oxford University Press for the World Bank, 1998.

References on Unites States foreign aid:

Baldwin, David A. *Foreign Aid and American Foreign Policy: A Documentary Analysis.* New York: Praeger, 1966.

Brown, William A., and Redvers Opie. *American Foreign Assistance.* Washington: Brookings Institution, 1953.

Bruton, Henry J. "Foreign Aid to the Less Developed Countries." In Joseph A. Pechman, editor, *Fulfilling America's Promise: Social Policies for the 1990s,* Ithaca, NY: Cornell University Press, 1992.

De Angelis, Manlio L. *U. S. Foreign Aid Programs.* Boulder, Col.: Westview, 1996.

Johnson, Harry G. *Economic Policies toward Less Developed Countries.* Washington: Brookings Institution, 1968.

Lumsdaine, David H. *Moral Vision in International Politics: The Foreign Aid Regime, 1949-1989.* Princeton, NJ: Princeton University Press, 1993.

Maizels Alfred, and Machiko Missanke. "Motivations for Aid to Developing Countries," *World Development* 12(9): 879-900, 1984.

Montgomery, John D. *The Politics of Foreign Aid: American Experience in Southeast Asia.* New York: Praeger, 1962.

Morss, Elliott R., and Victoria A. Morss. *U.S. Foreign Aid: An Assessment of New and Traditional Development Strategies.* Boulder, Co.: Westview, 1982.

Ohlin, Goran. "The Evolution of United States Aid Doctrine." in Benjamin J. Cohen, editor, *American Foreign Economic Policy,* New York: Harper and Row, 1968.

Rostow, Walt Whitman. *Eisenhower, Kennedy, and Foreign Aid.* Austin: University of Texas Press, 1985.

Rubin, Jacob. *Your Hundred Billion Dollars: The Complete Story of American Foreign Aid.* Philadelphia: Chilton, 1964.

Ruttan, Vernon W. *United States Development Assistance Policy: The Domestic Politics of Foreign Economic Aid.* Baltimore: Johns Hopkins University Press, 1996.

Sewell, John W. "Foreign Aid for a New World Order." In Brad Roberts, editor, *U.S. Foreign Policy after the Cold War,* Cambridge, Mass.: MIT Press, 1992.

White, John A. *The Politics of Foreign Aid.* New York: St. Martin's Press, 1974.

Wilhelm, John, and Gerry Feinstein. *U.S. Foreign Assistance: Investment or Folly?* New York: Praeger, 1984.

The history, politics and economics of the Marshall Plan:

Arkes, Hadley. *Bureaucracy, the Marshall Plan, and the National Interest.* Princeton, NJ: Princeton University Press, 1972.

Donovan, Robert J. *The Second Victory: The Marshall Plan and the Postwar Revival of Europe.* New York: Madison Books, 1987.

Fossedal, Gregory A. *Our Finest Hour: Will Clayton, the Marshall Plan, and the Triumph of Democracy.* Stanford, Cal.: Hoover Institution Press, 1993.

Hoffmann, Stanley, and Charles Maier, editors. *The Marshall Plan: A Retrospective.* Boulder, Co.: Westview Press, 1984.

Hogan, Michael J. *The Marshall Plan: America, Britain, and the Reconstruction of Western Europe, 1947-1952.* New York: Cambridge University Press, 1987.

Mayer, Herbert Carelton. *German Recovery and the Marshall Plan, 1948-1952.* Bonn and New York: Edition Atlantic Forum, 1969.

Mee, Charles L. *The Marshall Plan: The Launching of the Pax Americana.* New York: Simon and Schuster, 1984.

Pelling, Henry. *Britain and the Marshall Plan.* New York: St. Martin's Press, 1988.

Price, Harry Bayard. *The Marshall Plan and Its Meaning.* Ithaca, New York: Cornell University Press, 1955.

Schmitt, Hans A. *The Path to European Union: From the Marshall Plan to the Common Market.* Baton Rouge: Louisiana State University Press, 1962.

Wexler, Immanuel. *The Marshall Plan Revisited: The European Recovery Program in Economic Perspective.* Westport, Conn.: Greenwood, 1983.

Wilson, Theodore A. *The Marshall Plan, 1947–1951.* New York: Foreign Policy Association, 1977.

Representative statistical studies on the effectiveness or ineffectiveness of foreign aid:

Bornschier, Volker, Christopher Chase-Dunn, and Richard Robinson. "Cross-National Evidence of the Effects of Foreign Investment and Aid on Economic Growth and Inequality: A Survey of Findings and Re-Analysis," *American Journal of Sociology* 84(3): 658-683, November 1978.

Burnside, Craig, and David Dollar. "Aid, Policies and Growth," *American Economic Review* 90(4): 847-868, September 2000.

Griffin, Keith B. "Foreign Capital, Domestic Savings and Economic Development," *Oxford Bulletin of Economics and Statistics* 32(2): 99-112, February 1970.

Michalopoulos, Constantine, and Vasant Sukhatme. "The Impact of Development Assistance: A Review of the Quantitative Evidence." In Anne O. Krueger, Constantine Michalopoulos, and Vernan W. Ruttan, eds., *Aid and Development*, Baltimore, Md.: Johns Hopkins Press, 1989.

Mosley, Paul, John Hudson, and Sara Horrell. "Aid, the Public Sector and the Market in Less Developed Countries" (*Economic Journal* 97(387): 616-641, September 1987);

Papanek, Gustav S. "Aid, Foreign Private Investment, Saving and Growth in Less Developed Countries," *Journal of Political Economy* 81(1): 120-130, January-February 1973.

CHAPTER 6
A WORLD ECONOMIC EQUALIZATION PROGRAM

Technical contributions by the author on the World Economic Equalization Program:

Yunker, James A. "A World Economic Equalization Program: Results of a Simulation," *Journal of Developing Areas* 10(2): 159-179, January 1976.

Yunker, James A. "A World Economic Equalization Program: Refinements and Sensitivity Analysis," *World Development* 16(8), August 1988.

Yunker, James A. *Common Progress: The Case for a World Economic Equalization Program.* Westport, Conn.: Praeger, 2000.

Yunker, James A. Could a Global Marshall Plan Be Successful? An Investigation Using the WEEP Simulation Model," *World Development* 32(7): 1109-1137, July 2004.

Yunker, James A. "Swords into Plowshares: Financing a World Economic Equalization Program," *Journal of Policy Modeling* 28: 563-593, 2006.

CHAPTER 7
THE ISSUE OF NATIONALISM

Contributions related to nationalism cited in this chapter:

Bodin, Jean. *Six Books of the Commonwealth*, translated and abridged by M. J. Tooley. Oxford: Basil Blackwell, 1955.

Breuilly, John. *Nationalism and the State*, second edition. Chicago: University of Chicago Press, 1993.

Franck, Thomas M., editor, *Why Federations Fail: An Inquiry into the Requisites for Successful Federalism* (New York: New York University Press, 1968).

Hayes, Carlton. *The Historical Evolution of Modern Nationalism.* New York: Macmillan, 1931.

Hobbes, Thomas. *Leviathan*. New York: Barnes and Noble, 2004.

Kohn, Hans. *The Idea of Nationalism: A Study of Its Origins and Background* (New York: Macmillan, 1944);

Shafer, Boyd. *Faces of Nationalism: New Realities and Old Myths*. New York: Harcourt Brace Jovanovich, 1972.

Additional contributions related to nationalism:

Anderson, Benedict R. *Imagined Communities: Reflections on the Origin and Spread of Nationalism*, revised edition. New York: New Left Books, 1991.

D. Smith, Anthony D. *Theories of Nationalism*. New York: Harper and Row, 1971.

Deutsch, Karl. *Nationalism and Its Alternatives*. New York: Alfred Knopf, 1969.

Gellner, Ernest. *Nations and Nationalism*. Ithaca, NY: Cornell University Press, 1983.

Hechter, Michael. *Containing Nationalism*. Oxford: Oxford University Press, 2000.

Hinsley, Francis H. *Nationalism and the International System*. Dobbs Ferry, New York: Oceana Publications, 1973.

Kamenka, Eugene, editor. *Nationalism: The Nature and Evolution of an Idea*. New York: St. Martin's Press, 1976.

Minogue, Kenneth R. *Nationalism*. New York: Basic Books, 1967.

Sathyamurthy, T. V. *Nationalism in the Contemporary World: Political and Sociological Perspectives*. Totowa, New Jersey: Allenheld, Osmun, 1983.

Tivey, Leonard, editor. *The Nation-State: The Formation of Modern Politics*. New York: St. Martin's Press, 1981.

Ward, Barbara. *Nationalism and Ideology*. New York: Norton, 1966.

Representative references on the nature and attributes of state sovereignty:

Caporaso, James A. *The Elusive State: International and Comparative Perspectives*. Newbury Park, California: Sage Publications, 1989.

d'Entreves, Alexander P. *The Notion of the State: An Introduction to Political Theory*. Oxford: Clarendon Press, 1969.

de Jasay, Anthony. *The State*. New York: Basil Blackwell, 1985.

de Jouvenal, Bertrand. *Sovereignty: An Inquiry into the Political Good*. Chicago: University of Chicago Press, 1959.

Fowler, Michael Ross and Julie Marie Bunck. *Law, Power, and the Sovereign State: The Evolution and Application of the Concept of Sovereignty*. University Park, Pa.: Pennsylvania State University Press, 1995.

Hashmi, Schail H. *State Sovereignty: Change and Persistence in International Relations*. University Park, Pa.: Pennsylvania State University Press, 1997.

Hinsley, Francis H. *Sovereignty*. New York: Basic Books, 1966.

Sassen, Saskia. *Losing Control? Sovereignty in an Age of Globalization*. New York: Columbia University Press, 1996.

Sharp, Gene. *Social Power and Political Freedom*. Boston: Porter Sargent, 1980.

Solinger, Dorothy, David A. Smith and Steven Topik. *State and Sovereignty in the Global Economy*. New York: Routledge, 1999.

Spruyt, Hendrik. *The Sovereign State and Its Competitors*. Princeton, NJ: Princeton University Press, 1994.

Stankiewicz, E. J., editor. *In Defense of Sovereignty*. New York: Oxford University Press, 1969.

Wesson, Robert G. *State Systems: International Pluralism, Politics, and Culture*. New York: Free Press, 1978.

CHAPTER 8
THE PROGRESS OF INTERNATIONALISM

History of diplomacy in international relations:

Degenhardt, Henry W. compiler. *Treaties and Alliances of the World*, third edition. Detroit: Gale Research Co., 1981.

Hinsley, Francis H. *Power and the Pursuit of Peace*. Cambridge: Cambridge University Press, 1963.

Holbraad, Carsten. *The Concert of Europe: A Study in German and British International Theory, 1815-1914*. London: Longmans, 1970.

Kennan, George F. *The Fateful Alliance: France, Russia and the Coming of the First World War*. New York: Pantheon, 1984.

Kissinger, Henry. *Diplomacy*. New York: Simon and Schuster, 1994.

Osgood, Robert Endicott. *Ideals and Self-Interest in America's Foreign Relations*. Chicago: University of Chicago Press, 1953.

Paterson, Thomas, Garry Clifford, and Kenneth J. Hagen. *American Foreign Policy: A History*. Lexington, Mass.: D. C. Heath, 1977.

Read, Anthony, and David Fisher. *The Deadly Embrace: Hitler, Stalin and the Nazi-Soviet Pact, 1939-1941*. New York: Norton, 1988.

Taylor, A. J. P. *The Struggle for Mastery in Europe, 1848-1918*. Oxford: Oxford University Press, 1954.

Webster, Charles. *The Congress of Vienna*. London: Bell, 1937.

Wheeler-Bennett, John W., and Anthony Nicholls. *The Semblance of Peace: The Political Settlement after the Second World War*. New York: St. Martin's Press, 1972.

Wight, Martin. *Power Politics*. New York: Holmes and Meier, 1978.

History of the League of Nations:

Barros, James. *The Corfu Incident of 1923*. Princeton, NJ: Princeton University Press, 1965.

Barros, James. *The League of Nations and the Great Powers: the Greek-Bulgarian Incident, 1925*. Oxford: Clarendon Press, 1970.

Bendiner, Elmer. *A Time for Angels: The Tragicomic History of the League of Nations*. New York: Alfred A. Knopf, 1975.

Dexter, Byron. *The Years of Opportunity: The League of Nations, 1920-1926*. New York: Viking Press, 1967.

Gill, George, and George L. Lankevich, editors. *The League of Nations from 1929 to 1946*. Garden City Park, NY: Avery Publishing Group, 1996.

Nish, Ian Hill. *Japan's Struggle with Internationalism: Japan, China and the League of Nations, 1931-1933*. London: Kegan Paul International, 2000.

Northedge, F. S. *The League of Nations: Its Life and Times, 1920-1946*. New York: Holmes and Meier, 1986.

Ostrower, Gary B., and George L. Lankevich, editors. *The League of Nations from 1919 to 1928*. Garden City Park, NY: Avery Publishing Group, 1996.

Scott, George. *The Rise and Fall of the League of Nations*. New York: Macmillan, 1973.

Walters, Francis P. *A History of the League of Nations*, second edition. New York: Oxford University Press, 1967.

Zimmern, Alfred. *The League of Nations and the Rule of Law, 1918-1935*, second edition. Oxford: Oxford University Press, 1939.

The United Nations:

Alger, Chadwick F., editor. *The Future of the United Nations System: Potential for the Twenty-First Century.* New York: United Nations University Press, 1998.

Baratta, Joseph P. *Strengthening the United Nations: A Bibliography on U.N. Reform and World Federalism.* Westport, Conn.: Greenwood Press, 1987.

Boulden, Jane. *Peace Enforcement: The United Nations Experience in Congo, Somalia and Bosnia.* Greenwich, Conn.: Greenwood, 2001.

Fenichell, Stephen S., and Philip Andrews. *The United Nations: Blueprint for Peace.* Philadelphia: John C. Winston, 1954.

Fromuth, Peter J. *A Successor Vision: The United Nations of Tomorrow.* Lanham, Md: University Press of America, 1988.

Goodrich, Leland M., and Anne P. Simons. *The United Nations and the Maintenance of International Peace and Security.* Washington, D.C.: Brookings Institution, 1955.

Gordenker, Leon, editor. *The United Nations in International Politics.* Princeton, New Jersey: Princeton University Press, 1971.

Kay, David A., editor. *The United Nations Political System.* New York: John Wiley and Sons, 1967.

Mingst, Karen A., and Margaret P. Karns. *The United Nations in the Post-Cold War Era.* Boulder, Col.: Westview Press, 1999.

Newman Edward, and Chandra Thakur, editors. *New Millennium, New Perspectives: The United Nations, Security and Governance.* New York: United Nations University Press, 2001.

Ostrower, Gary B. *The United Nations and the United States.* New York: Macmillan, 1998.

Righter, Rosemary. *Utopia Lost: The United Nations and World Order.* New York: Twentieth Century Fund Press, 1995.

Ryan, Stephen. *The United Nations and International Politics.* New York: St. Martin's Press, 2000.

Sarooshi, Danesh. *The United Nations and the Development of Collective Security.* New York: Oxford University Press, 1999.

Simon, Geoffrey L. *UN Malaise: Power, Problems and Realpolitik.* New York: St. Martin's Press, 1995.

Stoessinger, John G. *The United Nations and the Superpowers.* New York: Random House, 1965.

Stoller, Ezra. *The United Nations.* Princeton, NJ: Princeton University Press, 1999.

Yoder, Amos. *The Evolution of the United Nations System.* New York: Taylor and Francis, 1989.

The European Union:

Bornschier, Volker, editor. *State-Building in Europe: The Revitalization of Western European Integration.* Cambridge: Cambridge University Press, 2000.

Burgess, Michael. *Federalism and European Union: The Building of Europe, 1950-2000.* New York: Routledge, 2000.

Corbett, Richard. *The Treaty of Maastricht: From Conception to Ratification: A Comprehensive Reference Guide.* Harlow, Essex, U.K.: Longman Group, 1993.

Cram, Laura. *Policy-Making in the European Union.* New York: Routledge, 1997.

Dinan, Desmond. *Ever Closer Union: An Introduction to the European Community.* Basingstoke, U.K.: Macmillan, 1994.

Green, Maria Cowles, and Michael Smith, editors. *The State of the European Union: Risks, Reform, Resistance, and Revival*. Oxford: Oxford University Press, 2000.

Haas, Ernst. *The Uniting of Europe: Political, Social and Economic Forces, 1950-1957*. London: Stevens, 1958.

Lister, Frederick K. *The European Union, the United Nations and the Revival of Confederal Governance*. Westport, Conn.: Greenwood Press, 1996.

McAllister, Richard. *From EC to EU: An Historical and Political Survey*. New York: Routledge, 1997.

Pagden, Anthony, editor. *The Idea of Europe: From Antiquity to the European Union*. Cambridge: Cambridge University Press, 2000.

Pond, Elizabeth. *The Rebirth of Europe*. Washington, D.C.: Brookings Institution Press, 2000.

Urwin, Derek. *The Community of Europe: A History of European Integration since 1945*. New York: Longman, 1991.

Weigall, David, and Peter Stirk, editors. *The Origins and Development of the European Community*. New York: St. Martin's Press, 1992.

Zurcher, Arnold. *The Struggle to Unite Europe, 1940-1958*. New York: New York University Press, 1958.

CHAPTER 9
TAKING THE NEXT STEP

Illustrative references on the concept and history of utopia:

Bloch, Ernst. *The Spirit of Utopia*. Stanford, Cal.: Stanford University Press, 2000.

Claeys, Gregory, and Lyman T. Sargent, editors. *The Utopia Reader*. New York: New York University, 1999.

Claeys, Gregory, editor. *Utopias of the British Enlightenment*. Cambridge: Cambridge University Press, 1994.

Cousins, A. D., and Damian Grace, editors. *More's Utopia and the Utopian Inheritance*. Lanham, Md.: University Press of America, 1995.

Erasmus, Charles J. *In Search of the Common Good: Utopian Experiments Past and Future*. New York: Free Press, 1977.

Gerber, Richard. *Utopian Fantasy: A Study of English Utopian Fiction since the End of the Nineteenth Century*. London: Routledge and Paul, 1955.

Goodwin, Barbara, editor. *The Philosophy of Utopia*. London: Frank Cass, 2001.

Hayden, Delores. *Seven American Utopias*. Cambridge, Mass.: MIT Press, 1976.

Jacoby, Russell. *The End of Utopia: Politics and Culture in an Age of Apathy*. New York: Basic Books, 2000.

Kateb, George. *Utopia and Its Enemies*. New York: Schocken Books, 1972.

Kaufmann, Moritz. *Utopias, or Schemes of Social Improvement, from Sir Thomas More to Karl Marx*. London: C. K. Paul and Co., 1879.

Kumar, Krishan. *Utopia and Anti-Utopia in Modern Times*. London: Blackwell Publishers, 1987.

Levitas, Ruth. *The Concept of Utopia*. Syracuse, NY: Syracuse University Press, 1991.

Manuel, Frank E., and Fritzie P. Manuel. *Utopian Thought in the Western World*. Cambridge, Mass.: Harvard University Press, 1979.

Manuel, Frank E., editor. *Utopias and Utopian Thought*. Boston: Houghton Mifflin, 1966.

Molnar, Thomas S. *Utopia, the Perennial Heresy.* New York: Sheed and Ward, 1967.
Morton,. Arthur Leslie. *The Story of Utopias.* New York: Viking Press, 1962.
Moylan, Tom. *Demand the Impossible: Science Fiction and the Utopian Imagination.* New York: Routledge, 1987.
Mumford, Louis. *The Story of Utopias, Ideal Commonwealths, and Social Myths.* New York: Viking Press, 1968.
Parrington, Vernon Louis. *American Dreams: A Study of American Utopias,* second edition. New York: Russell and Russell, 1964.
Richter, Peyton E., editor. *Utopias: Social Ideals and Communal Experiments.* Boston: Holbrook Press, 1971.
Theodore, Olson. *Millennialism, Utopianism, and Progress.* Toronto: University of Toronto Press, 1982.
Tuveson, Ernest Lee. *Millennium and Utopia: A Study in the Background of the Idea of Progress.* New York: Harper and Row, 1964.
Walsh, Chad. *From Utopia to Nightmare.* New York: Harper and Row, 1962.
Wheeler, Ian Michael. *Utopia.* New York: Harmony Books, 1978.

Need for a "new way of thinking" to cope with the problems of the world:

Allott, Philip. *Eunomia: New Order for a New World.* New York: Oxford University Press, 1990.
Archibugi, Daniele, and David Held, editors. *Cosmopolitan Democracy: An Agenda for a New World Order.* Oxford: Blackwell Publishers: 1995.
Archibugi, Daniele, David Held, and Martin Kohler, editors. *Re-Imagining Political Community: Studies in Cosmopolitan Democracy.* Stanford, Cal.: Stanford University Press, 1998.
Cleveland, Harlan. *Birth of a New World: An Open Moment for International Leadership.* San Francisco: Jossey-Bass, 1993.
Dilloway, James. *From Cold War to Chaos? Reviving Humane Development, or Remaking Market Man.* Westport, Conn.: Praeger Publishers, 1999.
Ekins, Paul. *A New World Order: Grassroots Movements for Global Change.* New York: Routledge, 1992.
Fahey, Joseph, and Richard Armstrong, editors. *A Peace Reader: Essential Readings on War, Justice, Non-Violence and World Order.* New York: Paulist Press, 1992.
Falk, Richard A. *Explorations at the Edge of Time: The Prospects for World Order.* Philadelphia: Temple University Press, 1992.
Falk, Richard A. *On Humane Governance: Toward a New Global Politics.* University Park: Pennsylvania State University Press, 1995.
Falk, Richard A., and Robert C. Johansen, editors. *The Constitutional Framework of World Peace.* Albany: State University of New York Press, 1993.
Held, David. *Democracy and the Global Order: From the Modern State to Cosmopolitan Governance.* Stanford, Cal.: Stanford University Press, 1995.
Rotblat, Joseph, editor. *World Citizenship: Allegiance to Humanity.* New York: St. Martin's Press, 1997.
Walker, Robert B. J. *One World, Many Worlds: Struggles for a Just World Peace.* Boulder, Col.: Lynne Rienner, 1988.
Weatherford, Roy. *World Peace and the Human Family.* New York: Routledge, 1993.

INDEX

multinational corporations (MNC), 208

Mutual Assured Destruction (MAD), 4, 200

Nagasaki, 3, 29, 120
Napoleonic wars, 117
Nationalism and the State, 272, 277
Nations, House of, 161-162
Nature and Function of International Organization, The, 24
negative feedback, 225
negative findings, 228
negative indicator, 180
neoclassical production function, 228
net transfers (WEEP model), 248-249
New Aid Policy for a New World, A, 211-212
New Cyneas, The, 115
Newfang, Oskar, 128
no plausible scenario, 370-371
non-experimental data, 227
non-market income, 180
non-payment of taxes, 81-82
Non-Union Affairs, Ministry of, 61
North Atlantic Treaty Organization (NATO), 194, 306
Norway, 312
Nuclear Nonproliferation Treaty, 78
nuclear war, 4-5, 35-36
nuclear warheads (number), 77
nuclear weapons, 150, 319

Official Development Assistance (ODA), 208-210
official language, 49
open door policy, 18
optimistic scenario, 186
Organization for Economic Cooperation and Development (OECD), 205
Orwell, George, 348-351
Ottoman empire, 110
Overseas Development Council, 213
Owen, Robert, 344

Papanek, Gustav, 223
paralysis, hysterical, 365-368
parameter values (WEEP model), 238
Paris Commune, 144
Parliament (U.K.), 52
passive risk-taking, 20
Pauling, Linus, 155
Peace Force, 168-170
peace-building vs. peace-keeping, 317
peacekeeping missions (U.N.), 323
People's Republic of China, see China
People's World Convention, 135
Peoples, House of, 161-162
per capita income growth, 181-183
Permanent Court of Arbitration, 309
Permanent Court of International Justice, 309
Perpetual Peace, 118-119
Persian Gulf War, 198, 201-202, 321
pessimistic scenario, 186, 363
Planning, Ministry of, 60
Point Four, 194
police state, 11
population vote, see dual voting
positive findings, 228
positive indicator, 180
Preliminary Draft of a World Constitution, 133
premature specificity, 12, 44
Preobrazhenskii, E., 148
Princip, Gavrilo, 355
Pritchett, Lance, 226
productivity differential source coefficient, 236, 251-253
Prohibition (of alcoholic beverages), 21-22
project assistance, 260
proletariat, 4
Protestant Reformation, 104
psychological displacement, 42
public expenditures on health, 179
pupil teacher ratio, 179
purchasing power parity (PPP), 190

ABOUT THE AUTHOR

James A. Yunker was educated at Fordham University (B.A., 1965), the University of California at Berkeley (M.A., 1966), and Northwestern University (Ph.D., 1971). He is currently Professor of Economics at Western Illinois University (Macomb, Illinois), where his principal teaching responsibilities include microeconomic theory, mathematical economics and econometrics. Over his 35-year academic career, Yunker has published eight books and 75 articles in professional periodicals. A special interest has been the application of economic methodologies to diverse real-world problems and issues ranging from the performance evaluation of college and university faculty to the potential effectiveness of capital punishment as a deterrent to homicide. An important component of Yunker's research and writing deals with visionary projects in the areas of socio-economic organization (pragmatic market socialism), foreign development assistance (a global Marshall Plan), and world government in the form of a supernational federation tentatively designated the Federal Union of Democratic Nations (the subject of *Political Globalization*). Although the great majority of people continue to regard these concepts as highly impractical if not downright dangerous, Yunker remains hopeful that his work might be planting seeds of thought that will ultimately germinate and develop into powerful instruments for securing the long-term prosperity and security of global human civilization.